THE BANYAN TREE

Essays on Early Literature in New Indo-Aryan Languages

THE BANYAN TREE

Essays on Early Literature in New Indo-Aryan Languages

(Proceedings of the Seventh International Conference on Early Literature in New Indo-Aryan Languages, Venice, 1997)

VOLUME II

Edited by

MARIOLA OFFREDI

MANOHAR
NEW DELHI

UNIVERSITÀ DEGLI STUDI DI VENEZIA
DIPARTIMENTO DI STUDI EURASIATICI
VENEZIA
2000

First published 2000

ISBN 81-7304-277-2 (Set)
ISBN 81-7304-343-4 (Vol. II)

Published by
Ajay Kumar Jain for
Manohar Publishers & Distributors
4753/23 Ansari Road, Daryaganj
New Delhi 110002

Typeset by
A J Software Publishing Co. Pvt. Ltd.
305 Durga Chambers
1333 D.B. Gupta Road
Karol Bagh, New Delhi 110005

Printed at
Rajkamal Electric Press
B 35/9 G T Karnal Road Indl Area
Delhi 110033

Contents

PART X
TEXTUAL AND ORAL TRANSMISSION

PART XI
SECULARIZATION OF RELIGIOUS MOTIFS
IN THE EIGHTEENTH CENTURY

PART XII
THE RITUAL AND THE POPULAR
TWO WAYS OF INTERPRETING DEVOTION
IN MODERN TIMES

GENERAL INFORMATION

PART VII
Mahābhārata Tradition in the Vernaculars

A Narrative Poet's View of his Material
Viṣṇudās's Introduction to his Brajbhāṣā *Pāṇḍav-carit* (AD 1435)

STUART McGREGOR

My paper at the Seattle conference was on Viṣṇudās of Gwalior's *Rāmāyaṇa* version dated 1442, called *Rāmāyan-kathā*. In that paper and in an earlier one of 1991 I considered the nature of *Rāmāyan-kathā* as a work of its time and place, as suggested by Viṣṇudās's introduction, by the structure of his adaptation, and by what he says about himself at different points in the text. In this paper I discuss the introduction to Viṣṇudās's earlier *Pāṇḍav-carit* from the same point of view.

At least four manuscripts of *Pāṇḍav-carit* have been recorded as extant during this century. Two were used by Hariharnath Dvivedi of Gwalior in his edition of the text with introduction, of 1973, which is indispensable for the study of Viṣṇudās. From it, *Pāṇḍav-carit* appears as a work of some 4,000 lines, mainly in *caupaī* metre. Its language, which is an early Brajbhāṣā, shows some Bundelkhandi and Rajasthani traits, and some modernization. The text may contain some added material. The extant text is an adaptation of some of the subject matter of Book I of the *Mahābhārata*, with additions from later Books. The intention behind this treatment was evidently to provide a representation of the ancient *Mahābhārata* tradition in the vernacular; but we may ask ourselves why this work, which is one of the oldest *prabandha* poems extant in Brajbhāṣā, appeared at just this time and place.

The introduction to the poem is surprisingly long and elaborate. With its 41 *caupaī*s and linking couplets, it rivals in length if not complexity those of Keśavdās, composed *c.*1600 as Brajbhāṣā reached its full literary development. Such an introduction must make a deliberate statement, whether bearing on the poet's intentions, or on attitudes or preoccupations of his society.

STRUCTURE

Sanskrit preamble

The Brajbhāṣā introduction has a Sanskrit preamble consisting of five ślokas, with a sixth verse in mixed Brajbhāṣā-Sanskrit. Verse 1 is addressed, like v.1 of the *Mahābhārata* text itself, to Nārāyaṇa, Devī, Sarasvatī and Vyās. This preamble is almost certainly not part of the original text, since Viṣṇudās's Brajbhāṣā text starts with its own invocations: to Bhagvān, Kṛṣṇa and Gaṇeśa. The Sanskrit preamble may be of some age, however, since we find from the *Mahābhārata* critical edition that one of its verses, v. 4, is to be found in a manuscript dated 1519, and only in that manuscript.[1] This verse is, moreover, prefixed along with several others to the 1519 Ms. in just the same way as the entire Sanskrit preamble we are now considering is prefixed to Viṣṇudās's Brajbhāṣā text of *Pāṇḍav-carit*. Yet the preamble, if it was old, probably suffered change over time. This is suggested by the sequence of its vv. 2 and 3.[2] Verse 2 is on the guru's dispelling the darkness of ignorance and opening the disciple's eyes, and it is followed in one of Dvivedi's Mss. (*kh*, of sv1814, which he thinks the more reliable) by a v. 3 which invokes the four-armed Viṣṇu; but in the other Ms. (*k*, of sv1785), v. 2 is followed by one on a Mādhava who does indeed show a Viṣṇu-like aspect, but in whom students of Sūrdās can also see clear Kṛṣṇa features.[3] This Mādhava's grace causes the lame to cross a mountain and the blind to see, exactly as we find in the well known, but late, opening verse of the Brajbhāṣā *Sūr-sāgar: carana-kamala bandauṁ harirāi | jākī kṛpā paṅgu giri laṅgai, andhe kauṁ saba kachu darasāi | bahirau sunai, gūṁga puni bolai. . . .* The Ms. *k* verse, then, could owe its presence in the preamble to knowledge of its content via the Sūrdās tradition. This would not rule out that an earlier form of the *Sūr-sāgar* verse could underlie the Sanskrit verse. It seems in any case that a *Mahābhārata* textual tradition and a Kṛṣṇa devotional tradition ran hand in hand with knowledge of Viṣṇudās's *Pāṇḍav-carit* for some time in the history of this text.

[1] Vishnu S. Sukthankar, The Ms. is from Sankheda, Baroda district, 1933, 3, xii.

[2] v. 2: *ajñānatimirāndhasya jñānāñjanaṃ śalākayā*
cakṣur unmīlitaṃ yena tasmai śrī gurave namaḥ

v. 3: *śuklāmbaradharaṃ viśnuṃ sasivarṇacaturbhujaṃ*
prasannavadanaṃ dhyāyet sarvavighnopasāntaye.

[3] v. 3: *mūkaṃ karoti vācālaṃ paṅgullaṅghayate giriṃ*
yat kṛpā tam ahaṃ vande paramānandamādhavam.

Brajbhāṣā text

The text is made up of four sections of from eight to twelve *caupaī / caupāī* verses, each section followed by a dohā couplet of 13 + 11 mātrās or a dohrā (extended dohā) of 13 + 12 mātrās. These couplets seem to be contracted from a longer couplet form called pālhurī, of 13 + 16 mātrās. The pālhurī couplets are given in Ms. *kh*, which typically shows older linguistic forms; they sometimes (as in the example discussed in n. 11 below) provide more meaningful or pointed readings than the dohrās, and to that extent deserve provisional acceptance in the text. They usually contain a phrase or two anticipating a phrase from the opening of the next caupāī section, or less often, repeating one from the end of the last. Pālhurīs or dohrās occur throughout the *Pāṇḍav-carit* text at intervals of from 10 to up to 30 couplets. They mark divisions in the composition having the same purposes as the dohās of *Candāyan*: to summarize or signpost the current topic and (more importantly, as Dvivedi thinks) to allow the singer to mark time and catch his breath.[4] Dvivedi believes that since Viṣṇudās's *Rāmāyan-kathā* does not contain *pālhurīs*, they will be later additions in the *Pāṇḍav-carit* text, but given their important purposes it seems they should date from very early in the public history of the text. If so, their content for its part reflects something like an original understanding of the text.

CONTENT OF VERSES, AND INTERPRETATION

The invocations of vv. 1-10 of the introduction establish a brahminical tone, and a specifically *Mahābhārata* context. The deities invoked are, first Gaṇeś, Brahmā and Hari, then, in a sequence containing additions to the list in the Sanskrit introduction, Devī, Śaṅkara, Nārāyaṇ, Jagdīś, and Śiva, with one more: the unnamed charioteer or *yantā* who will, when thought of in battle, defeat men's enemies,

जे नर सुमिरहिं रन महं जनता ते बैरीदल जितहि अनन्ता.[5]

Viṣṇudās's use of the word *nara* in this well known Kṛṣṇa context may recall the *Mahābhārata* use of the compound, *nara-nārāyaṇa*, in reference to Arjuna and Kṛṣṇa as avatar; but the tone of the verse, and its plural pronouns (*je nara...te*) suggest that a more modern context is also involved.

At the end of this set of verses the poet addresses the king, Dūṁgarsī, who is also yet to be identified by name, and to whom he will now 'tell the

[4] Details of Mss. *kh* and *k* in Dvivedi 1973, pp. 32-4.
[5] v. 9.

Bhāratha at length' (*bhāratha bhākhaum̐ tohi pasāī*) in the hearing of an assembly, *sabhā*. This poem will be a chronicle of praise, *khyāti*. The *khyāti* is a genre of older Rajasthan poetry celebrating the history of states and dynasties and the deeds of kings, inevitably partly in terms of legend and mythology. We may be entitled to assume that where ancient legend rather than recent (if romanticised) history is a poet's avowed subject, and the poet speaks to a modern, successful king, some topical relevance should be read into the ancient story. More on that anon. Before we leave the performance aspect of the poem, it is worth noting that Viṣṇudās describes his subject here as the 'origins' *utpātī*, of the Kauravas and Pāṇḍavas. This description agrees well with the content of the extant text of *Pāṇḍav-carit*, a fact which strengthens the credentials of the Dvivedi Ms. It also suggests that Viṣṇudās, in daring to select from his vast prestigious source in the drastic way his project demanded if it were to be practicable, was a poet of some experience, one who knew from example how to plan, and what might be achieved in an existing genre of narrative poetry: whether in the *khyāti*, or in other precedents in an emergent Brajbhāṣā.

This (it may be said) is conjecture: but Viṣṇudās proves to be very adequately versed in literary convention. At the end of his introduction he says he has no command of metres or *lakṣaṇa*, *chandu na lacchanu bidyā jānū*,[6] but this is over-modest: he is versed in a number of literary conventions. The standard beauties of a heroine become novel to a degree when it is Sarasvatī in whom they are found displayed (section 2 of the Introduction), and Sarasvatī's standard attributes, too, are given pointed novelty when she is described as *pustaka-pāni* 'holding a book'.[7] The purpose of this is apparently, as I suggested in discussing *Rāmāyan-kathā*, to make Sarasvatī the patroness of the vernacular *prabandha*. Similarly (in Section 1) Viṣṇudās hypes up Gaṇeś's charm to make him the quintessence of *rasa, bīnā sāra karai rasa-sārū*; and Viṣṇudās reflects that worshipping Gaṇeś brings sweetness to one's Sanskrit, *pranavata hohi madhura sura-bānī*.[8] A literary man is speaking here, and the problems of use of Sanskrit vocabulary (of which there *is* some in his Brajbhāṣā text) are on his mind.

I return now to the main point taken up in this paper. A feature of Viṣṇudās's references to Devī, Śaṅkara, Nārāyaṇ and Kṛṣṇa in the opening set of verses is that these deities, whatever their overall powers may be, are all shown as involved in the overcoming of mythological enemies.[9] Devī

[6] v. 41.

[7] v.17.

[8] vv. 2-3.

[9] vv. 5, 6, 9.

kills Mahiṣāsur; Śaṅkara apparently kills Tripura the demon (although it should have been his city Tripura that Śaṅkara destroys)[10]; Nārāyaṇ (that is to say, Viṣṇu) tricks Bali decisively, *bali chalyau patālā*; and the unnamed charioteer grants victory.

The above deeds are all well attested in *Mahābhārata* and Purāṇa contexts. Care must therefore be taken in reading special significance into references to them in later contexts. Yet it is noteworthy that immediately after referring to the Tripura and Bali episodes, Viṣṇudās invokes, first Viṣṇu as Jagdīś in the role of beneficent initiator of the cosmic drama, and then Śiva as cosmic dancer. It seems that Viṣṇudās may have wished to bring out the larger salvific functions of Viṣṇu and Śiva more specifically in the present context than might be suggested by references to divine destructive agency. Viṣṇudās's apparent error of emphasis in interpreting the Tripura reference (which diverges from *Mahābhārata* and is not much represented in Purāṇas[11]) appears as more understandable, if we consider the possibility that his opening references to Mahiṣāsur, Tripura and Bali are loaded ones, having a significance going beyond that of the old mythology. There is, again, a particular pointedness in Viṣṇudās's final reference to Kṛṣṇa as charioteer, for it is men's need of help rather than that of Arjuna the Pāṇḍava that is prominently emphasized here by its wording. The gods are of course regarded as surrogates of men and women, but it is actual needs of men and women that are important to Viṣṇudās (though this is not made explicit), and are referred to Kṛṣṇa's agency for solution.

Let us look now at the *pālhurī* couplet that follows this set of verses. It speaks first of Gaṇeś but chiefly of Sarasvatī who is the sole subject of the next set of verses. Reverence is to be shown to Śārdā 'by remembering whom *that* tale has been brought to completion which destroyed (or destroys) the gods' fear of the asura army':

भक्ति विनायक की करौ पुनि सारद के लागौ पाई
असुर बहिनि सुर भौ हरिनि जा सुमिरंतहि कथा सिराई [12]

[10] *saṅkara . . . tripura saṁghāryau*, v. 5. The Brajbhāṣā verb *saṁghār-* is usually used of living beings.

[11] Sörensen 1904, Dikshitar 1952, s.vv.

[12] The text of the corresponding dohrā in Ms. *k* is less convincing. It reads: *bhakti vināyaka kī karau puni sārada sira nāī, sura-racchaka asvara-nikara jinhataiṁ kathā sirāī*. The second line of this dohrā does not contain the verb *sumirant*— although there is every reason that this verb (since it is present in Viṣṇudās's following verse 11) should have occurred in the original *pālhurī*. Similarly the Ms. *kh* wording of the end of the first line of the *pālhurī* (*ke lāgau pāī*) is preferable to that of the *dohrā* since it reproduces that of the preceding verse 10. The semi-tatsama compounds of the Ms. *k* text do not have the immediacy of the

Given that this verse is a *pālhurī* interposed in the narration, it must refer to Viṣṇudās's composition of his own *Pāṇḍav-carit* (of which he has just spoken to Ḍūṁgarsī) as much as to composition of the *Mahābhārata* itself. Its first line contains imperatives addressed clearly to the *Pāṇḍav-carit* audience ('revere Gaṇeś, and bow to Sarasvatī's feet'). Viṣṇudās, or the *pālhurīkār* speaking on his behalf, closely relates his own position here to that of the gods in their fear of asuras, speaking in present time. The implication is that Viṣṇudās saw a modern relevance in the story, despite the covert, source-bound way he goes about suggesting it. As the gods were freed from fear of their enemies, so is long-embattled Gwalior freed in Ḍūṁgarsī's time from some of the pressures from Delhi and from nearer states. Ḍūṁgarsī had had increasing success during the years preceding 1435 in resisting incursions from, and perhaps in avoiding tribute to, Mubārakśāh of Delhi, to the point where in 1435 he was able to launch an attack on the fort of Bhander and its neighbourhood.[13] Gwalior was indeed at this time, as Viṣṇudās says to Ḍūṁgarsī at the end of the introduction, a thorn in its enemies' side, *gaṛha gopācala vairinī sāl.* The tone of the *pālhurī* is to be related to this resistance, and the king's success.

In the third section of the introduction Viṣṇudās invokes a series of major and minor icons of brahminical religious culture.[14] Starting with the guru, he proceeds via Hari and Īśa/Śiva to the Vedic Indra and Amarāvatī, thence to the rishis and eventually to Agni, mentioning tīrthas, the *dikpāl* elephants, the sun, planets and zodiac and other standard items on the way. An informal syncretistic statement about roots of the culture and their extent can be seen here. But in the middle of this statement, introduced seemingly at random after a reference to the rishis and before one to the planets, a more meaningful reference intrudes, to Kṛṣṇa as child and youth.[15] This Kṛṣṇa lives in Mahāban in Braj; he breaks bonds, and by his grace gives deliverance to those who think of him:

नगर महाबन जाकौ बासू बन्धन तोरै देइ खलासू
सुमिरत तोरै लोह जजीर जा पसाइ सुखु होइ सरीर.

Ms. *kh* reading *asura bahini sura bhau harini* [*hārini*]. Stylistically they resemble the usage of the sixteenth-century Brajbhāṣā Kṛṣṇa poetry and seem likely to be replacements in the text made at a time when the particular Gwalior context had been forgotten.

[13] Misra 1993, pp. 40, 56: *Tārīkh e Muḥammadī*, ff. 463b-464a, tr. Rizvī 1959, p. 42.

[14] vv. 22-33.

[15] v. 30.

The words *khalās*, which I have rendered here as 'deliverance', and *jajīr* 'chain' in the following line, are the only Arabic or Persian loanwords in Dvivedi's text of the introduction. Mahāban is often mentioned in the *Mahābhārata* as the name of a forest of Braj, but neither there nor in the *Harivaṃśa* does it seem to have the senses of Nanda's encampment, or of Gokul village, which it later acquired.[16] Alan Entwistle traced its later history.[17] The site of a fort and so an identifiable locality by the tenth century, Mahāban was captured by Mahmūd Ghaznī; after the time of Alā'uddīn, and so within 140 years of Visṇudās's time, it became a local Muslim centre and military headquarters. The tone of Viṣṇudās's reference to Kṛṣṇa and Mahāban in an otherwise general context of cultural piety suggests an awakened sense of Indian or Hindu cultural identity in the Gwalior of his time.

Finally, in the last part of his introduction Viṣṇudās speaks again of the origin of *Pāṇḍav-carit*.[18] But it is the king's status, lineage and power that is really at issue here as much as the history of his 'kavidās''s poem. Ḍūṁgarsī is the upholder of the Tomar dynasty in the lineage of the Pāṇḍavas, *paṇḍu-baṃsa tauvara dhura-dhīrū*; his fame has spread far, *para-bhumi jānā*, and his Gwalior is rich in steeds and elephants, its fort a thorn to his enemies. The king, who is also a 'Bhīm' in strength and harsh resolve, throws down a challenge in a shape of a betel-leaf (*tamor*) to Viṣṇudās. The challenge is one couched in *Mahābhārata* terms: tell me why and how Duryodhan died, asks the king, — one of a hundred Kauravas against five Pāṇḍavas?[19] This question is the pretext that launches Viṣṇudās on his narration. It had gone unasked by the *Mahābhārata* poets, who needed no gloss on the power of divine ordinance.[20] It is posed here in a local society for whom the *Mahābhārata* articulates a major segment of traditional culture, yet in this society the Sanskrit epic, adapted into vernacular language, can now convey a modern message. In the light of Viṣṇudās's poem the answer to the king's question can only be that the gods have favoured Gwalior as they did the Pāṇḍavas.

[16] A computer printout of *Mahābhārata* citations kindly provided by J.D. Smith strongly suggests this interpretation. Langlois's translation of *Harivaṃśa* gives no indication that the word *mahāvana* is regarded in that text as a proper name.

[17] Entwistle 1987, p. 423.

[18] vv. 34-41.

[19] v. 39.

[20] Cf. IX.58.19 (Yudhiṣṭhira's consolation to Duryodhana):
nūnam etad balavatā dhātrādiṣṭaṃ mahātmanā
yad vayaṃ tvāṃ jighāṃsāmas tvaṃ cāsmān kurusattama.

REFERENCES

Dikshitar, V.R. Ramachandra, *The Purana Index*, Madras: University of Madras 1952.

Dvivedi, Hariharnath, *Mahābhārat (Pāṇḍav-carit)*, Gwalior: Vidya Mandir Prakashan, 1973.

Entwistle, Alan W., *Braj, Centre of Krishna Pilgrimage*, Groningen: Egbert Forster, 1987.

Langlois, M.A., tr., *Harivaṃśa*, Paris and London: Oriental Translation Fund of Great Britain and Ireland, 1833-4, 2 vols.

McGregor, R.S., 'An early Hindi version of the Rāma story', in Diana L. Eck and Françoise Mallison (eds.), *Devotion Divine: Bhakti Traditions from the Regions of India*, Studies in honour of Charlotte Vaudeville, Groningen: Egbert Forster, 1991, pp.181-96.

Miśra, B.D., *Forts and Fortresses of Gwalior and its Hinterland*, Delhi: Manohar, 1993.

Rizvī, Saiyyid Athar Abbās, *Uttar taimūrkālīn bhārat*, Aligarh: History Department, Aligarh Muslim University, pt. 2, 1959.

Sörensen, S., *An Index to the Names in the Mahabharata*, London: Williams Norgate, 1904

Sukthankar, Vishnu S., *The Mahābhārata*, Poona: Bhandarkar Oriental Research Institute, 1933.

The Vaiṣṇava Parvan of the Assamese *Mahābhārata*

W.L. SMITH

The Assamese *Mahābhārata* is an assemblage; its various *parvans* (*parbba*) and sub-*parvans* were written by different poets at different times, some in more than one version, and two and a half centuries passed before it was complete. Work on it began at the initiative of king Naranārāyaṇa who reigned over Koch Bihar between 1540 and 1587. A great patron of learning, he assigned the task of supervising the rendition to Rāma Sarasvatī who contributed to nine different *parvans* himself, most notably the greater part of the longest and most popular of them, the *vana parvan*[1] (*bana parbba*) which makes up half the bulk of the vernacular epic, running to nearly 30,000 verses[2] in its printed version.[3] The first part of the *banaparbba*, known as the *ādi bana parbba*, numbers fifty printed pages and deals rather summarily with the episodes from the original Sanskrit epic while the remaining thousand pages are concerned with apocryphal matter. Much is omitted from the original, including the stories of Śibi, Sagara, Yayāti, Nala and Damayantī, Sāvitrī and of Rāma.[4] As its alternate name, *vaiṣṇava parvan*, announces, this a devotional work which describes the wanderings of the five Pāṇḍavas and their common wife Draupadī as exiles in 'the very terrifying, most horrible forest'[5] where they undergo twelve years of suffering.[6] Surrounded by numerous dangers,

[1] This is the name by which the *araṇyaka parvan* is known in the eastern recension of the *Mahābhārata*.

[2] Verses 3930-18770. The verses, chiefly couplets (*pada, payāra*), are not numbered couplet by couplet by the editor, as is the usual practice, but in pairs of couplets.

[3] Aṣṭadaś Parbba Asamīya *Mahābhārata*, edited by Harinārāyaṇ Dattabaruvā, Guvāhāṭī: Dattabaruvā aṇḍ Kompanī, rpt. 1993 (1955). This is the only printed edition.

[4] Rāma Sarasvatī begins a short version of the *rāmopakhyāna* on page 310, but soon abandons it.

[5] *durghora araṇya iṭo mahā bhaẏaṅkara*; v. 14043.

[6] *bāṛhaẏa batsara āmi bhuñjibo dukhaka*; v. 5443.

their sole support is their devotion to Kṛṣṇa. As Yudhiṣṭhira says, 'No one has suffered as much as we. We have only survived because of the mercy of Kṛṣṇa.'[7] Divine help is certainly needed since the brothers and their wife are constantly beset by monstrous demons, carnivorous beasts, poisonous *nāgas* and barbarian armies.

The apocryphal portions of the *bana parbba* consist of a number of very loosely linked independent episodes. The *puṣpaharaṇa parbba* relates how Bhīma destroys mustard plants in the garden of the sage Kanva and is forced to labour for him in recompense, while the *Bhīma caritra* describes how Śiva decides to become a rice farmer and takes on Bhīma as a farmhand.[8] The *maṇicandra ghoṣ parbba* tells how Bhīma clashes with *nāgas* of the underworld and the *bijaya parbba* contains the odd story of how King Dhṛtarāṣṭra temporarily regains his eyesight and sets off on a *digvijaya*, a campaign of universal conquest. The *yajña parbba* deals with the story of the *dharmacandra* sacrifice of the Pāṇḍavas and the slaying of Mahiṣa Dānava, the *kurmmavalī badha* recounts the horse sacrifice of Duryodhana, and the final episode, the *sindhu yātra*, tells of Arjuna's fight with Sindhu Rājā who turns out to be his elder (and apocryphal) brother fathered on Kuntī by the moon god Candra. The other episodes, *kulācala badha, jaṅghāsura badha, khaṭāsura badha, aśvakarṇa badha* and *baghāsura badha*, as their titles announce, describe the killing, *badha* (i.e. Sanskrit *vadha*), of various demons and belong to a popular genre of early Assamese literature known as *vadha kāvya*. Interspaced between these major episodes are minor ones describing the killing of yet other demons and wild animals.

The poets claim that this apocryphal material is taken from a number of different sources. At the very beginning of the *bana parbba* Rāma Sarasvatī tells us that his intention is to compose verses 'mixing [matter of] the *Haṁsa kākī* and *Yāmala saṁhitā*',[9] and he as well as the other poets[10] repeatedly refer to these two works, sometimes adding a third, the *Śiva rahasya*. They also claim that the *Yāmala saṁhitā* and the *Haṁsa kākī* were used by Vyāsa when he compiled his original Sanskrit *Mahābhārata*.[11]

[7] *āmāra samāna dukhabhāgī nāhikaẏa | kṛṣṇakṛpā nimittese jīva rahichaẏa*; v. 9542.

[8] The *Bhīma caritra*, the most popular of the episodes, has not been included in the printed edition. It is, however, often printed independently.

[9] *haṁsakākī saṁhitā yāmala miśra kari | racibo payāra*; v. 4529

[10] These include his son Gopinātha Pāṭhaka, Kaṁsāri Kāyastha and Dāmodara Dāsa.

[11] *byāse kathā kahe haṁsakākī purāṇara* (v. 5835): 'Vyāsa recites the matter of the Haṁsa kākī purāṇa'; *dvaipāyana nahāmuni | karilā śāstraka jāni |*

The *Haṁsa kākī* and *Yāmala saṁhitā*[12] are otherwise completely unknown. There are several Sanskrit works titled *Śiva rahasya* but none of them seems to be concerned with this material.[13] Rāma Sarasvatī and his fellows also cite the *Purāṇa saṁhitā* as a source; this is a legendary work, supposedly the original Purāṇa composed by Vyāsa divided into the present versions.[14] The sage Mārkaṇḍeya is also mentioned a number of times and the lengthy *kulācala badha* is recited to the sage Jaimini by 'wise birds' *dharmapakṣī*, rather than to Janamejaya as is the rest of the *parvan*. This is an echo of the *Mārkaṇḍeya purāṇa* (which is not named) in which Jaimini, the disciple of Vyāsa, asks the sage for information about points of the *Mahābhārata* he is unsure of and is referred by him to 'four wise birds' who recite the Purāṇa to him.[15] The Assamese scholar S.N. Sharma suggests that the *Yāmala saṁhitā* and the *Haṁsa kākī* 'probably formed parts of some Upabhārata which is irrevocably lost to us.[. . .] Considering the popularity of Jaimini's *Asvamedhaparvan* in Assam, it may not be altogether absurd to hold that the so-called *Haṁsa-kākī* or *Śiva-rahasya* might have been parts of the lost portion of Jaimini's work.'[16] The *Jaimini bhārata*, as the *Jaimini aśvamedha* or *Jaimini aśvamedhaparvan* is also known, is a devotional text from South India and written around the twelfth or thirteenth centuries which describes the horse sacrifice of Yudhiṣṭhira. This work was very popular everywhere in eastern India as versions in Maithili, Assamese, Bengali and Oriya can attest. An Assamese rendering of the *Jaimini bhārata* also serves as the fourteenth *parvan* of the Assamese *Mahābhārata* to which it was added centuries after the death of

---

yāmala saṁhitā cāi | *ekatra kariẏā taya* || (v. 13867): 'The great sage Vyāsa, considering the *Yāmala saṁhitā*, composed the *śāstra*, putting it together'. See also vv. 10032-3.

[12] Monier Monier-Williams, in *A Sanskrit-English Dictionary*, rpt. Oxford, 1971, notes that *Yāmala* is the name of a class of Tantric works.

[13] There is a *Śiva rahasya khaṇḍa* in the *Skandha purāṇa*, see Ludo Rocher, 'The Purāṇas: A History of Indian Literature', vol. II, fasc. 3, Wiesbaden: Otto Harrasowitz, 1986, p. 236. A *Śiva rahasya* in 50,000 verses was published in the Kannada script with a Kannada translation in 30 vols. in the 'Maharaja Jayachamarajendra Granthamala', series no. 32 in 1950; among other matters, it contains a life of the Sanskrit philosopher Śaṅkara; see *Śrīśaṅkaravijaya*, edited by N. Veezhinathan, University of Madras, 1971, pp. ivff. The Assamese poets also mention the *Bhāgavata, Dharmottara* [*sic*] (v. 12653), and *Brahmavaivartta purāṇas* (vv. 5728 and 12653).

[14] Ibid., p. 45; note verses 9349, 9856, 16540, etc.

[15] Ludo Rocher, op. cit., p.192.

[16] S.N. Sarma, *Epics and Purāṇas in Early Assamese Literature*, Pratima Devi, Gauhati, 1972, p. 67.

Rāma Sarasvatī.[17] According to tradition, Jaimini, a pupil of Vyāsa, wrote a version of the *Mahābhārata* superior to that of his guru Vyāsa who was so jealous of his skill that he ordered it to be destroyed; somehow its fourteenth *parvan* survived to be circulated under the name *Jaimini bhārata*. There is, however, no evidence that the *Jaimini bhārata* was ever part of a larger work and the text itself gives no indication of this.

Before considering the question of sources more closely, we can take a more detailed look at the apocryphal episodes of the *vaiṣṇava parbba*. Most conform to a simple pattern: the Pāṇḍava brothers leave forests bearing names such as *bhasma bana, bhavārṇa bana* and *tarāga bana* to enter a new ones where they encounter new foes. The demons they face are usually cephalically remarkable: the demon Suraketu has two heads, Surajita five, Jaṅghāsura one thousand; Baghāsura sports a tiger's head, Kulācala a goat's, Gajaketu an elephant's, Mahiṣa Dānava a water-buffalo's and Kālukuñja and Ṣoṣaka have needle-shaped mouths (*sūcī ākāra mukhagoṭa*) like giant mosquitoes. Like their classical protypes these demons perform austerities and are given boons (*bara*) of near invincibility as a result, but the boon always has a loophole, *bara chidra*, which brings about their doom. Accounts of the battles of the Pāṇḍavas with these demons, their ministers, brothers, sons, generals and their armies fill thousands of verses and make up the overwhelming bulk of the matter in the *parvan*. In one feature these stories differ from similar battle descriptions in other epic works: here the Pāṇḍavas lose many of their battles and they not only lose them, but they are repeatedly killed by their enemies. In the *maṇi chandra ghoṣ parbba* Draupadī and four of the brothers are killed by the serpent Puṇḍarīka and their bones lie bleaching in the forest for nine months while Bhīma goes to the underworld in order to find a magic jewel to revive them with, only to be killed there in his turn. In the next episode all five brothers are killed by the blood-sucking demons Kālukuñja and Ṣoṣaka, and they suffer the same fate again at the hands of the Tiger-demon, Baghāsura, only soon thereafter to be captured in the venomous snake-net (*nāgpāśa*) of the demon Khaṭāsura and then in that of the demon Jaṅghāsura. After this misfortune Bhīma is swallowed by the buffalo demon whereafter all the brothers are killed by Kulācala and, finally, in the concluding story four of the brothers are slain by the *kālakuṭa* weapon of king Sindhu. After every death the Pāṇḍavas are brought back to life — by the gods, by forest hermits, with the help of magic or by the direct intervention of Kṛṣṇa. Once brought back to life they resume the fight and finally prevail.

[17] For these see W.L. Smith, *The Jaimini-bhārata and its Eastern Vernacular Versions*, Studia Orientalia, vol. 85, 1999.

In two episodes it is Draupadī who defeats and kills the demons. After Kālakuñja and Ṣoṣaka slay her five husbands, Draupadī sits reciting the name of Kṛṣṇa whereupon she finds herself invested with great strength and a breastplate (*kavaca*) and a turban (*ṭupī*) fall from the sky as a celestial voice (*ākāśī bacana*) commands her to arm herself. Draupadī then picks up Arjuna's bow and quiver and marches into battle against the demons and their army, asking Kṛṣṇa's aid all the while. When she begins slaughtering the demons, Meghī, the wife of Kālakuñja, becomes enraged and takes the field invoking the help of Durgā (*durgāka smarante*) and Draupadī transforms herself into a kṣatriya to face her.[18] Meghī responds by transforming herself into a fly (*makṣikāra śarīra*), enters Draupadī's womb (or stomach) (*garbha*) by way of her nostril and begins drinking her blood. Draupadī faints from the pain. When Viṣṇu sees this, he commands his discus (*cakra*) to enter Draupadī's womb and frighten Meghī away. The battle then resumes and Draupadī kills the demons, one after the other using a woman-shaped (*nārīra ākāra*) arrow. In another episode all the Pāṇḍavas are ensnared in the poisonous snake-net of the amorous demon Khaṭāsura who attempts the seduction of Draupadī who again appeals to Kṛṣṇa. This time Kṛṣṇa himself appears to tell her that she need have no fear and that the demon can be killed by the bracelet (*hastar kaṅkaṇa*) given her by the sage Agastya; so, when the demon approaches her, she flings the bracelet at him and decapitates him.

With the exception of the *Bhīma caritra*, a theme popular all over eastern India,[19] the majority of the episodes in the *bana parbba* do not seem to occur elsewhere. Nevertheless, many of them have an air of familiarity about them. The *maṇicandra ghoṣ parbba* is modelled on an episode in the *Jaiminī bhārata* taken in its turn from the *aśvamedhikā parvan* of the *Mahābhārata*: Babhruvāhana, king of Maṇipura, kills his father, Arjuna, in battle and in order to bring him back to life, he, like Bhīma, goes to the underworld, defeats the *nāgas* and returns with the magic life-reviving jewel *mṛtasaṃjīvako maṇi*, as it is also called in the *bana parbba* story. One also notes how the *nāgas* Puṇḍarī and Dhṛtarāṣṭra play roles in both works.[20] This particular episode from the *Jaimini bhārata* was rendered into Assamese by the poet Harivara Bipra who may have done so before

[18] *meghī dekhi pāṇḍavī kṣatriya rūpa dhari | strī ki puruṣa eko cinite napāri ||* (v. 8208) 'Seeing Meghī she took the form of a Pāṇḍava warrior; one could not distinguish whether it was a man or woman'.

[19] For this theme see W.L. Smith, 'Śiva Lord of the Plow', in Rahul Peter Das (ed.), *Studies in Middle Bengali*, Calcutta, forthcoming.

[20] *Śrījaiminīyāśvamedhaparva*, with com. by Rāmādhār Śukla Sāstrī, Gorakhpur: Gītā Press, vs 2050, *adhyāya*s 38-9.

Rāma Sarasvatī, but his date, unfortunately, remains uncertain. The story of king Dhṛtarāṣṭra's campaign of conquest has a parallel in the *Śatruñjaya*, a work by the Assamese poet Raghunātha Mahanta on another equally apocryphal epic adventure, the *digvijaya* of the monkey king Vālin.[21] The *aśvakarṇa badha*, subtitled the *pātāli khaṇḍa*, tells how a rākṣasī pulls Arjuna and Bhīma down through a well into the underworld of *vitala* where they exterminate the demons plaguing its inhabitants. Similar themes are the subjects of two Assamese works: the *Adbhuta Rāmāyaṇa* (which is unrelated to the Sanskrit work of the same name), also by Raghunātha Mahanta, and the *Pātāli khāṇḍa* by the poet Pañcānana. These two works describe Hanumān's war against *nāga* armies in the underworld, another theme apparently not found outside Assam. It is interesting that Raghunātha repeatedly claims that he has taken the matter in his *Adbhuta Rāmāyaṇa* from the *Adbhutakāṇḍa* of the *Rāmāyaṇa* as narrated by Mārkaṇḍeya to Yudhiṣṭhira, a source, like the *Yāmala saṁhitā* and the *Haṁsa kākī*, otherwise quite unknown.[22] One also notes many echoes of Vālmīki in the various episodes of the *bana parbba*: the demon Kālajaṅgha shows Draupadī the false heads *(māyā śirā)* of her five husbands, just as Rāvāṇa shows Sītā those of Rāma and Lakṣmaṇa; both Khaṭāsura and Jaṅghāsura capture the brothers with a snake-net, the same weapon used by Indrajit to fell Rāma and his brother; and there is a also mighty monkey warrior, a 'servant of Rāma', with the unlikely name of Sarbbagajara, an obvious echo of Hanumān. Other illusions to Rāma's war with Rāvaṇa are also frequent.

The *bana parbba* is a devotional interpretation of the epic. Here the Pāṇḍavas slay monsters for the benefit of mankind, to 'rid the earth of its burden' as the familiar phrase has it,

> The five sons of Paṇḍu are supreme Vaiṣṇavas.
> They all will certainly benefit the earth
> by waging war with the utmost exertion
> and putting an end to the great sufferings of the triple world.[23]

In devotional reworkings of the Rāma and Kṛṣṇa stories the foes of the gods are transformed into devotees, as, for example, Rāvaṇa in the

[21] For this theme see W.L. Smith, *Rāmāyaṇa Traditions in Eastern India: Assam, Bengal, Orissa*, 2nd revd. edn., New Delhi: Munshiram Manoharlal, 1995, pp. 154ff.

[22] S.N. Sarma, op. cit., p. 50.

[23] *parama baiṣṇava pāñca pāṇḍura tanaya | lokara hitaka sabe sādhanta*

Rāmcaritmānas of Tulsīdās.[24] This same motif appears in the *kalācala badha* where the demon Kulācala is a devotee of Kṛṣṇa who only slays the Pāṇḍavas in order to provoke a battle with and be killed by the object of his devotion. In all the other episodes of the Assamese epic, however, the enemies of the Pāṇḍavas are genuine villains, not devotees pretending to be enemies. The *Jaimini bhārata* is also a devotional reinterpretation of a *Mahābhārata* theme but it provides no instructive parallels since the mode of *bhakti* it illustrates is quite different than that in the Assamese version of the epic.[25] What we seem to see there is Rāma Sarasvatī's grafting of a *bhakti* gloss on a common feature of regional epic literatures. The heroes of these works, in stark contrast to the near invincible protagonists of the ancient Sanskrit epics, often tend to be relatively hapless and consequently in continual need of rescue by the deities they worship. This can be seen in the various Hindi versions of the Lorikī theme, the Bengali folk epics and the Oriya works of Śaraḷā Dāsa. This is at the same time a familiar *bhakti* notion: that of the inadequacy of the individual devotee, one which can only be offset by a total reliance on Kṛṣṇa. Bhīma, Arjuna, Yudhiṣṭhira, Draupadī and the others cannot even survive, much less conquer without his constant help. Without faith they are doomed, with it they need fear no one.[26]

If Rāma Sarasvatī and his fellows had not repeatedly claimed they had taken their stories from the *Haṁsa kākī*, the *Purāṇa saṁhitā* and other such unknown texts,[27] one might well have presumed that they had relied upon their own imaginations, adapting regional motifs to the epic theme and animating them with the spirit of *bhakti*. This is what other Assamese poets later did with the *Rāmāyaṇa*. But if texts such as the *Haṁsa kākī* and the

---

niścaẏa || *prāṇa pariśrame tente samara kariba* | *tiniyo lokara mahā dukhaka khaṇḍiba* || v. 9956.

[24] For this motif in Rāmāyaṇa literature see W.L. Smith, *Rāmāyaṇa Traditions*, pp.113ff.

[25] For a discussion of this mode of *bhakti* see W.L. Smith, *The Jaimini-bhārata.*

[26] *pāñcabhāi pāṇḍavar tumise jīvana* | *śaṅkaṭa samaẏe rākhi phurā sarbbakṣaṇa* || *putrara snehata yena mātṛ nachāṛanta* || *āmāsāka nerā tumi prabhu bhagavanta* || v.13295 'You are the life of the Five Pāṇḍava brothers. You always protect them in time of peril, like a mother does not leave the son she loves, you, Lord, do not forsake us'.

[27] The fact that the *bana parbba* is a devotional work has other implications. The devotional movement had been introduced into Assam by Śaṅkaradeva, a contemporary of Rāma Sarasvatī, thus any texts *banaparbba* may have been based upon, cannot have been Assamese since there were no earlier Assamese devotional works.

Yāmala saṁhitā had not existed, why would Rāma Sarasvatī have said that they did and that he consulted them? One notes that it is only in the *bana parbba* that such claims are made and this must be a consequence of the fact that so very much of it consists of apocryphal material. Rāma Sarasvatī had been commissioned by king Naranārāyaṇa to produce an Assamese rendering of the *Mahābhārata*. Naranārāyaṇa's court was graced by the reformer Śaṅkaradeva and many other prominent scholars and poets of both Sanskrit and Assamese.[28] We know from biographies of Śaṅkaradeva that many of the Brahmins at Naranārāyaṇa's court were highly critical of the reformer, his Assamese rendering of the *Bhāgavata purāṇa* and the devotional movement in general and had urged the king to suppress it.[29] The *Mahābhārata* of Rāma Sarasvatī was another Assamese rendering of another Sanskrit *śāstra* and a rendering, morever, that radically deviated from the original. The hostile Brahmins at Naranārāyaṇa's court, one suspects, would not at all have been unwilling to point this fact out. One way to deflect such potential criticism would have been to claim that the deviant matter was from other, perfectly respectable sources which also had been used by Vyāsa himself. And if any listener would wonder why he had never heard of the *Yāmala saṁhitā*, the *Śiva rahasya*, the *Haṁsa kākī* or the stories found in them, there was another ready answer: these were secret tales. Our poets repeatedly refer to the 'secret' nature of their material: these were 'most secret stories', *parama rahasya kathā*, only known to a fortunate few since the days of Vyāsa.[30] This is an old and familiar ploy which has often been used in India to invest novelties with an aura of hoary legitimacy. Such statements also bring out another point: if the *Yāmala saṁhitā* or *Śiva rahasya* had been familiar to Rāma Sarasvatī's audience, there would not have been any reason to describe them as 'secret'. Most likely the *Yāmala saṁhitā* and the other texts named so often were just as imaginary as the *Purāṇa saṁhitā* or Jaimini's full-length *Mahābhārata*. They were just camouflage designed to obscure the fact that what Rāma Sarasvatī and his fellow poets were doing was what anonymous contributors to the *Mahābhārata* had been doing for thousands of years: enriching it with new materials thereby ensuring that it remained a living part of Hindu tradition.

[28] Maheswar Neog, *Early History of the Vaiṣṇava Faith and Movement in Assam: Śaṅkaradeva and his Times*, Delhi: Motilal Banarsidas, rpt. 1985 (1965), p. 62.

[29] This is described in the biographies of Śaṅkaradeva: the *Mahāpuruṣa śrī śaṅkaradeva āru śrīmādhavadeva carita* by Daityāri Ṭhākur and the *ŚrīŚrī Śaṅkaradeva* of Bhūṣaṇa Dvija.

[30] See verses 10033, 16733, 17332, 17775, 18720, etc.

PART VIII

Kṛṣṇa Cult in the Braj Region

A New Appraisal

Little Kṛṣṇa's Play with the Moon

HANS BAKKER

Within the collection of hymns (*Tirumoḻi*) attributed to Viṭṭucittaṉ, also known as the 'Great Saint,' Periyāḻvār (ninth century AD), we find 'a series of independent songs, [in which] Periyāḻvār envisages the childhood of Kṛṣṇa through various games and ceremonies such as a real south Indian child would play and go through' (*VB* 406). Friedhelm Hardy, from whose *Viraha-Bhakti* I derive this information, styled this section the *Bālacarita*. It contains folk-songs which, Hardy observes, afterwards came to form part of the genre styled *piḷḷaitamiḻ*, 'songs accompanying the games, etc., of children' (*VB* 406),'depicting the child-life of a hero or god' (Zvelebil 1974, p. 102). In one of the ten stages which constitute this genre, the mother, Yaśodā, calls the moon to play with the child, Kṛṣṇa.[1] 'Whence,' Hardy asks, 'did Periyāḻvār derive the inspiration for his *Bālacarita*?' This scholar points to the *Harivaṃśa* (60.15), in which, just as in one of the Āḻvār's songs (III.5), Kṛṣṇa is said to eat a 'lake of curds' with a 'whirlpool of ghee'/'marsh of ghee', and Hardy concludes 'that in the two common *rūpaka*s we can safely assume direct literary dependence' (VB 407).[2] How 'safe' is it, we may ask, to assume literary dependence on the basis of only two interconnected, and rather obvious metaphors (*rūpaka*): 'a lake of curd' and 'a whirlpool/marsh of ghee'? Hardy continues,

> Northern cultural values have deeply influenced and transformed the Southern awareness. Yet this is only one aspect of Viṭṭucittaṉ's work. Much of Tamil culture has remained and in certain respects even developed further with him. [. . .] The mythical events are seen through the eyes of the mythical actors, particularly Yaśodā, and their literary treatment stylizes them in such a way (by using genres of folk-songs) that a real mother can identify herself with these emotions, and can sing the songs, for example when playing with her child. Again, many of the themes depicted (like the *ciṟṟil*}, the sand-houses) are typical of older Tamil poetry, just

[1] *Nālāyirativiyappirapantam*, book I (*Mutalāyiram*), *Periyāḻvār Tirumoḻi* I.5 (*VB* 406).

[2] *HV* 60.15cd: *dadhihrado ghṛtāvartaḥ payaḥkulyāsamākulaḥ* ||15||; *Periyāḻvār-Tirumoḻi* III.5.1: *cōṟṟu pparuppatamum tayir vāviyum neyy aḷaṟum aṭaṅka* (quoted from *VB* 407, n. 24).

as the connection of particular folk customs with mythical songs (which, we might say, are acted out in the custom), has been detected already in the *Kalittokai* and the *Āycciyarkuravai*. In language and idiom, Periyâlvār comes closer to ordinary people than any other Āḻvār. It is a difficult problem to find an overall explanation for the clear Northern influence on the one hand, and the closeness of our brahmin priest to the ordinary people and his deep roots in Tamil culture on the other hand. I shall not attempt an answer here. (*VB* 411f.)

I cannot try to solve this problem, first and foremost because I do not have access to the source material, Tamil literature. However, we may observe that the alleged influence from the north does not necessarily entail literary dependence; the arguments adduced by Hardy for such dependence are rather flimsy and they are not corroborated by our investigation into the origin of one of the themes of the *piḷḷaitamiḻ*, baby Kṛṣṇa's play with the moon.

As one might expect, the topic of Kṛṣṇa's play with the moon became connected with those currents in the bhakti movement that cultivated the emotions associated with motherhood, in emulation of Yaśodā, the *vātsalyabhāva*. These emotions were beautifully expressed in a poem ascribed to Sūrdās, and we may assume that by the sixteenth century this and similar songs were sung all over India. I present to you *Sabhā* 809 of the *Sūrsāgar* in the translation of Kenneth Bryant.

Again and again, Yaśodā coaxes:
'Come, Moon! Moon, my little one's calling you!
He's going to eat honey and fruit and nuts and sweets,
and he might give you some too!
He 'll play with you in his hand, and he won't
even drop you once;
Just come down and live in this bowl of water
I 've got here in my hand . . .'
She set the bowl upon the ground, and took him
and showed him the moon;
And Sūr's Lord laughed and dipped his two hands
again and again and again.[3]

If this topic originally hailed from the north, we could hope to find allusions to it in the early Sanskrit literature dealing with Kṛṣṇa's childhood;

[3]Bryant, 1978, pp. 170.
bāra-bāra jasumati suta bodhati, āu caṃda tohiṃ lāla bulāvai |
madhu-mevā-pakavāna-miṭhāī, āpuna khaihai, tohiṃ khavāvai |
hāthahiṃ para tohiṃ līn he khelai, naiku nahīṃ dharanī baiṭhāvai |
jala-bāsana kara lai ju uṭhavati, yāhī maiṃ tū tana dhari āvai |
jalapuṭa āni dharani para rākhyau, gahi ānyau vaha caṃda dikhāvai |
sūradāsa prabhu haṃsi musakyāne, bāra-bāra doū kara nāvaiṃ |.

the first text to investigate is the *Harivaṃśa.* However, neither here nor in the *Viṣṇupurāṇa* have I been able to find the topic. Bhāsa's *Bālacarita* does not mention it either and even the *Bhāgavatapurāṇa*, which is certainly inspired by the south Indian tradition, does not seem to contain this theme.

A well-known collection of Sanskrit devotional verses in honour of Kṛṣṇa is the one ascribed to the poet Līlāśuka Bilvamaṅgala, the title of which in the south Indian Mss. is *Kṛṣṇakarṇāmṛta*. The identity of its author, who probably was a south Indian and who might have lived in the fourteenth century, is problematic,[4] but an anthology named *Kṛṣṇakarṇāmṛta* was reportedly brought from south India to Bengal by Caitanya in *c.* AD 1510.[5] Neither in the south Indian nor in the Bengali recension of this anthology do we find a verse dealing with the topic at issue. However, in addition to the Bengali one there exist other north Indian anthologies that are attributed to Bilvamaṅgala. In Wilson's critical edition they are represented by his Mss. Y. About these Mss. Wilson remarks:

> The Y version (Northern mss.) shows that the KK (*Kṛṣṇakarṇāmṛta*) collection reached West India and Madhyadeśa and was popular there from c. 1400-1700 AD. From a descriptive point of view the Y version is not a version of the KK: except for Y50 mss. the mss. of the Y version do not arrange the verses into centuries; no Y version is named *Kṛṣṇakarṇāmṛta*; finally, about one half the verses in any Y ms. are not found in the mss. named KK and about one half the verses in the mss. named KK are not found in any Y ms.[6]

Among the half that is not found in Mss. titled *Kṛṣṇakarṇāmṛta* is a verse that refers to our topic in a slightly varied form. It is preserved in a Ms. kept in the Chandra Shum Shere collection of the Bodleian Library (d 843), titled *Śrīgopālabālastuti* by Bilvamaṅgala, in an India Office Ms. (d 564), titled *Sumaṅgalastotra* by Bilvamaṅgala, with a commentary called *Kṛṣṇakarṇāmṛtaṭīkā*, in a Ms. used for a Bengali edition of 1817,[7] and in four Mss. used in the so-called Assamese version edited by M. Neog; two of the latter Mss. are dated, namely, AD 1803 and 1837, all other Mss. are undated.[8] Wilson presents this verse among his *Additional Verses*:

[4] Wilson 1975, pp. 16ff.; Gonda 1977, p. 31.

[5] Wilson 1975, p. 4.

[6] Wilson 1975, p. 5.

[7] Given in S.K. De's edition of the *Kṛṣṇakarṇāmṛta.*

[8] See Wilson 1975, p. 439. The same author mentions (ibid., p. 315) a Ms. in the Scindia Oriental Institute (Ujjain) (no. 6523) as a source for this verse (his Y31), which seems to take the place of the Oxford and London Mss. (his Y13 and Y33) that are mentioned as sources on p. 439.

Kṛṣṇa who, seeing the moon reflected in the waters of a pot, dipped his fingers into it to taste, thinking it was fresh butter: bewildered he was, when he found none; may he protect us.[9]

It would seem that in this Sanskrit version the original character of the topic as reported in the Tamil tradition and preserved in Sūrdās' poem, namely, that of a lullaby in which the moon is the object of Kṛṣṇa's fancy, has been assimilated to the famous theme of Kṛṣṇa's appetite for butter, for which he takes the moon's reflection by mistake.

Wilson reports that around Ujjain Bilvamaṅgala is identified with Sūrdās,[10] and though this may be just a local tradition, it may indicate the affinity that was sensed between this Sanskrit anthology and the *Sūrsāgar* tradition. Both verses, the Sanskrit and the Braj, may have come into existence independently at about the same period, articulating the popularity of the topic in circles of Kṛṣṇa bhaktas of the fifteenth and sixteenth century.

With respect to the origin of the topic, the verse ascribed to Bilvamaṅgala adds little to the testimony of the *Sūrsāgar*. We must conclude that our literary survey has not yielded any evidence that the topic of Kṛṣṇa's play with the moon was known in northern India before the fifteenth century.

We could leave it at that were it not that Indian archaeology has its own story to tell. For that reason I take you to a village called Paunar on the right bank of the river Dham, 70 km south-west of Nagpur in Maharashtra. It has several mounds testifying to a long-standing occupation of the site. Excavations were carried out in 1967 under the supervision of S.B. Deo of the Department of Ancient Indian History, Culture and Archaeology of the University of Nagpur. Among other things this excavation brought to light that Paunar enjoyed its days of prosperity during the Vākāṭaka period, i.e. fifth century AD, and consecutive period, the first quarter of the sixth century, when the Viṣṇukuṇḍins held sway over this area.[11]

The major findings in Paunar, however, did not emerge from the excavation, but were recovered during the building of the Paramadhāma Āśrama of Vinoba Bhave on the left (northern) bank of the Dham.The sculptures and panels found 'while digging in the fields round Śrī Vinōbājī's *āśrama*' are preserved in the Ashram.[12] They attest to the existence of

[9] *ghaṭodakeṣu pratimāśaśāṅkaṃ vilokya kṛṣṇo navanītabuddhyā | ādātum antar nihitāgrahastaḥ pāyāt tadaprāptisamākulo naḥ* || (Wilson 1975, p. 227).

[10] Wilson 1975, p. 6.

[11] Bakker 1997, pp. 89ff.

[12] *CII*, V, 1x.

several sanctuaries on the bank of the river, among which at least one large Viṣṇu temple. From the beginning, however, there has been controversy over their iconography and date. Mirashi, who was the first to give a systematic interpretation of the panels, thought they depict scenes of the *Rāmāyaṇa*.[13] This view has proved to be untenable and it is now generally believed that the majority of the panels (if not all) represent *līlā* scenes of Kṛṣṇa and his associates, for instance: 'Kaṃsavadha' (Plate I),[14] and 'Dhenukāsuravadha' (Plate II).[15]

Considerations of style would suggest that many of the findings preserved in the Ashram, including the panels, do not belong to the Vākāṭakas, but may date from a somewhat later period. Walter Spink ascribes them to 'a period (*c.* AD 500) of Viṣṇukuṇḍin rule over Vidarbha'.[16] The Viṣṇukuṇḍins, whose homeland was the Guntur district (A.P.) and the region to the north of the Śrīśaila Hills (the present Mahbubnagar district, A.P.), became, when their kingdom began to emerge at the end of the fourth century, heirs to the artistic tradition of Amarāvatī and Nāgārjunakoṇḍa (third century AD), the sculptural style of which may be characterized as 'lithe and slender'.[17] It is this legacy that we may recognize in the slender, natural but sensuous figures of Paunar; it may account for the stylistic undercurrent that is responsible for the 'south-Indian flavour' that art-historians savour when they examine these sculptures.

One of the panels (Plate III) was interpreted by Mirashi (1954, p. 4) as 'the birth of Rāma. The prominent male figure is Daśaratha who has taken the baby in his hands and is looking affectionately at him.' Joanna Williams (1983, p. 229) surmises that it 'may represent Vasudeva

[13] Mirashi 1954.

[14] The story covers Kṛṣṇa disposing of an elephant, named Kuvalayāpīḍa, Kṛṣṇa and Balarāma entering the arena and killing the wrestlers Cāṇūra and Muṣṭika, and finally Kṛṣṇa dragging Kaṃsa by holding his hair.

[15] Balarāma hurling the ass-demon Dhenuka on to a palmyra tree, from which he falls down, his back broken and, dying, transmutes into his anthropomorphic demon form (Bakker 1997, pp. 157f.).

[16] Spink 1981, p. 123 n. 8.

[17] 'The sculptural style at Nāgārjunakoṇḍa, like that at Amarāvatī, is known from the carved stone slabs that were part of the veneer of the major *stūpas*, as well as from free-standing images. By and large, the Nāgārjunakoṇḍa carvings are closely tied to the latest sculptures from Amarāvatī in style as well as range of subjects. If anything, the compositions of the reliefs are often more animated, the figures more *lithe and slender*, and the spatial arrangements more sophisticated'. (Huntington 1985, p. 180)

transporting the baby to Gokul'. Yet another identification has been proposed by Chandrashekhar Gupta, who describes the panel as follows:

The main figure standing in the centre facing right (head mutilated) is shown carrying a child. Two persons are standing on his either [*sic*] side and a female attendant is seated in the *Garuḍakrama* posture, holding an oval object in her hands in the lower right corner. One of the male figures is an attendant holding the staff of an umbrella and the other is some elderly person in the *varadamudrā*. The scene is described [by Mirashi] as Daśaratha receiving Rāma, brought to him by the female attendant, after the birth. The child does not appear to be a newly born one. On the other hand he looks like a 2-3 years old boy. It can be identified with the story of Kṛishṇa's obstinacy for getting the moon. The oval object in the hands of the female attendant can be identified as a mirror or a pot filled with water to reflect the image of the moon to satisfy Kṛishṇa. (Gupta 1992, pp. 146f.)

Though I find it difficult to assess the precise age of the boy held by the main male figure, I think Gupta's identification of the panel is the correct one. At variance with Sūrdās' description, the infant Kṛṣṇa in the Paunar relief is held by Nanda, while Yaśodā kneels in front of him to hold the mirror. The two male bystanders in the background may be inhabitants of Gokula.

Combined with the evidence of our literary survey the Paunar panel thus seems to endorse our hypothesis that the topic of Kṛṣṇa's play with the moon originated in south India. The south Indian Viṣṇukuṇḍins brought it with them when their influence spread over Maharashtra during the last phase of Vākāṭaka rule, when Pṛthivīṣeṇa II was king of Vidarbha. In order to defend his kingdom against the Nalas of the Bastar region (M.P.), the latter king had probably summoned the assistance of his son-in-law, the Viṣṇukuṇḍin king Mādhavavarman II Janāśraya in the last decade of the fifth century. As I have argued in my *The Vākāṭakas: An Essay in Hindu Iconology* (Bakker 1997, pp. 55-7) the Viṣṇukuṇḍins succeeded the Vākāṭakas after the collapse of the Vākāṭaka kingdom. Mādhavavarman II declared himself emperor (*sārvabhauma*) in his Khanapur Plates which were found in the Satara district of Maharashtra.[18] In the inscriptions of his descendants Mādhavavarman II's kingdom is said to have adjoined the waters of the Revā, i.e. the Narmada river.[19]

In conclusion it may be said that the materials that we have been able to survey all point to south India as the cradle, to use this apposite

[18] *EI* XXVII, 316 1.3

[19] *JIH* 43 (1965), 734 II, pp. 8-9, *revāsaritsalilavalayavibhūṣaṇāyā bhuvo bhartur mahārājaśrīmādhava-varmaṇaḥ.*

metaphor, of the topic of Kṛṣṇa's play with the moon. Of course it is very well possible that we have missed an early Sanskrit passage containing this topic. Moreover, further research is needed of the ancient Tamil tradition of folk-songs or lullabies from which Periyāḻvār may have derived his inspiration. If our interpretation of the Paunar panel is correct, such a song must already have been around in the fifth century AD.

ABBREVIATIONS

CII *Corpus Inscriptionum Indicarum*
EI *Epigraphia Indica*
HV *Harivaṃśa*
JIH *Journal of Indian History*
VB *Viraha-Bhakti* see Hardy 1983

REFERENCES

Bakker, Hans T., *The Vākāṭakas: An Essay in Hindu Iconology*, Gonda Indological Studies 5, Groningen, 1997.

Bryant, Kenneth E., Poems of the Child-God. Structures and Strategies in the Poetry of Sūrdās, Berkeley/Los Angeles/London, 1978.

Corpus Inscriptionum Indicarum, vol. V: *Inscriptions of the Vākāṭakas*, edited by Vasudev Vishnu Mirashi, Ootacamund, 1963 [= *CII* V].

Gonda, Jan, *Medieval Religious Literature in Sanskrit*. A History of Indian Literature II.1, Wiesbaden, 1977.

Gupta, Chandrashekhar, 'Paunar under the Vākāṭakas', in A.M. Shastri (ed.), *The Age of the Vākāṭakas*, New Delhi, 1992, pp. 119-53.

Hardy, Friedhelm, *Viraha-Bhakti. The early history of Kṛṣṇa devotion in South India*, Delhi, 1983.

Harivaṃśa, The Harivaṃśa being the Khila or supplement to the Mahābhārata. For the first time critically edited by P.L. Vaidya, Poona, 1969-71, 2 vols.

Huntington, Susan L., *The Art of Ancient India. Buddhist, Hindu, Jain.* With Contributions by John C. Huntington, New York, Tokyo, 1985.

Kṛṣṇakarṇāmṛta, edited by S.K. De., Dacca: University of Dacca, Oriental Publication Series No. 5, 1938.

———, Bilvamaṅgala's *Kṛṣṇa-Stotra,* edited by Maheshwar Neog, Gauhati, 1962.

———, See Wilson 1975.

Mirashi, Vasudev Vishnu, 'Pravarapura, an ancient capital of the Vākāṭakas', in *Sarūpa Bhāratī* or the Homage of Indology being Dr Lakshman Sarup Memorial Volume, Hosiarpur, 1954, pp. 1-9 [rpt. in *Studies in Indology* II, pp. 272-82].

Spink, Walter M., 'Ajanta's Chronology: Politics and Patronage', in J.G. Williams (ed.), *Kalādarśana*, Leiden: American Studies in the Art of India, 1981, pp. 109-26.

Sūrdās, *Sūrsāgar*, edited by Nandadulāre Vājpeyī, Kashi, vs 2033-5 [AD 1976-8] (5th printing).

Williams, Joanna Gottfried, 'Vākāṭaka Art and the Gupta Mainstream', in B.L. Smith (ed.), *Essays on Gupta Culture*, Delhi, 1983, pp. 215-33.

Wilson, Frances, *The Love of Krishna. The* Kṛṣṇakarṇāmṛta *of Līlāśuka Bilvamaṅgala.* Edited with an Introduction [and Translation], Haney Foundation Series 14, Philadelphia, 1975.

Zvelebil, K.V., *Tamil Literature.* A History of Indian Literature X.1, Wiesbaden, 1974.

Plate I: Kaṃsavadha (Paunar).

Plate II: 'Dhenukāsuravadha' (Paunar).

Plate III: Little Kṛṣṇa's play with the Moon (Paunar).

Uneasy Partners
Balarāma as Embodiment of Wilderness

A. WHITNEY SANFORD

INTRODUCTION

Most people see Balarāma, Kṛṣṇa's often eclipsed elder brother, in association with Kṛṣṇa or as somehow aiding him. What remains unclear is why Kṛṣṇa needs a foil and what aspects of Balarāma's character necessitate his relegation to subordinate. Devotees of Balarāma, particularly those at the Daujī (elder brother) Temple, elevate him to a position of centrality, a practice which contradicts textual accounts and challenges assessments of Balarāma as mere foil to Kṛṣṇa. Balarāma's associations with Nāgas (semi-divine serpent-like beings), for example, his irascibility, fondness for drink and connections to water, agriculture, and fertility, in relation to Kṛṣṇa's pastoral image have determined both Balarāma's elevation and subordination. The structure of this relationship has enabled Kṛṣṇa's persona as it is popularly known. This pattern is not only replicated in sectarian Vaiṣṇavism, but also in Jainism and Buddhism, for example, the relationship between Kṛṣṇa and Balarāma-*Nāga* recapitulates Buddhism's subordination and incorporation of the Nāgas.[1] The Jaina Purāṇas reinterpret the Vaiṣṇava account of the relationship of Balarāma and Kṛṣṇa to support the Jaina hierarchy.[2] I will examine the historical construction of the subordinate deity Balarāma and his relation to the dominant deity Kṛṣṇa of Braj in terms of what this has to tell us about the larger issue of complementary pairings and maintenance of subordinate traditions within dominant ones in the Indian culture.

The qualities of Balarāma have historically been conflated with those of the Nāga cults which have been active in the Braj region since at least the fourth century BC. The precise nature and cause of Balarāma's

[1] J. Ph. Vogel, *Indian Serpent Lore*, New Delhi: Asian Educational Services, 1995, p. 2.

[2] S. Jaini Padmanabh, 'Jaina Purāṇas: A Purāṇic Counter', in Wendy Doniger (ed.), *Purāṇa Perennis*, Albany: State University of New York Press, 1993, p. 230.

identification with the Nāga cults is at present unclear, although one can quickly see some obvious (and perhaps misleading) connections, such as Balarāma's fondness for liquor and his connections to fertility and water. Clarifying this conflation would not only explain the persistence of the Nāga tradition as it manifests in sectarian Vaiṣṇavism, Jainism and Buddhism, but also help to explain how Balarāma's Nāga associations render him appropriate as Kṛṣṇa's foil and essential for Kṛṣṇa devotion.

In the centuries after the growth of devotional Vaiṣṇavism in the sixteenth century, Balarāma emerged within sectarian Vaiṣṇavism as Kṛṣṇa's supporter. Empirical evidence of Balarāma's continued Nāga associations in relation to the theme of hierarchical subordination is provided by sectarian groups who see their leaders in these same terms of Kṛṣṇa and Balarāma. In the Vallabha Sampradāya (one of the two major doctrinal communities within Vaiṣṇavism), Balarāma is identified with Gopīnātha, Viṭṭhalanātha's eclipsed elder brother.[3] In the Gauḍīya Vaiṣṇava tradition, Balarāma is regressively understood through Nityānanda, Caitanya's disciple who is assigned the role of Caitanya's elder brother and the incarnation of Balarāma.[4] In both sectarian traditions, the subordinate as Balarāma mediates crises of authority, a narrative strategy which allows the leader as Kṛṣṇa to operate free of contention. In both groups, Balarāma emerges as a central figure through his relation to Kṛṣṇa, yet the two groups have radically different forms of organization. While the Vallabha Sampradāya has a centralized organization built around Vallabha and his descendants, Gauḍīya Vaiṣṇavism has no such central authority. Balarāma's complementary role in these sects suggests that his Nāga-related qualities provide a necessary structural completion, thus insuring their survival.

This paper investigates the Nāga (and related) themes within the poetic corpus of Paramānand (a sixteenth-century poet-singer traditionally considered to be one of the *aṣṭachāp*) which are expressed and maintained by Balarāma. Significantly this paper explores the (continued) relationship between Balarāma and his cultic origins and the poetic structures which mediate these origins. Balarāma's function within the Braj tradition suggests a pattern in which local traditions continually reassert themselves within a larger tradition. This pattern of re-assertion seems not only to exist within the dominant strain of Kṛṣṇa bhakti, but also to enable its very

[3] Richard Barz, *The Bhakti Sect of Vallabhācārya*, Faridabad: Thomson Press (India) Limited, 1976, pp. 38, 222.

[4] S.K. De, *Early History of the Vaishnava Faith and Movement in Bengal from Sanskrit and Bengali Sources*, Calcutta: K.L. Mukhopadhyaya, 1961 (2nd edn.), pp. 78, 565.

existence. Vaudeville, for example, has aptly documented Balarāma's relationship to his Nāga heritage and his connections to agriculture and fertility as Saṃkarṣaṇa and Halayudha (the one with the plough).[5]

Sāgar 64 Rāga-bilāval

नंद घर आए गरग मुनि ग्यानि।
राम कृष्ण कौ नाम करन हित जदु कुल के सनमानी।
गजमोतिनि के चौक पुराए नाम करन विधि ठानी।
मंगल गीत गबावति जसुदा बोलति अमृत बानी।
प्रथमै सुनहु बडे ढोटा के नाम राम बलदेव।
अब कहौं नाम तुम्हारे सुत के सुनो चित्त दै नंद।
कृष्ण नाम नाराइन कसौ औ हरि परमानंद।
पद्मनाभ माधौ मधुसूदन वासुदेन भगवान।
और अनंत नाम हैं इनके कहौं कहाँ लौं आन।
नंद सुवन त्रिभुवन के ठाकुर तिनके नाम धराए।
परमानँद प्रभु अखिल लोकपति गोप भेष धरि आए।

The learned sage Garga has come to Nanda's house.
For the name ceremony of Rāma-Krṣṇa, the honored ones of the Yadu family.
The 'elephant-pearl' *chauk* is done; the Brahmans begin the ceremony.
Yaśodā has auspicious songs sung and speaks sweet words.
Listen first to the name of the elder son: Rāma, Baladeva.
Haladhar and Saṃkarṣaṇa; no one knows these secret names.
Now, I say the name of your son; listen, Nanda pay attention.
The Krṣṇa, Narāyaṇa, Keśava and Hari, Paramānand.
Padmanābha, Mādhava, Madhusūdan, Vāsudeva, Bhagavān.
These endless names: how could anyone know all of them?
The Ṭhākura of the three-worlds, yet, in Nanda's house, he holds these names.
Paramānand says, the lord of all the worlds has come in the guise of a *gopa*.

BALARĀMA: DEVELOPMENT AND SECTARIAN ROLE

Balarāma first appears in the *Arthaśāstra* and continues to appear in post-sixteenth century sectarian developments. The *Bhāgavata Purāṇa* situates Balarāma in his connection to the following: (1) the Pañcarātra Bhāgavata doctrine of Saṃkarṣaṇa (another name of Balarāma) as *vyūha* (emanation);

[5] The epithet *lāṃgūlīn,* meaning 'furnished with a plough' also appears in the *Mahābhārata* and the *Purāṇas.* The word also means penis, suggesting the [raw] sexuality associated with Balarāma. Charlotte Vaudeville, 'The Lord of Govardhan Hill', in Gunther Sontheimer and Hermann Kulke (eds.), *Hinduism Reconsidered*, New Delhi: Manohar, 1991, p. 112.

(2) the Brahminical doctrine of Balarāma as the *avatāra* (incarnation) of Śeṣanāga, the serpent upon which Viṣṇu rests; (3) Balarāma as heroic *vīra* of the Vṛṣṇis; and (4) Balarāma as brother and play-mate of Kṛṣṇa-Gopāla. In the following centuries, this representation of Balarāma spreads from the south to the north with the ecstatic Kṛṣṇa bhakti influenced by the Āḻvār saints, although north Indian devotion develops independently of that in the south.

In the sixteenth century this pastoral Kṛṣṇa-Gopāla Vaiṣṇavism flourished in the Braj region, particularly among urban elite newcomers, and incorporated local Braj traditions. 'Pastoralization' (ironically an urban phenomenon), more adequately describes the dialectic between elite and folk cultures than Sanskritization or Brahminization.[6] (Despite the obvious parallels to German Romanticism, Braj pastoralization encompasses a different set of conflicts.) This urban elite imposed an idealized notion of nature upon a non-cooperative reality, setting up privileged hierarchies between urban and rural, sophisticate and rustic. This process, I argue, seems to have concentrated in Balarāma those elements which do not easily fit into the pastoral mode, and his persona seems to reflect the disparity between human experience and the pastoral construct. Conveniently Balarāma's earthy image frees Kṛṣṇa to exist in that pastoral ideal in which nature never presents danger, and erotic dalliances have no unwanted consequences. It is Balarāma who seems to provide balance and a vent for forces not reconcilable to Kṛṣṇa. Or so it seems to me at this point. It will take further study to develop or reconfigure this point.

Although Sanskritic and other Brahminic sources inform much of Braj bhakti, local pre- and non-Aryan influences, such as the Nāga and Yakṣa influences, are incorporated into Brahminical Vaiṣṇavism, a historical process possibly beginning as early as the Kuṣaṇa period (first century AD).[7] In the period prior to the sixteenth century, Śiva, Balarāma, Yakṣas and forms of the Goddess were important deities, and Nāga worship and wandering ascetics had greater influence on local peasants than did Vaiṣṇava orthodoxy.[8] Vaiṣṇava worship focused on four-armed

[6] Alan Entwistle, 'The Cult of Krishna-Gopāl as a Version of Pastoral', in Diana Eck and Françoise Mallison (eds.), *Devotion Divine. Bhakti Traditions from the Regions of India*, Studies in Honour of Charlotte Vaudeville, Groningen: Egbert Forsten, 1991, p. 88.

[7] N.P. Joshi, *Iconography of Balarāma*, New Delhi: Abhinav, 1979, p. 18; Alan W. Entwistle, *Braj, Centre of Krishna Pilgrimage*, Groningen: Egbert Forsten, 1987, p. 118.

[8] Entwistle, *Braj*, p. 136.

representations of Viṣṇu/Vāsudeva resting upon the serpent Śeṣa rather than the two-armed images of Kṛṣṇa seen later.[9]

Balarāma's association with the Nāga cult is well-represented in text and practice by his irascible temper, fondness of drink and palmyra leaf emblem—all Nāga traits. Like Nāgas, Balarāma is closely associated with fertility and agriculture and is usually depicted carrying a *mūsala* (pestle) and a *hala* (plough).[10] Popular iconography depicts Balarāma right hand up-raised, *madirā* (wine) in the left and frequently with a hooded Nāga canopy.[11] Local ritual practices suggest a strong identification between Nāgas and Balarāma, e.g. Braj folk songs link Balarāma and the healing of snakebites.[12] Balarāma is portrayed as the consummate master of all that is rustic and uncultured.

Though the pastoralization process radically transformed Braj devotion, Balarāma retains many of his pre-Vaiṣṇava associations. While Kṛṣṇa largely reflects the concerns of an urban elite, e.g. the Bengali and south Indian presence of the sixteenth century in Braj, Balarāma maintains his archaic Nāga associations and reflects the concerns of a rural and agrarian populace. Balarāma's habits such as drinking and wrestling render him the embodiment of aggression and sexuality. With his plough, he forcefully relocates the river Yamuna, an act which appears somewhat antithetical to pastoral representations of Braj. (Though such terms might automatically invoke Freud, they do not necessitate a Freudian analysis.) Balarāma mediates the Nāga affinity for wine, a multivalent symbol in sectarian concerns. Saṃkarṣaṇa, the second of the Pañcavyūha, represents the inebriation, or self-delusion, similar to the role of Yogamāyā, a role necessary for creation to unfold from divinity.[13] The Pañcarātra depicts the vyūha Saṃkarṣaṇa to be the *tāmasik* form of Viṣṇu (Kāla, or the destroyer), an essential component of the cycle of existence. Balarāma's association with intoxication is also expressed through Nityānanda and embodied by the Chaubes of Mathura.[14]

[9] Vaudeville, 'Lord of Govardhan Hill', pp. 113-14.

[10] Entwistle, *Braj*, p. 121.

[11] Vaudeville, 'Lord of Govardhan Hill', p. 113.

[12] Entwistle, *Braj*, p. 288.

[13] Dennis Hudson, 'Vāsudeva Kṛṣṇa in Theology and Architecture: A Background in Śrīvaiṣṇavism', *Journal of Vaiṣṇava Studies*, 2,1, Winter 1993, p. 151.

[14] Owen Lynch, 'The Mastrām: Emotion and Person Among Mathura's Chaubes', in Owen Lynch (ed.), *Divine Passions*, Delhi: Oxford University Press, 1990, pp. 91-115.

In the centuries after the devotional Vaiṣṇava explosion of the sixteenth century, Balarāma while retaining his Nāga associations — emerges within sectarian Vaiṣṇavism still in the role of foil. In the Vallabha Sampradāya, Balarāma is identified with Gopīnātha, Viṭṭhalanātha's eclipsed elder brother.[15] In the Gauḍīya Vaiṣṇava tradition, Balarāma is regressively understood through Nityānanda, Caitanya's disciple who is assigned the role of Caitanya's elder brother and incarnation of Balarāma.[16] The Caitanya/Nityānanda and Viṭṭhalanātha/Gopīnātha pairs function analogously to Kṛṣṇa/Balarāma; in both sectarian traditions, the latter's persona mediates crises of authority and identity, a narrative strategy which allows the former to operate free of contention. Empirical evidence of Balarāma's continued Nāga associations is provided by these sectarian groups who see their leaders in these same terms of Kṛṣṇa and Balarāma. Nityānanda corresponds to Caitanya as Balarāma to Kṛṣṇa in the Bengali tradition which has no central authority; at the same time, Gopīnātha is central to the Vallabha Sampradāya, a group which has a radically different authority structure. Even in such different groups, Balarāma emerges as a central figure through his relation to Kṛṣṇa.

Further, the Vaiṣṇava tradition has used the Nāga traits of Balarāma, e.g. association with liquor and aggression, to enunciate sectarian tensions, such as conflicts of authority. In the Vallabha Sampradāya, Balarāma is identified with Gopīnātha, Vallabha's elder son and Viṭṭhalanātha is considered an *avatāra* of Kṛṣṇa. Śrīnāthjī commanded Vallabha to marry and have children so that he might incarnate himself as Vallabha's son. Both sons were able to pass on the Brahmasambandha mantra, yet Gopīnātha's line ended with the sudden (and ambiguous) death of his only son Puruṣottama. The subsequent identification of the brothers as Balarāma and Kṛṣṇa reflects conflicts with the Puṣṭimārga about sectarian leadership. Gopīnātha is accused of favouring the *maryādā* over the path of puṣṭi, and Puruṣottama was involved in both the expulsion of the Bengalis and the barring of Viṭṭhalanātha from *darśana* of Śrīnāthjī for six months.[17]

In Bengal, Nityānanda's activities, when understood as those of Balarāma, exemplify these patterns, and he plays off of these and other

[15] Barz, op. cit., pp. 38, 222.
[16] De, op. cit., pp. 78, 565.
[17] Barz, op. cit., 1976, p. 38.

facets of Balarāma's personality.[18] By Caitanya's command, Nityānanda spread the doctrine to and is noted for 'converting' the Tāntrikas.[19] In his proselytizing, he consorted with prostitutes, drunkards and others of dubious character, activities normally considered outside Brahminical standards; yet these acts could be accommodated, if not sanctioned, by Nityānanda's association with Balarāma. Balarāma's power of greatness (*bala*) renders appropriate these actions as examples of saintly 'morality beyond morality'.[20]

THE PASTORAL AND THE NATURAL

A common theme in Braj bhakti is the unfavourable comparison between the sophistication of the city with the rusticity and simplicity of rural life, a theme that Alan Entwistle noted in his discussion of Braj as a version of the pastoral.[21] Typically this genre includes an emphasis on the beauty of nature, music and affairs with simple girls.[22] The pastoral genre constructs the rural as a haven — both physical and emotional — from society. Nature and human passions are always tempered; no danger lurks in the pastoral construct. As a form of pastoral, Braj Vaiṣṇavism 'sweetens' the *līlā*. Paramānand's *pada*s depict a delightful sylvan paradise in which Kṛṣṇa sports with the gopīs, enjoying a life free from the complexities of society and the city.

> The lovely *kusuma* flower, a languorous breeze scented with sandalwood, the shade of the *kadamba* tree. (*Sāgar* 708)

The cooperation of nature and a beautiful landscape are some of the constitutive elements of Braj as pastoral. Forest animals and natural conditions are not only backdrops to Kṛṣṇa's pastimes but actively support these activities. Nature, rather than a force to be reckoned with, enhances the passion of Kṛṣṇa and the gopīs. The following *pada*s illustrate nature's fascination with Kṛṣṇa.

[18] Within Gauḍīya Vaiṣṇavism, Nityānanda's identification with Balarāma remains central but is used for different purposes by those of Advaita's and Nityānanda's lineage.

[19] De, op. cit., p. 447; Edward C. Dimock, *The Place of the Hidden Moon,* Chicago: University of Chicago Press, 1989, pp. 91-5.

[20] John S. Hawley, 'Morality Beyond Morality in the Lives of Three Hindu Saints', in John S. Hawley (ed.), *Saints and Virtues*, Berkeley: University of California Press, 1987, pp. 55-9.

[21] Entwistle, *Braj*, pp. 96-101. 'The Cult of Kṛṣṇa-Gopāl', p. 78.

[22] Entwistle, 'The Cult of Kṛṣṇa-Gopāl', pp. 74-5.

Sāgar 344 Rāga-āsāvarī

गावै गावै घनस्याम कान्ह जमुना के तीरा।
नाचत नट भेषु धरें मंडली अभीरा।
लोल नैन चारु बैन अधर धरें बैना।
आवर्त्त कमलनयन की छबि मंडित कच रैना।
जल कि गति मंद भई-सुरभी तृन लीना।
बछरा नहिं छीर पिवत नादहिं मन दीना।
मोहे मृग पंछी द्रुम मधुकर मुनि ज्ञानी।
परमानँद प्रभु गोपाल लीला बन ठानी।

Rāga-āsāvarī

Ghanaśyām Kānha sings and sings on the banks of the Yamuna.
He poses like a dancer and dances in a circle of Abhīrās.
Sweet eyes, beautiful voice, his lower lip holds the flute.
They circumambulate the beauty of the one with lotus-eyes,
his body smeared with dust.
The flow of water slows, the grass remains [unchewed] in the cows' mouths.
The calves won't drink milk, helpless at the sound.
Deer, birds, trees, bees, sages and jñānīs: all are captivated.
Paramānand's lord Gopāl performs his *līlā* in the forest. (*Sāgar* 344)

Sāgar 347 Rāga-sārang

जब कर बेनु गहत।
पासंग ही पूजत नहिं जासों ऽब ब्रह्मानंद कहत।
खग मृग चित्त लिखे से ठाढे बदनु चहत।
सुनि धुनि धेनु ठगी दंतानि क्षिनु मौन रहत।
रोम हरष तरुवर मधु बरषत जलु न बहत।
परमानंद धन्य ब्रजवासी सुखु जे लहत।

Rāga-sārang

When he takes his flute in his hands.
There is no equal to his worship; now the Brahmānanda speaks.[23]
Birds and deer stand with this tableau watching his face.
The white cow hearing his voice, remains silent, straw in her teeth.
Hair standing on end; the tree rains honey, and the water does not flow.
Paramānand, blessed are the Brajavāsīs who take pleasure [in him]. (*Sāgar* 347)

[23] The word translated as equal is *pāsanga*, meaning the difference between two weights on a scale. The image is a balance-scale; there is no counterweight for Kṛṣṇa.

Sāgar 574 Rāga-sārang

बिहरत वृंदावन गोविंद।
गोप मंडली मध्य बिराजित स्याम मनोहर पूरन चंद।
बरुहापीड दाम गुंजामनि पीत कर्निका स्रवन बिराजनि।
लोचन लोल कपोल सुचिक्कन सुंदर बेनु मधुर धुनि गावनि।
नाचत गावत आनँद मूरति नटवत गति नाना रस रूप।
बरनत गोपी पावन लीला गोप भेष हरि त्रिभुवन भूप।
रटत पसु पंछी सुर बनिता अपनौ जन्म कृतारथ मानत।
परमानंद स्वामी सुख दाइक गोपी गोप सबै सचु पावत।

Rāga-sārang

Govind sports in Vṛndāvan.
He sits radiant amidst a circle of gopas, alluring Śyām,
the full moon [among the stars].
A peacock feather, a garland of *guñjāmani*, a golden earring adorns his ear.
Wandering eyes, smooth cheeks, his beautiful flute sings the sweet sounds of a song.
He sings and dances, the image of bliss, with the gait of an acrobat, many forms of *rasas*.
The gopīs speak of his pure *līlā*, Hari, the lord of the three-worlds, in the guise of a gopa.
Birds, animals, gods and women chant, accepting his appearance
as the fulfillment of their births.
Paramānand's lord, the giver of joy, gopīs and gopas all obtain the truth. (*Sāgar* 574)

Even the trees, once feared as the Yakṣis, now are considered bhaktas of Kṛṣṇa.[24] The interesting comparison here is between this 'glorification' of nature and the earlier Braj tradition that Vaudeville calls the 'worship of nature'. We see a contrast between a nice and tame nature and the nature that must be appeased and propitiated. This is similar to the conception of nature that one desires during a restive sojourn through a National Park compared to a trip into the back-country in which one deals with grizzlies that might eat you as an appetizer.

The crucial distinction articulated in this genre is the contrast of the simple and innocent pleasures of country life with the fast and loose pace of city life. Kṛṣṇa's choice of Braj over Vaikuntha reflects this contrast which is later portrayed in comparisons between Vṛndāvan and Mathura,

[24] Owen Lynch, 'Pilgrimage as Darśana', *Journal of Vaiṣṇava Studies*, 1, 4, Summer 1993, pp. 99-100. Lynch shows that the trees are just like the gopīs: perfect bhaktas. All thoughts and feelings are focused on Kṛṣṇa.

a distinction Jack Hawley discusses in relation to the Braj *līlās*.[25] Uddhava's debate in the *Bhramargīt* with Uddhava illustrates the latter contrast. Uddhava's sophisticated philosophical thought can not compare with the gopīs' simple devotion. *Padas* describe Kṛṣṇa's enjoyment of simple pleasures and his wooden flute, for example, in contrast to the courtly wealth that is his by birth. Qualities such as lack of guile, simplicity and steadfast devotion are esteemed over erudition and sophistication.[26] The Braj ethos stresses the rustic, yet this rusticity must be constructed with some sophistication. It is not the so-called 'natural' rusticity of peasants that is valued, but something that must be consciously constructed. Similarly this distinction is also relevant to bhaktas becoming 'female' in relation to Kṛṣṇa; a constructed femininity is valued over 'natural' femininity.

This rusticity is portrayed as 'natural,' but, that, too, is a social construct. The urbane and pastoral are delineated as a dichotomy, but, actually, the two are both expression of sophistication. One must be urbane and cultivated to participate in the pastoral as a rustic. The happy, cheerful peasant is a construct created as a foil for the urban sophisticate. This contrast, however, implies a third category: the rough 'natural' peasant with none of the social graces of the *rasika* rustic. This construct is the 'other' which collapses the pastoral urban/rural dichotomy into a singular category: *rasika*. This urbane vs. natural rustic also reinforces the male/culture and female/nature dichotomy. This ideal nature is constructed and encultured. It is important to remember that much of Braj bhakti was developed by elite urban Brahmins.

Owen Lynch's fieldwork with the Chaubes of Mathura illustrates this discussion of the 'constructed rustic'. Lynch discusses *mastrām* as a Braj ideal of personhood:

> without cant or servility, straight-forward, proud, independent, without care or concern (*lāparvāh*) for how others might see them. In short they are *mast*.

The Chaubes perceive of themselves as rustic and unhampered by the rules that inhibit life in the city. They idealize the mischievous boy Kṛṣṇa,

[25] Entwistle, 'The Cult of Kṛṣṇa-Gopāl', p. 79. A. Whitney Sanford, 'Teaching the Teacher: The Sakhī's Role in Paramānand's Kṛṣṇa Poems', *Journal of Vaiṣṇava Studies*, 1, 4, Summer 1993.

[26] In *At Play in Vrindavan*, Jack Hawley discusses the interaction between the simple rusticity of the rural and the urbane sophistication of the city and how this contrast is played out in the *līlās*.

though their fondness for wrestling and intoxication reveal Balarāma as a more appropriate exemplar for their behaviour.

According to Lynch, the *mastrām* is the folk version of the *rasika*. In traditional Indian aesthetics, the *rasika* (connoisseur of *rasa*) cultivates taste for the *rasa*s or emotional states, as one would art or fine wine through the arousal of *bhāva*, the personal and particular emotion. *Pada*s frequently depict Kṛṣṇa as the *rasika-rāja*, the highest *rasika* or as the jewel of the *rasika*s. Among the connoisseurs of emotion, he is the crown jewel, the *śiromaṇi* (*Sāgar* 1166). While Kṛṣṇa represents the constructed and pastoral ideal, Balarāma — as an ambivalent figure — manifests aspects of both the peasant and the rustic construct, but it is Balarāma's less-discussed anti-pastoral qualities that I will focus on.[27] Contrasting Balarāma and Kṛṣṇa's sexuality bears out this point: Although critics have called Kṛṣṇa wanton in reference to his erotic dalliances with the gopīs, Kṛṣṇa's sexuality fits into the pastoral mode; references to his sexuality are always nuanced and discreet, veiled in the guise of *rasa* and aesthetics. As the exemplar of the cultivated rustic, Kṛṣṇa reveals the softer edges of the refined rustic, while aspects of Balarāma illustrate the 'unconstructed' rustic. Balarāma's love of wine and his lust, for example, deviate from the pastoral, the urbane *rasika*, and represent those qualities which are less urbane and less benign. In Balarāma lurks those dangerous qualities and urges which are not constructed and sanitized by the Braj pastoral mood.

BALARĀMA'S NĀGA (AND CULTIC) HERITAGE

Both textual and iconographic evidence delineate Balarāma's ancient and cultic heritage. This ancient deity — (probably) older than Kṛṣṇa-Gopāl himself — is most often depicted holding a plough and pestle and thus is associated with agriculture. The oldest representation of this deity holds the plough in one hand, a goblet in the other, and rests upon a Nāga. Most representations of Balarāma depict him with the right hand in the *abhayamudrā* position over a Nāga canopy and *madirā* (a drink) in the left.[28] The serpent Ānanta/Śeṣa supports the earth, below the seven *pātāla*s where the Nāgas reside, and holds the pestle and plough that are considered attributes of Balarāma. Balarāma is also linked to Varuṇī, the goddess of

[27] Lynch, 'The Mastrām', pp. 99, 110.

[28] Vaudeville, 'The Cowherd God in Ancient India', p. 95, n. 6. Vaudeville cites V. Agarwal in claiming that this image is not later than the second century BC and predates any images of Kṛṣṇa-Govardhanadhara by at least several centuries. Also Vaudeville, 'The Lord of the Govardhan Hill', p. 113.

wine, who arose from the churning of the ocean. According to the *Viṣṇu Purāṇa*, Viṣṇu himself is incarnated as Śeṣanāga and lies below the seven *pātāla*s, supporting the world. Accompanying him are Varuṇī and Balarāma's familiar implements, the plough and the pestle. This suggests that these elements were present in the Vaiṣṇava tradition and were later grafted onto the cultic [Balarāma] deity who also had these characteristics.[29] This image presents an integrated view of those qualities associated with Balarāma: his affinity for wine and his association with Nāgas and agriculture. These Vaiṣṇava qualities have merged with the local and ancient Balarāma, and these qualities give those cultic forces a vehicle to reassert themselves.[30]

In Paramānand's *pada*s and in Vaiṣṇava bhakti, the incorporation of these Nāga cultic elements into the Vaiṣṇava tradition is such that the Nāga elements are not completely obliterated but appear subordinate to the dominant Kṛṣṇa tradition. The serpent protects Kṛṣṇa (or Viṣṇu) — just as Balarāma supports Kṛṣṇa in the Braj-līlā. At one time, worship of Balarāma surpassed that of Kṛṣṇa-Gopal which accounts in part for the preponderance of episodes and motifs which depict the superiority of Kṛṣṇa-Gopāl.[31]

[29] William Crooke, *The Popular Religion and Folklore of Northern India*, vol. II, Delhi: Munshiram Manoharlal, 1896, p. 125. One of the earliest literary mentions of the Kṛṣṇa-Gopāl myth appears in Kālīdāsa's *Meghadūta*. A yakṣa mentions 'a fair-skinned god who is fond of strong drink with his wife Revatī and also, dark as the rain-cloud, "Viṣṇu in the garb of a cowherd" adorned with peacock feathers', Vaudeville, 'The Cowherd God', p. 111.

[30] Vaudeville mentions a Braj tradition concerning a group called the Kalārs or Kalāvars who were once dominant in the Braj area. This group is reputed to be linked with the *Nāga* and *Yakṣa* cults and to be 'fond of strong liquor', Vaudeville, 'Braj, Lost and Found', *Indo-Iranian Journal*, 18, 3-4, 1976, p. 209. Such evidence suggests that there were appropriate local and cultic traditions upon which to integrate the Vaiṣṇava Balarāma.

[31] Vaudeville, 'The Cowherd God in North India,' p. 100. The cult of Kṛṣṇa-Gopāl was obscure in North India until the influx of Vaiṣṇava bhakti from the south. Vaudeville believes that the pastoral castes, the Abhīras, spread Kṛṣṇa-Gopāl worship throughout India, but claims that no evidence suggests that they were Vaiṣṇava or had any affiliations with the Brahmin cult of Viṣṇu-Nārāyaṇa or the teachings of the *Bhagavad-Gītā*. The Kṛṣṇa-Gopāl and Viṣṇu-Nārāyaṇa legends probably were first confused in the sixth-seventh century. Vaudeville, 'Cowherd God', pp. 104-6. Vaudeville also discusses the ancient Śaivite evidence in the Braj area and the connection of Śiva to the worship of trees and cattle. See also Sudhir Jaiswal, *The Origin and Development of Vaiṣṇavism*, Delhi: Munshiram

During Kṛṣṇa's escape from Mathura, Śeṣa shields Kṛṣṇa from the driving rain.

Sāgar 7 Rāga-sārang

भादौं की रायनि अँधियारी।
गरजत गगन दामिनी कोधंति गोकुल चले मुरारी।
सेस सहस फन बूँद निवारत सेत छत्र सिर तान्यों।
वसुदेव अंक मध्य जग दीवन कहा करैगौ पान्यों।
जमुना थाह भई तिहि औसर आवत जात न जान्यों।
आनँद भयो दास परमानँद देव मुनिन मन मान्यों।

It was a dark night of Bhādõ.
Thunder and lightning fill the sky. Kṛṣṇa is carried from Gokul.
Śeṣa's head spanned like a white umbrella; the hoods of his thousand heads repelled the drops.
The life of the world in Vasudeva's embrace. What could the water do?
Just there at that moment, the Yamuna stopped. Who knows why it rose and fell?
The servant Paramānand was in bliss. The gods and sages have accepted him in their hearts and minds. (*Sāgar* 7)

Frequently serpent Ānanta/Śeṣa sings the praises of Kṛṣṇa, an ubiquitous image of one tradition asserting dominance over another, yet even Śeṣa — with his thousand mouths — can not adequately praise Kṛṣṇa. Kṛṣṇa's infinitude of virtues are so great that they are beyond the serpent's ability to comprehend or speak.

Kīrtan 131 Rāga-sārang

देखी गोपाल की लीला ठाटी।
ब्रह्मा महादेव विस्मित भए जसोमति हाथ लिये रजु साटी।
ए सब बालक प्रगट कहत हैं स्याम मनोहर खाई माटी।
बदन उघारि आभ्यंतर देख्यो त्रिभुवन रूप वैराटी।
केसव के गुन वेद बखानत सेस सहस मुख लाई लाटी।
लख्यो न जाई अंत अंतरगति बुधि न प्रवेस कठिन घाटी।
जनमुकरमुगुनग्राम बखानत समुझि न परतगूढपरिपाटी।
ताके सरन गये भय नाही निसंदेह परमानंद डाटी।

Manoharlal, 1967, pp. 58-9; for a discussion of Saṃkarṣaṇa worship and its eventual subordination by the Nārāyaṇa-Viṣṇu cult, Vaudeville, 'Braj, Lost and Found', pp. 210-11.

Rāga-sārang

Look at the splendid play of Gopāl.
Brahmā and Mahādeva are amazed; Mother Yaśodā took a stick and rope in her hands.
Hey, the boys told her what happened; the enchanting Śyām ate dirt.
She lifted his face and looked in his mouth; the form of the expanded three worlds.
The Vedas narrate the qualities of Keśava; the 1,000 mouths of Śeṣa became exhausted.
All of these cannot even be written; knowledge cannot ascend this difficult pass.
The totality of his karma, qualities and birth are narrated; but the depths of this esoteric tradition cannot be comprehended.
Who takes refuge in him has no fear; he, Paramānand says, destroys doubt. (*Sāgar* 131)

Sāgar 550 Rāga-gaurī

सोभा सिंधु अनत रही री।
नंद भवन भरि उमडि सखी री।
ब्रज की बीथिनि फिरति बही री।
देखि जु आजु गई हुती सजनि बेचनी गोकुल माँझ दही री।
कहा कहि कहों सुनि चतुर सखी री।
कहत न मुख सहस हुँ न निबही री।
जसोमति उदर अगाध उदधि तें।
उपजी इन्है जु सबहीनि कही री।
परमानँद प्रभु इंद्रनीलमनि ब्रज जुवतिनि उर लागि रही री।

Rāga-gaurī

The ocean of beauty has no limits.
Filling the house of Nanda, it swells, oh *sakhī,*
it flows, running through the streets of Braj.
Oh look friend, today we went to Gokul to sell the curd.
What can we say, listen wise *sakhī*, the thousand mouths cannot say it all or stem the flow.
All speak of what was produced from the womb of Mother Yaśodā,
this fathomless ocean.
Paramānand's lord, the blue jewel of Indra,
the Braj women keep him in their hearts. (*Sāgar* 550)

Further Balarāma is conspicuously absent or has a reduced role in the *Kālīyadāmana* episode, a prime example of Vaiṣṇava domination over the Nāga-cult forces. Vaudeville shows that instead of killing the serpent-demon, Kṛṣṇa merely subdues him which could represent subjugation or accommodation. Meanwhile, Balarāma is absent or acts as an agent, as in the *Bhāgavata Purāṇa* version.[32]

Sāgar 259 Rāga-sārang

कोलाहल जमुना के तीर।
कालीनाग कहत हैं नाथ्यो संकरषन के बीर।
लागी पुकार सकल ब्रजबासी नंद जसोमति संग।
उछटत परत सीस कच छूटत रुदै बिरह के दुँद।
संकट जाइ भयो इक ठौरे हा हा सबद उचार।
परमानंददास कौ ठाकुर जीत्यों नंदकुमार।

[259] There is a great uproar on the banks of the Yamuna.
Kālīnāga speaks to the brother of lord Saṃkarṣaṇa.
Nanda and Yaśoda call all the residents of Braj together.
A head broke through the surface. The sucking sound is released, the pain of separation.
This place has become dangerous. Hey, these words were said.
Long live Nandakumār, the lord of Paramānand.

Although Balarāma's relationship with the Nāgas is the most prevalent of the cultic themes, the *pada*s also illustrate his relationship with the themes of mountain, cattle and agriculture. In Balarāma, the Nāga elements appear in a triad of inter-related concepts: Nāga, cattle and mountain. Closely related (and subordinate) to these themes are those of fertility and agriculture.[33] *Pada*s invoking the themes of nurturing the cows and the midday meal highlight Balarāma's connection to these motifs. Balarāma is frequently portrayed in the *pada*s as caring for the cows and meals.

[32] Vaudeville discusses the relationship between the Kālīyadāmana and Govardhanadharana episodes. Both are conspicuous in the absence of Balarāma and in both Kṛṣṇa reveals his cosmic form, suggesting his affiliation with Vasudeva as 'He who pervades all'. Further, both these episodes belong to the cowherd god legend of Braj. Vaudeville, 'The Govardhan Myth in Northern India', *Indo-Iranian Journal*, 22, 1980, pp. 10-11.

Norvin Hein discusses Kṛṣṇa's *coṭī* in the *līlā*s. He suggests that this motif 'with its obvious resemblance to a snake' represents Kṛṣṇa's besting of Kalinaga or the subjugation of some *naga* cult. Hein, *The Miracle Plays of Mathurā*, Delhi: Oxford University Press, 1972, p. 140.

[33] Vaudeville discusses the strong connection between snake- and cattle-worship and fertility rites. She also discusses the connections between Govardhana-*pūjā* and snake-worship. Vaudeville, 'The Govardhan Myth in Northern India', pp. 3-5.

Balarāma's epithets *Saṃkarṣaṇa* and *Haladhar*, 'the one holding the plough', invoke a connection to agriculture and suggest the connection of human fate to the uncontrollable forces of nature, weather and the earth.

Sāgar 263 Rāga-sārang

मैया गाँइ चरावन जैहौं।
तू कहे नंद महर बाबा सों बडौ भयो न डरैं हौं।
श्रीदामा आदि सखा सब अपने अरु दा[उ] संग लैहौं।
दह्यो भात कावरि भरि लैहों भूखें लागै खैहौं।
बंसीवट की सीतल छहियां खेलत अति सुख पैहों।
परमानंद तब साथ खेलहु जौ जमुना जल नैहों।

[263] Ma, I'm going to graze the cows.
Tell Nanda and mother: I'm big and I'm not afraid.
I'll go with Śrīdāmā and the other boys and with my big brother.
I've eaten my fill of full of curd, rice and kavri. I'll eat when I get hungry.
Playing under the cool shade of the banyan tree gives me such great joy.
Paramānand says, then they played together and bathed in the waters of the Yamuna.

This *pada* presents a relatively benign portrait of Balarāma and his connections with the plough and fertility, one appropriate to the Braj aesthetic.[34] Balarāma's implied relationship to agriculture and fertility is positive in this context. Other episodes, particularly Balarāma's post-Braj interaction with the Yamuna, also use the images of the plough, yet in a less benign context. Themes of sexuality and lust are re-contextualized to violate the Braj pastoral and the pervasive sweetness.

The following *pada* suggests the danger or malevolence that the *nāga* represents and illustrates the contextualization of danger.

Sāgar 1129 Rāga-sārang

बिरचि मन बहुरि न राचत आहि।
टूट्यो जुरै बहुत जतननि पे ऐंच्यो तउ न जाहि।
फाट्यौ दूध भयो जब कँजी कहा स्वाद दिखराइ।

[34] Balarāma's placement in these themes is, of course, also a result of the *sakhya bhāva*; it is in Kṛṣṇa's daily activities of eating and cow-herding that the *sakhya bhāva* is most evident. Balarāma as the chief of Kṛṣṇa's friends would necessarily be present in these activities. Yet, I do not think that the bhava explanation is sufficient, or perhaps these cultic affiliations and themes underlie Balarāma's presence with the *sakhya bhāva* and relative absence from the *vātsalya* and *mādhurya bhāva*s.

कपट कौ हेतु प्रीति ऐसी ज्यों बोथि चुकाई गाइ।
स्वाति बूँद जो परै फनग मुख अचवत बिष हूवै जाइ।
केरा पास जु बेरि लगाई छिनु परसि चिराइ।
ऊधौ हम हेत कियो हरि जल सों मीनहीं बूझौ जाइ।
परमानंद दिगंबरपुर में रजक कहा ब्यौसाइ।

Rāga-sārang

He [Hari]made our hearts, he won't again make them like that.
Once broken, even if mended with great effort, with one tug,
they won't hold.
When a plate of milk goes bad, how can the true taste be shown?
This love was founded on deceit, as the calf given
a small amount to taste.[35]
If a drop from *svāti* should fall into the mouth of a snake,
then the snake tastes it as poison.
If a soft plant is near a thorny bush, then every moment
they touch, it becomes torn.
Uddhava! We love Hari as a fish loves the water.
Paramānand, in a city of Digambaras,
what business is there for washerman? (*Sāgar* 1129)

This *pada* not only hints at the dangers of the serpent, but suggests the subjectivity of danger, the relative danger of forces depending on the recipient. The snake's wicked nature changes the rain drop from nectar to poison by virtue of his evil. The reference to the snake and poison invokes the *svāti* constellation which offers different gems depending on the recipient. While the *cātaka* tastes the raindrop as a pearl, the snake experiences it as venom. Thus, while Kṛṣṇa's passions are constructed through the *rasika* paradigm and support the pastoral, instead Balarāma as a Nāga represents uncontrolled erotic and aggressive urges. Fear of nature, the Nāga forces and fear of rampant passion are manifest in the *padas* through the context of Balarāma.

Other *padas* invoke Balarāma's identification with wine, lust and intoxication. Kṛṣṇa, too, is linked with sexuality and intoxication, but

[35] The more literal and precise translation of this line is something like '[his] love, intended to deceive, was like the small amount [of milk from the] cow fed [to the calf simply to get the milk flowing so it can be milked]'. The gopīs claim that Kṛṣṇa offered his love on the premise of deceit; he gave them a small amount to get the love flowing, but never intended to continue giving them this love. *Both(i)* which translates as 'unmeasured amount or rough estimate' is not easily defined and not to be found in Braj dictionaries. I am grateful to Alan Entwistle for his suggestion of Lala's Rajasthani dictionary.

these themes manifest differently in regard to Kṛṣṇa. While the motif of intoxication in regard to Kṛṣṇa upholds the pastoral or *rasika* construction, Balarāma's intoxication is more problematic. The gopīs are often drowning or intoxicated with love for Kṛṣṇa. They may lose their minds or their rational faculties, but the end result is a gain — a relationship with Kṛṣṇa. Further, Kṛṣṇa himself does not get intoxicated: he is the one who intoxicates. The following is an example of intoxication regarding Kṛṣṇa in the pastoral mode.

Sāgar 749 Rāga-sārang

तेरौ नाँऊ लैलै तू चलि भामिनि स्याम बोले।
वे बैठे देखौ वृंदावन की सोभा ठौर ठौर द्रुम फूले।
कोकिला नाद मन आनँद भवँर बिहंगम भूले।
नाना पच्छी सब्द रासि रचि सकल बेलि केसू फूले।
उनमद जोवन मद कोलाहल यहि औसर है नीकौ।
परमानंद स्वामी प्रथम समागम मिल्यो भाँवतौ जी कौ।

Rāga-sārang

Let's go woman, he sings your name again and again,
Śyām is calling.
See him seated [in] the beauty of Vrindavan,
everywhere the trees bloom.
The cuckoo's call creates bliss in the heart, the birds and bees have
lost their consciousness.
Different birds create a panoply of sounds, all the creepers and
red flowers are blooming.
Intoxicated with passion, the youths are exuberant,
this is a great situation.
The first union with Paramānand's lord pleased her heart.[36] (*Sāgar* 749)

Sāgar 827 Rāga-sārang

कहा फूली आवति है राधे।
मानहुँ मिले अंक भरि माधौ प्रगटित प्रेम अगाधे।
बार बार मुसिकाति बदन छबि बिकसित पदम जु आथे।
लोचन चारु बंक अवलोकिन काम नचावित ताधे।

[36]This last line has either skipped ahead into the resolution of the *māna* and portrays the union of the lovers or recalls the first meeting of the lovers and appeals to her nostalgia and desire to re-experience the good times. The latter reading seems to make more sense and is more likely. The word *samāgama* meaning union indicates sexual intercourse.

इहि रास मत्त फिरत मुनि मधुकर संभु रहत दिन साधे।
सोई रसु दियो दास परमानँद श्रीनिकेतन राधे।

Rāga-sārang

Rādhā, what makes you blossom?
I think that you met and embraced Madhava,
your unfathomable love is manifest.
Again and again, your beautiful face smiles, like a lotus half bloomed.
Your eyes are beautiful with a crooked glance;
desire makes you dance, 'tadhe.'
The *rasa* maddened sages wander like bees,
Śiva always practices meditation.
Dāsa Paramānand, that very *rasa* of the abode of Śrī,
[he] gave [to] Rādhā. (*Sāgar* 827)

Kṛṣṇa's erotic exploits support the pastoral theme; there is no suggestion of violation or danger. Kṛṣṇa's sexuality is seen as a gift to his bhaktas; he responds to them according to their needs. The gentle forces of Kṛṣṇa's passion reinforce Kṛṣṇa's characterization as a *rasika* and perpetuate the pastoral mode. In contrast, *pada*s depicting Balarāma's sexuality and intoxication subvert this pastoral and represent Balarāma as the rustic 'other'. Further Kṛṣṇa's sexuality is devoid of any connection to fertility and procreation; lust has no unwanted consequences.[37] All Kṛṣṇa's lust is for the sake of *bhāva*. But Balarāma's sexuality produces results, as in the following discussion.[38]

The following *pada* describes Balarāma's forced relocation of the Yamuna. His drunkenness reflects his pre- and Vaiṣṇava affinity for wine and invokes themes of danger, raw aggression and violation.

Sāgar 1162 Rāga-sārang

करत गोपाल की दुहाई।
मात्यौ हलधर बदत न काहु जमुना उलटी बहाई।

[37]Frederique Marglin discusses the issue of Kṛṣṇa's non-procreative sexuality in her essay in *Divine Consort*. Because Kṛṣṇa's activities occur in the *alaukika* realm of *prema*, they are exempt from their natural consequences. Procreation results from the sexuality of *kāma*, which suggests seed is spilled only in this context.

[38]Dennis Hudson discusses the connection between the plough and sexual fertility in the Bhāgavata context. As the 'plower', Vasudeva 'plowed his own womb to bring forth his son', like an earthworm. Hudson, 'Vraja Among the Tamils: A Study of the Bhāgavatas in Early South India', *JVS* 3, 1, Winter 1994, p. 115.

घूमत नयन चलत डगमगत जनु ऽब रुप कौ कूट।
अंबर नील अटपटे ओढ़ें कनक कटोरिया घूँट।
जुवती सहस्त्र संग इक लीनों बन बन गावति गीत।
मार्‌यो द्विविद कंस कौ साथी कर बलभद्र पुनीत।
जय जय राम करत देवांगन बरषत कुसुम अपार।
परमानँद स्वामी के भ्राता फनि मनि धरनि अधार।

Gopāl sent out a call.
Proud Haladhar does not speak to anyone. He changed the course of the Yamuna.
His eyes spin. His movements lurch. Just as if he took the form of a mountain.
He wears blue cloths, his blouse hangs. He swallows from a gold cup.
He brings 1,000 young women with him, singing songs from forest to forest.
The pure hand of Balabhadra killed Dvivid, the kin of Kaṃsa.
Jay-jay Rāma, the gods say. Countless Kusum flowers rain down.
Paramānand says, the brother of the lord, his support, carries the snake's gem.

This *pada* recounts Balarāma's changing the course of the Yamuna. Balarāma becomes drunk on the wine of the Kadamba tree and demands that the Yamuna come to him so he can bathe.[39] The Yamuna refuses, Balarāma takes offence and drags a new course for the Yamuna with his plough. Balarāma's act has obvious connotations of rape, and the plough represents a penis, both linguistically and thematically. Balarāma's aggressive sexuality — represented by his use of the plough — implies his connection to fertility and agriculture, but is far removed from Kṛṣṇa's gentle sexuality. This episode delineates the ambivalence of Balarāma and similarly the ambiguity of the relationship between the pre-Vaiṣṇava to the Vaiṣṇava tradition. The Yamuna river is clearly identified with Kṛṣṇa (if not an incarnation of Kṛṣṇa). Is this episode, perhaps, an example of the subordinated tradition reasserting its authority against the dominant tradition?

Also, in this *pada*, Balarāma is also likened to a mountain, a representation which generally applies to Kṛṣṇa. Balarāma usually has no role in the Govardhanadharana episode in the *Bhāgavata Purāṇa*.[40] The relationship depicted in this *pada* between Balarāma as the mountain (Govardhana)

[39] Balarāma's affinity for wine appears in the Purāṇas. According to the *Viṣṇu Purāṇa*, Varuṇa, hoping to entertain Balarāma/Śeṣanāga, sent his wife Varuṇi to please Balarāma, She hid herself in the Kadaṃba tree, and Balarāma drank the wine, then changed the course of the Yamuna. Shakti M. Gupta, *Plant Myths and Traditions in India*, Delhi: Munshiram Manoharlal, 1991, pp. 17-18.

[40] Hawley, 'A Feast for Mount Govardhan', in *Devotion Divine. Bhakti Traditions from the Regions of India*, p. 177, discusses Balarāma's role in the Govardhana-dharana episode in Braj *līlā*. Herein Balarāma has a role similar to his 'agent' role

and the Yamuna can be explained by the Annakūta ritual in which Brajavāsīs, folk and Brahmin, sculpt a Govardhan made of cowdung. Thus Govardhan has a *lāṃgūla* (meaning both plough and penis) hanging between the parallel feet or off to the side. The double meaning of *lāṃgūla* suggests an obvious connection between the plough and fertility, a connection further established by Balarāma's later interaction with the Yamuna. Although the Govardhan effigy is most clearly associated with Kṛṣṇa, Vaudeville makes a strong case for its identification with Balarāma; she suggests that its iconographic pattern with the right arm raised is most similar to local Baladev images, not images of Kṛṣṇa.[41] The *lāṃgūla* draws milk which is offered to the effigy of Govardhan downward through his navel to feed the snakes in the nether world and then water is drawn upwards again through the *lāṃgūla* to irrigate the upper regions during the dry season.[42] Vaudeville associates this irrigation with Balarāma's dragging the Yamuna with his plough. I do not think one can ignore the significance of the *lāṃgūla* and its connections to Balarāma's fertility and sexuality — which seems to be categorically different from the pastoralized Kṛṣṇa.

Balarāma's wanton sexuality also shapes his actions during the spring festival Holi, of which intoxication is no small part.

Sāgar 1210 Rāga-basant

हो हो होरी हलधर आवै।
ऐसी प्रीति स्यामसुंदर सों हरि लीला अपने मुख गावै।
पिये बारुनी मत्त संकरषन नैन रस मसे कच कछु ढीले।
भौंह चढी सिर पाग लटपटी
  बचन गँभीर अधर पुट गीले।
नील बसन ठवि डगत चरन गति
  सुभ्र सरीर रोहिनी नंदन।
परमानँद राम जुबती प्रिय कुंडल एक चढाए चंदन।

---

as in the Kālīyadāmana episode. Hawley further notes that this Balarāma in the *līlā* is not the liquor-swigging Balarāma of the Chaubes.

[41] This raised right arm offers protection to Braj and appears closest to the *Nāga* deities representation. Vaudeville, 'The Lord of Govardhan Hill', in *Devotion Divine. Bhakti Traditions from the Regions of India*, p. 112.

[42] Vaudeville, 'The Lord of the Govardhan Hill', p. 111. The word can also mean tail. In my photos, it looks much more like a tail. Vaudeville also discusses a group of *Lāṃguriyā* songs sung at a Kaila Devi shrine in Rajasthan during Daśahrā. Many of the songs are sexually explicit. The *Lāṃgūlīn* which most likely means 'the fellow with the [powerful] penis', is an epithet that well fits Balarāma. Vaudeville, 'The Lord of Govardhan Hill', p. 112.

[1210] Hey, it's Holi. Haladhar is coming.
Such love of Śyāmasundar. He sings of Hari's *līlā* with his own mouth.
Saṃkarṣaṇa drinks wine and is intoxicated.
His eyes are full of *rasa*, and his hair — now untied — dangles.
His eyebrows are raised, and his turban hangs off his head.
With slurred speech, his lower lip is wet and heavy.
With his beautiful blue cloths and a lurching gait, the body of the son of Rohinī is radiant.
Paramānand says, Rāma, the young beloved, has one earring smeared with sandal-paste.

While Kṛṣṇa might be lusty and intoxicated with love, he is usually seen as articulate, able to spar with the gopīs, but Balarāma, intoxicated, staggers and slurs his speech. Contrast this depiction of Balarāma's lower lip to that of Kṛṣṇa's. Kṛṣṇa's lower lip is the site of bliss, with nectar falling from it, not wine. Balarāma appears less the 'constructed' or *rasika* rustic, than the rustic other.[43] Balarāma also plays Holi with Rādhā. According to one story, once after seeing Kṛṣṇa play Holi with Rādhā, Balarāma approached Rādhā afterwards in a lustful manner. Rādhā, however, loved only Kṛṣṇa, so after she danced for Balarāma, she and the gopīs 'stripped him and flogged him with his own lust'.[44]

Although the majority of the *padas* depict Balarāma within the pastoral mood — a sweet little boy who gets into typical Braj boyhood trouble, many *padas* illuminate Balarāma's rustic side, revealing elements closer to the pre-Vaiṣṇava Balarāma. These *padas* reveal a Balarāma who appears far less the *rasika* than we see in most of the *aṣṭachāpa padas* which offer a pastoral or 'sweet' construction of Braj. Kṛṣṇa's nature — often described as 'bent' and 'crooked' — suggests none of the threat seen in Balarāma's involvement with wine. Kṛṣṇa is often depicted as 'bent' and that seems to be a preferred Braj way of looking at life — seeing things from a slightly skewed perspective. For example, Kṛṣṇa's perpetual tormenting of the gopīs is not malicious but mischievous and ultimately explained as for their own benefit. Balarāma, though, embodies these less

[43] In an episode in the *Mahābhārata* based on a spring festival, Phalguna, also seen as Arjuna, is clearly identified with Balarāma depicted as the 'fair god of spring'. The legend of this festival is probably based on Holi (Phāgu). Vaudeville suggests that the integration of the heroic (Kṛṣṇa of Dwarka) and the cowherd (Kṛṣṇa-Gopāl of Braj) had begun by the time of the *Mahābhārata*. Vaudeville, 'The Cowherd God', p. 110.

[44] David Haberman, *Journey Through the Twelve Forests*, New York: Oxford University Press, 1994, p. 211.

sanitized strains of Braj culture — a non-Vaiṣṇava Braj that is wilder and more violent than the majority of *pada*s illustrate.

BALARĀMA AS ANTI-PASTORAL

This assertion and maintenance of Balarāma's cultic and anti-pastoral nature fills multiple roles in the Braj tradition. First, maintaining Balarāma's cultic and less-refined roots furthers the superiority of the Kṛṣṇa-Gopāl tradition over the Balarāma-*Nāga* elements. We have already seen this operative in the episodes regarding the role of the Nāga. In this case, does portraying Balarāma as a drunken boor or a ruffian advance the cause of the urbane *rasika*? The Braj pastoral construct was created by 'foreigners'. chiefly those associated with the Caitanya and Vallabha traditions who 'rediscovered' Braj; they imposed. Clearly there was tension between these outside Brahmins and the local Brajavāsīs. Vaudeville alludes to this tension in the worship of Śrīnāthjī. Though Paramānand, according to his Vārtā, was a Brahmin, his Braj origins and folk connections manifest in the *pada*s. Vaudeville suggests that when Braj bhakti became Brahminized, there was a clear difference between those chosen for elite service, i.e. *pūjā* of Śrīnāthajī and those chosen to sing *kīrtana*. This 'class' distinction suggests that those with greater folk connections were chosen to sing *kīrtana*, and it is largely through them that these cultic ties are maintained. The Brahmins had a stake in maintaining the superiority of the *rasika* over and against the local rustics, the Brajavāsīs. The elite tradition created these social categories, the *rasika* and the 'unconstructed rustic', and thereby could control these rival forces. The implied hierarchy between the illustrations of Balarāma and Kṛṣṇa's sexuality fosters the superiority of Kṛṣṇa's devotion to his bhaktas over Balarāma's anti-social qualities.

Balarāma also functions as the representative by which pre-Braj Vaiṣṇava themes are maintained, and the pastoral structures questioned. Again, the question is who maintains or subverts these constructions? Who gains and who has the authority? Balarāma's unconstructed rusticity invalidates the city/rural dichotomy assumed by the pastoral genre and exposes these concepts, including the 'natural' rustic, as socially-created and negotiated constructions. Through Balarāma we see two cultures competing for superiority and an authoritative voice. From the elite perspective, Balarāma's representation as the ruffian can be a rhetorical device for controlling local cultic elements. Yet, from the cultic perspective, Balarāma struggles to maintain those cultic themes which have been 'sweetened' and subjugated by the occasionally saccharine Braj

Vaiṣṇavism. The cultic features that have been amalgamated into Balarāma function as vehicles for the reassertion of cultic themes and concerns.

The Braj of Kṛṣṇa and the Vaiṣṇava tradition is a delightful 'paradise' with none (or few) of the threats of the natural world. It is far closer to the Walt Disney Fantasia evocation of nature as a pastoral scene into which one might withdraw to escape culture and society. Nature and humanity have been purged of violence and dangerous urges, and the dangers once present in the cultic heritage are not really present in the pastoral Braj. The Nāgas, Yakṣas and natural forces which had to be appeased and propitiated in pre-Vaiṣṇava times reassert their authority through Balarāma. The pastoral genre cannot account for the vagaries and dangers of nature and humanity, so how could it account for the apparent malevolent forces which, for example, manifest in pre-Vaiṣṇava times as Nāgas. Perhaps the resurgence and/or maintenance of cultic themes of danger and uncontrollable forces delineates a world-view which can account for malevolence and uncertainty. Balarāma—as mediator—for these forces speaks for both the Vaiṣṇava and the pre-Vaiṣṇava voices, allowing both a voice.

The primary intellectual construct regarding the relationship of Kṛṣṇa to Balarāma is one of a hegemonic tradition appropriating a peripheral tradition for its own ends. In fact, evidence suggests that Balarāma enables the Kṛṣṇa complex by incorporating within itself elements which conflict with the pastoral image. Rather than appropriation, this relationship might be more properly termed symbiosis, suggesting a system of interdependence. Frequently such dialectics between peripheral and hegemonic traditions are envisioned as invasions (i.e. the Āryan invasion), a motif which suggests a unilateral imposition of a dominant culture upon a subordinate other. Yet, the Nāga cults continued survival through Balarāma — as a quasi-independent figure complete with cultic praxis — suggests otherwise: that peripheral traditions can and do persist through less recognized strategies of subversion and appropriation from within, and perhaps might prove to be the more enduring cultural form.

Understanding the dynamics between peripheral and hegemonic traditions is not only important for Vaiṣṇavism, but for the broader field of Religious Studies. Previous scholarship has concentrated on hegemonic traditions and powerful figures within traditions, yet, as indicated by Balarāma and the Nāga tradition, subordinate traditions not only persist but are essential to the existence of dominant traditions. Maintained traditions, such as the Nāga cult, perpetuate themselves through the paradigms of other traditions, replicating their own discourses using the motifs and symbols of more powerful traditions. This pattern also exists in global traditions, such as Buddhism, Christianity and Islam, which absorb and incorporate the motifs and practices of local traditions and reinterpret those practices within their own frameworks. Yet, through the structure of complementary pairings, subordinate traditions — often represented in dominant traditions by a foil or overshadowed character — persist by expressing those qualities which provide completion. In their obscurity, peripheral traditions gain an unrecognized measure of power, not only perpetuating their own existence but constituting and enabling the existence of a seemingly more powerful tradition.

global traditions, such as Buddhism, Christianity and Islam which absorb and incorporate the motifs and practices of local traditions and reinterpret those practices within their own frameworks. Yet, through the structure of complementary pairings, subordinate traditions — often represented in dominant traditions as lacking or as of a shallow character — persist by expressing those qualities which provide completion. In their often implicit presence, subordinates gain an unrecognized measure of power, not only by entailing their own existence but ensuring and enabling the existence of a seemingly more powerful tradition.

PART IX
Bhakti in Rajasthan

Kabīr and Mīrābāī in Folk Traditions of Western Rajasthan: Meghwāl and Māṅganiyār Repertoires

NANCY M. MARTIN

Who actually sings the songs of Mīrābāī and Kabīr? We speak easily of 'oral traditions', but when we turn to serious study, a number of questions immediately arise. Who are the carriers of these traditions? Where are the reservoirs of memory, what are the systems of classification for that which is remembered and performed, and how might we map the contours of change? In terms of song content, what particular songs are being sung by whom for whom, and what role might social factors, regional differences, and religious affiliations play? Further, as performance rather than written text, how do performance contexts and musical considerations impact such traditions? These are some of the issues I set out to explore as I embark on a study of the repertoires of singers from specific caste groups in Rajasthan. In so doing, I follow in the footsteps of others who have begun to examine oral and popular traditions of these two saints — Edward O. Henry and David Lorenzen in the case of Kabīr and Parita Mukta in the case of Mīrābāī.[1]

* The field research for this paper was carried out with funding provided by the American Academy of Religion and Chapman University for which I am very grateful. The work has been done in collaboration with Komal Kothari of Rupayan Sansthan, the Rajasthan Folklore Institute (Jodhpur, Rajasthan), whose insights and knowledge gleaned over forty years of fieldwork in Western Rajasthan inform my study at multiple levels, and to him I want to express my the deepest gratitude and thanks for the great pleasure of working together. Any errors herein, however, are purely my own.

[1] Edward O. Henry, *Chant the Names of God: Music and Culture in Bhojpuri-Speaking India*, San Diego: San Diego State University Press, 1988; Henry, '*Jogīs* and *Nirguṇ Bhajans* in Bhojpuri-Speaking India: Intra-Genre Heterogeneity, Adaptation, and Functional Shift', *Ethnomusicology*, 35, 2, Spring/Summer 1991, pp. 221-42; David Lorenzen, 'Kabīr's Most Popular Songs', in his book *Praises to a Formless God: Nirguṇī Texts from North India*, Albany: SUNY Press, 1996, pp. 205-23; Parita Mukta, *Upholding the Common Life: The Community of Mirabai*, Delhi: Oxford University Press, 1994.

The choice to look at both Kabīr and Mīrā deserves some explanation, given that Kabīr is clearly a *nirguṇ sant* and Mīrā a *saguṇ bhakta*. However, in Rajasthan both saints are extremely popular, and the songs of both are sung by most groups, irrespective of religious affiliation. Further, *nirguṇ* and *saguṇ* do not seem to be primary categories used by the majority of singers I interviewed to differentiate between these two saints or to classify devotional songs, with a few notable exceptions. The clear contrast between the renunciant royal lover of Kṛṣṇa and the iconoclastic low-caste devotee of the Lord Beyond Form, as well as similarities that emerge in the songs sung in their names, can provide fruitful insights into those elements which characterize these traditions generally, and those which are particular to each saint, as well as revealing more about the religious milieu of the people who sing their songs.

When we turn to the actual repertoires of specific singers, many factors come into play — the caste, region, gender, religious affiliation, and personal preferences of both the singers and the patron(s) and audience(s); the venue of performance and the instruments used; the singer's skill, musical training, level of education, and exposure to media and written sources; and the caste, gender, religious affiliation, and level of knowledge of the singer's guru(s) or *ustād*(s). The sophistication of individual singers' musical and religious understanding of the material also varies considerably from one singer to another as does the depth and feeling of their devotion and personal religiosity. Unique features of a particular field recording session also play a role in the selection of songs performed on a given occasion. Here, I will offer a preliminary comparison of the repertoires of selected singers who belong to two quite different groups: the Mānganiyār and Meghwāl castes of Western Rajasthan.[2]

The Mānganiyārs are professional musicians by caste, with sophisticated musical capabilities (although not all members of the caste are active musicians and singers). Their traditional patrons or *jajmān* are said to be Rajputs, but also include people of other castes who serve these particular Rajput families. The Mānganiyārs themselves are Sunni Muslims, although their religious practice is clearly not rigidly orthodox and warrants further investigation, and they can be separated into two groups — those who play *kāmāichā* and have only Hindu patrons and those who play *pyāledār* or *sindhī sārangī* and perform for both Muslims and Hindus.[3] The patronage

[2] Neither group belongs to the religious contexts of Henry or Lorenzen, and though Mukta focused to some degree on Meghwāls, she used examples from many castes.

[3] Komal Kothari, 'Musicians for the People: The Manganiyars of Western

situation can also become more complex, because there is a procedure for 'divorcing' one's hereditary patrons if some very serious problem arises between the groups, and other caste groups without traditional musicians are highly motivated to pick up an unattached Mānganiyār family since musicians are an absolute necessity for ritual life and full caste recognition.[4] In the case of one of the singers whose repertoire is presented here, his family left the Solaṅkī Rajputs and Solaṅkī Muslims who had been their patrons and have now become attached to Viṣṇois.[5]

The presence of these professional caste musicians is required during each aspect of the life-cycle rituals of birth, marriage, and death, and patrons may call them for major festivals and private gatherings as well.[6] Their performances of Mīrābāī and Kabīr songs, however, fall outside the formal ritual space on such occasions.[7] Mīrābāī's songs might be played on the morning following the formal marriage ritual or on other mornings of a wedding celebration, during devotional sessions referred to as *paḍavā* in which Kṛṣṇa *bhajans*, especially those recounting his youthful sporting with the gopīs and Rādhā, are particularly popular.[8] In the evenings also people assemble for sessions called *kacheṛī*.[9] At these times, audience attention is acute with a focus on the performers' musical skill, artistic merit, and breadth of repertoire. The types of songs played during such a session are diverse, including songs telling of love and romance, of feminine and natural beauty, and of heroic, compassionate, or virtuous actions and self-sacrifice, as well as philosophical reflection and devotion

---

Rajasthan', in Karine Schomer, Joan L. Erdman, Deryck O. Lodrick, and Lloyd I. Rudolph (eds.), *The Idea of Rajasthan: Explorations in Regional Identity*, vol. I, New Delhi: Manohar, 1994, pp. 211-12. The *kāmāichā* is a bowed instrument with a hollowed-out round wooden belly and four main gut strings and eight sympathetic steel strings, and the *pyāledār* or *sindhī sārangī* used by the Mānganiyārs is a bowed instrument having a carved wood belly with concave sides, two gut and two steel main strings, and 25 sympathetic strings in two sets.

[4] Komal Kothari, 'Patronage and Performance', in N.K. Singhi and Rajendra Joshi (eds.), *Folk, Faith and Feudalism*, Jaipur: Rawat Publications, 1995, pp. 56-7.

[5] Both the Hindu Solaṅkī Rajputs and the Solaṅkī Muslims trace their lineage to the same Solaṅkī Rajputs, but one branch of the family converted to Islam while the other remained Hindus.

[6] Kothari, 'Musicians for the People', p. 208.

[7] For a detailed description of their performance responsibilities on such ritual occasions, see Kothari, 'Musicians for the People', pp. 216-19.

[8] Komal Kothari, personal communication, 30 July 1997.

[9] Kothari, 'Musicians for the People', pp. 217-21.

and praise of God in multiple forms including folk deities.[10] In addition, Mānganiyārs might be invited to perform for *jāgaraṇs* or all-night devotional performances not associated with life-cycle rituals during which songs of Mīrā and Kabīr might also be sung.

When performing devotional songs, Mānganiyārs generally play the melody on *kāmāichā* or *sārangī* with the rhythmic pattern created by bowing and an accompanying *ḍholak* and sometimes *khartāls* and *manjīrā*. *Jagtārā* or *tandūro* are also sometimes played instead of *kāmāichā* or *sārangī* during jāgaraṇs, and the *tandūro* may be accompanied on the *ghaṛā* (a clay pot wind rhythm instrument).[11] The Mānganiyārs play many other instruments as well including *ḍhol, surnāī, nagārā,* and *muralī,* but these instruments are not generally used to accompany devotional singing.[12]

The Meghwāls, in contrast, are not professional musicians by caste, but weavers and leather workers with a very low social status. Until very recently they have been subjected as a group to intense social oppression, including forced labour and socially sanctioned restrictions on innumerable aspects of daily life such as the type of houses they might construct, the jewellery they could wear, and how they might practise their religious traditions.[13] Among the caste members are some who perform regularly, primarily for jāgaraṇs or all night singing which may be held for a variety of reasons — to celebrate the completion of a new house or well, to give thanks for recovery from an illness, to fulfil a particular vow regarding some desired outcome, or the like as well as to express deep devotion.[14] In the past, performers were not paid for this service (although this has changed in the last decade and many do now accept monetary compensation), and they could not refuse if someone called them to

[10] Ibid., p. 220.

[11] *Tandūro*, also called *cautāro*, is a four or five stringed instrument with a rounded or sometimes rectangular belly and a long neck. The strings are tuned to the first and fifth, and the instrument is strummed with the right hand. It serves only as a drone, and the melody must be carried by the singer.

[12] Kothari, 'Musicians for the People', pp. 222-9. Further details regarding these instruments can be found in Kothari, *Folk Musical Instruments of Rajasthan: A Folio*, Borunda: Rajasthan Institute of Folklore, 1977.

[13] For further details, see Mukta, *Upholding the Common Life*, pp. 75-86. She draws her information from the *Rajputana Census* of 1901 and the *Rajasthani Census of Marwar* (1891), as well as other sources.

[14] Komal Kothari, 'Performers, Gods, and Heroes in the Oral Epics of Rajasthan', in Stuart Blackburn, Peter Claus, Joyce Flueckiger, and Susan Wadley (eds.), *Oral Epics of India*, Berkeley: University of California Press, 1989, pp. 102-8.

perform.[15] Such singers and musicians provide a service to the village as a whole, called by and performing for people from a wide range of castes, though many engage in other work as well, such as farming or weaving. They may also perform in mixed caste groups, with Meghwāls and Māṅganiyārs sometimes performing together.[16] Singing is accompanied by the *tandūro* which serves as a drone with *ḍholak* and *manjīrā* providing the rhythm. These days in urban areas and larger townships harmonium, which can render the full melody, rather than *tandūro* has become the instrument of choice (for both singers and audience), but *tandūro* still predominates at the village level.[17]

The religious milieu of the Meghwāls is complex and fluid, without a rigid institutional structure. Most affirm a devotion to Rāmdev, a Rājput saint and miracle worker who probably lived in about the same time as Kabīr and Mīrābāī and who, Dominique-Sila Khan argues, may actually have been a proponent of Isma'ili Islam, although the tradition today is considered a thoroughly Hindu devotional one and Rāmdev said to be an incarnation of Viṣṇu/Kṛṣṇa.[18] Certainly he has had both Hindu and Muslim followers, and the traditions surrounding him reflect a number of elements from both traditions. Temples to Rāmdev exist, most built only in the decades since independence, with Kāmaḍs generally serving as priests to the Meghwāl devotees, though upper caste reappropriation of Rāmdev is occurring as well.[19] All night singing sessions, in this particular case referred to as *jama jāgaraṇs*, are regularly organized in relation to Rāmdev, and Mīrābāī and Kabīr's songs are sung at this time along with songs in the name of Rāmdev and others. A number of more organized Vaiṣṇava, Śaivite, and *nirguṇ* panths and sampradāys also exist in addition to devotion to Rāmdev and tantric practices, and caste members may be affiliated with, for example, the Kabīr Panth, Dādū Panth, Rāmānandīs or

[15] The motivation for taking up this responsibility warrants further investigation, given that it can be quite demanding and at least until recently did not provide material compensation. Some singers follow in the footsteps of family members, but what might motivate others to take up this vocation remains to be explored.

[16] Komal Kothari, personal communication, 30 July 1997. Such mixed caste devotional singing sessions are sometimes also referred to as *sangat*.

[17] Komal Kothari, personal communication, 30 July 1997. It seems, however, that harmonium is becoming increasingly popular.

[18] Dominique-Sila Khan, *Conversions and Shifting Identities: Ramdev Pir and the Ismailis in Rajasthan*, Delhi: Manohar, 1997, pp. 60-96.

[19] Dominique-Sila Khan, 'The Kāmaḍ of Rajasthan — Priests of a Forgotten Tradition', *Journal of the Royal Asiatic Society*, Series 3, 6, 1, April 1996, pp. 29-56.

related Vaiṣṇava sects, Nāths, or Dasnāmis (although all of the Meghwāl singers whom I interviewed claimed not to have any formal association with such groups). Singers sing songs attributed to a number of other saints, together with songs praising a variety of forms of the divine. Hindu saints and Muslim pīrs are revered by Hindus and Muslims alike, and songs attributed to both sung, although there are trends toward both Hinduization and Islamicization operating as identities coalesce along oppositional religious lines. Islam, too, takes multiple forms with interweaving and sometimes opposing strands of Sunni, Sufi, Twelver Shia, and Isma'ili traditions, and there are a number of deified heroic figures in addition to Rāmdev who are revered. Clearly the religious fabric of the Meghwāl community and of rural Rajasthan in general is richly textured and diverse and has been at least since the medieval period, and those Meghwāls I interviewed seemed to move freely within this milieu. Their multiple audiences also necessitate an ability to address the preferences of patrons with diverse religious leanings.

How then do Mīrā and Kabīr fit into this religious milieu, and from whom do the singers learn the songs they sing in their names? Among those I interviewed, there seemed to be an appreciation for both saints that crossed all religious boundaries. A Kālbeliyā Jogī guru did say that within his community Mīrā was not revered because she was a *saguṇ bhakta* and they, being Nāths, followed the *nirguṇ* path.[20] However, he also sat before a Rāmdev Temple (of which he was the priest), richly decorated with paintings of Rāmdev, Śiva, Durgā, Śrī Nāthjī (Kṛṣṇa), Raidās, Kabīr, the nine Nāths, and himself — a perhaps unanticipated element of their '*nirguṇ*' practice for those trying to make sharp distinctions between these devotional perspectives — and he affirmed that singers within his caste and community did sing Mīrā as well as Kabīr. Neither saint seemed to have been constrained by boundaries separating *nirguṇ* and *saguṇ* or even Hindu and Muslim, at least until the recent past.

Mīrā and Kabīr's songs form only a small part of the full repertoires of the singers and the songs actually performed at jāgaraṇs. Within the devotional context their songs are sung along with those of Tulsīdās, Narsī Mehtā, Sūrdās, Dharmidās, Gorakhnāth, Jasnāth, Meghrī, Candrasakhī, Rūpāṅdev, Harirām, Acaldās, Mānsingh, Rohil, Sādūl, Sadarām, and literally hundreds of other poet saints who have composed across the centuries. Present-day gurus and devotees continue to compose and other singers to pick up their songs, providing a constant source of new material as well.

[20] Jetunāth, Interview, 19 July 1997.

With reference to how they learned the songs, the Meghwāl singers I interviewed reported a variety of sources including attending many jāgaraṇs. They learn both the melody and the words directly from other singers and generally do not compose independently in a conscious way. In response to direct questioning, one singer first said that, when he was around sixteen, his guru had been a Kabīrpanthī Meghwāl who sang mostly the songs of Kabīr. However, further questioning revealed that, although he considered this man to be his guru, he no longer remembered songs learned from this source. Rather he was singing songs he learned primarily from another jāgaraṇ singer of the Rāwat caste.[21] Additionally, his father had been a jāgaraṇ singer and a priest of Rāmdev and his older brother continued to sing for jāgaraṇs as well. His wife, who sings with him, learned from her father whom she accompanied until her marriage. A third singer, a Kāmaḍ priest of Rāmdev, had learned from his older brother, and he sang with another singer, a Meghwāl man who had learned from his grandfather. All affirmed that they also learned new songs during other jāgaraṇ performances.

A fifth singer by the name of Padmarām is a somewhat more unusual case and is a particularly gifted singer with an unusually large repertoire of Mīrā songs. His teacher was a Sādh woman, Sahaja Bāī, and they sang with 'open hands/arms' (*khulo hāth*), that is without any kind of instrumental accompaniment. He only took up playing the *tandūro* much later. The term Sādh (derived from sadhu) or Vairāgi is used to refer to a number of groups but most in western Rajasthan are Vaiṣṇavas.[22] Initially open to initiates from multiple castes, they have come to form caste groups, who perform rituals for lower middle level peasant castes with whom food and water can be shared, where no Brahmins are available. They often serve as the priests of temples dedicated to Chārbhuja or Ṭhākurjī (forms of Kṛṣṇa) for which the land and resources for building and maintenance have been donated by middle and lower caste villagers (in contrast to the temples formerly funded by the ruling jāgīrdārs and now supported by the government which are dedicated to Lakṣmī Narāyan and manned by Brahmin priests).[23] Additionally, in western Rajasthan they traditionally had the responsibility of going to the homes of their jajmāns and announcing the day of the week

[21] The Rāwats are a low-caste community who are said to be the descendants of Rajput men and Mina (tribal) women and claim Rajput status.

[22] Gahlot, Sukhvir Singh and Banshi Dhar, *Castes and Tribes of Rajasthan*, Jodhpur: Jain Brothers, 1989, pp. 49f; *Marwar Census of 1891*, rpt. by Sri Jagdish Singh Gehlot, Jodhpur: Shodh Sansthan, 1997.

[23] Komal Kothari, personal communication, 30 July 1997.

and the date, a service for which they received flour, sugar, ghee, and various other uncooked foodstuffs on particular designated days. These days Sādh women are also called to perform *vrat kathās*.[24] It was a woman from this community from whom Padmarām learned much of his extensive repertoire of Mīrābāī and Kabīr.

These responses and those of other singers I interviewed suggest the following. Most singers learn from other jāgaraṇ singers, very often first by accompanying older family members, as jāgaraṇs provide not only worship space but also a training ground for singers and a song pool available to people from multiple castes. Among jāgaraṇ singers, particular individuals are also known by the community to be especially knowledgeable with respect to Mīrā and/or Kabīr. In addition, the householder priests who serve middle and low caste groups including Kāmaḍ priests of Rāmdev, Sādh priests of Chārbhuja or Ṭhākurjī, and Nāth priests in temples devoted to Śiva are regularly called on to organize jāgaraṇs, and among these religious specialists are also some who seem to know a wider range of songs, which find their way into the repertoires of Meghwāl and other jāgaraṇ singers, providing a second reservoir of material.[25] Professional musician castes such as the Mānganiyārs but also including Langās, Ḍholis, Ḍhāḍhīs, and Damāmis form a third pool, both performing and passing on knowledge of these traditions in varying degrees to family and fellow caste members and beyond. A fourth possible pool may lie in the hands of renouncers of various types, whether affiliated with particular panths or orders or not, whose individual vocation includes devotional singing.[26]

These reservoirs of tradition are not isolated but interrelated and cross-fertilizing, and their boundaries are permeable, with elements from written and electronic sources also contributing to singers' repertoires. Vast

[24] This information was provided by Komal Kothari based on his field inquiries during the past four decades (personal communication, 30 July 1997).

[25] When searching for those who might sing Mīrā in particular, I was very often referred to Sādhs and Kāmaḍs as well as Meghwāls generally. I was also told that women would know many of her songs but have not yet found examples of women from any caste with large repertoires with the exception of Padmarām's guru. Such priestly groups are open to people from other castes who might choose to take up this work, but they have also come to function as hereditary castes.

[26] One professional caste musician's family source turned out to be a maternal uncle who had renounced the world to become a *fakīr* and taken up *tandūro* playing. The Kabīrpanthī Meghwāl guru of another Meghwāl singer and the Nāth guru of a Kālbeliyā Jogī singer I interviewed offer additional examples.

collections of manuscripts exist, documenting the traditions in written form beginning in the seventeenth century and increasing exponentially in number by the nineteenth century, indicating the strength of past traditions and providing a written reservoir of material as well. With the introduction of the printing press, a multitude of song books and collections are also readily available in the market. Commercial cassette tapes of compositions of Mīrā and Kabīr sung in classical, *filmī*, and folk versions are played over the radio and village loudspeakers and are also easily purchased in the market. In addition, singers are now recording themselves, or villagers the groups popular in their village or community, and these tapes too are being circulated.

Meghwāl jāgaraṇ singers' repertoires are not generally directly affected by written sources because they learn songs as a whole (text and melody) from the performances of other singers (either live or recorded). To limit the influence of popular commercial recordings, only those songs sung to the accompaniment of *tandūro* will be analysed here (since most popular recordings employ harmonium), and thus the songs discussed do not necessarily include all the songs actually performed by Meghwāl singers when and if they use harmonium.

The Mānganiyārs, in contrast to the Meghwāl singers, are quite capable of taking a text and composing music for it on the spot. To increase their repertoires, they need only find a text, either from another singer or a written source. Then, choosing an appropriate *rāg* and rhythmic pattern, they can create a melody, using elements from existing melodies or composing entirely new ones. Many singers keep diaries or notebooks in which they write down texts they gather from various sources. One singer's diary I examined resembled some of the manuscripts I have seen, with variable writing size and penmanship reflecting the accumulation of songs over a period of time. He used this diary for reference to expand his performance repertoire, and he is clearly an active collector of new material. Another singer referred to a book his father had kept that he now draws on, although he did not seem to carry one himself. Other singers had single sheets of paper with a song or two written on them, and I watched one singer teach another a song simply by giving him the words and *rāg*. The second singer immediately performed it and also carefully wrote down the text, as the field recording session was transformed into a site of transmission.

Without exception, the Mānganiyār singers with whom I worked referred to *rāg*s with respect to the songs of Mīrā and Kabīr, with morning *rāg*s and those associated with devotion predominating, such as Āśā and

Bhairavī. Komal Kothari has discussed the Mānganiyār use of *rāgas* in considerable detail, and it is clear that these *rāgas* differ considerably from those of the north Indian classical music.[27] With respect to performance, the *rāg* sets the parameters of the notes but not the specific melody, and each performer improvises according to his own style, with no two performances of a particular song by the same singer being identical. All their musical improvisation is outside the body of the text, however, and they do not change the text (unless they mistakenly combine verses from several songs) except by adding repetitions and substitutions such as varying names for God — Girdhāri, Sāṃvarā, Rām, Hari — or for the *rāṇā* or ruler of Mewār into whose family Mīrā married — Mewāri rāṇā, Udaipur rāṇā, — and the like. But such changes generally occur only in the refrain or the final verse containing the saint's characteristic signature or *chāp*.[28] According to Komal Kothari, this lack of textual expansion stands in considerable contrast to the folk songs Mānganiyārs sing in which they improvise freely within the text as well as outside it, adding nonsense syllables, etc. Theoretically they could do this type of expansion with Mīrā and Kabīr, but do not, with one possible limiting factor being the shorter rhythm phrases of the *bhajans*. A further consideration is the structure of the songs themselves. They generally have a set form with a refrain and four verses, the last of which contains the *chāp*. This set structure requires rote memorization of the text unlike the more free form structure of other folk songs.[29]

Mānganiyār singers also almost always begin a song with one or more *dohās* that may be only peripherally related to the content of the song that follows, more often relating to the *rāg* in which the song is performed. The singers have a large number of *dohās* in memory from which to draw, however, including some referring directly to Kabīr, Gorakhnāth, and other saints (although I am not aware of any that specifically refer to Mīrā).

Meghwāl singers and other jāgaraṇ singers of Mīrā and Kabīr may also give *rāg* designations for the songs (and such designations regularly appear in the manuscript traditions), but most are unable to improvise in the way that the Mānganiyār musicians do, and they are more likely to refer to the songs in terms of another classification system based partly on musical structure and partly on the content of the individual songs. Even

[27] Kothari, 'Musicians for the People', pp. 231-4.

[28] According to Komal Kothari, the *chāp* is also referred to as *mudrā*, as *nānvau* or *sirainānvau* in western Rajasthan, or *thavau* in the Jaisalmer/Barmer region (personal communication, July 1996).

[29] Komal Kothari, personal communication, July 1996.

the term *bhajan* is seldom used. Mīrā's songs are generally called *harjas* or praise and the songs of Kabīr more often generically referred to as *vāṇī* or 'speech' with a further breakdown of types of *vāṇī* based on content.[30] *Vāṇī* also refers to a particular type of song, however, which differs musically from the *harjas* or *bhajan* form with a more limited note range (five to six notes, an octave at most), a strong rhyme scheme, and a musical elongation of the syllables at the end of text lines. Other categories are defined by content as well as musical structure. In *helī* songs the refrain always addresses a *helī* or close woman friend, and often the song includes an extended metaphor of some type. A third class, *fakīrī*, includes this (Muslim) term for renunciation in the refrain, and the verses focus on this theme. Musically, *fakīrī* songs include slower segments without rhythmic accompaniment that begin each verse followed by sections with rapid tempo and strong rhythm. Moments of complete silence also occur between verses. Additional categories include *parbhātī* (morning songs often in particular *rāgs*) as well as songs dealing with various types of love such as *virahaṇī*, *matwāl*, and *pyārī*, and songs in praise of gurus, called *guru mahimā*. If we compare songs within each category, for example, *fakīrī* songs attributed to Kabīr and Mīrā, we will be able to further elucidate the distinctive nature of the traditions surrounding each poet-saint. A systematic study of these categories requires drawing examples from many singers' repertoires, however, and goes beyond the scope of our discussion here. In general these categories apply in devotional settings such as those of Meghwāl jāgaraṇ performances, while the songs performed by Mānganiyārs in *kacheṛī* sessions tend to fall in the *harjas* or *bhajan* forms that allow for more free musical improvisation.

Precisely what songs of Mīrā and Kabīr are being sung by these singers, and what characteristics of each saint emerge from them? Rather than analysing the actual songs sung in specific jāgaraṇs or *kacheṛī* sessions for specific audiences (an interesting and immense project well worth doing), I will confine my discussion here to the full repertoires of Mīrā and Kabīr songs known to selected Meghwāl and Mānganiyār singers. Distinct differences do emerge in terms of content and the specific songs sung, both in relation to each other and the wider traditions associated with the saints.

Turning first to Kabīr, we find that much of the existing academic work has largely been textually based with an eye toward establishing his

[30] One Ḍhāḍhī singer I interviewed referred to four types of *nirguṇ vāṇī* based on content: *madā*, *bekharī*, *parā*, and *pacchantī*. These categories are also found within the literary tradition and warrant further investigation with respect to how they are being used within oral and performance traditions.

authentic works and the historical facts of his life. With respect to popular and folk traditions of Kabīr, however, Edward O. Henry and David Lorenzen have offered us detailed studies. Henry provides song texts and translations of *nirguṇ bhajans* of Kabīr sung by mendicant Jogīs in the Bhojpuri-speaking region of eastern Uttar Pradesh and western Bihar, including analysis of both content and performance, and Lorenzen's extensive and excellent work on Kabīr includes a presentation of Kabīr's most popular *bhajans* predominantly among Kabīr Panthī sadhus and bhagats in the Banaras region.

Both Henry and Lorenzen observe that although the songs that emerge in these contexts are consonant with the themes within the written corpus, there is a softening of the social and religious critique found in the verses of the *Bījak*, and the predominant themes emphasized include the immanence of death, the equality of all in this regard, and the impermanence or passing nature of this life, coupled with a stress on inner religiosity rather than outward forms of practice.[31] Henry further notes a stress on *bhajan* singing as a means of spiritual emancipation and an emphasis on detachment from the things of this world which so easily delude human beings, coupled with noticeably little development of concepts such as karma or *mokṣa* or of specificity with regard to the nature of the divine.

What do we find when we turn to the repertoires of singers in Rajasthan? Padmarām (the fifth singer cited above) has thirty songs of Kabīr within his repertoire, providing us with an excellent example of material performed within the Meghwāl community, and I will limit my discussion here to these songs although comparison with other Meghwāl singers' repertoires also can and should be made.[32] The Kabīr who emerges here is in many ways consonant with the observations of Lorenzen and Henry, but there is very little overlap in the actual material performed. Kabīr appears as a weaver of protest and dignity, though his social and religious critique is embedded in what is praised and what devalued, lacking the *Bījak*'s directness, and he speaks not to the religious elite or to those of high caste with purity concerns but rather his words address ordinary people of middle and lower castes and sadhus. The cloth he weaves reflects a variety of themes and influences.

Within the songs of Kabīr performed by Padmarām, Kabīr does speak of the immanence of death, crying out to all equally 'Wake up! Death is

[31] Lorenzen, *Praises to a Formless God*, p. 207; Henry, *Chant the Names of God*, pp. 183-5.

[32] This recording was done in the professional studios of the *Patrikā* newspaper in Jaipur, Rajasthan, in 1993.

dancing on your head!' In so doing he calls the listeners to take control of and responsibility for the precious human birth that each has been given. Youth, wealth, the love of family, lovers, friends — all these are transitory, and things over which one ultimately has no control, whether powerful and wealthy or poor and socially and politically powerless (though it is perhaps easier for the rich to maintain the illusion of control). The search for and remembrance of God are what in the end truly make life meaningful and bring an end to birth and death, and the relationship with the guru is finally the only true and necessary one.

The body is a gift, crafted over time by a master artisan, though at the same time not something to take pride in. The body and the soul are to be kept clean, not weakened in senseless pursuits, and washed by the *satguru* Dhobī (as God becomes washerman, weaver, potter, spinning woman in successive songs). A particularly telling song speaks in an extended metaphor of a forest in which a sandalwood tree takes root, pleasing all the other plants because the air will be filled with its scent. Bamboo also takes root, a notorious plant that will lead to the whole forest burning. Sure enough a fire starts, and flames spread rapidly. The birds fly away escaping, but the swan soul (*haṃs*) remains. 'Why do you not fly?' cries the sandalwood. 'We must burn because we have no feathers, but you could escape.' The swan soul replies that it has played in the branches of the tree, rustled its leaves, and eaten its fruit. 'How much life will I have in leaving anyway?' she says. Rain suddenly begins to fall, coming from the south and extinguishing the flames. The soul and the body move through this world as one. Here again we hear a call to self-respect and an honouring of oneself, yet without unwarranted pride or a false sense of 'me' and 'mine'. The latter critique undercuts others' claims to wealth, power, and status, as well.

Knowledge is the only real possession, and it is not in the hands of those who think they know. The knowledge that matters is that which cannot be spoken, the hidden meaning, not understood by those from 'another country' in the east who do not speak the same 'language'. Only a few truly understand — Kabīr, the guru, and by implication those who sing Kabīr's songs hold the inner knowledge which is the key to this true power over life and death, over this endless coming and going. The blind cannot give the blind directions; the fly who wants more honey becomes mired in sticky sweetness, unable to depart. We all have a *pallā* (corner of a cloth or scarf) filled with treasure, yet few untie the knot and examine its contents, preferring instead to wander driven by desire and calling out 'Ruby, Ruby' even as they walk carelessly over diamonds.

The reality to which Kabīr points lies outside of time, and in one song he asks (in a rather koanic Zen style): who were we in this time before all that is? He speaks also of a place in the vault of the sky where there are no mountains, no winds, no rivers; no hunger or thirst; no Brahma, Viṣṇu, Śiva or Pārvatī; no rituals and no meditation or concentration. Such songs express alternately a place beyond or before distinction or a place of abundance, a paradise where there is no longer concern for needs of any kind. In so doing, he invokes a world where the rules of this *saṃsāric* realm do not hold, an alternate reality which is 'our country', belonging to the singers and their audience. All are invited to join in this surprising or strange game of reversals and to draw water from the upside down well in the sky without a pot and without a rope if only they know how.

He speaks as well in one song, of a sadhu who meditates in the sky and in a second of a cosmic man (Alakh Puruṣ) who lies sleeping in space. Kabīr cries, 'Tell me the hidden meaning!' — Brahma, Viṣṇu, and Śiva serve him, Alakh offers *ārati* while Nirañjan fans him, but Kabīr says to concentrate only on this man. In another song Kabīr speaks of himself as existing from the beginning, taking up various accoutrements of the sadhu renouncer across the four yugas, suggesting as Kabīr Panthīs affirm, that Kabīr is an incarnation of the divine or that even this distinction of human and divine is transcended. Still other songs are *ulaṭbāṃsī* or carefully encoded with meanings comprehensible to 'one who speaks our language' but not so readily to the uninitiated or one from 'another country'.[33]

This is no easy path of consolation for those who must suffer in this world. It is narrow and hard, and many fail to see it; instead, they wander here and there like an ox, never even for a moment remembering or singing the praises of God or looking inside where indeed God is to be found. This path cannot be followed half-way either. Sesame seeds are useful if whole or fully crushed to yield oil, but being half crushed is of no value. Having once tasted the fruit of bitterness, we should leave it and keep ourselves apart, or we will burn even as the bitter vine does when the heat comes. Māyā, the one who has cheated rishis and gods, must also be avoided. Kabīr invokes images of the heroic warrior who never retreats though his body may be hacked to pieces and of the satī who chooses to die on her husband's pyre without fear to stress both the courage and the dedication that are required. We must attach ourselves to Rām with the same desire that a barren woman has for a child and with the same single-minded concentration that parrots show in devouring sweet fruit. Kabīr is the drummer on the battlefield urging us forward to victory.

[33]Linda Hess, *The Bījak of Kabīr*, San Francisco: Northpoint Press, 1983, pp. 135-61.

Many other images from everyday life are woven through the songs as well — the Dhobī and the spinning wheel, the acrobat, the special stone and iron used by nomadic people to make a fire, the game of *caupaḍ*, the bellows and anvil of the ironsmith, churning and the contrast of ghee and buttermilk, the gourd (of karma) that the thief cannot force into hiding beneath the water's surface, the purifying fire of the kiln. Wedding imagery is used to speak of preparing the soul to unite with God and the *gaunā* (when the groom comes to fetch the bride to take her to his home), to speak alternately of renunciation leading to union and the coming of death which none can avoid. A mother asks the approaching stranger to spare her innocent, young daughter, but he has his orders from Rām. The girl is first allowed to prepare herself for the holiday of Tīj with her companions, but ultimately everyone must go to this *sasurāl*, and the family sends her off to go alone. Henry has also noted the use of the *gaunā* in this latter sense in the Jogī songs he recorded, though not in the former.[34] The world of the singers and their patrons forms the metaphorical warp and woof of many of these songs.

Specific critiques and references to both Hindu and Muslim practices and beliefs are limited in Padmarām's Kabīr repertoire. There is an emphasis on singing the praises of God, on remembering the name of Rām, and on the inner meaning of religion and the indwelling God. One song speaks of the Muslim Maulvī within the heart-mind (*man*) and the mosque which lies in the mouth, where 'Adam' is saying prayers (*namāz*). Listen to what this inner Maulvī is saying, Kabīr counsels, implying perhaps that an outer Maulvī is less important but also internalizing (and thus affirming) these Muslim images. Similar verses can be found attributed to Pīr Shāms and Guru Nānak.[35] This particular song also negates the value of the Vedas, Śāstras, Gītā, and other holy books, so Hindu traditions are also critiqued and inner realization rather than book knowledge affirmed. In particular that knowledge which was forbidden and inaccessible to people of the lowest castes is rejected. The only other song with an explicit reference to Islam speaks of Rām as the God of all the gods and the Pīr of all the *pīr*s, suggesting an ultimate unity of these two paths.

Elsewhere other Hindu practices are questioned — bathing in Kāśī or Mathurā and meditation, for example — but the emphasis again seems to be on a state that in some sense precedes such distinctions and an inner religion which does not necessitate such outward actions. The final

[34] Henry, *Chant the Names of God*, pp. 174-5.

[35] Cited by Dominique-Sila Khan in *Conversions and Shifting Doctrines*, pp. 236-7.

signature lines of the songs generally address 'brother sadhus' or Kabīr's disciple Dharmidās, and several also mention Kabīr meeting Rāmānanda, placing them well within the Hindu fold none the less. The divine is also referred to in a variety of ways, including Alakh and Nirañjan as well as Rām.

Turning to the Kabīr repertoires of three Mānganiyār musicians, we find a much smaller selection of songs. One singer sang eight songs in the name of Kabīr although the final two were incomplete and combined verses from several different songs, suggesting that he had stepped beyond what he really knew.[36] Among the first six he sang was one which corresponds to a song of Padmarām — without the guru, who will be one's companion? The body gives sorrows to the soul — blood relations stay away and the beloved wife loses her temper. Only the guru remains true. A second song parallels one cited by Lorenzen as the most popular of all Kabīr songs, but the verses of the song differ somewhat.[37] The body is compared to a finely woven cloth, dyed in the colour of Rām, which took eight months to weave on the eight lotus spinning wheel. This cloth has covered the poor person; the brave one, the prostitute who taught the parrot to repeat Rām's name, Mīrābāī, Dhruv, Prahlād, Vibhīṣaṇ and Śukdev, all have used it. The foolish ones make it dirty, but all these people named (as well as Kabīr) take care to keep it in its original pure form. Again the *satguru* is the Dhobī with full knowledge. The refrain of a third song speaks of youth and wealth being a guest who stays only four days — to have pride in them is foolish. The body is only a cage of bones and flesh filled with filth, though it has been given a beautiful appearance by a master artisan. Animals' skins can at least be used to make instruments — of what use is human skin? Rāvaṇ and other brave ones die like all the rest, and the world passes as quickly as drops of dew. The refrain of a fourth asks why we search for God who is always within. A critique of outward religious (mostly Hindu) practices follows — God is not in images (*mūrti*) or pilgrimage places (*tīrtha*), not in Kāśī or Kailāś, not in temples or in mosques, not in recitation (*japnā*) or in meditation (*tapasyā*), not in fasting, whether you take one meal or none, not in yoga or renunciation (*sannyās*), not in the breath or soul, in the material form, or in space. Instead God lies within all, dwelling not in Vaikuṇṭh but within the inner

[36] These recordings were made in Jodhpur in July 1996 with material on Mīrābāī and Kabīr being recorded during the same sessions. The Langā singers who are discussed within this essay were recorded during the same period, and interview material also was collected at this time.

[37] Lorenzen, *Praises to a Formless God*, p. 208.

'dark cave' and easily available within seconds to anyone who looks. This song is seemingly spoken by God in the first person, again suggesting that Kabīr is an incarnation rather than an ordinary person. A fifth song speaks of the need for desire or interest in order for things to get done, of the emergence of multiplicity from the singular reality of Alakh, and of a world where there is no Brahma, Viṣṇu or Śaṅkara Dev. 'Who will remember God there?', Kabīr asks. A sixth song shares elements with one song of Padmarām, speaking of a world in which there is no mother to give Kabīr birth, no water in which to bath, no earth on which to place his feet, no direction in which to go. In a time before Pārvatī and Śiv, Kabīr met the guru (who in the last verse is identified as Rāmānanda) and in each age acquired some new item marking the sadhu — wooden sandals, a staff, a characteristic cross-tied robe. Now in this Kali Yug he wanders in the four directions. Again there is an implication that Kabīr has taken incarnation in all these ages, reflecting Kabīr Panthī views, and the Kabīr emerging here is more consonant with the one found in the popular songs translated by Lorenzen within the Kabīr Panth, emphasizing the themes of death and impermanence as well as inner religion.

A seventh song is a fragment of a narrative song about Kabīr's wife Loi, referring to the incident in which she agrees to trade her virtue in order to get provisions for Kabīr from a merchant who has been eyeing her, to offer hospitality to visiting holy men. When she tells Kabīr (at his insistence) how she has been able to get the provisions, he offers to carry her to the merchant himself, but when the latter asks how she reached him through the rain without getting wet and she explains, he repents and becomes Kabīr's disciple. I had asked specifically if he knew this song, and although he seemingly had heard it and could reproduce a portion of it, he did not know the full text.[38] As Lorenzen observes, this legend 'combines protests against economic and sexual exploitation of poor low-caste people by local merchants with an insistence that even the poor owe charity and hospitality to religious ascetics',[39] and it is interesting that this particular episode should make its way into song. I do not know of any other narrative songs about events related to Kabīr's life, although there are many about Mīrā including extended ones of near epic proportions.

[38]The existence of such a song tradition had been reported to me by Manohar Lalas and Komal Kothari who had heard it performed once many years ago in their work at Rupayan Sansthan.

[39]David Lorenzen, *Kabīr Legends and Ananta-Dās's Kabīr Parachai*, Albany: State University of New York Press, 1991, p. 49.

However, the *dohās* sung by the Mānganiyārs and sometimes also by Meghwāl singers before the actual songs attributed to Kabīr also contain a wealth of material about him that is sometimes more narrative in nature, and this additional well of oral tradition about the saint also warrants further investigation. One set of *dohās* sung by a Mānganiyār singer first has Kabīr addressing Gorakhnāth and advocating the *Śabd* or Word followed by an answering *dohā* in which Gorakhnāth addresses Kabīr in support of the *Nām* or name of God as the way for the soul to cross over this ocean of *saṃsār* — quite a different encounter from the miracle contest between the two found in written sources and with no clear winner.[40] I have also heard a Kālbeliyā Jogī guru speaking the songs of Kabīr (and others very similar but attributed to Nāth gurus) within his spontaneous teaching in an alternate form of performance. He incorporated a large body of legendary material as well, including stories of Kabīr's daughter Kamali (consistent with Kabīr Panthī accounts)[41] and of an encounter between Raidās and Kabīr in which Raidās appears as the spiritually superior of the two (in contrast to the outcome of the written debate in the text attributed to Sain and translated by Lorenzen).[42] This Kālbeliyā Jogī guru spoke much of 'Hindu and Mussalman' as well, and of the senseless disputes between the two, advocating a *nirguṇ* path that transcended these distinctions and outward practices (although the Kabīr songs he recited did not deal so directly with this theme).[43]

Several other Mānganiyār singers I worked with could offer only one or two songs of Kabīr. A second singer sang a popular song about the swan soul having to leave this world alone and the regret that people will feel in the end who have spent their time pursing wealth at the cost of the body and building castles in the sand, adamantly claiming them as 'mine' when the world and life pass so quickly. The guru, too, will die, his future determined by his deeds, and the disciple will be left alone. Better then to plant a garden and pursue the ultimate fruit. This singer also sang three other songs in the name of Kabīr, but all were clearly Kṛṣṇa *bhajans*, with references to Rādhā and to the world of Vṛndāvan. He did not, however, see the contradiction, suggesting that he did not have a clearly defined idea of what songs might be consistent with Kabīr based on *saguṇ* and *nirguṇ* distinctions. A third singer sang two songs, one paralleling songs cited by Lorenzen and sung by Padmarām relating how we search outside for what we already

[40] Ibid., pp. 54-5.

[41] Ibid., pp. 50-1.

[42] Lorenzen, *Praises to a Formless God*, pp. 169-203.

[43] Jetunāth, Interview, 19 July 1997.

have, using images like the thirsty fish in the sea and the deer searching everywhere for musk.

When I asked a Langā singer also to perform songs of Kabīr, he was able to sing five songs. The Langās are professional caste musicians who are very close to the Mānganiyārs except that they tune their *sārangīs* differently and their patrons are Muslims–Sindhī sepoys. This singer sang of renunciation and the variable nature of a sadhu's life — sometimes well provided for and sometimes living as the poorest of the poor. The song concludes with an admonition not to walk the walk of wealthy people. A second song also focusing on *fakīrī* or renunciation speaks of the great degree of happiness that comes from singing Rām's *bhajan*s rather than from wealth. The sadhu is the landlord of all the four directions in his wandering. A third critiques the hypocrisy of mistreating parents while they are alive but making ancestral offerings eaten by crows after they are gone, of making stone images of snakes to which sweet offerings are given but chasing away real snakes, and of making icons of God that will be sold for hard cash or provisions in case of drought or famine. In a fourth, Kabīr challenges the way we waste our lives — talking endlessly without taking the name of Rām, earning great sums of money but never being satisfied or sitting in the company of sadhus, spending our youth in the pursuit of sensual pleasure, weakening ourselves in senseless activities. A final song reminds us of old age — the eyes will go blind, the ears deaf, the knees weak, our grip feeble. Your 'wife', he says, 'will lose respect for you; your children and grandchildren will speak without concern, asking when you will die. Remember then the name of God, leaving wealth, affection, and anger.'

The Langās are interesting precisely because both they and their patrons are Muslims, and yet they sing both Kabīr and Mīrābāī. Their repertoires of both were smaller even than those of the Mānganiyārs singers with whom I worked, but the singers reported that their predecessors had larger repertoires.[44] Further questioning revealed that a generation ago, Langās were including Mīrā and Kabīr in performances for their Sindhī sepoy patrons, but now these Muslim patrons generally insist on only the songs of Muslim saints. Clearly this trend is reflective of changing times and of religion becoming a primary component of identity, but this

[44] One singer said that his elder brother, now deceased, knew many songs, and the singer had learned the three he could remember from him (2 of Mīrā; 1 of Kabīr). The singer whose Kabīr songs are reported above said that his father also sang, and when he moved to Jodhpur, he began associating with Brahmins and learned a few songs from them.

is a recent phenomenon. In the past the boundaries between Hindu and Muslim have clearly been much more fluid and not oppositionally defined with Mīrā and Kabīr easily moving across them. Though the Langās are not attached to Hindus as jajmāns, they do perform for some Hindu caste groups, and thus still find an audience for these songs even today.

In turning to the songs of Mīrābāī, Parita Mukta offers us an alternate vision of Mīrā and the traditions surrounding her, through an extensive examination of the songs sung among low-caste groups in Rajasthan and Saurashtra during jāgaraṇs.[45] She identifies three overriding themes in the songs of her 'People's Mīrā': (1) a rejection: the rāṇā (the king and feudal lord)'s authority coupled with a critique of caste oppression and advocacy of an alternate egalitarian society, (2) a challenge to an arranged or forced marriage and widowhood, and (3) an expression of the suffering that afflicts those who must live under these systems, as well as the itinerant singer and those exiled from society because they dared to challenge its norms.

In a small portion of my own earlier work on Mīrābāī, I have also presented an overview of folk traditions of Rajasthan, attempting both to survey the range of themes within songs attributed to her and to examine narrative traditions about her.[46] Some of the songs I surveyed (sung by singers from a variety of castes) confirm the themes identified by Mukta, reflecting resistance to feudal domination and caste oppression as well as arranged marriage primarily through the language of renunciation and rejection. Other songs, however, reflect more directly the longing for God, using the language of love and the seriousness and utter dedication required to follow the path of bhakti, with some corresponding to well-known songs from the wider Mīrābāī traditions. A clear appropriation of Mīrā is found as well, as Mukta also notes. She is alternately a weaver woman abandoned by her husband, a village woman going for water at the

[45] Mukta, *Upholding the Common Life.*

[46] Nancy M. Martin-Kershaw, 'Dyed in the Colour of Her Lord: Multiple Representations in the Mīrābāī Tradition', dissertation, Graduate Theological Union, 1995, pp. 254-337. The narrative traditions I surveyed included *Mīrā Janma Patrī* (or Mīrā's Horoscope) sung by Meghwāls, *Kumbhā Rānā rī Bāt* sung by Turi Bhāts in the Sirohi region (a more complete version of which I recorded in January 1997), and the *Mīrā Maṅgal khyāl*s or folk dramas by Lacchirām and Punimchand Sikhwāl. The song texts I used did not constitute a comprehensive survey but rather examples drawn from my own recordings in 1992-3 and from material collected by Komal Kothari and Rupayan Sansthan, beginning in the 1960s. Both Mukta and I had access to the latter, and she, too, briefly discusses *Mīrā Janma Patrī*.

well, a *tandūro*-playing *bhajan* singer, and a Kumār potter, as people make her over into their own image (even as high caste people do in other contexts). Many of the songs reflect elements from other types of folk songs and oral epics, and there is clear continuity between these traditions. Folk traditions are far from monolithic, however, and the traditions not limited to those songs most commonly sung in jāgaraṇ settings. In order to see patterns of difference within this realm and to explore the breadth of material attributed to Mīrā, we must turn to a more specific examination of the full repertoires of singers from specific groups who perform in a variety of different contexts.

An excellent example of the Mīrābāī repertoire of a Meghwāl singer is provided by a set of forty-two songs again performed by Padmarām, together with Maganrām who regularly sings with him and a third singer Maheśarām who joined them in a joint recording session.[47] Some of the songs are versions of material found in the wider tradition, though the texts differ, for example, from those in popular recordings, suggesting an alternate route of transmission. Some of these songs also appear in early manuscripts and later printed collections with sometimes only minor and sometimes considerable variation. Padmarām sings the quintessential Mīrā song, *Dūsarā na Koī* (There is no other), but it is the name of Rām rather than Girdhar Gopāl himself that is without compare for the saint. Mīrā buys the Dark Lover Sāṃvarā (rather than Govind) in the market to the beat of the drum and for a good price in a rendering of this familiar song and cries out to Kṛṣṇa as a *jogī* renouncer in a rendering of *Jogī Mat Jā* (Jogī, don't go), begging him not to leave her behind and, indeed if he must go, to build a fragrant fire of sandalwood and aloe, lighting it by his own hand, that she might burn and her ashes be spread upon his limbs. In another, Mīrā calls her own heart-mind (*man*) to the banks of the Ganga and Jamuna rivers for classic views of Kṛṣṇa, seated beneath a parasol, adorned with his peacock feather crown and diamond earrings, and roaming in the forest with his brother Balvīr as they graze the cows. Mīrā's dream marriage to Gopāl is also recounted but with more details of the wedding ceremony than are generally found in written traditions and commercial recordings. Such songs, with considerable variation, form a kind of common core of Mīrā material found in both written and oral traditions, although, I would argue, there is no 'original' form of any one song traceable back to a historical Mīrā of which the others are variants but rather a series of related renderings.

[47] Recorded in the *Patrikā* studios, Jaipur, Rajasthan, in November 1993.

A second set of songs speak of renunciation, reflecting both Mīrā's rejection of authority (feudal and patriarchal) which Mukta has highlighted, and the rejection of Mīrā by both her royal husband and society because of her religiosity and rule-breaking behaviour. In a number of such songs Mīrā appears as a woman of passion and strength who chooses to renounce her life of privilege, voluntarily taking up a life of poverty and embracing a low-caste guru, the Camār Raidās (also called Rivdās, Rohidās, or Ravidās). In one song she adamantly refuses to wear the shoes or royal dress the rāṇā gives her, choosing instead the wooden sandals and saffron cloth of a renouncer. She will not eat or drink from metal utensils but will carry the gourd and black bowl of the sadhu and refuses to sit in a high palace, choosing to live instead in the company of holy men. She does not want the things the rāṇā has to give, and thus he has no power over her. The same can be said of the singers in relation to those who would oppress them, and Mīrā's voluntary rejection of her life of privilege shows her solidarity with them and devalues the things that wealth and privilege can provide or deny to another.[48]

Further, Mīrā appears to reject the idea of absolute parental authority in arranged marriages and to question the ideology that says a husband should be treated as a god, when she says to the rāṇā in another song, 'Why should I wed a man who will die in birth after birth?' She will marry Shyām instead, and her wedding bangles will never be broken. She begs her mother to marry her to God and to bring her joy rather than sorrow. Clearly her mother does not listen, however, for the rest of the song recounts the rāṇā's attempts to kill her with a cup of poison said to be *caraṇāmṛt* and a venomous snake which she takes as a garland for her Lord. Mīrā is unharmed, but the very real and violent opposition to behaviour that challenges these social norms is clearly portrayed. These trials are repeated in a number of songs as fundamental elements in Mīrā's story and identify her as one who suffered deeply at the hands of members of her own family because of her love of God, her public behaviour breaking the rules for womanly propriety, and her crossing of caste barriers by taking a low-caste guru and interacting freely with devotees of all castes. (The latter theme is made particularly explicit in *Mīrā Janma Patrī*, an extended narrative song sung by Meghwāls although not part of Padmarām's repertoire and about

[48] Padmarām does not sing some of the popular songs sung by other Meghwal and low-caste singers who recount Mīrā's embrace also of the dry pieces of *roti* and simple hut that mark the life of the poor and her defiant cry, 'What can the Mewari Rana do?' See Mukta, *Upholding the Common Life*, pp. 90-105 and Martin-Kershaw, 'Dyed in the Colour of Her Lord', pp. 280-302.

which I have written elsewhere.)[49] She is also quintessentially one who survives such torments and thus a harbinger of hope and a source of courage in resistance, with God clearly on her side. Indeed in many songs she addresses Kṛṣṇa as Dīnānāth, the Lord of the Poor.

In other songs, Mīrā's renunciation seems less voluntary, and it is the rāṇā or Kṛṣṇa who seems to reject her. In folk songs, Winifred Bryce has observed, women sometimes refer to their husbands as raja or king, and it is not too great a leap to suggest that the songs of Mīrā that refer to the rāṇā might also reflect other women's experiences.[50] Within Padmarām's repertoire is a song suggesting that it is the rāṇā who turns away from Mīrā and that he does so because of her religiosity, a theme which Ann Gold has highlighted in her presentation of women's stories such as that of the *junglī rāṇī* where women's religious power lives in an uneasy tension with the marital state.[51] *Mīrā Janma Patrī* reflects a similar theme, and the life stories of women renouncers often highlight such struggles.[52] Mīrā speaks of the ripe mangoes, raw green ones, and lemons that grow in her land and then asks the rāṇā why he has abandoned this country. In subsequent verses she addresses Kṛṣṇa, saying that it is because of him that she has become a jogin, putting on saffron clothes, weeping bitterly, and letting loose her hair. The song concludes ironically with the line 'Rādhā's Lord is but a child', suggesting that from the singer's point of view there is no necessary competition between husband and God, though clearly the rāṇā sees things differently. In being forced to embrace renunciation because she holds fast to her sense of herself, Mīrā comes into even deeper solidarity with those who suffer similar torments without the real freedom to choose.

In another song she also addresses the rāṇā asking him why he as wounded her with the dagger of love, and begs for compassion. She

[49] Nancy M. Martin, '*Mīrā Janma Patrī*: A Tale of Resistance and Appropriation', in *Religion, Ritual and Royalty*, edited by N.K. Singhi and Rajendra Joshi, Jaipur: Rawat Publications, 1999.

[50] Winifred Bryce, *Women's Folk-songs of Rajputana*, Delhi: Ministry of Information and Broadcasting, Government of India, 1961, p. 18. For further examples, see also William Archer, *Songs for the Bride: Wedding Rites of Rural India*, New York: Columbia University Press, 1985, pp. 149-50; and Henry, *Chant the Names of God*, p. 72.

[51] Ann Grodzins Gold, 'Devotional Power or Dangerous Magic?' in Gloria Goodwin Raheja and Gold, *Listen to the Heron's Words*, Berkeley: University of California Press, 1994, pp. 149-63.

[52] Nancy M. Martin, 'Mīrābāī: Inscribed in Text, Embodied in Life', in Steve Rosen (ed.), *Vaiṣṇavi: Women and Devotion to Kṛṣṇa*, Delhi: Motilal Banarsidass, 1996, pp. 7-46.

recounts that in her courtyard she has done meditation until she grew tired, drawn water from a step-well endlessly with dedication, and spent all her energy guiding the elephant who walks there with a goad — images which also suggest a serious religious practice in which she takes pride but to which he responds only by hurting her. In this portrayal, Mīrā is still far from the good wife we find in much of the Hindi literature — she is a religiously powerful woman who must give up much to follow her calling. This sense of regret or sorrow at the rāṇā's behaviour is not a dominant theme in Padmarām's repertoire, for many more songs suggest that Mīrā wants nothing to do with him. It is only Ram who interests her, no other — all the rest has little meaning and only burdens her.

That Mīrā has become a jogin because of Kṛṣṇa and taken up the life of a sadhu is repeated in a number of songs with varying refrains, including one where she tells her mother clearly that she takes on saffron dress expressly with the aim of meeting Rām. Renunciation is a fundamental characteristic of the Mīrā who emerges in Padmarām and other jāgaraṇ singers' repertoires, and her defiance and rejection of the world and its set of values introduces another form of community in the *satsang* of the saints where religious experience is valued over socially-sanctioned inherited authority or the power that comes from wealth. The refrain of one song has her running to join the community of devotees, and in another she speaks of all the *tīrtha*s or pilgrimage places being found at the feet of the saints who are for her Kāśī, Mathurā, and Ganga in an internalization of religion reminiscent of Kabīr, but with its centre in the community rather than the individual heart.

We find, as well, an emphasis on the immanence of death and the short time we have in this world, though this theme is less pronounced than in Kabīr. We are only here for a little while and then we must die, so why not spend our time as Mīrā does in singing praises to Hari? Life is so short, yet we waste our energy on senseless pursuits. If we engage in the business of selling, then the goods are gone. If we make a cup of paper, it collapses when the first water hits it. Dew evaporates quickly as the earth heats up, and though the pots on the water wheel fill on the way up, they are all emptied on the way down. Even so with our lives. Such a song might as easily be sung under Kabīr's *chāp*, but is attributed to Mīrā. I have observed a number of discussions among singers about whether a particular song belongs to this saint or that; 'correct' attribution is not always easily determined, and there is not always consensus.

Other songs of Mīrā speak of devotion to God in traditional metaphors of love and longing, with detailed descriptions of Kṛṣṇa and references to

Vṛndāvan and to the rainy season of desire and union, as images from everyday village life blend with those of more classical Kṛṣṇa devotion in a way characteristically attributed to Mīrā. In one song she speaks of receiving *darśan* of Kṛṣṇa after sweeping the path and covering it with flowers, comparing herself to a *papīya* bird waiting in the cool shadows, a bee in a flower singing of its beauty, and a dark cuckoo in the garden enjoying the blossoms' perfume. In other songs she speaks of the pain of love in separation and abandonment, begging Kṛṣṇa not to turn his back on her after having shot her with the arrow of love and longing, comparing her agony to that of a fish out of water. But he is unaware or uncaring of her plight. In still others she invokes classic images of the rainy season when lovers should lie in each others arms and when separation is that much harder to bear — thunder rumbles, dark clouds gather and the peacocks, frogs, and cuckoos call as Indra fills the sky with a seething storm. She finds joy, finally, at Kṛṣṇa's feet. In yet another, she sends a parrot to carry a message to her lover, promising to cover its beak with gold and silver and put golden bells on its feet in return for making her again a happily married woman.

Images from the world of Vṛndāvan and the gopīs also blend with those of village life. With the irresistible call of Kṛṣṇa's flute, renunciation is given another twist as Mīrā tells a friend how she heard this sound and abandoned everything — the water pot, the task of cleaning her teeth, the work of churning milk, the baby swinging in the cradle, the elephant and the horse ready to ride, the lamp burning and with it, all hope of living in a palace. Without Hari, she weeps bitterly, withering like an unwatered vine. In another the identities of Mīrā, Rādhā, the gopīs, and village women fetching water merge when she tells Kṛṣṇa not to block her way, burdened as she is with heavy pot upon her head. In successive verses she speaks of planting a garden for him in which he will be the ripe mango and she the unripe green one, of digging a step well in which he will be the pot and she the rope, of building a palace where he will be the pillars and she the lattice work screen, and of laying out the *caupaḍ* game in which he will determine the moves and she will be the game piece. In the end he wins and she loses in this playful interchange, but in yet another song, it is she who wins, for she claims to have enchanted the Renouncer Kṛṣṇa. She invites him to come as a milkseller to taste the curds she has churned, as a gardener's wife to enjoy the flowers she has collected, as a carpenter's wife to admire the sandalwood spinning wheel she has made, and as a tailor's wife to take the gold needle and silk thread she offers.

Such songs are filled with images of everyday life, and reflect longing at multiple levels — for human love, for union with the divine, to be known and loved utterly and without question by another — as well as the joy of love fulfilled. Those which speak particularly of the world of Vṛndāvan, recounting for example Kṛṣṇa's childhood games and youthful wanderings with the cows, also mark a kind of boundary of the tradition, as *bhajan*s from the wider traditions of Kṛṣṇa devotion receive Mīrā's *chāp*.

Beyond these characteristic themes we also find songs in which images of love and those of meditative concentration and yoga merge. Though the refrain of one invites the resident of Dwarka to come to her home, it also stresses the value of taking the name of God and speaks in the first verse of a shoot emerging from the lotus of the navel and reaching to the house of eternity. Mīrā offers to lay out a beautiful bed for Kṛṣṇa in the sky, covering it with flowers, to build a sacred fire that he might come to her temple, and to dig a well and become his water carrier. In a particularly beautiful song, she draws first on the image of the acrobat — holding the bamboo pole of knowledge that has penetrated her body, the intoxicated lover climbs up on the rope of love that has been pulled tight. Having smashed the pot of ego balanced on her head, she comes to her Lord with a dancer's graceful steps, snapping out the rhythm with joy. The spout of the pleasure palace will open with a thousand drops cascading down as the cuckoo of love calls. These she says are the things worth tasting. The refrain stresses that she sees and loves only Hari's name. She claims to take the path of earlier traditions, though people say she has gone astray, wounding her and taking no account of how she feels. Old books, old scripts — why get hung up on these things, she says in a clear critique of book religion coupled with an affirmation of the authority of religious experience, and thus of the religiosity and wisdom of the poor so often devalued by those in positions of authority and power.

The royal renouncer who emerges in these songs and others in Padmarām's repertoire is multidimensional, and her renunciation is coupled with overpowering and unswerving devotion. Defiance and joy as well as deep suffering and sorrow mark the verses, as Mīrā becomes a model of courage and hope as well as a voice to articulate pain and resistance. The events of her life emerge much more clearly than do those of Kabīr, and are the vehicle for this modelling, forming the ground of shared experience that makes her such a powerful and well-loved figure. A number of songs refer to both the importance of the community of saints and to the *satguru* as well as to Mīrā's earthly guru Raidās, an affiliation that explicitly brings Mīrā much suffering in the *Janma Patrī*, and places her in solidarity with the experiences of all those who suffer caste oppression. She is also a dancer, a singer of God's praise, and a player of a variety of instruments. Further, she is a woman struggling in a world that does not readily allow her to determine the course of her life, and a lover who draws the community with her into all the shades of love in ever-deepening devotion.

When we turn to the Mānganiyār singers, we find the range of Mīrā material considerably more limited, though one singer was able to perform nineteen songs. His repertoire of Kabīr was also larger than other Mānganiyār singers, and this seems to be directly related to a difference in patronage. His Viṣṇoi patrons often call him to perform in devotional contexts, and he has actively worked to enlarge his repertoire in this area. More than half of the songs he sings are beautiful renderings of songs popular in the written and recorded tradition of Mīrā such as *Koī kahiyau rai Sānvariyau Ghar Āvan Kī*, *Jal Jamanā rī Tīr*, *Mhāne Cākar Rākhau jī*, *Dūsarā na Koī*, *Rām Ratan Dhan Pāyau, Darasan Bin Dūkhaṇ Lāgau Nain*, *Mharau Ghar Āau Kānha jī*, and *Prem Divāṇī Darad na Jāne ko*. A second Mānganiyār singer could perform seven songs and a third five, again with the majority being well-known texts from popular, written, and folk traditions with strong poetic forms. For example, one such song speaks of the addiction to Hari's name — like the water carrier always conscious of the pot on her head and the acrobat who dare not take her eye off the rope, she is always conscious of this 'opium' without which she cannot survive.[53] In a second Mīrā addresses an old Brahmin astrologer, begging him to tell her when she will meet Rām who has kept his promises to others and offering him all kinds of rewards. In general we find much more overlap in the singers' repertoires of Mīrā than of Kabīr, suggesting that the range of material attributed to Kabīr is much wider.

In terms of content, we find no mention of Raidās in any songs performed by the Mānganiyār or Langā musicians I recorded. References to the world of Vṛndāvan appear, with some songs being Kṛṣṇa *bhajans* that might be sung without Mīrā's *chāp*, and most songs are in the language of love, paralleling themes of love and romance that mark other songs sung in *kacheṛī* sessions and offering an emotional range that reaches well

[53] In addition to appearing in the repertoire of many singers from many castes, similar songs dealing with opium addiction are found in Anand Swami Swarup's *Mīrā Sudhā Sindhu*, Bhilwara: Śrī Mīrā Prakāshan Samiti, 1991, pp. 873-4; Harinarayan Purohit (Sharma)'s *Mīrā Bṛhatpadāvalī*, vol. 1, Jodhpur: Rajasthan Oriental Research Institute, 1989, 1st published 1968, p. 195; and Shekhawat's *Mīrā Bṛhatpadāvalī*, vol. 2, Jodhpur: Rajasthan Oriental Research Institute, 1975, p. 173.

beyond the devotional sphere. Lively and biting songs addressing the rāṇā also occur as do some relating events from Mīrā's life — a good story and a kind of divine human romance in itself. Defiantly Mīrā says that she has the affection of the Dark Lover and tells this crazy person with whom she has no relations to go away. In the ensuing dialogue between her and the rāṇā, he tries to get her to give up her renunciation, and join him in his world, but she rejects the necklace of diamonds and jewels he offers, threatening to burn it, and takes up a *tulsī mālā* of God and her guru's name. The royal dress he would have her to wear instead of saffron cloth and his invitation to leave her wood hut and join him in his royal bedchamber (*raṅg mahāl*) are rejected with the same blatant disregard. In another, Mīrā says straight out that she will lose her credibility, her integrity, her self-respect, if she keeps trying to explain herself to the rāṇā. It is like giving a mirror to a blind person—what beauty will he see? How will a mute person describe what he hears? How will a fool judge the jewel put before him? Why keep company with snakes, she asks. You may feed them milk and sugar, but they will still turn and bite you. A more complete rejection and humiliation of the rāṇā is hard to imagine, and clearly such a song could be generalized to refer to other 'rāṇās'.

We might conclude that Mānganiyār repertoires are closer to the textual tradition, in part because textual sources are a viable means of learning new material for them, but also perhaps because these songs are popular with themes that resonate with life as well as devotion and are poetically well constructed, meeting the performance demands of the *kacheṛī* context. In another sense, text is less important to the Mānganiyār singers than to devotional performers, with musical virtuosity and entertainment taking precedence over the cultivation of love for the divine or even the articulation of resistance and suffering that must be veiled as the words of the saints rather than spoken directly. More wide-ranging repertoires are found among expert Meghwāl singers whose skill lies in their ability to elicit a multifaceted love of God, to call people to act with dignity and focus their lives on what really matters, and to give voice to the longing, suffering, defiance, and wisdom of those traditionally silenced. Clearly musical performance elements have a profound effect on repertoire as do social and religious factors, and the Mīrās and Kabīrs who emerge in the fluid realm of oral performance are multiple, reflecting the rich religious heritage and diverse life experiences of those who sing the songs of the renunciant *rāṇī* and the weaver of protest.

Kabīr: Recited and Sung Today in Rajasthan

BAHADUR SINGH

In almost every Rajasthan village I went to in 1995 there were people reciting Kabīr texts to musical accompaniment on *tānpurā*, *dholak*, *khartāl*, *mamjīrā*, *iktārā*, *jogiyā sāramgī*, even on a harmonium at times, though I avoided this, because it is not traditional and introduces film melodies. The Rajasthan I am referring to includes the north, the west and the south, and though the east is not included, nevertheless even the above diffusion is altogether remarkable.

Let me emphasize here that all my recordings were done in an entirely natural context, at the homes of the singers or of patrons organizing a session, even though on our behalf. That is to say, in my collection there are no studio recordings whatsoever.

Of interest in terms of Sociology of Religion is the fact that most of the reciters/singers belong to the so-called low castes, namely meghwāl/chamār, nāyak, kolī, tūrībhāṭ, nāyī, telī, etc. The relevance of this is that the patrons of such recitals are high caste Hindus, with the result that, a very few exceptions apart, the texts recited are not such as criticize Hindu scriptures or brahmins; that is to say, the repertoire of the reciters lacks precisely such texts we have all been taught to look upon as the authentic words of Kabīr.

Similarly, there is scarcely any criticism of the Muslim priesthood, though naturally enough the patrons are not Muslims. We can only speculate on the reasons for this: were perhaps the relations between the Rajput rulers and Muslims very cordial? Perhaps this was so also among the people in general in Rajasthan?

I could collect 500 texts, and surprisingly enough hardly any of them is found in the collections we already have, those of Tiwārī or Vaudeville or Callewaert, though we do find a few in H.P. Dvivedī's Kabīr-Vāṇī.

Again, we have all been taught that the *sākhī* is a literary form essential to Kabīr. And yet in my collection there are only a few, recited as

* The paper is based on a project for collecting Mīrā and Kabīr oral recitation in Rajasthan today. The project was financed by the German Research Society (Deutsche Forschungsgemeinschaft), to which I am really obliged for its help.

introduction to the *vāṇī* or *pad*. Note too that the few *sākhīs* in my collections are not those considered authentic.

And this applies in principle to the *ulaṭbāṃsī* form also — I have only one sole example in my collection.

How does one explain this divergence from the written tradition? I am afraid I have no convincing answer at the moment.

The type of text I have come across most often while recording is the *helī*, again not to be found in our printed collections of Kabīr. Let me cite only a few lines from a typical *helī*:

rain samāī bhāṇ maiṃ mhārī helī
bhāṇ akāsāṃ māṃy mhārī helī
akās samāyau sūn meṃ mhārī helī
sūn sabad gai māṃy mhārī helī . . .
kaive kabīro dharmīdās nai mhārī helī
sāheb samtāṃ rai pās.

O my lady friend (*helī*), night
merges in the sun, the sun merges
in the sky, o my *helī*, the sky merges
in emptiness, o my *helī*, emptiness
merges in the Word. . . .
O my *helī*, Kabīr tells / teaches Dharmīdās
that the Master [resides] with the Sants.

Instead of going into various problems of interpretation even these few lines pose, problems characteristic of all *nirguṇ* literature — I mean of course the juxtaposition of contraries overcome gradually, and yet we have Sāheb and Sants in the end — let me merely point out the formal elements of the *helī*. Thus, it is the *helī* who is repeatedly addressed, and in the end, it is Dharmīdās, Kabīr's pupil, it is said, who is taught a truth from Kabīr's own experience.

A slightly different type of text is the *fakīrī*. In my recordings it is less frequent than the *helī*, but I know that it is very common and in this sense important too. Like *helī*, the word *fakīrī* too is repeated at the end of each line, and its theme and language too are those of *nirguṇ* bhakti.

In the Jaisalmer and Baṛmer areas I also found the *pyārī* form. In this case, the *pyārī* is addressed repeatedly, and there is no difference as to theme and language. What is important is that the *helī*, the *fakīrī* and the *pyārī* each have a different musical form.

Let me conclude these short remarks on formal characteristics of texts ascribed to Kabīr with the so-called *mangaḷ*, 'the auspicious'. This is a rather long type of composition, the recitation too is different from that of the others, it is often sung in the early hours of the morning, and after it, the jāgaraṇ, the *satsang* comes to an end. The theme is the marriage of *surati* as the bride, and *sabad* as the bridegroom. The metaphor contains all that precedes and follows a normal wedding ceremony, but it ends with philosophy: the bride meets *niranjan*, the ultimate, the undefiled.

The foregoing remarks refer to questions of form. Let me now give an example of what concerns belief. Some of the singers I met, spoke of speech as having four faculties. To quote Mr. Vasudev, village Bargaoṃ, Sirohi district: the faculties are *parā, pasantī, madā* and *bekarī*. Each is bound to a specific time of the jāgaraṇ and also to a specific type of text: the *parā* is linked to the *gurumahimā*, recited between 9 and 10; the *pasantī* to *vārtā*s or religious stories, told from 10 to 12; the *madā* to *helī, sajnī* and *pyārī*, recited after midnight; finally the *bekarī* is bound to the *prabhātī*, that is, Kṛṣṇa-Rādhā songs, for example, and sung early in the morning.

Let me give one final example of belief at times motivating the reciter. Mr. Bhīkhārāmjī Śarmā, of Mokaḷsar, district Suratgarh, recited a text in which the journey to the city of immortality and the journey to the city of death are described as journeys by train, the body being considered an 'engine' (*anjan*) or a train (*tan gāḍī*). The passenger (*jīv*) is warned not to lose the ticket (*ṭigaṭ*), the time is short (*ṭem jarāsī hai*), etc. Now I was careless enough to point out that Kabīr himself could scarcely have composed this text. But Mr. Śarmā was deeply hurt, and he replied that Kabīr was after all a seer and it was most natural that he should have perceived things to come. And I realized that I had committed a real error and hurt him in an entirely gratuitous manner.

Such beliefs call for extensive study, and all I wish to indicate here is how interesting and varied are the questions that this field of research poses.

For us who are interested in Sant literature the most important question is of course that of authenticity. Let me give only one sole example of the type of problems this poses. Paṇḍit Kumār Gandharv sings a text included by Hazārī Prasād Dvivedī in his edition of *Kabīr-Vāṇī.*

On my part I could record two versions of this very text, recited by Gomandrāmjī Harijan and Sohanlāl Harijan, both of Suratgarh district (see appendix). Now Paṇḍit Kumār Gandharv begins with *sakhiyāṃ vā ghar sab se nyārā*: that is to say, it is women who are being addressed. But in Gomandrāmjī's text, it is the *avadhū* who is addressed, and Sohanlāl's version begins with philosophy, for the first words are *vāṃ nahīṃ dukh sukh*, and only after two further lines do we find a vocative, but now it is *sādho*. Now let us assume for the moment that Kabīr himself did indeed compose this text; but even if this were true, how does one decide which of these three variants is the original one? And this is equally true of the other lack of uniformities found in these three versions, though I am now adding only two examples.

Paṇḍit Kumār Gandharv has this at one point:

oham soham ardh urdh nahīṃ
pāṭh lekh na ko hai.

[Where the *pūrṇ puruṣ*, 'the perfect being',
resides], there are no [such categories like]
'I am that', 'below', 'above', 'recitation' and 'writing'
[*oham* and *ardha* are of course conditioned by alliteration.]

Now in Gomandrāmjī's text we find instead:

ovai sovai ardh urdh vic,
svāṃsā levat koī,

on which he himself says that Kabīr wishes to make a point here, namely, that only a person most exceptional can breathe in the states mentioned; and Goṃandrāmjī adds, among other things, that only the *guru* knows what exactly these states are.

And this is Sohanlāl's version, completely lacking *oham soham* and reciting instead:

aisā hai ard urd vic
bāsā levat hai vāṃ koī.

It is thus: somebody lives
there, between below and above.

Now of course *svāṃsā levat* and *bāsā levat* are essentially phonetic variations, leading to different ideas, but how does one choose objectively from these three variants?

In the versions of Gomandrāmjī and Sohanlāl we find the following four lines which are absent in that of Paṇḍit Kumār Gandharv:

nā andar nā avagat kahiyai
nā saksam asthūlā
nā nirguṇ nā surguṇ kahiyai
tāṃtak man rī bhūlā.

Call him not the inward [one], not
[the one] not comprehended, neither subtle
nor gross, call him not as having qualities or
without qualities — all this is the mind's error.

The text recited by Sohanlāl is different only in that he has *ye sab* instead of *tāṃtak*. Again we have no criteria to prove that these four additional lines are not genuine.

Now Sohanlāl did indeed forget four lines of his text while reciting them, but he remembered them when I requested him to repeat the text without reciting it. Suppose somebody had simply recorded his text as he recited it, in such a case, we would have had another version of the text and the problem of authenticity would have been there again.

Let me conclude with lines of Sohanlāl's once more:

vāṃ nahīṃ dukh sukh sāc jhūṭh nahīṃ
pāp punn nahīṃ pasārā
candar sūr devas nahīṃ rajanī
binā jot ujiyārā
sadho bo ghar sab syūṃ nyārā
jāṃ rahtā hai prūs hamārā . . .
pāṃc tant guṇ tīnūṃ nāhīṃ
surat sabad vāṃ nāhiṃ . . .

There is no happiness or suffering there,
no truth, no lie, no evil, no merit is present
[there], no moon, no sun, no day, no night,
[there is] light [there] without [a source of]
light. O *sadhu*, that abode is enterely different,
there lives my Master (?) . . . .
The five *tattvas*, the three *guṇas, surat*, word
are not there.

These words and those already cited in the context of the *helī* and the *mangaḷ* are common to much of Nāth and Sant literature. And the problems are substantially the same in both the written and the oral traditions. How then can we decide as to who was the author of the one or the other text? As I have already pointed out, a fundamental aim of future research has to be to develop criteria of authenticity.

APPENDIX

Text 1 Paṇḍit Kumār Gandharv

sakhiyāṃ vā ghar sab se nyārā, jahāṃ pūraṇ puruṣ hamārā
jahāṃ nahīṃ dukh sukh sāṃc jhūṭh nahīṃ, pāp na punn pasārā
nahīṃ din rain cand nahīṃ sūraj, binā jyoti ujiyārā
nahīṃ tahāṃ jñān dhyān nahīṃ jap tap, ved kitāb na vāṇī
karnī dharnī rahnī kahnī, ye sab jahāṃ hirānī
dhar nahīṃ adhar na bāhar bhītar, piṇḍ brahmāṇḍ kachu nāhīṃ
pāṃc tattva guṇ tīn nahīṃ tahāṃ, sākhī śabd na tāṃhī
mūl na phūl beli nahīṃ bījā, binā bricch phal sohai
oham soham ardh urdh nahīṃ, pāṭh lekh na ko hai

jahāṃ puruṣ tahṃvā kachu nāhī, kahai kabīr ham jānā
hamrī sain lakhai jo koī, pāvai pad nirvānā.

Text 2 Gomandrāmjī

avadhū vo ghar sab se ī nyārā, jahāṃ rahatā puruṣ hamārā
jahāṃ nahīṃ sukh dukh sāc jhūṭh nahīṃ, pāp punya nahīṃ pasārā
candramā sūraj divas nahīṃ rajanī, binā jyoti ujiyārā
gyān na dhyān jap tap sādhan, ved kurān na vāṇī
rahnī gahnī karanī kaṃthanī, tāṃsau sab harānī
dhar nahīṃ adhar bāhar nahīṃ bhītar, piṇḍa biremāṇḍ nāhīṃ
pāṃc tant guṇ tīnūṃ nāhīṃ, surat sabad vahāṃ nāhīṃ
mūl na phūl bīj na belī, binā barach phal hoi
ovai sovai ardh urdh vic, svāṃsā levat koī
nā andar nā avagat kahiyai, nā saksam asthūlā
nā nirguṇ nā surguṇ kahiyai, tāṃtak man rī bhūlā
jahāṃ hai puruṣ vahāṃ kachu nāhī, kahai kabīr ham jānī
jo koī lakhai sain hamārī, milāūṃ puruṣ nirbāṇī

Text 3 Sohanlāl

vāṃ nahīṃ dukh sukh sāc jhūṭh nahīṃ, pāp punn nahīṃ pasārā
candar sūr devas nahīṃ rajanī, binā jot ujiyārā
sādho bo ghar sab syūṃ nyārā, jāṃ rahtā hai prūs hamārā
gyān dhyān jap tap nahīṃ sādhan, ved kurāṇ nahīṃ bāṇī
rahaṇī gahaṇī karṇī kathaṇī, tāṃsyū hai sabhī hairānī
dhar nahīṃ adhar pavan nahīṃ pāṇī piṇḍ brihmāṇḍ vahāṃ nāhīṃ
pāṃc tant guṇ tīnū nāhīṃ, surat sabad vāṃ nāhīṃ
mūl nahīṃ phūl bīj nahīṃ bālī, bin birach phal sohvai
aisā hai ard urd vic, bāsā levat hai vāṃ koī
nā andar nā avigat bhāyā, nāhīṃ suksam asthūlā
nā narguṇ nā sarguṇ kahiye, e sab man rī bhūlā
vahāṃ hai prūs tahāṃ aur kuch nāhīṃ, kahai kabīr ham jānī
je koi sain lakhai hamārī, miljai purus nirvāṇī.

Mīrā's Yoga

MAYA BURGER

INTRODUCTION

This paper aims to explore a so far neglected aspect of Mīrā's work: the exploration of her spiritual path, which one may qualify as her yoga. Yoga is certainly not the term that immediately comes to mind when one hears the name Mīrā or even when one reads her poetry. The purely devotional side of her unique love for Kṛṣṇa has played a central role in the apprehension and comprehension of the poet. The scrutiny of the texts attributed to her shows, however, a more complex image of Mīrā that will be presented here by emphasizing her yogic side and her unique spiritual path. Yoga has to do with experience. What has been handed down to us, are however, the poetic expressions of her experience or her yoga. These expressions have entered the history of bhakti literature in a peculiar way. I will start with a first chapter on the traditional image of Mīrā (I), the reception of her work (I.1. and I.2) and some methodological consequences and a working hypothesis (1.3). Chapter 2 will be consecrated to her yoga.

THE TRADITIONAL IMAGE OF MĪRĀ

About the sources: critical evaluation of the editions and commentaries

The state of research on Mīrā has so far been quite stagnant in western Indology. She has however been much worked on in the Indian context.

Much has been said about the difficulty of knowing exactly who Mīrā was. It is commonly admitted now that she lived around 1498 to 1547[1] and that she was a Rajput.[2]

[1] These dates are as uncertain as others.

[2] She might have been the daughter of Rav Ratansi, born in Bajoli; married to Kunwar Bhojraj of Cittor, who died early (1522?). She is supposed to have undergone torture by her in-laws who did not appreciate her behaviour. At a certain time (around 1531/2) she is supposed to have left Cittor to become an itinerant pilgrim to settle finally in Dwaraka, where she died in 1547. An early mention of her life is made in the *Bhaktamāla* of Nābhājī (dating back to the beginning of the sixteenth century).

Her work also is a true puzzle, no consensus has been established concerning her work and its authenticity. Researchers admit by now, that most probably her work lies in the *pada*s (*padāvalı*);[3] they constitute the material of this paper. There are innumerable collections (around fifty?) that do contain her *pada*s, some of them in different languages. Editors claim to have collected the material from old manuscripts (from the last century), but these manuscripts are themselves collections of material that belongs to the oral tradition, so that it is very difficult to establish their authenticity, or to establish a criteria of selection.[4] A systematic investigation into the early manuscripts has been done by W. Callewaert to whom we owe much in this respect.[5] He has pointed to the difficulty of establishing a valid corpus for Mīrā, as her verses were written down only after the eighteenth century. He gives a selective bibliography of editions of the songs of Mīrā.[6] According to Hiralal Maheshvari, for example, there are about 2000 *pada*s (other estimates are much larger)[7] that are ascribed to her, out of which at the most, 250 may be termed authentic.[8] I have concentrated my investigations on mainly three editions, the one by Caturvedi (*Mīrāṃbāī kī padāvalī*, 1966), the more recent Jodhpur edition by Harinarayanji Purohit (*Mīrāṃ bṛhatpadāvalī*, 1989) and the more extensive *Mīrāṃ Sudhā-Sindhu*, 1992) by Svarupa.[9] Compared to the immensity of Mīrā's work, this may be a modest, but nonetheless representative selection.

The corpus of texts on which we may work has no solidly defined source. The different editors of Mīrā have their established criteria to evaluate the authenticity of the collected songs, among which the philological criterion is by far not the dominant one. One can even ask if such a criterion makes much sense in her case (there are of course certain

[3] See for instance, Hiralal Maheshvari, *History of Rajasthani Literature*, New Delhi: Sahitya Akademi, 1980, p. 150.

[4] One finds, for example, the same or similar *pada*s in different collections and sometimes intermingled texts.

[5] Winand M. Callewaert, 'The "Earliest" Song of Mīrā', *Annali*, vol. 50, 1990, Naples: Istituto Universitario Orientale.

[6] Callewaert 1990, pp. 372-7.

[7] Tivari mentions over 5000 songs. Bhagvandas Tivari 1974, quoted in Callewaert 1990, p. 364.

[8] Hiralal Maheshvari, *History of Rajasthani Literature*. See also, Harinarayanji Purohit, *Mīrāṃ bṛhatpadāvalī*, Jodhpur: Rajasthan Oriental Research Institute, 1989, Bhūmikā, pp. 4-12.

[9] Other collections have not been considered, either because they were not available or because of their very unsatisfactory character as compared to the work of Harinarayanji Purohit, Parashuram Caturvedi and Ananda Svarupa.

elements which can be said to be based on the language, such as the use of Persian, Braj, Gujarātī, more or less archaic expressions, etc., but it is also recognized that these elements are necessarily insufficient). The criteria of selection and also of the commentaries of her work occur more on the basis of religious convictions.[10]

It is interesting to notice how most of the commentaries of Mīrā treat the poems which do not neatly fall into the picture they have drawn of Mīrā. Either they are spoken of in a negative way, considered as spurious or simply distorted.[11] Alston's work is a good example of this approach.[12] Whenever the name Rāma appears in Mīrā's poetry, he translates it by Kṛṣṇa, arguing that in fact it is Kṛṣṇa to whom the poetess refers. Yet, the name Rāma, as we shall see, occurs in a very specific context of Mīrā's utterings, and this stresses the necessity to remain very close to the text, if one wants to draw a complete picture of her utterances.

Caturvedi has for instance put into an appendix, the poems that mention the name of Raidās as her guru. Neither the language nor the style of these poems show enough diversion from other selected poems to allow for an exclusion from the collection. She does not say anything which she does not also say in other poems (see for instance poem 18 of the appendix which contains so many expressions found in the selected poems, from among which one may quote (C, 18, 174, 194). The reason for exclusion appears to be just the mention of Raidās. However, there is no way, in the present stage of research, to decide in favour of, or against the guruship of Raiḍās. On the other hand, Caturvedi includes (in his last edition) poems as doubtful as the ones he has put into the appendix.

The *rāga*s mentioned at the top of the poems[13] which could have been a source of knowledge concerning her spiritual experience and the transmission of the text (musical memory) differ from edition to edition

[10] Hawley states in an article of which I became aware once my own paper was already written, that many poems attributed to Mīrā are in fact created songs about her, relating her life and imitating her style. They are of a more hagiographical nature. John S. Hawley, 'Mīrābai as wife and yogi', in Vincent L. Wimbush and Richard Valantasis (eds.), *Asceticism*, New York: Oxford University Press, 1995, p. 309.

[11] For example, see Shambhusinh Manohar, *Mīrāṃ padāvalī*, Jaipur: Research Publishers, 1969, Chapter 7, pp. 92-5.

Nicole Balbir, for instance, does not mention the question of yoga, *Chants mystiques de Mīrābāī*, Le Monde indien 6, Paris: Les Belles Lettres, 1979.

[12] A.J. Alston, *The Devotional Poems of Mīrābāī*, Delhi: Motilal Banarsidass, 1980.

[13] Caturvedi and Harinarayanji Purohit have quoted *rāga*s for the poems, which are supposed to have come down through tradition (most probably they had been

and hence fail to constitute a source of information other than to inform us in which *rāgas* devotees liked to sing Mīrā's poetry in the last century.[14]

To state it briefly, the collections we are presently working on are as much Mīrā as the reception-history of Mīrā.

MĪRĀ'S RECEPTION

Mīrā has emerged over the years as the embodiment of a type of devotion. The historical figure has vanished underneath a certain perception of what she is supposed to represent, mostly a devotee of her beloved and personal God, Gopāla Giridhara Nāgar. This stereotyped way of perceiving Mīrā and of putting her into a definite category has led, on the one hand, to collecting material that corresponds to this image. Many stereotyped songs of a conventional style have been attributed to her on the sole basis that they are a very common trend of love poetry. On the other hand, it has led to a misleading and one-sided interpretation of a far more complex poetical material and spiritual path. The ongoing tradition has chosen to retain from her work pure bhakti in its simplest and very popular form of expression. Many other poems have remained more inaccessible and have not attracted the attention of the devotional audience. The history of her *padas* has framed the image we have of Mīrā. She is remembered as the gopī, as Rādhā, as the pure lover, the *virahiṇī*, the crazy lover and singer of absence, but why is she not remembered also as the one who expresses a very interesting *sādhanā*, a yogic way that has transcended worldly boundaries and constitutes an unique way. This remains a very important question for which we have to try to find an answer.

METHODOLOGICAL CONSIDERATIONS AND WORKING HYPOTHESIS

Mīrā and her work form a typical case which defies any kind of rigid classification, where a positivistic approach fails and a complex construction

written on the consulted manuscripts). For most of the poems checked in the two editions, the indicated *rāgas* differ. The same poems have been recorded in different *rāgas*. This also is an important indication that no *rāga* was prescribed for the poems, but that the singer himself, or herself, sang it most probably according to his mood or some more sophisticated criteria such as time or *rasa* prescriptions. We don't have in this case all the reliable indications that we do with the *Guru Granth*.

[14]The *rāgas*, as mentioned for instance in the *Guru Granth*, that were prevalent at the time of Mīrā, do not appear in these collections. A precise history of the *rāgas* in the nineteenth century would bring a decisive answer to the problem.

of religious perception is called for. The challenge is to include, in the epistemology, the nature of the object that is religious experience and poetry, as well as the projection of what 'Mīrā should be'. Both these religious experience and reception-history escape by definition the rigidity of premoulded models.

There is not much that we can do insofar as the collections of the works of Mīrā are concerned, except include the fact as a particular trend of the Mīrā research and history of the figure. What has been handed down to us, is more of an attitude, more of a prevalent tradition than a person, at least in the reception of her history.

If we accept that the collected material does include a variety of religious experiences and many layers of intermingling traditions, the interpretation of her work should include all the facets of her spirituality, also the yogic one.

I would like to contribute to this broadening of her spirituality by working on what I call her yogic side. I do so with the assumption that traits preserved in her works which contradict the cliché are likely to point to a historical reality. Mīrā was a yoginī before she was made into a bhakti model.

MĪRĀ'S YOGIC SIDE

Mīrā's work shows the confluence of many traditions in which one recognizes the trends prevalent in her time and in her surroundings.[15] She is neither a philosopher nor a theologian; she is a poet, a singer, a devotee, a yoginī. Her yoga cannot be simply classified as belonging to either the classical line of yoga or to the more popular Nātha tradition, but shows a very personal character.[16] In the collection of Caturvedi (C) out of the 200 poems attributed to Mīrā, almost a quarter have some explicit reference to yoga;[17] Svami Ananda Svarupa has dedicated one chapter to poems that speak explicitly of yoga (*jogi ke pada*) in the *Sudhā-Sindhu* (*SS*).

I will start to depict her yoga by quoting lines that explicitly speak of yoga (II.1). I will then present and analyse her experience and her vision of God (II.2) and conclude with her yogic path (II.3).

[15] For a good discussion on Mīrā's heritage, see Rama Bhargava, *Bhakti kāvya kī paramparā meṃ Mīrāṃ*, Jodhpur: Kusumanjali Publishing House, 1991, pp. 64-89.

[16] Mīrā's yoga also yields much information about yoga and its evolution in that period.

[17] Besides, the eighteen poems of the appendix (chosen because they are said to be not authentic) have many yogic references.

Yogic terminology

In many poems Mīrā says she has taken the way of a yogi (C, 188): 'having become a jogi, I wander through the world' (*SS*, 632,28); here she speaks of herself as a *vairāgī* (C, 68), who has given up everything in order to obtain God; she wears the yogi beads (C, 80); there she sits in *āsana* in a cave and meditates on Hari (*dhyāna*); more generally *dhyāna* is a key attitude with Mīrā and has to be practised day and night (C, 88), in the heart; she speaks of attributes that belong to the yogi and that she uses, such as *selī*, *rudrākṣa*; she has chosen the company of the saints and sādhūs (C, 33); she is an outsider who has overcome worldly shame and opted for renunciation, *tyāga* (C, 93). She has taken the begging bowl and wanders as an ascetic through the world (*SS*, 630); very often she also calls her God a jogi, as well as *avadhūt* (*SS*, 632,35).

In more indirect, yet very explicit words, she states elements that indicate the way of the yogi and renouncer. First of all, body and senses have to be overcome: 'First of all your body is crushed, when you want to offer love, be eager [to cut off] and make a seat (*āsana*) with your head' (C, 191); senses do not allow for detachment (C, 158). Repeatedly she speaks of the necessity to purify oneself to obtain the divine. She speaks for instance of her activity of sweeping to calm her disturbed mind (*cit*), which incidentally is a sign of the greatest detachment for a person of her status. She says: 'Expel lust, anger, pride, greed and infatuation from my mind (*cit*)' (C, 199, transl. Alston). She implores her God to cut her knots (*gāṃsī*), in order to permit the presence of God (C, 195). Her way is so intense and resolute, and utterly opposed to the rest of the world that she often speaks of her craziness: she is intoxicated with love for the divine (C, 178); if she cannot live in his presence, it is a question of life and death ('my body is pervaded by pain, my heart is in state of intoxication' C, 174); she uses the term *prāṇa* (C, 4/5) to show the intensity and the ontological necessity to live in the presence of the divine. If she cannot see him, it is her life, i. e. her *prāṇa* that goes. She is not searching for an exterior yogic path: there is no need to put on the external attributes if the heart is not clean (C, 158), and if one is not able and wanting to pierce the secret, '. . . they are jogi, but they don't know the [real] purpose' (C, 195).

Mīrā's experience and her vision of God

The basis of her thought is a deep divine experience or realization (*samādhi*). This is the starting point from which all the other elements of her life and spirituality derive. She has had what one may qualify as a yogic experience: she has seen and met her God, in the sense of a profound meditative trance or absorption accompanied by a visionary contemplation of the absolute pure spirit, brilliant light, divine love. She hence possesses his supreme and direct knowledge. In her own formulation:

'My love for Śyāma has set in and my eyes have enjoyed his sight' (C, 201); 'My beloved dwells in my heart, I have seen the abode of joy' (C, 194, transl. Alston); she had the perception of a cosmic body, she is in fact the universal consciousness:

> . . . I already have Hari for my necklace, I will have Him for my ear-rings too, Him, my bride-groom, Viṭṭhal Nāth. My crest-jewel is the Four-armed Vishnu, whose image revolves in my mind. I need not to go to a goldsmith, my anklets are composed of Him who is the Life of the Universe. Krishna is my armband and my foot-band too. My foot-rings and dancer's anklets are Rāma Nārāyaṇa, the ring on my big toe the Inner Ruler. I will have a casket fixed to my belt, made from the Supreme Spirit [*puruṣottama*], a lock from the Name of Trivikram, a key from Him whose Joy is compassion. There I will keep my treasure safe. Now I am seated in the bride-groom's house, Arrayed in finery and quite without shame. . . .[18]

The yogic *samādhi* is not only a visual experience, but also an acoustic one. She hears the divine word (*śabda*), revealed as a sweet voice (C, 103);[19] the use of terms like thunder, lightning, drumming calls to mind the riddled language used by the Nātha-yogins to announce realization (C, 142: 'Nandanandan has entered my heart, and the clouds have obscured the sky. Thunder roars, clouds quake, and flashes of lightning terrify'). In a terminology very close to Kabīr,[20] she speaks of the terrible arm (*kaṭārī*) that has stricken her (C, 38, 155, 174), the arrow that inflicts a wound of such love that it is absolutely total and irrevocable, and allows for no return (C, 173).

The notion of vision of God (*daraśana*, *daras*) is central to almost all her poems. If one was to count the expression that arises the most frequently in her songs, I think it would be the quest of Mīrā for the vision of God, her thirst to see her God. This demand is so omnipresent in her work it is even difficult to single out an example: Once again, only once would be enough, 'Give me your sight once, and all troubles are over', she asks, 'again and again' (C, 89); she implores her jogi to provide her with

[18] Translation by Alston 1980, p. 92.

[19] It is interesting to note that Alston, for instance, intercalates the word 'fancy' in his translation in order to explain hearing that voice, Alston 1980, p. 76.

[20] See *Kabīr vāṇī, recension occidentale avec concordances*, établie par Charlotte Vaudeville, Pondichéry: Institut Français d'Indologie, no. 64, 1992, poems such as in *satguruī mahimā kau aṅg*, 1.21 and 1.22.

his *daraśana*, as she has abandoned all for him (*SS*, 632,28). In another poem she announces that she wants to become a yoginī to be able to get his *daraśana* (C, 94). It is hence not the ordinary vision of the God, as known in temple worship or through the statue that is meant here, but something else that points to the difficult path to (re-) attain the realization of the divine. Mīrā's spirituality and her search is only understandable in the light of the fact that she has had a spiritual realization. The notion of *daraśana*, as used by her, is a quest for something she has actually experienced. She is literally incapable of living without the vision (C, 66). If she were only a ritualist or the worshipper of a statue there would be no need to claim *daraśana*, because she can have it all the time (one knows that the statues have played most probably an important role in her life).[21] Mīrā's bhakti is a visual knowledge, it is *daraśana*; the notion of *daraśana* is a question of survival (C, 66). As she says (C, 76) it is not the outer vision (figurative) she is interested in, but the inner: 'your statue is in my heart' (*SS*, 632). *Daraśana* seems to be the experience, a mystical realization of the Lord: *tum bic ham bic antar nāhiṃ* (C, 114).

In its abstract or absolute form she uses words such as the indestructible principle (*abināsī*) (C, 201); in this context she often calls him Hari; another abstract concept is *antarjāmi* (C, 84); she speaks of him as 'all there is' (C, 202); he is all pervading, '. . . where shall I go' (C, 39). She says 'the coarsest bread is the *nirguṇa* one and I feed on this' (*SS*, 28).

On the level of the manifestation of the divine her description is more complex. The most frequently used name is Giradhara Lāl, meaning Kṛṣṇa. Mīrā has innumerable ways to name Kṛṣṇa. But this is by no means her unique way of describing her God.[22] Often she calls him a yogi, which is not the habitual way of the bhakti poets to apprehend Kṛṣṇa, but could refer to a tradition closer to the *Bhagavadgītā*; sometimes he is described in a way that resembles Śiva (C, 55); mostly, however, she uses the term Rāma. As I have already said, the use of the name Rāma occurs more frequently in poems which are close to expressions found in the Sant tradition. Other expressions echo with memories from the Upaniṣads: 'There is no difference between you and me, just like [there is no difference] between the sun and the heat' (C, 114). There are however poems where Rāma is also invoked in the folk traditional context of *viraha*

[21] These statues are Viṣṇu and Kṛṣṇa. Some verses talk about how these were destroyed by her family members. But we do not have any evidence of this.

[22] See for instance the different names used for the divine as stated by Harinarayanji Purohit, pp. 62-5. The author gives however no explanation and puts together names which are abstract and concrete (*antaryāmī*/Gopāl).

songs (more usually addressed to Kṛṣṇa) (C, 92). Both names may occur in the same poem (C, 133). Sometimes the two names appear in opposition (C, 67,[23] C, 55-9). This might suggest that the signature she uses, which often contains the name of Giradhara Nāgar, is really nothing other than a signature, or a poetical device rather than an expression that carries the meaning of the song. It could also be an indication that other singers composed these poems and added the well-known signature of Mīrā. As we know it did actually happen.

Her concept of God is multiple, in spite of what is generally said. She has not one name and she has not one God. Of course, her chosen deity is Kṛṣṇa, but her God is also far above it. Lines such as the ones quoted here are important in this matter. To substitute Rāma simply by Kṛṣṇa and say that it is the same is to miss the specificity of her religious experience.

In a certain way it is true that bhaktas do have an exclusive love for one chosen deity.[24] But the belief in the oneness of the ultimate in no way hinders the fact that its manifestation is multiple. Mīrā is a very good example of this. It could also be an indication that Mīrā's spirituality had periods of very different intensity and nature and cannot be closed up in a one-sided category of a defined religious trend once and for all.

To understand *daraśana*, we also need to remember what the aim of Mīrā's spirituality is. It is, in fact, to see her divine lover. Another term for this liberating effect is *milan*, as for Kabīr, which translates in other words that she wants to see, meet, him. Mīrā also uses the term of *sahaja*, a term by which she indicates the return to a natural state of being.[25] It is a state where one does what one has to do; Mīrā says, 'Hari has bound me with a thin thread of love, where ever he draws me there I go' (C, 173, transl. Alston). 'Let my light dissolve in your light, jogi' (C, 46). Over and over she craves to unite with her divine lover; she and her beloved are united, inextricably in one body:

> I am dyed in the love of Giridhara My beloved . . . I am playing hide and seek with him robed in his smock of five colours. Disguised as I was, he caught me, and beholding his beauty I made myself over to him, body and soul. . . . (C, 23, trans. Alston)

[23] The description of Rāma in this poem is in fact a description of Kṛṣṇa.

[24] This exclusiveness appears for instance strongly in poem C, 60.

[25] Her sense of *sahaja* comes, I think, close to how the Nāthayogīs, or Kabīr uses it. I disagree with the translation of 'simple' by Alston. See for instance my article, Maya Burger, 'Kabīr et la répétition du nom de Rāma', *Etudes asiatiques*, XLVII. 4, 1994, Berne: Peter Lang, p. 1051.

The question of liberation also shows the complexity of Mīrā's spirituality. On the one hand she states that liberation (*daras/milan*) can only happen because of God (C, 156), but on the other side she emphasizes very strongly, that it does happen according to one's own actions (C, 196). The terms of *anugraha* or *prasāda*, so familiar with other poets of her time, are singularly absent from her collections. She very rarely uses the term of *bhagavān*. She has taken refuge (*śaraṇa*) at the feet of her *satguru* (C, 111). In the relation to her God, she calls herself a slave (*dāsī)* and a servant (*cerī*), terms which one has to understand as the one who has given up her own will, and who acts in an attitude of service (C, 45); her personal will is replaced by the will of God (C, 153). On the other hand, she describes her being only dependent on herself and her actions (like for instance the fruits of her previous lives). Her Lord is of a totally unpredictable nature (C, 53-7); he does what he wants (C, 85): 'To love a jogiyārī is source of pain. When you are with him he speaks sweet words, but then he goes and forgets you'(C, 54).

Mīrā knows the result and expresses in her poems the conditions for obtaining the vision of God: these are her path. Mīrā has to renounce the world, the senses. In the ordinary condition the Absolute God is not visible, he can be seen only when he takes form and this depends on the path of the searcher. The divine vision asks to go beyond the ordinary life and to bypass worldly attachments. Renunciation is central to Mīrā and her vision, *daraśana* is in fact for Mīrā seeing God which is the only aim of life.[26] Her aim, her path, her ritual all indicate the strong yogic side of Mīrā's unique bhakti.

SOME MORE ELEMENTS ON HER YOGIC PATH

On the assumption that the experience is at the beginning of her spiritual life, her path (*sādhanā)* appears as attempts to recreate this experience. Having had the experience, she finds herself in the condition of *viraha.*

Her path, which she describes as difficult and high (*ūcāṃ*) (C, 106) proposes different ways to reach the goal, which all derive from her experience.

[26] This comes very close to what Peter Schreiner says in the context of the Nārāyaṇīya, '*Darśana* bezeichnet die Belehrung über die Gestaltwerdung der Gottheit, welche Ausdruck göttlicher Zuwendung zur Welt sind; diese Zuwendung ist Gegenstück zu einer "Antwort" auf einen Weg menschlicher Abwendung von der Welt, deren Ziel die teilhabende Schau des transzendenten Geistesprinzip ist.', Peter Schreiner, 'Die Schau Gottes', in *Nārāyaṇīya-Studien*, p. 191.

The recitation of the name

The recitation of the name is a strong element of her path (*japna*); 'drink the nectar of his name' (C, 199); however *japna* is not practised with the lips (C, 63) but in her heart ('Day and night, I have practiced remembrance of thy name in my heart'). The name is in fact the possibility to obtain liberation ('I will sail the boat of the name Śyāma and cross the ocean of becoming'), the name takes her to the other shore (C, 31). The name can even act as a magical device for being saved (C, 140). In the absolute majority of the poems that use the glorification of the force of the name, it is the name Rāma which is used (for example, C, 63). She goes as far as to say, that liberation can only be obtained by the name of Rāma: *Rāma nāma bini mukuti na pāvāṃ* (C, 156).

The yogic path of the absence, Mīrā virahiṇī

Many poems of Mīrā are dedicated to singing the absence of her beloved. It is a path of purification, where the absence has to go as far as to reach the state of complete nudity and emptiness, this seems the only way to allow the presence of God to re-emerge and fill her totally: '. . . Enchanted by your form, beloved, I offer to you my body, mind and life. I have lost all appetite for food and drink and my eyesight has faded. Oh Murari, day and night I dream of meeting you, when shall I have your sight?. . .' (C, 69). *Viraha* is not a state of despair,[27] but the state of certainty that the spiritual realization is possible and that the only urge in life lies in the desire to recreate it on and on. The certitude of a realized experience abides deeply in Mīrā. *Viraha* certainly indicates the absence, but the more the divine is absent, the more it becomes present, till the moment when the union is consumed in silence or pure praise. Bhakti is far more than a simple love, it is the yogic path of giving up all personal perception ('what ever he says I shall do', C, 153) and being filled, after emptying each corner of the body by the divine nature, acquiring a new body, this time divine 'Mīrā is dyed in the colour of Hari' (C, 17). 'Only she whose beloved is abroad has to

[27] It is very instructive to see that most of the *viraha* songs are recorded in light *rāgas*, that point rather to the *ṭhumrī* style, hence to a style of singing that is emotional, certainly, but that is also light. Peter Manuel has for instance shown in his book on *ṭhumrī*, that on the Muslim side the *gazal* takes on a far more dramatic tone than on the Hindu side, where it is always accompanied by an optimistic and 'happy end mood'. Peter Manuel, *Thumri. A Historical and Stylistic Perspective*, Delhi: Motilal Banarsidass, 1989, p. 18.

write and send letters, my beloved rests in my heart, nor does he go, nor does he come' (C, 23).

Music and dance

Having heard the sound of Kṛṣṇa's flute, she imitates it by singing his praise. According to the traditional image, Mīrā is a singer for her beloved Kṛṣṇa and a dancer in front of his statue. However, even these more ritualistic elements can be viewed according to a yogic state. Music and dance are actually *the* ritual of Mīrā. It is how she expresses and builds her religious experience. Sound and rhythm are also in a certain way a yoga, they corroborate to build the physical and mental fabric that constitutes the religious experience.

Methodologically speaking, it is very difficult to approach a religious experience that is expressed not in a discourse on God, but in poetry, rhythm and sound. Yet these are most probably stronger elements to convey and express religious experiences than words.

To understand Mīrā's *pada*s and spirituality, the musical part plays a crucial role. If reading her poems may bring about a feeling of repetition, the musical element is exactly what transforms these poems into a unique experience converted into the subtle knowledge of the wedding of sound/rhythm and meaning. It is in fact the music that makes the poems of Mīrā, that gives them their full shape and constitutes the core of the experience. Her spiritual path converges with the expression of singing and dancing, which is sculpting the modal melodies in space. Mīrā does not sing or dance to bring about an altered state of consciousness. In her case it is the reverse that seems true: 'Wherever I put my feet on, there I praise you' (C, 21), sound and rhythm are the perfect, at least most accurate state of love and praise, and pure unity with the divine: 'All I can see is Śyāma, all I can think of is Śyāma' (C, 21). As she says, even her Lord is under the charm of the seven notes (C, 167). It is a cosmic knowledge of the power of music. Kṛṣṇa's flute is an expression of the fact that this state comes from outside and corresponds to a cosmic order which she reproduces, as well as Kṛṣṇa does. Mīrā loses consciousness, i.e. she gives up the ordinary way of perception, when she hears the flute: 'The sound of the flute has driven me crazy...on hearing the sounds I lose consciousness' (C, 167).

Mīrā's music is related to her land and environment. This again is an essential clue to her work. In the first place it is not classical music. It is the music of the region of her homeland, intimately related to the folklore of the women of that state.[28] It is a music that emerges in the land, from the earth, that is in the wind, that is captured and rendered by those who choose music as their means of expression.

It turns out to be classical music when it shifts to the city and the world of culture. That is what has happened to the music of Mīrā. It is rendered now in almost every repertoire of singing in a *rāga* chosen for the occasion and it is built into the classical frame of aesthetic and musical experience. There is hence an important shift, which is significant, but this would be an entirely different topic. It would have been interesting to trace the original *rāga* used by Mīrā, for that would have been a very helpful insight into the religious experience of Mīrā according to the postulate that the music expresses her experience in the deepest sense. Yet this has proven an unfruitful investigation, as there is no connection to be traced between the *rāga*s, the recension and Mīrā's living musical rendering. A very important clue to her work remains silent.

CONCLUDING STATEMENTS

Besides her recourse to yogic words, in her general attitude, as described in her poems, yogic elements are much present. Mīrā turns her back on the ordinary world, she opts for renunciation (*tyāga*, *vairāgya*); life is shown as source of suffering: 'In pain I wandered from door to door, but could not find any doctor' (C, 70); her devotion is absolutely firm and fixed on one goal centred on the vision and union with her God. She accentuates the importance of her personal contribution to achieve the goal, the necessity to transform herself and the role of actions. Further, her path is based integrally on personal experience and direct knowledge. All these elements may be accepted as defining yoga.

I hope I have been able to demonstrate how much Mīrā's bhakti is determined by yoga. To conclude I quote a poem which juxtaposes the world of yoga and the world of bhakti.

Go to the unreachable land (*agam vā des*), that death himself trembles to look at. There is a watertank of love, with swans (*haṃs*) playing on it. There is the assembly of holy men who realize knowledge. There one can meditate on the beloved and the mind (*cit)* becomes clean (bright) (*ujalo*). There the ankletbells of good

[28] Charlotte Vaudeville has shown the interrelation between the religious experience and the folksongs of the seasons of the year. Charlotte Vaudeville, *Bārahmāsā in Indian Literatures*, Delhi: Motilal Banarsidass, 1986.

behaviour can be tied on and the dance of satisfaction (delight) (*tos*) be danced. There one may get a headpiece of gold and the sixteen kinds of adornment. Let there be love for the beloved only, and indifference to all else. (C, 193, transl. Alston, with modifications).

REFERENCES

Alston, A. J., *The Devotional Poems of Mīrābāī*, Delhi: Motilal Banarsidass, 1980.

Balbir, Nicole, *Chants mystiques de Mīrābāī*, Le Monde indien 6, Paris: Les Belles Lettres, 1979.

Bhargava, Rama, *Bhakti kāvya kī paramparā meṃ Mīrāṃ*, Jodhpur: Kusumanjali Publisher House, 1991.

Bhati, Narayanasinh, *Mīrāṃbāī rī parcī ya parcīkāvya paramparā*, Jodhpur: Rājasthānī Śodh Saṃsthān (dna).

Burger, Maya, 'Kabīr et la répétition du nom de Rāma', *Etudes asiatiques*, XLVII. 4, 1994, Berne: Peter Lang.

Callewaert, Winand M., 'The "Earliest" Song of Mīrā', *Annali*, vol. 50, 1990, Naples: Istituto Universitario Orientale.

Caturvedi, Parashuram, *Mīrāṃbāī kī padāvalī*, Prayāg: Hindī Sāhitya Sammelan, 1966.

Harinarayanji Purohit (Sharma), *Mīrāṃ bṛhatpadāvalī*, Jodhpur: Rajasthan Oriental Research Institute, 1989.

Hawley, John S., 'Mirabai as wife and yogi', in Vincent L. Wimbush et Richard Valantasis (eds.), *Asceticism*, New York: Oxford University Press, 1995.

Kabīr vāṇī, recension occidentale avec concordances, établie par Charlotte Vaudeville, Pondichéry: Institut Français d'Indologie, no. 64, 1992.

Khan, Alam S., *Mīrāṃ: Lokatāttvika adhyayan*, Jaipur: Sandhī Prakāśan, 1989.

Les Duhā de Dhola Mārū, une ancienne ballade du Rājasthān, traduction et édition par Charlotte Vaudeville, Pondichéry: Institut Français d'Indologie, 1962.

Maheshvari, Hiralal, *History of Rajasthani Literature*, New Delhi: Sahitya Akademi, 1980.

Manohar, Shambhusinh, *Mīrāṃ padāvalī*, Jaipur: Research Publishers, 1969.

Manuel, Peter, *Thumri. A Historical and Stylistic Perspective*, Delhi: Motilal Banarsidass, 1989.

Shukla, Dinesh Candra and Ankor N. Sinh, *Rājasthān kī bhakti-paramparā tathā saṃskṛti*, Jodhpur: Rājasthānī Granthāgār, 1992.

Sharma, Madan Lal, *Mīrā*, Delhi: Rajesh Prakashan, 1990.

Schreiner, Peter, 'Die Schau Gottes', in Peter Schreiner (ed.), *Nārāyaṇīya-Studien*, Wiesbaden: Otto Harrassowitz, 1997.

Sri Guru Granth Sahib (English) trans. by Gurbachan Singh Talib, Patiala: Publication Bureau Punjabi University, 1985.

Svami Narottamdas, *Mīrāṃ-muktāvalī*, Agra: Śrīrām Mehrā, 1963.

Svami Ananda Svarupa, *Mīrāṃ Sudhā-Sindhu*, Bhilvara: Sarasvatī Vihār, 1992.

Vaudeville, Charlotte, *Bārahmāsā in Indian Literatures*, Delhi: Motilal Banarsidass, 1986.

PART X

Textual and Oral Transmission

A *Vajrasūcī* in Hindi

DAVID N. LORENZEN

In 1994 and 1996, I spent a total of about three months cataloguing the Hindi and Sanskrit manuscripts stored in the library of the Kabir Chaura monastery in the city of Varanasi.[1] Four of the nearly 250 manuscripts I catalogued contained a short text called the *Vajrasūcī*. Three of these *Vajrasūcī*s were written in Hindi (nos. 012, 104, 171) and one in Sanskrit (no. 030). Two of the manuscripts (nos. 012, 104) were definitely copied by Kabīr Panthī sadhus, and probably the other two as well. Since these texts evidently contained a detailed discussion of the *varṇa* system, I was immediately intrigued and took photographs of the four manuscript texts, but then put these away in a drawer while I worked on other projects. Later in 1996, Patricio Nelson, a graduate student in El Colegio de Mexico asked my advice about possible topics for his master's thesis. I suggested that the *Vajrasūcī* might be a good choice. He agreed and is now working on this project. His main interest is in the Sanskrit versions of this text and their reception by nineteenth and twentieth century Indian and British intellectuals. My main concern in this essay will be the Hindi version of the text found in the Kabir Chaura manuscripts. A translation is included at the end of this essay.

There are in fact two separate Sanskrit compositions called the *Vajrasūcī*. One, called simply the *Vajrasūcī*, is attributed to the famous first century Buddhist scholar Aśvaghoṣa. Unfortunately this attribution is quite doubtful. The second composition is often given the title, the *Vajrasūcy-upaniṣad* and is often attributed to Śaṅkara, presumably the famous Advaita author Śaṅkarācārya. This attribution is even more doubtful. Although the Buddhist *Vajrasūcī* and the *Vajrasūcy-upaniṣad* are distinct works, the thematic contents, and even some of the language, is similar in both. It is clear that one must have inspired the other, but there is no easy way to decide which was written first, when either of them were written, or which has had greater popularity and influence.

[1] The catalogue of the first 195 manuscripts was published in 1994. The remaining manuscripts will be integrated into a forthcoming second edition of the catalogue. A draft of the complete catalogue and the original manuscripts are available at the Kabir Chaura monastery in Varanasi.

Aśvaghoṣa's *Vajrasūcī* and the *Vajrasūcy-upaniṣad* are important because, among all pre-colonial Sanskrit texts, they present virtually the only sustained philosophical attacks against the division of human beings into the four social classes (*varṇa*s) determined by birth: the Brahmins, Kshatriyas, Vaishyas and Shudras. Other Sanskrit texts do, of course, chip away at the margins of the *varṇa* system. I am thinking here of some tantric texts and, more consistently, of many *bhakti* texts starting from the *Bhagavad-gītā* and including, above all, the *Bhāgavata-purāṇa*. In Aśvaghoṣa's *Vajrasūcī* and in the *Vajrasūcy-upaniṣad*, however, the attack on *varṇa* is not relegated to the thematic margins; it is the central message of the texts.

The modern publication history of both the Buddhist *Vajrasūcī* and the *Vajrasūcy-upaniṣad* is quite interesting. The Sanskrit text of the *Vajrasūcy-upaniṣad* was first published in 1827 by no other than Rammohun Roy, who also published a Bengali translation of the text (Killingley 1977). In 1831, the English Resident in Nepal, Brian Hodgson, prepared a translation of the Buddhist *Vajrasūcī*, on the basis of a single manuscript, and sent it to the Royal Asiatic Society in London where it was read at a meeting of the society. In 1839 Lancelot Wilkinson published the Sanskrit text of the Buddhist *Vajrasūcī*, based on a manuscript from Bhopal, together with Hodgson's English translation (of the Nepali manuscript) and a harshly critical Sanskrit commentary by a local Brahmin scholar. In 1860, Albrecht Weber published Sanskrit texts of both the Buddhist *Vajrasūcī* and the *Vajrasūcy-upaniṣad* together with German translations. The texts then seem to have passed into relative obscurity — apart from a 1921 Adyar edition of the *Vajrasūcy-upaniṣad* — until they were re-edited and translated by Sujitkumar Mukhopadhyaya in 1950. S. Radhakrishnan also included a text and translation of *Vajrasūcy-upaniṣad* in his 1953 publication, *The Principal Upaniṣads.*[2]

Although, as we shall see, Aśvaghoṣa's *Vajrasūcī* is of less interest for this essay than the *Vajrasūcy-upaniṣad*, we should note that a relatively early Chinese version of Aśvaghoṣa's text still exists. According to Patricio Nelson, this version is either a loose paraphrase of Aśvaghoṣa's text or a translation of a now lost Sanskrit commentary on it. This Chinese version dates from about the end of the ninth century. This is the earliest confirmed date for either the *Vajrasūcī* or the *Vajrasūcy-upaniṣad.*

[2] The references to these works can be found in the bibliography. Killingley's thesis contains a minutely detailed analysis and comparison of Rammohun Roy's Sanskrit text and Bengali translation.

As for the Sanskrit *Vajrasūcy-upaniṣad*, Nelson has found that there are at least two somewhat different recensions of this text and that some manuscripts of one of these recensions add a second part to the text whose contents are quite different from the first part. This second part criticizes the views of various philosophical schools and religious sects other than Advaita and also analyses the *mahāvākya* '*tat tvam asi*' in Advaita fashion.[3] It has not so far been published or translated, but Nelson is preparing an edition and translation for his thesis. The oldest manuscript of the Sanskrit *Vajrasūcy-upaniṣad* to which we have so far found a reference is one dated 1723 VS (CE 1666) listed in the catalogue of the Rajasthan Oriental Research Institute in Jodhpur (Jinavijaya 1967: 274-5, no. 15984[2]). Another manuscript from this institute contains a critical Sanskrit commentary on the Upanishad entitled the *Vajra-mudgara* or 'Hammer to the Vajra'.[4]

The three manuscripts of a Hindi *Vajrasūcī* found in the Kabir Chaura library are almost identical versions of a single composition whose basic source is the Sanskrit *Vajrasūcy-upaniṣad.* Only one of these manuscripts is clearly dated (no. 171), and this is a quite recent manuscript, with a date equivalent to CE 1877. The Hindi text was probably composed considerably before this date, but exactly when is impossible to judge.

The relation between the Hindi text and the Sanskrit Upanishad is more that of a loose paraphrase than that of a close translation, but they are clearly different versions of roughly the same composition. Likewise, the Sanskrit *Vajrasūcī* found in the Kabir Chaura library is a rather short version of the same Sanskrit *Vajrasūcy-upaniṣad.* This Sanskrit text is also somewhat closer to the Hindi version than is the Sanskrit text edited by S. Mukhopadhyaya (1950). In general the readings of the Kabir Chaura Sanskrit text correspond more closely to those of the earlier edition by A. Weber (1860).

The Hindi text in all three manuscripts claims that the original Sanskrit text was composed by Śaṅkara and the Hindi (*bhāṣā*) version by a Sant Rām. Another manuscript containing a Hindi *Vajrasūcī* attributed to Sant Rām is listed in the catalogue of the library of the Jaipur Palace (Bahura

[3] Nelson has located three manuscripts containing this second part in the University of Pennsylvania collection of Indic manuscripts (Poleman's nos. 761, 762, and 4150). This collection is available on micro-fiche in many libraries.

[4] Jinavijaya 1967, pp. 59, 294-5. Excerpts from the beginning and end of this manuscript are found on p. 59 of the catalogue. I thank Patricio Nelson for this reference.

1976: 196). It is undoubtedly the same text, although I have not yet had a chance to examine it. It is not dated. The same catalogue also lists a Hindi *Vajrasūcī* attributed to a Dhurandhar Kavi in a manuscript dated 1778 vs (ibid.). I have not found references to other compositions by either author.

That both a Hindi and a Sanskrit *Vajrasūcī* should be found in the Kabir Chaura library is perhaps not surprising since arguments against caste distinctions, and against the *varṇa* system itself, abound in Kabīr's own Hindi songs and verses and in the later literature of the Kabīr Panth. What is interesting, however, is the fact that the Kabīr Panthī scribes who copied these texts chose to ground their anti-*varṇa* position in this relatively obscure older text originally composed in Sanskrit.

Also interesting is the fact that two other Sanskrit texts that attack aspects of the *varṇa* system are found in three of the same Kabir Chaura manuscripts that also contain the *Vajrasūcī* (both texts in one manuscript, one each in the other two). The first of these associated texts is the *Brāhmaṇo ke lakṣaṇa*, also attributed to Śaṅkarācārya (in nos. 012 and 104). The second text is the *Sāra-candrikā* and its short eleven-verse summary called the *Ādi-purāṇa* (in nos. 104 and 030 respectively). The *Sāra-candrikā* also appears in five other Kabir Chaura manuscripts (nos. 115, 121, 129, 132, 141). All but one of these manuscripts (no. 129) includes a Hindi commentary to the Sanskrit text. Either the text itself or the commentary is attributed to a man named Kiśorī Alī.

In this essay, I would like to look at two questions connected with the texts of the *Vajrasūcīs* found in the Kabir Chaura manuscripts. First is the question of the nature of their relationship to Mukhopadhyaya's and Weber's published versions of the *Vajrasūcy-upaniṣad*. Second is the question of which specific arguments against *varṇa* are used in the Kabir Chaura *Vajrasūcīs* and the relation of these arguments to those in the associated *Brāhmaṇo ke lakṣaṇa* and *Sāra-candrikā*.

The close mutual relations among the different versions of the *Vajrasūcy-upaniṣad* can easily be seen in the following short passages from near the beginning of the text. The only significant difference among the versions is the inclusion of only six items in Mukhopadhyaya's text (*jīva, deha, jāti, jñāna, karma, dhārmika*) as opposed to eight in the other texts (*jīva, deha, jāti, varṇa, paṇḍita, karma, dharma, dhārmik[y]a*). Succeeding sections of the text do not correspond as closely as this, but the similarities are close enough to show that all the texts are versions of roughly the same composition.

OPENING LINES OF THE *VAJRASŪCY-UPANIṢAD*

A. Mukhopadhyaya (Sanskrit): *brahma-kṣatriya-vaiśya-śūdrā iti catvāro varṇas*
B. Weber (Sanskrit): *brāhmaṇaḥ kṣatriyo vaiśyah śūdraś catvāri varṇānām |*
C. Kabir Chaura (Sanskrit): *brāhmaṇa-kṣatriya-baiśya-śūdrāś catvāro varṇās*
D. Kabir Chaura (Hindi): *brāhmaṇa kṣatrī vaiśya śūdra | cyāri varṇa ye jānī |*

A. *teṣāṃ brāhmaṇa eva pradhāna iti veda-vacanānurūpaṃ smṛtibhir apy uktam |*
B. *teṣāṃ brāhmaṇaḥ pradhāna iti veda-vacanān nirūpitaṃ smṛti-niruktam |*
C. *teṣāṃ vrahmaṇyaṃ pradhānyaṃ veda-vacanāt nīrupītaṃ | smṛtirbhir uktaṃ*
D. *tini ke madhe hai kahyau | brāhmaṇa muṣa baṣāni ||3|| beda māṃhi brāhmaṇa mūṣa kahyo | tyo hi smṛti pramāna so lahyo |*

A. *tatra codyam asti ko vā brāhmaṇo nāma |*
B. *tatra codyam asti ko vā brāhmaṇo nāma*
C. *tatra yo 'yam asti ko brāhmaṇo nāma*
D. *yeha to jñāna kaho so jānyo | aba brāhmaṇa so kauna baṣāṇyo ||4|| brāhmaṇa nāma so kauna prakāra sunāīye |*

A. *kiṃ jīvah kiṃ dehaḥ kiṃ jātiḥ kiṃ jñānaṃ*
B. *kiṃ jīvaḥ kiṃ dehaḥ kiṃ jātiḥ kiṃ varṇaḥ*
C. *ko jīvah ko dehaḥ kā jātiḥ ko varṇaḥ*
D. *jīva ke deha ke jāti ke varṇa batāīye |*

A. *kiṃ karma kiṃ dhārmika iti |*
B. *kiṃ pāṇḍityam kiṃ dharmaḥ kiṃ dhārmikyam kiṃ karmety aṣṭau vikalpāḥ |*
C. *kaḥ paṃḍitaḥ ko dharmmaḥ kiṃ dhārmmikyaṃ kiṃ karmma ceti iti aṣṭau vikalpāḥ*
D. *paṃḍita karma ke dharma ke dhārmika jāniye | aṣṭa vikalpana māhi jo soī basāniye ||5||*

The basic philosophical tactic of both the Buddhist *Vajrasūcī* and the *Vajrasūcy-upaniṣad* is to deconstruct *varṇa* by showing that there exists no single essential intrinsic trait or substance in which *varṇa* distinctions can be located and legitimized. Various alternative essences are proposed — seven in Aśvaghoṣa's text, six or eight in the Upanishad — and each of them is shown to offer an inadequate basis for *varṇa* distinctions. Since Buddhist doctrine does not accept the existence of a soul or self, Aśvaghoṣa's text implicitly allows the deconstruction of *varṇa* to reach its ultimate consequence, the denial of any permanent substrata of individual persons.

In the Upanishad, on the other hand, the deconstruction of *varṇa* leads to the explicit claim that Ātman-Brahman is the immanent substrata of all persons. Either way, there is no ontological ground on which to build innate distinctions of *varṇa*. The only legitimate basis for *varṇa* distinctions is personal conduct. A person who acts as a Brahmin becomes a Brahmin; a person who acts as a Shudra becomes a Shudra. The Upanishad adds to this the Advaita argument that enlightenment itself is achieved only through the mystical realization of the truth of Ātman-Brahman. By this reckoning, only a knower of *Brahman* can be considered to be a complete Brahmin. Although the Upanishad is sometimes attributed to Śaṅkarācārya and shows the influence of Advaita, Śaṅkara's arguments that *varṇa* distinctions are valid in the context of *vyāvahārika* reality and that Shudras have no right to hear the Vedas or take *saṃnyāsa* (and hence have virtually no chance to reach enlightenment, much less become Brahmins) are nowhere mentioned (Lorenzen 1987).

These six or eight items analysed as possible essences or bases of *varṇa* and caste in the *Vajrasūcy-upaniṣad* are precisely those mentioned above. Each in turn is proposed as a possible source of Brahmin status and each is found wanting according to the following arguments:

1. The individual soul (*jīva*) cannot be the essence of the Brahmin because the individual soul has the same characteristics, including omniscience, in all human beings.
2. The body (*deha*) cannot be the essence of the Brahmin because all bodies have a similar composition. All are subject to old age and death. Also, when a son cremates his parents, he would, if they were Brahmins, be guilty of the sin of harming a Brahmin.
3. One's birth (*jāti*) cannot be the essence of the Brahmin since 'history' tells us that many famous Brahmin sages were originally born in other castes and *varṇa*s. Among them are Ṛṣyaśṛṅga, Kauśika, Gautama, Vālmīki, Vyāsa, Vasiṣṭha, Viśvamitra, Agastya, and Jāmbūka. Also, according to the 'Puruṣa Sukta' of the *Ṛg-veda*, all the different *varṇa*s are said to have been born from one single Puruṣa.
4. Colour (*varṇa*) cannot be the essence of the Brahmin since the different colours associated with the different *varṇa*s — white for Brahmin, red for Kshatriya, yellow for Vaishya, and black for Shudra — can in fact be all mixed together. Here the logic of the text is perhaps a little weak. The idea seems to be simply that all have roughly the same ontological status.

5. Erudition (*paṇḍita*) cannot be the essence of the Brahmin since all men, regardless of *varṇa*, are capable of learning and of sharing the truth (as even Śaṅkarācārya admits).
6. Karma cannot be the essence of the Brahmin since if this were true then one would expect that Brahmins would live twice as long as Kshatriyas, Kshatriyas twice as long as Vaishyas, and Vaishyas twice as long as Shudras. In fact this does not happen.
7. Dharma cannot be the essence of the Brahmin since each *varṇa* is associated with a particular dharma. No *varṇa* is without dharma in this sense.
8. Generosity (*dhārmika*) cannot be the essence of the Brahmin since Kshatriyas, Vaishyas and Shudras all give gifts.

All these rather different arguments share a single deconstructive purpose. If it can be shown that there is no permanent ascribed essence or location of Brahmin status, then one can propose that Brahmins are made, not born. It is restrained behaviour leading to direct mystical knowledge of *Brahman* that makes a Brahmin a Brahmin. As the Hindi *Vajrasūcī* says (vss. 26, 30):

One abandons all desires, passions, and hates. Through the discipline of making self-control, one gets satisfaction. One abandons thirst, envy, pride, confusion, illusion. One abandons doing harm, wicked killing, and the *ātman* is adorned with wisdom. [...] He who is a knower of *Brahman* is a Brahmin. No other is a Brahmin.

The argument concludes with a statement of the idea that *Brahman*, or God, is the unitary substrata of all the universe, implicitly including the four *varṇas* (vs. 33): 'You are present in all, all is in you, warp and woof, whatever exists.' The Hindi text concludes with the statement that the text was originally written in Sanskrit by Śaṅkara and rendered into dialect (*bhāṣā*) by Sant Rām (vs. 34).

As we have noted, the *Brāhmaṇo ke lakṣaṇa*, also attributed to Śaṅkarācārya, is found in two of the four *Vajrasūcī* manuscripts (nos. 012, 104) in the Kabir Chaura library. In both manuscripts, the *Brāhmaṇo ke lakṣaṇa* immediately precedes the *Vajrasūcī*. Evidently, the basic messages of these two compositions by Śaṅkara were thought to be complementary.

Despite the Hindi title found in the manuscripts, the *Brāhmaṇo ke lakṣaṇa* is written in Sanskrit. Unfortunately, the Sanskrit of the two manuscripts is quite defective, and at several points I have not managed to fully decipher it. I have also been unable to find the text in the published works attributed to Śaṅkara. None the less, the basic line of argument is clear enough. The text lists nine marks (*lakṣaṇa*) of a true Brahmin. Those who do not have these nine marks are considered to be Shudras. The marks include a variety of moral virtues, the restraining of senses and bodily pleasures, and, as the ninth mark, a standard set of six practices (*ṣaṭkarman*) that includes study (*adhyayana*), teaching (*adhyāpana*), performing sacrifices (*yajana*), sponsoring sacrifices (*yājana*), charity (*dāna*), and accepting gifts (*pratigraha*).

As we have noted above, six Kabir Chaura library manuscripts (nos. 104, 115, 121, 129, 132, 141) — including one of those with the Hindi *Vajrasūcī* (no. 104) — contain a text entitled the *Sāra-candrikā*. In addition, the manuscript with the Sanskrit *Vajrasūcī* (no. 030) includes a text called the *Ādi-purāṇa,* which is in fact a selection of verses from the same *Sāra-candrikā.* The full *Sāra-candrikā* consists of Sanskrit verses together with a Hindi commentary. The Sanskrit verses are almost all said to be taken from other sources, especially from several Purāṇas. The manuscripts attribute either the compilation of the Sanskrit verses, the Hindi commentary, or both to a man named Kiśorī Alī. I have only partial photographs of the manuscript versions of this text, but an edition of this text has recently been published (*Graṃtha-sāra-candrikā* 1989). This edition, however, does not mention Kiśorī Alī or give any other name of the compiler or author. The published text contains somewhat fewer Sanskrit verses than the manuscript texts, but almost all the published verses are apparently included in the manuscript texts, but not in the same order. The published text also has a Hindi commentary, written in verse, but this is different from that of the manuscripts.

The opening verses of the published *Sāra-candrikā* claim that sincere devotion is the mark of a superior person, no matter what *varṇa* or caste he or she was born into. Here is a translation the first six Sanskrit verses, all attributed to the *Padma-purāṇa*:

Whether one is a Brahman, a Kshatriya, a Vaishya, a Shudra, or other, one should consider the best of all these to be the one who is dedicated to devotion to Brahman. (1)

Even a Caṇḍāla may become the best of sages, if he is dedicated to worship of Brahman. He who is without devotion to Vishnu, even if he is a Brahmin (*dvija*), is lower than a Dog-eater (Śvapaca). (2)

A person who knows the four Vedas, if he is not my devotee, is not dear to me. A Dog-eater who is my devotee is dear to me. To him offerings are to be given, from him offerings are to be accepted. He is to be worshipped as I am. (3)

If persons are devotees of the Lord, they are not Shudras, they are the best of the followers of the Lord. Among people of all the *varṇa*s, those who are not devotees are the real Shudras, o Janārdana. (4)

I consider a Dog-eater better that a Brahmin (*vipra*) who is endowed with the six virtues, has a lotus-navel but has his face turned away from the Lord's lotus-feet. [. . .] (5)

He who sees my devotee — be he Shudra, Niṣāda, or Dog-eater — as the same as his caste (*jāti*) will go surely to hell. (6)

One other text associated with the Sanskrit *Vajrasūcī* in Kabir Chaura manuscript no. 030 merits further comment. In this manuscript, fourteen Sanskrit verses taken from the *Manu-smṛti* immediately follow the *Vajrasūcī* and immediately precede the *Ādi-purāṇa* excerpts from the *Sāra-candrikā*.[5] Why are verses taken from the text that contains the most authoritative defense of the *varṇa* system found here, between two texts that challenge this system? Obviously it is not easy to find verses in the *Manu-smṛti* that argue against caste by birth. The text does contain verses prescribing the proper conduct for Brahmins that could be used to defend the idea that such conduct is what defines a true Brahmin. What the compiler does instead, however, is to select verses that mostly deal with issues other than caste.

The first five verses, taken from Chapter 2, inculcate respect for one's guru and warn against the sexual attraction of women, even one's mother, sister or daughter. Two verses from Chapter 3 warn against sexual relations between a Brahmin man and a Shudra woman. The original intention of the verses was undoubtedly to warn Brahmin males against the risks of the pollution and miscegenation that results from such relations. Here, however, it is quite possible that the compiler reads the verses as a warning against the sexual exploitation of low-caste women by Brahmins. One curious verse from Chapter 2 relates the benefits from eating while facing in different directions. Five verses from Chapter 5 proscribe eating meat and promise heavenly bliss for those who refuse to eat it. Vegetarianism is, of course, an essential virtue for a good Brahmin, a good Vaiṣṇava, and a good devotee of the Kabīr Panth. The last verse, from Chapter 8, warns against the dire consequences of not speaking the truth.

The inclusion of these *Manu-smṛti* verses in the present context can be reasonably be regarded as an attempt to disguise and subvert the dominant message of the text. The Kabīr Panthī sadhu who probably organized and copied the manuscript has sandwiched these miscellaneous *Manu-smṛti* verses between the *Vajrasūcī* and the *Ādi-purāṇa* in order, I think, to co-opt the text for socially subversive aims of the Kabīr Panth while avoiding

[5] The verses correspond to the following verse numbers in Buhler's translation (*The Laws of Manu* 1988): 2.200; 2.201; 2.214; 2.215; 2.218; 3.17; 3.19; 2.52; 5.45; 5.46; 5.48; 5.51; 5.53; 8.89.

a flagrantly skewed and out-of-context reading of any *Manu-smṛti* verses more directly concerned with the defence of caste and *varṇa*.

The presence of three manuscripts containing a Hindi *Vajrasūcī* and one of a Sanskrit *Vajrasūcī* — as well as texts of the *Sāra-candrikā* and the *Brāhmaṇo ke lakṣaṇa* — in the Kabir Chaura library in Varanasi, provides good evidence of the basically egalitarian but partially ambiguous social and religious ideology of the Kabīr Panth. On the one hand, these texts explicitly reject the idea of a *varṇa* status based on birth, in keeping with Kabīr's own radical attacks on the *varṇa* and caste systems. On the other hand, the sadhus who copied the texts implicitly, and probably consciously, were appealing to the traditional authorities of the Sanskrit language itself, Advaita metaphysics, and even the great Brahmin proponent of Advaita, Śaṅkarācārya.

SANT RĀM'S HINDI *VAJRASŪCĪ*

1. Joining hands and bowing my head, I praise the lotus feet of my Guru. They are always helpful, remove obstacles, and create an auspicious condition.[6]

2. *dohā*:
I will describe the *Vajrasūcī*. The Śāstra that pierces ignorance;[7] it always is the destroyer of ignorance and the ornament of the wise knowers of truth.[8]

3. Brahmin, Kshatriya, Vaishya, and Shudra: these are known as the four *varṇa*s. Among the other three, it is said that the Brahmin is the head.

4. *caupāī*:
In the Veda the Brahmin is said to be the head. Just so also is the view of the Smṛti.
[...] Now we will explain who is really a Brahmin.

5. *arilla*:
Who is he whose name is Brahmin? The ways of explaining this should be told. It should be indicated if the Brahmin is (1) the *jīva*, (2) the body, (3) the *jāti*, (4); the *varṇa*; if he should be known as, (5) learning,

[6] I thank Neelima Shukla-Bhatt for her help with this translation.

[7] This translation is taken from the Sanskrit version. The readings in the three Hindi manuscripts are not satisfactory.

[8] I have interpreted *tajña* as *tattva-jña*.

(6) *karma*, (7) *dharma*, (8) or *dhārmika*. The correct view among these eight alternatives should be indicated.

6. *soraṭhā*:
Doubt will not be erased simply if you say that, among these eight, this is the Brahmin. The exact determination must be made.

7. First is the determination if the *jīva* is the Brahmin.
arilla:
If you say that the *jīva* is the Brahmin, then you have to also acknowledge that the *jīva* is omniscient. It then follows that the Kshatriya, Vaishya, and Shudra also do not have limited knowledge. From this, this all-knowing *jīva* is not the Brahmin. Considering again and again, this is seen [*or* is not seen] in the texts.

8. Next is the determination if the body is the Brahmin.
arilla:
If you say that the body is the Brahmin, then one has also to admit that all bodies are one in composition. Up to the limit of the Caṇḍāla, the taking form of the same sort of body is seen. In all is to be known the same getting old [no. 171, birth] and death. If you say the body is the Brahmin, in what way is this to be accepted?

9. Again, if the body is the Brahmin, then when one of his parents dies and the son takes that body and does the rite of cremation, then the son acquires the sin of doing harm to a Brahmin. If you say that the Brahmin is the body, how is this possible?

10. Next is the determination if *jāti* is the Brahmin.
arilla:
If you say that the *jāti* is the Brahmin, then one has also to admit that this is not possible. Many Brahmins have been manifested from other *jātis*. This is the case of the *ṛṣis*, *munis*, and *tapasīs* who made the Vedas and Sastras. [. . .[9]]

11a. *manaharaṇa* metre:
Ṛṣyaśṛṅga was born from a female deer. Kauśika appeared from Kuśa grass; Gautama from a hare; Vālmīki is considered to be from a *vāmī*(?). Veda-vyāsa is from a female boatman, Vasiṣṭha from a prostitute. It is

[9] This *caraṇ* can be taken to mean: 'Creating strength and manliness, you/they dried up the oceans.' If this is correct, the connection with the rest of the verse is not clear.

accepted as completely proved that Viśvamitra was from a family of Kshatriyas.

11b. The *muni* Agastya is said to have been manifested from a pot. The *muni* Jāmbūka is known to have been born from the womb of a jackal. These all are seen as having appeared from various *jātis*, but they are called Brahmins in the Smṛtis and Purāṇas.

12. *dohā*:
If you say that the *jāti* is the Brahmin, how can such a determination be made? Those called Brahmins have arisen from other *jātis*.

13. In who else's heart is there this pride. One says that the Lord Himself made the Brahmin from the head of the Puruṣa.

14. *arilla*:
The Brahmin came from the head; the Kshatriya is known to be from the arms. The Vaishya came from the thighs, the Shudra is considered to be from the feet. All these people were manifested from one Puruṣa. [. . .]

15. *dohā*:
These four *varṇas* have arisen from one Puruṣa, as if from one tree has been produced many different fruits.

16. *arilla*:
It is as if there is one tree and many fruits are seen, with some in the branches, some on the roots, some on the trunks. If it is considered that among these some are high and some low, it would be known to be absurd.[10] If you say that *jāti* is the Brahmin, in what way can this be accepted?

17. Next is the determination of *varṇa* as the Brahmin.
caupāī:
If it is said that the Brahmin is *varṇa*, this is not found anywhere. Without finding it, one can't understand it, even if it is explained in millions of attempts.[11]

18. *arilla*:
The Brahmin is said to be white *varṇa* and the Kshatriya red. The Vaishya

[10] The sense of this verse is not completely clear. The word *tīna/tina* may mean 'three'. The word *hāsyapada* (no. 171) probably became *hāsyaṣada* (no. 012) through an orthographic confusion of *pa* and *ṣa* and then became *hāsyakhada* (no. 104) through a correction of *ṣa* to *kha*.

[11] The translation of this verse is somewhat speculative.

is the yellow *varṇa* and the Shudra gets black. It is known that white, black, yellow, and red get all mixed together. If you say that *varṇa* is the Brahmin, in what way can this be accepted?

19. Next is the determination of learning (*paṇḍita*) as the Brahmin.
arilla:
If you say that learning is the Brahmin, this is not a correct determination. The Kshatriya, Vaishya and Shudra: all are have a share in [or can read] the truth. All are known to have knowledge of categories of objects. If you say that learning is a Brahmin, in what way can this be accepted?

20a. Next is the determination of *karma* as the Brahmin.
manahara metre:
If you say that the Brahmin is he who is known through *karma*,[12] how can the proof of this be brought to mind? All say that the proper life span of a Brahmin is 100 years, the span of a Kshatriya should be 50 years.

20b. The life span of a Vaishya is thought to properly be 25 years. The span of a Shudra is known to properly be 12 years. This is made baseless, since no such rule is seen in practice. How can *karma* be accepted as the Brahmin?

21. Next is the determination of dharma[13] as the Brahmin.
arilla:
If you say that dharma is the Brahmin, the best cannot be the inferior. However, the Kṣhatriya, the Vaishya, and the Shudra: who is without dharma? No one in the world is known to be without a form of proper service (*upāsanā*). If you say that dharma is the Brahmin, in what way can this be accepted?

22. Next is the determination of *dhārmika* as the Brahmin.
arilla:
If you say that *dhārmika* is the Brahmin, then no good reason comes to mind. The Kshatriya, the Vaishya and the Shudra give many gifts. The gift of maidens, gift of cows, and that consisting of gold [*or* gold and female buffaloes] are seen. If you say that *dhārmika* is the Brahmin, in what way can this be accepted?

23. *dohā*:
Among these eight alternatives, none can be known as the Brahmin. I now will tell the marks of a Brahmin. Having made this determination, it should be accepted.

[12] The sense of *prasiddha he ju* is not competely clear.
[13] Nos. 012 and 104 wrongly read *karma* here.

24. Next is the description of the marks of a Brahmin.
dohā: [. . .]

25. *arilla*:
As one sees directly what is in one's hand, so one should see oneself directly as Brahman. He who has such wisdom is known to be a true Brahmin. There is no other *varṇa* and *āśrama* of Brahmins than that.

26. One abandons all desires, passions, and hates. Through the discipline of making self-control, one gets satisfaction. One abandons thirst, envy, pride, confusion, illusion. One abandons doing harm, wicked killing, and the *ātman* is adorned with wisdom.

27. *dohā*:
[. . .], he should be known as a Brahmin. I cannot say anything about other texts, but the Vedas say that the Brahmin is the head.[14]

28. Anyone who gets these marks among the four *varṇa*s, he is to be known as a Brahmin. The *varṇa* is not the Brahmin.

29. *arilla*:
As soon as one is born, one is called a Shudra; by the rite of initiation one becomes known as a twice-born (*dvija*) when the sacred thread is put on. After reciting the Veda one gets the name of 'vibrator' (*vipra*); when one knows oneself as Brahman, then one becomes a real Brahmin.

30. *dohā*:
He who is a knower of Brahman is a Brahmin. No other is a Brahmin. [. . .]

31. Since there is no rule about who can be a knower of Brahman, why can't anyone become one? A Caṇḍāla [. . .], he is said to be a Brahmin.

32. *sorațhā*:
[. . .]. He should be known as a Brahmin.

33. *dohā*:
In all You exist. All are in You. Warp and woof this condition prevails. The dualist view does not appear as correct. He is said to be a Brahmin.[15]

34. *sorațhā*:
This text, the *Vajrasūcī*, was told in Sanskrit by Śaṅkara. Having understood the path, Sant Rām made a dialect version.

[14] The sense of much of this verse is not clear.

[15] The last *caraṇ* does not seem to be logically connected with the rest of the verse.

35. This resolve was created, that the determination of the Brahmin be made. For that reason the description of the eight options was made in dialect.

This ends the eight alternatives of the honourable *Vajrasūcī* in dialect.

REFERENCES

Aśvaghoṣa, 1839, *The Wujra Soochi or Refulation [sic] of the Arguments upon which the Brahmanical Institution of Caste is Founded.* Edition of L. Wilkinson with a translation by B. Hodgson. Also with the Sanskrit text of 'The Tunku' by Soobajee Bapoo. No publishing information apart from date.

Bahura, Gopal Narayan, *Literary Heritage of the Rulers of Amber and Jaipur*, Jaipur: Maharaja Sawai Man Singh II Museum, 1976.

Gramtha-sāra-candrikā, Fatepur, Shekhavati: Śrī Sarasvatī Pustakālaya, 1989.

Jinavijaya, Muni, *A Catalogue of Sanskrit and Prakrit Manuscripts in the Rajasthan Oriental Research Institute (Jodhpur Collection)*, pt. III(A), Jodhpur: The Rajasthan Oriental Research Institute, 1967.

Killingley, Dermot Hastings, 'Rammohun Roy's Interpretation of the Vedanta', Ph.D. thesis for the School of Oriental and African Studies of the University of London, 1977.

The Laws of Manu, trans. by G. Bühler, Delhi: Motilal Banarsidass, 1988, 1st published in 1886.

Lorenzen, David N., 'The Social Ideologies of Hagiography: Śaṅkara, Tukārām and Kabīr,' in M. Israel and N.K. Wagle (eds.), *Religion and Society in Maharashtra*, Toronto: Centre for South Asian Studies, University of Toronto, 1987, pp. 92-114.

———, *A Catalogue of Manuscripts in the Kabir Chaura Monastery*, Mexico City: El Colegio de México, 1994.

Mukhopadhyaya, Sujitkumar, 1950, *The Vajrasūcī of Aśvaghoṣa*, Santiniketan: The Sino-Indian Cultural Society. Contains the Sanskrit texts of Aśvaghoṣa's *Vajrasūcī* and the *Vajrasūcy-upaniṣad*, each based on several manuscripts, and a translation of the former text.

Radhakrishnan, S. (ed. and trans.), *The Principal Upanisads*, London: George Allen & Unwin, 1953.

Vajrasūcy-upaniṣad, in A. Mahadeva Sastri (ed.), *The Samanya Vedanta Upanishads with the Commentary of Sri Upanishad Brahma Yogi*, Adyar, 1921.

Weber, Albrecht, *Vajrasūcī des Açvaghosha*, Berlin, 1860.

The *Ādi Granth* of the Sikhs: A Canon?

WINAND M. CALLEWAERT

An analysis of the method by which the *Ādi Granth*[1] of the Sikhs was compiled around AD 1600, in no way suggests a lack of respect for the sacredness of the scripture. Human hands and memories were indeed needed to give a form to the divine inspiration and in this article I try to describe the genius of the human medium which put that inspiration into writing. It was not only an inspiration of a moment or of a few months, but of several centuries, as is testified by the numerous songs of Bhagats prior or contemporary to Guru Nānak. Drawing from my experience when studying huge anthologies of the same period in Rajasthan, I try to analyse the methods Guru Arjan applied to bring all the songs — nearly 6,000! — together, and I ask the following questions: were the songs of the Gurus copied from existing written material, or dictated by Guru Arjan or by someone else, or were they written straight from the memory of the secretary Bhāī Gurdās? I wonder whether the canonical status attributed to the *Granth* was indeed part of the project in 1604, or could it have to do with a newly defined identity of the Sikhs at the end of the eighteenth century?

THE REDACTION OF THE *ĀDI GRANTH* ACCORDING TO TRADITION

Let us first see what tradition says about the redaction of the *Ādi Granth* (called *Guru Granth* when it was installed as such by Guru Gobind Singh).

[1] For the *Ādi Granth* as 'neutral title' and other names for the sacred book of the Sikhs, see Hew McLeod, *Sikhism*, Penguin Books, 1997, pp. 166-7.

The *Granth* is an anthology of 5,894 songs (roughly 12 lines each) and 500 couplets: a total of approximately 55,000 lines or 1,430 pages in the standard edition. This takes about 2.8 Mbyte in my computer; see my *Śrī Guru Granth Sāhib*, with complete index (in Devnagari, 2 vols.), Delhi: Motilal Banarsidass, 1996. For a comparison, we note that in the *Dādū-Vāṇī* we find 433 songs and 2539 couplets. In Tivari's *Kabīr-granthāvalī* 403 songs and 811 couplets of Kabīr are given.

The bulk of the songs (4,957) are by the first 5 Gurus: Nānak (976 songs), Angad (61), Amardās (907), Rāmdās (679) and the compiler himself Arjan (2,216). The 118 songs and couplets by the ninth Guru, Tegh Bahādur, were added

It is often taken for granted that, as early as AD 1550, writing down songs was a common and ordinary enterprise in the Sikh environment. *It was not* so in Rajasthani Santa circles or in Banaras. The conviction about writing by the early Sikhs is evident in the publications of recent Sikh scholars. I quote only a few examples. Talib writes about the meeting of Nānak and Farīd, which is most probably an anachronism: 'After a considerable stay with Farīd, whose compositions the Guru must have obtained from the Saint, *written no doubt in the Persian script, in which all Punjabi writing by Muslims was done,* [my italics] Nānak continues on his travels.'[2] Harbans Singh notes: '. . . it could perhaps be speculated that Farid's compositions were, *inscribed by Guru Nānak in the book which he was believed to carry with him* [my italics]. This book, no longer extant, or a copy made from it, might have been one of the sources utilized by Guru Arjan in preparing the Granth.'[3] In a letter to me, 11 March 1989, my dear friend the scholar Prof. Pritam Singh, Patiala, wrote: 'The collection of Guru Nānak's compositions must have been made during Nānak's own time. He could not have composed the longer poems, characterized by great architectural finesse and conceptual sequence, *without committing them to writing.*' [my italics]

Some sources suggest that written collections of Nānak's songs were produced as early as during the lifetime of Angad, the second Guru.[4] In Fauja Singh, we read about Guru Angad: 'Not only did he *write his own compositions in this new script* [Gurmukhi, my italics], but he is also believed to have rendered a transliteration of his Master's writings in the same characters. . . . *He wrote a large number of hymns* [my italics] which were later incorporated in the *Ādi Granth.*'[5]

Guru Nānak died in AD 1538 and in 1581 Arjan became the fifth Guru. More than twenty years later it was decided that songs be brought together and written down in a canonical edition. We note 1604, a landmark in Sikh

---

in AD 1675. Besides these we have a total of 937 songs by non-Sikh bards and Bhagats; a.o. Jaydev (2; twelfth century), Sheikh Farīd (112 songs and 130 couplets; *c.* AD 1200), Trilocan (4; *c.* AD 1300), Nāmdev (61; *c.* AD 1300), Kabīr (217 songs and 241 couplets; see Ch. Vaudeville, *Kabīr-Vāṇī*, Pondichéry, 1982, p. VI; fifteenth century), Raidas (40; *c.* AD 1500).

[2] Gurbachan Singh Talib, *Guru Nanak. His personality and vision*, Delhi: Gur Das Kapur & Sons, 1969, p. 61.

[3] Harbans Singh, *Guru Nanak and origins of the Sikh faith*, Bombay: Asia Publishing House, 1969, p. 136, n.

[4] See Surinder Singh Johar, *The Sikh gurus and their shrines*, Delhi: Vivek Publishing Company, 1976, p. 51.

[5] *Guru Amar Das*, New Delhi: Sterling Publishers, 1979, p. 10.

history and in the history of Santa literature in north India. Traditionally the following reason is given why Arjan decided to compile 'orthodox' literature. Guru Arjan's enemies (the Minas led by his elder brother Prithi Cand) were circulating copies of songs not acceptable to the 'orthodox' branch lead by Arjan.[6] If that was the reason, it is not clear why — and this has been pointed out by even Sikh authors — the songs of the non-Sikh Bhagats were included in the *Granth*, if the purpose was to standardize the Sikh songs![7]

According to tradition, all available manuscripts were brought before Arjan. He examined every single song and instructed his secretary to write whatever was in agreement with orthodoxy. Some manuscripts had even to be brought from Sri Lanka, where Guru Nānak is supposed to have been. Sahgal argues that Nānak himself wrote down each song he had composed, for fear that one day he might forget it (that is in *c.* AD 1520).[8] On the occasion of the appointment of his successor, he solemnly gave him that book. Each of the following gurus did exactly the same with his own compositions, and this manuscript came into the hands of Arjan. This belief is taken for granted till today.

Finally, I should mention the account which attributes the compilation of an important collection of songs to Mohan or to somebody in his family. This is the famous *Mohan-Pothī*.[9] Mohan was the son of the third Guru, Amardās, who died in 1574. He was frustrated because the succession of the Guru was given to his son-in-law Rām Dās. As a result, Arjan had great difficulty in obtaining the famous, two-volume, *Mohan-Pothī*. He did, however, after he had composed a song in praise of 'Mohan' and sung it in front of Mohan's house. Both this account and the song seem to be legendary. McLeod accepts that the volumes were used by Arjan, but the present location of (copies of?) that text is not certain.[10] He further states,

[6] For a description of the enterprise, see W.H. McLeod, *The Evolution of the Sikh Community*, Delhi: 1975, p. 60. Also Hew McLeod, *Sikhism*, Penguin Books, 1997. W. Owen Cole and Piara Singh Sambhi, *The Sikhs: Their Religious Beliefs and Practices*, New Delhi: Vikas, 1978, pp. 25-6; and Surinder Singh Kohli, *A Critical Study of Ādi Granth*, Banaras: Motilal, 1961, rpt. 1976, pp. 11ff.

[7] Manmohan Sahgal, *Guru Granth Sāhib: Ek sānskritik sarvekṣaṇ* (Hindi), Patiala: Bhasha Vibhag, 1971, pp. 42ff.

[8] Ibid., pp. 49ff.

[9] See Gurinder Singh Mann, *The Goindval Pothis: The earliest extant source of the Sikh canon*, Harvard Oriental Series, vol. 51, Harvard University Press, 1996 and the recent work of Prof. Pritam Singh, Patiala.

[10] *The Evolution of the Sikh Community*, New Delhi: Oxford University Press, 1975, p. 61.

in his usual extremely cautious style: 'If the two volumes still exist and can be located, we may well discover that they are not the original *Goindvāl pothīs*. We may even discover that they bear insufficient resemblance to any collection which could have served as a source for the *Ādi Granth*.'[11]

LITERARY EVIDENCE ABOUT THE COMPILATION

So much for tradition. But what literary evidence do we have to support this description of the event of compilation and to corroborate the reasons why the *Granth* was compiled. In what source do we read for the first time about Nānak carrying a book with him? Here we enter the minefield of hagiographical writing about the early Sikh Panth. I quote extensively from the earliest attested source, the *Gur Nānak Prakāś* by Santokh Singh.[12] Many of the 'traditional' theories current now are clearly formulated in it. In this account we read the dialogue which supposedly led to the decision to compile the *Ādi Granth*:

> Prithia (the elder brother of the compiler guru Arjan) and others are circulating their compositions together with the authentic works of the Gurus (*gurbānī*). Such compositions reflect their misconceived notions. . . . Cannot learned Sikhs as Gurdās (the scribe of Arjan) guide us? He is himself a writer. . . . The works of Gurdās are filled with the Guru's praises. Read them attentively . . . Mohan has in his possession the works of the first four Gurus. He holds the entire collection and he must somehow be persuaded to part with it. It must all be recorded in a single volume so that it may be safely preserved for the benefit of mankind.[13]

If, with the respect due to oral traditions, we try to argue only from evidence available in literary sources, I should point out that the *Gur Nānak Prakāś* — and the earliest description of the compilation — was written by Santokh Singh in 1823. McLeod states: 'references by modern authors to incidents in the lives of the gurus (after Nānak) can often be traced no further than the statements by Santokh Singh'.[14] And that work, he says, relies heavily on an 'untrustworthy source', that is, the *Bālā Janma*

[11] See also W.H. McLeod, 'The Sikh Scriptures: Some Issues', in M. Juergensmeyer and N.G. Barrier, *Sikh Studies. Comparative Perspectives on a Changing Tradition*, Berkeley Religious Studies Series, Berkeley, 1979, p. 99.

[12] For a Hindi edition, see Jagbhagvan Goyal, *Guru Nānak Prakāś*, Patiala: Bhasha Vibhag, 1972, 2 vols; vol. I: 683 pp., vol. II: 463 pp.

[13] W.H. McLeod, *Textual Sources for the Study of Sikhism*, Manchester University Press, 1984, pp. 29-30.

[14] *The early Sikh tradition*, p. 46.

Sākhī.[15] This text is very popular — and each fresh edition is an enlarged version — because of the claim that it was dictated in the presence of Guru Angad by Bhāī Bālā, a companion of Guru Nānak.

One could — hypothetically — suggest that accounts about the early Sikh Panth not only describe certain events, but also add nuances of interpretation due to sectarian developments some time before Santokh Singh, that is at the end of the eighteenth century or 200 years after Guru Arjan and his compilation of the *Granth*. As a result, what is given in Santokh Singh's dialogue quoted above, may reflect a sectarian interpretation meant to give more importance to the redaction of the *Ādi Granth* by Arjan Dev. Was there any political reason for that, around 1780? With due respect for oral traditions, it would appear that the 'first' (?) literary evidence about the redaction of the *Ādi Granth* — and the scribal claims about it — was written 219 years after AD 1604, relying to a great extent on an ever expanding version of the *Bālā Janma Sākhī*.

For the purpose of the present paper I should remind the reader of the immense importance of the musical structure of the *Ādi Granth*. All songs — with a few exceptions — are classified according to the *rāg*. Each *rāg* group has distinct sub-groups and the arrangement generally follows a uniform pattern (with negligible exceptions). Three norms emerge as basis for assigning a song to a particular group within a *rāg*.

1. the number of *pād*s or stanzas a song has (*caüpade, asaṭapadīā, dupade, tipade and pañcapade*),
2. its *gharu* and/or its *sankar rāg*,
3. its author.[16]

[15] W.H. McLeod, *Guru Nanak and the Sikh religion*, New Delhi: Oxford University Press, 1968, pp. 23-4.

[16] Authorship is an important basis for distinguishing groups of songs within a *rāg*. One major division is between *mahalā* and *bhagat* songs. The *mahalā* songs always come first, beginning usually with the *caüpade* of *mahalā* 1. If *mahalā* 1 has no *caüpade* in that *rāg*, then the *caüpade* of the second *mahalā* take precedence over those of the third or the fourth *mahalā*, as the case may be. The *dupade*, if any, are usually placed together with the *caüpade*, after which come the *asṭapadī*s. Here, too, the same logic is followed as with the *caüpade*: songs of *mahalā* 1 come first followed by those of his successors, in numerical order. These are followed by '*chant*' (Skt. '*chanda*') songs and '*Vār*s'. Then follow the compositions of the *bhagat*s or saints other than the gurus. An arrangement according to author is followed here too. The songs of Kabīr, if there are any in a given *rāg*, always come first, followed usually by Nāmdev and Raidās.

For a detailed analysis of the (musical) structure of the *Ādi Granth*, I refer to Callewaert 1996, vol. II, pp. 15-28, 161-98.

I conclude that at the time of the composition of the *Ādi Granth* (or of the written sources underlying it), there was a very strong link with the oral tradition and with singers' repertoires. This is evident when we look at the very musical structure of this huge text, at the *rāgs*, at the *rāg-mālā* at the end,[17] etc.

THE *ĀDI GRANTH* AND THE RAJASTHANI COLLECTIONS

The compilation of a huge corpus like the *Ādi Granth* was in no way a unique phenomenon around AD 1600. We have several Rajasthani collections of enormous size and, like the *Ādi Granth*, all are closely connected to the singing tradition. Even more, in early copies of these anthologies we find clear traces of scribes tampering with the text because of a link with the ongoing oral tradition. Looking at what happened to similar huge repertoires in Rajasthan, it should not amaze us if the text of the *Ādi Granth* was not as sacrosanct as tradition wants us to believe; and that it also was much more in close contact with an ongoing oral tradition than is generally accepted.

One unique work in Rajasthan is the thematic compilation called *Sarvāṅgī*, one compiled by Dādū's disciple Rajab and another by the Dādūpanthī Gopāldās.[18] I (proof)read the complete *Sarvāṅgī* of Gopāldās and it is not only a fascinating product of a seventeenth century memory, or a marvellous synthesis of Bhakti literature: it is a wonderful experience if you can sing it — in long sessions — or have someone to sing it for you. As we sang, immediately the good songs stood out, even before we saw the *bhaṇitā*: Sūrdās, Kabīr, Dādū. When I first discovered this huge manuscript I was baffled by the neatness of its handwriting, the immense variety of the

[17] For the controversy about the origin of this *rāg-mālā*, see S.S. Kohli, *A critical study of Ādi Granth*, Delhi: Motilal Banarsidass, 1976 (1961), pp. 101f. Also D.S. Narula, *Guru Nānak saṅgītagya* (Hindi), Jalandhar: New Book Co., 1978, pp. 47-8.

Most of the *rāgs* named in that *rāg-mala* are not found in the *Ādi Granth*. The *rāg-mala* has no relevance in the Granth, except perhaps as a kind of tribute to the importance of music for it. Another and more specific tribute is paid by the gurus themselves, especially the third Guru, Amardās. He wrote verses in praise of various *rāgs*. Songs praising *rāgs* were not uncommon in the literature of this period and the attempts of Amardās fall within an established genre. The difference is that in his praise of a *rāg*, *bhakti* takes precedence over music.

[18] For a detailed analysis of the first work, see Callewaert 1978. The second *Sarvāṅgī* has been edited by me and published by Manohar, New Delhi, 1993.

Bhaktas quoted in it and its size — 1.6 Mbyte, or more than half of the size of the *Ādi Granth*![19] The variety of songs makes one wonder how a person could be acquainted with so many repertoires. Of the total of about 26,800 lines in the complete work, about 13,900 lines are with *pād*s of 138 different, identified Bhaktas. There are further 4,413 lines with literature of (so far) unidentified poetry (of which some *sākhī*s are no doubt of Dādū and Kabīr, but without a *bhaṇitā*).

It has taken me years to dismiss the notion that Gopāldās compiled his anthology from existing manuscripts lying on the floor in front of him. It was hard to imagine that without manuscripts a person could produce such a wonderful selection of songs and couplets and classify them according to theme. The singers' repertoires he must have known by heart were not classified according to theme, but according to *rāg*! Slowly, as I made progress in the wonderful world of performers emerging before me from the manuscripts, I started to imagine a Bhakta of the Dādūpantha with a fabulous memory. He must have spent many days of many months listening to travelling singers and storing in his memory whatever he heard.[20] It is not only amazing that Gopāldās could store such an amount of literature in his memory. How could he make a selection based on 126 different themes? It is clear that he received his material from the singers' single repertoires. With only two exceptions all *pād*s have the *rāg* to which a singer would perform the *pād*. We have shown in our studies of Nāmdev and of Raidās[21] that the *rāg*-tag was an essential part of the 'text' of a *pād*, and that variation in the *rāg* takes the researcher back to the period of oral transmission. In the singers' repertoires *pād*s appear to have been classified in *rāg*-clusters: in the *Sarvāṅgī* too of Gopāldās (and of Rajab) the *rāg*-tag is preserved, but the *pād*s do not appear in clusters of identical *rāg*s. On the contrary, we often find in one chapter as many *rāg*s as there are Bhaktas quoted. Only towards the end of the work Gopāldās seems to copy more

[19] Only when the input of the text in the computer was completed, could I grasp the importance of this document: 1,669 *pād*s and 6,568 *sākhī*s of 138 identified Bhaktas and approximately 640 *ślokas*. Of Kabīr alone, the compiler Gopāldās quotes — in AD 1627! — 358 *pād*s and 609 *sākhī*s, of Dādū 401 *pād*s and 1,452 *sākhī*s.

[20] In the colophon of his *Sarvāṅgī* Gopāldās states that he was 37 years of age when he completed the collection and wrote it down on paper (in AD 1627). He must have been fourteen years old when Dādū died in 1603, and he declares himself to be a disciple of Santadās, a disciple of Dādū. If he does not call himself a disciple of Dādū, we may perhaps presume that Gopāldās was initiated into the Dādūpanth after 1603.

[21] Callewaert and Lath 1989; Callewaert and Friedlander 1992.

directly from one singer's repertoire; there it appears that more songs of a particular Bhakta are given under the same *rāg*. It is also amazing how the compiler remembered, according to the content, songs which in existing repertoires must have been classified under a different *rāg*. In Chapter 61, e.g. he quotes 8 *pād*s of Sūrdās, and each *pād* has a different *rāg*, which each must originally have belonged to a different *rāg*-cluster. It is further to the credit of Gopāldās' memory that — as far as I could see — not a single line is given twice.

There seems to be a regular pattern in the way Gopāldās arranged the material available to him. The basic frame is a selection of *pād*s, interspersed in most chapters with *sākhī*s. However, there are also chapters with only *sākhī*s.[22] Very frequently one can discover a kind of mnemonic device in the fact that a similar keyword occurs in (the first lines of) consecutive *pād*s or *sākhī*s of different poets. Even with these obvious devices, one keeps wondering how Gopāldās could link one *pād* to another. It would appear also that at times the *rāg* is the mnemonic device, and this is especially so when a particular *rāg* is otherwise not frequently found. In not a few chapters Gopāldās gives subtitles. This is clearly the result of scribal editing as singers would not have used subtitles during their performances.

During the same period of search for manuscripts in 1973, I managed to copy four manuscripts with the *Sarvāṅgī* of Rajab, a disciple of Dādū.[23] A comparison of the two *Sarvāṅgī*s confirms the notion that early in the seventeenth century the Dādūpanth was an important nucleus of literary activity in northern India. The results of that activity were rivalled only by the endeavours of Guru Arjan in Panjab, but the relevance of both traditions for later generations is equal. In the *Sarvāṅgī*s we find a treasure trove of, to a great extent, unpublished material; for the material that was already published I found the recension of both *Sarvāṅgī*s to be very accurate and well preserved. If we accept that a copying tradition may undergo fewer intentional changes in a work of compilation than in a

[22] Not all chapters are equally long. Chapter 12 has only 44 lines and Chapter 82 has 18 lines, while Chapter 17, *Sādh mahimā*, has 33 *pād*s and 83 *sākhī*s or *ślokas*. Similarly, Chapter 35 is very small but Chapter 36 is huge. Chapters 62-4 are again huge and Chapter 78 has 94 *pād*s of 15 Bhaktas. Often Gopāldās gives first a *pād* of Kabīr, followed by one of Dādū. If Gopāldās was a Dādūpanthi, this would confirm how high was the esteem for Kabīr in the early Dādūpanth.

[23] See Callewaert 1978. In this work Rajab has grouped thematically, in 144 *anga*s, *sākhī*s and *pād*s from his own *vāṇī* and of 88 identified Bhaktas 'writing' in Hindi, Persian and Sanskrit. About 102 titles are identical with titles of chapters in Rajab's own *vāṇī*. In the colophon the work is said to contain 8,000 verses.

sectarian text of just one poet, it becomes evident that the *Sarvāṅgī*s are important for a text-critic, wishing to study a Bhakta of the period. It is a well-known fact that for modern editions of Bhakti literature, often only a few and not the oldest manuscripts have been consulted. In these anthologies we have a text reflecting a particular set of singers' repertoires written down early in the seventeenth century. When we look at the structure of the two *Sarvāṅgī*s, we note that both works are independent products of compilation, differing both in the amount and the choice of the material and in the way it has been arranged. It is clear that the *Sarvāṅgī* of Gopāldās is based on sources which are very different from those underlying the *Sarvāṅgī* compiled by Rajab.

To conclude: The *Sarvāṅgī*s are impressive products of an exceptional memory and, looking at them we should, at least theoretically, not consider it impossible that memories were the most important basis for the compilation of the *Ādi Granth*.

THE *PAÑC-VĀṆĪ*

For a study of the Bhagats (Nāmdev, Kabīr and Raidās), quoted abundantly in the *Ādi Granth* I made a detailed study of the songs of these Sants in manuscripts found in Rajasthan.[24] Many manuscripts written in Rajasthan around AD 1600 originated within the Dādūpanth, which appears to have been a nucleus of literary activity. As a result, we find the songs of five Bhagats, revered in the early Dādūpanth, put together in one collection called *Pañc-vāṇī*: Dādū, Kabīr, Nāmdev, Raidās and Hardās. All the *Pañc-vāṇī* Mss. record the *pāds*, *sākhī*s and *ramainī*s of the *Pañc-vāṇī* saints in the order noted earlier. The works of Kabīr, Nāmdev, Raidās and Hardās follow those of Dādū in an unbroken sequence. All *Pañc-vāṇī* manuscripts are copied within the Dādūpanth, as is indicated not only by the prominence given in them to Dādū's writings, but also by the fact that they include many works of Dādū's followers. With the hypothesis that the *Pañc-vāṇī* tradition in the Dādūpanth started around AD 1600, we face the amazing fact that there must have been several *Pañc-vāṇī* compilers, each working separately either from existing manuscripts or in direct contact with the oral tradition (or both). We can no longer speak of *one* Rajasthani *Pañc-vāṇī* recension or Western *pāṭh* tradition for Kabīr and so on. We have as many recensions, going back to different singing traditions, as there are (early) *Pañc-vāṇī*s.

When we compare the songs of Kabīr or of Nāmdev there is a difference

[24] See Callewaert and Lath 1989.

in the *rāg* under which these songs are classified in the Rajasthani manuscripts and in the *Ādi Granth.* But the difference in *rāg* when comparing the Rajasthani versions is much smaller than the difference noted when we compare the Rajasthani manuscripts and the *Ādi Granth.* This fact goes parallel with the following observation: the text of those songs which have a different *rāg* in the Rajasthani and the *Ādi Granth* texts is much more variant than in the songs which appear to have the same *rāg.* Further, the variety in the musical repertoires reflected in the Rajasthani manuscripts points to a musical development in Rajasthan which takes us further back in history than so far has been accepted. What we find in the seventeenth century Rajasthani manuscripts is a variant musical version which may well be as old as the musical version from which the Panjabi singers drew their inspiration, if not older. This is an important hypothesis for the text-critic of the Bhagat songs.

SEVERAL FACTORS DISTINGUISH THE RAJASTHANI COLLECTIONS FROM THE *ĀDI GRANTH*

The *Ādi Granth* — we are told — was given a canonical status, as an extreme development of the *nirguṇ* devotion for the Word of God in the Book. It was regarded as the only and correct version recognized by Sikh orthodoxy. 'Dissident' copies like the 'Banno Manuscript' were ostracized and orthodox Sikh scholars are anxious to avoid the question of variant readings and interpolations.[25] A critical comparison of the earliest written versions of the *Ādi Granth* has till now been hardly possible.

The Rajasthani collections of the Dādūpanth aim at collecting all available songs of the major Sants, like Dādū, Kabīr, Nāmdev, Raidās and Hardās, and many others. No attempts were ever made to compile a canonical and final collection, nor is there any evidence that such a claim was made in the tradition. As a result the text-critic meets with considerable diversity in these collections. There is clear evidence that in Rajasthan different compilers made individual collections, each of them going back to his own oral tradition. These collections proliferated in different manuscript traditions which, in turn, underwent a certain degree of contamination in the scribal period.

In Rajasthan the manuscript tradition does *not* seem to have stopped the continuity of the oral tradition. The oral tradition in Rajasthan has

[25] See Pritam Singh, 'Bhai Banno's Copy of the Sikh Scripture', in Monika Thiel-Horstmann 1983, pp. 325-41.

remained dynamic and has continued to be a vital source for Santa songs and sayings, even after a rich manuscript tradition was established. The two traditions have run parallel, up to the present day. The oral tradition remained alive and active, till perhaps two generations ago, adding to and modifying the earlier material. Proof of this lies in the fact that manuscripts dated after 1750 give 'new' songs of early Sants, especially Kabīr and Nāmdev. Some songs also appear in larger editions. The Rajasthani manuscripts dated after AD 1700, give excellent material to study the symbiotic relation between the scribal and oral traditions (as is still to be seen in Hindustani music). As a result, the oral tradition in Rajasthan should not be thought of as monolithic. There was as much variety and creativity in it as in any institution which transmits knowledge, art or literature. Unlike the case of the Sikhs and their *rāgī*s, other *nirguṇ* poets relied on institutions outside the sampradāy for their more professional *bhajan* singing. This does not deny the presence within the sampradāy of skilful musicians and singers.

In the *Ādi Granth* too we have a very conscious and meticulous arrangement of songs with a musical criterion in mind. (If my information is correct, there seems to be only one *rāg*-pattern in both the 'Kartarpur' version and the 'Banno' version of the *Ādi Granth*.) *Rag*s are assigned to a song in the singing tradition (not in scribal collections) and looking at the scant information so far available, we may perhaps conclude that songs were already well defined under particular *rāg*s before the *Ādi Granth* was compiled in 1604. This suggests a strong 'Nānak' singing tradition from at least AD 1520 onwards. By then, the songs of Bhagats like Nāmdev or Kabīr may have acquired a very well-defined *rāg* pattern, quite distinct from the Rajasthani pattern.

SUMMING UP

Compilations of huge collections of Santa literature became quite a fashion in the early seventeenth century in north-west India. In Rajasthan these collections were to a great extent written from memory or from unorganized notes of musicians. The pattern of classification of the songs also points to a close link with the musical tradition. If we argue that the *Ādi Granth* was (to a great extent) written from memory and not (only) from written documents compiled earlier, we may ask the following questions. Is the reason for compilation necessarily as sectarian as later accounts seem to suggest? Even if the original copy prepared under the direction of Guru Arjan is still available, we know that copies were soon made. Was the collection 'canonical' from the very start, making changes and additions by early copyists impossible? Often, many scribes were singers. They knew the songs by heart. Have they left traces of their interference in the early manuscripts? Can we accept the hypothesis of oral contamination during the first scribal days of the *Ādi Granth*? In the Rajasthani manuscripts of the *Pañc-vāṇī* and the *Sarvāṅgī*s we clearly see the interference of singers changing their repertoires and of scribes copying earlier collections. Would it have been very different in Punjab? Was there any sectarian reason at all for a different situation, as tradition seems to suggest?

REFERENCES

Callewaert, W.M., 'A Seventeenth Century Anthology of Hindi Poetry', *Orientalia Lovaniensia Periodica*, Leuven, 5, 1974, pp. 187-96.

———, *The Sarvāṅgī of the Dādūpanthī Rajab* (Orientalia Lovaniensia Analecta, 4), Leuven, 1978, 446 pp.

———, *The Hindī Biography of Dādū Dayāl*, Delhi: Motilal Banarasidass, 1988.

———, W.M., *Sri Guru Granth Sahib, with complete Index*, 2 vols:, New Delhi: Motilal Banarsidass, 1996, vol. I: 1430 pp., vol. II: 967 pp.

Callewaert, W.M. and Mukund Lath, *The Hindī Songs of Nāmdev* (Orientalia Lovaniensia Analecta, 29), Leuven, 1989, 432 pp.

Callewaert, W.M. and B. Op de Beeck, *Devotional Hindi Literature: Nirguṇ bhakti sāgar*, New Delhi: Manohar, 1991, 1175 pp.

Callewaert, W.M. and P. Friedlander, *The Life and Works of Raidas*, New Delhi: Manohar, 1992, 335 pp.

Caturvedi, P., *Dādū Dayāl Granthāvalī*, Benares, 1966.

Iraqi, S., *The Sarbāṅgī of Rajjabdās*, Aligarh, 1985, 632 pp.

Monika Thiel-Horstmann (ed.), *Bhakti in Current Research 1979-82*, Proceedings of the Second International Conference on Early Devotional Literature in New Indo-Aryan Languages, St. Augustin, 19-21 March 1982, Berlin: Dietrich Reimer Verlag, 1983.

Narayandas Svami, *Śrī dādū panth paricay*, 3 vols., Pushkar, Jaipur: Śrī Dādū Mahāsabhā, 1979.

Tivari, P.N., *Kabīr-granthāvalī*, Allahabad, 1961.

Varma, V., *Rajjab-Bānī*, Kanpur, 1963.

Vaudeville, Ch., *Kabīr*, New Delhi: Oxford University Press, 1974.

———, *A weaver called Kabīr: Selected Verses, with a detailed biographical and historical introduction*, New Delhi: Oxford University Press, 1993.

———, *Kabīr-Vāṇī*, Pondichéry: Institut Français d'Indologie, 1982.

Different Voices, Different Songs
Early Anthology Versions of Songs by Harirām Vyās

HEIDI PAUWELS

INTRODUCTION: PURPOSE OF THE PAPER

In this paper, I will investigate in detail a few early Braj Bhāṣā 'hit songs' by Harirām Vyās, a sixteenth century Rādhā-Kṛṣṇa devotee (*bhakta*). These previously untranslated songs (*padas*) seem to have been widely popular by the end of the sixteenth and mid-seventeenth century, as they appear not only in collections of Rādhā-Kṛṣṇa bhaktas from the Braj area but also in those of Rājasthānī bhaktas devoted to God-without-attributes (*nirguṇa* bhaktas).

Harirām Vyās probably hailed from Orcchā (in present Madhya Pradesh) but spent a good deal of his life in Vrindāban, the very site of Rādhā and Kṛṣṇa's love play. Inspired by the company of like-minded *bhakta* poets, Hit Harivaṃś and Svāmī Haridās, Vyās was engaged in composing devotional songs or *padas* in Braj Bhāṣā. He seems to have been a very prolific composer,[1] judging by the amount of songs that are available in

* I want to acknowledge gratefully all the help I have received with this paper, in the first place from my Ādiguru, Dr. Winand Callewaert of KU Leuven, Belgium. At the very beginning of my Ph.D. project, he made me aware of the *nirguṇi* anthologies used here, and kindly allowed me to consult and copy the valuable microfilms of Mss. he has made. Thanks also for his comments on a draft of this paper. For help with he translation of the poems quoted, I am much obliged to Prof. Monika Boehm-Tettelbach. During the wonderful year 1989-90 I had the chance to study with her in Cologne, Germany, thanks to a stipend of the DAAD. I also am grateful *kṛpāpātra* of Buddhi Prakāś of Vrindāban, India, who patiently worked with me through the *padas* quoted here in 1987-8, which was made possible by a scholarship of the Indo-Belgian Cultural Exchange Programme.

[1] Mss. of Vyās's collected oeuvre vary in giving anything from about 550 to over 800 *padas*, and from about 84 to nearly 150 *sākhīs*, in addition to a work called *Rāspañcādhyāyī* (which I have edited and translated Pauwels 1996b).

several Mss. of *Vyās Vāṇī,* anthologies exclusively devoted to him.[2] However, my intention in this paper is to report on my search for poems by Vyās as they occur, not in *Vyās Vāṇī* collections, but in early non-Vyās-specific anthologies (*pada-saṃgraha*). I will concentrate here on the earliest available collection, namely, the sixteenth-century Fatehpur manuscript (referred to as Fms.).

What is the general purpose behind studying such early non-poet specific *pada-saṃgraha*s? Investigating this type of early anthologies is useful for several reasons. In the first place, it brings to light previously unknown poems, which have not made it into the standard author-specific editions. In the case of Vyās, as I believe is also true for other sixteenth-century bhaktas, the Ms. material for the extant *Vyās Vāṇī* does not go back any further than the early eighteenth century. In trying to get beyond that, we need to turn to earlier anthologies. Of course, if we are lucky and find previously unknown poems, we cannot accept at face value such 'new' (or in fact more correctly — older) poems. They may bear the signature or *chāpa* 'Vyās', but that does not guarantee they are indeed by Vyās. So, one purpose is to find 'lost' poems, and to assess the case for their being attributable to Harirām Vyās.

Secondly, looking through anthologies is important for studying the reception of a given author's poems. In a way one can see these anthologies as a kind of 'hitparade', reflecting to a certain extent the popularity of *pada*s in the circles in which the anthologies were compiled and written down. At the very least, they represent the script of a performance and very likely a script for future performances. That makes them valuable material for a study of the reception of *pada*s, especially when the anthologies were compiled in geographical and religious circles different from those in the immediate vicinity of the poet. In other words, these anthologies provide us with a glimpse of the spread of the *pada*s. In the case of Vyās, where most of the *Vyās Vāṇī* material comes from Rādhā-Kṛṣṇa circles in Vrindāban, it is refreshing to look through Rājasthānī and *nirguṇī* Mss. Nowadays Vyās may not be known outside of the Braj-Bundelkhand area, but there was a time when some of his poems travelled well beyond Vrindāban and Orcchā. First, we need to determine which poems by Vyās had a wide circulation in non-Vyās specific collections. As soon as we find

[2] A Vulgate recension of *Vyās Vāṇī* is available in three editions of the early half of this century. The first was a Rādhāvallabhīya edition by Akhil Bhāratvarṣīy Śrī Hit Rādhāvallabhīy Vaiṣṇav Mahāsabhā 1934, and in response came a Mādhva-Gauḍīya one by Gosvāmī 1937, and a more scholarly one by Gosvāmī 1952.

out which poems made it into the 'hitparades', we can start speculating why they did so. As always, one has to wonder by whom the hitparade was compiled and for what purpose.

Thirdly, sometimes we find in *pada-saṃgrahas* poems that we already know from author-specific anthologies, yet with interesting variants that warrant a close textual analysis. In the case of Vyās, the extant versions of the poems in *Vyās Vāṇī* do not go back beyond the eighteenth century. The earlier *pada-saṃgrahas*, however, bring to light different and older versions of the 'hit' songs of Vyās. A comparison of the earlier versions with the later ones may perhaps allow us to get closer to what Vyās himself sang or wrote. However, we have to keep in mind that such a study will say less about Vyās and his times than about the collectors of the anthologies and their interests. In any case, we can offer new versions for poems that so far had only been available in one 'Vulgate' version. This is interesting because it informs us of the way in which different milieus have transformed the songs they have transmitted.

In short, this paper presents the results of my investigation of early *pada-saṃgrahas*. In the process I discuss the newly discovered songs by Vyās, the spread of Vyās' songs in the late sixteenth and early seventeenth century, and the question of how the different interests of the communities, in which the songs were transmitted, influenced their selection from Vyās's oeuvre, and coloured the version of the songs they present. Hence the title of the paper: it is an investigation of how different voices chose and sang different songs.

The relevance of this study is not limited to matters concerning the relatively obscure Vyās alone. Its findings raise questions that regard the recent rethinking and re-evaluation of the *saguṇa-nirguṇa* distinction. In how far are we justified to classify bhaktas as those devoted to God-without-attributes (*nirguṇa*) on the one hand, and those devoted to God-with-attributes (*saguṇa*), such as Rāma, Kṛṣṇa, Śiva, on the other?[3] Recently, Prof. J. Hawley (1995) called into question the rigidity of a strict subdivision between *saguṇa* and *nirguṇa* bhaktas and pointed out directions

[3] The publications of, among others, Prof. D. Lorenzen have contributed much to expanding and refining our knowledge of these categories and what they stand for, see in particular his recent publication (Lorenzen 1996), part of which is devoted to a comparative study of a *nirguṇī* retelling of a *saguṇī* source text. Lorenzen also reflected on the issue in the introduction to the proceedings of a conference he organized (Lorenzen 1995). The article by Prof. J. Hawley referred to next was published in that conference volume.

for future research in the form of a three-fold study. In order to determine to what extent *saguṇa* and *nirguṇa* bhaktas saw each other as part of distinct or even opposing movements, we should in the first place look at the poems by early bhaktas themselves, next at the early hagiographies, and finally we should decide what we can glean from the anthologies, the collections of songs of the type I am looking at here.

I am trying to contribute to this broader question by means of a micro-study with reference to Harirām Vyās. I will relate my findings for Vyās to Hawley's for Sūr, so as to help integrate the picture of the early generation of Kṛṣṇa devotees settling in the Braj area. And I would like to support Hawley's call for more detailed studies of this type: it is only when we manage to collect many such micro-studies, that we can achieve a more accurate broader picture.

This paper is in a way a sequel to the one I presented at an earlier chapter of this conference in 1991 in Paris (Pauwels 1994a). There too, the central question regarded the scholarly division of bhaktas in *saguṇa* and *nirguṇa* camps. The point I made was that Harirām Vyās regarded bhaktas of either side as belonging to one family (the only people excluded from the happy bhakti family, are what Vyās refers to as *śāktas*). I compared Vyās's case with that of Sūr and it turned out that Vyās was more explicit in including names like Kabīr and Nāmdev, as members of this family. However, later *saguṇī* hagiographers felt uneasy with poems in which Vyās expressed reverence for Kabīr and his like. They felt compelled to overcome what they saw as a contradiction by ascribing such poems to a pre-conversion stage in Vyās' life. One could say that in that paper, I was addressing the first and second of Hawley's directions for further research, that is, internal evidence of bhaktas, and the picture emerging in the hagiographies, with respect to Harirām Vyās. In the present paper I will concentrate on the third issue, and show how a *saguṇa* poet created some poems which have a *nirguṇī* ring and which became incorporated in *nirguṇī* anthologies.

PART 1. DESCRIPTION OF THE MANUSCRIPT MATERIAL

Vyās Vāṇī manuscripts

At the outset, I should provide a description of the manuscript material used for this study. I shall first introduce the *Vyās Vāṇī* manuscripts, the Vyās-specific anthologies, that I collated for my Ph.D. research. All of them belong to what one may call a Vrindāban Vulgate recension. In a previous study of the manuscript material I have found that the Vulgate has two different sub-recensions (Pauwels 1994b, pp.135-48). Hence, for each poem under investigation here, I give a representative version of each of those sub-recensions. Representative of the first sub-recension is the oldest *Vyās Vāṇī* manuscript, called J. This Ms. is preserved in Jhānsī,[4] but was written in Vrindāban. It is a non-sectarian manuscript, and is dated 1737 (vs 1794). Representative of the second sub-recension is VN, which is preserved in Nimbārk Koṭ in Vrindāban (available on microfilm in VRI reel no. 136, serial no. 1693). This undated manuscript was probably written between 1780 and 1830, and is of Rādhāvallabhīya sectarian origin. (References will be to an assigned 'serial number' for the *padas*; for more details about these Mss., see Pauwels 1996b, pp. 22-4.)

Lastly, I will make reference to the standard edition of *Vyās Vāṇī,* the only one readily available nowadays, which was published in 1952 by Vāsudev Gosvāmī, a descendant of Vyās. This edition is referred to as VG. It is in effect a summary statement of manuscript material preserved in Datiya, in Gosvāmī's personal collection and in the former royal library. The poems in this edition are divided in two subsections, the first one containing poems on the theme of *siddhānta*, or: 'theory', the second one *śṛṅgāra rasa vihāra,* or: 'play of erotic *rasa*'. (References will be to the sequential *pada* number as assigned by the editor.)

Manuscripts of anthologies (pada-saṃgraha)

With regard to non-Vyās specific anthologies, I did an extensive search for early dated *pada-saṃgraha* Mss. in India, in the areas where he lived (Braj, and Bundelkhand), and in major Mss. collections (in Banaras, Allahabad, and Rajasthan). I scanned the anthologies I gained access to for songs by Vyās, and I hope to have occasion to report my findings elsewhere. However, I did not find any Ms. older than what other scholars have made available already. In view of the scope of this paper, I will concentrate here on those earliest anthologies only, and present the picture of Vyās that emerges from the famous Fatehpur Ms. (Bahura and Bryant 1984) and compare it with some Dādūpanthī material that has been collected and published by Winand Callewaert.

[4] I want to express my gratitude to Ghanśyām and Lalit Prasād Gosvāmī, Mohanlāljī kā mandir, Manik Cauk, Jhānsī, for kindly allowing me to photograph the manuscript in their possession.

Fatehpur manuscript

The Fatehpur Ms. is an early *pada-saṃgraha* which goes back to the late sixteenth century; it is dated 12 *sudi Jyeṣṭha* vs 1639 or 3 June 1582 (Bahura and Bryant 1982, iv). This anthology includes five poems by Vyās, which is exciting, because it must have been written down shortly after Vyās's death, or perhaps even while he was still alive. All sources agree that Harirām Vyās died at an advanced age; he definitely survived most of his friends. We know that he must have come to Vrindāban before 1552 and was in his mid-forties at the time he arrived (Pauwels 1996b, pp. 4-5). So, when the Fms. was written down in 1582, Vyās must have been at least seventy-five, if indeed he was still alive.

Given the early date, the picture of Vyās that appears from Fms. is particularly significant, yet, it has to be evaluated in the context of what Fms. stands for. This collection contains a large proportion of poems by Sūrdās, as the anthology title *Pad Sūrdāsjī kā* indicates. It represents a non-sectarian tradition, apparently free of Vallabhan influence, and it is not a liturgical Ms. or *varṣotsava* collection, which would be arranged according to the festivals throughout the year. In fact, its principle of organization is not very clear.

Even more interesting: the content of the poetry is not undiluted *saguṇa.* This is the case in particular for the middle section, which contains most of the so-called *vinaya* poems by Sūrdās himself (Hawley 1984, 121), but also songs by poets whose affiliation is usually considered to be *nirguṇa.* This section starts out with a poem by Kabīr (no. 107; other poems are nos. 177-8, 191-2, 211, 218, 228 [Callewaert & Op de Beeck 22.64], 229, 248-9, 251-2, 254 [ibid. 22.39]), and incorporates poems by Raidās (nos. 195 [ibid. 4. 66], 196 [ibid. 4.34], 205 [ibid. 4.86], 255-8 [ibid. 4.33], 213), and Nāmdev (nos. 170 [ibid. 3.62], 171 [ibid. 3.232], 175 [ibid. 3.257), 176, 181, 187, 203, 223-6 [the last = ibid. 3.258]).

Which poems by Vyās are included and where do they fit in this manuscript? All five poems by Vyās are written by the anonymous scribe of the first two sections of the manuscript, who is not the writer of the colophon. Poems with *chāpa* 'Vyās' are the following:

Poem one: no. 49, *pada* 49, fol. 17v. Refrain: *kisorī deṣī vana maiṃ jāta*, or: 'Did you happen to see a young lady walking in the wood?' (Bahura and Bryant 1982, p. 34).

Poem two: no. 186, *pada* 82, fol. 70r-v. Refrain: *hari sauṃ prītamu bhayau na hvaihai*, or: 'No one dearer than God has been nor will be' (Bahura and Bryant 1982, pp. 139-40).

Poem three: no. 190, *pada* 86, fol. 71v-72r. Refrain: *sācoī gopāla gopāla raṭibau*, or: 'Repeat in truth "Gopāl, Gopāl"' (Bahura and Bryant 1982, pp. 142-3)

Poem four: no. 207, *pada* 102, fol. 77r. Refrain: *hari hūṃ te haridāsa lāgata pyāre*, or: 'Better than God Himself, I like His servants' (Bahura and Bryant 1982, p. 153)

Poem five: no. 214, *pada* 109, fol. 79r-v. Refrain: *rasanā syāmahi naiku gāi rī*, or: 'Sing a little "Śyāma", O tongue of mine' (Bahura and Bryant 1982, pp. 157-8).

Surprisingly, out of those five poems by Vyās, four occur in the middle section of Fms., in which the *nirguṇīs* are most heavily quoted (cp. their numbers with the ones for Raidās, Kabīr and Nāmdev quoted above). Only poem one is found in the first section of Fms. As one would expect from its refrain, this poem is on the bucolic-erotic theme of Kṛṣṇa's dalliance with Rādhā. As it turns out, that is also the only poem by Vyās on that theme to be found in the whole of Fms.

Dādūpanthī material

In search of more poems by Vyās in early anthologies, I checked also anthologies of *nirguṇa* origin, such as those compiled in the Dādūpanth. An important early one is the *Sarvāṅgī* anthology compiled by Gopāldās (GDS) some forty-three years after the Fms., in 1627. A relatively early Ms. of the anthology, dated 1724 (vs 1781 in *Bhādoṃ sudi*), was preserved in the Dādū Mahāvidyālay in Jaipur, and has been published by Winand Callewaert (1993). This collection has several songs with *chāpa* Vyās, and, interestingly, two of these are the same as two poems from the *nirguṇī* section of Fms. The song with *ṭeka: sācoī gopāla gopāla raṭibau* (Fms. no. 190) is found in GDS Chapter 11, no. 9 (Callewaert 1993, p. 55) and *rasanā syāmahi naiku gāi rī* (Fms. no. 214) is found in GDS Chapter 8, no. 50 (Callewaert 1993, pp. 139-40). Since I shall discuss these poems in detail, it is worthwhile briefly sketching their context in the Dādūpanthī anthology.

The song with *ṭeka: rasanā syāmahi naiku gāi rī* is found in the GDS chapter entitled *sumiraṇa kau aṃga*, or: 'Chapter of remembrance' (GDS 8.50). The main topic that the poems of this chapter share is an urgent reminder that remembrance of God brings salvation, helps to cross the ocean of existence, and eradicates sins. The poems recommend remembrance in the company of like-minded devotees and plead urgency in view of human mortality and man's being caught in the eternal cycle of *saṃsāra.* The world of the senses and human relations are sheer *māyā* or illusion, useless and unstable when compared to the bliss of salvation and the eternal love of God. Role models from mythology for turning to God are occasionally quoted as an illustration. Favourite referees are sages, such as Nārada and Dhruva, Brahmā's sons (Sanaka and his brothers), and Prahlāda, as well as redeemed sinners, such as Ajāmila, the elephant, the hunter and the prostitute (see Nāmdev *pada* 9 and 10; Kabīr *pada* 20; Sūr *pada* 24 and 53, Trilocan *pada* 25, Vidyāpati *pada* 47). The poem by Vyās has all these themes in a nutshell, though it does not give any mythological examples.

The other song by Vyās that occurs in both anthologies, *sācoī gopāla gopāla raṭibau,* is found in the GDS chapter entitled *nāma mahimā kau aṃga,* or: 'Greatness of the Name' (GDS 11.9). The poems in this chapter recommend recitation of the Name of God as the most efficient method to gain salvation. This method is a short cut, preferable to all other religious means, such as ritual, asceticism, *pūjā* of any god, pilgrimage, recitation of scriptures, ritual bathing, etc. Some poems in this chapter also stress that reciting the Name gives far superior results compared to magic and legendary wishing cows and trees. Vyās' poem has the same theme: the Name is most important and other religious methods miss the point. Vyās draws simple but powerful analogies from real life, rather than alluding to mythological events, as some other poets quoted in this chapter do (see Nāmdev *pada* 2 and Sūr *pada* 11).

Both these songs from Fms. have, with some variants to be discussed below, basically the same text in GDS. In addition, for a third song by Vyās in Fms., the one with refrain *hari sauṃ prītamu bhayau na hvaihai,* a close parallel can be found in GDS. However, though on a similar theme, the song is not exactly the same and its *ṭeka* is different: *hari kau sau hita na kiyau aba kāhūṃ,* or: 'No one ever loved like God'. This poem is quoted in GDS 62.15 (Callewaert 1993, p. 319) in the chapter entitled *saguṇa sādha milata gobiṃdajī kā guṇāṃha kau aṃga,* or: 'Chapter on [singing] the qualities of Govindajī together with *saguṇa* holy men.' The meaning of the title is unclear,[5] but the poems included under this heading share the common theme. They all stress the ineffability of God's wonderful power of grace, which saves even those who have fallen lowest. God's endless

[5] One might expect the title to refer to the inclusion of *saguṇa* poets in this chapter, but, although there are several poems by Sūr, the bulk of the poetry in this chapter is by Dādū, while some by Kabīr and Nāmdev are included too. Even more puzzling for understanding the title is the fact that this chapter is certainly no exception in quoting poems by *saguṇīs*. Sūr is well-quoted throughout GDS.

mercy is contrasted with human ungratefulness. The perfection of God's love makes it abundantly clear how imperfect even the best examples of human love remain.

Finally, a parallel in Dādūpanthī material can also be found for a fourth poem by Vyās in Fms., the one with refrain *hari hūṃ te haridāsa lāgata pyāre*. The Dādūpanthī poem is on an identical theme, though it has a rather different *ṭeka: janama janama ke pāpa gaye*, or: 'The sins of life after life [washed] away.' The poem is not found in GDS, but in another Dādūpanthī anthology by an anonymous compiler. A manuscript of this anthology, dated 1676 (vs 1733), was also preserved in the Dādū Mahāvidyālay in Jaipur, hence it is further referred to as DM2.[6] The contents of this anthology (described in detail in Callewaert 1980, pp. 29-31) are an interesting mix: starting with *Dādū Vāṇī* and Garībdās's *Anbhay Prabodh*, it includes several shorter works, among others, reworkings of excerpts from *Purāṇas* and *Bhagavadgītā*, hagiographic works (*paricaīs*), Nāth-yogic exposés, bhakti sermons and *kathās*. In addition, there is a fair number of independent poems, including poems by such stalwart *saguṇīs* as Sūrdās, Vidyādās, and Mādhaudās Jagannāth. The poem by Vyās with *ṭeka: janama janama ke pāpa gaye* is the second of two with *chāpa* Vyās found under the heading *Vyāsa ke pada* (DM2, fol. 162 r-v), however, it is followed by a *pada* that has *chāpa* Syāmdās. Then follows a new heading with songs by Tursī, the same author whose *chāpa* occurs in the poems before Vyās's.

The scope of this paper does not allow for more than a discussion of Vyās's poems in these different anthologies. However, the relevance of, in particular, the Dādūpanthī anthologies for the question of *saguṇa-nirguṇa* divide warrants more research of this type. Suffice here merely to draw attention to the fact that Vyās is only one of the many *saguṇa* poets quoted in these Mss. that are clearly of *nirguṇa* origin.[7] A lot of songs quoted are by two other *saguṇīs* associated with Braj, namely Sūrdās and Parmānand (both claimed by the Vallabha Sampradāya). GDS has also one quote from Vidyāpati, one from the Nimbārka-follower Śrī Bhaṭṭ (GDS 17.14: *aba gopāla sarani terī āyau*, which is basically the same as the first poem in his *Yugal Śatak*: with *ṭeka*: *madana gopāla sarana terī āyau*).[8]

[6] This manuscript has been preserved on microfilm by Winand Callewaert (film no. 2).

[7] Nāmdev (and others) associated with the Vārkarī sect, has an interesting position in that he is associated with a particular temple image, but belongs at the same time to the 'big five' of the *nirguṇī Pañc Vāṇī* collections.

[8] Incidentally this poem is also quoted in the middle section of Fms. (no. 219,

GDS also has a considerable amount of poems by Mādhavdās, who seems to be the Gauḍīya Mādhavdās Jagannāthī (e.g. 8.4, which corresponds to Kṛṣṇadās s.d., *pada* 4 [*phuṭkar*]). Hopefully other scholars will take up study of these poets. I will limit my discussion to the poems by Harirām Vyās.

PART 2. VYĀS'S HIT SONGS

1. An Erotic Poem

Fatehpur manuscript poem on the theme of Rādhā and Kṛṣṇa's dalliance

The first poem by Vyās in Fms. is found in the first section of the Ms. (no. 49, *pada* 49 on fol. 17v, see Bahura and Bryant 1982, p. 34). This is his only poem in the collection dealing with the Rādhā-Kṛṣna theme. It occurs in the midst of a sequence of songs on the bucolic-erotic theme, immediately following a song describing Kṛṣṇa's beauty after a night of unfaithfulness and preceding a song warning an unnamed Gopī not to wander into Kṛṣṇa's territory near the Yamunā.

Vyās's poem seems to have been very popular. It is also found twice in manuscripts of Vyās's collected work, *Vyās Vāṇī*, in both recensions of the collection (J 441 fol. 194v and 451 fol. 199r. and VN 489 and 487 fol. 62v-63r), as well as in the two early editions. In each manuscript the poem occurs once with a shorter and once with a longer version of the *ṭeka* and with some minor variants[9] (see Table 1).

---

pada 114 on fol. 80v: *giridharalāla sarani terai āvau,* Bryant and Bahura 1982, p. 160). Interestingly both anthology versions omit the more orthodox sounding lines *dhani dhani māta pitā suta baṃdhu dhani jananī jina goda khilāyau; dhani dhani caraṇa calata tīratha kauṃ dhani guru jini haṛi nāma sunāyau*, or: 'Hail to parents, sons and relatives, hail to the one who gave birth and fed [me] on her lap. Hail to the feet that walked in places of pilgrimage, hail to the guru who initiated [me] in the name of Hari.'

[9] The version with the longer *ṭeka*, the *textus ornatior,* is given as *pada* 68 in Pauwels 1994b. In VG the double occurrence of this poem is reported for one manuscript (Gosvāmī 1952, p. 335), but only the *textus ornatior* is provided. In my dissertation, I have included its variants for comparison in the apparatus of both *padas* 58 and 68.

राग सारंग[10]

किसोरी देषी वन मै जात[11]
जा[12] विनु दीनु षीनु भयौ[13] डोलतु कोऊ न वूझतु[14] वात
तेरी सी अनुहारि नारि[15] के सवै लुभानै[16] गात
वोलत हसत[17] अधिक छवि उपजति कोटि मदन शर घात
तू अपनौ व्यौरो कहि मो सौ अधर[18] नयन मुसक्यात
व्यास स्वामिनि वार न लागी स्याम[19] कंठ लपटात

Did [you] happen to see a young lady walking in the wood?
Without her [I'm] roaming lost and lonely.[20] No one understands [my] mood.[21]

[10] The *rāga* is not specified but the preceding poem is in Sāraṃg, hence I have assumed the same for Vyās's poem. Other Mss. give for variants Devgandhār for the short version (VN, J), and Gaurī for the longer one (VN, J). P1, a Ms. dated 1839, preserved in Prayāg (Allahabad) at Hindī Sāhitya Sammelan, which belongs to the first sub-recension of the Vulgate, and is probably of Rādhāvallabhan sectarian provenance, gives Jaitśrī (short version in) and Kamod (long version).

[11] The longer version in the *Vyās Vāṇī* Mss. adds सुनि गोरी तैं एक before किसोरी, some have मह for में in the longer version (VN).

[12] A corrector has crossed out the superscript to correct जा for जो. VN and J give ता, P1 has तो.

[13] The longer version in the *Vyās Vāṇī* Mss. has हौं or होइ. The former could be taken as a first person pronoun.

[14] This follows the variant of the longer version in the *Vyās Vāṇī* Mss. The variant for the shorter version is वूझै. A corrector of Fms. has changed कौऊ to कोऊ and clarified the second *akṣara* of वूझतु.

[15] The longer version in the *Vyās Vāṇī* Mss. has ऊनहारि भारि (or: ता भारि [VN] or वा सोभा [P1]).

[16] Variant for the two first words in most Mss. is लुभारे (लुभ्मीर in VN's long version).

[17] This follows the variant of the longer version in the *Vyās Vāṇī* Mss. The variant for the two first words in the short version is चितवत चलत 'When she glances and moves.'

[18] Again, this follows the variant of the longer version in the *Vyās Vāṇī* Mss. The variant for the short version is कहि मो सौं व्यौरौ तू अपनें.

[19] This follows the variant of the longer version in the *Vyās Vāṇī* Mss., न लागी बार, except in word order. The variant for the short version is वार न लाई. Note also that VN has in its long version व्यास स्वामि स्वांमिनी.

[20] Literally: '[I]'ve become dependent and emaciated, roaming around.'

[21] If one takes this poem to be the words of a *sakhī*, or Kṛṣṇa in disguise of a *sakhī*, one could substitute 'he' and 'his', meaning 'Kṛṣṇa(’s)', for 'I' and 'my'. However, note that one of the variants has हौं instead of भयौ, which refers more clearly to a first person.

She looks a bit like you do:[22] a woman whose body entices all [hearts].
When [she] talks and smiles, she displays such beauty![23] [I'm] hit by thousands of Cupid's darts.
[But how about] you, tell me your story, with smiling lips and winks.
Vyās's Lady doesn't hesitate a moment: around Śyāma's neck she clings.

There are several ways to interpret this poem. A straightforward reading is to see it as the words of Kṛṣṇa addressing Rādhā, but failing to recognize her because he is so obsessed with finding her. This is the classical theme of *prema vaicittya.* However, in the available *Vyās Vāṇī* Mss., all versions of the poem are in a subsection that is called *māna kī śṛṅkhalā*, or: 'Chain of [Rādhā's] *pique*'. In accordance with this classification by tradition, the poem can be interpreted as a practical joke of Kṛṣṇa's. As is his wont, he is trying to fool Rādhā out of her *pique* by pretending not to recognize her and complaining he has been dumped by 'a lady', who, he then specifies looks a lot like her. Needless to say, those tricks of Kṛṣṇa always work, and Rādhā cannot help but smile and embrace him lovingly. Áll *pique* is duly forgotten.

Table 1: Comparison of Fms. version and *lectio simplicior and lectio ornatior* from the Vulgate for *kisorī deṣī vana maiṃ jāta* (bold for most significant variants, underline for different word order).

Fms. 49
राग सारंग

किसोरी देषी वन मै जात
जा विनु दीनु षीनु **भयौ** डोलतु कोऊ न **वूझतु** वात
तेरी सी **अनुहारि नारि** के सवै लुभानै गात
वोलत हसत अधिक छवि उपजति कोटि मदन शर घात
तू अपनौ व्यौरो कहि मो सौ अधर नयन मुसक्यात
व्यास स्वामिनि वार न **लागी** स्याम कंठ लपटात

Vāṇī: Mān kī śṛṃkhalā
(VG 544; VN 489 and 487 resp.)

J 441*simplicior (saṣī ke vacana śrī priyājū prati)*	J 451 *ornatior (saṣī ke vacana śrī priyājū prati coja ke)*

[22] The variant of the second sub-recension उनहारि 'similar' seems better, but the manuscript evidence is in support of the *lectio difficilior* अनुहारि.

[23] Literally: 'manifold splendour is manifested.'

राग देवगंधार	**राग गौरी**
किशोरी देषी वन में जात	**सुनि गोरी तें एक** किसोरी वन मह देषी जात
ता विनु दीनु <छ>ीन **भयौ** डोलत कोऊ न **वूझै** वात	ता विनु दीनु छीन **हौं** डोलतु कोऊ न **वूझतु** वात
तेरी सी **अनुहारि नारि** के सवै लुभारें गात	तेरी सी **उनहारि भारि** कै सवै लुभारे गात
चितवत चलत अथिक छवि उपजति कोटि मदन सर घात	**वोलत हसत** अधिक छवि उपजति कोटि मदन सर घात
कहि मो सौं व्यौरो तू अपनें अधर नेंन मुसकात	तू अपनौं व्यौरौ कहि मो सौं अधर नेंन मुसक्यात
व्यासि स्वांमिनि वार न **लाई** स्यांम कंठ लपटात	व्यासि स्वांमिनि**हि** वार न **लागी** स्यांम कंठ लपटात

For easy comparison, table 1 shows three versions of the poem: the Fms. and both Vulgate versions, the *lectio simplicior* and *ornatior* (both are from J; VN has only minor variants). The poem as attested in Fms. turns out to be a mixed version: it has variants from both. However, with the significant exception of the *ṭeka*, and the beginning of the first stanza, it follows mostly the longer version. It may come as a surprise that the readings associated with the longer version are attested closer to Vyās's times than those of the simpler one. Perhaps the simpler version is secondary to the more elaborate one? Even if the simpler version is primary and a singer in the chain of oral transmission of Vyās's poem is to be held responsible for the elaboration, this singer must have been at work very early on, possibly while Vyās was still alive. Would perhaps even Vyās himself have sung different versions of his own song?

If the compiler of Fms. intended to provide a representative poem by Vyās, he did a good job in picking this one. It is representative of a significant part of Vyās's oeuvre, namely, the section on Rādhā's *pique* (*māna*). This occurs in all recensions of *Vyās Vāṇī,* as a substantial subdivision of about seventy poems. These poems concentrate on a moment of estrangement between Rādhā and Kṛṣṇa, but typically they have a happy ending. Mostly, Rādhā's anger is shown to have been unsubstantiated or feigned. Even where that is not the case, in the end all anger is dissolved by some clever stratagem devised by one of the confidantes (*sakhī*s) or by Kṛṣṇa Himself. Precisely that is the theme of the first poem by Vyās that the compiler of Fms. chose to quote.

[24] In the first sub-recension, the short version is classified as 'the *sakhī*'s plea to Rādhā', in the second, both versions are classified as 'the *sakhī*'s joking words' (and so is the longer version in the first sub-recension). It is indeed possible to imagine that Kṛṣṇa is disguised as a *sakhī* so as to better approach Rādhā, or so as to trick her out of her quarrelsome mood by playing this joke on her. Yet another possibility is to interpret it as the words of Kṛṣṇa when talking to a *sakhī* and being overheard by a hidden Rādhā.

2. Poems on the Theme of Hari's Incomparable Love

Fatehpur manuscript poem by Vyās on Hari's incomparable love

The second poem by Vyās in the Fms. is on the topic of God's incomparable love. It occurs in the *nirguṇī* middle section of the manuscript (no. 186, *pada* 82 on fol. 70r-v, see Bahura and Bryant 1982, pp. 139-40). The poem is part of a sequence of songs dealing with the theme of exclusive devotion for Hari-Kṛṣṇa (some evoke the same images, cp. especially, the song by Kṛṣṇadās, Fms. no. 183). Vyās's song incorporates references to the *saguṇa* mythology of Viṣṇu, but does not remain restrained to the Kiśora-Kṛṣṇa phase.

राग सोरठी

हरि सौं प्रीतमु भयौ न ह्वैहै
देष्यौ सुन्यौ न अैसौ कोऊ कलि मै रह्यौ न रहिहै
जा अजामिल अधम उधारयौ क्यौं नर ताहि भुलैहौं
पतित पिंगुला की महिमा कौ अपनै मुष कहिहै
(राजुसभा के चरण धोइ करि)[25] जूठनि कौन उठैहैं
को अभिमानी दासी सुत पै भात मांगि फुनि षैहै
को चेरी को चंदन रुचि करि अपनै अंगि चढैहौ
को अरजुन को सारथी ह्वैहै उग्रसेन की पन हीं गहिहौ
रंक कुचील सुदामा कौ तन को उर स्यौ लपटैहौं
आरति गर्भ परीषित झारत हाथ चक्र को लैहै
. . . लौ कवि् महि बिभौ कहैहै
नीच पोच अपराधी व्यासहि हरि हूं कै पेटि समैहौ

No one dearer than God has been nor will be!
No one like Him is seen or heard of in Kali, there hasn't been nor will be.
He uplifted the vile Ajāmila! How could man forget Him?
The fallen woman Piṅgalā! [Who] will get her praise over his lips?
Who will have his feet washed in the royal council, and sprinkle the water around?[26]

[25] Added in the margin by a later hand.

[26] The second part literally means: 'who will lift the leftovers'. I am stretching the meaning in the first half of the line, which more naturally would mean: 'Having washed the feet of the royal council'. However, there does not seem to be any incident fitting that description. The allusion might be to Kṛṣṇa drinking the footbath water of the brahmin Sudāmā at His court in Dvārkā, but that does not quite fit the bill. More likely, the reference is to an event during Yuddhiṣṭhira's

From a slave's proud son (Vidura), who will beg rice to eat?[27]
Who will desire a maidservant's (Kubjā's) sandal paste, and have it massaged on his limbs?[28]
Who will become Arjuna's charioteer? [Who] will grasp Ugrasena's feet?[29]
Poor, ragged Sudāmā, who will press his body to his chest?[30]
Parīkṣit is burning desperately in the womb. Who will take the disc in his hand [to save him]?
. . . among poets [who] will speak of His glory?[31]
Low and simple, Vyās the sinner. Will he prove too much to stomach for God?

This poem elaborates on the theme that God's grace saves the low and distressed, those on whom society has given up. It is built around a more or less chronological pattern (with the exception of Vidura) of examples from *Bhāgavatapurāṇa*, where Viṣṇu-Kṛṣṇa showed kindness without expecting anything back. Interestingly, Vyās does not make any references to the Braj episode. Each reference is phrased as a rhetorical question, with the implication that no one but God would care to show mercy on those miserable creatures. The purpose of this enumeration of mythological antecedents of Kṛṣṇa's grace becomes clear in the last stanza, which is again a rhetorical question: is there any sinner too bad for God to have mercy? Vyās himself, with all his human shortcomings will surely be saved too.

---

rājasūya, where Kṛṣṇa was accorded the first place of honour in the assembly and Yuddhiṣṭhira washed his feet and sprinkled the waterdrops on those present (see *Bhāgavatapurāṇa* 10.74.26-27). This may be interpreted as an act of grace on the part of Kṛṣṇa to bless the Pāṇḍava family and their allies.

[27] This is likely a reference to Kṛṣṇa's foregoing Duryodhana's hospitality when visiting Hastināpura in favour of taking his meals at Vidura's home (*Bhāgavatapurāṇa*, 3.1.1-16; and *Mahābhārata* 54.89 [91], see Van Buitenen 1978, pp. 372-4).

[28] Reference to the well-known incident told in *Bhāgavatapurāṇa* 10.48.1-11.

[29] This may refer either to Kṛṣṇa's instrumentality in reinstalling Ugrasena on the throne of Mathurā (*Bhāgavatapurāṇa* 10.45.12-14), or, given the reference to Arjuna in the same line, it may refer to the respect he showed Ugrasena and his elders upon their meeting in Kurukṣetra on the eve of the big battle (*Bhāgavatapurāṇa* 10.82).

[30] The reference is to the poor brahmin who was Kṛṣṇa's boyhood friend and fellow-student, whose reunion with Kṛṣṇa is described in *Bhāgavatapurāṇa* 10.80-81. Interestingly, the word Vyās uses to describe him, *kucīla,* evokes Śuka's *kucaila* (*Bhāgavatapurāṇa* 10.80.7).

[31] The line is incomplete, but may have been intended as a reference to *Bhāgavatapurāṇa* 10.87, in which the personified Śrutis sing Kṛṣṇa's praise.

Vulgate poem by Vyās on Hari's incomparable love

The poem *hari sauṃ prītamu bhayau na hvaihai* is not attested in any of the extant collections of *Vyās Vāṇī.*[32] So, the question of attribution to Harirām Vyās needs to be addressed first. Interestingly, some oral formulae occurring in this poem are found elsewhere in Vyās's attested poems (*nīca poca* as applied to the poet himself, and the expression *peṭa samā-* with reference to God, occur both in VG 269, a poem not attested in J, but in VN 261 fol. 39v).

Attribution of the Fms. poem to Vyās can be affirmed more convincingly, with reference to other poems by Vyās on this general theme. Such poems are attested under the section *śrī kiśora-kiśorī jū kī stuti*, or: 'Praise of the young couple', in the VG edition, especially *padas* 65-7. The refrains (*ṭeka*) of these poems are very similar to the one in Fms.: *hari sau dātā bhayau na āhi*, or: 'No one as generous as God has been nor exists' (VG 65), *bhayau na hvaihai hari sau pyārau,* or: 'No one has been nor will be as dear as God' (VG 66), and *hari kau sau hita na kiyau aba kāhū*, or: 'No one ever loved like God' (VG 67). All three poems are found in the oldest Mss. of *Vyās Vāṇī* I collected.[33] Especially the first of these poems is close to the Fms. poem, so it makes sense to provide the poem for comparison.

राग सारंग

हरि सौ दाता भयौ[34] न आहि
सुख करिवे कौं दुख हरिवे कों सब जग देष्यौ चाहि
भक्तन के बस हरि ह्वै जानत जसु दीनौं जसुदाहि
जाहिं भक्त की लाज बडाई दीनीं द्रुपद सुताहि

[32] The index in Bryant and Bahura 1984, for reasons unclear to me, ascribes this poem to Vyāsdev. Perhaps intended is Harivyās Devācārya of the Nimbārka Sampradāya, who is often confused with Vyās. However, that poet's *chāpa* or signature line is Haripriyā (used throughout his *Mahā Vāṇī*, see also Mītal 1968, p. 348).

[33] Two of these poems occur in J under the heading *prema bhakti nirdhāra ke pada*, or: 'Poems on the establishing of loving devotion' (J 107-8 fol. 39v-40r), and one under the heading *śrī kiśorī kiśorajū kau mādhuja*, or: 'The sweetness of Rādhā and Kṛṣṇa' (interpreting *mādhuja* as a variant for *mādhuya*) (J 63 fol. 24r-v). However, the latter poem seems a bit out of place under that heading, in that it does not mention Rādhā, nor makes reference to any of Kṛṣṇa's childhood pranks as the other poems in that section do. In VN, all three poems occur under the heading *śrī kiśorajū kī stuti prakarṇa*, or: 'Section on the praise of Kṛṣṇa' (VN 62-4 fol. 14r-15r).

[34] J has भायौ.

जाकी दान मान की महिमा सकत न वेद सराहि
जिहि चिरवा लै कमला[35] दीनी मंद न माँगत ताहि
पतित[36] पिंगलहिं आलिं(ग)न[37] दै रूप दियौ कुबजाहि
हरि न पाइयतु व्यास[38] भक्ति बिनु मिटै न मन की ढाहि[39]

No one generous as God has been nor exists.
To provide joy and relieve sorrow, of the whole world, He keeps eager watch.
To His devotees He surrendered willingly: He brought Yaśodā glory.[40]
He transformed His devotee's shame to fame: [take] Drupada's daughter.
The glory of His grace and fame, [even] the Vedas cannot acclaim.[41]
In exchange for some rice, He gave fabulous wealth (to Sudāmā)![42] [Only] idiots don't ask for His [favour]!
He embraced the fallen woman Piṅgalā and made (the hunchback) Kubjā look smart!
Says Vyās: except by devotion, it's tough to find God,[43] or put to rest the fire in the heart.

As the poem in Fms., this one too is built around an enumeration of famous antecedents of Kṛṣṇa's grace. An overlap in stories alluded to is found in the last stanzas, with reference to three figures: Sudāmā, Piṅgalā, and Kubjā. (Perhaps also in common is the reference to the Vedas singing Kṛṣṇa's praise.) However, in addition, Yaśodā is mentioned, which extends the Kṛṣṇa cycle covered in the poem to the Braj episode. The reference to rice (*ciravā*) with regard to Sudāmā is also reminiscent to the

[35] This word is illegible in J, but the reading is confirmed by VN.

[36] This word is partly illegible in J, it seems to be ending on -त्या, but the reading is confirmed by VN.

[37] Emendation on the basis of VN, J seems to confirm this but is difficult to read.

[38] Confirmed by VN, though difficult to read in J.

[39] J and VN have डाहि.

[40] Pun on name of Kṛṣṇa's foster-mother, that can be analysed as a compound of *yaśas* and *-dā:* 'giver of praise'.

[41] Reference to *Bhāgavatapurāṇa* 10.87, in which the personified Śrutis sing Kṛṣṇa's praise.

[42] *Ciravā* is probably to be taken as *ciḍavā* [*cipiṭa*], a rice preparation. This refers likely to the story of Sudāmā who visited Kṛṣṇa, without having much to offer, but who nevertheless came home rich (see *Bhāgavatapurāṇa* 10.80-1). Throughout the story (esp. in Chapter 81), there are several references to Kamalā or Śrī-Lakṣmī, such as Śrī eating the poor man's rice preparation and expressing satisfaction (*Bhāgavatapurāṇa* 10.81.10-11). When Sudāmā returns home and finds his hut transformed in a palace, his wife is compared to Śrī (*Bhāgavatapurāṇa* 10.81.25). Also, throughout the episode Lakṣmī is mentioned in epithets of Kṛṣṇa.

[43] Literally, 'God cannot be found...'

one to rice (*bhāta*) in the context of Vidura in the Fms. Notwithstanding these similarities, the focus of both poems is slightly different. The poem last quoted stresses that it is only via bhakti that Kṛṣṇa can be reached (cf. the words *bhaktana* and *bhakta* in the first stanza). The poem in Fms. is more intent on communicating the message that there is no condition for God's grace, just being a sinner should be plenty.

Poem by Vyās on Hari's incomparable love from a Dādūpanthī collection

Of the three thematically related poems in *Vyās Vāṇī* referred to above, also the third one is worth looking at in detail, especially because it is also attested in the Dādūpanthī anthology, Gopāldās' *Sarvāṅgī* (62.15, see Callewaert 1993, p. 319). An overview for comparison of the GDS and Vulgate versions (the poem corresponds to VG 67, J 63 fol. 24r-v, and VN 64 fol. 14v) is available in table 2. Most of the variants can be attributed to oral transmission, these are the so-called *geyavikāras*. A clear example is the switched sequence of certain lines. The translation given here is based on the text of Gopāldās (variants from the Vulgate are indicated in the footnotes).

राग धनाश्री[44]

हरि कौ सौ हित न कीयौ अब कांहूं और सबै दुषदाता
लातनि मारत लागत पांऊं लूटि लग रिसहु षाता[45]
अैसौ सुष सुपिनैं हूं न[46] दीनौं ग्रभि बसत माता हूं
स्वार्थ निपुन भरम पोषन लग[47] कीनौं कपट पितां हूं
अपनैं काजि पतब्रत लीनौं बसि कीनौं अबला हूं[48]
बोल तोतरा बोलि चोरि चित बित लानौं बेटां हूं

[44] V specifies Sāraṃg for the *rāga* of this poem, which is apparently confirmed by VG.

[45] In J, VN and VG the *ṭeka* is shorter and slighlty different: हरि कें सौं हितु न कीयौ अव कांहू। और सवै दुषदाता लातनि मारत लागत पाहू॥ (Note: VN has it garbled: हरि कौ सौहि सुन कियौ . . .)

[46] Both J and VN, as well as VG share the variant सुपनैं नहि.

[47] Very interesting variant shared by J, VN and VG: अपनों बिषै भोग पोषन लगि or 'For satisfying his own sensual enjoyment.'

[48] In J, VN, and VG this line comes after the next one. VG also gives the fem. form of the perfective participle: कीनी.

भई बिपरीते संमींपि मिले मांनूं धंन लीनौं भइयां हूं[49]
ब्याह बराती मिस रूंट्यौ करि[50] घर लूट्यौ सजनां हूं
कपट प्रीति परतीति बंधाई[51] अपनैं काजि सषां हूं
रिण कारंनि मनुहारि करी सब[52] स्वार्थ लग राजां हूं
हरि गुण बिमल अगाध स्यंध को जांनैं सीवां हूं
कूड[53] कुटिल कांमीं अपराधी ब्यास बिमुष सेवां हूं

No one ever loved [you][54] like God, nowadays; everyone else will disappoint.
They bow to the feet that kick them, hoping for spoils they suffer [your] anger.
Even mother?
Even she could not give such joy, not even in a dream while [you] stayed in her womb.
Even father?
Good for his own sake, his care a charade, [all] fraud what he did.
Even a wife?
Loyal to her husband for reasons of her own: she's got [you] under her thumb.
Even a son?
With cute little words he stole [your] heart and made off with your money.
Even a brother?
Turning against [you], when [you] thought he'd stand by: he too took [your] money.
Even in-laws?
At the wedding festivities[55] they made a show of anger and looted [your] house.
Even a friend?
With fake friendship he made [you] trust him; for his own gain.
To oblige [you], everybody is congenial, even the king['s attention] is self-serving.
[Only] God['s love] has the traits of a vast, clear ocean, no one can find its limits.
Base, wretched, lustful, sinner. Vyās, though indifferent, can still [join] His service.[56]

[49] The variant shared by J and VN (mostly confirmed by VG): भाईप प्रति समीति मिलै चितु धरू लीनौं भैयाहूँ means 'Brotherhood, (भाईप = भायप), love, friendship, [my] heart got attached, but my brother took the house.'

[50] The variant in J, VN, and VG read: ब्याह वरैति मिस रुठयौ करि.

[51] J reads: बढा, VG has बढाई, VN has वढी. Note also that J, VN, and VG have this line reversed with the previous.

[52] J, VN, and VG read धन कारन मन हरयौ करयौ सव.

[53] J, VN, and VG read: कूर.

[54] I have translated the poem throughout with reference to a second person, as appropriate for a sermon. However, one could also translate it with reference to the first person, and read it as a confession of Vyās about his disenchantment with the world. These approaches are not mutually exclusive.

[55] Literally: 'the wedding ceremony and procession'.

[56] Or 'Vyās has also turned away from devotion', or: 'Vyās says: you have

Table 2: Comparison of VG and GDS version for *hari keṃ sauṃ hitu na kīyau ava kāṃhū* (bold for most significant variants, underline for different word order).

Vāṇī: VG 67 (VN 64, J 63)	GDS 62.15 (*saguṇa sādha milata gobiṃdajī kā guṇāṃha*)
सारंग	**राग धनाश्री**
हरि के सौ हितु न कीयौ अब कांहूं	हरि कौ सौ हित न कीयौ अब कांहूं और सबै दुषदाता
और सबै दुषदाता लातनि मारत लागत पाहू	लातनि मारत लागत पांऊं **लूटि लग रिसहु षाता**
अैसौ सुष सुपनैं नहि दीनौं गर्भ बसत माता हूं	अैसौ सुष सुपिनैं हूं न[46] दीनौं ग्रभि बसत माता हूं
अपनों विषै भोग पोषन लगि कीनों कपट पिता हूं	**स्वार्थ निपुन भरम** पोषन लग कीनौं कपट पिता हूं
वोलि तोतरे बोल चोरि चितु वितु लीनौं बेटा हूं	अपनैं काजि पतब्रत लीनौं बसि कीनौं अबला हूं
अपनैं काज पतिवृतु लीनौं वस कीनौं अवला हूं	बोल तोतरा बोलि चोरि चित बित लानौं बेटां हूं
भाइप प्रीति समीति मिलै **चितु घरु** लीनौं भैया हूं	**भई बिपरीते** संमींपि मिले **मांनूं धंन** लीनौं भइयां हूं
कपट प्रीति परतीति बढा(ई) अपनैं काजि सषा हूं	ब्याह बराती मिस रूंट्यौ करि घर लूट्यौ सजनां हूं
व्याह वरैती मिस रूठ्यौ करि घरू लूट्यौ सजना हूं	कपट प्रीति परतीति बंधाई अपनैं काजि सषां हूं
धन कारन **मन हर्‌यौ** कर्‌यौ सव स्वारथ लगि राजा हूं	**रिण** कारंनि **मनुहारि** करी सब स्वार्थ लग राजां हूं
हरि गुन विमल अगाध सिध की को जांनैं सीवा हूं	हरि गुण बिमल अगाध स्यंध की को जांनैं सीवां हूं
कूर कुटिल कामी अपराधी व्यास विमुष सेवा हूं	कूड कुटिल कांमीं अपराधी ब्यास बिमुष सेवां हूं

This poem too is on the theme of the superiority of God's love. However, it has quite a different slant compared to the other two translated earlier. Its focus is not on illustrating its theme by reminding the audience of God's glorious mythological deeds, but rather on bringing out God's greatness by contrast with human meanness. The pattern of the poem is built on a sequential degradation of all worldly love, starting with the strongest family bonds. Each kind of worldly love is unmasked as ultimately selfish and hence not comparable to that of God. In a way, the Fms. is getting at the same point, by highlighting the unusual character of Kṛṣṇa's mythological actions, and the fact that they are rarely seen in the world: who would have compassion with sinners (Ajāmila), paupers (Sudāmā), prostitutes (Piṅgalā), or hunchbacks (Kubjā) and associate with them? Who would swallow his pride and show himself subservient to those who have a lower social rank (Vidura, Arjuna)? Who would take risks to help weak allies (the unborn child Parīkṣit and the dethroned Ugrasena)? Though there is no systematic contrast with different forms of

turned away from devotion.' Alternatively the last words could be read: *vimukha se vāṃhu* which could be taken to mean '[draws away] a helping hand from the godless'.

worldly love, the Fms. poem can be seen as the reverse of the coin, the shadow version of the one quoted by Gopāldās.

In support of such an interpretation, the context of this poem in Fms. is relevant: the poem is immediately followed by another one in which the contrast between divine and worldly love is quite explicit. This poem is Nāmdev's *tūṃ jina barajai māī*, or: 'Don't be angry with me, mom' (see also the variant edited by Callewaert and Lath 1989, p. 375), in which the (presumably) child-author pleads with his mother to let him go to the temple. To convince his mother, Nāmdev says: *mātā bina bālake kisau tyāu hama kṛṣṇa binā* (Bahura and Bryant 1982, p. 141), 'How is a child without a mother? Such, I am [lost] without Kṛṣṇa.' Ironically, Nāmdev uses the strong image of love between mother and child to convince his mother that love for God is more important than his love for her.

It is clear that there are several well-attested poems by Vyās on the theme of God's unequalled love, which resemble the Fms. poem with *chāpa* Vyās on that theme. Hence, the Fms. poem may plausibly be ascribed to Harirām Vyās. Out of that available pool of Vyās's poems on the topic, the compiler of Fms. has chosen a poem which is essentially *saguṇī,* in that it gives examples of God's unexpected grace from the mythology of Kṛṣṇa. On the other hand, the compiler of GDS, the *nirguṇī* anthology, has for the same theme selected a poem that compares God's selfless love with the selfish motives of mundane attachment. This difference of selection is interesting in itself. It is consistent with the theory that the *nirguṇa* agenda prefers mundane images above orthodox mythical ones and is more often interested in the genre of sermons of admonition (*cetāvnī*), rather than mythology or praise of God (Gold 1992).

Fatehpur manuscript poem by Sūr on Hari's incomparable love

At this point, it may be better to broaden the picture, by comparing Vyās's poems on the theme of God's generosity with one by Sūrdās on the same topic. Such a poem by Sūr is found in Fms., preceding Vyās's by only a few folios (no. 179, *pada* 76 on fol. 68r-v, Bahura and Bryant 1982, p. 135):

राग मारू

पतित पावन हरि नामु तिहारौ कौनै हो धर्‌यै
हौ तो दीन दुचित संश्रित रङ्ग[57] द्वारै रटतु[58] पर्‌यै

[57] A later hand has added the character श above the last two syllables of संश्रित.
[58] The original had रटति which is corrected by a later hand.

जोनिज तन[59] जीव रुधिर जल जब जव जरठ जर्‌यै
तब हीं तै तौ[60] निकट तज्यौ हरि[61] सत अपराध भर्‌यै
गज गनिका नृप विप्र व्याधि ते मै घटि कहा कर्‌यै
विद्यमान भवसूल सहत हौं काल कुलिसनि (ड)दर्‌यै़ (ौ)
औरै कोट कोटि करुनामय तिन्ह तै कहा सर्‌यौ़
ना जानौ या सूर महासुठु कौन दोष बिसर्‌यौ

'Saviour of the poor', God, who has given You that name?[62]
[Look at] me, desperate and pained: a refugee's plight,[63] reduced to begging at Your door.
[My] body is born from a womb, [I am] a living being of water and blood; whenever I am consumed by old age,
Just then, You desert [my] presence! God, You commit libel against [Your own] honour!
Elephant and prostitute, king, brahmin, and hunter [were saved].[64] Why, have I done less than them?
Alive, I suffer the pains of existence, I'm in fear of Death's sudden lashes.[65]
To thousands of others You are graceful. Compared to them, what did [I] get?
I can't think, of this foremost fool Sūr,[66] which sins You have overlooked.

[59] A later hand has added the graph इ to fit before तन, this would be metrically slightly better and could be translated as: 'So many souls are born from the womb, of water and blood...'

[60] The original had तैतिो, an impossible combination.

[61] A later hand has made a clearly irenical emendation: न हरिहि.

[62] The expression *nāma dhar-* can be neutral: 'to give a name', or negative: 'to defame' (OHED).

[63] One of the meanings of *raṃga* can be 'condition' (OHED). Alternatively, one might be tempted to read *raṃka,* 'poor'.

[64] These are legendary characters, who where saved by Viṣṇu. The elephant is the mythological creature saved from the crocodile by Viṣṇu's timely coming to his rescue upon utterance of the name (*Bhāgavatapurāṇa* 8.2.27-33). The prostitute was saved by utterance of the name (*Bhāgavatapurāṇa* 11.8.22-44). The brahmin may refer to Kaṃsa's ally, the ruthless Śrīdhara (BBSK). The hunter may be a reference to the Niṣāda king Guha, a low-caste tribal, at whose place Rāma spent his first night away from home (*Vālmīki Rāmāyaṇa* 2.50-52). The enumeration is close to another poem by Sūr (NPS 138, p. 38, translated and annotated by Hawley 1984, pp.151, 199-200).

[65] Literally: 'thunderbolts' (*kulisa* as *kuliśa*, see BBSK).

[66] I have translated *suṭhu* as *saṭha* (see also the last line of the poem with refrain: *merau mana matihīna gosvāmī* (Snell 1991, pp. 86-7). Alternatively *mahāsuṭhu* can mean 'foremost' (taking *suṭhu* as derived from *suṣṭhu*).

Like Vyās's Fms. poem, Sūr's poem is about God's saving grace. However, Sūr dwells more on the debasedness of human existence and on the need for God's grace, whereas Vyās concentrated on praising God's never-failing grace itself. Vyās gave a series of examples where God's grace has worked for sinners, contrasting this with the shortcomings of human love. For Sūr it is God's performance that has been poor, especially given the expectations raised by His title 'Saviour of the poor'. Sūr gives a few examples where those expectations were fulfilled, but without elaborating, merely alluding to the stories, and squeezing all references into one single line (l. 5). The only example overlapping with Vyās is that of Piṅgalā, the prostitute.

The Fms. poem by Sūr has a famous, but later variant (NPS 133, p. 37), with more or less the same *ṭeka,* but quite different stanzas. In the more famous poem, 'Sūr' dwells much less on mundane sorrows, and more on heartening mythological antecedents of God's grace. This comes much closer in spirit to Vyās's poem. As in the latter, Sudāmā and Draupadī are mentioned, and so is, in addition, Sandīpana, Kṛṣṇa's guru:

राग धनाश्री

पतित पावन हरि बिरद तुम्हारौ कौनै नाम धर्‌यौ
हौं तौ दीन दुखित अति दुरबल द्वारैं रटत पर्‌यौ
चारि पदारथ दिए सुदामा तंदुल भेंट धर्‌यौ
द्रुपद सुता कौ तुम पति राखी अंबर दान कर्‌यौ
संदीपन सुत तुम प्रभ दीने बिद्यापाठ कर्‌यौ
बेर सूर की निठुर भए प्रभु मेरी कछु न सर्‌यौ

'Saviour of the poor', God, is Your fame. [Now,] who has given You that name?
[Look at] me: desperate and pained, utterly weak, reduced to begging at your door.
You gave Sudāmā [fulfillment of] the four goals [of human life], and he had brought [You] some [plain] grain for a gift.
You preserved the honour of Drupada's daughter, You gave her cloth for cover.
To Sandīpana You gave back his son, he had instructed You in learning.
But for Sūr You delay! You have become cruel, Lord. Nothing has worked for me.

There are several other poems by Sūr in a similar vein (see Hawley 1984, pp. 148-56 and Hawley 1992 for some other examples from early Ms. materials, among which the poem with *ṭeka: jā kau mohana aṃga karai*, or: 'Whom Mohana embraces', comes closest in spirit to Vyās's poems). An important poem of this type has the *ṭeka: syāma garībana hūṃ ke grāhaka*, or: 'Śyāma is a customer of those who are poor' (NPS 19, p. 6). This poem is very close to Vyās's in that it too mentions Sudāmā,

Arjuna, Vidura, and in one version even Kubjā. However, this poem is attested only from relatively late Mss. (see Hawley 1984, pp. 137, 149 and 196).

Comparison of the Fatehpur manuscript poems by Sūr and Vyās

The poems by Vyās and Sūr are similar and quite close, both in space in the Fms. and in terms of theme. It seems appropriate to compare them so as to define differences in approach between the two bhakta poets. (This is an elaboration on the general thoughts at the end of my paper at a previous conference, Pauwels 1994a, pp. 40-1.) Sūr is addressing his poem directly to God and his tone is that of challenge and complaint. He asserts his right to divine grace and basically tries to blackmail Kṛṣṇa into granting him His mercy. In that sense his poem fits the type of *binatī* or *vinaya:* it is a petition to God. Vyās, on the other hand, addresses his fellow seekers among human beings. He has a message to deliver, namely asserting the power of Hari to save sinners. Vyās's poem is classified as *upadeśa* or instruction. He is trying to convince others of what he himself has no doubt is true. In a way, he is more self-confident about his eligibility for divine grace than Sūr. The last line of the Fms. poem ('Low and simple, Vyās the sinner. Will he prove too much to stomach for God?') is a purely rhetorical question. Though Vyās too refers to himself as a sinner, he does not portray himself as the biggest of all. His tone is less self-accusatory than Sūr's. Or is this perhaps merely a difference in style of convincing the audience: Vyās is more straightforward about his message, his poem is didactic, he is clearly giving a sermon. Sūr's poem may function as an indirect invitation to the audience to identify with him, but on the surface it remains a monologue, directed to God.

Interestingly, both poets make use of the technique of enumeration of precedents of the recipients of God's grace. The main difference, however, is in the way they use this technique. Vyās's list serves to strengthen his case of reassuring his audience. Sūr, on the other hand, seems to be engaged in creating a kind of 'Schindler's list' of those 'saved' among whom he is eager to include himself (see also Hawley 1992).

The difference in style observable in the case of the poems of Fms. may hold good more in general. Recent research has established that the early Sūr poems mostly challenge God Himself, using a kind of blackmail of self-deprecation (see Hawley 1984, pp. 148-56). Sūr addresses God with his complaints, rather than lashing out against others. Although the available Mss. of *Vyās Vāṇī* are later than the 'early Sūr', it is nevertheless interesting to explore to what extent they confirm the attitude that appears from the one poem from Fms. What immediately stands out, is that there is no section on *vinaya* in the Vulgate *Vyās Vāṇī.* One might turn to the poems under the titles *madhyama sādhaka bhakta lakṣaṇa*, or: 'Characteristics of intermediate devotional practitioners' and *kaniṣṭha pravartaka bhakta lakṣaṇa,* or: 'Characteristics of novice promoter devotees.' Upon inspection, they turn out to be mainly aimed at directing others to the path of true bhakti.[67] Granted, there is some scope for ambiguity, especially in the *chāpa* lines, and one could read some of the poems under the aforementioned titles as self-castigating.[68] A rare example of a song which is quite clearly a self- reproach is VG 116 (VN 113, fol. 21v, J 131, fol. 50r-v), the last line of which reads *vyāsadāsa kī binatī suni puni kṛpā karī naṃdalāla*, or: 'Listen to Vyās's plea (*binatī*), and have mercy, darling of Nanda.' On the other hand, in J, this poem falls under the heading *bhakti gyāna upadesa ke pada*, or: 'Poems of instruction in knowledge of devotees', implying that the tradition regarded it as a vehicle for instruction, rather than a plea to God.

We can conclude that both Vyās and Sūr stress the miraculous saving power of God's grace by enumerating recipients of this grace. In contrast to Sūr, Vyās is more interested in convincing his audience in a straightforward sermon, rather than Sūr's style of challenging God and self-castigation. Vyās's tone is more self-assured, one of self-confidence rather than self-reproach.

3. Poems on the Theme of Satsaṅga

Fatehpur manuscript poem by Vyās on the theme of satsaṅga

The other three poems by Vyās in Fms. have all a strong *nirguṇī* ring. First,

[67] Clear examples of self-confident sermons are VG 113 [J 165, VN 109], VG 118 [J 125, VN 114], VG 119 [J 69, VN 115], VG 129 [J 190, VN 115], VG 135 [VN 131]. These appear in J under the titles *kapaṭa nirvāraṇa ke pada*, or: 'Poems to avert deceit', *bhakta gyāna upadesa ke pada*, or: 'Poems of instruction in knowledge of devotees', and the last under *kalikāla pravāha*, or 'Current of bad times'. In VN they appear under the same titles as in VG.

[68] Cp. esp. VG 114 (VN 110, J 68, under the title *śrī kiśorī-kiśorajū kau mādhuja* or especially the *ṭeka*, though less the *chāpa* line of VG 115 (VN 111, J 124, under the title *bhakta gyāna upadesa ke pada*).

I will discuss a poem on the topic of *satsaṅga* or 'good company', which is a favourite theme of much bhakti poetry, both *saguṇa* and *nirguṇa.* Vyās's poem in Fms. (no. 207, *pada* 102 on fol. 77r, see Bahura and Bryant 1982, p. 153), however, is not simply a poem in praise of *satsaṅga*; it is a very strong affirmation that Vyās is interested in the here-and-now, as opposed to the abstract, aspect of God's grace. In his refrain, Vyās affirms plainly that he likes God's bhaktas better than even God Himself.

राग धंन्याश्री

हरि हूं ते हरिदास लागत प्यारे
देषत मिलत परम सुषु उपजत होत सकल दुष न्यारे
जिन के चरन कमल सेवत है (ह)म (कह)[69] कहौं त सारे
तिन कै सरन गयो काकै डरु जिन कै हरि रषवारे
तन के तन मन हू के मन नैननि हू के तारे
यह जीय जानि साध संगति पर व्यास प्रान धन वारे

Better than God Himself, [I] like God's servants!
Beholding and meeting them, is [my] highest joy, all sorrow falls away.
The servants of His lotus feet, how could I tell about all of them?
When I have sought refuge with them, whom should [I] fear? They have God for their protector.
They are the body of my body, the heart of my heart, they are the apple of my eye.
This is what my heart tells [me to do],[70] so, for the company of holy men, Vyās has surrendered money and life.

Like the previous one, this poem is not found in any of the printed editions or Mss. of *Vyās Vāṇī* as available to me. So far, no other version of this poem has been attested. So again, first the likelihood of attribution to Harirām Vyās needs to be discussed. The theme is not at all unusual for Vyās, who seems to have indeed felt strongly about his fellow-devotees, as he has several songs on the theme of his ardent devotion for bhaktas. Many poems on this theme are attested under the heading *sādhani kī (a)stuti*, or: 'Praise of holy men' in the Mss. (*bhakta praśaṃsā*, or: 'Praise for devotees', section 14 in VG). A good example of this kind of song is VG 22 (corresponding to J 22 fol. 8r, VN 22 fol. 7v) with *ṭeka*: *mere bhakta haiṃ deī deū,* or: 'For me, devotees are like gods and goddesses.'

[69] As it stands in the Ms., the second *pāda* of this line is deficient, very likely due to a case of haplology from the scribe. I have tentatively reconstructed the line on this basis, restoring metre and meaning.

[70] Literally, 'Knowing this in the heart.'

The *chāpa* line of this poem is very similar to the one in the Fms. poem quoted above: *vyāsadāsa ke prāna jīvana dhana harijana bāla baḍeū*, or: 'Vyāsdās's life, soul, and wealth are the devotees of God, both great and small.' Another example is VG 227 (not in J; VN 221 fol. 35r) with *ṭeka*: *karau bhaiyā sādhuna hī soṃ saṃga*, or: 'Brother, associate only with holy men.' The second line of this poem reads: *hari teṃ haridāsana kī sevā parama bhakti kau aṃga*, or: 'The most important part of devotion is service of God's servants, rather than that of God.' Another argument in favour of attribution to Vyās is the occurrence of exactly the same second half of the *chāpa* line, *vyāsa prāna dhana vāre*, in another, well-attested poem, namely, VG 346 (J. 294, fol. 127v-128r). The topic of that poem is, however, quite different: it is a description of the beauty of Rādhā's eyes.

Poem by Vyās on the theme of satsaṅga from a Dādūpanthī anthology

A poem on a similar theme is also attributed to Vyās in the other Dādūpanthī anthology introduced above, DM2, the Ms. of 1676, preserved in the Dādū Mahāvidyālay in Jaipur (see above part 1; this poem is found on fol. 162 r-v) This poem is not attested elsewhere either.

जनम जनम के पाप गये
हरि भगतन के दरस परस तैं मंगल आज भये
धंनि सोइ धांम धरणिं धनि सो जहां संतनिं चर्ण[71] दये
देव पित्र मुनिं त्रिपति भये है चरणोदिक अंचये
आजि कीये हरि काज हंमारे संत भवंन पठये
जिनि की क्रिपा क्रिपाल होत हंरि व्यास जनिंज जंनए

The sins of life after life [washed] away:
By the sight and touch of God's devotees, today, [sins] turned auspicious.
Hail to that place, hail to that earth, which the saints have blessed with their feet.
Just a sip from the water [that washed] their feet, and forebears, sages, and gods are satisfied.[72]

[71] Probably for चरण to remain within the boundaries of the page (it is the last word of the line).

[72] A reference to the traditional three 'debts' or *ṛṇas*: to *devas*, *ṛṣis*, and *pitṛs*. Vyās intends to say that there is no need for special ceremonies such as that of offering *piṇḍas* for ancestry worship. It is much more important to revere devotees.

Today, at last, God was of use to me: He has sent holy men to my house
It's by their grace that God is gracious: to Vyās they are [brother,] son of his mother.[73]

Like the previous poem, this one proclaims Vyās's respect for holy men, devotees of God, and makes it clear that Vyās loves them even more than God Himself. The first poem does so quite explicitly in the *ṭeka*, the second in its last stanza where Vyās states in so many words that it is only via holy men that God is of use and can show His mercy. Thus, the theme of both poems is very similar, but nevertheless each has a different slant. The poem quoted in Fms. stresses the good qualities of *satsaṅga*, the joy and bliss of meeting like-minded devotees in the flesh, whereas the poem quoted in DM2 sets up comparisons. It stresses the superiority of *satsaṅga* over traditional Hindu ritualism, such as that of paying off the three debts, and elaborates on the superiority of saints over God, which is done only in the refrain in Fms.

In both cases, in placing devotees above God, Vyās is going quite a bit further than just a formulaic recommendation of *satsaṅga.* This avowed fervour of Vyās for paying obeisance to true devotees of God is supported by the occurrence of many poems by Vyās in praise of bhaktas (for more examples, and also of Vyās's promoting the feeling of belonging to the same family, see Pauwels 1994a, pp. 26-31). Interestingly, this trait of Vyās's devotion is also confirmed by the famous hagiographer Nābhādās. In his *Bhakt Māl* (probably finished before 1600), he devotes one song (*chappāī* 92) to Vyās, which has in its refrain: *bhakta iṣṭa ati vyāsa ke*, or: 'The devotee was the object of his special devotion' (see Gaṇeśdās and Rāmeśvardās 1986, p. 124). Later hagiographers pick up the theme with much gusto (see Pauwels 1994b, pp. 22-5), but suffice it here to determine that poems on this topic are vintage Vyās.

Finally, one might have wanted to compare the Fms. poem by Vyās with similar ones by Sūr. Quoted in the same section, are Sūr's poems *jo pai aura bīyau koū pāvai* (Fms. no. 201, *pada* 96 fol. 75r; NPS 201, p. 55) and *vai dina visari gaye īhā āyau* (Fms. no. 209, *pada* 104 fol. 77v-78r; NPS 320, pp. 87-8). However, neither of those poems touches on the theme

[73] I have interpreted *janija* as from *janī* ('mother') + *ja* 'born' and *janae* as a perf. part. of the trans. verb 'to give birth'. Alternatively, a pun on the *chāpa* 'Vyās' could be intended: 'Those in the line of Vyās (*vyasaja*) are my own people (*nija jana e*).' In any case, Vyās intends to make the point that *bhakta*s are his true family, as in his song with *ṭeka: meraiṃ bhakta haiṃ deī deū* and further on: *mātā pitā bhaiyyā mere bhakta damāda sajana bahneū* (VG 22, J22 fol. 8r).

of *satsaṅga*. Both are about the traps of *saṃsāra*, and the need to get out of it via God's grace.

4. Poems on the Theme of the Importance of the Name of God

The two remaining poems by Vyās in Fms. are on the theme of the importance of the Name of God. Given that this too is a universal *bhakti* theme, dear to *saguṇī*s and *nirguṇī*s alike, it is perhaps not all that surprising that precisely these two poems from Fms. are the ones that are also attested in the Dādūpanthī anthology GDS. The availability of different versions of the same poems in ideologically different anthologies warrants a close study of the variants in the different versions of these poems, including the Vrindāban Vulgate version.

At the outset, it is useful to discuss the context of these poems in Fms. They occur among poems that have in common the theme of God's grace. The first poem (*sācoī gopāla gopāla raṭibau*) is followed by Kabīr's *rāmabāna aniyāre tīra*, or: 'The sharp arrows from God's bow' (which is with some variants, the same as *rāma bhagati aniyāle tīra*, poem 8 in the *Granthāvalī*, see Callewaert and Op de Beeck 1991, I, p. 303). The second poem (*rasanā syāmahi naiku gāi rī*) is followed by Parmānand's *jaba goviṃdu kripā karai taba saba bani āvai*, or: 'When Govinda is gracious, then all falls into place' (which is the same as Śarmā 1959, p. 584, *pada* 1303). Interestingly, no poems by Sūr are quoted on these themes. The nearest poem by Sūr in the Ms. concentrates less on the reviving power of God's grace, but rather on the miseries of human existence (cp. *vai dina bisari gaye īhā āyau*, or: 'Those days were forgotten [when] you came here'; no. 209, *pada* 104 on fol. 77v; Bahura and Bryant 1982, pp. 154-5).

First Fatehpur manuscript poem by Vyās on the importance of the Name

The poem I will discuss first is Fms. no. 190, *pada* 86 on fol. 71v-72r (Bahura and Bryant 1982, pp. 142-3), which corresponds to Gopāldās's *Sarvāṅgi* 11.9. The poem is also found in the Vulgate, where it is classified under the heading *upadesa prakaraṇa*, or: 'Chapter on instruction' (VG 175 and VN 169 fol. 30v-31r) or *paṛhive ke pada*, or: 'Songs for reading/recitation' (J 170 fol. 67v-68r).

राग धंन्याश्री[74]

साचोई[75] गोपाल गोपाल रटिबै[76]
[रूप सील गुन कौंन कांम के][77] राम भगति[78] बिनु पटिबौ
जोग जग्य तीरथ तप यह़ सब[79] कलई कौ सौ[80] मढिबै
नाम कुठार बिना को काटै पाप बधि[81] कौ बटिबै
जैसौ अन [ि]ब[न] भूस क[ू]टत[82] बारू मै तेल ना कढिबै[83]
अैसे करम धरम (धरम) करि[84] हरि बिनु बिनु बैसांदर [डढि](कटि)बौ[85]

[74] All manuscripts and editions agree on the *rāga* of this *pada* being Dhanāśrī.

[75] GDS has साचौ.

[76] Most versions give consistently rhyme words on -ढिवौ with voiced aspirate ढ-. The Fms. seems to waver between -ढ- and the unvoiced unaspirated -ट- but in general those graphs are tough to distinguish. Some of the verbs, such as this one occur in both forms: both रट- and रढ- are attested with the same meaning.

[77] Supplied from GDS, nearly identical in J, VN, and the edition VG.

[78] GDS has a near identical reading. J and VG share an interesting variant: हरि की भक्ति (discussed below).

[79] GDS's and J-VG's variants are similar and poetically better, in that they continue summing up devotional practices instead of saying 'all those': J and VN: जोग जग्य जप तप संजम वृत, GDS जोग जग्य जप तप तीरथ बरत. GDS has the best of both: the rhyming formula जप तप as well as alliterating तीरथ. The peculiar reading of Fms. might have resulted from a misreading of a model जोग जग्य तीरथ जप तप बरत; the scribe of Fms. may have read यह for जप and सब for बरत.

[80] GDS has के सौ.

[81] Fms. reading is unclear, may also be ब्यध. GDS and the Vulgate (J, VN, VG) agree on the variant: पाप बुंद/वृंद (resp). Interestingly, GDS has reversed the last two lines with the following two.

[82] Probably a case of haplology on the part of the scribe of Fms., who left out the न in बिन. Emendation of this and the verb कूटत for कटत on the basis of GDS, confirmed by the Vulgate (J and VG)'s variant: अन्न बिना तुस कूटत. The reading तुस (for तुष 'husk') can be explained as a synonymous variant for भूस with reference to graphic probability. VN also reads कटत.

[83] In fact the rhyme word in Fms. looks more like कटिबौ, but the other versions agree on कढिबौ, which also makes most sense. VN leaves out the first syllable of तेल.

[84] Poetically inferior variant in GDS and VN: अैसें भरम करम सब and J-VG: अैसैंहिं करम धरम सव.

[85] Very likely कटिबौ is a case of *homoeographon* (see end of previous line). I have emended it to the reading of J, VN, and VG: डढिबौ, GDS has जढिबौ, but no such verb is attested for Braj nor Rājasthānī. It may be a contamination with जल- 'to burn,' which would make good sense in context, but is a *lectio facilior* compared to VG's variant. VN has only once बिन, probably a case of haplology.

जैसे परदार स्यौ रति करी[86] पति बिनु रासभ चढिबौ[87]
अैसे ब्यास निरास भये है कह बातनि कौ[88] [गढि](कटि)बौ[89]

Repeat[90] in truth 'Gopāla, Gopāla'.
What good is beauty, talent, training, recitation without love for Rāma?
Yoga, ritual, pilgrimage, and fasting amount to applying a coat of polish.
What would cut sharply, but the axe of the Name, which knot of sin could one demolish?[91]
Try threshing chaff without grain! No oil is pressed from sandy soil![92]
Without God, what karma-dharma would transpire? Do you get burning without the fire?[93]
If another man's wife for a lover you've taken: you'll parade on an ass, honour-forsaken.[94]
So, Vyās has given up aspiration[95]: why crafting words [for obfuscation]?

The theme of this song is recitation of the Name of God, and contrasting this with other, traditional and less efficient, religious praxes. The point is, Vyās asserts, that any religiosity without true feeling for God is fruitless

[86] GDS has परदारा सूं रूचि मांनत है. The Vulgate's variant seems metrically better: जैसैं परदारा कों रति करि (shared by VG, VN, and J).

[87] In Fms. this line is repeated twice.

[88] GDS reads: अैसैं ब्यास निरास भये सब, का बातनि कौ. The Vulgate (J, VN, and VG) has: अैसेंही व्यास निरास भए विनु कहा वातानि कौ.

[89] Fms.'s कटिबौ is another case of *homoeographon* (see end of some previous lines) and has been emended to the reading on which GDS and the Vulgate agree: गढिबौ.

[90] The rhyme words are all verbal forms in *-ibau* or (*-ibai*), which can be taken as verbal nouns ('doing') or as gerundives ('is to be done').

[91] In fact, this is an intransitive verb, meaning 'to come apart'. The variants could be translated as: 'Who would hack down ... the flourishing of the bush of sin.'

[92] Literally, 'oil is not drawn from sand.'

[93] Literally, 'Doing karma and dharma without God, [is like] burning without fire.' The word used for fire, *baisaṃdara*, is etymologically related to *vaiśvānara*, which means 'that which belongs to all people', a title of Agni, god of fire. This creates a nice parallel with the first half of the comparison, where Hari is portrayed as the one force which pervades all people.

[94] Reference to a type of punishment, in which a culprit is paraded on a donkey to be humiliated by the whole village. This line aims at ridiculing religious praxis without sincere love for God. As long as one is still engrossed in the world of the senses, talking about God, or pretending to be religious, is as pointless and contemptible as making love to a woman who is not one's own.

[95] The alternative readings of VG and GDS could be translated as 'Similarly, without giving up (mundane) ambition, Vyās [says], ...'

and pointless. As long as worldly goods are pursued, there can be no room for God, and all claims to the contrary are false. This message is brought home in a very effective manner, with simple examples from day-to-day village life (threshing grain, pressing oil, burning fire). In case anyone would still have missed the point, Vyās is sure to get his audience's ear when he uses strong language and brings up scandalous sexual affairs, turning adultery into a metaphor for turning away from God. This nicely sets up the audience for the last line where Vyās urges abandonment of all worldly desire and discourse, except that of God's Name.

Table 3: Comparison of Fms., GDS, and Vulgate version for *sācoī gopāla gopāla raṭibau* (bold for most significant variants, underline for different word order).

Fms. 190	GDS 11.9 *(nāma mahimā)*
राग धंन्याश्री	**राग धंन्याश्री**
साचोई गोपाल गोपाल रटिबै	साचौ गोपाल गोपाल रढिबौ
राम भगति बिनु पटिबौ	रूप सील गुन कौंन कांम के **राम** भगति बिनु पटिबौ
जोग जग्य तीरथ तप **यह सब** कलई कौ सौ मढिबै	जैसैं अंन बिन भुस कूटत है बारू मैं तेल ना कढिबौ
नाम कुठार बिना को काटै पाप **बधि** कौ बटिबै	अैसैं **भ**रम **क**रम **सब** हरि बिन बिन बैसंदरि जढिबौ
जैसौ अन ब भूस कटत बारू मै तेल ना कढिबौ	जोग जग्य **जप** तप तींरथ **बरत** कलई के सौ मढिबौ
अैसे **करम धरम** धरम **करि** हरि बिनु बिनु बैसांदर कटिबौ	नांव कुठार बिनां को काटै पाप **बृंदं** कौ बढिबौ
जैसे परदार स्यौ **रति करी** पति बिनु रासभ चढिबौ	परदारा सूं **रुचि मांनत है** पति बिन रासिब चढिबौ
अैसे ब्यास निरास भये़ **है** कह बातनि कौ कटिबौ	अैसैं ब्यास निरास भये **सब** का बातनि कौ गढिबौ

Vāṇī: J 170: *paṛhive ke pada;*
VN 169, VG 175: *upadesa prakaraṇa*

धनासिरी रागे

सांचौइ गोपाल गोपाल रढिवौ
रूप सील गुन कौंन काम कों **हरि की** भक्ति विनु पढिबौ
जोग जग्य **जप** तप **संजम वृत** कलई कौ सौ मढिवौ
नाम कुठार विना को काटै पाप **वृंद** कौ वढिवौ
जैसें अंन विना तुस कूटत वारू में तेल न कढिवौ
अैसेंहि करम धरम **सव** हरि विन विन वैसांदर डढिवौ
जैसें परदारा सौं **रति करि** पति विन रासभ चढिवौ
अैसेंही ब्यास निरास भए **विनु** कहा वातनि कौ गढिवौ

Since three different versions of this song are available, a textcritical study is possible. Table 3 facilitates a comparative overview. A major variant occurs right in the second part of the refrain. The Fms. reading, *rāma bhagati,* is confirmed by GDS, but J, and with it the whole Vrindāban recension, has instead *hari kī bhakti.* The main difference is in the epithets referring to God. The epithets have also a different metrical value: *hari* is one *mātrā* shorter than *rāma.* This has been accommodated by adding the possessive *kī* and then shortening the three-syllabic *bhagati* as two-syllabic *bhakti.* Since the reading of Fms. is also confirmed by GDS, it seems that the Vulgate reading is secondary. Its variant may reflect an uneasiness on the part of the Vulgate line of transmission with the non-Kṛṣṇaite epithet *rāma.*

Other variants are less important, but notable too is the Vrindāban Vulgate's substitution of *tīrtha* with *saṃjama.* The reading of Fms. here is not very satisfactory and may stem from a misreading (see also footnote 79), but it shares with GDS the formulaic combination of alliterating *tīrtha* and *tapa.*[96] Hence, it seems clear that the Vrindāban Vulgate's dropping of *tīrtha* and insertion of *saṃjama* is secondary. The question then is why this happened. The scribes of the *Vyās Vāṇī* were mostly writing in Braj, where pilgrimage was and is one of the major sources of income. Hence, one might speculate, Vyās's statements minimizing the merit of pilgrimage were not very welcome. Nevertheless, the scribes of the Vulgate have preserved other instances in Vyās's poetry, where he points out the limited value of *joga jagya tīratha brata* as long as one is still caught in the web of worldly desire (VG 147, 173, 192, 211, 240 [with also *saṃjama* in the list], 279), or its inferiority when compared to bhakti or keeping company of saints (VG 153). Most of these poems are attested in J. So, it would be safest to assume that the variant with *saṃjama* is merely an alternative formula without much ulterior motives.

In conclusion, we can say that the poem *sācoī gopāla gopāla raṭibau* by Vyās seems not only to have been very popular, but also to have remained fairly stable in its transmission in different milieus. This is affirmed by the relative lack of significant variants and by the unanimity in the Mss. regards the *rāga* in which this poem is to be sung.

Second Fatehpur manuscript poem by Vyās on the Name

The next poem by Vyās on the topic of the Name of God in Fms. is no. 214, *pada* 109, fol. 79r-v (Bahura and Bryant 1982, pp. 157-8), which corresponds

[96] Interestingly, the same combination occurs in the next poem in GDS (11.10, see Callewaert 1991, pp. 155-6), which is by Sūrdās (*soī to bhalau jo rāmahi gāvai . . . joga jagya japa tapa tīratha brata, jahāṃ jahāṃ jāi jāi tahāṃ ḍahakāvai*).

to GDS 8.50. The poem is also found in the Vulgate under the section *sādhaka avasthā*, or: 'The condition of the practitioner' (VG 252; VN 246 fol. 38r), or *utkaṇṭhā ke pada*, or: 'Poems of longing' (J 70 fol. 26v-27r).

राग गूजरी[97]

रसना स्यामहि[98] नैकु गाइ री[99]
चढि बैकुंठ निसरनि[100] हरिपद प्रेम प्रसाद पाइ री[101]
छाडि बिरानी निदां तूं गोबिदा कौ जंसु गाइ री[102]
या देही बेही कौ कारन[103] छिन छिन घटत आव् री[104]
भौंसागर[105] तिरबे कै कारन[106] पावन (राम)[107] नाम नाव् री[108]
इहि कलिकाल गुपाल भजन बिनु सुपनै सचु न पाइ री[109]

[97] The *rāga* is Gandhār in GDS, Devgandhār in J, VN, and VG.

[98] GDS has for *ṭeka*: रसनां तूं रांमहि नैंक गाव री. VN's *ṭeka* is incomplete: रसना स्याम हैं ने.

[99] J and VG read the more poetical लडाउ री. In Fms., throughout the poem, the rhyme fluctuates between -आइ री, -आउ री , or -आव री. Most editions have cleaned this up in favour of one or the other.

[100] This reading, निसरनि, is confirmed in GDS, whereas J, VN, and VG have नसैंनी/निसैनी.

[101] In J and VN's version the second *pāda* of this line works out better metrically: प्रेम प्रसादहि पाउरी.

[102] J, VN, and VG agree on the more Sanskritic पराई, and are poetically better: छाँडि पराई निंदा विंदा गोविंदा गुन गाउ री. Similarly, but with a different epithet for God, in GDS: छाडि पराई निंद्या ब्यंद्या भगवंत सुजस सुनाव री.

[103] GDS has इहि देहि षेही कैं करन; VG, VN, and J share: वेही काजें या देही की.

[104] J and VG fill out the metre: छिन छिन घटति जु आउ री. Note also that this line and the previous one are switched around in the Vulgate (in all three, VG, VN, and J).

[105] J, VN, and VG share the more Sanskritic भवसागर.

[106] This time, J, VN, and VG share the less Sanskritic काजै/काजें.

[107] I have made an emendation based on metrical considerations and supported by the reading of GDS: पांवन नांव नाव री. The latter reading adds a stylistic feature to the line, by introducing a *yamaka* or apparent repetition of the same word, but with twice a different meaning: here नाव meaning 'name' the first time, and 'ship', the second.

[108] Totally different variant of the second *pāda* in the Vulgate (J, VN, and VG): नाहिंन आन उपाउरि, or 'there are no other means.'

[109] GDS has the hypermetrical सुपिनै हू सुख न री, whereas all Mss. of the Vulgate (J, VN, and VG) share reversed word order: सुष सपनें नहिं पाउ री.

[हरि][110] बिमुषनि कौ जलु न्याजु ते[111] काली धार[112] बहाउ री
भगत अनन्यनि की जूठनि परि[113] ब्यासहि [रु](र)चि[114] उपजाइ री

Sing a little 'Śyāma', O tongue of mine,[115]
God's feet are the staircase[116] to heaven above, climb it to get to the banquet of love.
Stop bringing others to shame, sing instead Govinda's fame.
This body is a jar of clay,[117] so minute by minute life seeps away.[118]
To cross life's ebb and flow, the Holy Name's the raft [to row].
In this age of Kalikāla, without singing the Name 'Gopāla', you won't find [of] bliss [a gleam], not even in a dream.
Food[119] and drink from non-believers, whip the stream of Death in waves,
Crumbs of bread from true believers, that's what Vyās's palate craves.

This poem again praises the efficacy of reciting the Name of God for the goal of transcending this world. Vyās urges his audience to change their life in the face of mortality. In addition to using the Name, he also stresses the importance of *satsaṅga,* or the company of true believers. Hobnobbing

[110] I have made an emendation on the basis of the reading shared by GDS and J-VG.

[111] The reading of J and VG आजु नाजु जलय (VN: अजु नाजु ललु) seems to be a combination of the one in Fms. and the one in GDS: अनं पांनी आज ते, with similar meaning.

[112] VG has the internally rhyming कारी धारि.

[113] J, VN, and VG share: रसिक अनंन्यनि. GDS has a different metrical structure दास अनिन की जूठनि ऊपरि.

[114] I have made an emendation on the basis of the reading shared by GDS and the Vulgate.

[115] Rhyme words throughout have the vocative particle *rī* and (except for l. 4 and 7) a verbal form which can be interpreted as and imperative, absolutive, or unmarked third person sg. pres-subj.

[116] *Nisaranī* and the other Mss. variants (*nisainī*) stand for Skt. *niśrayaṇī.*

[117] *behī,* according to OHED, is an earthen vessel presented by the potter community of a village to a newly wedded couple. It seems to apply here in a less specific meaning. The alternative reading from GDS *ṣehī,* 'dust', works well and one could contemplate emendation on the basis of meaning and graphical probability (confusion of ष and ब).

[118] I have interpreted *āva* as equivalent to *āyu,* see also HŚS 476.

[119] *Nyāju* may be taken as a combination of *nyāda* (food) and *nāja* (grain) both attested in OHED, HŚS and RSK. This understanding is more or less confirmed by the variant from GDS: *ana pānī* 'water and grain'. The compound *jala nāja* is found elsewhere in Vyās' oeuvre clearly with the meaning 'food and drink', see VG 228 (not in J, but VN 222 fol. 36r).

with godless people is never advisable. Even making a living should be secondary to turning to God. Vyās makes this clear by stressing that for him leftovers (*jūṭhana*) of true devotees are worth much more than all the food and drink of those who do not worship God.

Table 4: Comparison of Fms., GDS, and Vulgate version for *rasanā syāmahi naiku gāi rī* (bold for most significant variants, underline for different word order).

Fms. 214	GDS 8.50 (*sumiraṇa*)
राग गूजरी	**राग गंधार**
रसना **स्यामहि** नैकु गाइ री	रसनां तूं **रांमहि** नैंक गाव री
चढि बैकुंठ निसरनि हरिपद प्रेम प्रसाद पाइ री	चढि बैकुंठ निसरनी हरिपद प्रेम प्रसाद पाव री
छाडि बिरानी निदां **तूं गोबिदा कौ जंसु गाइ री**	छाडि **पराई** निंद्या **व्यंद्या भगवतं सुजस सुनाव** री
या देही बेही कौ कारन छिन छिन घटत आव री	इहि कलिकाल गुपाल भजन बिन सुपिनैं हूं सुष न पाव री
भौंसागर तिरबे कै कारन पावन **राम नाम नाव** री	इहि देही षेही कैं कारन छिन छिन घटत आव री
इहि कलिकाल गुपाल भजन बिनु सुपनै सचु न पाइ री	भौंसागर तिरबे कै कारनं पावनं **नावं नाव** री
बिमुषनि कौ जलु न्याजु ते काली धार बहाउ री	**हरि बिमुषनि कौ अंन पांनीं आज ते** काली धार बहाव री
भगत अनन्यनि की जूठनि परि ब्यासहि रुचि उपजाइ री	**दास** अनिन की जूठनि ऊपरि ब्यासहि रुचि उपजाव री
रसना स्यामहि नैकु गाइ री	

Vāṇī: J 70: *utkaṇṭhā;* VN 246, VG 252: *sādhaka avasthā*
राग देवगंधार
रसना **स्यामहि** नैंक लडाउ री
चढि वैकुंठ नसैंनी हरि पद प्रेम प्रसादहि पाउ री
छाडि पराइ निंदा **विंदा गोविंदा गुन गाउ** री
भवसागर तरिवे के काजै **नाहिन आन उपाउ** री
वेही काजें या देही की छिन छिन घटति जु आउ री
इहि कलिकाल गुपाल भजन विनु सुष सुपनें नहि पाउ री
हरि विमुषनि कों आजु नाजु जलु कारी धार वहाउ री
रसिक अनंन्यनि की जूठिनि पर व्यासहि रुचि उपजाउ री

Again, three different versions of this song are available, which makes a text critical study possible. Table 4 facilitates a comparative overview. The first major difference that jumps to the eye regards again the epithets used for referring to God. This time, however, Fms. shares its variants with the Vulgate: both have *syāma* (in the *ṭeka*) and *govindā* (in the first stanza). The Dādūpanthī version stands alone with its readings *rāma* and *bhagavaṃta.* As in the previous poem, the selection of different epithets has necessitated metrical adaptations: whereas *govindā,* has the 6 *mātrā*s required for the metre, *bhagavaṃta* has only 4 *mātrā*s. In order to avoid a hypometrical line, two *mātrā*s have been added by reading *sujasa* instead of *jasa*, and *sunāu* for *gāi.* However, in this case it is the GDS reading that seems to be secondary. So, this time the textual change is the opposite of what happened in the previous poem: a certain measure of metrical accommodation has served to help substitute *saguṇī* epithets with more preferable *nirguṇī* ones.

A second interesting variant is found in the last line. Here all three versions show different readings: Fms. has *bhagata ananyana*, GDS has *dāsa anina*, and J (and Vulgate) has *rasika ananyana.* The term *rasika ananya* is used frequently throughout the Vulgate *Vyās Vāṇī*, especially with reference to Vyās's fellow-bhaktas Hit Harivaṃś and Haridās, but it is also applied to such important connoisseurs as Jayadeva and Prabodhānanda, as well as to the inhabitants of both supernatural and worldly Vrindāban. The term seems well-established and nearly *cliché.* How are the variants to be interpreted? There are two ways to look at the textual evidence of this *pada.* The existence of the variants may cast some doubt on how fixed the term was in Vyās's times. May be the text of Vyās's *pada*s was less stabile than is assumed now on the basis of the Vulgate *Vyās Vāṇī*, and the term became *cliché* only later. Alternatively, it is possible that the formula was indeed there early on, but, since it was less meaningful for the non-Vrindāban crowd, it was less fixed in those routes of transmission. Evidence of a formula *rāma rasika* can be found in the *nirguṇī* works, such as in the corpus of Dādū (Callewaert and Op de Beeck, I *sākhī* 8.82 and *pada* 51, 1.3) and Kabīr's Bījak (ibid. I *pada* 20, *ṭeka*). The term *ananya* on its own, in a positive sense of exclusively devoted to God, is also used by *nirguṇī*s, as it is found in Dādū's *sākhī*s (e.g., ibid. I *sākhī* 2.84) and Raidās' *pada*s (e.g., ibid. I *pada* 15, *ṭeka*). However, at least in the poems by the most famous *nirguṇī* poets Dādū, Kabīr, Nāmdev, Raidās, Hardās, the Siddhas, Gorakh, and Sundardās (as collected by Callewaert and Op de Beeck), there is no evidence of a formula *ananya rasika.* This raises an interesting point: some oral formulaic expressions seem to be milieu-specific, and do not travel well outside the immediate context from which they derive their meaning.

In comparison to the previous poem, *rasanā syāmahi naiku gāi rī* has more significant variants in the different milieus in which it was transmitted. Interestingly, this goes hand in hand with a greater variability in the *rāga* assignation.

CONCLUSION: FINDINGS OF THE PAPER

To conclude, the major findings of this investigation of Vyās's poems in Fms. will be summarized and their relevance for the *saguṇa-nirguṇa* question will be evaluated. Finally, the case of Vyās will be compared to that of Sūr, so as to provide a more complete picture with regard to how the early generation of Braj Kṛṣṇa bhaktas regarded their *nirguṇī* colleagues.

Out of the five poems by Vyās quoted in Fms., only the first poem (*kisorī deṣī vana mai jāta*) deals with Kṛṣṇa's adolescent romances. This is also the only poem by Vyās to be found in the first portion of the Ms. It is quite a popular *māna* poem, and a good representative of a significant section of Vyās's collected works (the subsection *Māna kī śṛṅkhalā*).

Of the four other poems attributed to Vyās in Fms., only one poem (*hari sauṃ prītama bhayau na hvaihai*) has references to the mythology of Viṣṇu-Kṛṣṇa, in order to illustrate God's amazing grace. This poem is not attested elsewhere, but a fair case for authorship can be made on the basis of other poems on this theme which are well-attested as attributed to Vyās, including one that is attested in GDS. The compiler of the latter, more *nirguṇī* anthology has chosen to include a poem that makes less reference to mythology, and contrasts instead God's grace and forgiving, selfless love with the selfish love of humans.

A third poem (*hari hūṃ te haridāsa lāgata pyāre*) is not attested elsewhere either, but we find similar poems attributed to Vyās in the *Vyās Vāṇī* and in a Dādūpanthī anthology. Also according to the hagiographers the poem's theme, praise of holy men and the superiority of their *satsaṅga* above all else, was dear to Vyās's heart. There is nothing particularly *saguṇī* about this poem, but again, it is a good representative of Vyās's concerns.

The two other poems (*sācoī gopāla gopāla raṭibau* and *rasanā syāmahi naiku gāi rī*) are very well attested elsewhere (in *Vyās Vāṇī* as well as in GDS) and could be called Vyās' greatest early hits. They are mainly on the theme of the importance of recitation of the Name, which is again, a favourite of both *saguṇī*s and *nirguṇī*s.

The picture of Vyās that emerges from Fms. then is different from the one currently prevalent. He appears less in the capacity of a singer celebrating Rādhā and Kṛṣṇa's love, not even as one concentrating on the theme of Kṛṣṇa's idyllic youth in Braj. Rather, Vyās comes across as a preacher, singing songs with a message. His poems are sermons on how to change one's life by trust in the grace of God, by recitation of the Name and by seeking out the company of other bhaktas. With those themes,

Vyās treads on ground that *nirguṇī*s and *saguṇī*s hold in common.

Perhaps this non-Kṛṣṇaite picture of Vyās should not come as too much of a surprise, given that four out of five of his poems are found in the section of Fms. that quotes *nirguṇī* poets most heavily. Similarly, it should not surprise us too much that two poems from Fms. find correspondents with minor variants and two others have close equivalents on the same theme in Dādūpanthī sources. Given the interest of the compilers of the latter anthologies, it is natural that such a picture of Vyās will emerge. Compared to the compilers of *Vyās Vāṇī*, who were devotees of Kṛṣṇa, they will naturally select different songs to sing.

The close textual study of different versions of the same songs shows that the most obvious variants are the epithets for God and to a lesser extent specific terminology. Predictably, the epithets are more *nirguṇī* in the Dādūpanthī material, and more *saguṇī* in *Vyās Vāṇī*. Fms., written in Rājasthān, with an equal measure of *nirguṇī* and *saguṇī* selections, seems to fall somewhere in between. Given its early date, it could be used to help determine what a likely 'original' version might have been. The results are mixed: sometimes there is stronger evidence for a primary *nirguṇī* reading (when the Fms. reading is confirmed in the early Dādūpanthī material), sometimes there is clear evidence for *saguṇī* epithets early on (when the Fms. reading is confirmed in the Vulgate *Vyās Vāṇī*). The most interesting endeavour is, however, not to search for Vyās's authorial intent, which has to remain always tentative and speculative, but to map out the differences in transmission between different milieus, a 'transformation' of the formulae of one into those of the other. Different voices tend to sing slightly different songs.

This confirms that Vyās's poetry is an excellent terrain to study where *nirguṇa* and *saguṇa* meet. I have shown before (Pauwels 1994a, pp. 24-31, 42) that Vyās had respect for bhaktas categorized nowadays as *nirguṇī*, and that he thought in terms of a bhakti family rather than in terms of lineage-alliance. However, such sectarian alignment and vertically oriented spiritual lineage came into the picture soon enough, as is clear from evidence in *saguṇī* hagiographies barely a generation after Vyās.

Still, at least Vyās seems to have straddled both sides of the spectrum. There is no doubt that he was a *rasika* devoted to Rādhā in particular. After all, the early Fms. has clearly one poem that supports an unambiguous *saguṇī* denomination. In addition, there is of course the weighty evidence of the (admittedly later) *Vyās Vāṇī* Mss., which amply illustrate Vyās's penchant for hard-core *saguṇa* stuff, especially that on the Rādhā-Kṛṣṇa dalliance theme. However, a significant part of Vyās's oeuvre, also attested in those Mss., consists of poems in a different genre. These poems seem to fall in the grey zone between *nirguṇa* and *saguṇa*. They are quoted in the *nirguṇī* anthologies, as well as in collections for personal reading, of which Fms. is the earliest example.

The question then is whether Vyās was the exception that confirms the rule. It turns out that he was not unique among the *saguṇī* Rādhā-Kṛṣṇa devotees of his generation; the other two bhaktas who are most heavily quoted in *nirguṇī* Mss. are Parmānand and Sūr. Interestingly, their songs are also included in the Ādi Granth, which was compiled in 1604 (McGregor 1984, p. 54). Vyās, however, does not get quoted among the *bhagatas* in the Sikh scriptures.

Only for Sūr a detailed study of his more *nirguṇī*-ringing poetry has been carried out so far, which makes it possible to compare Vyās's case with his. There are many similarities between Sūr's and Vyās' *nirguṇī* type of poems. Both have poems on the amazing saving grace of God, both contemplate death and the need to abandon the world of sensuality and to seek refuge with God before it is too late. This was illustrated above in the detailed comparison of one of Vyās's poems in Fms., *hari saum prītamu bhayau na hvaihai*, with one by Sūr in the same section, *patita pāvana hari nāmu tihārau*. The analysis shows that Sūr's poetry has a self-accusatory tone, or rather, one of priding himself in his debasedness in order to prepare the ground for his being saved (see also Hawley 1984, pp. 138-41, 148-56), and shows that this is lacking in Vyās's poems, which are more self-confident. Or one could put it this way: Vyās does not use Sūr's tactics of self-deprecation (*vinatī*, *vinaya*) in order to make his audience come around (Hawley 1984, pp. 156-7), rather he attacks his listeners directly in no ambiguous terms. Sūr and Vyās both make it a point to stress that God is caste-blind (Hawley 1984, pp. 136-7), but Vyās can be said to be more direct in his making fun of hypocritical bhaktas and Brahmins alike (for some examples of his rather strong disapproval, see Pauwels 1994a, pp. 33-8).[120]

Vyās pays much more attention to the Name of God, than does Sūr (for the latter, see Hawley 1984, pp. 170-1). This is clear by the absence of poems by Sūr to that effect in the section of Fms. that includes Vyās's two hits on the theme of the Name. Perhaps the most important difference

[120] On the basis of a word check of VG, it can be said that references to *sabada* and 'the arrow' are more common in Sūr (Hawley 1984, pp. 135-6) than in Vyās on the other hand, both poets are similar in neglecting to identify the *guru* (Hawley 1984, p. 146 for Sūr) and abstaining from references to the *sadguru* (Hawley 1984, p. 147 for Sūr).

between them is that Sūrdās hardly mentions any of the great Sants of the *nirguṇī* persuasion by name, in contrast to Harirām Vyās (several poems are discussed in Pauwels 1994a, pp. 26-31). Even more, while for Sūr *satsaṅga* is a means to a goal (Hawley 1984, pp. 141-8), Vyās loves the company of *haridāsa*s, and he goes as far as to say that he loves them even more than God.

Another significant contrast with Sūr is that Vyās does not have any 'songs of the bee'. I have drawn attention to this in another context, in connection with the lack of *viraha* or songs on separation in Vyās's oeuvre context (Pauwels 1994a, p. 41 and 1996a, pp. 37-9). Whereas many *bhramaragīta* poems are attested for the early Sūr, Vyās shies away, not only from the particular theme, but from *viraha* in general. He describes the love of Rādhā and Kṛṣṇa always as one of happy fulfilment. In general, Vyās' confident tone can be described as that of the optimistic mystic: he is quite confident in the possibility of ultimate salvation and feels well-entitled to criticize people who are on what he considers to be the wrong track.

It is appropriate to bring up the absence of *bhramaragīta* songs again, in this context, because it is a genre in which usually the philosophical concept of god as *nirguṇa* is mocked. Is it sheer coincidence that not a single poem in the genre is to be found for Vyās, who has such strong *nirguṇī* affinities? Is it accidental that the word *nirguṇa* itself does not occur anywhere in the Vulgate edition of Vyās's collected work? May be not. On the other hand, it needs to be stipulated that the mockery of *nirguṇa* in the *bhramaragīta* poems (e.g. Sūrdās's) seems to be more directed against philosophical discourse of the *advaita* type, rather than *nirguṇa bhakti per se.* This is well illustrated by an important, though later, hagiographical polemic work of the Vallabha Sampradāya, *Caurāsī Baiṭhak Caritra* (probably after the early eighteenth century, see Entwistle 1987, p. 263). In that work Vallabhācārya is portrayed as making a *digvijaya* with main intent to convince and convert Śankara's followers (*māyāvādī*s), and to counter their denial that the world can be a manifestation of God.

In any case, as with Sūr, there is no evidence of Vyās's opposing *nirguṇī*s. The people to whom Vyās reacted adversely were in fact the same as those whom for instance Kabīr loathed so much: the *śākta*s (see Pauwels 1994a, pp. 33-8). For the rest, Vyās was an outspoken fellow, and did not hesitate to ridicule whomever deserved it in his eyes: he quite snidely makes fun of fake yogīs, of arrogant Brahmins and also of insincere bhaktas.

It may be appropriate to venture to extrapolate the limited conclusions of this investigation onto the broader framework of the general *saguṇa-nirguṇa* 'divide', which of course stands to be modified or corrected as new material will be forthcoming. Vyās's case confirms what had been found about Sūrdās: the categories *saguṇa* and *nirguṇa* were not always watertight. At least two of the early *saguṇī* bhaktas creating poems in the vernacular Braj owe (and avow) quite a bit of their inspiration to the *nirguṇī*s. This entails influence in ways of thinking and ways of expression. In fact, this should not be reason for big surprise, given that the genre in which those poets worked, devotional songs and distychs in the vernacular, was the same as that of the (earlier established) *nirguṇa* tradition. If the *saguṇī*s composed poems in the same vein, it is small wonder that those songs made it into *nirguṇī* anthologies.

Of course, the *saguṇī*s cannot be reduced to this type of didactic sermon. They had other sources of inspiration in the form of folk genres, other vernacular literatures, and Sanskrit devotional and secular literature. In any case, it makes most sense not to speak about a divide, let alone diametrically opposed groups, but to think in terms of a continuum. On the one hand are poems that are clearly *saguṇī* about, e.g. Kṛṣṇa's dancing and flirting with Rādhā or the Gopīs; or about the exploits of Rāma of Ayodhyā. On the other hand are poems affirming the discovery of the unqualified divine within, poems which strongly reject all depiction in mythological terms. In between we find an overlapping area, one in which fit the *vinaya* poems of Sūr, as Hawley has shown. In addition, now we know about those of Vyās, and, apparently, there are also quite a few by Parmānand. This still blurry area needs to be mapped out more clearly, and it is to that topography that I hope to have made a contribution.

REFERENCES

Abbreviations of dictionaries

OHED McGregor, Ronald Stuart. 1993. *The Oxford Hindī-English Dictionary*. Oxford: Oxford University Press.

BBSK Gupta, Dīndayālu and Premnārāyaṇ Taṇḍan. 1974 (vs 2031). *Braj-bhāṣā sūr-koś*. 2nd ed. 2 vols. Lucknow: Viśvavidyālay Hindī Prakāśaṇ.

HŚS Sundardās, Śyām, ed. 1965-75. *Hindī śabd-sāgar*. 2nd ed. 11 vols. Banaras: Nāgarī Pracāriṇī Sabhā.

RSK Lāḷas, Sītārām. 1962-79. *Rājasthānī sabad-kos*. 9 vols. Jodhpur: Caupāsanī Śikṣā Samiti.

Editions of Vyās Vāṇī

Akhil Bhāratvarṣīy Śrī Hit Rādhāvallabhīy Vaiṣnav Mahāsabhā (ed.), *Śrī vyāsvāṇī*, 2 vols., Vrindāvan: Śrī Vrajendra Machine Press, 1934 (vs 1991).

Gosvāmī, Rādhākiśor (ed.), *Śrī vyās vāṇī: Siddhānta aur ras sahit*, Mathurā: Agravāl Press, 1937 (vs 1994).

Gosvāmī, Vāsudev, *Bhakta kavi vyāsjī*, Mathurā: Agravāl Press, 1952 (vs 2009).

Other editions of primary sources

Bahura, Gopal Narayan and Kenneth Bryant, *Pada Sūradāsajī kā: The padas of Surdas*, Maharaja Sawai Man Singh II Memorial Series 6, Jaipur: Maharaja Sawai Man Singh II Museum Trust, 1982.

Bhāgavatapurāṇa. Goswami, C.L, and M.A Śāstrī, *Śrīmad Bhāgavata Mahāpurāṇa (with Sanskrit text and English translation)*, 2 vols., Gorakhpur: Gītā Press, 1971.

Gaṇeśdās, Bhaktmāḷī and Rāmāyaṇī Rāmeśvardās, *Śrīmad gosvāmī śrīnābhājī kṛt śrībhaktmāl: Śrīmatpriyādāsjī kṛt kavittmayī ṭīkā sahit*, vol. 3, Vrindāban: Śrīrāmānandpustakālay, 1986 (vs 2043).

Kṛṣṇadās, Bābā. s.d. *Śrī mādhavdāsjī kī vāṇī tathā ādarśjīvanī*, Gauḍīya-granthagauravaḥ 115-16, Kusum Sarovar: Gaurhār Press.

Mahābhārata. See: van Buitenen, 1978.

NPS Vājpeyī, Nanddulāre, *Sūrsāgar*, vol. 1, 5th edn., Nāgrīpracāriṇī Granthmālā 25, Benares: Nāgrīpracāriṇī Sabhā, 1978 (vs 2035).

Vālmīki Rāmāyaṇa. Śrīmad Vālmīki-Rāmāyaṇa: With Sanskrit text and English translation, vol. 1, Gorakhpur: Gītā Press, 1978 (vs 2035).

Śarmā, Brajbhūṣaṇlāl, Kaṇṭhmaṇi Śāstrī, and Gokulānand Tailang, *Parmānand-sāgar: Śrīmadbhāgavata-daśama skaṃdha par ādhārit nitya-bhagavallīlāeṃ*, Lucknow: Lakhnaū Viśvavidyālay, 1959 (vs 2016).

Other references

Callewaert, Winand M. and Lieve de Brabandere, 'Nirgun literature on microfilm in Leuven, Belgium', *IAVRI* 9, December 1980, pp. 28-48.

Callewaert, Winand M. and Mukund Lath, *The Hindī Padāvalī of Nāmdev: A critical edition of Nāmdev's Hindi songs with translation and annotation*, Delhi: Motilal Banarsidass, 1989.

Callewaert, Winand M. and Bart Op de Beeck, *Nirguṇ-bhakti sāgar devotional Hindī literature: A critical edition of the Pañc-Vāṇī or five works of Dādū, Kabīr, Nāṁdev, Rāidās, Hardās, with the Hindī songs of Gorakhnāth and Sundardās, and a complete word-index*, 2 vols., South Asia Institute, Heidelberg, South Asian Studies 25, New Delhi: Manohar, 1991.

Entwistle, Alan W., *Braj: Centre of Krishna Pilgrimage*, Groningen: Egbert Forsten, 1987.

Gold, Daniel, 'What the merchant-guru sold: social and literary types in Hindi devotional verse', *JAOS* 112.1, 1992, pp. 22-35.

Hawley, John Stratton, *Sūr Dās: Poet, Singer, Saint*, Seattle: University of Washington Press, 1984.

———, 'Creative Enumeration in the *vinaya* poetry of Sūrdās', in R.S. McGregor (ed.), *Devotional literature in South Asia: Current research, 1985-1988*, University of Cambridge Oriental Publications 46, Cambridge: Cambridge University Press, 1992, pp. 225-36.

———, 'The Nirguṇ-Saguṇ distinction in early manuscript anthologies of Hindi Devotion', in David Lorenzen (ed.), *Bhakti Religion in North India: Community, identity and political action*, New York: SUNY, 1995, pp. 160-80.

Lorenzen, David, (ed.), *Bhakti Religion in North India: Community, identity and political action*, New York: SUNY, 1995.

———, *Praises to a formless God: Nirguṇī texts from North India*, Albany: SUNY Press, 1996.

Mītal, Prabhudayāl, *Braj ke dharma-sampradāyoṃ kā itihās*, Delhi: National Publishing House, 1968.

Pauwels, Heidi R.M., 'Harirām Vyās and the early bhakti-milieu', in A. Entwistle and F. Mallison (eds.), *Studies in South Asian Devotional Literature: Research Papers 1988-1991*, Paris: École Française d'Extrême-Orient and New Delhi: Manohar, 1994a, pp. 24-50.

———, *Harirām Vyās's Rās-pañcādhyāyī* and *Mān kī Śṛṇkhalā: A critical interpretation*, Ann Arbor: University Microfilms, 1994b.

———, 'The Great Goddess and fulfilment in love: Rādhā seen through a sixteenth-century lens'. *Bulletin of the School of Oriental and African Studies*, vol. 59.1, 1996a, pp. 29-43.

———, 'Kṛṣṇa's Round Dance Reconsidered: Harirām Vyās's Hindī *Rās-pañcādhyāyī'*, London Studies on South Asia 12, London: Curzon Press, 1996b.

Snell, Rupert, *The Hindī classical tradition: A Braj Bhāṣā Reader*, London: School of Oriental and African Studies, 1991.

van Buitenen, J.A.B., trans., *The Mahābhārata*, vol. 3, Chicago: University of Chicago Press, 1978.

The Tradition of *Varṣotsav-pad-saṅgrah* A Different Perspective on Brajbhāṣā Devotional Poetry

GALINA ROUSSEVA-SOKOLOVA

It is generally agreed upon that, applied to Mediaeval devotional literature, the concepts of 'author' and 'authenticity' tend to lose the unequivocal meaning they usually have in other contexts.[1] The bigger the popularity of a poet is, the more likely is his work to be expanded during the centuries after his death by enthusiastic followers signing with his name. This is particularly obvious with the huge modern-day editions of compilations like the *Sūrsāgar*.

This situation has led scholars to favour the broader term 'tradition' when referring to one famous poet's name rather than dealing with the uncertainties of authorship *stricto sensu*. Even so, existing studies have so far been predominantly focused on particular names. Thus fairly consistent, though heterogeneous (as far as authorship is concerned) traditions of Brajbhāṣā devotional poetry anthologies have been neglected as independent objects of study, even though they have been referred to occasionally for supplying additional evidence material in support of different philological arguments.

This line of ideas was inspired by one such particularly conspicuous tradition which I happened to run across in the library of the Vrindaban Research Institute[2] in 1995.[3] It consists of a large number of both manuscript

*This paper does not aim at an exhaustive and complete presentation. Its purpose is rather to draw the attention on a tradition which has not, so far, been studied for its own sake, as well as to make some methodological considerations on the scholarly treatment it could, or should, get.

[1] See John S. Hawley, 'Author and Authority in the *Bhakti* Poetry of North India', *The Journal of Asian Studies* 47, no. 2, May 1988, pp. 269-90.

[2] See *A Catalogue of Hindi Manuscripts in the Vrindaban Research Institute*, Vrindaban: VRI, vol. 1, edited by R.D. Gupta and M.L. Gupta, 1979; vol. 2, edited by R.D. Gupta and N.C. Bansal, 1986.

[3] I would like to thank the International Association of the Vrindaban Research Institute for granting me the fellowship which made this research possible.

and printed compilations of devotional *pad*, designed for use during religious ceremonies in temples and private homes, and structured according to the temple yearly festivals, the eight watches of the day, and, within these divisions, according to the appropriate *rāg*.

A. Entwistle mentions that each sect in Vrindaban uses its preferred compilation of *pad*.[4] Actually all of them, except the Caitanya Sampradāy have edited their own compilations. The Caitanya Sampradāy uses at present those of the Puṣṭimārgīya and the Rādhāvallabha Sampradāy (though Ms. 757 of the VRI library, donated by the Rādhādamodar temple suggests that at some point in the past at least this temple was using its own anthology, which differs in structure and content from those of the Puṣṭimārgīya Sampradāy).

My focus in this paper will be on the collections of the sect of Vallabhācāryā for two main reasons:

1. they definitely outnumber all the others, both in terms of printed editions available on the market and among the manuscripts sample of the VRI library;
2. in usage and content they reach beyond the sectarian boundaries.

This last point needs clarification. In the Puṣṭimārgīya collections along with the *pad* of the *aṣṭchāp* poets, one can find, both in manuscript and printed editions, *pad* bearing the *chāp* of Gadādhar Bhaṭṭ, Mādhavadās and Sūrdās Madanmohan (from the Gauḍīya Sampradāy), as well as some signed by Svāmi Haridās and Harirām Vyās. The festive calendar, reflected in the chapter titles, incorporates, together with the specific Puṣṭimārgīya festivals, such as the birthdays of leaders and saints of the sect, about every Vaiṣṇava festival celebrated in Braj, as well as different popular traditions, drawn into the gravitation field of Kṛṣṇa bhakti. Rādhā, her birth and early childhood are given due attention, which is far from Vallabha's orthodoxy, but probably reflects the general concern of this important sect to answer the expectations of a large number of devotees. In fact there seems to be a general tendency that the smaller the sect, the more exclusively they will tend to stick in the temples to their own poetry.[5]

[4] Alan W. Entwistle, *Braj Centre of Krishna Pilgrimage*, Groningen: Egbert Forsten, 1987, p. 482. Ronald S. McGregor also acknowledges the existence of such hymnaries (Ronald S. McGregor, *Hindi Literature from its beginnings to the nineteenth century*, Wiesbaden: Otto Harrassowitz, 1984, p. 158).

[5] The Rādhāvallabha Sampradāy being in this case the exception: in their compilations they use quite a lot of poetry coming from other sects, including many *aṣṭchāp* signed *pad*. The most recent and available edition is *Śrīrādhāvallabhajī*

A further evidence of functional trespassing of sectarian boundaries is supplied by the fact that the Puṣṭimārgīya editions are regularly being used during *samāj* performances at Rādhāraman temple in Vrindaban, which is affiliated to the Caitanya sect. This makes them a favourite with the two biggest Kṛṣṇa cult sects, thus confirming once again their dominant position among the other existing devotional anthologies.

There are three main types of Puṣṭimārgīya hymnals:

1. *Varṣotsav ke pad* — covering the whole of the yearly festive cycle, starting from *janamāṣṭami* (dark half of the month of *bhādoṁ* (August-September) to *rākhī-bandhan* (*rakṣābandhan*) in the bright half of the month of *śrāvan* (July-August);
2. *Vasanta-dhamār ke pad* — collecting specific *pad* appropriate for spring-time festivals, including Holī;
3. *Nitya-pad* — 'eternal' *pad*, following the daily *aṣṭayām* routine of the temple deity.

These types can be found both among manuscript and printed edition hymnals. The names I have given correspond to generic appellation.[6] The actual titles may vary.

Especially among manuscripts, one can also find a type of 'integrated' *varṣotsav* compilations, incorporating at the appropriate place, spring-time songs and, within particular *utsav* chapters, different *aṣṭayām* oriented *pad*. Among the printed anthologies an impressive example of this type of hymnal is the 1941 Mumbai edition of a 822 pages *Kīrtan saṅgrah*.[7] However, since modern editions are compilations of manuscript compilations and so tend to be extremely voluminous, they come most often in a three-parts division.

About thirty devotional anthologies are being kept in the manuscript funds of the VRI library. Most of them are only a few pages long and partially damaged. Three are of Rādhāvallabha origin, one is Gauḍīya. Out of the remaining relatively voluminous manuscripts (more than seventy folios) two deal exclusively with *nitya pad*, one with *vasant-dhamār ke*

---

kā varṣotsav: braj-vṛndāvan ke prācīn rasikoṁ kī vāṇiyoṁ kā saṅgrah, edited by Śrī Lalitācaraṇjī Gosvāmī, 2nd edn., Vṛndāvan: Śrīrādhāvallabha Mandir Vaiṣṇav Kameṭī, vol. 1, 1991; vol. 2, 1994; vol. 3, 1996.

[6] Actually the name I have assigned to the tradition itself has, to some extent, a conventional character. The manuscripts, if they bear any title at all, feature *pad-saṅgrah*, *bārahmāsī utsav ke pad*, *varṣotsav kīrtan ke pad*, etc. The same goes for printed editions.

[7] *Kīrtan saṅgrah*, edited by Jagannāth Murlīdhar, Mumbai, 1998.

pad. Two of the manuscripts that seemed the oldest did not have any internal divisions and I could not positively identify their structure.

Among the important Mss remaining I have selected six (Mss. 1007, 1103, 1108, 2610, 2611, 2613) and have compared their structure and partially their content with the existing printed editions. Out of the six only one (Ms. 1007) had a preserved colophon, according to which its year of completion was 1826. As a whole, judging from external appearance and general state of preservation, my supposition is that none of them goes further back than the latter half of the eighteenth century and that most of them were written during the first half of nineteenth century.

The earliest printed anthology, available in that same library is a three-volume Mumbai edition named *Puṣṭimārgīya pad-saṅgrah.*[8] The first volume, containing *varṣotsava ke pad* is dated 1908/9. The second and third volumes, devoted, respectively, to *vasanta-dhamār* and *nitya pad* bear an even earlier date — 1895/6. The prologue to the first volume mentions the existence of even earlier editions, containing, according to the editor, 'many inaccuracies'. These early dates allow us to make the assumption that for a certain period of time manuscripts and printed editions were used in parallel, and that printed editions are the direct prolongation of the manuscript tradition.

After the three-volume edition, published by the turn of the century, comes the above mentioned one-volume *Kīrtan saṅgrah* of 1941. These two old editions are printed on a large page format with an imposing design suitable for sacred books. Present-day editions are numerous and come in all shapes and sizes. Some may contain *pad* from the repertoire of some famous *kīrtankār* or *pad*, devoted only to one particular festival. As a whole, modern editions are never simple re-editions of older ones. In fact, ever since the first one, there seems to be a tradition of criticizing everything that was published before as *aśuddha* and to present one's own production as the ultimate one.

The standard layout of manuscript editions includes big-sized *akṣara* aligned in continuous text flow, with verses separated by *daṇḍa*, and *pad*, chapter titles and *rāg* names, by double *daṇḍa. Daṇḍa* and chapter titles (or first letter of chapter titles) are sometimes marked with red ink. Within the chapters the different *pad* are numbered. As a whole the layout shows a general concern to facilitate the task of the temple singers.

[8] *Puṣṭimārgīya pad-saṅgrah*, Mumbai, vol. 1, 1965; vol. 2, 1952; vol. 3, 1952. I recently learned that a new reprint in four volumes of this edition has appeared on the market.

The oldest printed editions follow the pattern set in manuscripts. Modern editions though tend to use a more 'literary' style of presentation, with smaller *akṣara*, a separate verse for each line and blank space between the *pad*. This may be interpreted as the beginning of a tendency to move the anthologies from the confinement of temple ceremony context to broader horizons.

In spite of the difference in the size of manuscript and printed hymnals this tradition appears to be reasonably consistent . Though I haven't had the opportunity to conduct an extensive study in that matter, it seems that most of the *pad*, included in manuscripts are locatable, sometimes in a slightly modified form, in the printed editions. The order in which they appear is also, more or less, preserved. This is particularly true for *pad* sequences, dedicated to important festivals, like Janamāṣṭamī. The main difference is that printed editions include much more internal divisions, i.e. more festivals, and, within each festival, much more *pad* than the manuscripts. Actually the *varṣotsava-pad-saṅgrah* tradition is supplying first class textual evidence of the process of gradual assimilation by Kṛṣṇa *bhakti* of various popular traditions for a period of almost two centuries up to present day.

What scholarly approach is appropriate to this huge amount of devotional texts? Though I presented it as a fairly consistent tradition, a classical philological treatment would be a tedious and frustrating experience. Nevertheless these texts can supply additional evidence material for critical editions. In appendix III to the critical edition of the *caurāsī pad* of *Hit Harivaṃśa*, R. Snell makes use of such text material, taken from the *Śṛṅgār ras sāgar*, the old compilation of the Rādhāvallabha sect and formulates the hypothesis that the inclusion of stanzas of one famous poet in sectarian anthologies may represent 'an initial stage in the accretion of new *pad* to an existing corpus'.[9] This idea deserves further research, especially if the manuscript background of the anthology allows a diachronical perspective on this process.

However, what makes these texts of significant value, is the fact that they represent the closest evidence we can ever expect to get on the evolution of Kṛṣṇa devotional practice. They can be particularly useful in illustrating how Kṛṣṇa bhakti has been assimilating over the centuries various popular traditions. One such tradition is the worship of Sāñjhī.

[9] Rupert Snell, *The Eighty-four Hymns of Hita Harivaṃśa*, Delhi: Motilal Banarsidass, 1991, p. 348.

Sāñjhī worship was originally a rural ritual, performed by unmarried and newly-wedded girls in order to secure themselves a good husband and a happy family life. It consists in the preparation and worshipping of a series of designs made of cow-dung, flowers, white flour, shells and other materials, drawn on the outer walls of houses during the Hindu month of Āśvin. Symbolically the designs represent the visit of the goddess Sāñjhī to her parents'home and her final return to her husband's palace. Since it was believed that Rādhā and her gopī friends also used to worship Sāñjhī, at some point in the past, Sāñjhī designs entered the temples of Braj. These were, however, quite different from the simple icons of the village girls — up to present day they are made by professional artists and priests on platforms on the temple floors and represent scenes of the Rādhā-Kṛṣṇa love games surrounded by intricate decorative motives, made out of coloured powder sprinkled through paper stencils.

When did Sāñjhī enter the temple? In a detailed study on the Sāñjhī tradition[10] Alan Entwistle draws evidence again from the *Śṛṅgār-ras-sāgar,* the printed edition of the anthology used by the Rādhāvallabha Sampradāy. He states that since the earliest poet included in this anthology to have composed *Sāñjhī ke pad*, is Gosvāmī Rūpalāl (born in 1683), Sāñjhī can be assumed to have become part of the temple calendar as early as the latter half of the seventeenth century. Now, one can find further evidence on this matter in the Puṣṭimārgīya compilations: the Sāñjhī chapter of the 1941 *Kīrtan saṅgrah* includes one *pad* bearing the signature of Haridās and another one from Harirām Vyās. So, following the same logic, the date of the establishment of temple Sāñjhī tradition should be pushed further back to the sixteenth century. But even if the attribution of these two *pad* proves to be uncertain, the fact that all the manuscripts from the VRI library contain a section on Sāñjhī, at least confirms beyond any possible doubt, Prabhudayāl Mītal's statement that Sāñjhī tradition had been reestablished in Braj temples by the beginning of nineteenth century.[11]

This is one example of how this type of text can prove useful for scholars, interested in the history of Kṛṣṇa devotional cults. On the other hand, to the the historian of literature they can give a larger perspective on Kṛṣṇa *pad* as a genre. Because of the specific functional orientation of

[10] Alan W. Entwistle, 'Sā̃jhī – Images for a Twilight Goddess', in *Visible Religion*, vol. 3, 1984, pp. 43-63.

[11] Prabhudayāl Mītal, *Braj kī kalāoṁ kā itihās*, Mathura: Sāhitya Saṁsthān, p. 566, cited by A. Entwistle, 'Sā̃jhī...', p. 56.

these *pad*, they tend to be even more formulaic than usual. Furthermore, being grouped in large clusters around the same theme, they make particularly evident the existence of internal structures and creative patterns. They are a reservoir of what Mukund Lath calls 'floating *antarās*',[12] i.e. a stock of ready-made phrases or verses which one can find with the *bhaṇitā* of different poets. One such famous *antarā* is the verse — *khelata maiṁ ko kāko gussaiy*[13] — which is also, at least in Braj, a popular saying. It is found, functioning as a *ṭek* in two very similar *pad* : one from the *Sūrsāgar*[14] (*pad* 863) and one from the *Parmānandasāgar*[15] (*pad* 233). One can also find it on p. 91 of the third volume of the *Puṣṭimārgīya pad saṅgrah,* published in 1895/6, this time as a real *antarā*, a line within a *pad* with no apparent signature in the last line. Finally, it appears again in a very recent, though undated edition of a *nitya pad* printed collection,[16] this time in Sūrdās' variant. One can imagine that at a certain point, the memory of the original *pad* having been lost, it had been recreated around this one very famous line. Then, in the modern edition, the old 'mistake' has been 'corrected' by the editor. Whatever the interpretation of such shifts may be, they help to enlarge our perspective on Kṛṣṇa devotional songs as a genre.

[12] Mukund Lath, '*Bhajan* as Song: towards an Oral Stemma of Nāmadev's *Padas*', in Monika Thiel-Horstmann (ed.), *Bhakti in Current Research 1979-1982*, Berlin: Dietrich Reimer Verlag, 1983, p. 233.

[13] Translating as 'In play who is the master of whom' — a very revealing verse, indeed, as far as the god-devotee relationship in bhakti context is concerned.

[14] Sūrdās, *Sūrsāgar*, edited by Nandadulāre Vājpeyī, Banaras: Nāgarī Pracāriṇī Sabhā, vol. 1, 1972; vol. 2, 1976.

[15] Parmānandadās, *Parmānandasāgar*, edited by Śrī Brajbhūṣaṇ Śarmā, Kaṅkarolī, 1959.

[16] *Nitya kīrtan: ras ratnākar*, Bikaner: Mūṁdharā Faunḍeśan (dna), p. 182.

PART XI
Secularization of Religious Motifs in the Eighteenth Century

Mundane and Divine Love in Ānandghan's Poetry
An eighteenth century literary debate

IMRE BANGHA

Is his poetry about mundane or divine love? This is one of the main questions that emerges among many western scholars concerning the poetry of such poets like Jayadeva, Vidyāpati or Ānandghan,[1] etc. But according to the general Indian opinion, Ānandghan's love is both mundane and divine. In this paper I am going to examine if this question has always been irrelevant in India.

According to the most popular legend about the poet,[2] Ānandghan was the mīr munśī, the chief scribe of Muhammadśāh 'Rangīle' of Delhi (r. AD 1719-48). He was in love with a courtesan whom he called Sujān. He even made a vow that he would sing only to her and no one else. When his enemies in the court learnt this, they entered into a conspiracy and told the emperor about Ānandghan's skill in singing. He was summoned but declined to sing. The conspirators suggested that Sujān order the mīr munśī to do so. Then Ānandghan sang, but he turned towards Sujān and not the emperor. Infuriated by such disrespect, Muhammadśāh exiled Ānandghan from the country. When the poet asked Sujān to accompany him, she

* I am indebted to Dr. Śaraṇbihārī Gosvāmī and Prof. Govind Śarmā for helping me to interpret the difficulties of the Braj texts.

[1] This poet is today known as Ghanānand, because in his *savaiyā*s to insert it into an anapaestic or dactylic metre, he used his *chāp* as *ghana ānāda*. Most of the modern scholars were acquainted or impressed only by Ānandghan's *kavitt*s and *savaiyā*s. Thus they became familiar with this *chāp*, which they often contracted as Ghanānand. This form, however, has not been used before the twentieth century except in cases of metrical constraint. The poet himself and his contemporaries usually used the name as Ānandghan 'Cloud of joy'. (GhanĀnand is the transcription of the impossible Hindi word घनआनंद)

[2] The first available reference to this legend is found in Rādhācaran Gosvāmī's (1859-1925) *chappay* about Ānandghan (published, e.g. in Viyogī Hari [ed.], p. 173). This legend was described in detail in Rāmcandra Śukla, p. 185, hence today it is widely known in India.

refused to. However, Ānandghan did not cease to write poems to Sujān. In his exile he went to Vrindaban, became a sadhu of the Nimbārk Sampradāy and the word *sujān* in his works came to mean Krishna himself or Radha and Krishna jointly. Until his death he wrote quatrains to Sujān. Rāmcandra Śukla quotes a *kavitt* addressed to Sujān, which according to the legend, was written by the poet when he was mortally wounded.[3]

The legend tries to interpret a distinctive feature of Ānandghan's poetry. The central theme of his quatrains is the love for Sujān (also put as *jān*, *jānrāy*, etc.), who in some places is a female (*pyārī sujān*) and sometimes a male (*pyāre sujān*). Moreover, in some poems the word *sujān* is an adjective of Krishna, Radha or Radha-Krishna and it can also denote the god without qualities. A closer look at Ānandghan's quatrains reveals the following principal ways of usage of this word:

1. It can stand for the heroine (*nāyikā*) of the traditional śṛṅgār poetry:

to kaṭi bhedahi kiṅkini jānati terī sā̃u erī sujāna hā̃u jānā̃u.

SH20 (GK222)

I swear, oh Sujān, I know that only the kinkini (tinkling belt) knows the secret of your waist.

2. It can stand for the hero (*nāyak*) of the śṛṅgār poetry:

rāvare gunani bā̃dhi liyau hiyau jāna pyāre
ite pai acambho chori dīnī ju surati hai. SH69 (GK453)

My heart has been bound by your virtues/ropes [*gunani*], my dear jān, still it is a wonder, that you abandoned my memory.

3. In some poems this word is an adjective of Krishna in a clear bhakti context:

rasamūrati syāma sujāna lakhẽ jiya jo gati hoti su kāsõ kahū̃;
cita cumbaka loha lā̃u cāyani cvai cuhaṭai uhaṭai nahī̃ jetau gahū̃;
. . .
ura āvati yā̃u chabi chā̃ha jyā̃u hā̃u brajachaila kī gaila sadāī rahū̃.

SH10 (GK417)

[3] SH 54. The numbers with SH refer to the numbers of the *Sujānhit* collection as published in Ā. Miśra 1952; while those with GK refer to the numbers of the *GhanĀnand-kabitt* as published by Miśra 1950.

Whom shall I tell the state of my heart when seeing the intelligent
Śyāma, the form of rasa incarnate.
Overwhelmed by desire my mind attaches to him like iron to magnet
and does not become detached, no matter how I seize it.
. . .
I keep thinking of staying for ever in the ways of the Child of Braj, like
the shadow of his light.

4. Sometimes *sujān* denotes the attributeless *nirguṇ* deity.

antara mā̃i bāsī pai prabāsī ko so antara hai
merī na sunat daiyā āpanīyau nā kahau;
locanani tāre hvai sujhāvau saba sūjhai nāhī̃
būjhī na parati aisẽ socani kahā dahau;
hau tau jānarāya jāne jāhu na ajāna yātẽ
ānãda ke ghana chāya chāya ughare rahau;
. . . SH271 (GK86)

Inhabitant of the heart, still distant like a far-dwelling one,
you neither listen to my words, oh my God [*daiyā*], nor tell yours.
As the pupil of the eyes, you make everything be perceived but you are
not perceived.
I cannot understand, why you torment me with these thoughts.
You are the King of knowledge, thus you cannot be known by one who
is without knowledge.
Cloud of joy, you clear away [*ughare rahau*] even when spread (over
the sky).

5. There are also poems where *sujān* is the object of a mystic experience:

ceṭaka rūpa-rasīle sujāna daī bahutai dina neku dikhāī;
kā̃udha mā̃i caũdha bhare cakha hāya kahā kahā̃u herani esẽ hirāī;
bātā̃i bilāya gaī̃ rasanā pai hiyo umagyau kahi ekau na āī;
sā̃ca ki sambhrama hau ghanaānāda socani hī mati jāta samāī.
SH353(GK167)

After many days, the wonder of the charming form of Sujān appeared
for a little while.
In this flash, my eyes got dazzled, alas, how can I express this loss of
sight!
The words vanished from my tongue, my heart overflowed,
not one (word) could be uttered.

'Are you real or an illusion, oh, Cloud of joy?' — my mind gets filled
with doubts.

These usages are sometimes combined. For example the word *sujān* can stand for a beloved who can either be a male or a female (a *nāyak* or a *nāyikā*):

kaisẽ suhāti sujāna tumhãĩ hitū māni daī koū aisẽ bisarāta.

SH74 (GK454)

How does it suit you Sujān that having considered someone to be friend,
you leave him/her alone?

Sometimes it is not clear whether the poet speaks about a mundane or a divine beloved. In the following example it seems to be divine love. However, the poet mentions Sujān's beauty and uses a metaphor (*locanani tāre*) that can traditionally refer to a mundane beloved, too, therefore the possibility of a mundane attachment cannot be excluded:

mohī dīṭhi kārana hau, dukha tama ṭārana hau,
prīti pana pārana hau kahā̃ lāũ kahāũ jasai;
locanani tāre aciraja bhāre jāna pyāre
tumahī tẽ piyata tihāre rūpa ke rasai;
. . .

SH90 (GK468)

You are the reason for my sight,
you are the remover of the darkness of suffering.
Pupil of my eyes, dear Jān, full of wonder,
only from you can I drink the juice [*rasa*] of your beauty.
. . .

Sometimes the beloved is both with and without attributes, depending on the point of view of the observer. In a quatrain for example, the eyes are not satisfied with a formless aspect of Sujān, which dwells in the soul:

naina kahe suni re mana kāna dai kyãu itane guna meṭi dayau hai;
sundara pyāre sujāna ko mandira bāvare tū hama hī tẽ bhayau hai;
lobhī tinhãĩ tanakau na dikhāvata eso mahāmada chāki gayau hai;
. . .

SH132 (GK491)

My eyes say: 'Listen, oh, soul, with your ears, why did you efface so
many virtues/attributes [*guna*]?
You dull, it is through us that you have turned to be the temple of the
dear beautiful Sujān;

You greedy, you have become drunk by great drunkenness in such a
 way that you do not show him [i.e. Sujān] for a moment;'

. . .

In the *Sujānhit* and the *GhanĀnand-kabitt*, the two most popular compilations of Ānandghan's quatrains, the poems with these various meanings of *sujān* are collected together without paying much attention to the different connotations of this word.

* * *

The object of Ānandghan's love might vary from poem to poem, but it shows some unity, too. That is why it is again and again called Sujān. This unity is the result of the continuity of the subject's sentiments. The most famous fact about Ānandghan's style is that even if he sometimes takes refuge behind a third person, *nāyak* or *nāyikā*, he mostly expresses his own personal feelings in love and not those of a heroine or a hero. In contrast with the majority of the poets of his time (the so called Rītikāl) he puts emphasis on the expression, and not on the description of sentiments. There are many poems about the difficulty or the impossibility of expressing these sentiments.[4] Ānandghan's poetry is centred around love itself and not around the object of this love. The multiple meaning of the word *sujān* shows that the love is the same both for a human being and the divinity. In a quatrain, the poet explains further that his own love for Sujān is a particle of the same 'ocean of love' that Hari and Radha's love belongs to.

Prema ko mahodadhi apāra heri kai bicāra
 bāpuro hahari vāra hī tẽ phiri āyau hai;
Tāhī ekarasa hvai bibasa avagāhaĩ doū
 nehī Hari Rādhā, jinhaĩ dekhẽ sarasāyau hai;
Tākī koū tarala taraṅga saṅga chūṭyau kana
 pūri loka lokani umagi uphanāyau hai;
Soī ghanaānãda sujāna lāgi heta hota
 aise mathi mana pai sarūpa ṭhaharāyau hai. (GK310)

Looking at the boundless ocean of love, the poor
 thought retreated embarrassed from this very side.

[4] See Ghanshyam Sharma's paper in this volume.

Two lovers, Hari and Rādhā (both) powerless, continuously (*ekarasa*, 'of one rasa')
plunge into it: seeing them (the ocean) was overwhelmed.
A particle escaped from one of its fickle waves
welled up and upsurged all the worlds.
That (particle) — stuck to the cloud of joy, Sujān — is love (for Sujān);
having thus churned (pondered) in the mind the character (of love)
has been put firm.

The idea of the oneness of the divine and human love has its roots both in Persian and Hindi poetry. On the Persian side, it is the Sufi idea[5] of the '*iśq-ī-haqīqī* developing into '*iśq-ī-majāzī*. In Indian literature, it is, on the one hand, the sixteenth-seventeenth century bhakti poetry, which uses the terminology of human love for the description of the relationship between the soul and God.[6] On the other hand, from the seventeenth century onward, even in secular Hindi poetry the Krishna mythology became a pretext for depicting aspects of human love. But in the philosophical bhakti literature the oneness of the divine and human love has never been stated explicitly.

* * *

Such a radical approach as Ānandghan's was novel in the Hindu religious poetry and it was not acceptable to a strong circle. It seems that both the poetry and the person were condemned.

[5] This idea is not at all new in the medieval Hindi poetry. Its foremost exponent was Muhammad Jāyasī. About his views on love see Vaudeville 1962a, pp. 351-67. '(Jāyasī) admet-il une distinction dans la nature même de l'amour, selon que celui-ci a le Créateur ou la créature pour objet . . .? Il faut remarquer que les poètes persans précurseurs de Jāyasī et ses maîtres dans l'art du *mathnavī* ne tiennent aucune compte de cette distinction fondamentale. La tradition persane dans l'ensemble l'ignore; pour elle tout beauté créée n'est qu'un reflet de la Beauté incréée et il n'y a pas de solution de continuité de deux amours: l'un conduit à l'autre, l'un anticipe l'autre, l'un figure et engendre de l'autre . . . Jāyasī paraît suivre la tradition persane.' Vaudeville 1962a, p. 364.

[6] Günther D. Sontheimer examining the Bhakti in the folk (oral) literature of Khandobā says that 'the borderline on the one hand, ordinary human love and emotions amongst humans, and on the other hand, divine love between god and devotee is fluid and permeable . . .' Sontheimer 1991, p. 239. This fact can shed light on the origin of this terminology, too.

Ānandghan had enemies throughout his life. It is enough to refer to the two best known events of his legend. His enemies set up a conspiracy against him in the court and at the time of the sack of Mathura and Vrindaban his enemies in Mathura sent the Pathans to loot the 'mīr munśī' in Vrindaban.

We can have a glimpse of the views of Ānandghan's opponents in the four so called *Bhaṛoā chand*.[7] All the four poems blame Ānandghan and mock at his love for the Muslim Sujān. The examples below show the style of all these verses.

karai gurunindā vaha hurakinī kau baṃdā mahā
niraghinī gandā khāta panīra au nāna hai;
baina ko curāvai tākau majamūna lāvai kūra
kabitā banāvai gāvai rijaulī sī tāna hai;
sūra ghaṭa sokhī deha m̃āsa hī sõ pokhī bipra
gaiyana ko doṣī rūpa dhare abhimāna hai;
pāpa ko bhavana karai agama gamana aisau
muṛiyā anandaghana jānata jahāna hai. (2)

That slave of prostitute blames his guru; very
shameless and dirty; eats paneer and naan.
Steals the words, takes their theme, composes
base/false/ poems and sings in a very indecent tune.
Feeds his body — dryer of liquor-vessels — only with meat; harasser
of Brahmins and cows, (he) is pride incarnate.
Abode of sin, goes to a forbidden woman; this is
how the world knows the shaven Ānandghan.

daphar̄ī bajāvai ḍauma ḍhāṛhī sama gāvai kāhū̃
turakai rijhāvai taba pāvai jhūṭhau nāma hai;
hurakinī sujāna turakinī ko sevaka hai
taji rāma nāma vākau pūjai kāma dhāma hai;
. . . (3)

Beats the tambourine, sings like a ḍom or a ḍhāṛhī; pleases
a Muslim and then gets false fame;
He is the servant of the prostitute Muslim Sujān,
leaves the name of Rām and worships her abode of desire.

The tone of these poems is so filled with anger that they must have been

[7]First published in Miśra 1952, *Vāṅmukh*, pp. 66-7.

written in circles that somehow were in close contact with the poet or with his poetry. According to Manoharlāl Gauṛ, the most influential monographer of Ānandghan, the *Bhaṛoā chand* were probably composed before 1755.[8] These verses must be interpreted as an attack both on the person and his poetry.

It is asserted in the *Bhaṛoā chand* that Ānandghan is a monk (*muṛiyā anandaghana*, 'shaven Ānandghan'), but he does not conform to the Vaishnava rules of purity and has respect neither for the Brahmins nor for his Vaishnava community (*karai gurunindā*, 'blames his guru'; *bipra... ko doṣī*, 'harasser of Brahmins'; *taji rāma nāma*, 'leaves the name of Rām'), he respects only himself (*rūpa dhare abhimāna hai*, 'he is the pride incarnate'). The author of the *Bhaṛoā chand* puts much emphasis on external Vaishnava and Brahmanic rules, which gives a hint that he might come from such circles.

These verses also refer to Ānandghan's association with Muslims. It is difficult to trace to what extent the poet was in touch with them in his lifetime, but as far as his quatrains are concerned, they show strong influence from Urdu and Persian poetry[9] and consequently, they were considered non-Hindu by the poet's opponents (cf. *kāhū | turakai rijhāvai taba pāvai jhūṭhau nāma hai*, 'pleases | a Muslim and then gets false fame'). Probably because of this Muslim association, his poetry was regarded as indecent and the poet himself base as Ḍoms and Ḍhāḍhīs.[10]

Similarly, Ānandghan's liaison with a courtesan must have been condemned: 'If he is a true Vaishnava, why does he use only an epithet of

[8] Gauṛ 1972, p. 7.

[9] The main features of this influence are the special accent on the one-sided love and the indifference of the beloved; straightforward expression of feelings; calling the beloved *jān* 'my soul'. Similarly the transcendentalization of mundane love is the basic teaching of Sufism. The Absolute both hidden, and revealed is also a Sufi idea. In style the use of idioms is the most characteristic sign of Persian and Urdu influence. See Miśra's *Paricay* to Gauṛ's *Ghanānand aur svacchand kāvyadhārā*, pp. 6-16, and also Gauṛ 1972, pp. 153-4, 159-60. Ānandghan writes in a pure Brajbhāṣā almost entirely free from words of Arabic and Persian origin. It also shows his consciousness about the Arabic and Persian origin of words in the Hindi vocabulary.

[10] On the Ḍhāḍhīs see Vaudeville 1962b, pp. 40-5, 123-5. The Ḍhāḍhīs are wandering musicians who are mostly in service of the Jāṭs. Today most of them are Muslims, but linked to the cult of the *devīs*, and usually sing without an instrument, but earlier they might have had a kind of tambourine (Punjabi *ḍhaḍh*) hence their name. Their relationship with the Ḍoms is an object of discussion among scholars.

Krishna instead of one of his real names? And this epithet is the name of a courtesan!' Such thoughts are reflected in the following line: *taji rāma nāma vākau pūjai kāma dhāma hai*, 'leaves the name of Rām and worships her abode of desire'.[11] Such sentences prove that Ānandghan's opponents did not consider his mundane love for Sujān identical with his bhakti for the divinity. They probably looked upon this identification as a pretext to write about the courtesan. It can be concluded that the identification of divine and mundane love was rejected as non-Vaishnava by the author of the *Bhaṛoā chand.*

* * *

The *Bhaṛoā chand* could not have been an isolated attack, but was probably the expression of the opinion of a religious and literary circle. Ānandghan's influence on certain poets, was enormous[12] and today he is considered one of the greatest poets of Hindi literature, even so, this antagonistic circle had such a strong influence that there is no appreciation of Ānandghan till the seventies of the last century and there is no mention of him in the old hagiography[13] or in the old literature, apart from being mourned for in the *Harikalā Belī* of 'Cācā' Vṛndāvandās,[14] praised in some quatrains of Brajnāth[15] and mentioned in a strophe in the *Sundarśyāmavilās* of Sundardās.[16]

[11] It is difficult to tell, to what extent this sentence refers to Ānandghan's life and to what extent to his poetry. Miśra (1952, *Vāṅmukh*, pp. 61-6), M. Gauṛ (1972, p. 9), Kiśorīlāl Gupta, etc., accepts the existence of Ānandghan's beloved called Sujān (K. Gupta 1967), while Mohan Avasthī rejects it (Avasthī 1972). About Sujān see also Bahuguṇā 1944, pp. 13-14 and Kṛṣṇa Candra Varmā 1966, pp. 75-7.

[12] For example, on some so called *svacchand* poets and on Hariścandra and Ratnākar. For a comparison with some authors see Gauṛ 1972, pp. 467-74.

[13] Kailāścandra Śarmā makes a survey of all the *sādhaka*s, *ācārya*s and *bhakta*s mentioned in the most important *bhaktamāl*s. Ānandghan's name is missing from this list. See Kailāścandra Śarmā 1983, pp. 160-290.

[14] The only published (abridged) version of this work can be found in Ṭhākurprasād Varmā (ed.) 1988, pp. 224-31. For a study of the *Harikalā Belī* and Ānandghan see Bangha 1997.

[15] See Miśra 1952, pp. 3-4.

[16] A Ms. of this unpublished work composed in vs. 1867 (AD 1810) can be found in the private collection of N.C. Bansal (no number). The verse concerning Ānandghan is on folio 202.

The influence of his opponents can also be the reason why Ānandghan repudiated his earlier works[17] in later life and gave up his ideas and ornate style, instead he started to write simple bhakti poetry:

rasanā Gupāla ke guna urajhī;
bahuta bhā̃ti chala chanda banda bakavāda phanda te surajhī;
(*Padāvalī:* 687)[18]

My tongue is entangled in Gopāl's virtues;
(and) disentangled from the various bounds of false poems (and) traps of twaddle.

* * *

Attacks on the poet and his poetry led to attempts to protect his reputation. Since Ānandghan became famous as a poet;[19] the beauty of his quatrains being undeniable, some people even tried to 'correct' the controversial quatrains.

In the oldest available dated Ms. of Ānandghan's quatrains,[20] an effort is made to eliminate the word *sujān* and to replace it either with a name of Krishna (*ju Syāma*, etc.) or with a direct reference to the female lover (*su pyārī*, etc.) who cannot be the divinity.

The nine works contained in this oldest Ms. were copied between VS 1783 (AD 1726) and VS 1794 (AD 1734). The first two works and perhaps also the sixth one[21] were copied by a certain Śvetāmbar Hemrāj. The place of the copying is given only in the colophon of the first work: Rupnagar, the old capital of the Kishangarh state in Rajasthan. Although some of these works were copied by different hands, the presence of Svetāmbar Hemrāj and two works by Sāvant Singh (Nāgarīdās), the heir to the throne of Rupnagar, suggests that all these works in the Ms. were copied in Rupnagar probably by the circle or workshop of Śvetāmbar Hemrāj.

[17] Gauṛ 1972, pp. 12, 153-4.

[18] Ānandghan's *Padāvalī* is published in Miśra 1952, pp. 329-584.

[19] It is enough to refer to the *Bhaṛoā chand* that says: *kāhū turakai rijāvai taba pāvai jhūṭhau nāma hai*, or to the event that in the Govinddev temple of Jaipur the Maharaja praised his poems (see Śyāmsundardās [ed.] 1937, p. 173) or to Sundardās' line *parama rasika auraṅga ke sāgara, desa desa me bahuta ujāgara.*

[20] Ms. no. 2437(4) in the Khāsmohor Collection of the Pothīkhānā of Jaipur dated from VS 1784 (AD 1727).

[21] If its scribe Śvetāmbar Rāy is identical with Śvetāmbar Hemrāj.

Almost all these works were written by bhaktas, about bhakti. The collection of Ānandghan's kabitts is also refashioned in a Vaishnava bhakti style. Although the order of the poems in most part of this collection loosely follows that of the *Sujānhit*, the first four quatrains of the AD 1727 Ms. do not fit into this order. These four poems (Prakīrnak32[P1],[22] SH82[P2], SH197[P3], SH130[P4]) are explicitly about bhakti. One of them (P3) figures later also as P188, which suggests that these four quatrains were taken from different parts of the original compilation, to emphasize bhakti in the beginning. In the case of P3, the scribe must have forgotten that he had already copied it once and written it down also in its original place.[23] It suggests that the scribe did not automatically follow his original, but prepared his own compilation.

This Ms. contains 218 different quatrains (*kavitts* and *savaiyās*).[24] In 28 poems the text in connection with Sujān is changed. Two main directions of these changes can be detected: when the context suggests that Sujān is a female, then the word is changed into *su pyārī*, etc., referring clearly to a female lover (as it happened in eleven cases) or into *Rādhe Sujān* which takes the poem into a bhakti context (in two cases). For example the above-mentioned line of SH20 was changed in the following way in P14:

to kaṭi bhedahi kiṅkini jānati terī sā̃u Rādhe sujāna hā̃u jānā̃u. P14

I swear, intelligent Radha, I know that only the *kinkini* (tinkling belt) knows the secret of your waist.

When the poem suggests that Sujān is male, then this word is changed into Śyām (or Mukund), that is Krishna, as it happened in the example below (and as it was done in twelve more quatrains).

rāvare gunani bā̃dhi liyau hiyau syāma pyāre
ite pai acambho chori dīnī ju surati hai. P56

[22] Prakīrṇak refers to the stray poems of the *GhanĀnand* (*granthāvalī*) not included into the *Sujānhit* or other old collections. P refers to the numbers of the Pothīkhānā Ms.

[23] The scribe did not do his work very carefully, because one more numbering mistake can be found. The number 43 is applied to two successive quatrains. In many places there are spelling mistakes too. Was this new compilation prepared in haste?

[24] As has been mentioned, P3 and P188 are identical and P43 is applied to two poems, thus the numbering at the end also arrives at 218, although there are 219 poems actually written down.

My heart has been bound by your virtues/ropes [gunani], my dear
Śyām,
still it is a wonder, that you abandoned my memory.

By these changes the multiple meaning of *sujān* is not prevalent in this collection, and the distance between *laukik* and *alaukik śṛṅgār*, mundane and divine love is better maintained. The poetic beauty, however, suffers a loss, not only because many suggested meanings disappear, but also because the poem sometimes becomes awkward as for example the words of an offended woman (*khaṇḍitā*) of SH23 seem to be addressed to a woman beloved in P17.

The Ms. found in the Pothīkhānā of Jaipur is not the only dated one from Ānandghan's lifetime. Apart from the No. 9431(2) Ms. of the Jodhpur branch of the Rajasthan Oriental Research Institute, which is dated from VS 1786 (AD 1729) and which is obviously a copy of the AD 1727 Ms., the No. 4789(4) Ms. of the Alwar branch of the Rajasthan Oriental Research Institute, also contains a dated collection of Ānandghan's quatrains, which is from VS 1800 (AD 1743). In this collection there are 209 *kavitt*s and *savaiyā*s in the same order as in the one from AD 1727, the only difference being that the first ten poems of that older collection are missing from the later one. The text is similar and most of the changes of the AD 1727 Ms. are preserved. The basis of the Alwar Ms. must have been the earlier mentioned older compilation or a copy of it. Still in this collection even more changes are made to eliminate the controversy concerning the word *sujān*. In 209 poems, 59 such changes can be found,[25] about twice as many as in the older one. It is not surprising that in its colophon, it is written that this collection was copied in Rupnagar by Śvetāmbar Hemrāj.[26]

The first Ms. was written in VS 1784 (AD 1727) with all probability in Rupnagar and perhaps by someone who belonged to the workshop or circle of Svetāmbar Hemrāj. The obvious reason for these changes was to defend Ānandghan's fame. It means that by AD 1727, Ānandghan was attacked

[25] Interestingly such changes occur almost exclusively in the first half of both Mss. (after the no. 100 poem only one or two such variants are found).

[26] This Śvetāmbar Hemrāj appears as the copyist of several Mss. between VS 1784 (AD 1727) and VS 1833 (AD 1776). From the name, he seems to be a Jaina but from a copy of a *Varṣotsav ke pad* from VS 1833 (AD 1776) it seems that he might have been a Rādhāvallabhī (Ms. no. 4400 in the VRI, Vrindavan. See *A Catalogue of Hindi Manuscripts in the Vrindaban Research Institute*, pt. I, p. 145). Śvetāmbar Hemrāj of Rupnagar is the author of the *Bainbattīsī* (from VS 1819) about Krishna's flute and the gopīs (see *Hastalikhit hindī pustakõ kā saṅkṣipt vivaraṇ*, p. 38).

on the ground of his identification of mundane and divine love. It is also very probable that the poet was in touch with Rupnagar at that time, otherwise there would not have been any necessity to defend his fame in that particular place. It is important to remember that in his *Paramahaṃs vaṃśāvalī*, Ānandghan, describing his guru-paramparā in the Nimbārk Sampradāy, speaks with great reverence about Vṛndāvandevācārya of Salemabad (AD 1697-1740) who was the leading religious authority of his times. According to Brahmacārī Bihārīśaraṇ[27] and Viśvanāthprasād Miśra[28] this reference to Vṛndāvandevācārya indicates that he was Ānandghan's guru. Moreover, Dr. Śaraṇbihārī Gosvāmī noticed a similarity between the poetry of Vṛndāvandevācārya and Ānandghan.[29] Salemabad being just a few kilometres away from Kishangarh and Rupnagar, Vṛndāvandevācārya had very close contacts with the royal family of this state. (Mahārājā Rāj Singh's second wife, the step-mother of Nāgarīdās, Rānī Bānkāvatī was the ācārya's disciple.[30]) All these coincidences indicate that around AD 1727 Ānandghan was living either in Rupnagar or in its vicinity in Salemabad.

The two Mss. mentioned do not represent all the efforts to defend Ānandghan's fame. In the SH collection the text of the above-mentioned philosophical poem (GK310 [P109; Alwar 99]) is changed.

Prema ko payodadhi apāra heri kai bicāra
bāpuro hahari vāra hī tẽ phiri āyau hai;
Tākī koū tarala taraṅga saṅga chūṭyau kana
pūri loka lokani umaṇḍi uphanāyau hai;
Soī ghanaānāda sujāna lāgi heta hota
aisẽ mathi mana pai sarūpa ṭhaharāyau hai.
Tāhi ekarasa hvai bibasa avagāhẽ doū
nehī Hari Rādhā, jinhaĩ herẽ sarasāyau hai. (SH116)

By the change in the order of the lines the philosophy is also changed: in SH the importance of the ocean of love is lessened by the importance of Hari and Radha. This version is in accordance with the legend that Ānandghan's love for Sujān has turned into love for Radha and Krishna. Nevertheless, this version seems to be more awkward because Hari and Radha plunge into the character and not the ocean of love, and the thought

[27] Bihārīśaraṇ (ed.) 1930, pp. 492-500.
[28] Miśra 1952, *Vāṅmukh*, p. 75.
[29] Gosvāmī 1966, p. 583.
[30] Mītal 1968, p. 357.

expressed in it does not give importance to Sujān, who is the most important theme of Ānandghan's quatrains. This poem has been mutilated by the compiler of the SH[31] to create a more pious image of the poet.

CONCLUSION

Concerning Ānandghan's poetic career, we can distinguish two important stages. In the first one he wrote quatrains about his love for Sujān. In these poems he was interested in both the mundane and the divine aspects of love. He wrote in an ornate style about the paradox of love. In these verses Sujān, the beloved, can be either a woman (*nāyikā*), a man (*nāyak*), or an undefined God, or Krishna. The poet does not let us decide whether Sujān is a human being or the Absolute. Ānandghan wants to show that the love is the same for both: it is a particle of 'the boundless ocean of love'. This love for Sujān — 'Sujānhit' — is the main theme of the poems.

In the second part of his life he discarded the ornamental style and the possibility of mundane love. He started to write simple poetry of explicit Vaishnava bhakti, and disregarded his early poems.

The motivation for this change was the attack on his poetry, first of all on his identification of the mundane love for Sujān and the bhakti for the *sujān* Krishna. The condemnation of this identification was so strong that very few people dared to praise Ānandghan and even those who wanted to defend his fame (Śvetāmbar Hemrāj of Rupnagar and his circle) did not dare to justify it, but tried to hide this peculiarity of the quatrains.

The second target of the attack was Ānandghan's association with Muslims and his 'disrespect' for the rules of Vaishnavism, although he was a monk, a disciple of Vṛndāvandevācārya. In fact, Ānandghan's identification of mundane and divine love reminds us Sufi ideas and Persian and Urdu poetry. In that philosophical bhakti all worldliness is left behind and all the sentiments of the bhakta shine with divine light.

Ānandghan's quatrains were condemned and even the poet himself discarded his style and ideas. Still the beauty and depth of the poems were stronger than any hypocrisy, and after a century of secret copying, Ānandghan's *kabitt*s gained popularity and recognition among the connoisseurs in India.

[31] Most probably at the time of the composition of the SH, because it reflects the idea of the whole collection emphasizing first mundane then divine love. V.P. Miśra thinks that the compiler belonged to the Rādhāvallabhī sect, because the followers of Hit Harivaṃś used to put the word *hit* into the title of their works or into their own names.

REFERENCES

Avasthī, Mohan, 'Ghanānand kī preyasī kā nām Sujān nahī̃ thā', *Sammelan Patrikā*, vol. 65 (1972), nos. 3-4, pp. 137-43.

Bahuguṇā, Śambhuprasād, *Ghanānand*, Allahabad: Sāhitya Bhavan, 1944.

Bangha, Imre, 'The *Harikalā Belī* and Ānandghan's death', *Annali*, Istituto Universitario Orientale di Napoli, 1997, nos. 1-2, pp. 1-10.

Bihārīśaraṇ, Brahmacārī (ed.), *Nimbārk mādhurī*, Vrindaban: Brahmacārī Bihārīśaraṇ, 1930.

Gauṛ, Kṛṣṇadev Prasād and others (eds.), *Hastalikhit hindī pustakõ kā saṅkṣipt vivaraṇ*, Banaras: Nāgarīpracāriṇī Sabhā, 1964.

Gauṛ, Manoharlāl, *Ghanānand aur svacchand kāvyadhārā*, Banaras: Nāgarīpracāriṇī Sabhā, 1972 (1st edn. 1958).

Gosvāmī, Śaraṇbihārī, *Kṛṣṇabhakti-kāvya mẽ sakhībhāv*, Banaras: Chowkhambha Vidyabhavan, 1966.

Gupta, Kiśorīlāl, 'Ghanānand kī preyasī kā nām Sujān thā', *Sammelan Patrikā*, vol. 63 (1967), no. 1, pp. 116-21.

Gupta, R.D. and M.L. Gupta, *A Catalogue of Hindi Manuscripts in the Vrindaban Research Institute*, pt. I, Vrindaban: Vrindaban Research Institute, 1979.

Mītal, Prabhudayāl, *Braj ke dharm-sampradāyõ kā itihās*, Delhi: National Publishing House, 1968.

Miśra, Viśvanāthprasād, *GhanĀnand (granthāvalī)*, Banaras: Vāṇī Vitān, 1952.

———, *GhanĀnand-kabitt*, Banaras: Vāṇī Vitān, 1950 (1st edn. 1943).

Śarmā, Kailāścandra: *Bhaktamāl aur hindī kāvya mẽ uskī paramparā*, Rohtak: Mantham Publications, 1983.

Sontheimer, Günther, 'Bhakti in the Khandobā Cult', in D.L. Eck and F. Mallison (eds.), *Devotion Divine. Bhakti Traditions from the Regions of India*, Groningen-Paris: Egbert Forsten—École Française d'Extrême Orient, 1991, pp. 232-42.

Śukla, Rāmcandra, *Hindī sāhitya kā itihās*, Banaras: Nāgarīpracāriṇī Sabhā, 1990 (1st edn. 1929).

Śyāmsundardās (ed.), *Rādhākṛṣṇadās granthāvalī*, Allahabad: Indian Press, 1937.

Varmā, Kṛṣṇa Candra, *Ghanānand*, Gwalior: Ravīndra Prakāśan, 1966.

Varmā, Ṭhākurprasād (ed.), *Yugyugīn Braj*, Banaras: Bhāratīy Itihās Saṅkalan Samiti, 1988, pp. 224-31.

Vaudeville, Charlotte, (a): 'La conception de l'amour divine chez Muhammad Jāyasī: virah et 'ishq', *Journal Asiatique*, 1962, pp. 351-67.

———, (b): *Les Duhā de Ḍholā-Māru*, Pondichéry: Institut Français d'Indologie, 1962.

Viyogī Hari (ed.), *Brajmādhurī-sār*, Allahabad: Hindī Sāhitya Sammelan, 1987, 16th edn.

Forms of Poetic Enunciation in Ghanānand

GHANSHYAM SHARMA

INTRODUCTION

Ghanānand (*c.* AD 1700-57) is one of the most important poets of the poetic current called *rītimukt kāvya*[1] (poetry free from *rīti*[2]). The so-called *rītimukt kāvya* is a common denomination popular with the historians of Hindi literature for a number of poets of Rītikāl (period of *rīti*) who did not simply write poetry to describe the subject matter of *nāyikā-bhed* (description and classification of heroines), *nakh-śikh varṇan* ('head-to-toe' description) and *alaṅkāraśāstra* (poetics, art of poetic embellishment) but, though attached to various courts, wrote poetry of great importance which was to a considerable extent free from *rīti*. Like the other contemporary *rīti* poets, these poets too were interested mainly in gratifying their patrons and therefore in search of a better form of genre and style full of poetic ornaments. However, at the same time they developed a form of vernacular poetry which dealt with the subjects of love and bhakti. Like his contemporaries Ghanānand too wrote poetry which was noticeably influenced by rhetoric and poetic conventions borrowed from Sanskrit poetics and *kāvya*, and made every use of the traditional themes and motifs common to almost all the authors of Rītikāl. Nevertheless his personal voice and an inherent emotional impact on every poetic image imbued his poetry with a distinct spirit and poetic sense that is not easily found in other poets of Rītikāl. Unlike other poets of Rītikāl, for Ghanānand poetry is neither a detailed taxonomy of hero and heroine (*nāyaka-nāyikā bheda*)

[1] The term is used by the historians of Hindi literature to refer to those poets who, unlike their contemporaries, wrote poetry that was to a great extent free from a mere description of topics in poetics such as *nāyaka-nāyikā bheda*, *śṛṅgāra rasa*, *alaṅkāra*, etc. The most important of these poets are Ghanānand, Bodhā, Ālam and Ṭhākur (1766-1823).

[2] 'The term *rīti* 'path, way, style' is used in Hindi criticism to refer generically to verse on all the above types of subject, suggesting a sense of working within a received literary tradition.' McGregor 1984, p. 123.

nor should its aim be to discuss and analyse different figures of speech. In his poetry the conventional themes and motifs are given a fresh imagery and become original, exploring aspects of emotions and love. He discards any devices a poet might use in order to keep pace with the poetic output of his time and he believes in a natural way of writing poetry. He says:

. . . लोग हैं लागि कबित्त बनावत मोहिं तौ मेरे कबित्त बनावत

(घनआनंद (ग्रन्थावली), *सुजानहित,* २२८)

People busy themselves creating poetry; my poetry creates me.

GHANĀNAND ON *THE BEING OF A POEM*

The distinctiveness of Ghanānand's poetry is due to the concept of poetic language and the meaning he has in mind. Poetry, for him, is an outpouring of love and springs from the heart of the poet, where it is hidden in a subtle form. It is born as a result of the emotional experiences of the poet and these experiences need to be accompanied by speech.[3] In a very carefully conceived metaphor Ghanānand tries to envisage the form of literary enunciation which will parallel the traditional Indian concept of literary meaning:

उर-भौन मैं मौन को घूँघट कै दुरि बैठी बिराजति बात-बनी।
मृदु मंजु पदारथ भूषन सों सु लसै दुलसै (हुलसै) रस-रूप-मनी।
रसना-अली कान गली मधि ह्वै पधरावति लै चित-सेज ठनी।
घनआनँद बूझनि-अंक बसै बिलसै रिझवार सुजान-धनी॥

(घनआनंद (ग्रन्थावली), *सुजानहित,* १९२)

Concealed in the veil of silence, the word-bride sits shining in the heart-palace,
graced by sweet charming ornaments of *padārth* (sound and meaning) she, the jewel of *ras* (essence) and *rūp* (form) rejoices.
Through the ear-lane the tongue-*alī* (bridesmaid) accompanies her (or him) to the decorated bed of consciousness,

[3] 'He who is a peerless lover | skilled in the Braj language | knowing well poetry's elegance | and all its sundry arts; who knows the secret of union | and of parting too, and what is hid deep | in human minds.

Who is forever drenched | in the sweet essence of love; whom meeting vexes | as much as parting does, because in meeting | the fear to part again | is ever present.

Who can master language | yet not be enslaved by convention.

Such a man alone | can expound | Ghanānand's verse.' (Translated by K.P. Bahadur 1977, p. 49.)

the cloud of joy (Ghanānand), she settles down in the lap of understanding and the fascinating, clever bridegroom takes pleasure.

In what seems to be a simple sustained metaphor, Ghanānand tries to put forward his theory of literary enunciation which gives him a distinct place in Brajbhāṣā poetry. According to him the poetry-bride, or rather the subtle form of poetry, remains in the heart of the poet but requires the speech-bridesmaid as an accompanying person who then takes her through the ear-lane to the consciousness-bed where the (sensitive) reader-bridegroom takes pleasure. It is not necessary to analyse and to establish the different sources of Ghanānand's concept of poetic enunciation in the context of the extremely rich Indian theories of literary meaning and philosophy of language, as that would require another paper. For our present purposes here it suffices to point out that Ghanānand's poetry is distinct in that it derives from the implied meaning, which is neither a secondary meaning nor simply a rhetorical *double entendre* (*śliṣṭārtha*) but is an 'implicit' meaning at utterance level in the form of an index of 'odd' situations which are almost always beyond the reach of a human sign system. In such cases, then, what remains for a poet to describe is the contrasting situations of life.

THE ROLE OF SILENCE IN LITERARY ENUNCIATION

According to Ghanānand, human language is equipped with a special power for 'implying' situations in every aspect of communication: it implies meaning even during silence. Needless to say, his poetic enunciations are in most cases embedded with this power of implying ('implicitating') poetic situations:

आँखिन मूँदिबो बात दिखावत, सोवनि जागनि बातहि पेखि लै।
बात-सरूप अनूप अरूप है, भूल्यौ कहा तू अलेखहि लेखि लै।
बात की बात सुबात बिचारिबो सूछमता सब ठौर बिसेखि लै।
नैननि-काननि बीच बसे घनआनँद मौन-बखान सु देखि लै।

(घनआनंद (ग्रन्थावली), *सुजानहित,* ४२४)

Closing the eyes reveals word (language), consider the word in sleeping, in being awake,
the nature of word is peerless and formless, how come you have forgotten it; contemplate the indescribable through it!
In one word, if good word is to be reflected upon, then you find its distinctiveness in subtleness,
it lies between the eyes and the ears, Ghanānand (cloud of joy), see it in the silence-speech.

Ghanānand now and again takes up the theme of silence in his poetry, referring to that implying power of verbal operation which is required for any poetical act to take place. From his repeated reference to this concept of linguistic function, one gets the impression of his very deep knowledge of Indian theories of meaning. He seems to expound the theory of Bhartṛhari in his poetry according to which 'There is no cognition in the world in which the word does not figure. All knowledge is, as it were, intertwined with the word (*Vākyapadīya* I: 123, p. 110)',[4] but, by the word 'silence' he points out the importance to the poetic enunciation of that inward looking sequence of different levels of language cognition that starts from *Vaikharī* (the lowest, outward, and most external level in language cognition which fully maintains the temporal sequence of words in an utterance: the language uttered, word-sounds) to *Madhyamā* (the second, upper level of language cognition: the inner word meanings are present *in toto*, but the sequence of words in an utterance is not totally retained) and to *Paśyanti* (the third and innermost level of language cognition: without any temporal sequence and without any distinction between the word and meaning) up to *Parā* (uppermost level of language cognition: the indivisible whole of the speaking act):[5]

कौन कौन अंगन के रंगन मैं राँचै मन,
    मौन होत सोई सुख मुख पुनि ल्यावई।
मौन मिहीं बात है समझि कहि जानौ जान,
    अमी काहू भाँति को अचंभै भरि प्यावई।
सोवनि जगनि याकी मूरछा सचेत सदा,
    रीझ घनआनँद निबेरै याहि न्यावई।
कहें कौन माने, पहचानै कान नैन जाके,
    बात की भिदनि मोहिं मारि मारि ज्यावई॥

(घनआनंद (ग्रन्थावली), *सुजानहित,* ४२३)

In the colours of what limbs my soul has been painted,
    he who is in silence in turn brings joy to the tongue;
    [the joy of being silent is expressed in turn by the tongue]

[4] Coward 1980, p. 126.

[5] Our observation about the nature of different levels of language cognition is based solely on Coward (1980) as ours is not an in-depth study of the subject; rather, we simply intend to highlight a similarity that can easily be observed between Ghanānand and Bhartṛhari as far as their ideas about language and its meaning are concerned.

silence is a subtle word which Sujān can understand and say,
 it makes one drink a kind of Amrit (nectar) full of wonder;
its sleeping is being awake and its consciouslessness is always conscious,
 the conscious cloud of joy wards it justly off with joy;
who can say it? Who can believe it? He recognises it whose ears are in the eyes,
 the piercing of words makes me live by killing over and over again.

This concept of silence is so dear to Ghanānand that he takes it up even in those stanzas dedicated to Bhakti, where his goal seems to be different from simply discussing the role of silence in language and indeed in poetic language:

मोसे अनपहचान कों, पहचानै हरि कौन।
कृपा-कान मधि-नैन ज्यों, त्यौं पुकार मधि-मौन॥
(घनआनंद (ग्रन्थावली), *सुजानहित,* ४५१)

Who can comprehend such an incomprehensible person like me,
as your ears of grace are in the eyes, so is my call in the silence.

THE LOCUS OF GHANĀNAND'S POETIC MEANING

This implying power of poetic enunciation to which Ghanānand occasionally refers in different contexts is, according to the theory of *dhvani*, based on the third verbal operation, namely *vyañjanā* (implicitation) — the other two being *abhidhā* (designation) and *lakṣaṇā* (indication). I shall digress from the topic for a while to clarify the concept of implied meaning to which Ghanānand refers again and again through expressions like 'call in silence', 'silence is a subtle word', etc. The three verbal operations of utterance meaning can be presented in the following formal way:

(a) Verbal Operation I: Designation
 Sentence *S* means that *P*
 Utterance *U* of *S* means that *P*
 where both the sentence meaning and utterance meaning are the same.

(b) Verbal Operation II: Indication[6]
 Sentence *S* means that *?P*

[6] The whole semantic phenomenon referred to by the term Indication (*lakṣaṇā*) can not be considered appertaining to the term metaphor, though there are many more similarities than differences between these two terms. While their nature of

Utterance U of S means that $?P$
Therefore, utterance U of S indicates that Q
where sentence meaning is obstructed and is different from the utterance meaning.

(c) Verbal Operation III: 'Implicitation' (Implication)
Sentence S means that P
Utterance U of S means that P but
Implies ('Implicitates') that $R_1, R_2, R_3...R_n; S_1, S_2, S_3...S_n$, *etc.*

According to the theory of *dhvani*, all forms of enunciation in a human communication system, keeping in mind the possible combinations of verbal operations, can be roughly grouped into four categories (G. Sharma 1996). There are in fact two types of the use of the second verbal operation, viz., Indication, one in which it gives the utterance meaning of its own, the second leading to the third verbal operation and thus giving further Implied meaning:

(1) Combination Type I
Sentence S means that P
Utterance U of S means that P

(2) Combination Type II
Sentence S means that P
Utterance U of S means that $?P$
Therefore, U indicates that Q

(3) Combination Type III
Sentence S means that P
Utterance U of S means that P
But implies that $R_1, R_2, R_3...R_n; S_1, S_2, S_3...S_n$, *etc.*

---

dealing with the so-called linguistic aberration is the same, their fields of application not. Under the term Indication fall even those examples which are generally accounted for in the domain of syntax. All examples of Indication require at the utterance level both semantic account as well as pragmatic explanations. Can the similarity theory of metaphor resolve the problems we encounter in the field of Indication? The answer is No. On the surface level, 'Man is a wolf' can be studied presenting a formal account, i.e., $(\exists F)\ (\exists G)\ \{SIM[F(S), G(P)]\}$, meaning 'There is some property F and some property G such that man's being F is similar to a wolf's being G.' (Searle criticizing Miller's similarity theory in Ortony 1993), the examples of Indication certainly require another level of explanation. We have therefore preferred the term Indication instead of Metaphor.

(4) Combination Type IV
Sentence S means that P
Utterance U of S means that $?P$
Therefore, U indicates that Q
and implies that $R_1, R_2, R_3 ... R_n$; $S_1, S_2, S_3 ... S_n$, *etc.*

Now, to understand the nature of meaning derived from the third verbal operation, namely, 'implicitation', let me very briefly discuss an example from Kālidāsa (*Kumārasambhava* 6.84) cited and analysed by Ānandavardhana (*Dhvanyāloka* 2.22) to show the nature of the meaning obtained through the Combination Type III in which the third verbal operation gives the meaning immediately after the first verbal operation; there is no place for any kind of intervention by the second verbal operation:

While the heavenly visitor was speaking, Pārvatī standing with lowered face beside her father, counted the petals of the lotus in her hand.

(D.H.H. Ingalls 1990, p. 311)

Here, without going into the details of the discussion among scholars on this example, we can notice clearly that in this utterance Pārvatī's 'shyness in the presence of her father' and 'curiosity to know about her future fiancé' are implied (implicitated) through the verbal operation called 'implicitation' which is not like any other categories we have at our disposal to study such phenomena. It is different from the seemingly similar logical term 'implication', or from some other terms that deal with that form of meaning which is either in addition to or different from the sentential meaning, viz., 'presupposition' and 'entailment'. This example, however, falls into the Combination Type III of the verbal operations discussed earlier in which the 'implied' (implicited) meaning is obtained through Designation (*abhidhā*) only. Having studied about 110 stanzas by Ghanānand for the present analysis it can be safely affirmed that his poetic utterances are endowed with implied meaning derived from the Combination Type IV of verbal operations in which the implied meaning of literary enunciation is arrived at through the verbal operation called Indication (*lakṣaṇā*) or to use the Western rhetoric term 'metaphor', though the locus of his poetic meaning remains in most cases without any doubt the implied (implicited) meaning. There is hardly any utterance the meaning of which is not derived from this kind of verbal operation. Nevertheless, unlike his contemporaries, his use of Indication is always full of implied poetic meaning. Gauṛ (1958) divides the use of Indication by Ghanānand into three major categories: firstly, those uses of Indication which are aimed at merely creating an atmosphere of a 'sudden delight' or 'rapture' (*camatkār*) in the reader with different charming uses of this verbal operation. Although not totally indispensable for the poet in his/her effort to give a poem an extra poetic meaning, such uses of Indication can be seen as an important element of the poetic repertoire of the period of *rīti*. This kind of usage of the verbal operation called Indication can further be seen as either related exclusively to the content of the poem or as a means of poetic expression. In the second place come those uses of this verbal operation which not only create in the reader an atmosphere of sudden delight but also add to the poem's content sensitivity of feelings and functions as a vehicle to express the poet's imagination. Thirdly, there are some uses of this verbal operation which serve neither of the poet's purposes: they do not create any poetic 'sudden delight' in the reader, nor do they help the poet express his/her feelings. Such uses can certainly be discarded in favour of poetic imagination. A list of Ghanānand's different usage of indication can be presented here:

(1) Use of Indication for the purpose of creating an atmosphere of 'sudden delight' or 'rapture':
   (a) the 'sudden delight' is sometimes due to the charming nature of the poet's imagination; there is no extra effort by the poet to add the expressions of Indication;[7]
   (b) the 'sudden delight' is arrived at through an extra effort by the poet to insert such uses of Indication; no damage would be done if such uses were discarded and were substituted with other expressions based on Designation. Gaur takes into consideration some uses where, in his opinion, Indication is the result of the poet's effort.[8]

(2) Use of Indication as an important instrument for expressing the poet's imagination; Indication is not employed to create an atmosphere of a 'sudden delight' in the reader, rather it is put into practice to convey the poetic intensity and becomes a fine example of the poet's knowledge of the subtleties of poetic thought. Poetic fineness could not otherwise

[7] Gauṛ cites different examples of this type of use of Indication: *SH* (*Sujānhit*) '. . . *jab hohu gharīk hū āp tẽ nyāre*' *SH* 177, '. . . *maribau anmīc binā jiy jībau*' *SH* 148, '. . . *jānai vei dinrāti, bakhānẽ te jāy parai dinrāti ko antar*' *SH* 207.

[8] For example, according to Gaur, the second part of the second line in *Sujānhit* 247, '. . . *ur gā̃ṭhi tyõ antar kholati hai*', can be considered such type of use of the second verbal operation, i.e. Indication.

be obtained. Ghanānand's poetry is a clear example of such uses of Indication in poetic enunciation.[9]

(3) Use of Indication does not in any way help to create an atmosphere of 'sudden delight', nor does it express any poetic feelings. They can be substituted by some simple expression without damaging the poetic nature of enunciation.[10]

WHAT KIND OF SPEECH ACT IS GHANĀNAND'S POETRY?

Although poetic enunciation is a special kind of speech-act (it has no real speaker-hearer which is a necessary condition for any utterance in ordinary oral communication) it is indeed a linguistic act and should therefore be studied also in terms of its illocutionary force. Poetic enunciation is said to employ the so-called 'mimetic' forms of illocutionary force which are responsible for the realization of 'quasi-speech acts', but can also be tackled as a special kind of speech act in a deep structure of the poem which should have this abstract form (S.R. Levin in van Dijk 1976, p. 150):

'I (poet) imagine myself in and invite you (reader) to conceive a world in which . . .'.

Now, if we look closely at the poetry of Ghanānand and compare it with that of his contemporaries, its surprisingly distinct quality emerges: Ghanānand invites the reader to conceive a world or, to use the modern term, a set of 'possible worlds' which is quite different from the 'possible worlds' created by other contemporary poets. In most cases it seems to be the poetry of 'expressive illocutions' in which the poet, no matter what strategies he/she employs, neither makes assertions to merely describe the

[9] This kind of use of the second verbal operation in the poet is quite frequent and is meant for different poetic purposes: '. . . *taraṅg uṭhai*' *SH* 32, '. . . *bharī virah ritaun kī*' *SH* 155, '. . . *khoybo lahā lahāũ*' *SH* 242, '. . .*maun hī sõ kachu bolati hai*' *SH* 247, '. . . *joi rāt pyāre saṅg bātan na jāt jānī, soi ab kahā̃ tẽ baṛhani liẽ āi hai*' *SH* 278, '. . . *kānh! pare bahutāyat mā̃i akilaini kī bedani jānau kahā tum*' *SH* 404, '. . . *jin hī barunīn sõ bedhyau hiyau tinahī dṛg-hāth sikhāvat ho*' *SH* 109, '. . . *jin ā̃khin rūp cinhāri bhai tinkī nit nīdahi jāgani hai*' *SH* 279, '. . . *lājani lapeṭī citvani bhedbhāy bharī*' *PR* (*Prakīrṇak*) 1.

[10] Gauṛ (1958, p. 130) cites some examples in which according to him the use of Indication does not add any further Implied meaning, nor can it be seen as a necessary tool to create poetic effect in the reader: '. . . *sūjhati būjh kī ḍīṭhi su tānau*' *SH* 20, '. . . *bhūl kāũ sāũpi sabai ju tabai sudhi*' *SH* 134, '. . . *jau lāũ jage na bhūl tau lāũ sovai surati sukh*' *SH* 396.

object of the stanza nor makes the reader think about complex romantic situations borrowed from the stock-in-trade of most *rīti* poets. Although the *rīti* tradition has handed down to him various descriptions of *śṛṅgāra* and women's beauty, Ghanānand manages to handle them with a fresh romantic imagery and a pleasant lyric form. In the following stanzas which seem to be a typical example of *rīti*, much in the same way as other *rīti* poets, Ghanānand describes situations in which the mind of the poet's persona goes up to the lady's toes and remains attached there, implying at the level of enunciation the charm of the lady's toes. But the apparently simple structure of the illocution employed gives it a poetic spirit that is rare in other *rīti* poets and is totally different from that of Bihārīlāl's *gāgar mẽ sāgar* 'an ocean in a pitcher' technique: its lyrical cadence and sensuality in the deep structure are the distinct poetic qualities which make Ghanānand's poetry remarkable:

अँगुरीन लौं जाय भुलाय तहीं फिरी आय लुभाय रहै तरवा।
चपि चायनि चूर ह्वै एड़िनि छ्वै धपि धाय छकै छबि छाय छवा।
घनआनँद यौं रस-रीझनि भीजि कहूँ बिसराम बिलोक्यौ न वा।
अलबेली सुजान के पायनि-पानि पर्‌यौ न टर्‌यौ मन मेरो झवा॥

(घनआनंद (ग्रन्थावली), *सुजानहित,* १६)

It goes up to the toes, there becomes bewildered and then remains lured under the sole,
crushed into powder by desires it touches the heel, runs and jumps satiated and takes shelter in the charm of the ankle;
in this way steeped in the joy of *ras* it nowhere gets (sees) rest,
my mind like a pumice fell at the hands of the charming Sujān's feet, and didn't move away.

The same could be argued about the following example in which Ghanānand's persona, impressed by the lady's beauty, talks to her of the redness in her face. Ghanānand uses a sustained metaphor in which the redness of the lady's face becomes the red powder used on the occasion of the Holi festival. This is certainly an example of mannerist poetry but its sensuality in the deep structure and its lyrical cadence give it a vibrant poetic quality:

देखि धौं आरसी लै बलि नेकु लसी है गुराई मैं कैसी ललाई।
मानौ उदोत दिवाकर की दुति पूरन चंदहि भैंटन आई।
फूलत कंज कुमोद लखें घनआनंद रूप अनूप निकाई।
तो मुख लाल गुलालहि लाय कै सौतिन के हिय होरी लगाई॥

(घनआनंद (ग्रन्थावली), *सुजानहित,* १९)

Take a mirror, I beg you, and have a look, how redness shines in whiteness,
as if the light of the rising sun came to embrace the full moon;
seeing the excellence of the peerless beauty, cloud of joy, both the red lotus by day
and white lotus by night bloom (together),
bringing red powder your face lights holī fire in the hearts of your co-wives.

GHANĀNAND'S SCHEMATA OF POETIC COMMUNICATION

Ghanānand has exploited all possible schemata of poetic communication in his stanzas. Very often he himself talks to an imagined reader as an inherently present speaker, sometimes in the form of an absent speaker. At times he creates a persona who talks either to another persona, who always remains a silent listener, or to some natural phenomena or to some animal; at other times he narrates or describes various situations. In the stanzas which have *vinay* (humble entreaty to God) as a major theme, he directly talks to God or describes his own miserable situation. But perhaps his favourite schemas of poetic communication is that in which a persona (usually a *virahī* or *virahiṇī*) talks to his/her beloved. The following is a tentative list of Ghanānand's poetic schemata of communication in stanzas:

(1) Poet ⇨ Persona ⇨ ------- ⇨ Reader[11]
(2) Poet ⇨ ------- ⇨ ------- ⇨ Reader[12]
(3) Poet ⇨ Persona$_1$ ⇨ Persona$_2$ ⇨ Reader[13]

[11] This category includes those stanzas in which the poet speaks to some imagined addressee (in most cases his beloved girl), though she is not an obvious hearer of the communication. It therefore becomes a sort of monologue whose addressee's presence is perfectly suggested by the poetic enunciation. The numbers given here refer to the stanzas we have analysed for this purpose and indicate their order in *Ghanānand granthāvalī*: *SH* 49, 207, 268, 269, 272, 256, 243, 21, 277, 178, 225, 78, 273, 280, 418, 190, 171, 223, 279, 283, 189, 218, 36, 183, 241, 284, 216, 255, 198, 38, 8, 206, 212, 24, 274, 270, 240, 7, 251, 246, 276, 221, 41, 224, 235, 209, 4; *PR* 3, 5, 6.

[12] We can cite as examples of this category those stanzas in which the poet, though engaged in conceiving some sort of dialogue between two imagined personas, does not create any apparent personas: (*SH* 196, 170, 215, 219, 179, 91, 203, 204, 136, 282, 240, 285, *PR* 2, 1; *PP* (*Prempatrikā*) 85.

[13] This class of stanzas is based on some form of clear dialogue between two personas, although in such cases the locus of poetic meaning remains an addressee which is not present in the poem: *SH* 271, 220, 67, 244, 164, 169, 257, 275, 260, 202, 187, 299, 278, 411, 226, 47, 266, 264, 263.

(4) Poet ⇨ Persona ⇨ ------- ⇨ Reader[14]
(5) Poet ⇨ ------- ⇨ God ⇨ Reader[15]

No matter what kind of poetic schemata Ghanānand envisages for his poem to convey the deep poetic meaning, his most efficient method to engage the reader is that of creating some kind of dialogue between two entities which are sometimes clearly present in the poem and sometimes absent. At times the participants of the dialogue are human beings, at times they are some natural entity.

If we look carefully at the structure of different kinds of enunciation employed by Ghanānand, his poetry can be divided into two categories: firstly, those *kavitt*, *savaiyā* and *pada*, etc., whose main themes are *vinay* (humble entreaty to God) or, like other bhakti poets, description of some form of Kṛṣṇa-bhakti. They are quite simple at the level of poetic enunciation: they are on a par with most bhakti literature as far as their subject matter is concerned, but their internal structure is simple, sometimes even banal as it describes the poet's own miserable situation towards the end of his life. Like Sūr's poems, they are seemingly self-contained *formal* units, yet parts of a long narrative already known to the audience, and thus not self-contained narrative units (Bryant 1978, p. 45). Ghanānand's second type of poetic enunciation — and perhaps the most important one — is most commonly used to express the theme of love. Its internal structure is based mainly on reporting and expressing incongruous situations of *virah* in complex enunciation. These stanzas are not a mere description of *virahiṇī*, as is common in Bihārilāl's *dohā*s. Their macro illocutions at the deep structure level are expressions of lamentation or simply of tragic situations:

अंतर उदेग-दाह, आँखिन प्रबाह-आँसू,
देखी अटपटी चाह भीजनि दहनि है।

[14] In this type of poetic communication the poet creates a persona who either talks to his/her mind (heart) or to some natural phenomenon (cloud, wind, etc.): *SH* 259 (wind), *SH* 258 (mind), *SH* 281 (mind), *SH* 194 (mind), *SH* 195 (heart, mind).

[15] In such type of examples the poet talks directly to God. We can cite from a vast range of such examples only a few. For example *SH* 451, *PD* (*Padāvali*) 2, 3, 4, 5, 6, 22, 78, 241, 136, 154, 242, 677.

सोयबो न जागिबो हो, हँसिबो न रोयबो हू,
खोय खोय आप ही मैं चेटक-लहनि है।
जान प्यारे प्राननि बसत पै अनंदघन,
बिरह-बिषम-दसा मूक लौं कहनि है।
जीवन-मरन, जीव मीच बिना बन्यौ आय,
हाय कौन बिधि रची नेही की रहनि है॥

(घनआनंद (ग्रन्थावली), *सुजानहित,* १९६)

In the heart burning passions, in the eyes streaming tears,
in this strange desire burning and drenching at the same time.
You can neither sleep nor awaken, neither can you laugh nor weep,
being lost in yourself you fall into a spell.
The dear Jān (beloved) lives in the heart (yet I suffer from *virah*, love in separation),
but describing this incongruous state of *virah* would be like words said by a dumb man.
Living without breath and dying without death,
alas, how strange the Lord has made the lover's state!

The poetic enunciation of this kind is the result of Ghanānand's technique of arranging two incongruous things or many contrasting situations in a single utterance, thereby placing an extra semantic load on the meaning of the expression. In the above example there are contrasting phenomena like 'burning passions in the heart' and 'streaming tears in the eyes' in which burning and drenching take place at the same time. Sufficient indications have been made about the clear influence of Persian literary genre and style on Ghanānand's poetic style — he was in fact fluent in the Persian language and is said to have written a book in that language. Without entering into a detailed enquiry of how much Ghanānand's style was influenced by Persian literary style, and how much was his own innovation, it can be said that Ghanānand's most beautiful stanzas are based on enunciation which contains arrangements of contrasting situations. The same could be said about the following examples in which Ghanānand creates some kind of contrasting situations — a style whose origins can be traced back into the Persian poetic genre:[16]

सुधा तें स्रवत बिष, फूल में जमत सूल,
तम उगिलत चंदा, भई नई रीति है।

[16] Many more examples can be cited here in support of the claim made by different authors about the nature of Persian influence on Ghanānand's poetry: *SH* 170, 206, 244, 269.

जल जारै अंग, और राग करै सुरभंग,
संपति बिपति पारै, बड़ी बिपरीति है।
महागुन गहै दोषै, औषदि हू रोग पौषै,
ऐसें जान ! रस माहिं बिरस अनीति है।
दिनन को फेर मोहिं, तुम मन फेरि डार्‌यौ,
एहो घनआनँद! न जानौं कैसें बीतिहै।

(घनआनंद (ग्रन्थावली), *सुजानहित,* २२४)

Nectar has turned into poison, flowers into thorns,
the moon spits heat, such has become this new situation (way of nature)!
Water burns the body, melody spoils the voice,
wealth (my riches) brings misfortune to me, such has become all this unfavourable!
The noblest virtues has turned into defects, medicine nurtures the disease,
such has been, dear Jān, your injustice upon me!
All these changing times (days), you too have changed your mind,
o Ghanānand, cloud of joy, what will happen to me next without you, who knows!

This kind of proclivity for taking the additional step of arranging two contrasting situations at the level of poetic enunciation, however, does not in any way affect the intensity the poet intends to bring about at the deep semantic level of the poem. Rather it serves as an instrument to intensify the different themes of *virah* (love in separation). Although not completely spontaneous in its imagination because of an eccentric love for contrasting situations, this kind of poetic technique is quite common in different literary traditions. At times this type of artificial arrangement in Ghanānand's poetry becomes quite obvious, thus suggesting poet's excessive effort in bringing about a parallelism or contrast in the poetic thought, aimed at creating a sense of 'sudden delight' (*camatkār*) in the reader. In quite a simple but succinct manner, in the following example Ghanānand creates a contrast between two situations, thus implying the excessive level of *virah*. The obvious parallelism is certainly effective, but requires the reader to recognise the structure of the stanza on which the poetic enunciation is framed. In the following example, the girl suffering from a critical stage of *virah* expresses her anguish comparing the night with the she-cobra and considering the damage caused by the night in absence of her lover much more venomous than a she-cobra's bite. This poetic motif is very much along the lines of the poetic conventions of the period,[17]

[17] Almost the same motif is found in the poetry by Sūrdās: *piyā bin nāgin kārī rāt* (*Bhramargītsār*).

nevertheless the lyrical cadence employed here by Ghanānand saves the verses from being a mere parallelism between two incongruous things which we are told have almost the same effect:

करुवो मधुर लागै वाकौ बिष अंग भएँ,
याहि देखें रस हू मैं कटुता बसति है।
वाके एक मुख ही तें बाढ़त बिकार तन,
यह सरबंग आनि प्राननि गसति है।
सुंदर सुजान जू सजीवन तिहारो ध्यान,
तासों कोटिगुनी ह्वै लहरि सरसति है।
पापनि डरारी भारी साँपिनि निसा बिसारी,
बैरिनि अनोखी मोहिं डाहनि डसति है।

(घनआनंद (ग्रन्थावली), *सुजानहित,* २६८)

Bitter tastes sweet when her (the she-snake's) poison spreads into the body,
nectar tastes bitter when I see this (night in separation!).
Hers (the she-snake's) is only the mouth to cause deterioration to the body,
this (night) bites me from all sides.
O dear handsome one, thinking of you gives me life,
but now (because of this night) it sends through me a charge of venom a million times more potent than the she-cobra's bite.
Sinful (wicked), fearsome, and venomous this cobra-night,
a strange enemy, it bites me out of jealousy (for the she-cobra).

It should be noted, however, that this kind of poetic imagery, no matter how appealing, requires an extra effort to understand the reasoning behind the poetic enunciation. Such an effort from the part of the reader is less required when the poet does not rigidly stick to his fervent desire of creating a 'sudden delight' or 'rapture' in the reader at the expense of the natural flow of poetic thought into poetic enunciation. His poetry in such cases becomes as marvellous as in any other context:

जगि सोवनि मैं जगियै रहै चाह वहै बरराय उठै रतिया।
भरि अंक निसंक ह्वै भेटन कौं अभिलाष-अनेक-भरी छतिया।
मन तें मुख लौं नित फेर बड़ो कित ब्यौरि सकौं हित की बतिया।
घनआनँद जीवन-प्रान लखौ सु लिखी किहि भाँति परै पतिया॥

(घनआनंद (ग्रन्थावली), *सुजानहित,* ४२८)

In sleeping, in being awake the desire remains awake: such is the desire that even the night starts babbling,
The heart is filled with many desires to meet and embrace you fearlessly.
There is always a big discrepancy between soul and mouth — How to express the words of love?

Look, cloud of joy, breath of life, how could they be written in a letter?

But, as soon as he is overpowered by his obsession to arrange the poetic enunciation according to a pre-planned strategy for creating a contrast or suggesting a similarity or simply putting an excessive stress on the semantic locus of a poetic utterance, his poetic enunciation becomes quite similar to a piece by any other *rīti* poet. In the following example the reader is not given, at the level of enunciation, any hint about the dialogue, which is in reality a sort of monologue in which questions and answers are arranged in such a way that no trace is found regarding who is asking whom. The reader is supposed to do a lot of mental exercise to work out that the hypothetical question raised in the first line and a well-planned answer given in the rest of the stanza have some kind of rationality:

कंत रमैं उर-अंतर मैं सु लहै नहीं क्यौं सुख-रासि निरंतर।
दंत रहैं गहैं आँगुरी ते जु बियोग के तेह तचे परतंतर।
जो दुख देखति हौं घनआनँद रैन-दिना बिन जान सुतंतर।
जानैं वेई दिन-राति, बखानें तें जाय परै दिन-राति को अंतर॥

(घनआनंद (ग्रन्थावली), *सुजानहित,* २०७)

(Should someone ask me)
'Since your lover roams in your heart, why aren't you constantly blessed with abundant joy?'
(I would say)
'Even those scorched by the fire of *viyoga* (love in separation) remain open-mouthed
on seeing the suffering that I experience day and night without my indifferent and wise Jān (the cloud of Joy),
only these days and nights can understand it; since describing it makes it totally a different thing: as a day is different from a night'

CONCLUSION

As we have seen in the last pages, it is the distinct use of poetic enunciation that gives Ghanānand's poetry its uniqueness. Other elements of his poetry, i.e. myths, themes, motifs, etc., do not differ greatly from those of his contemporaries, except for his excellent use of the theme of love. Nevertheless, Ghanānand did not make use of popular themes and motifs just for the sake of using them. In his poetry they become an integral part of the poetic structure of the stanzas, giving implicit meaning to utterances. His poetry does not arise merely from an amalgamation of myths and themes, as was the case in the work of most *rīti* poets, in relation to which

Ṭhākur has made a strongly-worded attack:

सीख लीन्हों मीनमृग खंजन कमल नैन,
  सीख लीन्हों यश औ प्रताप को कहानो है।
सीख लीन्हों कल्पवृक्ष कामधेनु चिन्तामणि,
  सीख लीन्हों मेर औ कुबेर गिरि आनो है।
ठाकुर कहत याकी बड़ी है कठिन बात,
  याको नहीं भूलि कहूँ बाँधियत बानो है।
डेल सो बनाय आय मेलत सभा के बीच,
  लोगन कबित कीबौ खेल करि जानो है।
(ठाकुर ठसक, १२ [मनोहरलाल गौड़ १९५८, पृष्ठ २८७ से उद्धृत])

They have learnt to say eyes as of a fish, deer, wagtail and lotus,
  they have learnt tales of fame and glory
they have learnt to say *kalpavṛkṣa* (the tree of all desires), *kāmadhenu* (the cow of desires), *cintāmaṇi* (the jewel of desires)
  they have learnt of the Mount Meru (the mythological golden mountain) and Mount Kuvera (the God of wealth);
says Ṭhākur, its (poetry's) subject is very difficult,
  speech can never ever (even) determine it by mistake,
They come to the gatherings having made it into a lump,
  they consider writing poetry like playing a game!

Certainly these attacks are not directed at Ghanānand's poetic work. It would be a biased approach to value Ghanānand's poetry by simply comparing it with the work of his contemporaries, for, though akin to their poetry as far as the poetical conventions of that time are concerned, his is a poetry extremely rich in the form of poetic enunciation. It is the incomparable quality of his poetic enunciation that makes his poetry unique in medieval Hindi literature.

REFERENCES

Bahadur, K.P., *Love Poems of Ghanānand*, Delhi: Motilal Banarasidass, 1991 (1st edn. 1977).

Bryant, K.E., *Poems to the Child-God, Structures and Strategies in the Poetry of Sūrdās*, Berkeley: University of California Press, 1978.

Coward, Harold G., *Sphota Theory of language*, Delhi: Motilal Banarasidass, 1980.

van Dijk, Teun A., *Pragmatics of Language and Literature*, Amsterdam: North-Holland Publishing Company, 1976.

Eco, U., *I limiti dell'interpretazione*, Milano: Bompiani, 1990.

Gaur̤, M.L., *Ghanānand aur svacchand kāvyadhārā*, Banaras: Nāgrī Prachāriṇī Sabhā, 1958.

Gerow, Edwin, *Indian Poetics*, Wiesbaden: Otto Harrassowitz, 1977.

Grice, P., *Studies in the Way of Words*, Cambridge, Mass.: Harvard University Press, 1989.

Ingalls, D.H.H. (ed.), *The* Dhvanyāloka *of* Ānandavardhana *with the* Locan *of Abhinavagupta* (trans. by D.H.H. Ingalls, J.M. Masson and M.V. Patwardhan), Cambridge Mass.: Harvard University Press, 1990.

Kunjunni Raja, K., *Indian Theories of Meaning*, Madras: The Adyar Library and Research Centre, 1977 (1st edn. 1963).

Manoharlal, *Ghanānand ke kāvy mẽ aprastut-yojnā*, Delhi: National Publishing House, 1980 (1st edn. 1974).

McGregor, R.S., *Hindi Literature of the nineteenth and early twentieth centuries*, Wiesbaden: Otto Harrassowitz, 1968.

———, *Hindi Literature from its beginnings to the nineteenth century*, Wiesbaden: Otto Harrassowitz, 1984.

Miśra, Viśvanāthprasād, *Ghanānand granthāvalī*, Banaras: Vāṇī Vitān, 1952.

Ortony, Andrew, *Metaphor and Thought*, Cambridge: Cambridge University Press, 1993 (1st edn. 1979).

Sharma, G., *Aspetti semiotici dello dhvani*, Ph.D. dissertation, University of Bologna, 1996.

Śukla, Rāmdev, *Ghanānand kā kāvy*, Delhi: Macmillan, 1976.

———, *Ānandghan*, Delhi: Vāṇī Prakāśan, 1993.

Singh, Bābū Amīr (ed.), *Raskhān aur Ghanānand*, Banaras: Nāgrī Prachāriṇī Sabhā, 1956.

Snell, R., *The Hindi Classical Tradition: A Braj Bhāṣā Reader*, London: School of Oriental and African Studies, University of London, 1993.

Tripāṭhī, Rāmpher, *Ghanānand-kāvya-kirīṭ*, Lucknow: Prakāśan Kendr, 1992.

PART XII

The Ritual and the Popular Two Ways of Interpreting Devotion in Modern Times

Devotional Poetry in Performance: *Samājagāyana* at the Temple of Śrī Rādhāramaṇa in Vrindaban

SELINA THIELEMANN

Music and singing are essential components of the ritual service in most religious traditions in the world. The musical practice of the Vaiṣṇava temples derives its legitimation from numerous instructions provided by the scriptures, in particular by the *Bhāgavata Purāṇa* which propagates singing and dancing as the primary modes of worship. According to the *Bhāgavata Purāṇa*, musical performances in the temple should include song, dance and instrumental music (11.11.36), and the repertoire of songs should comprise both hymns found in the ancient texts and verses in the current language (11.27.45). Narration and enactment of the deeds of the Lord represent further significant elements of the ritual service (11.11.23, 11.11.36, 11.19.20, 11.27.44), besides various kinds of offering that are normally accompanied by songs of praise (11.3.52-3). The present paper shall provide insights into the practical realization of the scriptural instructions with regard to music, exemplified in the musical tradition of the temple of Śrī Rādhāramaṇa in Vrindaban.[1]

In the Vaiṣṇava temples of Vraja, musical performances take place in the setting of congregational singing known as *samājagāyana*, conveniently

[1] This paper is presented in the form of a report rather than as an analysis for two reasons. Firstly, the aim is to disprove the widespread but wrong notion that the Caitanya Sampradāya does not own a musical tradition other than *saṃkīrtana* in Bengali style. It is my intention, therefore, to fill the gap in the hitherto existing academic study of Vraja music by introducing the tradition of daily *kīrtana* and congregational singing (*samājagāyàna*) in a Caitanyite temple of Vraja. Secondly, the temple of Rādhāramaṇa has maintained the practice of *kīrtana* singing to accompany the ritual worship throughout the entire day. Daily *kīrtana* is otherwise performed only in temples of the Vallabha Sampradāya. The documentation contained in this paper points thus at a unique tradition not found in any other non-Vallabhite temple. Detailed analyses of the collected material, including transcriptions of selected musical examples into Indian and Western notations, are presented in my new accounts (Thielemann 1999, pp. 50-133; and in preparation).

shortened *samāja*. *Samājagāyana* involves a relatively small group of musicians, comprising the lead singer or mukhiyā, and a chorus of five to ten other singers called samājīs, who provide also the instrumental accompaniment of the performance. Three instruments are indispensable in every *samāja*: a harmonium to support the melody, frequently played by the lead singer himself, furthermore the wooden double-conical drum *pakhāvaja* or *mṛdaṅga* to provide the rhythmic accompaniment, and a pair of small cymbals called *mañjīrā*, *jhāñjha* or *kinnarī* to indicate the metric beat. *Samājagāyana* is performed on the basis of comprehensive poetic repertoires compiled in printed textbooks or *pada saṃgraha*s as well as in temple manuscripts; these repertoires contain the appropriate verses for the daily ritual service as well as for seasonal events and major religious festivals. The verses are sung on the basis of musical compositions consisting of strophic sections. Each song is set to a specific melody type or *rāga*, and composed within the frame of a metric cycle or *tāla*. In the course of the performance, the verses are presented line by line, first by the lead singer and thereafter repeated by the chorus of samājīs.

Samājagāyana in the setting just described takes place in the five major Vaiṣṇava communities that use Vrajabhāṣā for their language. Among these, the *samājagāyana* tradition of the Caitanya Sampradāya represents a branch of the *samāja* tradition in Vraja that has been given rather little scholarly attention so far. This negligence may have initially resulted from a tendency of overemphasizing the Bengali element within the musical tradition of the Caitanya Sampradāya. Nevertheless, the Sampradāya not only owns an abundant tradition of devotional poetry in Vrajabhāṣā, but has also a flourishing tradition of *samājagāyana* that continues to the present day. In Vrindaban, *samājagāyana* of the Caitanya Sampradāya is performed at the temples of Bhaṭṭa-jī and of Rādhāramaṇa. At the former, *samāja* takes place on a daily basis during the festive seasons; this tradition is maintained by the descendants of the sixteenth century Caitanyite poet Gadādhara Bhaṭṭa whose poetry features prominently in the performances. *Samājagāyana* at the temple of Rādhāramaṇa-jī — the subject of the present paper — is conducted by Shri Purushottam Goswami-jī Mahārāj, the foremost leader of the Caitanya Sampradāya. The performances are held twice a year, during the festivals of Holī and Janmāṣṭamī, and each series of *samāja* performances lasts for seven days concluding on the day on which the respective festival proper is celebrated.[2] The seasonal

[2] The performances for Janmāṣṭamī begin officially in the evening of the first day of the dark half of Bhādrapada (August-September), but in practice, the

samājagāyana apart, musical performances accompany also the daily ritual service at the temple of Rādhāramaṇa. The present paper shall not, as the title suggests, limit itself to the seasonal *samāja* performances, but is intended to provide as comprehensive as possible an overview over the various types and styles of music presented at the temple of Rādhāramaṇa in the daily service as well as on seasonal occasions.

The seasonal *samāja* performances at Janmāṣṭamī and Holī are held during the early evening period, between *utthāpana* and *sandhyā āratī*, lasting for about one hour. The poetic repertoires sung in these performances comprise both verses of Caitanyite poets handed down in manuscripts kept by the Gosvāmī families, and verses of the *aṣṭachāpa* and other Vallabhite poets taken from printed verse collections. Interestingly, no printed editions other than the *kīrtana saṃgraha*s of the Vallabha Sampradāya are accepted for reference; thus, Shri Purushottam Goswami-jī Mahārāj rejects for example the *Śṛṅgāra-rasa-sāgara* of the Rādhāvallabha Sampradāya as being *aśuddha*.[3] For the *samāja* performances at Janmāṣṭamī, a *sevā* manual titled *janmāṣṭamī ki badhāī* is used, which contains the *maṅgalācaraṇa* and a number of significant verses that are repeated every day. There is no such manual for the performances at Holī; here, the *maṅgalācaraṇa* is taken from a manuscript, and the other verses can be found in the various Vallabhite textbooks. The concrete choice of verses sung on a specific day may be determined by a particular event taking place on that day—thus, a verse referring to the Holī festival at Barsana will be sung on the actual day when Holī is celebrated in Barsana—but in many cases the verses are chosen according to spontaneous inspiration, though always within the proper repertoire. A typical *samāja* performance for Holī is opened with a verse of *maṅgalācaraṇa*, followed by one or two extended verses lasting for about twenty-five minutes to half an hour each. Thereafter, one or more shorter verses may be presented before the performance is concluded with a few *rasīā* songs, the characteristic genre for the season of Holī. The *samāja* at Janmāṣṭamī, too, opens with the

---

opening performance is held in a rather private setting the night before, after *śayana āratī* on the full-moon day of Śrāvaṇa. On this occasion, only the *maṅgalācaraṇa* is sung.

[3] Though Shri Purushottam Goswami-jī Mahārāj did not mention explicitly as to why he regards the textbook in question as *aśuddha*, the reason has to be looked for in readings of some of the verses contained in *Śṛṅgāra-rasa-sāgara* that differ considerably from the readings of the same verses contained in manuscripts kept by the Gosvāmī families of the Rādhāramaṇa temple.

maṅgalācaraṇa, followed by *badhāī*s or songs of congratulation. As regards the Janmāṣṭamī performances, a change in the structure could be observed during the past three years. Thus, during the 1994 sequence of performances, about six to eight verses lasting for five to fifteen minutes each were sung per day, whereas in recent years the tendency changed towards centring the performance around one extended verse, which is thereafter followed by one or two shorter songs, as in the Holī performances. The following brief example may suggest an impression of the singing style in *samāja* performances at the Rādhāramaṇa temple. The verse belongs to the poetic repertoire sung for Janmāṣṭamī and was recorded during the 1994 sequence of Janmāṣṭamī *samāja* performances.

Example 1. *nanda rāya jū kī paurī badhāī lāī māliniyā*
0:50 Rādhāramaṇa samāja, 29 August 1994
recording: collection Selina Thielemann
Śrī Caitanya Prema Saṃsthāna

The remaining part of this paper shall deal with musical performances in the daily ritual service at the temple of Rādhāramaṇa, illustrated on the basis of musical examples. In order to obtain a complete impression, both the daily schedule and the musical examples are taken from the twenty-two days of service performed by Shri Purushottam Goswami-jī Mahārāj, during which a maximum variety of musical activities was offered, exactly in accordance with the instructions given by the *Bhāgavata Purāṇa*. Both local singers and guest musicians took part in the celebrations. The daily *samāja kīrtana*, i.e. the songs to accompany the ritual worship throughout the day, was performed by Pandit Chandra Prakash from Ajmer in Rajasthan, one of the leading singers of devotional music in *havelī saṃgīta* style. A group of about 30 musicians performing *saṃkīrtana* had come from Orissa. Hindustānī classical music was represented by *dhrupada* singer Pandit Vidur Mallik from Vrindaban and his son Prem Kumar from Allahabad. The list of local musicians included *rāsadhārī* Svāmī Fatekrishna Sharma from Vrindaban and the *havelī saṃgīta* performer Haribabu Kaushik from Mathura, as well as a number of singers who perform at the temple of Rādhāramaṇa on a daily basis. Professional musicians apart, the devotees, too, took their turn in rendering *bhajanas* and songs of praise. Thus, from the early morning to the late evening, every single ritual act was accompanied by music. The textual basis for the daily *kīrtana* was provided by a thirteen-page manual or *nitya-sevā praṇālī* (system of daily worship) compiled by Shrivatsa Goswami, which contains the most important verses for *aṣṭayāma sevā* as well as verses for *phūla baṅgalā* (flower throne), *snāna yātrā* (festival of bathing) and *ratha yātrā* (chariot festival), i.e. the major seasonal celebrations held during the period of the temple service. This *nitya-sevā praṇālī* forms the textual basis for daily *kīrtana* at the temple of Rādhāramaṇa throughout the year. For each verse, both the time of singing and the *rāga* are indicated. In addition to the *nitya-sevā praṇālī*, printed verse collections of the Vallabha Sampradāya were consulted.

The daily schedule presents itself as follows:

The temple opens at about 4:30 a.m. The Bengali temple servant presents a few songs to awaken the deity, in Bengali language, accompanying himself on cymbals and the double-conical drum *khola*, during the pre-*darśana* period before *maṅgalā āratī*.

Example 2. Bengali verse sung by the temple servant before
0:48 *maṅgalā āratī*
Rādhāramaṇa sevā, 4 July 1997
recording: Śrī Caitanya Prema Saṃsthāna[4]

At the middle gate of the temple compound, a *śahanāī* (oboe) begins to play tunes in rāga Bhairava, a melody type for the early morning period, while drums play at the outer entrance gate of the temple.

Example 3. *śahanāī* playing at the middle gate before *maṅgalā*
0:24 *āratī*, rāga Bhairava
Rādhāramaṇa sevā, 4 July 1997
recording: Śrī Caitanya Prema Saṃsthāna

Just before *maṅgalā āratī*, the group of musicians from Orissa render a song, in Bengali language, to awaken the deity. They accompany their performance on *khola*s, cymbals, clappers and other idiophones.

Example 4. *saṃkīrtana*: song (in Bengali) to awaken the deity
0:52 Rādhāramaṇa sevā, 1 July 1997
recording: Śrī Caitanya Prema Saṃsthāna

Maṅgalā āratī takes place at about 5 a.m. Thereafter, the women devotees sing the second composition (*prabandha* 2) from Jayadeva's *Gīta Govinda*, in Sanskrit.

[4]The recordings were made by me on behalf of Śrī Caitanya Prema Saṃsthāna. I am very grateful to Shrivatsa Goswami for giving his consent to present these musical examples at the conference.

Example 5. verse from *prabandha 2* of the *Gīta Govinda*, sung after
0:30 *maṅgalā āratī*
Rādhāramaṇa sevā, 4 July 1997
recording: Śrī Caitanya Prema Saṃsthāna

From 6 a.m., the *Bhāgavata Purāṇa* is read by about forty pandits sitting in the temple courtyard. The reading continues until 8:30 a.m., followed by twenty minutes of congregational singing to the accompaniment of harmonium, cymbals and *khola* performed by the pandits. The verses sung during this presentation are in Sanskrit, such as the *Madhurāṣṭakam* of Vallabhācārya, or the *Gopī Gīta* from the *Bhāgavata Purāṇa*, but the textbook referred to is written in Bengali.

Example 6. recitation of the *Bhāgavata Purāṇa* (beginning of *Gopī*
0:40/0:44 *Gīta* and *kīrtana* after *Bhāgavata* recitation (*Gopī Gīta* repeated)
Rādhāramaṇa sevā, 6 July 1997
recording: Śrī Caitanya Prema Saṃsthāna

Following the recitation of the *Bhāgavata Purāṇa*, the daily *samāja kīrtana* in the style of Vaiṣṇava devotional music known as *havelī saṃgīta* opens with *maṅgalācaraṇa* and verses for *bāla āratī* (also referred to as *dhūpa āratī* because incense is offered to the deity), which is performed at about 9 a.m. These verses are sung in morning *rāga*s such as Bhairava, Ahīra Bhairava, Devagandhāra, Rāmakalī, Bilāvala, Āsāvarī and Bhairavī. The singer renders these verses soloistically, supporting himself melodically on the harmonium and accompanied by the bowed lute *sāraṅgī*, the drum *pakhāvaja* and the *jhāñjha*, or cymbals. Two verses are compulsory at *dhūpa āratī*. The first verse, of Guṇamañjarī, is sung immediately after the ceremony:

अगर धूप कौ धूम सुहायौ।
चन्दनचूर कपूर उसीरन, मिलि कुञ्जन नव घन सों छायौ।
हेम आरती बाती बिजुरी, रव घंटा गरजन मनभायौ।
गुणमञ्जरी मोर कुहकत हैं, निरखि श्री राधारमण सचु पायौ।

The pleasant smoke of aloe incense,
sandalwood powder, camphor, grass — these are mixed in the groves in the shade of fresh clouds.
A golden *āratī* [is arranged with] lamps of lightnings, the sound of a bell of roaring thunder appears pleasing to the mind;
peacocks are crying, Guṇamañjarī attains delight at lord Rādhāramaṇa's sight.

It is common to render this verse in rāga Bilāvala. The second verse, that follows afterwards, is an invocation directed to Śrī Caitanya (*gaura-candrikā*), which is most often sung in rāga Bhairava:

महाप्रभु तुम परम उदार।
अद्भुत रीति तुम्हारी देखी, पतितन के तुम अति रिझवार।।
ये ही आसा लागि रही प्रभु, और नहीं मेरे आधार।
जगन्नाथसुत परदज बन्दीं, दीजै प्रेम भक्ति विस्तार॥

O great lord, you are of utmost generosity;
your sight is of remarkable kind, you feel extreme delight at the fallen ones.
May this base take root, O Lord, I need no other support;
[I am wearing] the dust of Jagannātha's son's feet as a forehead ornament,
may you grant loving devotion to expand.

Around 9:30 a.m., *darśana* closes for *śṛṅgāra bhoga*, the morning meal, for which the singer presents a number of *kalevā* verses. The *nitya-sevā praṇālī* quotes three verses for *śṛṅgāra bhoga*. The first two verses, both of Guṇamañjarī, are sung in rāga Bilāvala:

भोग मधुर आयौ श्रृंगार, जेंवत श्री राधारमणलाल।
मोतीचूर मगद के लड्डू, गुझिया मठरी फैनी सुहार॥
सेब सकरपारे तिरकोना, मधुर सलौने कंचन थार।
बूँदी मोहनभोग जलेबी, सरस इमरती अति रुचिकार॥
बेढई बेसन टिकिया टेंटी, कचरी लौंजी बिबिध अचार।
प्राणपियारी श्रीकर परसत, गुणमञ्जरी नव स्वाद अपार॥

The sweet morning meal has come, darling Rādhāramaṇa partakes of food:
sweets of crystallized sugar, flour sweets, sweet flour balls, pastries, sweet cakes,
fried pastries and triangular pastries;
apples, all placed in triangular shape on a sweet, charming, golden plate;
drops of soft sweet, pretzel-shaped sweets, juicy pulse-sweets very much to
stimulate the appetite;
different varieties of bread-cake, *karīla* fruits, small melons, pickled mango slices
and various kinds of pickles;
with his fair hand, he serves the food to his beloved — Guṇamañjarī [delights
himself] in unbounded fresh relish.

भोग श्रृंगार श्री राधारमणजू, आरोगत कुञ्जन संकेत।
अपनी प्राण पिया कू निरखत, परसत त्रिस नहीं द्रिग चेत॥
दाड़म नारंगी आदिक फल, मेवा माखन सिता समेत।
कछुक लै श्रीजमुनाजल, सुवरन झारी भर मुख लेत॥
अचमन के श्रीमुख हस्तन पद, पोंछत हैं सुंदर पट स्वेत।
नवनागरी रहस अधरामृत, चाखत कछु गुणमञ्जरी देत॥

Lord Rādhāramaṇa enjoys his morning meal in the grove's meeting-place;
the eye cannot feel satiation in seeing his beloved.
Pomegranates, oranges and other fruits, dry fruit, butter, together with candied sugar;
take a little Jamunā water — he takes a mouthful from a golden pitcher.
He rinses the mouth, fair face, hands and feet, and wipes them with a beautiful white cloth;
the young skilful one, merrily with the nectar of his lips, relishes the food and gives a little to Guṇamañjarī.

The third verse, of Sūrdāsa Madanamohana, is sung in rāga Āsāvarī, Bhairava or Bhairavī on completion of the first two verses:

छगन मगन प्यारेलाल कीजिये कलेवा ॥
छींक सों माखन दधि, ऊखल चढ़ि काढ़ि लेओ।
पहरि लेओ झंगुलि फेंट, बाँधि लेओ मेवा ॥
ग्वालन संग खेलन जाओ, खेलत खेलत न अघाओ।
कौंन सी परी है लाल, निसदिन की टेवा ॥
सूरश्याम मदनमोहन, घरहि क्यों न खेलौ लाल।
भौंरा चकडोर देंहों, हंस मोर परेवा ॥

Tasting and relishing, the darling boy eats his morning meal —
take butter and curd from the pot, thickened with the mortar;
put on garment and waistband, having tied them, take dry fruit;
go to play together with the cowherds, and do not grow tired in the course of playing.
Which beautiful girl is it, darling, written in your horoscope day and night?
O Sūra's Śyāma, enchanter of Madana, why don't you play at home, darling — seeing the whirling of the top makes laugh peacock and dove.

Example 7. verse *chagana magana pyāre lāla kījiye kalevā* (Sūradāsa
0:40 Madanamohana, rāga Āsāvarī)
samāja kīrtana by Pandit Chandra Prakash and party
Rādhāramaṇa sevā, 29 June 1997
recording: Śrī Caitanya Prema Saṃsthāna

Śṛṅgāra āratī takes place around 10 a.m., accompanied by *saṃkīrtana*. Thereafter, the musicians from Orissa continue to perform *saṃkīrtana* as long as *śṛṅgāra darśana* remains open.

Example 8. *saṃkīrtana* after *śṛṅgāra āratī*
0:32 Rādhāramaṇa sevā, 6 July 1997
recording: Śrī Caitanya Prema Saṃsthāna

As *śṛṅgāra darśana* closes, Shri Purushottam Goswami-jī Mahārāj comes to the rear platform to give a sermon of about one hour until *rājabhoga āratī*, which is again accompanied by *saṃkīrtana*. (In case there is no sermon after *śṛṅgāra darśana*, this period is reserved for *samāja kīrtana* in which *rājabhoga* verses in rāgas Dhanāśri and Sāraṅga are sung to accompany the midday meal.) Following *rājabhoga āratī*, the *kīrtana* singer presents a daily verse, *baiṭhe hari rādhā saṅga*, in rāga Sāraṅga. The verse belongs to the *kuñja* repertoire describing the divine couple enjoying each other's company in the bower.

बैठे हरि राधा संग कुँज भवन अपने रँग, कर मुरली अधर धरें सारंग मुख गाई।
मोहन अति सुजान परम चतुर गुण निधान, जानबूझ एक तान चूक कें बजाई॥
प्यारी तब गह्यौ बीन सकल कला गुण प्रवीन, रूप सोहत अति नवीन तान वह सुनाई।
श्रीवल्लभ गिरधरनलाल रीझ दई अंक माल कहत भलेजू भले सुंदर सुखदाई॥

Hari sits together with Rādhā in his beautiful forest abode, with his hands holding the flute to his lower lip, singing a charming tune.
Mohana, very wise and extremely clever, a treasure of virtues, with knowledge and understanding, oversees one note in his play.
At this, the beloved woman grasps the *vīṇā*, and, proficient and accomplished in all arts, she renders a very new melody, full of beauty.
Śrīvallabha's darling boy Giridhara, with delight, embraces her, saying 'very well, excellent and pleasant indeed'.

Thereafter, at about 12:30 p.m., the temple closes for the afternoon siesta. During the entire morning period, as well as during the evening services, oboe and drums play at the outer temple gate to announce that ritual worship is taking place inside the temple. This practice, which is still compulsory in south Indian temples, is nowadays no more common in north India. In Vrindaban, it can be observed at the temple of Rādhāramaṇa at least on festive occasions.

Example 9. oboe and drums playing at the outer gate, after
0:42 *rājabhoga darśana*
Rādhāramaṇa sevā, 6 July 1997
recording: Śrī Caitanya Prema Saṃsthāna

Around 5 p.m., the temple re-opens, and verses in the afternoon *rāga* Pūrīya are sung during the pre-*darśana* period before *utthāpana*. At that time, it is common to render the *dhrupada* (*āge gāya pache gāya*), based on a verse of Chītasvāmī.

आगें गाय पाछें गाय इत गाय उत गाय गोविंदकों गायनमें बसवौई भावै।
गायनके संग धावें गायनमें सचुपावें गायनकी खुररज अंग लपटावें॥

गायन सों वृज छायो वैकुंठ विसरायो गायनके हेत गिरि करलें उठावै।
छीतस्वामी गिरधारी विट्ठलेश वपुधारी ग्वालिया को भेषधरें गायनमें आवै॥

Cows ahead and behind, cows here and there — it suits Govinda to dwell with the cows.
He roams together with the cows, he attains delight amidst the cows, he smears his limbs with the dust of the cows' hooves.
Because of the cows he has settled in Vraja and forgotten about Vaikuṇṭha, for the cows' sake he lifted the mountain with his hand.
Chīta's lord Giridhārī, who has taken the body of Viṭṭhaleśa, comes in the disguise of a cowherd, surrounded by the cows.

Example 10. verse *āge gāya pache gāya* (Chītasvāmī, rāga Pūriyā)
0:44 *samāja kīrtana* by Pandit Chandra Prakash and party
Rādhāramaṇa sevā, 1 July 1997
recording: Śrī Caitanya Prema Saṃsthāna

The evening *dhūpa āratī* (i.e. *utthāpana*) is performed around 5:30 p.m. Thereafter, verses for *utthāpana* and *āvanī* are sung. The *nitya-sevā praṇālī* quotes two verses for this period, *kadamacaṛha kānha bulāvata gaiyā* of Govinda Svāmī, in rāga Gorī, and *dekhau gopāla ki āvanī* of Paramānanda Dāsa, in rāga Pūrvī.

कदमचढ़ कान्ँह बुलावत गैया॥
मोह न मुरली कौ शब्द सुनतही जहाँ तहाँते उठ धैया।।
आवो आवो सखासंग के सब पाईहें इक ठैया।।
गोविन्द प्रभु बलदाऊ सों कहन लागे अब घरकों बगदैया॥

Kānha steps out to call the cows;
without bewilderment, hearing the sound of the flute, from here and there, [all] get up and set themselves into motion;
they are coming, together with the companions, all feet plunging into [one movement];
it appears as if Govinda's lord says to Balarāma: let us return home.

देखौ गोपाल की आवनी॥
कमलनेंन श्यामसुंदर सूरत मन भावनी॥
वरुहा चंद सीस मुकट गुंजा मन लावनी॥
परमानंद स्वामी गुपाल अंग अंग नचावनी॥

Look at Gopāla's coming —
the beautiful, lotus-eyed, dark one's embodiment delights the heart;
peacock-feathers and the moon on his head, [wearing] a crown and earrings, he appeals to the mind;
Paramānanda's lord Gopāla sets every limb a-dancing.

At *sandhyā āratī*, the verse *laṭakata calata juvatī sukhadānī* of Caturabhuja Dāsa is sung. The *nitya-sevā praṇālī* indicates rāga Sāraṅga for this verse, but the song may be rendered in other *rāga*s such as Kalāvatī, Malhāra (during the rainy season) and Gaurī.

लटकत चलत जुवती सुखदानी ।।
संध्या समें सखा मंडल में सोभित तन गोरज लपटानी ॥
मोर मुकट गुंजा पियारो पट मुख मुरली गुंजत मृदुबानी ।।
चत्रभुजप्रभु गिरधारी आये बनते लै आरती वारत नँदरानी ॥

The pleasant young women walk with swinging gait;
at evening twilight time, the beautiful, fair bodies come together in the circle of friends.
The beloved [wears] the peacock-feather crown, earrings and garment, the flute at his mouth resounds in sweet tunes;
Nanda's queen offers *ārati* to Caturabhuja's lord Giridhārī who arrives from the forest.

Sandhyā āratī takes place after 7 p.m. and is followed by about ten minutes of *kīrtana* in praise of Gopāla Bhaṭṭa, the Gosvāmī to whom the deity of Rādhāramaṇa revealed himself in the 16th century. This hymn is sung by the devotees.

Example 11. *kīrtana* singing by the devotees, after *sandhyā āratī*
0:40 Rādhāramaṇa sevā, 5 July 1997
recording: Śrī Caitanya Prema Saṃsthāna

Thereafter, the musicians from Orissa take their turn once more to perform *saṃkīrtana*. Meanwhile, *aulāī darśana* is prepared, at which Rādhāramaṇa-jī can be seen in his informal household dress (*aulāī*), before taking his evening meal. As *aulāī darśana* opens, around 8:30 p.m., the *kīrtana* singer reassumes his performance by presenting a verse of Guṇamañjarī that describes the beautiful appearance of Rādhāramaṇa in his casual dress, followed by *phūla* verses describing the beauty of the deity seated in a palace of flowers. These verses are sung in evening *rāga*s such as Hamīra and Yamana. The verse of Guṇamañjarī is compulsory at *aulāī darśana*:

बनी है आज अनुपम झांकी।
राधारमणलालजी की सखि औलाई तनयाँकी।
अँग अँग भीजे अतरन में धारी कुलही बाँकी।
गुणमँजरी हिये में बैठी चपल नैन अनियाँ की॥

How beautiful is this unparalleled sight today! —
dear Rādhāramaṇa's intimate household dress has been put on;
every limb is wet from perfumes, he wears a smart cap;
Guṇamañjarī [says] the restless eyes of his face settle down in the heart.

Example 12. verse *banī hai āja anupama jhāṃkī* (Guṇamañjarī, rāga
0:44 Yamana)
samāja kīrtana by Pandit Chandra Prakash and party
Rādhāramaṇa sevā, 22 June 1997
recording: Śrī Caitanya Prema Saṃsthāna

Around 9 p.m., *darśana* closes for *vyālū bhoga*, the evening meal, for which two verses, *mohana lāla viyārū kījai* of Āsakarana and *rādhāramaṇa biyālū kījai* of Guṇamañjarī, are sung, both in rāga Bāgeśrī. Like the verses for *sṛṅgāra bhoga* quoted earlier, these verses, too, consist of an enumeration of various kinds of food offered to the deity for his meal.

Example 13. verse *mohana lāla viyārū kījai* (Āsakarana, rāga Bāgeśrī)
0:56 *samāja kīrtana* by Pandit Chandra Prakash and party
Rādhāramaṇa sevā, 15 June 1997
recording: Śrī Caitanya Prema Saṃsthāna

The remaining period until *darśana* re-opens is reserved for *rāsa* verses in rāga Kedāra. *Bhoga kā darśana* is followed by *dūdha bhoga* and *bīrī bhoga*, the offerings of milk and betel. For the former, two verses are sung: *aba dūdha lāī jasodā maiyā* of Āsakarana and *hãsa hãsa dūdha pīvata nātha*, both in rāga Bihāga.

अब दूध लाई जसोदी मैया।
आछो नीको औट सिरायो तामें मधुर मलैया।
पान करो मेरे कुँवर लाढिले बैनी बढ़ेगी तेरी छैया।
आसकरन प्रभु मोहन नागर प्रात करूँगी उठ धैया॥

Now, mother Yaśodā has brought the milk;
well-boiled and cooled down, with a sweet skimming on it.
Drink, my darling son, it will make you grow;
o skilful Mohana, Āsakarana's lord, in the morning I shall wake you up in time.

हँस हँस दूध पीवत नाथ॥
मधुर कोमल वचन कहि कहि प्राण प्यारी साथ॥
कनक कटोरा भर्‌यौ अमृत सों लिये ललिताजु हाथ॥
लाढ़िली अँचवाय पहिलै पाछें आप अघात॥
चिंतामणि चित बस्यौरी सजनी नाहिंन और सुहात॥
श्रीराधारमण जुगलछवि पै, रसिकजन बलि जात॥

Smilingly, the lord drinks the milk;
together with his beloved, they converse in sweet, gentle words.
He takes a golden bowl full of nectar from Lalitā's hand;
the darling girl rinses her mouth, before and afterwards, with self-satisfaction.
Having placed the wish-granting jewel in her heart, the sweetheart does not cherish any other desires —
the devotees offer themselves up at the beauty of the couple with lord Rādhāramaṇa.

For the offering of betel, one verse is compulsory: *bīrī leo mere karasõ lālana*, again in rāga Bihāga (occasionally, this verse is sung in rāga Bāgeśrī). Thereafter, about 10 p.m., the last *darśana* of the day opens and *śayana āratī* is performed, accompanied by tunes in rāga Bihāga. After *śayana āratī*, two verses of Śrībhaṭṭa Deva and Vīṭhala Vipula Dāsa respectively are sung: *basaũ mere nainana mẽ doū canda* and *padhāriye piya paīyā*. Finally, the daily cycle is concluded with a number of *āśraya* and *binatī* verses such as *bharõso dṛṛha ina caranana kero* of Sūradāsa, *piyā toya nẽnana hī mẽ rākhõ* of Harirāya (Rasika Prītama), and *aho bidhinā topẽ añcarā pasāri mā̃gõ* of Chītasvāmī. These verses are rendered in rāga Bihāga, since no other *rāga* is permitted to be sung after *śayana āratī*.

Example 14. verse *bharõso dṛṛha ina caranana kero* (Sūradāsa,
0:48 rāga Bihāga) sung by Pandit Chandra Prakash
Rādhāramaṇa sevā, 6 July 1997
recording: Śrī Caitanya Prema Saṃsthāna

The schedule of daily musical items accompanying the ritual worship leaves yet enough space for guest musicians to perform. Thus, during Shri Purushottam Goswami-jī Mahārāj's *sevā*, Pandit Vidur Mallik gave regular presentations of classical *dhrupada* and *khyāla* singing, both in the morning and in the evening. Time for such additional performances is available particularly during the pre-*darśana* periods before *śṛṅgāra āratī* in the morning and before *sandhyā āratī* in the evening, as well as during the more extended *darśanas* such as *bāla* and *utthāpana*. On festive days, the evening schedule is slightly modified. On such days, an additional *utsava āratī* takes place before *sandhyā āratī*, and there is no *aulāī darśana*. During the extended *darśana* lasting for about one and a half hours from *utthāpana* until *vyālū bhoga*, specific verses referring to the concrete festive occasion are presented, and at Holī, the *samājagāyana* performances are held during that period.

It was said earlier that the schedule of musical events accompanying the ritual service at the temple of Rādhāramaṇa in the form just presented offers a maximum variety of items, and that it had been specifically arranged during the twenty-two days of service performed by Shri Purushottam Goswami-jī Mahārāj. However, at other times, too, music accompanies the worship during most periods of the day even without special arrangements. In the early morning, the Bengali temple servant performs *kīrtana* during pre-*darśana* before *maṅgalā āratī*. The daily *kīrtana* verses sung between *śṛṅgāra bhoga* and *rājabhoga* in the morning and from *sandhyā āratī* to *śayana āratī* in the evening are rendered by a temple singer who attends to the service every day. The compulsory verses at *bāla darśana* and after *rājabhoga āratī*, as well as the *utthāpana* verses are sung by one of the Gosvāmīs. For these daily items, there is no instrumental accompaniment available, and the singers confine themselves to melodic support on the harmonium. The only exception is the period before *sandhyā āratī*, when a larger group of musicians, including an old temple singer and a number of instrumentalists contributing accompaniment on *tablā*, flute and cymbals, gather to perform evening songs.[5] The *āratī* ceremonies are generally accompanied by *kīrtana* singing by the devotees. *Sandhyā āratī* is followed by the daily *kīrtana* in praise of Gopāla Bhaṭṭa, following which the devotees sing Bengali *kīrtana* to the accompaniment of *khola* and cymbals while circumambulating the two tulasī stands in the courtyard for another approximately five minutes. At *śayana āratī*, one of the Gosvāmīs plays tunes in rāga Bihāga on the flute.

To conclude this paper, I would like to present one musical example to demonstrate the expressiveness in Shri Purushottam Goswami-jī Mahārāj's performances. The verse belongs to the daily repertoire, and is sung in the evening at the time of *bīrī bhoga*, the offering of betel, just before the last *darśana* opens. The verse reads as follows:

बीरो लेओ मेरे करसों लालन। बीरी . . .
नागर पान सुगन्ध सुपाड़ी तुमहि को लाई में धरकैं।
मुक्ता को चूना कत्था इलायची लोंग सुपाड़ी धरकैं।

[5] Since August 1997, all daily verses from *bāla* to *śayana* are sung by Tarun Krishna Das, a senior disciple of *dhrupada* artist Pandit Vidur Mallik. He accompanies himself on the harmonium; *tablā* accompaniment is provided at most times by the temple musician who originally used to sing the verses between *śṛṅgāra bhoga* and *rājabhoga* and between *sandhyā āratī* and *śayana āratī*. With the introduction of Tarun Krishna Das, for the first time, a singer is available who attends to the entire daily cycle on a regular basis. He renders the daily verses on the basis of the *nitya-sevā praṇālī* compiled by Shrivatsa Goswami, which contains selected texts for all periods of the day.

लालन आछौ पावो मुख भरके दासन कों दीजै उगार प्रभु।
विनती करूँ पग परकै॥ लालन बीरी . . .

Take the folded betel leaf from my hand, darling.
Just for you I have kept and brought courtly betel leaves and fragrant betel nuts;
pearls of lime, catechu, cardamom, cloves and betel nuts.
Eat well, darling, filling the mouth, and give the spittle to the slaves, O Lord;
I bow at thy feet.

The song is set to rāga Bihāga and its presentation lasts for about five minutes. In the present performance, it is rendered jointly by Pandit Chandra Prakash and Shri Purushottam Goswami-jī Mahārāj, accompanied by cymbals, *pakhāvaja*, harmonium, *sāraṅgī* and *śahanāī*. In the course of the performance, the respective verse-lines are repeated several times in order to enhance the effect of the poetic word, and, as a peculiarity of the present performance, the text is altered at times for the sake of utmost expressiveness.

Example 15. verse *bīrī leo mere karasõ lālana* (rāga Bihāga)
7:14 Rādhāramaṇa sevā, 4 July 1997
recording: Śrī Caitanya Prema Saṃsthāna

In conclusion, it may be appropriate to draw attention once again to the scriptural instructions regarding the performance of music and dance in the temple. Verse 11.11.36 of the *Bhāgavata Purāṇa* indicates that the ways of worship on festive occasions should include the recitation of 'pleasing stories of me and my incarnations and deeds' as well as the celebration of 'festivals in my temple with song, dance, instrumental music and discourses': *maj-janma-karma-kathanaṃ mama parvānumodanam, gīta-tāṇḍava-vāditra-goṣṭhībhir mad-gṛhotsavaḥ*. The daily schedule of ritual service at the temple of Rādhāramaṇa contains recitation of the *Bhāgavata Purāṇa* and discourses, as well as a rich variety of musical presentations. Among the latter, song forms the principal component. Instrumental music is represented by the instrumental accompaniment of the song performances, by the signal instruments (*śahanāī* and drums) that play at the outer temple gate to announce the ritual worship inside the temple, and by occasional soloistic performances of melody instruments such as *sitāra*, *sāraṅgī* or flute. Dance, too, takes many forms, ranging from classical *kathaka* dance presented in soloistic setting to spontaneous dancing of the devotees at the sight of the deity. *Saṃkīrtana* is attributed particular significance inasmuch as it comprises all three essential components of worship, i.e. song, dance and instrumental music. The *Bhāgavata Purāṇa* (11.27.45) prescribes further that the songs presented in praise of the deity should include 'hymns found in ancient texts as well as in the current language': *stavair uccāvacaiḥ stotraiḥ paurāṇaiḥ prākṛtair api*. This indication, too, is followed in the daily ritual service at the temple of Rādhāramaṇa. The repertoire of songs comprises Sanskrit verses, including texts from the *Bhāgavata Purāṇa* such as the *Gopī Gīta*, as well as devotional poetry in Vrajabhāṣā and Bengali, and each repertoire is sung in its own characteristic musical style. The temple of Rādhāramaṇa is in fact the only temple in Vraja that maintains two parallel poetic and musical traditions, namely the Bengali tradition and the *samāja* tradition in Vrajabhāṣā, and an in-depth study of the rich musical heritage of this temple will be worthwhile and is intended to be undertaken and completed within the next two years.

REFERENCES

Thielemann, Selina, *Musical traditions of Vaiṣṇava temples in Vraja. A comparative study of samāja and the dhrupada tradition of North Indian classical music*, New Delhi: ABC Publishing House, 1999.

———, in preparation: *Songs of Worship. A musical anthology of the temple of Rādhāramaṇa in Vrindaban.*

Bhakti in Hindi Folktales

TEIJI SAKATA

FOLKTALES IN SOUTH ASIA

Story telling is still a living tradition in South Asia. Folktales are told, listened to and retold. We may observe folktale sessions in Hindi and other language areas of South Asia when we visit the courtyards of village folks and the living rooms of extended families in the cities, where menfolk enjoy adventure and fortune making stories and mothers tell animal folktales to their children for their behaviour guidance.

We have already a good amount of Hindi folktales published both in their original languages / dialects and in English translation. In addition to them, we find new collections of Hindi folktales being published from time to time. The present author has been colllecting and studying Hindi folktales since 1973 in the areas of the Khari Boli, Braj, Awadhi and Bhojpuri dialects. Some of them were translated into Japanese and warmly received by Japanese readers.

Some Hindi folktales are structurally very simple: the cunning jackal deceives innocent poeple and enjoys undue profits, but he is punished by the people. Some tales are comprehensive with a grand frame story including three to five episodes, which reminds us of Sanskrit story books such as *Śukasaptati, Hitopadeśa.*

The topics of Hindi folktales are various and will be studied later. Among the various topics of Hindi folktales, we sometimes come across topics which illustrate bhakti, one important way of the Hindus to obtain liberation from *saṃsāra*.

IMPORTANT TERMS TO BE EMLOYED IN THIS PAPER

Bhakti is to be understood as the devotional path, the doctorine of liberation as opposed to *karma*, *jñāna* (Stutley 1977: 41).

Devotional observances as aids to *bhakti* consist of *śravaṇam* — 'hearing' the praises of the deity; *vandanam* — 'praising' the deity and chanting his name; *smaraṇam* — 'remembering' deity at all times;

sevanam — 'serving' the deity by worship and doing good deeds in his name (Walker 1963, pp. 138-40).

As for the term Hindi, in general, the languages and dialects spoken in the so called Hindi belt from Rajasthani to Bhojpuri and Maithili are included, and more specifically the Hindi dialects covered by the source books given at the end of this paper are included. All the source books are published in either standard Hindi or one of the Hindi dialects except Sakata's books in Japanese translation. Sakata's books are based on his personal collection of Hindi folktales in tape-recorded form. Thus, all the material upon which this paper is based is originally told and published (recorded) in Hindi or its dialects.

POSITION OF BHAKTI IN THE WHOLE SCOPE OF FOLKTALES

It is of some interest for us students of South Asian devotional literature to examine and confirm the role bhakti plays in folktales. Although bhakti is a very important phase of present-day religious life of the Hindi-speaking people and the folktale is a living tradition of the people, the folktales related with bhakti occupy a rather limited portion.

We have an excellent handbook to survey the whole scope of South Asian folktales edited by Stith Thompson and E. Robert, titled *Indic Oral Tales* (Helsinki, 1960). In this handbook, 'Religious Tales' including folktales related with bhakti occupy only the types from 750 to 849B in the whole system extending from 1 to 2399.

Seven types of Hindi folktales are mentioned in Satyendra's *Braj lok sāhitya kā adhyayan* (Agra, 1957) as follows:

Extraordinary and entertaining tales — There was a king . . .
Tales related with castes — There was a Jāṭ and his wife . . .
Religious tales — Generosity of Śiva and Pārvatī.
Tales related with festivals — On the festival day of Karwā Cauth . . .
Tales related with faith — From where has Mount Govardhan come.
Tales explaining the meaning of proverbs.
Tales in or containing verses.

According to Satyendra, 'Religious Tales' (*dhārmik kathāẽ* in Satyendra's Hindi term) occupy one-seventh portion, and the third sphere of his classification.

The actual number of folktales related with bhakti is much more limited as we will see in the next section.

FOLKTALES ILLUSTRATING BHAKTI

Of the four hundred or so Hindi folktales reviewed in preparing the material for this paper, only the following fourteen folktales remain as having something to do with bhakti. Details of the sources are given at the end of this paper. It is quite clear that the proportion of bhakti folktales is very limited both in classification and actual number.

Here given are: the 'titles' (tentative ones by the present author to present the notion of the tales at a glance), (dialects in which the tales are told or recorded), and the synopses of the tales classified mainly by the central deity who appears in each tale. KB here is the abbreviation of Khari Boli dialect.

Indra

1 The faithful wife (Braj): Newly-wed daughter of a merchant washes Indra's garment. Indra gives her *amṛta.*

Viṣṇu

2 'Ṭhākurjī's idol enjoys the food' (Bhojpuri): The poor boy offers food for the first time to the idol. Living Ṭhākurjī appears in front of him and blesses him.
3 'The pious Vikramāditya' (Braj): The king becomes poor by giving away everything generously. Bhagvān (Viṣṇu?) extends help to him.

Śiva, Pārvatī and *Gaṇeśa* (Śiva often referred to as sādhu)

4 'Newly-wed brahman's wife' (KB): The wife offers food to Śiva, but she is murdered by a princess. Śiva gives magic medicine to her husband with which he revives his dead wife.
5 'Dead son recovers his life' (Bhojpuri): A merchant offers *khīr* to Śiva / sādhu (referred to in these two terms). The sādhu orders the dead son of the merchant to wake up and the son revives.
6 'Wealthy family of a Jāṭ' (KB): A Jāṭ offers the *khīr* prepared in the manner a sādhu requests. The sādhu / Śiva assures wealth to the Jāṭ's family.
7 'Poor younger sister' (KB): In the evening of Gaṇeś Cauth, the poor sister receives a poor boy in difficulty. The excrement of the boy/Gaṇeśa changes into gold the next morning.
8 'Poor younger brother' (Malvi): Even though short of fuel for cooking, the younger brother hesitates to burn the wooden idol of Gaṇapati. Gaṇapati blesses him with plenty of sweets.

9 'Faithful youngest sister' (Malvi): On the elder brother's advice, the younger sister worships Gaṇapati. Gaṇapati gives her magic power and fame.

Bhagvad Gītā
10 'Choose either Silver coins or the Holy Book' (Marwari): The youngest servant of a merchant choses the Book as gift. A gold coin happened to be contained in the BOOK, and he receives the coin also.

Viṣṇu is greater than Brahmā
11 'Brahmā in disguise as a frog' (Bhojpuri): In giving meaningless ill fortune to a poor farmer, Brahmā in disguise as a frog is caught and beaten by the farmer. Viṣṇu persuades the farmer to set Brahmā free.

Vaiṣṇava is more pious than Śaiva
12 'Who is pious?' (Braj): A wealthy devotee of Śiva rejects the humble request of two deities in disguise as wandering mendicants. A poor devotee of Viṣṇu does his best to give comfort to the two.

Man persuades the Goddess of Fate and succeeds in changing his fate
13 'Baimātā's decision changed' (Rajasthani): The goddess of fate determines the miserable lives of two princes. The family priest successfully persuades her to give them better future.
14 'Vidhātā Mātā's blessing' (Malvi): The king destined to die soon, is advised by a poor elderly lady to welcome and entertain the goddess of fate. The goddess allows him to live longer for the benefit of the people.

All this material reads as follows in the case of folktale no.1: The faithful wife or newly-wed daughter of a merchant washes Indra's garment, and Indra gives her *amṛta*. This tale was told in the Braj dialect.

Oversimplified synopsis fails to tell that (1) the newly-wed wife washed the garment of a stranger without knowing that he was Indra: she just served the stranger to relieve his difficulty, and (2) the *amṛta* given to her by Indra was served to her dead husband to give life again to him.

It will be worth noticing that the wife belongs to the merchant caste (not to lowly ranked washerman caste). The connotation may be that she served the stranger neglecting her caste restrictions, or sacrificing her dignity to some extent without expecting any reward. In this tale, we can see the case in which *sevanam* or *sevā* among the devotional observances is given light to.

In this single case, we observed the importance of examining each folktale in its own context and minute expression. Keeping this observation in mind, we will examine some more folktales given above.

In folktale no. 2: Ṭhākurjī's idol begins to enjoy the food offered by a poor and innocent boy to fulfil his hope. Thus the boy was able to see the supreme one personally . The folktale ends stating that when other people came to the spot, the living Ṭhākurjī assumed the form of the idol again and stood still. It is clear that innocent and sincere devotion is highly valued in this tale.

Śiva and his family members are popular as central characters of Hindi folktales. Among the nine folktales apparently related with deities in the above list, we find six folktales of Lord Śiva, his consort Pārvatī and their son Gaṇeśa. As seen in the folktales nos. 4, 5 and 6, Śiva often gives life again to those who were killed due to no fault of their own. His consort Pārvatī, though not mentioned in the above given synopses, usually accompanies Lord Śiva and advises him to take care of the people in distress. Gaṇeśa /Gaṇapati is known to the people as the god who removes obstacles and brings wealth. This popular faith is well expressed in the folktales given above: he gives wealth to the poor, warm-hearted wife by changing his excrement into gold (no. 7) ; he gives plenty of sweets to the man who has no fuel to prepare them (no. 8); and he gives fame to a girl who worships him (no. 9).

We find cases which may suggest that Viṣṇu is superior to other deities: he has more influence over people than Brahmā (no. 11), his devotees are more virtuous than Śiva's devotees (no. 12).

We also find some folktales in which people express a hearty wish to have better fortune. According to popular Hinduism, Lord Brahmā writes the fortune of a new-born baby on its forehead, which is exemplified in folktale no. 11: Brahmā allocates quite a severe life to a farmer and he is not ready to change what he has once decided. This stubborn way of Brahmā's behaviour brings about his own ill fortune. He is caught and beaten by the farmer.

In the folktales nos. 13 and 14, tender people negotiate with the Goddess of Fate (Baimātā / Vidhātā Mātā) on behalf of the virtuous and noble characters for their good fortune, and succeed in winning the mercy of the Goddess for them. The last two folktales may be interpreted to say that people are stronger than deities in that they can persuade deities for their sake. But this interpretation is too superficial. We should note that negotiation was made not by the ill-fated characters, but by the tender people who are concerned about the former. This warm-hearted negotiation causes the Goddess to show mercy.

We should take note of another point in these folktales : these tales are the product of the very faith that whatever a God / Goddess decides is usually not changed by the wishes or efforts of human beings. These tales never claim that a human being is superior to a deity, but illustrate that people are quite humble and weak in front of a deity. This notion is most central to devotion.

VARIOUS PHASES OF BHAKTI FOUND IN HINDI FOLKTALES

Although Hindi folktales of bhakti are not great in number, they offer us material to understand the popular form of bhakti.

Characters in Hindi bhakti folktales are very often poor or are in distress, but they are virtuous and helpful to others. They just adore deities and extend warm hands to those in need of help without expecting any reward. When offered such simple-hearted devotion and behaviour, deities are often deeply influenced and give boons to the faithful. In some folktales, though not described in the synopses, greedy and impious people, in contrast to innocent people, are punished by a deity. In this way, the importance of bhakti is narrated in order to reach the hearts of the common people, and the miserable situation of ill-natured ones are illustrated with exaggeration. Thus, these folktales function to confirm and reinforce the importance of bhakti in the manner simple people will understand and accept.

It is interesting to find that Lord Śiva and his family members are the most popular deities in Hindi folktales. But, in everyday life of the present-day Hindus in the Hindi language area, we know the fact that Lord Viṣṇu in the incarnations of the hero Rama and the playful cowherd Kṛṣṇa, is much more popular than Śiva and his family members. This fact may suggest that the strong faith in Śiva is remaining in folktales as the trace of previous religious concepts in the area. Or, this fact may also be interpreted very simply that magic power of Śiva and his family members is appreciated and expected by those who enjoy Hindi folktales: Śiva, Pārvatī and Gaṇeśa have the power to revive dead persons or to give wealth to needy people.

In most of the folktales examined above, *sevā* is the most popular form among various devotional observances. *Sevā* here means, principally, serving deities. Human beings in the form of poor travellers are also served and entertained. In such cases, the travellers are often revealed as deities at the end of the tales. By serving various deities sincerely, the central characters of Hindi folktales may be helping poor people who unexpectedly come into their contact.

* A single term *sevā* in Hindi folktales includes both serving deities and serving/helping people. Hindi folktales related with bhakti are very much folk oriented with myths in their background.

REFERENCES

Ādarśkumārī, *Puṇya kī jaṛ Harī* (Braj), New Delhi: Sastā Sāhitya Maṇḍal Prakāśan, 1976.

Birlā, Lakṣmīnivās, *Lakhṭakiyā* (Rajasthani), New Delhi: Sastā Sāhitya Maṇḍal Prakāśan, 1978.

Dube, Candrśekhar, *Satvantī* (Malva), New Delhi: Sastā Sāhitya Maṇḍal Prakāśan, 1978.

Grierson, G.A., *Linguistic Survey of India*, Calcutta, 1903-22.

Sakata, Teiji, Folktales from the Khari Boli and Bhojpuri areas collected personally and translated into Japanese in four books, Tokyo, 1983-97.

Stutley, Margaret and James Stutley, *A Dictionary of Hinduism*, London: Routledge & Kegan Paul, 1977.

Walker, Benjamin, *Hindu World*, London: George Allen & Unwin, 1968.

Yaśpāl, Ādarśkumārī, *Braj kī lok-kathāẽ*, vol. I, Delhi: Rajkamal Prakāśan, 1964.

General Information

Researches on Early Literature in New Indo-Aryan Languages in Japan after 1980

TAIGEN HASHIMOTO

In the first proceedings of the international Middle Hindi Bhakti Conference, Teiji Sakata (1980) had contributed a brief sketch of research activities on the middle Hindi *bhakti* literature in Japan. In his paper, he had regretfully mentioned that, because our Indological studies in Japan have generally been focused on the history of classical Indian thoughts and Buddhism, the scope and method of study on this subject were still in their infancy. It can hardly be said that, since then, this whole situation has remarkably changed. The main reason for this perhaps may lie in the extreme inclination to studies on the ancient Indian philosophies, which are expected to greatly contribute to Buddhist studies. This means that, in Japan, Indological studies have still been estimated as subsidiary sciences of the Buddhist studies. On the other hand, a few researchers in the Modern Indo-Aryan languages and literatures, at present, stoically limit their subjects only within modern literatures and linguistic issues. Yet the main languages studied here are Hindi, Urdu and Bengali. Japanese researchers on the New Indo-Aryan languages and literatures, therefore occupy only the smallest part of Indological studies in Japan.

But it may be said that against these unfortunate tendencies, our researchers are making steady progress in this field. In the last seventeen years, both in terms of philology and philosophy, full-fledged studies on the saint-poets have appeared. Hashimoto (1983a) made an attempt to determine the original verses of Kabīr by comparing, in terms of their style and contents, the *Granthāvalī* and the *Bījak* and successfully pointed out the greater approximation of the *Bījak* to his original verses. Hashimoto (1986) then, studied a philosophical continuity from the *siddhas* of Buddhist-Sahajayāna to Kabīr, focusing on their concept of *sahaja* (an ultimate state beyond the duality). Sakata, continuing his study on Tulsīdās, developed his range into the study of manuscripts of *Rāmcaritmānas* in the possession of the library of Rāmnagar Fort, Banaras (1985a). In this paper

Sakata analysed some characteristics of several manuscripts dating AD 1705 from view-point of the written transmission. In his other paper, Sakata (1985b), from a socio-religious stand, presented a bird's eye-view on historical development of bhakti movements in Gaṅgā-Yamunā plain, describing the relation between expansion of the Brajbhāṣā and activities of the Vallabha Sampradāya.

On the Quincentenary of Śrī Kṛṣṇa Caitanya, fortunately invited by the director of Caitanya Prem Sansthan, Vrindaban, Sakata and Hashimoto (1989a), with two other members, one of whom is a social anthropologist, the other being a ethno-musicologist, carried out extensive fieldwork on the pilgrimage arranged by Caitanya Prem Sansthan to celebrate the Quincentenary in the summer of 1988. During the twenty-one days of this pilgrimage, Sakata, Hashimoto and others, closely observing the daily religious activities of the pilgrims, conducted a questionnaire with them, asking about their social conditions and their religious concerns. In this paper, Sakata, Hashimoto and others, describing the results of the observation and the questionnaire, analysed several sociological features of this group pilgrimage and also discussed the Caitanyan doctrine which highly acclaims the sacredness of Kṛṣṇa's homeland, Vrajamaṇḍala and prescribes the conduct of any pilgrimage in it. After carrying out this fieldwork, Sakata and Hashimoto (1988), jointly wrote a paper discussing an effective contribution of their pilgrimage to the formation of Caitanya's and Vallabha's doctrine.

Along with these studies of the *bhakti* movement and its literatures, a full-fledged study of *rīti* literature has been started. Mizuno (1987), clearly showed how the *rūpaka* metaphor of the classical Sanskrit had been preserved in the *Satsaī* of Bihārīlāl and extended this comparative method into the study of *upamā* metaphor which Daṇḍin and Keśavdās (1993) preferred. Out of many works of Keśavdās, Mizuno is preparing a critical version of *Kavipriyā* based on about a dozen of manuscripts.

With some development of researches on early Hindi devotional literature, the other New Indo-Aryan devotional literature naturally came into our research field. Hashimoto (1989b) searched for the devotional thought of Caitanya by analysing thoroughly his most important biography written by Kṛṣṇadāsa Kavirāja in the medieval Bengali, which was well mixed with the Brajbhāṣā of that time and, therefore, later called Brajbuli. Mizokami (1986), a linguist of the modern Indo-Aryan languages, specializing in Punjabi, included direct translation of some verses from the *Gurū Granth Sāhib* in his Japanese translation of *Sikhism*, by W. Cole and P.S. Sambhi. Since she had submitted to the University of Poona her Ph.D. thesis entitled 'Social Implications of Bhakti: with Special Reference to the Philosophy of Jñāneśvara', Koiso has been working on the *bhakti* movements in Maharashtra and trying to define the characteristics of Jñāneśvara's bhaktism and its influences on saints of Vārkarī sect (1996).

Researches on the bhaktism in south India should be reasonably added here. Out of the Dravidian languages, Tamil is the main subject as well as in Japan. A comprehensive study of the poetics of ancient Sangam literature has been made by Takahashi (1995). While Yamashita (1994), summarizing prior arguments about the social history of ancient and medieval Tamil Nadu, clearly pointed out a reactionary feature of bhaktism. According to his analyses of the medieval Tamil literature, although, generally accepted that bhakti has some revolutional aspects as a religious thought, bhaktism structurally has a reactionary feature as a theory of slavery, which tends to identify the personified God with a mundane king.

Last but not least, our steady progress in studies in the New Indo-Aryan languages and literature along with studies on medieval bhaktism in various regions, has attracted the attention of historians of pre-modern India, and also of researchers in the other foreign literatures. Consequently, we have recently contributed to the largest Japanese encyclopaedia of the world literature (6 vols.) published by Shūeisha, and to a series entitled *The Caste System and the Oppressed People* (5 vols.), the first volume of which contains our articles on Ālvārs, Deccan-saints, Kabīr and Vallabha sect.

REFERENCES

Although Sakata distributed at the conference a complete list entitled 'A Chronological List of Studies in the Medieval Devotional literature of north India in Japan after 1980', prepared by me and Mizuno, I think it would be better to present some notable articles with their brief introductions. The bibliography as below is in alphabetical order of the authors' name. Almost all the articles were published in Japanese, though, those with * contain a summary in English.

Hashimoto, Taigen, 'A Comparative Study of *Kabīr-Granthāvalī* and Holy *Bījak* — in Consideration of the Original Verses of Kabīr', *Journal of Indian & Buddhist Studies*, 32/1, 1983, pp. 497-9.

———, 'On *Sahaja*, the Traditional Concept accepted by Kabīr', *Memoirs of the Society for the Buzan Study*, 14, 1986, pp. 194-202.

———, 'Religious Leaders; their Pilgrimage and Doctrines in Medieval India', *Journal of Historical Studies*, 582, 1988, pp. 33-49, 61.

———, 'Pilgrims Aspiring toward Unity with Kṛṣṇa; the Hindu Deity of Justice and Love', **Journal of Asian and African Studies*, 37, 1989a, pp. 69-121.

———, 'The Devotional Thought of Caitanya as Reflected in his Biography', *Journal of Indian and Buddhist Studies*, 37/2, 1989b, pp. 938-42.

———, forthcoming (A Japanese translation of the whole *Bījak*).

Koiso, Chihiro, 'The Bhakti of Jñāneśvar and Vārkarī Sect', *Journal of the Association for the Study of the International Relations*, 5/2, Asia University, 1996.

Mizokami, Tomio, *Sikhism — Its Doctrine and History* (Japanese Translation of *The Sikhs — Their Religious Beliefs and Practices* by W. Owen Cole & Piara Singh Sambhi), Tokyo: Chikumashobō, 1986.

Mizuno, Yoshibumi, 'Rūpaka in Satsaī — A Tradition of Classical Sanskrit Literature preserved in Indian Modern Literature', *Journal of Indian and Buddhist Studies*, 36/1, 1987, pp. 23-7.

———, 'Upamā; Daṇḍin and Keśavadās (in English)', *Journal of Indian and Buddhist Studies*, 42/2, 1993, pp. 1-6.

Sakata, Teiji, 'Research on Middle Hindi Bhakti Literature in Japan—A Tentative Report', in Winand M. Callewaert (ed.), *Early Hindi Devotional Literature in Current Research; Proceedings of the International Middle Hindi Bhakti Conference* (April 1979) organized by the Katholieke Universiteit Leuven, New Delhi: Impex India, 1979, pp. 152-3.

———, 'Correction and Addition in the AD 1705 Manuscripts of *Rāmcaritmānas*', *The Annals of Takushoku University*, 8, 1985a, pp. 1-16.

———, 'Development of the Bhakti Movement in Gaṅgā-Yamunā Plain', in N. Karashima (ed.), *Historical Image of the Indian World*, Tokyo: Yamakawa Publishing Co., 1985b, pp. 188-206.

———, 'Religious Leaders: Their Pilgrimage and Doctrines in Medieval India', *Journal of Historical Studies*, 582, 1988, pp. 33-48, 61.

———, 'Pilgrims Aspiring toward Unity with Kṛṣṇa; the Hindu Deity of Justice and Love', *Journal of Asian and African Studies*, 37, 1989, pp. 69-121.

Takahashi, Takanobu, *Tamil Love Poetry and Poetics* (Brill's Indological History no. 9), Leiden: E.J. Brill, 1995.

Yamashita, Hiroshi, 'Lower Caste and Bhakti — Lower Caste People depicted in Ancient and Medieval Tamil Literature', in M. Sato and G. Yamazaki (eds.), *History, Ideology and Structure* (1st vol. of the Series: *The Caste System and the Oppressed People*), Tokyo: Akashishoten, 1994, pp. 185-224. This volume also includes Hashimoto's 'Caste Criticism in the Original Text of Kabīr', Shima's 'The Deccan Bhaktism and the Untouchables', and Sakata's 'The Upholders of Religious Sects; The Roles and Origins of Important Figures in the Early History of the Hindu Vallabha Sect'.

Śraddhāñjali

Śraddhāñjali
श्रद्धांजलि

ALAN ENTWISTLE (1949-1996)

For almost two decades now it has been a moment of happiness to meet every three years to put in common our research and labour. Ever since the session at Seattle in July 1994 this joy is overshadowed. Günther Sontheimer (1933-92) who having left us too early had been missing. But how to imagine that the convenor at Washington University, Alan Entwistle, was not to be at Venice, taken away much too early from the affection of his colleagues. As one of them confided to me, 'Alan nevertheless was very much among us'. His pupils Heidi Pauwels and Alessandra Consolaro, his colleagues and friends, Naseem Hines and Svapna Sharma succeeded in recalling Alan's wit and the mood, his kindness and his gifts. Listening to the *Alan caritra,* as they sang it for us, our sadness grew lesser.

HEIDI PAUWELS

A new-found manuscript: Alan-caritra (bhāv-dīpikā sahit)

While working on my Ph.D. dissertation under the supervision of Professor Alan Entwistle, I kept up an extensive search for manuscripts in the Braj area. As experienced researchers know, for this kind of research to be successful, it often takes many long rural tonga or public carrier rides and a liberal dose of tea drunk in the delightful company of custodians of manuscript treasuries. Once one gains access to any such collection, one is well advised to take good note of all the material it contains, even if it is not the direct goal of one's research. So, when I hit by accident on a manuscript with a work I had never heard about before, with colophon *Alan caritra bhāv-dīpikā sahit,* I quickly overcame my *vismaya bhāva,* and undauntedly started making extensive notes on its contents. I was delighted to find that this manuscript offers significant textual variants of well-known poems, that has been hitherto attested in one recension only.

I tried hard, but unfortunately, I did not succeed in obtaining the permission to photograph the text. In conformity with the rules of copyright, I was granted permission to photograph only a limited portion of the manuscript, and of course I decided on the pictures, with which the manuscript was lavishly illustrated. These pictures, reproduced below, are of immense value because they were all done by the famous artist *Alanjī Kalākār* whose fine eye for detail and wonderful sense of humour is doubtlessly known to all of you.

Needless to say, my Indological zeal inspired me to pay the collection owners a follow-up visit. However, it turned out that the manuscript had disappeared. I was informed that there were several theories that explained this disappearance, but likely it had been eaten by a peculiar kind of bookworm (an even more dreaded threat to manuscripts than visiting scholars). Unfortunately, the destruction was of the type that even famous alchemists would deem 'irreversible'. However, since the manuscript is so exceptional, I will, for the benefit of all *rasika*s devoted to textual studies, along with the reproduction of the pictures, also provide the text based on my field notes. It has to be understood though, that these notes are limited in their accuracy. With the invaluable help of Dr. Svapna Sharma of Vrindāban and Dr. Naseem Hines from University of Washington in Seattle, grammatical and metrical inaccuracies have been straightened out to some extent. All remaining incompletenesses are entirely my own, and I would like to urge the reader not to draw any definite conclusions until further manuscript versions will be forthcoming.

श्री गणेशाय नमः। श्री गुरुवे नमः। श्री एलन चरित्र भाव टीका सहित लिष्यते।

॥ गुरुवन्दना ॥

श्री गुरु चरन सरोज रज, निज मनु मुकुर सुधारि।
बरनउ श्री एलन विमल जस, रवि सम मिटै अंधियारि॥
ज्ञान के सागर जानिकै, हम सुमिरे आचारि।
बल बुद्धि बिद्या दिये हमें, हर्‌यौ कलेस विकारि॥

॥ सवैया ॥

पोथी मैं दूरयौ पुरानन, गानन, हस्थलिखित तो चौगुने चायन।
लोहबन महि मिली प्रति एक, जु एलन चरित वो नीके मो भायन॥
लेन तो देत न चींटिन मीटी, तौ लौट न ला सकैं पाँडे रसायन।
भेद जो हुतौ प्रगट बखानौं, ब ध्यान तें सुनौ रे लोग लुगायन॥

मेष वृंद जहँ चरत हैं, हरी रहत नित घास।
सागर तट नियरे तहाँ, सुन्दर कुटी निवास॥

इक रात महा तुफान में, प्रगट भयौ विद्वान।
श्री एलन जी महाप्रभू, जनम लियौ इंग्लिस्तान॥

॥ भाव प्रदीपिका ॥

सो एलन विद्वान म्लेच्छ हुतौ। सो काहे तें?

सो पिछले जनम में वह रसखान रसिक हुतौ।

सो इक दिन बिना छानैं बीयर पान कियौ।

तामैं इक गाय कौ रोम पेट में गयौ।

सो ता अपराध तें वह म्लेच्छ भयौ।

॥ दोहा ॥

अति सयान बाललीला, माखन चाखन हार।
लंडन मंडन ह्वै गयौ, करत किशोर बिहार॥

पूर्व जनम के करम तैं, लंडन तें ह्वैं न्यारे।
युगल किशोर कृपा करी, सो ब्रज धाम पधारे॥

॥ चौपाई ॥

भयौ महमान गुप्ताजी कौ, पोथी पुरानी लागत नीकौ
गोप जूथ संग धूम मचायौ, बृज जीव-जंतु ताकौ भायौ

॥ सवैया ॥

धूर भरे अति सोभित एलन जू तैसी बनी पहिरै वे कछोटी।
पूछत बात फिरै ब्रज गोकुल खींचत नक्शा बनावत कोटी॥
वा छबि को हौं बिलोक्यौ जो चाहत, सुन्दर हो पै चढ़त न बोटी।
बानर भाग कहा कहिये एलन हाथ सों लै गयौ माखन रोटी॥

॥ दोहा ॥
बृज में रमकै एलन जू, लेत रहत रस स्वाद।
शोध कर्‌यौ रुचि तें बडी, केवल कवि अनुवाद ॥

शोध ग्रन्थ के गुनन कौ, कोउ न करै बषान।
किया विदेसिन कूँ प्रगट, केवल रास व मान॥

बीच बीच कियौ भ्रमन, पहुँचे राजस्थान।
बिरह सहित बीते दिवस, राजकुमार समान॥

समर नीति के चित्त में, खडे तोप के पास।
पर एलन जू लौटे सदा, गोपि चरन के दास॥

आरता री आरता, मेरी सांझा माई आरता।
काहे कौ दीबला, काहे की बाती?
काहे कौ तेल जलै सारी राती?
एलन कौ दीबला, बिलियम की बाती।
एंटविसल तेल जलै सारी राती।

॥ दोहा ॥
वेनिस में जैसे बीएनाले, तैसे बृज में साँझी।
इंट्रीगिंग दीज़ैन गोबर में तैसे बनावत भांझी॥

॥ सार ॥
परम मुदित है ब्रज की छोरी, घर घर साँझी काढत।
मोदक बाँटत बाँटत एलन जी, अपनौ शोध बढावत॥

॥ दोहा ॥
वेनिस में जैसे कानाले, बृज में साँकरी खोर।
भूल भुलैया कौ नक्शा बना, लिखत रहत सिरमोर॥

॥ कवित्त ॥

ग्वालन सँग जैबो बन ऐबो सु गायन सँग, हरि तान गैबो हा हा नैन फरकत हैं।
ह्याँ के गज मोती माल वारौं गुंजमालन पै, कुंज सुधि आए हाय प्रान धरकत हैं॥
गोबर को गारो सु तौ आप लगै प्यारौ कहा, भयौ महल सोने को जटत मरकत हैं।
मंदर ते ऊँचे यह मंदिर हैं पश्चिम के, बारज के खिरक एलन हिय खरकत हैं॥

॥ फिल्मी ॥

वाकौ जूता अमरीकानी
हॉलैंड, फ्रांस जानै जुबानी।
अंगरेज़ तो तन-मन तें
फिर भी दिल है हिन्दूस्तानी॥

॥ सवैया ॥

केसौ–ब्रजेस–सुरेस–गोपेस–राधेसोपदेस सदाहि पढावैं।
जो ही अनादि अनन्त अखंड अछेद अभेद सुभेद बतावैं॥
इंग्लैंड तें हॉलैंड रहे पचिहारि तऊ कोउ राखि न पावै।
वोही शितालय कौ विश्वविद्यालय करुना वरुनालय शोध बढावै॥

॥ कवित्त ॥

तैसे तिलक बनायौ मधुर मधुर तैसे, बंक चितवन मंद मंद मुसकान री।

गोरज बिराजै भाल लहलहै रुद्रमाल, सिर पै लाल टोपी रूसी हौं कहाँ बखानौं री॥

एलन जी को लगी लत साधु भयौ सटपट, पाछै आयौ झटपट एलन को लगान री।
रस बरसावै तन तपन बुझावै नैन, प्राननि रिझावै वो विराजे एलन शान री॥

॥ सवैया ॥

मानुष हौं तो वही रसखानि बसौं ब्रज गोकुल गाँव के ग्वारन।
जो खग हौं तो बसेरो करौ मिलि कालिंदी कूल कदंब की डारनि॥
पाहन हौं तौ वही गिरी को जो धर्यौ कर चक्र पुरन्दर धारन।
जो पशु हौं तो कहा बस मेरो चरौं नित नंद की धेनु मंझारन॥

॥ पुष्पिका ॥

यह बिराग संदीपनी, सुजन सुचित सुनि लेहु।
अनुचित बचन विचारि कै, जस सुधारि तस लेहु ॥

As the *Alan caritra* might have suggested, the part of Alan Entwistle in the foundation of the Vrindavan Research Institute was an essential one. His *magnum opus*: *Braj, Centre of Krishna Pilgrimage* (Groningen, 1987) testifies to this. But one of the founders of the Vrindavan Research Institute, Dr. Ramdas Gupta, untimely passed away the day before we started our conference at Venice. Dr. Rupert Snell briefly evoked his memory among us.

For those who knew Alan less, I enclose a list of his articles and books:

1977: 'Cultural Material in Kaman', in *Journal of the Vrindavan Research Institute* 2 (pp. 49-51, 65-71).

1980: 'Manuscripts of the Eighth Gaddī of the Vallabh Sampradāy', in *Early Hindi Devotional Literature in Current Research*, edited by W.M. Callewaert, Leuven: *Orientalia Lovaniensia Analecta* 8 (pp. 55-65).

1981: edited with H.T. Bakker, *Vaiṣṇavism: the history of the Kṛṣṇa and Rāma cults and their contribution to Indian pilgrimage*. Groningen: Instituut voor Indische Talen en Culturen. Co-editor of the volume (vi-206 pp.) and sole author of the chapters entitled 'Vaiṣṇavism up to A.D. 1000' and 'Vaiṣṇavism since A.D. 1000' (pp. 1-55), and Appendix 2: 'Notes on the Hindu Calendar and Vaiṣṇava Festivals' (pp. 57-163).

1982: 'Vaiṣṇava Tilakas: *Sectarian marks worn by worshippers of Viṣṇu*', London, *IAVRI Bulletin* 11-12 (ii-81 pp.).

1983: 'Kailā Devī and Lāṃguriyā', in *Indo-Iranian Journal* 25 (pp. 85-101) ['The Goddess Kailā and (her male attendant) Lāṃguriyā'].

——— 'The Transmission and Authorship of Poetry attributed to Kevalarāma of Dera Ghazi Khan', in *Bhakti in Current Research 1979-82*, edited by M. Thiel-Horstmann, Berlin: Dietrich Reimer Verlag (*Collectanea Instituti Anthropos*, vol. 30, pp. 123-31).

1984: 'Sā̃jhī: Images for a Twilight Goddess', in *Visible Religion* 3 (pp. 43-79).

1985: 'An Introduction to Indian Historiography', in *Groniek* (*Gronings Historisch Tijdschrift*) 90 (pp. 4-15).

1986: *Kevalrām kṛt rās mān ke pad*, Vṛndāvan: Vṛndāvaṇ Śodh Saṃsthān. ['Kevalrām's Songs of Dalliance and Wounded Pride'; abridged version of the Ph.D. dissertation with introduction in Hindi], xiv-62 pp.

1987: *Braj, Centre of Krishna Pilgrimage*, Groningen: Egbert Forsten, xviii-554 pp. and 3 maps.

1988: 'Rediscovering 'Braj', *IAVRI Bulletin* (14). Editor of the whole issue (32 pp.) and author of the article entitled 'From *vraja* to Braj' (pp. 14-18).

1990: 'Māhātmya Sources on the Pilgrimage Circuit of Mathurā', in *The History of Sacred Places as Reflected in Traditional Literature*, edited by H.T. Bakker. Leiden: E.J. Brill (pp. 5-28).

1991: 'The Cult of Kṛṣṇa-Gopāl as a Version of Pastoral', in *Devotion Divine. Bhakti Traditions from the Regions of India*, edited by Diana Eck and

Françoise Mallison. Groningen: Egbert Forsten / Paris: École Française d'Extrême-Orient (pp. 73-90).

1993: 'Indian Prosody II: The Modern Indian Vernaculars', in *The New Princeton Encyclopedia of Poetry and Poetics*, edited by A. Preminger et al., Princeton: Princeton University Press, 1993 (pp. 602-3).

——— 'Synaesthesia in Poetry and Ritual of the Puṣṭimārga', in *Journal of Vaiṣṇava Studies* 1.3 (pp. 84-103).

——— Revised edition of the Ph.D. thesis (see 1983), Gronigen: Egbert Forsten.

1994: *Studies in South Asian Devotional Literature Research Papers 1988-1991*, co-edited with Françoise Mallison, Delhi: Manohar, xiv-585 pp.

In press: *Representations of 'Alā'uddīn Khaljī.*

SHANKAR GOPAL TULPULE (1914-1994)

Professor Tulpule regularly attended our conferences but his health had not permitted him to come to Seattle in July 1994 to join the 'clan' (as Alan called us, using a term coined by Daniel Gold to describe the group of the Sants !). Professor Tulpule died in August 1994 at Poona having worked almost upto the last day on the dictionary of Old Marathi in company of Anne Feldhaus, one of his numerous foreign students, colleagues and friends he initiated into the study of medieval devotional literature in Marathi. Some of them present at Venice could informally tell about him or send their own personal testimonies which are speaking for themselves on the personality and scholarship of our old friend. I could start like my colleague: 'I first met Professor Tulpule in 1969 . . .' But I was not the first, Professor Charlotte Vaudeville introduced me to him. She and Günther Sontheimer were the first. Professor Tulpule retired early in 1968 from the University of Poona where he had been heading the Department of Marathi. From that time he started working with foreign scholars and students opening up for them not only the treasures of his scholarship but also the world of a Maharashtrian Brahmin household while at the same time opening himself up to the Western world. This mode of mutual exchange led to many a warm friendship such as our two families experienced when we were living in Poona from 1971 to 1977.

I enclose the account sent by Anne Feldhaus, and some of the recollections from our commemorative session at Venice, by Eleanor Zelliot, Irina Glushkova and Catharina Kiehnle, followed by a short list of the publications of S.G.Tulpule.

ON S.G. TULPULE, BY ANNE FELDHAUS

I called him 'Dada' ('Elder Brother'), the name by which he was called at home. Asking for 'Dr. Tulpule', especially on the telephone, was always too confusing — there were too many Drs. Tulpule in the house.

Before I met Dada, I met his father. In October 1974, the father of a friend of a friend of mine in America, learning that I was to be writing a thesis on Old Marathi literature, marched me to the door of Dr.Tulpule's House in Sadāśiv Peṭh, Pune. Dada was out of town, on a trip through the Himalayas, but other members of the family let us in, his father, lying on what was to be his death-bed, met us graciously, though briefly. By the time I visited the house again, Dada's father had died.

Portrait of Professor Shankar Gopal Tulpule taken in February 1993 at the Memorial Conference for Günther Sontheimer, at the Bhandarkar Oriental Research Institute, Pune. It was his last public appearance. (Copyright Henning Stegmüller, Clemensstrasse 80, D-80796 München)

I had hoped to be able to ask Dr. Tulpule about passages in my dissertation text that I had difficulty understanding. He insisted on reading with me not only those passages but the whole text. This was to prove typical of the generosity with which he would work with me for the next two decades. We subsequently read all of the *Govindaprabhucaritra (The Deeds of God in Ṛddhipur)* together, and then all of the Mahānubhāvs' religous-geographical literature. One summer, with no particular project in mind, we read *Smṛtisthal*; later we published our translation as *In the Absence of God* (Honolulu University of Hawaii Press, 1992). When I was working on religious materials about the rivers of Maharashtra, Dada read through all the literature of the Vārkarī poet-saints for me, picking out the passages that had to do with rivers or with religious geography more generally; and then he read all those passages with me. We also read some Nāmdev together, and tried some Tukārām, but I found Tukārām too hard. Dada suggested that I work on Bahiṇābāī (I did) and on Rāmdās (I couldn't bear to). And he kept me abreast of the latest developments and controversies in the field of Old Marathi literature — in many of which he himself played a role.

For the next twenty years, Dada would spend a couple of hours reading and talking with me for most of the days that I was in Pune. When both Günther Sontheimer and I were there, he would get the mornings and I the afternoons, when Günther was not there, I would sometimes be moved up to the mornings. I remember our sessions together with pleasure. Dada had the good teacher's instinct for telling me what I needed to learn, and for not boring me with things I already knew. With him, as with all other Marathi speakers, I insisted from the beginning on using Marathi, and he went along with this. As we worked together, usually translating Marathi texts into English, we developed our own mixture of Marathi and English. I was so comfortable with Dada linguistically that I was often not aware of which language we were using — a rare experience for me.

Besides Günther Sontheimer and me, there were also many other scholars, mostly foreign, whom Dada helped with Old Marathi and sometimes Middle or modern Marathi. Charlotte Vaudeville claimed to be the first of them — and Dada dedicated one of his books to her, calling her 'my first French friend'. In his several visits to Heidelberg, Dada helped a number of Sontheimer's students and other scholars to read Old Marathi texts. He even went to California once, to read *Jñāneśvarī* with a young man who called himself Narad Muni.

And yet, despite all this, Dada remained extremely productive, churning out books and articles, working steadily and regularly, on a relaxed and satisfying daily schedule. He began the day early, with yoga and meditation, then did a 'walk-jog' (ten steps walking alternating with ten steps jogging) before sitting down until lunch time at his desk on the third floor of his house in Sadāśiv Peṭh. After a mid-day rest, he would work again until evening. By the time I met Dada, his poor eyesight kept him from working at night. During the day, an army of women guarded Dada's time and space in his attic study. His wife, his daughters-in-law, his grand-daughters, and various domestic servants took telephone messages, kept out unwanted visitors, and prepared seemingly endless cups of tea for Dada and his students and guests.

During the last five years of his life, Dada's steady work routine was dedicated to his *Dictionary of Old Marathi*. He first told me of his interest in such a project in 1983, and invited me to collaborate with him on it. Not until 1989 could we get the necessary funding and permissions in place. We (mostly he) started work on the dictionary at the end of August, 1989 ; when he died, at the end of August 1994, his part of the work was essentially complete. Now, in August 1998, my part of the work is also finished, and the dictionary is scheduled to be published before the end of this year.

In the last months of his life, Dada reduced his daily walk-jog to a walk; in his final weeks he could not even do that. He quoted Eknāth on the subject of old age: You reach a point where 'even your courtyard is a foreign land', he said. For one who had taken much pleasure as Dada had in living and working abroad, Eknāth's words held special irony.

A TRIBUTE TO SHANKAR GOPAL TULPULE, BY ELEANOR ZELLIOT

I went to Dr. Tulpule in 1975 with some hesitancy, since what I wanted to work on were the *barudes* (drama poems) of Sant Eknāth, a sixteenth century poet of great imagination. The *bharudes* were not Eknāth's high religious works, they were poems in the mouths of all non-Sanskritic men and women (and animals) if the town of Paithan: Untouchables, Muslims, acrobats, unhappy wives, dogs, spiders — all teaching the religion of *bhakti*, devotional religion. The empathy of this unorthodox Brahmin was a constant challenge and a constant delight and Tulpule entered into the translations with great spirit. Only once did he falter — and that was the Hindu-Turk dialogue, much of which was in Deccani Hindi/Urdu. He found a delightful school teacher of Hindi for me to work with, and so we finished the entire book of Eknāth's remarkable work.

My next venture with this indefatigable scholar was the poetry of fourteenth century Mahar Untouchable poets, and this too was undertaken with constant interest. One of my memories is that of Tulpule stopping in the middle of a song by Nirmalā, the sister of Cokhāmeḷā, and exclaiming, 'Why, this is a very intelligent woman!'. I think the contact with Dr. Tulpule through the years was one of the most rewarding a scholar could have. He entered into the works of these medieval Maharashtrian poets with technical skill for their spare image-filled poems but also profound interest in their religious life.

Going to Tulpule's *wada* in the old city of Pune, just near 'Nagnath par', a tree in the middle of the street and the benchmark for finding his home, was a real treat. I photographed him with a solid background of books in his library and his wife in the kitchen near the god-house. He also visited in my home in Northfield, Minnesota, uncomplainingly eating my (at that time) amateur Indian cooking. Except when I made *urad* dal, which he pronounced too full of protein. He was a proper Brahmin, but with a remarkable love of life and spirit of adventure. I miss him most dreadfully, not only for translation but as a dear friend. But he is still of help through my translations and through his invaluable *Classical Marathi Literature* (Otto Harrassowitz) which still astonishes me with its thoroughness and its broad compass.

SOME MEMORIES OF SHANKAR GOPAL TULPULE, BY IRINA GLUSHKOVA

For the first time I met Professor Tulpule in 1973 when I had come to Pune to study Marathi. I remember feeling shy as I could yet not articulate much and was still a student of the Moscow State University. So we communicated in a mixture of English and Hindi — both foreign to me, and after an introductory conversation he asked me to stay for dinner. On hearing that I was planning to make a tour to Delhi, Agra, Jaipur, etc., in January, Professor Tulpule left the room and returned with a woollen blanket — 'Better you take it with yourself, it is very cold in the North of Pune during the Indian cool season and you will need something to keep you warm'. It was the memory of the warmth of this blanket that made me call Professor Tulpule the moment I came to Pune for the second time–after a gap of twelve years.

This time with my position as a teacher of Indian languages, linguistics and literature at the Moscow State University we were more like equals, though I never stopped to experience the boundlessness of his knowledge, especially after becoming a sort of pupil again attempting to master the medieval Marathi of the Maharashtrian poet-saints under his guidance. Since then and upto the time of his death we met regularly, reading systematically the poems of Tukārām. What stuck me during our two-hour sessions (every Tuesday and Friday during my stays in Pune) was the eagerness of the old scholar to learn — both of us tried to discover patterns in the disarrayed grammar and excited style of the most popular saint of the seventeenth century. We argued constantly and enjoyed it immensely.

Since our first meeting Professor Tulpule became an essential part of my life, I had missed him a lot after 1973, and I have been missing him daily since his death.

ON S.G. TULPULE, BY CATHARINA KIEHNLE

When I was for the first time in India in 1979, I had just moved into a new flat when the bell rang. In the doorway stood a smallish elderly gentleman who introduced himself as Professor Tulpule. He had been teaching Marathi to my predecessor in the house and was just curious to know whether he could continue his tuitions with me. At that time my Sanskrit studies kept me too busy to do so, but nevertheless a friendship developed with this inquisitive scholarly globe-trotter that lasted until his death. It was he who first took me to my future *bhajan* teacher, it was he who came to Germany to teach me the language of the Vārkarī songs and it was he who talked in Marathi until I started liking this language more than my own one. It was he who read passages with me from the scriptures of Jñāndev, Nāmdev, Eknāth, Tukārām, Rāmdās and other poets of Maharashtra, and a comedy on a false guru guru by Ācārya Atre. So in my memories he is not only connected with the holy scriptures, but also with the laughter of Maharashtra. During long walks along the banks of river Main he told me about his life and his own attitude towards the Sants whom he loved and admired. But in those days he was not sure whether or not he could completely trust their words. In this way, he said, he was a typical Konkanastha Brahmin, a member of a community who (also according to him) had always been too intellectual to produce saints. Yet, it seems, Marathi *bhajan*s accompanied him right to the end. It is good to know that during his lifetime he had studied something that was useful even then. However, those of us who were his friends and who are students of Marathi would have welcomed a much longer period in this world for him to doubt.

Books by Shankar Gopal Tulpule, a list of important publications, compiled by himself:

——— *An Old Marathi Reader*, Pune, 1960.
——— *Ranade – A Modern Mystic*, Pune, 1961, in coll. with S.R.Sharma.
——— *A Corpus of Old Marathi Inscriptions* (in Marathi), Pune: University of Poona, 1963.
——— *The Lila-Caritra of Cakradhar*, edited with Introduction and Notes, in five parts (in Marathi), Pune, 1968-1973.
——— *The Pathway to God in Marathi Devotional Literature* (in Marathi), Pune, 1969.
——— *A Linguistic Study of Yadav-Marathi* (in Marathi), 2nd edn., Pune, 1970 (1st edn. 1942).
——— *A History of Book-Production in Marathi* (in Marathi), Pune, 1972
——— *The Mahanubhava Sect and its Literature* (in Marathi), Pune, 1976
——— *Classical Marathi Literature*, Wiesbaden, 1979 (vol. 9, fasc. 4 of *A History of Indian Literature*, edited by Jan Gonda).
——— *R.D. Ranade – Life and Philosophy* (in Marathi), 3rd edn., Pune, 1982.
——— *Mysticism in Medieval India*, Wiesbaden, 1984.
——— *Five Poet-Saints of Maharashtra* (in Marathi), 3rd edn., Pune, 1984.
——— *A History of Marathi Literature, vol. 1 (From the Early Beginnings to 1350 A.D.)* (in Marathi), Pune, 1984.
——— *The Divine Name in the Indian Tradition: A Comparative Study*, Shimla: Indian Institute of Advanced Study, 1991.
——— *In the Absence of God: The Early Years of an Indian Sect*, Honolulu, 1992, in coll. with Anne Feldhaus.

Contributors

ALI S. ASANI: Committee on the Study of Religion, Harvard University, Phillips Brooks House, 3rd floor, Cambridge, MA 02138, USA, fax: +1-617-496-5798, e-mail: aliasani@husc.harvard.edu

HANS BAKKER: Institute of Indian Studies, University of Groningen, P.O.Box 716, 9700 AS Groningen, The Netherlands, fax: +31-50-3637263, e-mail: BAKKER@LET.RUG.NL

IMRE BANGHA: The Oriental Institute, University of Oxford, Pusey Lane, Oxford, 0X1 2LE, UK, e-mail: imre.bangha@oriental-institute.oxford.ac.uk [Imre Bangha, 9028 Györ, Zichy Otto u. 4-b, Hungary, e-mail: banim@arrabonet.gyor.hu]

HARIVALLABH C. BHAYANI: 25/2 Vimanagar, Satellite Road, Ahmedabad 380 015, India

MANDAKRANTA BOSE: Dept. of Religious Studies, Institute of Asian Research, University of British Columbia, Vancouver, BC V6T 1Z2, Canada, e-mail: mbose@interchange.ubc.ca [Mandakranta Bose, 4166 West 10th Avenue, Vancouver, BC V6R 2H3, Canada]

MAYA BURGER: Département interfacultaire d'histoire et de sciences des religions, Faculté de Théologie, BFSH 2, Université, 1015 Lausanne, Switzerland, e-mail: Maya.Burger@dtheol.unil.ch

WINAND CALLEWAERT: Dept. of Oriental Studies, Blijde Inkomststraat 21, 3000 Leuven, Belgium, fax: +32-16-324932, e-mail: winand.callewaert@arts.kuleuven.ac.be

THOMAS DE BRUIJN: Zuster Meijboomstraat 81, 2331 PE Leiden, The Netherlands, telephone: +31-71-5316417, e-mail: PVENTHB@XS4ALL.NL

PETER GAEFFKE: 343 Llandrillo Road, Bala Cynwyd, PA 19004, USA, fax: +1-215-573-2138, e-mail: pgaeffke@sas.upenn.edu

IRINA GLUSHKOVA: Center for Indian Studies, Institute of Orientology, 12 Rozhdestvenka, Moscow 103753, Russia, fax: +7-095-4704094 (or 9752396)

KATHRYN HANSEN: 189 Grove Street, Montclair, NJ 07042, USA, e-mail: kghansen@aol.com

TAIGEN HASHIMOTO: Dept. of Indian Philosophy, Toyo University, 5-28-20 Hakusan, Bunkyo-ku, Tokyo 112-8606, Japan, fax. +81-3-3945-7357, e-mail: hasimoto@hakusrv.toyo.ac.jp

NASEEM HINES: Dept. of Asian and Near Eastern Languages and Literatures, Washington University in St. Louis, Campus Box 1111, One Brookings Drive, St. Louis, MO 63130-4899, USA, e-mail: nhines@artsci.wustl.edu

BALVANT JANI: Dept. of Gujarati Language and Literature, Saurashtra University, University Road, Rajkot 360 005 (Gujarat), India, fax: +91-281-77633

DAVID N. LORENZEN: CEEA, El Colegio de Mexico, Camino al Ajusco 20, Mexico, D.F. 01000, Mexico, e-mail: lorenzen@colmex.mx

FRANÇOISE MALLISON: Les Montèzes, 30170 Monoblet, France, fax: +33-466852606

NANCY M. MARTIN: Religion Department, Chapman University, 333 N. Glassell Street, Orange, CA 92866, USA, fax: +1-714-532-6078, e-mail: nmartin@chapman.edu

STUART McGREGOR: 79 Thornton Road, Girton, Cambridge, CB3 0NR, UK, e-mail: rsm3@hermes.cam.ac.uk

ZAWAHIR MOIR: 20 Denning Road, London NW3 1SO, UK, telephone: +44-171-435-0588

GANGADHAR MORJE: 'Morjai', Behind Sahakari Bank, Sahakar Sabhagrih Marg, Phule Chowk, Ahmednagar 414 001 (MS), India, telephone: +91-241-24602, fax: +91-241-41517, e-mail: pmorje@hotmail.com

MARIOLA OFFREDI: Dipartimento di Studi Eurasiatici, Università degli Studi Ca' Foscari di Venezia, San Polo 2035, 30125 Venezia, Italy, fax: +39-41-5241847, e-mail: offred21@unive.it

SHYAM MANOHAR PANDEY: Dipartimento di Studi Asiatici, Istituto Universitario Orientale, Piazza San Domenico Maggiore 12, 80134 Napoli, Italy, fax: +39-81-5517852

HEIDI PAUWELS: Dept. of Asian Languages and Literature, University of Washington, Seattle, WA 98195-353521, USA, e-mail: hpauwels@u.washington.edu

José Pereira: 330 Hawthorne Avenue, Yonkers, NY 10705-1831, USA, fax: +1-718-817-5787

Carla Petievich: Dept. of History, Montclair State University, Upper Montclair, NJ 07043, USA, fax: +1-201-655-7225, e-mail: petievichc@saturn.montclair.edu

Galina Rousseva-Sokolova: Département interfacultaire d'histoire et de sciences des religions, Faculté de Théologie, BFSH 2, Université, 1015 Lausanne, Switzerland, e-mail: Galina.Rousseva-Sokolova@dtheol.unil.ch

Teiji Sakata: 124-34 Aoyagi, Sayama City, Saitama-ken 350-13, Japan, fax: +81-3-3947-5333, e-mail: tsakata@ner.takushoku-u.ac.jp

A. Whitney Sanford: College of Liberal Arts and Sciences, Religious Studies Program, 402 Catt Hall, Ames, Iowa 50011-1306, USA, e-mail: wsanford@iastate.edu:

Ghanshyam Sharma: Dipartimento di Studi Eurasiatici, Università degli Studi Ca' Foscari di Venezia, San Polo 2035, 30125 Venezia, Italy, fax: +39-41-5241847, e-mail: sharmave@unive.it

Christopher Shelke, SJ: Pontificia Università Gregoriana, Piazza della Pilotta 4, 00187 Roma, Italy, e-mail: shelke@unigre.urbe.it

Varsha S. Shirgaonkar: c/o Dr S.A. Dange, Girnar, Gokhale Road, Mulund (East), Mumbai 400 081, India, e-mail: sanjay@diversion.com

Bahadur Singh: Institut für Kultur und Geschichte Indiens und Tibets, Neue Rabenstr. 3, 20354 Hamburg, Germany, fax: +49-40-4123-6267

Pritam Singhvi: 4-A, Ramya Apartment, Polytechnic, Ambawadi, Ahmedabad 380 015 (Gujarat), India, e-mail: singhvi@ad1.vsnl.net.in

Bożena Śliwczyńska: Oriental Institute, Warsaw University, Krak. Przedmiescie 26/28, 00-927 Warszawa, Poland, fax: +4822-8263683, e-mail: bozka@orient.uw.edu.pl [Bożena Śliwczyńska, ul. Chelmia 14 m 19, 00-020 Warszawa, Poland]

William L. Smith: Dept. of Indology, University of Stockholm, Stockholm 106 91, Sweden, e-mail: William.Smith@orient.su.se

Selina Thielemann: c/o Swami Fatehkrishna Sharma, Shri Radha Madhava Raslila Sansthan, Shri Radhakrishna Bhavan, 410 Bankhandi, Vrindaban 281 121 (UP), India, telephone: +91-565-422-296 (or 422-927)

DONNA M. WULFF: Dept. of Religious Studies, Brown University, Providence, RI 02912-1927, USA, fax: +1-401-863-3109, e-mail: Donna_Wulff@brown.edu

HASU YAJNIK: 3, Sheetal Plaza, Near Lad Society, Vastrapur, Ahmedabad 380 054, India, telephone: +91-272-6750362, fax: +91-272-6753624

ELEANOR ZELLIOT: Dept. of History, Carleton College, Northfield, Minnesota 55057, USA, fax: +1-507-646-4204, e-mail: ezelliot@carleton.edu

Index

THE BANYAN TREE

Essays on Early Literature in New Indo-Āryan Languages

THE BANYAN TREE

Essays on Early Literature in New Indo-Aryan Languages

(Proceedings of the Seventh International Conference on Early Literature in New Indo-Aryan Languages, Venice, 1997)

VOLUME I

Edited by

MARIOLA OFFREDI

MANOHAR
NEW DELHI

UNIVERSITÀ DEGLI STUDI DI VENEZIA
DIPARTIMENTO DI STUDI EURASIATICI
VENEZIA
2000

First published 2000

ISBN 81-7304-277-2 (Set)
ISBN 81-7304-342-6 (Vol. I)

Published by
Ajay Kumar Jain for
Manohar Publishers & Distributors
4753/23 Ansari Road, Daryaganj
New Delhi 110002

Typeset by
A J Software Publishing Co. Pvt. Ltd.
305 Durga Chambers
1333 D.B. Gupta Road
Karol Bagh, New Delhi 110005

Printed at
Rajkamal Electric Press
B 35/9 G T Karnal Road Indl Area
Delhi 110033

To
the memory of
Alan Entwistle
(1949-1996)

Contents

PART III
MODERN INDIAN ISMAILISM

PART IV
SOCIAL VALUES AND MODES OF DEVOTION IN BENGAL

PART V
MODES OF TRANSMISSION OF RELIGION IN GUJARAT

PART VI
RELIGIOUS AND LITERARY TRADITIONS IN MAHARASHTRA AND THE KONKAN

Preface

Following six conferences of different title, held in Leuven (1979), Bonn (1982), Leiden (1985), Cambridge (1988), Paris (1991) and Seattle (1994), the Seventh International Conference on Early Literature in New Indo-Aryan Languages, which took place in Venice from 6 - 8 August 1997, was attended by more than sixty academics hailing from Europe, India, Canada, the United States, Mexico, Japan, and South Africa.

This book, which is published in two volumes, contains most of the papers presented at the Venice conference. They are grouped in part by geographical area, in part by subject matter, in a crossing of boundaries that sharpens the exchange between the two. In fact, they share a common feature which goes beyond regional specificities. This consists of the dialectical relationship between two elements, such as popular devotion as opposed to erudite religious faith, and their respective literary outputs; or the Muslim and Hindu religions, modified by Hindu-Muslim synthesis, and the revival of the more specifically Hindu spirit. From another point of view, where papers have been grouped according to topic, those imbued with religious sentiment may be read in contrast with those in which religious sentiment is on a fundamentally aesthetic level.

There are varying degrees of Islamization and, consequently, the cultural assimilation of Hinduism and Islam has produced different results. The nine papers on this topic dwell not only on the cultural synthesis of Hinduism and Islam in northern India and the Deccan — whether it be of a religious, or, as in the case of the Muslim courts, a sophisticated and aesthetic nature. We also learn how, even in the intensely Islamized province of Sind, many centuries after the Arab conquest of AD 711-12, the voices can be heard of poets who directly take up, or at any rate echo, the themes of religious literature of northern India. Even at the start of the twentieth century, Indian Ismaili writers continued to question the religious syncretism of the community to which they belonged.

Three papers are devoted to the subject of Bengal, where, according to Suniti Kumar Chatterji ('Purāṇa Legends and the Prakrit Tradition in New Indo-Aryan', in *Select Papers*, vol. I, Delhi: People's Publishing House, 1972, pp. 27-38), around AD 500, the figure of Rādhā — the married Rādhā, seed of the sixteenth-century 'spiritual translation of the *Parakīyā* idea' (ibid., p. 35) — first entered pre-vernacular folk tradition. In these writings, Bengal emerges as a region in which the female element is pre-eminent in both popular and high religion, in both spiritual and social contexts; and because it is pre-eminent, it is capable of freedom of judgement and behaviour and, in many cases, even of predominance over the male element.

The papers dealing with Gujarat reveal it to be a dualistic region, with its combination of learned tradition and fertile ground for folk culture. The subjects range from the Kakka genre, analysed in a thirteenth-century didactic text in old western Gujarati-Rajasthani, in which every line starts with a letter of the Sanskrit alphabet (a genre that crept into other forms of medieval Indian literature) to religious folk songs in honour of the Goddess, and the devotional songs (again, deriving from the Muslim-Hindu synthesis) that are widespread among the low castes and the untouchables of Saurashtra; and to writings by Muslim saints and preachers from Gujarat that are strongly influenced by Yoga and the Vedānta.

The articles on Maharashtra are linked by the evidence they provide of popular culture which, when connoted by anti-Brahmanism, is inspired by spiritual devotion; alternatively, imbued with eroticism, it portrays the lavish lifestyle enjoyed in the Maratha courts, contrasting depiction of everyday life with the polished elegance of the court. Topics include the results of the merging of Vedic and Tantric traditions, and various thoughts on the Vārkarī saints' worship of Viṭhobā, touching on a number of women saints who achieve true freedom, ranging from the two untouchable women who attribute equal importance to household life and devotion to God, to another woman who gives more weight to her personal spiritual experience and that of other saints.

One article deals with the area in which Konkani, a close relation of the Marathi language, is spoken. The most southerly region in which new Indo-Aryan languages are found, its literary history came to a temporary halt in 1684 when the Portuguese Viceroy of Goa abolished the language, which only in 1987 was declared the official language of the State of Goa.

It is clear from those articles in the book that are devoted to Kabīr and Mīrā, that the oral tradition is significant in Rajasthan, serving to modify and extend the literary heritage; alternatively, especially in the case of Mīrā, it is a source of literary tradition.

The stereotypical perception of Kṛṣṇa in the Braj region is altered by the demonstration, on the one hand, of the influence of southern Indian themes and, on the other, with the perpetuation of traditional local themes. With regard to devotees of Rādhā-Kṛṣṇa in the Braj region, a challenge to the current distinction between *sagun̩* and *nirgun̩* is supported by material found in handwritten collection of poems.

Outside the Braj region, more openly critical of the new orthodoxy which has built up around Kabīr on the one hand, and the *Ādi Granth* on the other, are the two articles dealing with these subjects.

The adaptation of Sanskrit epic poems to various vernaculars bears witness to the perpetuation of tradition on one hand and, on the other, to the modification and use of tradition for diverse purposes. The two articles on this subject reveal two different techniques of re-working epic material: one is the modernization of material in order to extol the virtues of the Rajput struggling against the Muslims, so that tradition is used to strengthen Hindu cultural identity; the other method sees the addition of fictional episodes which emphasize the superiority of devotional religion and therefore promote anti-Brahmanism.

It is a well-known fact that the dalliance of Kṛṣṇa in Braj was instrumental in the secularization of divine love. Two complementary articles demonstrate the development of the theme in the eighteenth century. The various nuances of love, in both religious and secular forms, added to personal experience of earthly love leading to outpourings from the poet's heart, is ideal material for profitable semantic analysis.

To turn to a more recent era, two articles deal with two ways of interpreting devotion, the ritual and the popular respectively, from an account of ritual in the Vaiṣṇava temples in Vrindavan to a study of devotion in Hindi folktales.

The General Information section contains a survey on the state of research into early literature in new Indo-Aryan languages in Japan.

The final section of the book is devoted to the memory of Alan Entwistle and Shankar Gopal Tulpule. The organizer of the Seattle Conference in July 1994, it was Alan Entwistle who wanted the seventh conference to be held in Venice. Instead of attending the event, he was with us as an intangible presence. The editor of the *Śraddhāñjali* is Françoise Mallison, to whom I am deeply indebted for her extreme kindness and helpful nature.

MARIOLA OFFREDI

Acknowledgements

I would like to thank the many persons in the Ca' Foscari University of Venice who have assisted me in the organization of the conference. My colleague Dr. Ghanshyam Sharma, who was always there to lend a hand, especially during the last hectic days of pre-conference organization. My thanks go also to Daniela Memo, who designed the poster and the programme, and to the secretaries and librarians from the Department of Euro-Asiatic Studies, Nadia Gropuzzo and Anna Camuffo, Adriana Stama and Patrizia Barbazza. My thanks are also due to the ESU (Students' Rights Board) of Venice District and the staff of the hostel 'Domus Soccorso' for their hospitality. Finally, I am most grateful to the Head of Department, Professor Giuliano Tamani, for the unstinting moral support that led to a substantial financial contribution. The Dean of the Faculty of Foreign Languages and Literatures, Professor Mario Sabattini, too, was responsible for the provision of funding. The present publication was assisted by awards from the Department of Euro-Asiatic Studies.

Note on Transcription

In view of the difficulties involved in using a single system of transcription for all the articles in the book, individual authors' decision as to method of transcription have been respected; for their part they were asked to maintain consistency in the transcriptions in their papers.

PART I

Hindu-Muslim Cultural Synthesis in North India and Sind

Qāẓī Qādan
A Pioneer Sindhi Poet

ALI S. ASANI

On 9 September 1976, All-India Radio's evening news bulletin announced that a two-hundred-year old manuscript, entitled *Santõ kī vāṇī* containing the poetry of 69 medieval sants had been discovered in a Dadupanthi monastery in the village of Ranila, state of Haryana. Among the contents of the manuscript, which included poems attributed to major poets associated with the bhakti and sant movements, such as Dādū, Nāmdev, Kabīr, Guru Nānak, were 116 verses attributed to the Sindhi poet Qāẓī Qādan (1463-1551). Although not well-known by scholars of the north Indian devotional literatures, Qāẓī Qādan had already been acknowledged, prior to this discovery, by Sindhi scholars as one of the earliest poets of classical Sindhi literature. This assessment had been largely based on the style and content of seven verses attributed to Qāẓī Qādan in a seventeenth century Persian work, the *Bayān ul-ᶜārifīn*. Lalsingh Ajwani, the author of the *History of Sindhi Literature*, describing Qāẓī Qādan as the 'first authentic Sindhi poet' lamented the fact that only seven gems should have been preserved from the treasury of verse written by him.[1] Allama Daudpota declared these seven verses, on account of their style and content, to be the 'shining stars' of Sindhi literature.[2] Clearly the discovery of over one hundred additional verses of this poet had significant implications for the history of Sindhi literature. As the Indian scholar Hiro Thakur, who later edited and published the newly-found verses, stated, 'a chapter of Sindhi literary history, which was submerged in the ocean of the unseen, had suddenly come to light'.[3]

In the years following the discovery of the manuscript, various scholars of Sindhi literature in India and Pakistan examined these verses with a view to preparing a critical edition. They also examined the important

[1] Lalsingh Ajwani, *History of Sindhi Literature*, New Delhi: Sahitya Akademi, 1970, p. 57.

[2] As quoted in Hiro Thakur, *Qāẓī Qādan jo kalām*, Delhi: Puja Publications, 1978, p. 27.

[3] Hiro Thakur, *Qāẓī Qādan jo kalām*, p. 30.

issue of authenticity: could all 116 verses be confidently attributed to Qāẓī Qādan? Answers to this question varied, especially since none of the newly-discovered verses indicated authorship by explicitly mentioning the Qāẓī's name or even a pen-name. Nabi Bakhsh Khan Baloch, in a two-part article published in the Sindhi journal *Mihrāṇ*, concluded that, on the basis of detailed linguistic and stylistic analysis, only 78 verses were authentic, the rest being attributable to other poets.[4] Hiro Thakur, who published an edition of the verses under the title *Qāẓī Qādan jo Kalām*, determined as many as 112 to be authentic.[5] Motilal Jotwani, in his article published in the *Panjab University Journal of Medieval Indian Literature*, was of the opinion that, with the exception of 2 verses, it was difficult to ascertain which of the verses were genuine and which were fraudulent.[6]

Qāẓī Qādan, to be sure, was not the first to write Sindhi poetry. There are several specimens of Sindhi verse believed to have been composed before his time. For example, an Arabic chronicle preserves a verse that is said to be in Sindhi and recited by a visitor to the Abbasid court in Baghdad, yet it is impossible to decipher it due to distortions.[7] Sufi biographies in Persian also quote a few verses in Sindhi recited by various shaykhs,[8] yet as these were usually employed during the ceremony of *samā*ᶜ, or mystical concert, to arouse mystical ecstasy, they were usually transmitted orally. Occasionally, spiritual masters also used verses to convey their personal approval or disapproval of the deeds of their contemporaries.[9] The Ismaili pīrs, or preacher-poets, also composed religious poems (*gināns*) to propagate Ismaili ideas, yet these are difficult to authenticate and generally tend to be a polyglottic mixture of Sindhi, Gujarati and Hindi.[10] Also predating Qāẓī Qādan's verses are a few folk romances and ballads, notably the mid-fourteenth century ballad of *Dodo Chanesar*, the sons of the Samma

[4] Nabi Baksh Khan Baloch, 'Qāẓī Qādan jā bait naĩ taḥqīq jī raushnī mẽ', *Mihrāṇ*, vol. 27, no. 4, 1978, and vol. 28, no. 1, 1979, p. 147.

[5] Hiro Thakur, *Qāẓī Qādan jo kalām*, p. 30.

[6] Motilal Jotwani, 'Sindhi Sufi Poet Qāẓī Qādan: His Poetry in Transliteration and Translation', *Panjab University Journal of Medieval Indian Literature*, vol. 5, nos. 1-2, 1981, p. 70.

[7] Nabi Bakhsh Khan Baloch, *Sindhīa ḇolīa jī mukhtaṣar tārīkh*, Hyderabad, Pakistan, 1962, pp. 45-7.

[8] Husam ad-Din Rashdi, *Sindhī adab*, Karachi: Idarah-i matbuᶜat-i Pakistan, n.d., pp. 19-22.

[9] Memon Abdul Majid Sindhi, *Sindhī adab jo tārīkhī jā'izo*, Sukkur: Ajaib Stores, 1976, p. 49.

[10] Ghulam Ali Allana, *An Introduction to Sindhi Literature*, Jamshoro, Sind: Sindhi Adabi Board, 1991, pp. 8-14.

ruler,[11] and the *Mamui* riddles, which were supposedly recited by the seven faqirs after they had been beheaded in the reign of Jām Niẓāmuddīn (d. 1509) or Jām Tamāchī.[12] Since most of these works are considered to be 'folk' in character, doubts have been raised concerning their authenticity. Qāẓī Qādan thus remains the first Sindhi poet to whom a substantial number of verses can be attributed with a considerable degree of certainty, largely on account of their being preserved in writing.

Qāẓī Qādan, as his title indicates, was a man learned in Islamic law and a master of Islamic religious sciences. He was also famous for the excellence of his writing in the *inshā* style of Persian, the language of *belles lettres* in Sind at the time. In the *Tārīkh-i Maᶜṣūmī*, written in 1600, he is described as a personage of great religious and political standing, especially as the Qāẓī of Bakkar, a strategically located town on the Indus famed for its sanctuary of the legendary Zinda Pir. He became the political and religious advisor to Shāh Beg Arghūn, the ruler of Sind. On Shāh Beg's death in 1522, his son, Shāh Ḥassan, appointed Qāẓī Qādan as Qāẓī of Bakkar, a post he held for 20 years.[13] A later chronicle, the *Tuḥfat al-kirām* (written 1767-8) throws light on Qāẓī Qādan's family history: his great grandfather served as the Qāẓī of Uch, the most important centre of Sufi learning in medieval Sind; his son, 'Abdul Ghafūr, was a renowned scholar who earned the title *Asad ul-ᶜUlamā* ('Lion of the Religious Scholars') while a grandson, Muḥammad Ẓāhir, was the Qāẓī of Thatta and Lahore;[14] his grandson through his daughter Bībī Faṭima, was none other than Miān Mīr, the renowned Qadiri Sufi shaykh who was the spiritual preceptor of the Mughal Prince Dārā Shikoh and his sister, Jahān Ārā.

Through ancestry and education, Qāẓī Qādan belonged to the intellectual elite of Sind. He was obviously well-versed in classical Arabic and Persian, the languages customarily employed in Sind at that time for administration, literature and scholarship. In contrast, the use of Sindhi language in official public circles was confined primarily to bards and minstrels who, through song, praised the bravery and generosity of local rulers and heroes or recounted local folk romances. We have no clear indication in the historical sources of what may have prompted Qāẓī

[11] Annemarie Schimmel, *Sindhi Literature*, vol. VIII of J. Gonda (ed.), *A History of Indian Literature*, Wiesbaden: Otto Harrassowitz, 1974, p. 8.

[12] Memon Abdul Majid Sindhi, *Sindhī adab jo tārīkhī jā'izo*, pp. 35-8.

[13] Sayyid Muḥammad Maᶜṣūm Bakkarī, *Tārīkh-i Maᶜṣūmī*, edited with introduction and notes by U.M. Daudpota, Poona: Bhandarkar Oriental Research Institute, 1938, pp. 200-1.

[14] Mir ᶜAlī Sher Qānīᶜ Thathawī, *Tuḥfat al-kirām* (Urdu translation), Hyderabad, Sind: Sindhi Adabi Board, 1959, pp. 669-70.

Qādan to take the bold and innovative step of composing poetry in Sindhi and employing it to express mystical and gnostic ideas. We can only surmise that he may have taken to writing in Sindhi as a result of a dramatic change in his life. According to the *Gulzār-i abrār*, the celebrated biographical compendium of Sufis (composed between 1605 and 1610), Qāẓī Qādan experienced a crisis of some sort after the completion of his formal education and as a result became more mystically-inclined, capable of perceiving the 'true realities' underlying material objects.[15] The *Bayān al-ᶜārifīn* specifically mentions that, for a brief time, Qāẓī Qādan lived in Dar Bela where he came in contact with an ascetic (*faqīr*) who initiated him into a new spiritual life.[16] One of Qāẓī Qādan's Sindhi verses may in fact allude to this spiritual initiation. He wrote:

I was asleep in a slumber, the jogi woke me up;
He cleansed my heart of dirt and showed me the essence. (35)[17]

The identity of this ascetic who became Qāẓī Qādan's spiritual mentor remains unknown. The *Gulzār-i abrār* suggests that after this change in his outlook, Qāẓī Qādan took to composing mystical verses in his native tongue Sindhi. These verses were said to be so beautiful that they could not be adequately translated into other languages.[18]

Qāẓī Qādan's turn towards spirituality may have also been a result of his association with the chiliastic movement of Sayyid Muḥammad Jaunpūrī, the Mahdi of Jaunpur (d. 1505), a mystic whose ideas reached even the Mughal Emperor Akbar through Abu'l Fazl and Fayzī, whose father Muḥammad Nagorī was a prominent follower of the Mahdi. According to the *Tārīkh-i Maᶜṣūmī*, Qāẓī Qādan's adherence to the Mahdi, 'brought on his head the criticism of the *ᶜulamā* of the time', who were bitterly opposed to this movement.[19] However controversial it may have been, the Qāẓī's affiliation to the Mahdawi movement may have also played a significant role in his decision to compose poetry in Sindhi, for the Mahdi and his followers frequently employed local dialects for their

[15] Muḥammad Ghauthī, *Gulzār-i abrār*, Urdu translation *Aẕkār-i abrār*, by Fạzl Ahmad, Ujjain: Alayar Khan, 1909, p. 275.

[16] Motilal Jotwani, 'Sindhi Sufi Poet Qāẓī Qādan', p. 47.

[17] The translations of Qāẓī Qādan's verses, unless otherwise indicated, are from Motilal Jotwani, 'Sindhi Sufi Poet Qāẓī Qādan'. The number indicated in parentheses after this and subsequent verses indicates the number of the relevant verse in the above article.

[18] Muḥammad Ghauthī, *Gulzār-i abrār*, Urdu translation *Aẕkār-i abrār*, p. 275.

[19] Sayyid Muḥammad Maᶜṣūm Bakkarī, *Tārīkh-i Maᶜṣūmī*, p. 201.

compositions in order to popularize their religious revivalist message among the masses.[20]

Some of the linguistic features of the verses composed by this pioneering writer are revealed in the style of his poetry which combines extreme density in meaning with an abundance of puns, word-plays and alliterations. He employs a wealth of grammatical forms and rich verbal structures to put together words in an intricate pattern, mainly by using a grammatical structure that is peculiar to the Sindhi language — the pronominal subject and object suffix which can be added to verbs as well as post-positions to create very compact constructions. According to Annemarie Schimmel, the resulting 'closely knit fabric of words, carrying different shades of meaning and ambiguous allusions makes a proper, and even more a poetical, translation of Sindhi poetry extremely difficult'.[21] All these features were to become common to later Sindhi mystical poetry. Another noticeable characteristic of Qāẓī Qādan's poetry is the almost total absence of influence of the Arabic and Persian languages or prosody on his Sindhi verse, a remarkable fact given his extensive familiarity with both languages. There are barely a handful of Arabic or Persian words in his verses, nor does he incorporate any Arabic verses from the Koran or explicitly allude to any verses from Persian Sufi poems such as Rūmī's *Maṣnawī*, as many later Sindhi poets were inclined to do. In terms of verse forms, he employs only traditional Sindhi ones, including the *dohā* (60), *soraṭhā* (44), *baro duho* (2), *tunverī duho* (1).[22] In short, Qāẓī Qādan appears to have been consciously keeping the Arabo-Persian literary tradition at a distance from the local Sindhi tradition, a tendency which becomes less pronounced over time as later Sindhi poets tend to draw freely from both traditions in their compositions, thus synthesizing them. On the other hand, Qāẓī Qādan does not write with a purely Sindhi vocabulary; he employs several Siraiki and Punjabi words and grammatical forms in his verses which is perhaps a reflection of the influence of these two languages on the northern Sindhi dialect with which he was most familiar.[23]

The genius of Qāẓī Qādan as a poet lies in the originality of his imagery. Instead of drawing from the traditional stock images and symbols of the Arabo-Persian tradition, he ventures into new territory by turning to nature

[20] Qamaruddin, *The Mahdawi Movement in India*, Delhi: Idarat-i Adabiyat-i Delhi, 1985, pp. 184-200.

[21] Annemarie Schimmel, *History of Sindhi Literature*, p. 12.

[22] Hiro Thakur, *Qāẓī Qādan jo kalām*, pp. 79-80.

[23] Hiro Thakur, *Qāẓī Qādan jo kalām*, p. 82.

and the physical world around him as a source of inspiration for his symbolism. In the process, he utilises images, symbols and idioms that are not evident in the folk poetic tradition that preceded him.[24] The results are stunning. In one memorable verse he proclaims:

There is a solitary banyan tree in the field; I love it very much;
The Beloved sits in its cool shade; a single tree, yet a forest in itself. (55)

In this imaginative verse, he tries to convey the ineffability of God:

Even if you gave me millions of bodies, and on each body millions of heads,
In each head millions of mouths, in each mouth millions of tongues,
And all those tongues sharp and articulate, sang as one,
How would I be able to praise you enough, O Lord? (70)

In another verse, he declares:

My (formal) studies only served to impede me (on the spiritual path).
Every word was a crocodile to battle with.[25]

Elsewhere he compares the spiritual guide or *pīr* to a graceful swan gliding on the lake of existence, feeding on the pearls of true knowledge (verses 14 and 16). He also likens the ignorant soul to a silly frog sitting in the sludge at the bottom of a pond, totally oblivious of the beautiful lotus floating above (verses 17, 18 and 19). The wayward soul is like a stubborn camel who, unable to abandon its habits, prefers coarse grass to the wheat spikes offered it (verse 62).

In terms of its themes, Qāẓī Qādan's poetry reflects many that occur in contemporaneous devotional poetry composed in other north Indian languages. Prominent are verses condemning the efficacy of formal learning and scholarship on the spiritual path:

However much you continue your studies, even if you were to read thousands of books
All that these will teach you is that you won't meet the Beloved this way. (2)

People study grammar, but I, I contemplate the Beloved
Whatever I read, I read again and again—the one and the same letter![26]
I haven't read the *Kanz*, *Qudūrī* and *Kāfiya*
It's a different place where I have met the Beloved. (3)

[24] Nabi Bakhsh Khan Baloch, 'Qāẓī Qādan jā bait', *Mihrāṇ*, vol. 28, no. 1, 1979, p. 149.
[25] L.H. Ajwani, *History of Sindhi Literature*, p. 57.
[26] Hiro Thakur, *Qāẓī Qādan jo kalām*, p. 58.

(The *Kanz* refers to the *Kanz ul-ᶜummāl*, a collection of traditions of the Prophet Muhammad, composed by the Indian scholar ᶜAlī al-Muttaqī; the *Qudūrī* is a traditional eleventh century handbook of Hanafi Sunni jurisprudence as taught in Indian madrasas; the *Kāfiya* is a poem by Ibn Ḥāgib (d. 1249) that summarizes the rules of Arabic grammar which students had to memorize.)

Although he was a religious judge, Qāẓī Qādan was open in his criticism of the religious establishment:

O Qazi! don't sermonize that much; you are knowledge from head to toe!
When the camel (of the last journey) leaves who will put the heavy bag (of your knowledge) upon his back? (59)

The Mulla eats wheat flakes by adding lots of butter and honey
Ask him if he loves God that much as well. (60)

He has many verses regarding the forgetfulness or heedlessness of the soul to its true destiny:

O you sleeping one; awake, arise, the night is all over
Your luck will change; don't forget the Beloved. (87)

You slept the whole night, covering your head like a corpse
Neither do you think of any preparations (for the journey ahead) nor do you have any anxiety (of how will you will meet the Beloved). (78)

The importance of the guide or mentor on the inner spiritual path, the idea of an interiorised religion, and the search for the Beloved in the inner wastes of one's self and the transformation of the ego are other concepts that are frequently echoed:

Lightning, clouds and wind; don't be afraid of the waves
Take an expert pilot, (then) there is no fear of the boat capsizing. (86)

You are the hero of heroes, a jogi. known all over the world
You are our Pir who helps us find Him within ourselves. (34)

He is not to the south or north; nor is he on this or that river bank
He for whom you search in confusion: see Him in yourself. (11)

Those who look into themselves and enter into the calm ocean of the soul
Will see with their own eyes the priceless pearls, deep down. (13)

Don't make a litany of your 'I' 'I' and thereby insult the Beloved
Even though you have ground your ego very thin, still hold the handle of the grinding mill. (73)

Finally, as with many Sufi poets in the subcontinent, Qāẓī Qādan's poetry is permeated by the doctrine of *waḥdat al-wujūd*, or 'unity of existence' popularized by the Hispano-Arab Sufi Ibn ᶜArabī (d. 1240).

It (the world) is a palace of millions of doors and windows
From wherever I look, my Beloved is in front of me. (31)

Like the water, I myself assimilated all colours;
The master Himself gives color: all colors are His. (101)

To what extent can Qāẓī Qādan be regarded as the pioneer of Sindhi poetry? In his symbolism, the themes he expounds and the poetic forms he employs, Qāẓī Qādan foreshadows many of the expressions used by subsequent generations of Sindhi poets. This is particularly true in the case of two important Sindhi poets who came after him: Shāh ᶜAbdul Karīm (d. 1623) and his grandson, the greatest of classical Sindhi poets, Shāh ᶜAbdul Laṭīf (d. 1752). Qāẓī Qādan's influence on Shāh ᶜAbdul Karīm is evident from the inclusion of seven of his verses alongside those of Shāh ᶜAbdul Karīm in the *Bayān ul-ᶜārifīn*, a Persian work written in 1630 and dedicated to preserving the spiritual teachings of Shāh ᶜAbdul Karīm. Shāh ᶜAbdul Karīm was apparently so affected by Qāẓī Qādan's verses that he used to recite them during the assemblies of the *samaᶜ* or mystical poetry concerts. Among the newly-discovered verses, many are echoed in the 93 verses attributed to Shāh ᶜAbdul Karīm in the *Bayān ul-ᶜārifīn*. As for Shāh ᶜAbdul Laṭīf, it is clear that several of Qāẓī Qādan's verses have been incorporated, with a few minor changes, into his *Risālo*, the great classic of Sindhi literature. In a few instances, it appears that Shāh ᶜAbdul Laṭīf borrowed hemistiches from Qāẓī Qādan's verses and then completed them with hemistiches of his own, a poetic device well-known in Persian poetics as *taẓmīn*.

Notwithstanding the above, there are some features of classical Sindhi poetry that are not prominent in Qāẓī Qādan's work and, therefore, are later developments. According to L.H. Ajwani, the culture of Sind is so permeated with folk tales and romances that they become a pivot around which the bulk of Sindhi literature revolves, regardless of form or theme.[27] Folktales provide a rich source of symbols for Sindhi poets. Typical in Sindhi mystical poetry is the use of the heroines of the folktales as the symbols of the soul on her spiritual quest, the soul who burns in divine love and frequently dies through intense longing. The tales themselves are not told in their entirety, rather the poet assumes that the audience is familiar with their plots and simply focuses on those dramatic events and moments

[27] L.H. Ajwani, *History of Sindhi Literature*, p. 40.

in the stories which best convey mystical stages and states.[28] The master of this technique was Shāh ᶜAbdul Laṭīf, whose poetry is replete with references to a whole cast of legendary characters from Sindhi folklore. Indeed, popular folk romances are so central to Shāh ᶜAbdul Laṭīf's poetry that they provide the framework on which to base the the major themes of most of the *Risālo*'s thirty chapters. In contrast, only two of Qāẓī Qādan's verses allude to folktales. One refers to the folktale of Sassui-Punhun, in which Sassui loses her beloved Punhun after he has been kidnapped and sets out on a long trying journey through the desert in search of him:

Following him closely and wailing, I go into the hills;
Let me meet that very Beloved for whom I am grieved. (39)

The other refers to the folktale Moriryo-mangarmachu, according to which the seven sons of Obahiyo, an experience fisherman, ignored the warning of their father that they were not to go in a certain direction and subsequently fell prey to a crocodile:

What Obahiyo said to them, they didn't lend a ear to;
This brought the hunters to a breach with the Beloved. (83)

Another noticeable difference between Qāẓī Qādan's poetry and those of later Sindhi poets concerns the use of the woman soul symbolism. In common with other Indian devotional literatures, Sindhi mystical poetry employs the yearning woman, particularly the *virahinī* as the symbol of the soul. This symbolism led classical Sindhi poets to draw extensively on imagery from songs sung by women not only as they lamented separation from their husbands but also as they engaged in a variety of daily activities such as spinning, weaving, grinding grain, singing lullabies and fetching water.[29] Frequently, skilled poets also introduced expressions used by women into their poetry to give them an authentic touch. For example, one of the chapters of Shāh ᶜAbdul Laṭīf's *Risālo*, titled *Kāpā'itī*, or 'The Spinning Wheel', imagines the soul as a woman at the spinning wheel and employs many idioms that are peculiar to women. This type of imagery, which pervades not only classical Sindhi but also Punjabi poetry,[30] is not so conspicuous in Qāẓī Qādan's poetry.

[28] See Ali Asani, 'Folk Romance in Sufi Poetry from Sind', in *Islam and the Indian Regions*, edited by A. Dallapiccola and S. Lallemant (Beiträge zur Südasienforschung, no. 145), Heidelberg: Südasien Institut Universität Heidelberg.

[29] Ali S. Asani, 'Sufi Poetry in the Folk tradition of Indo-Pakistan', *Religion and Literature*, vol. 20, no. 1, 1988, pp. 81-94.

[30] See Lajwanti Rama Krishna, *Panjabi Sufi Poets*, AD *1460-1900*, London and Bombay: Oxford University Press, 1938.

Let us now turn to a brief consideration of the contextual aspects of Qāẓī Qādan's verses. By this I intend the relationship of these verses to the context of performance. We can be certain that these verses were meant to be sung, most likely to musical accompaniment. The *Gulzār-i abrār* records the impact of Qāẓī Qādan's verses on listeners by remarking that their beauty cannot be adequately expressed,[31] while their inclusion in the *Bayān ul-ᶜārifīn* suggests that Shāh ᶜAbdul Karīm, with his great proclivity for concerts of mystical poetry,[32] was greatly affected by recitations of Qāẓī Qādan's poetry. The relationship of Sindhi devotional poetry to its performance in a musical context becomes explicit in later poets such as Miān Shāh ᶜInāt (d. *c.* 1700) and Shāh ᶜAbdul Laṭīf whose verses are actually arranged into chapters according to the *sūr*s, or musical melodies, in which they were intended to be sung. The inclusion of Qāẓī Qādan's verses in the Dadupanthi manuscript, *Santõ kī vāṇī*, indicates that his verses were sung well-beyond the borders of Sind. Several contemporaneous sources from neighbouring regions, such as Saurashtra and Gujarat, indicate that Sindhi performers had developed a fine reputation for the beauty and sweetness with which they sang mystical poetry.[33] Even Badāūnī, the chronicler in the court of the Mughal Emperor Akbar, writes that he experienced a spiritual state when he heard two Sindhi Sufis singing a melody in mournful and grating tones.[34] Significantly, even during Qāẓī Qādan's lifetime, a group of Sindhi mystics, on account of political turmoil in their homeland, migrated to Burhanpur where records indicate that they used to recite Sindhi verses during *samāᶜ* sessions.[35] It is quite likely that they may have recited some verses composed by the Qāẓī, especially since a close associate and friend of his, Shaikh Ibrahīm Sindhī, whose tomb is to the north of Burhanpur, was among the immigrants.[36] Nabi Bakhsh Khan Baloch suggests that the presence of Qāẓī Qādan's poetry in the manuscript *Santõ kī vāṇī*, housed in a Dadupanthi monastery, indicates

[31] Muḥammad Ghauthī, *Gulzār-i abrār*, Urdu translation *Aẑkār-i abrār*, p. 275.

[32] Motilal Jotwani, *Shāh Abdul Karīm: A Mystic Poet of Sindh*, Delhi: Kumar Brothers, 1970, pp. 15-17, describes Shāh ᶜAbdul Karīm's fondness for the Sufi *samāᶜ* based on hagiographic accounts of the mystic's life recorded in the *Bayān ul-ᶜārifīn.*

[33] Memon Abdul Majid Sindhi, *Sindhī adab jo tārīkhī jā'izo*, pp. 7-8.

[34] 'Abdul Qādir Badāūnī, *Muntakhab at-tawārīkh*, trans. by Wolseley Haig, rpt., Patna: Academia Asiatica, 1973, vol. III, p. 39.

[35] Rashid Burhanpuri, *Burhānpūr ke sindhī auliyā*, Karachi: Sindhi Adabi Board, 1957.

[36] Muḥammad Ghauthī, *Gulzār-i abrār*, Urdu translation *Aẑkār-i abrār*, p. 275.

that Dādū, himself, may have spent some time in Sind and that he must have been so affected by Qāẓī Qādan's poetry that his disciples recorded it alongside that of other north Indian poet-saints.[37] Indeed, poetry attributed to Qāẓī Qādan appears in several other manuscripts containing devotional verses of medieval poets of the *nirguṇ* tradition.[38] This occurrence raises significant questions concerning the relationship of medieval Sindhi literature to the broader corpus of north Indian devotional literatures, questions which hopefully will be addressed in future research.

[37] Nabi Bakhsh Khan Baloch, 'Qāẓī Qādan jā bait', *Mihrāṇ*, vol. 28, no. 1, p. 148.

[38] See W.M. Callewaert and L. De Brabadere, 'Nirguṇ Literature on Microfilm in Leuven, Belgium', *IAVRI Bulletin*, vol. 9 (1980), pp. 28-48. Qāẓī Qādan's poetry appears in the following manuscripts: nos. 2 (dated AD 1676) and 12 (dated AD 1636), at the Dadu Mahavidyalay, Jaipur; nos. 12 (dated 1664) and 34 (dated AD 1658) in the Vidya Bhusan Collection, Jaipur; and no. 875 (dated AD 1675) in the film collection of the GND University in Amritsar.

In Quest for the Correct Combination
The Home-coming Episode in Maulana Daud's Indo-Sufi Masnavī *Candāyan*

NASEEM HINES

MAULANA DAUD AND HIS *CANDĀYAN*

Little reliable information has come down to us about the life of Maulana Daud. What information there is about his life is based on extremely limited sources. These sources are the text of *Candāyan* itself, which may be analysed for details about its author, official documents (*malfuzāt*), of the Sufi orders with which Daud was associated; information about *Candāyan* in Badauni's (d. 1596) *Muntakhab ut-Tawārīkh*; and references in *Candāyan* to other contemporaneous historical personages about whom some biographical information is available. Of these sources, *Candāyan* itself is the major one upon which our understanding of Daud's life, limited as it is, is founded.

Regarding Daud's date of birth and death, Mataprasad Gupta, in the introduction to his edition of *Candāyan*, writes:

> Daud has given the date of composition as Hijri 781 which is approximately 1436 Vikram Saṁvat. Therefore it can be construed that he was born in approximately 1400 vs. and died in approximately 1475 vs. (AD 1343-1418). (M. Gupta 1967, p.1)

From the text of *Candāyan* we learn that *Candāyan* was composed in Hijri 781 (AD 1379), when Firoz Shah was the Sultan of Delhi, and Jauna Shah was Firoz Shah's chief minister. In addition, we can surmise that Daud lived in a place which he refers to as 'the nine-coloured Dalmau' located on a hill on the banks of the Ganges in Uttar Pradesh.

Daud is also mentioned briefly in Shaikh Muhaddis Dehlavi's *Akhbārul Akhiyār*, written in Akbar's reign (1546-1605), which mentions that Shaikh Zainuddin was the nephew, successor, and chief attendant of Nasiruddin Chiragh Dehlavi (d. 1356) and was also the spiritual preceptor of Maulana Daud, the author of *Candāyan*. This is a significant piece of information regarding the life of the author.

Al-Badayuni, a contemporary of Akbar (1556-1605), mentions Maulana Daud and the popularity of his *Candāyan* in his chronicles *Muntakhab ut-Tawārīkh*, which was completed in 1591 (AH 999). M. Gupta recaptures it as follows:

In 1370 Feroz Shah's prime minister Khan-i-jahan died. His son Jauna Shah succeeded him as the prime minister. In *Candāyan*, the well-known Hindi *masnavī*, the love of Lorik and Cāndā is described. This *masnavī* was composed by Maulana Daud and was dedicated to Jauna Shah. The *masnavī* was so famous throughout the region that it was deemed unnecessary to praise it. On one occasion Makhdūm Shaikh Wāiz Rabbanī read some parts of it and the listeners were immensely pleased. When some of the prominent scholars asked the Shaikh whether so much importance should be accorded to a Hindi *masnavī*, the Shaikh replied to them that the entire *masnavī* is filled with the divine truth and symbols. It is an interesting composition and in it is contained food for thought for those who love God and are spiritually inclined. It successfully explains the mystic meaning of some of the *āyāt* of the Quran and is a repository of the sweet songs of India. (M. Gupta 1967, p. 3)

The key words in the above statement are 'divine truth and symbols, and the interpretation of their mystic meaning'. By definition, the *masnavī* is a literary genre in which a long story is narrated in a designated metre. It often is an allegorical romance; a tale of love, quest, adventure, suffering and subsequent redemption. Often there is a one-to-one correspondence between certain mystical themes, and the characters and the elements of the story. In *Candāyan*, the hero, Lorik represents the human soul in quest of the cosmic soul represented by Cāndā.

A BRIEF STORYLINE OF *CANDĀYAN*

The folktale of Chanda and Lurak, which served as the basis for the masnavī *Candāyan* was quite well known in its oral form throughout the north-eastern region. The story begins in the lovely north Indian city of Govar which is ruled over by Mahar Sahdev. His queen Phulārānī gives birth to a beautiful daughter who is actually an *avatāra* of the moon (Cānd), wherefore she was given the name Cāndā. When Cāndā is but four years old, she is married off and sent to live in her father-in-law's household. However, twelve years pass after Cāndā's marriage but her husband Bāvan is incapable of consummating the marriage. Finally, Cāndā returns back to Govar to live with her parents at age seventeen. Here, at a festive occasion, brave Lorik and Cāndā see each other and fall in love at first sight. Lorik's devoted wife, Mainā, is very hurt when she learns of her husband's affair with Cāndā. During a chance encounter between the two women a physical struggle occurs. Shortly after this incident, Lorik, who is forced to make a choice between the two women, elopes with Cāndā across the Ganges. After a long journey and many adventures, Lorik returns home to live with Mainā along with Cāndā. Once again, there is a conflict between Mainā and Cāndā but Lorik successfully resolves it.

All in all, 397 stanzas or *kaḍvak* of this composition are available; at which point, the narrative stops and the reader is left to resort to the oral traditions of *Lorikī* to guess how the story may have come to an end. Nevertheless, it should be kept in mind that because none of the available manuscripts are complete, the concluding stanzas of the masnavī *Candāyan*, are missing. The available text of *Candāyan* has been divided by Mataprasad Gupta in his edition of *Candāyan* into twenty-seven parts. Throughout this paper the numbers following the quotes from *Candāyan* refer to the *kaḍvak* and line numbers in M. Gupta's 1967 edition of *Candāyan*. This paper focuses on the events described in the twenty-sixth part of the narrative entitled the Home-coming Episode, गृहआगमन खण्ड, where Lorik's journey comes to an end.

In the Home-coming Episode Lorik comes back to Mainā after an adventuresome journey, bringing Cāndā along with him. At this point, the question is, since eventually Lorik returns with Cāndā to live with Mainā, why did he decide to go away from Govar in the first place? He certainly would have saved himself from enduring a great deal of hardship away from home. What is the special value of the Home-coming Episode?

My analysis is as follows. Although on the surface *Candāyan* seems to be an interesting love story, *premākhyān*, a more careful reading reveals that even though it contains the 'masālās', such as the portrayal of fights between armies as well as women, detailed description of the female form, recounting of an extra-marital affair, to keep the general audiences entertained, in reality it is an Indo-Sufi *masnavī*, adapted as a vehicle to transport the Sufi doctrine to the uninitiated audiences. Maulana Daud, as mentioned earlier, was a disciple of Shaikh Zainuddin of the Chishty Sufi order and it was not uncommon for a Sufi *murīd* to perform missionary work in such a capacity.

Actually, as an evangelist, Maulana Daud had significant goals to accomplish. First of all he had to introduce the idea of Sufism to his audiences who came from all walks of life. He needed to impress upon the layman that the spiritual aspect of one's existence is just as important as a person's physical existence. He wished to illustrate to his audiences that a Sufi disciple must undertake a spiritual journey in order to infuse enlightenment into his life. He wanted to explicate the various experiences or the different stages through which a Sufi must travel to achieve spiritual fulfilment. In short, Daud had to teach the basics of the Sufi philosophy without boring or scaring his audiences away.

To realize this objective, Daud composed his *Candāyan*. He selected a popular folktale merely as a point of reference. The changes Daud brought into the story and the sophisticated form he gave his composition, altered its focus. From being a simple engaging folk tale, it was transformed into an elevated literary work to transmit Sufi doctrine. Daud was not the first one who used an interesting story to illustrate a point. However, story telling is an art and Daud deserves to be recognized for telling a popular story with skill to keep the audiences in sustained suspense till the very end. The literary genre of *masnavī*, as mentioned above, is an allegorical mystical poem in which certain characters and elements represent specific ideas and doctrines. In other words, the story can be interpreted on a secular as well as on a metaphysical level. Metaphorically, the journey of Lorik in *Candāyan* is the symbol of the spiritual journey of the individual self in search of the universal self. His sojourns in *Candāyan* are an embodiment of a Sufi's spiritual voyage in quest of Eternal Beauty. For a better understanding of *Candāyan* and its purpose it becomes essential to closely examine the Sufi symbols and their meanings.

Cāndā, the heroine of *Candāyan*, is a fitting symbol for divine majesty and glory. In Hindi her name Cānd, means the moon, a source of light and beauty in the firmament. But more importantly, the moon reflects a greater source of light. Therefore, princess Cāndā is a reflection as well as the representation of the divine brilliance. In the Sufi texts, light or brightness is often equated with knowledge. By the same token darkness represents ignorance or an indiscriminate mind. The human soul is likened to a mirror which reflects the light emanating from the eternal source of light. The Koran says: *Allahu Nurussamawati wa-alarz* (24:35), i.e. God is the light of the firmaments and the earth. Among the Sufis, it is believed that the more a Sufi works towards purifying and polishing the mirror of his soul, the better prepared he would be to receive and transmit the celestial light. The hero of *Candāyan*, Lorik, is the symbol of a Sufi novice who has embarked on a quest for spiritual enlightenment.

In *Candāyan* the spiritual journey of Lorik, begins when he sees Cāndā for the first time and swoons. The title of this chapter reads as: आमदने चान्दा बर कस्र व दीदने लोरिक व बेहोश शुदन लोरिक, i.e. Cāndā's arrival at the balcony, Lorik catching a glimpse (of her) and fainting (M. Gupta 1967, p.150). The incidents of this episode may remind the audience of the Biblical story when Moses insisted that he be granted a glimpse of God at Mount

Sinai, but not being able to bear the sight of God's majesty, he faints.

In this episode, Lorik who is invited to a feast at Cāndā's father's house, sees her at her balcony and is convinced that he has seen a nymph (*apsarā*) Lorik falls unconscious and is so disabled that he is carried home on a stretcher or *ḍāṇḍ*. लोरु लीन्ह कइ डांडी, बिसम्भर कछु न संभार (153:7), i.e. 'some carried Lorik on a stretcher as the unprepared one lost consciousness'. After this incident, Lorik declines all interest in the daily pleasures of life. In his mother, Kholin's words: अब न खाइ अन पानी, दीनहि जाइ कुंबिलात (156:7), i.e. now he neither eats food nor drinks water; day by day he wastes away. Lorik now has no recourse but to seek out Cāndā. At this juncture in the story, Lorik represents a Sufi novice who has seen a glimpse of the Eternal Beauty and is ready to embark on a mystical journey in quest of her.

In the context of a Sufi monastery (*khanqah*), a Sufi novice begins his spiritual journey by taking the first step towards a solitary place (*maqām-i-khalwat*), where he retreats in order to practise constant meditation, prayer and vigil. Here he concentrates on God and repeatedly chants His names or a formula of prayers he has been recommended to do, by his Sufi master. The practice of meditation in solitude, *khalwat*, equips a novice to accomplish a state of permanent inward retreat. The practice of remembering by repetition/chanting, *zikr*, promotes the Sufi to a different plane of consciousness. Sufi orders believe that these initial stages are the most significant experiences of a mystic's spiritual journey. Entering a solitary retreat frees the novice from his daily cares and the distance from his immediate environment grants him a different perspective. Once the novice accomplishes this, he is generally considered to be ready to progress to the next stages of his spiritual voyage.[1]

In *Candāyan*, after seeing Cāndā for the first time, relinquishing the comforts of domestic life, Lorik retreats to a shrine in a forest. He holds up the picture of Cāndā in his mind and trusting her name to be the only essence, remains in seclusion for one whole year, practicing austerities: चितहि चांदा मुख चित्र उपावइ, चांद नाम तत सार। एक बरिस लोरिक मढ्ढु सेवा (164:5,7; 165:1). At this point, in his spiritual journey, Lorik has experienced the stages of solitude (*khilwat*), remembrance (*zikr*), and asceticism (*zuhd*).

According to Carl Ernst, the stations or stages, *maqāmāt*, of internal experiences of a Sufi seeker are the result of his soul's striving to attain the qualities of God. According to Ernst, these stages can be considered the station of the creature before God, in terms of where one stands from

[1] Mir Valiuddin, in *The Quranic Sufism*, writes that if entered into and embraced with sincerity, the stage of the spiritual retreat, *khilwat*, has the potential to open the door to the next stage of the mystic journey (Mir Valiuddin 1987, pp. 152-4).

devotions, exertions, meditations, and concentrating on God. Ernst mentions repentance (*tawbā*), asceticism (*zuhd*), poverty (*faqr*), patience (*sabr*), trust in God (*tawakkul*) and satisfaction or submission to the will of God (*rida*), as being some of the principal stations (*maqāmāt*) in a Sufi's spiritual journey (Ernst 1992, pp. 9-10).

In *Candāyan*, after practising austerities for a year at the temple, Lorik does meet Cāndā again. However, Lorik's wife Mainā, the symbol of his worldly existence, finds out about the affair. A short time later, Mainā and Cāndā run into each other at a shrine where they engage in a physical fight. Lorik, who intervenes between the two women is now faced with making a choice between the two. Lorik takes the next step. Leaving behind his family, his land, material wealth and cattle, he elopes with Cāndā to the regions across the Ganga. His decision to renounce his wealth in order to be with Cāndā spontaneously leads Lorik into poverty the next stage of his journey. *Faqrī fakhrī*, a well known Sufi concept can be translated as, 'my poverty is my pride' (Schimmel 1992, p.103).

In the course of their travels, Lorik and Cāndā stop over at a Brahmin's house. In the night, Cāndā succumbs to a snake-bite. Lamenting her loss, Lorik blames his own actions for this predicament लोरिक बीर बहु कारनु करइ। चाह कटारइ कंठ दइ मरई॥ 'Brave Lorik cried ruefully and wished to die by cutting his throat with an axe' (310:3). He repents for his sins over and over again and says that he deserves what he got, जस कीन्हेउं तस पाएउं (316:6). Fortunately, a snake-charmer (*gāruṛī*) arrives at the scene at this time. In exchange for bringing Cāndā back to life he takes away all of their ornaments: कर कंगन अभरन सभ दीहा। अउ सो गारुरि मांगि कइ लीहा। (Lorik) gave the bangles on the wrists and all the other ornaments to the gāruṛī. Whatsoever remained, the gāruṛī demanded and took. At this moment in *Candāyan*, it can be said that the impoverished Lorik has repented for his sins, and has experienced the stage of *tawbā* (repentance).

Unfortunately, soon after being revived from the first snake bite, Cāndā succumbs to a second one. Even though Lorik is overcome by grief, nevertheless, he reiterates his staunch faith in God's compassion in the following words: दया गुसाई सिरजनहारा। तोहि छाहि किसु करउं पुकारा॥ 'Have compassion (on me) O my Maker, except for you, who can I call upon?' (316:5). दुसर न कोउ जो कर उपगारा, सिरजनहार देइ निस्तारा। 'Please tide me over this difficulty for there is no one else capable of doing me this favour' (320:3). After Cāndā's demise, Lorik grieved at Cāndā's side for several hours, इकु दिनु दूसरी रइनि निरबही 'One day and the second night passed' (325:1). Finally he surrenders to the will of God (*rida*), and cuts sandalwood for Cāndā's funeral pier, चंदन काटि कइ चियहि संवारा, i.e. cutting the sandalwood, he arranged the funeral pyre' (325:3). The prospect of living out his life without Cāndā becomes unacceptable to him. Holding Cāndā in an embrace he is about to set fire to the pyre. At this time, Lorik's mind is free of all carnal desires. He is ready to give up his body to be with Cāndā in spirit. The Sufis believe that the ultimate station, *fana*, is experienced when a seeker loses his self in the Self. The seeker's final orientation is towards total receptivity. One of the most famous sayings of the Prophet Muhammad is 'Die before you die'. The day of death of the Sufi saints all over the world is celebrated as their wedding anniversaries (*urs*), because on that day their worldly existence is annihilated in the unity of being (*wahdat-alwajūd*). At this point in *Candāyan*, Lorik has advanced on to the spiritual stages defined by the Sufis as *tawakkul*, i.e. trusting and expecting compassion and mercy from God alone, and ultimately he has experienced *fana*.[2]

The concept of getting rid of the body to facilitate spiritual fulfilment is a prominent theme in Maulana Rumi's *Masnavī.* One fine example of this is the 'Qissa-i-Tuti' or the 'Tale of the Parrot' (Nicholson 1977, p. 101). It goes as follows:

Once upon a time a Persian merchant had a very accomplished Indian parrot encaged. When the time came for the merchant to go to India again on business, he came to the parrot and asked what it would like the merchant to bring back from India as a gift. The parrot sent a message with the merchant to the free flocks of parrots in India. In this message he told his free fellow birds of his feelings of suffering and woe in captivity.

When the merchant reached India and chanced upon a flock of parrots which appeared to be similar to his own bird, he delivered the message which his parrot had entrusted him with. Upon hearing this message, a parrot from this flock became afflicted, trembled and fell. The good merchant was extremely remorseful and cursed himself for bearing such a fatal message.

Returning home the merchant narrated the entire episode to his parrot. As soon as the bird in captivity heard about what had happened in India, it also trembled and fell from its perch. Seeing this the distracted merchant released the listless bird. To his surprise, the bird which he had discarded,

[2] Annemarie Schimmel describes the state of *tawakkul* as follows:

'For the first noted ascetic of the East, Ibrahim ibn Adham (d. 777) and his compatriots, one of the most important aspects of true religious life was absolute trust in God, *tawakkul*. For the early Sufis it meant to refrain completely from carrying any money or food when travelling. One trusts in God because there is no bestower of goods but Him. He is the One Who nourishes and has promised that He will care for all the needs of His creatures.' (Schimmel 1992, p. 103)

taking it to be dead, flew to a high branch. The merchant asked the parrot to explain this mystery.

The bird told the merchant that it had asked the free birds in India to send it a formula for its release from captivity. The free bird had sent the captive bird a message by example. So long as one serves another, he remains a captive. Only by being indifferent and ignoring the external world, does one find true freedom. The merchant appreciated this new lesson and vowed to follow a new path.

A famous Urdu poet Mirza Asad Allah Khan Ghalib encapsulates this concept in one of his couplets:

न था कुछ तो खुदा था, कुछ न होता तो खुदा होता
डुबोया मुझ को होने ने, न होता तो मैं क्या होता

When there was nothing, God was there.
He would still be there, if there was nothing.
It is my existence which has done me in.
Guess what would I be if there was no 'me'. (*Dīwān-ē-Ghalib*, no. 32)

Tracing the spiritual journey of Lorik to the high point of *fana*,[3] one realizes that Lorik actually reaches that state where he can distinguish the difference between the true essence and the mirror which merely reflected the Divine Reality. He realizes that he does not wish to survive Cāndā. Without her he feels that his own physical existence is extremely painful and unbearable:

जरमि न छूट पिरम कर बांधा, पिरम खान्ड आहइ बिस सांधा
जेहि यह चोट लागि सो जानि, कइ लोरिक कइ चान्दा रानी
कोइ न जान दुख काहु केरा, सो पइ जान परइ जेहिं बेरा (323:1-3)

In life, there is no escape from the noose of love.
Love (hurts) like a wound from a poisoned axe

[3] Annemarie Schimmel defines the concept of *fana* as follows:
'*Fana* is in the first place an ethical concept, i.e. the renunciation of human qualities and increasing spiritualization; it has nothing to do with Indian concepts of *nirvana* since it does not mean the attempt to be rescued from the painful cycle of birth and rebirth but rather the return of the creature to the state he was in, before he was.' (Schimmel 1992, p. 106)

With reference to the great Persian mystic Bayezid Bistami and his experiences of *fana*, Annemarie Schimmel, in *Islam* writes:

'Bayezid was the first to use the symbolism of the heavenly journey when speaking of his raptures and has described his longing for *fana* in highly poetical images, as well as his inexplicable disappointment at the end of his experiences.' (Schimmel 1992, p. 106)

Only those who take the wound know the pain.
  Be it Lorik or be it Lady Cāndā.
Nobody knows the pain of another person,
  Except those on whom (trying) times have descended.

A couplet from a poem attributed to Mira Bai which begins: हे री मैं तो प्रेम दीवानी मेरा दरद ना जाने कोय (Chaturvedi 1966, p.121), captures the essence of this thought. It goes as follows:

घायल की गति घायल जाने, कि जिन घायल होय
जौहरी की गति जौहरी जानी, की जिन जौहर होय

Only the one who has endured a wound may fathom the pain of the wounded. Only the one who has already immolated herself on the funeral pyre may claim to know and understand what another woman, who has also performed the Rājpūt ritual of *Jauhar*, has experienced.

In *Candāyan*, when Cāndā dies from the second snake-bite, Lorik decides that he would rather die in order to accompany Cāndā where their souls could be together: कवनिहु भांति न छुटत देखेउं तेहि पिरम कइ झेल। पिरम खेल सोई पइ खेलइ जो सिर सेती खेल॥ Lorik says: 'I have never seen any body free himself, no matter how he tries, from enduring the pain of love. Love is not for everybody, only those who are willing to wager their heads, (lives), should dare play this game' (324:6-7). As Lorik prepares to burn himself on the funeral pyre, he is prepared to make the ultimate sacrifice, i.e. the sacrifice of his life, his ego, his self. At this moment Lorik is devoid of all carnal desires and his mind is pure. In actively embracing self annihilation, the ultimate sacrifice, we realize that Lorik has actually moved towards his ultimate goal of union with eternal beauty and joy represented by the heroine in the story. In *fana* he has found the life everlasting. In other words, the success of the individual soul in attaining union with the universal soul lies in the seriousness of his pursuit and his complete commitment and readiness to sacrifice everything to achieve his goal. Self sacrifice, then, is the key to *fana*.[4] Lorik's adventures away from home and

[4] In Ibn Farid's words,

'Existence is a veil in the beginning of the mystic life, and also in its middle stage, but not in its end. The mystic is veiled in the beginning by the outward aspect of existence (created things) from the inward aspect (God), while in the middle state, he is veiled by its inward aspect from its outward aspect. But when he has reached his goal, neither do created things veil him from God nor does God veil him from created things, but God reveals Himself to the mystic in both His aspects at once as the Creator and as the universe of created things, so that the mystic sees with his bodily eye the beauty of the Divine Essence manifested under the attribute of the Outward.' (Laleh Bakhtiar 1976, p. 95)

his various experiences and actions mirror his spiritual progress to the point when he completes his formal training and has successfully accomplished his spiritual goals.

In most allegorical stories, the life of a Sufi remains conventional to a certain degree till the moments of mystic experience imbue it with a quality that makes it quite different from the life of common people. For example, when the mystic eats, drinks, sleeps and tends to the daily routine of his life, his life is similar to that of a common man, but when he is experiencing spiritual ecstasy, it is the high point in his life. Nevertheless, the mystic cannot remain on this high point for a long time and has to descend from the high moment of ecstasy to the mundane.

Therefore, after being absent from home for six seasons, or approximately a year, Lorik returns back to Gover along with Cāndā. It is by no means an easy task for him to re-enter the life of Gover. However he cajoles Maināinto forgiving him for the pain he caused her. When Lorik and Cāndā arrive home, Lorik's mother Kholin also embraces both her daughters-in-law and takes them into the house.

At this point in the story, one could ask why Lorik could not have accomplished this before the elopement because this would have saved him from enduring the constant dangers, numerous battles and injuries, unbearable sufferings and countless hardships of the journey?

Perhaps, a Sufi's answer would be that in order to infuse his life with meaning, Lorik had to experience the *maqāmāt* of *khalwat*, *zikr*, *zuhd*, *faqr*, *rida* and *tawakkul* which finally guide him to the stage of *fana*. Without successfully completing such a spiritual journey he could not come back to his family life.

In conclusion, unlike many religious denominations and orders, Islam does not impose celibacy on the Muslim clergy. Nevertheless, believers are advised that they should strike a balance between their spiritual and material existence. God says in the Koran that the world along with its beneficial plants, bountiful fruits and animals has been created for the enjoyment of the people, however one should be cautious of extremes and should partake of the pleasures of the senses only in moderation.

The journey of Lorik is essentially symbolic of his spiritual growth which ultimately guides him to *fana*. The experiences of spiritual retreat, asceticism, renunciation, patience, submission to the will of God and ultimately the total orientation towards spiritualism are such experiences which will remain in Lorik's mind permanently. In *Candāyan*, the Home-coming Episode is the harbinger of the message that it is time now for Lorik to return to his family life. He has to concentrate on finding the correct combination to create a sense of balance and harmony in the spiritual and physical aspects of his existence. Lorik must enjoy in moderation the worldly bounties which are gifts from God. Cāndā, is the symbol of Lorik's spiritual accomplishments and Mainā, of his worldly blessings. The struggles between Cāndā and Mainā are symbolic of the initial struggle between the spiritual and physical forces in Lorik's existence. By striving to bring harmony to his household, he is actually trying to strike a balance between the material and spiritual aspects of his life.

In conclusion I would like to reiterate that the most important lesson Daud wished to teach his readers and audiences is visible only in the Home-coming episode. In this chapter Daud demonstrates that renouncing the worldly pleasures of this world in pursuit of spiritual fulfilment is admittedly a difficult task but it is even more difficult to re-enter the world of phenomena without breaking away from one's spiritual accomplishments and aspirations. In other words, Daud is teaching his audiences that even though seeking the correct combination to achieve a sense of balance and harmony in the spiritual and the physical aspects of life is like walking a tight rope; for a mystic, it is the only way to go.

Clearly, in the above context, the Home-coming episode of *Candāyan* contains the true essence of the didactic aspect of this *masnavī*. It demonstrates that Daud was not interested in merely telling an entertaining tale to his audiences. His true agenda was to communicate to his audiences that one must strive to bring spiritual fulfilment in life to make it meaningful. When *Candāyan* is appreciated as an Indo-Sufi *masnavī*, only then is its correct spirit and message realized. Placing the Home-coming episode in the above context, I believe that it is the perfect end to Lorik's story. In fact, it will hardly be an exaggeration to claim that the story could not have culminated in a more appropriate manner.

REFERENCES

Bakhtiar, Laleh, *Sufi Expressions of the Mustic Quest*, New York: Thames and Hudson, 1987.

Chaturvedi, Parashuram, *Mīrāṁbāī kī padāvalī*, Prayag: Hindi Sahitya Sammelan, 1996.

Ernst, Carl, *Aeternal Garden: Mysticism, History & Politics at a South Asian Sufi Center*, Albany: State University of New York Press, 1992.

Gupta, Mataprasad (ed.), *Candāyan*, Agra: Agra Printing Works, 1967.

Nicholson, R.A. (ed.), *Mathnavi of Jalaluddin Rumi*, 4 vols., Cambridge: University Printing House, 1977 (reprint).

Schimmel, Annemarie, *Islam*, New York: State University of New York Press, 1992.

Valiuddin, Mir, *The Quranic Sufism*, Delhi: Motilal Banarsidass, 1987, 3rd edn.

Nakh-śikh in *Candāyan*

SHYAM MANOHAR PANDEY

Candāyan[1] is the first Sūfī text in Hindi in which Maulānā Dāūd makes an attempt to describe the beauty of the heroine, Candā, from head to foot. This description of beauty clearly demonstrates that Candā's beauty is divine in its nature. Later most of the Hindi Sūfī poets such as Kutuban in *Mirgāvatī* (1503), Malik Muhammad Jāyasī in *Padmāvat* (1540) and Manjhan in *Madhumālatī* (1545) follow this tradition. A Sūfī text *Kanhāvat*, attributed to Jāyasī and which describes Kṛṣṇa as divine, also includes milkmaids *nakh-śikh* in details. These Sūfī poets suggest that their heroines are not ordinary human beings; they are symbols of divine beauty on earth.

In *Candāyan*, Bājir[2] who is a beggar and a mendicant from Ujjain, struck by Candā's beauty in Govar comes to Rūpcandra, a king of Rājpur and describes her *nakh-śikh* before him and he is sunk in love for her. The description in *Candāyan*[3] begins from the parting of Candā's hair *(māng)*, and then the poet portrays her forehead, eyebrows, eyes, nose, lips, teeth, tongue, ears, cheeks, arms, breast, stomach, back and feet, etc.

MĀNG

Bājir says

I am describing the *māng* (parting of hair) which is blessed and the whole world plays the festive Phāg with her (64/1). She has put vermilion in her *māng* as if a centipede of golden colours is creeping there (64/2). It seems as though a lamp is burning during the night. Her parting looks as bright as the brightness of the rays

[1] *Candāyan* was composed in AD 1379. The author Maulānā Dāūd was a disciple of Shaikh Zainuddīn, a Chishti saint who was a disciple and nephew of Shaikh Nasiruddīn Chirāgh-i Dehlī who died in AD 1356.

[2] For a detailed study see 'Candāyan meṃ Bājir Murchā kā Prasang' in Shyam Manohar Pandey, *Hindī aur Fārsī Sūfī Kāvya*, Allahabad: Lokbhārtī Prakāśan, 1989.

[3] All the references in this article, unless otherwise stated are from the edition of M.P. Gupta, who has also been referred to as MPG in this article, Agra: Prāmāṇik Prakāśan, 1968.

of the rising sun through the darkness (64/4). Pearls are embellished on the parting of her hair which illuminate the whole world (64/4).

Rūpcandra the king of Rājpur, insists that Bājir sing this episode of *nakh-śikh*. He is so enmeshed in love that he finds himself helpless and cannot come out of it.

In Kutuban's *Mirgāvatī*[4] the *māng* has been described differently. A maid servant describes the beauty of Mirgāvatī to prince Rājkuvār. Here, the parting of her hair has been described 'as beautiful as white sandal paste'. Pearls are studded there as if a group of white cranes are appearing in among dark thick clouds. According to Kutuban, Mirgāvatī's *māng* is the 'edge of a sword which can cut anybody to pieces'.

In *Padmāvat*[5] there are two descriptions of the *nakh-śikh.* One from verse 99 to 118 and the other from verse 470 to 484. In the first *nakh-śikh*, a parrot describes Padmāvatī's beauty to Ratnasen. Padmāvatī is then unmarried. In the second one Rāghavcetan comes to Alāuddīn and describes her beauty to the king of Delhi, Alāuddīn. Here Padmāvatī is married. In the first *nakh-śikh,* the *māng* is portrayed as a golden line on a touchstone (100/3). It looks like lightning which flashes through the dark night. Like in *Mirgāvatī,* the *māng* has been compared to the edge of the sword in *Padmāvat* too (100/5). In *Candāyan* this imagery is not found but the *māng* brings light to the world both in *Mirgāvatī* and *Padmāvat*. The *māng* is compared with the rays of the sun as in *Padmāvat*.

In *Madhumālatī*,[6] Manjhan borrows some comparisons from *Candāyan* as do the other texts, such as the *māng* is a burning lamp (78/4). and is resplendent like the rays of the sun (78/1).

[4] Mātā Prasād Gupta (ed.), *Mirgāvatī*, Agra: Prāmāṇik Prakāśan, 1968. See also the critical edition of D.F. Plukker, Amsterdam, 1981. In the present article Gupta's edition has been used mostly but where the texts differ, I have applied my own judgement to select the words or the verses between the two editions.

[5] Here V.S. Agravāl's text has been used which is based on M. P. Gupta's edition of *Jāyasī Granthāvalī*, Allahabad: Hindustānī Academy, 1952. V.S. Agravāl's, Hindi commentary and culural notes are very exhaustive. His first edition was published in vs 2012 (1957) from Cirgā̃v, Jhā̃sī. Since then several editions have appeared. The second revised edition appeared in vs 2018 (1961). Later, Mātā Prasād Gupta published his own commentary in 1963, but he has given very few notes. Before these critical editions came out, the vulgate edition of R.C. Shukla, *Jāyasī Granthāvalī*, Banaras: Nāgarī Pracāriṇī Sabhā, 1924 (2nd revd. edn. 1935), was very popular. A.G. Shirreff has based his English translation on this text. See *Padmāvatī*, Calcutta: Royal Asiatic Society of Bengal, 1944.

[6] See M.P. Gupta (ed.), *Manjhan kṛt Madhumālatī*, Allahabad: Mitra Prakāśan, 1961.

In *Kanhāvat*,[7] a Kṛṣṇaite Sūfī text attributed to Malik Muhammad Jāyasī, the beauty of the milkmaids has been described. In their *māng*, *muktāhal* (pearls) look like *nakṣatras* (planets) (SP 234/3). As in *Candāyan*, the *māng* has been described like the rays of the rising sun (SP 234/4). In *Candāyan*, the vermilion in the parting of the hair looks as though a *kanakkhajurā* (centipede) of the yellow colour is creeping. Here in the *Kanhāvat*, the *māng* resembles the red *ghunghucī* (abrus precatorius). In *Kanhāvat*, this *māng* has also been portrayed as a golden pillar, which is surrounded by serpents. Even a magician does not have a cure if one is bitten by the curls which circle the *māng* (SP 234/7).

HAIR

After the *māng* in *Candāyan*, Candā's dark bee-coloured hair has been described. Her black hair is like serpents who roll on a store of nectar. A magician can not cure those who are bitten by these serpents, nor any medicine or mantras work on them. When she loosens the locks of her hair, then darkness prevails upon the day. The king Rūpcandra becomes unconscious when he hears about Candā's dark hair. Maulānā Dāūd says, 'How one can be cured if one is affected by snake poison just by hearing about it?' (65/7).

Following *Candāyan* Kutuban also describes Mirgāvatī's hair which is as black as bees. Mātā Prasād Gupta has reconstructed the text here as *megh baran* for *bhāvar baran* (colour of the bees) which does not seem to be very appropriate (*Mirgāvatī* MPG 51/1). Plucker's text reads here as *bhāvar baran* (51/1). Just as in *Candāyan*, hair in *Mirgāvatī* has been compared to serpents. People are smitten when they see Mirgāvatī's hair. When she loosens the locks of her hair, the dark and the thick night of the *Bhādon* (August-September) month pervades the day time. This line is not found in MPG but Pluckker has included this in his text (51/ 2).

[7] *Kanhāvat* is a text by a Muslim poet who uses the story of Kṛṣṇa to depict the Sūfī philosophy of love. For a detailed study on *Kanhāvat* see my article, '*Kanhāvat*, A Kṛṣṇaite Sūfī Text Attributed to Malik Muhammad Jāyasī', *Orientalia Lovaniensia Periodica*, vol. 26, 1995, pp. 187-98. The famous author of the *Padmāvat*, Malik Muhammad Jāyasī, is supposed to be the author of this text. There are two different editions published in Hindi, one by P.L. Gupta, *Malik Muhammad Jāyasī kṛt Kanhāvat*, Varanasi: Annapūrṇā Prakāśan, 1981 and the other by Ś. Pāṭhak, *Kanhāvat*, Allahabad: Sāhitya Bhavan, 1981. Both the texts have been used in this study. P.L. Gupta has been referred to as PG and Ś. Pāṭhak as SP in this article.

In the first *nakh-śikh* of *Padmāvat*, Padmāvatī's tresses are black bees as in *Candāyan* and in *Mirgāvatī*. When she loosens her hair, darkness spreads over the universe from Heaven to Hell. Her hair is as poisonous as the serpent as has already been described in the early two texts.

Following *Candāyan*, Manjhan also describes Madhumālatī's black hair. The locks on her head are poisonous serpents (79/1). The day darkens when she loosens her locks. Manjhan, at the end of the verse says that the God of love has spread his net to ensnare the souls of grieving lovers (80/7).

In *Kanhāvat*, hair is not described. Candā, Mirgāvatī, Madhumālatī are divine symbols. They symbolize divine power which can radiate light and set in darkness. Hyperbole is the strategy through which Hindi Sūfī poets purport to convey their message. Since in *Kanhāvat* Kṛṣṇa is the male divine symbol, it was not necessary to describe his long hair.

FOREHEAD

Candā's forehead attracts the gods and leaving their families and the world, they serve Candā. This forehead is like the moon rising on the second day (*dūj kā cā̃d*). It seems that pure gold has been tested on the touchstone. It is to be remembered that this metaphor has been used later by Jāyasī in the description of the *māng* (*kancan rekh kasauṭī kasī* 100/3). Drops of perspiration on Candā's face look like planets (*nakṣatra*) in the moon. Her forehead is the sun rising on the sky. Maulānā Dāūd compares her forehead with a hot melting iron also which nobody could see from the front.

Bājir describes Candā's forehead to king Rūpcandra and he gives him gold as a gift. When he hears the description of the hair which was like the serpents, he suffers from the poisonous effect, but now this effect has declined.

In *Mirgāvatī* (52/1) as well as in *Padmāvat*'s two descriptions (101/1, 472/2) the forehead has been compared with the second day's moon. Kutuban describes Mirgāvatī's drops of perspiration which are akin to *nakṣatra*s (52/3). Here *Mirgāvatī* follows *Candāyan*. In *Madhumālatī* as in *Candāyan,* and subsequent Hindi texts the forehead of Madhumālatī brightens the nine parts of the universe and the three worlds. Drops of perspiration here have been portrayed as the *kṛttikā nakṣatra* (the third lunar mansion) obliterating the moon.

Padmāvat's author Malik Muhammad Jāyasī does not mention drops of perspiration which are like the *nakṣatra*s, although he is very detailed in his other descriptions. The moon is inferior to Padmāvatī's forehead as he is not spotless and Rāhu grabs him in the eclipse. Padmāvatī's forehead like the moon, is always illuminated. Ratnasen loses his senses like Rūpcandra of *Candāyan* when he hears the description of Padmāvatī's (forehead) *lalāṭ* from the parrot Hīrāman. Later, Tulsīdās in his *Rāmāyaṇa* describes Rāma's lunar face in a similar style (Laṅkā 12b-13a) .

Kanhāvat, attributed to Malik Muhammad Jāyasī, describes the foreheads (SP 235) of the milkmaids in the *nakh-śikh,* but the drops of perspiration which are like the *nakṣatra*s are not mentioned here either.

EYEBROWS

Her eyebrows look like a bow completely drawn which she is holding in her hands. Fully ready, she is aiming to kill some one with the poisonous arrows of her glances. They are sharpened on a lathe and like a fowler she goes on hunting. Maulānā Dāūd says that Candā's arrows have all the qualities of Arjuna's[8] arrows. When she uses them on some one he falls to the ground immediately and cannot move from that place. Candā aims and kills and she never fails.

Rūpcandra hears about the bows and like a deer he becomes so infatuated that he cannot help moving towards her to be killed. The poet suggests here the divine glances which wound the devotees on the path. *Mirgāvatī*, *Padmāvat*, and *Madhumālatī*, all use this symbol.

In *Mirgāvatī* the eyebrows are like the bows and like *Candāyan* her glances are like Arjuna's arrows (53/1). Again the poet says 'it is not known from where she obtained these sharp arrows of Karṇa which are soaked in poison'(53/3). She uses her eyebrows when she shoots her arrow-like glances on some one, he falls to the ground and there is no remedy for him. No magic and no magic formula work on he who is wounded by her. The prince Rājkuvār says 'I am a deer and like a hunter she has killed me with her poisonous arrows'. According to the poet

[8] Arjuna's miraculous bow has been mentioned in the *Mahābhārata* in the chapter 'Burning of the Khāṇḍava Forest'. Thereupon he (Agni) gave him (Arjuna) the miraculous, powerful gem of a bow that would increase his fame and renown, unassailable by any weapon, wreaking havoc on all weapons, great lord of all arms that menaced the enemy forces, by itself the equal of hundred thousand, enhancer of the realm, colourfully shining with many-fold hues, smooth and unscratched, which for eternities had been worshipped by Gods. For details see *Mahābhārata* (1. The book of the beginning), English translation, J.A.V. Van Buitenen, Chicago, 1973, p. 416.

Mirgāvatī's bows compare with Paraśurām's[9] bow, but when she kills someone neither the wounds nor the blood stains are visible (53/6).

Padmāvat's images are more detailed. Padmāvatī's two eyebrows, black bows are ready, strung, from which she speeds mortal shafts at whomsoever she casts but a glance (Shirreff, pp. 73, 74). This is the bow which Kṛṣṇa bore; this was the bow which was gripped by Rāma's hands. With this bow was Rāvaṇa slain. With this bow Arjuna smote the fish (Shirreff, p. 73, verse 4).

Like Candā and Mirgāvatī, Padmāvatī is a huntress. It becomes clear that Jāyasī elaborates upon the metaphors borrowed from *Candāyan* and *Mirgāvatī*. It is obvious that *Mirgāvatī* owes many elements to *Candāyan* as do many other Sūfī poets in Hindi.

In *Madhumālatī*, eyebrows are bows but descriptions are different here. It is the God of love who has brought this bow and placed it there. With this bow Madan (Kāmdeva) conquered the three worlds and then he brought it as a gift to Madhumālatī (verse 82).

In *Kanhāvat,* the eyebrows who kill people have not been described since the divine power of killing in love rests in Kṛṣṇa; therefore, milk-maids' eyebrows as hunters and killers have naturally been ignored. It is the same case with tresses. They have the power to diffuse light and the darkness, and this capacity has been invested in Kṛṣṇa who is a divine symbol. In *Kanhāvat*, the milkmaid's tresses have been described very briefly. These tresses are not poisonous serpents here as in other Sūfī texts. Heroines are divine symbols endowed with the power of giving light, darkness and killing and infusing life.

EYES

In *Candāyan*, Candā's beautiful eyes are whitish-black (*makarāre*) and they change their colour to reddish every moment. It seems as though they are pieces of mangoes filled with pearls which have been placed below the eyebrows. These eyes move about as though they are deeply drunk. It

[9] Paraśurāma, the sixth incarnation of Viṣṇu. Literally Paraśurāma means Rāma with *paraśu* (an axe). He was a Brāhmaṇa, the fifth son of Jamadagni and Reṇukā, and descended from Bhṛgu and for this reason he is called Bhṛgunāth also. Many stories are told of him in the *Mahābhārata* for his murder of his mother in obedience to his father and restoring her to life again. His conflict with Rāma is narrated in the *Tulsī Rāmāyaṇa* as well. He is considered to be an enemy of the Kṣatriyas and he cleared the earth of Kṣatriyas twenty-one times. Paraśurāma is not very famous for his bow still Kutuban compares Mirgāvatī's eyebrows with Paraśurāma's bow. It does not seem to be a very appropriate simile.

seems they are lamps put out by the morning air. The poet also compares them with the jewels thrown out by the sea waves. Kings try to get them unsuccessfully. These eyes are the fathomless sea. Boats sink into them and they cannot cross it. Many kings live in her eyes. She is the moon sitting on the sky.

Kutuban describes the eyes as whitish and red (55). They are bees buzzing on a lotus. Like Candā's eyes Mirgāvatī's eyes also move about and fluctuate. They are never stable (55/2). They are intoxicated in *virah* and like the sea they are overflowing. Eyes have been compared to the sea in *Candāyan* also. They are unstable, move and fluctuate like Candā's eyes. They are sharp and bright and the prince Rājkuvār was pierced by them.

Candā's eyes are not intoxicated in *virah* as Mirgāvatī's, but in Candā's eyes dwell many kings of the world and she herself lives in the sky.

In *Padmāvat*, Malik Muhammad Jāyasī as usual is elaborate and detailed. Padmāvatī's eyes are the ocean whose waves rise and fall. When these two eyes turn from side to side, the sea also moves in waves. Her eyes put the *khanjan* bird and deer to shame. Their eyes do not look as beautiful as Padmāvatī's. Jāyasī uses these traditional Indian metaphors very often here. It is to be noted that like *Candāyan*, Jāyasī also depicts eyes resembling the ocean filled with gems (*māṇikya*). Just as in *Candāyan* these eyes move and dart around.

In *Madhumālatī*, her eyes were arrows black, white and red in colour. There is no comparison of the eyes here with an ocean but they are arrows which could pierce through a person's heart. These eyes are never still. Here Manjhan uses the *Candāyan*'s metaphor of a hunter who kills people, the only difference being that *Candāyan* uses this metaphor in the context of eyebrows as mentioned above. Both the *Candāyan* and *Madhumālatī* texts use the word Pāradhī for the hunter.

In *Kanhāvat* also eyes are unstable and they dart about. They have been compared to an ocean. They are sharp and beautiful as the *khanjan* bird's eyes. Here eyebrows are like the hunter who goes out in the forest hunting. It has to be remembered here, that milkmaids in *Kanhāvat* go to the forest hunting Kṛṣṇa. The word used here is *aherī* (hunter) and not *pāradhī* who is a violent killer. Milkmaids keep sharp arrows in their eyes, which are the sidelong glances of Kāmadeva.

NOSE

After the eyes Maulānā Dāūd describes the beauty of her nose. People praise the parrot's beak in this world but Candā's nose is more attractive than that. Like the beauty of the sesamum flower, her nose is soft and delicate but again the poet compares her nose with a golden sword. From her nose she enjoys the fragrance of *khas*, and other flowers. Hearing this Rūpcandra sometimes loses consciousness and then comes to life again.

In *Mirgāvatī*, Mirgāvatī's nose is well-formed. It is neither big nor small. The great artist, the creator has shaped it well with his own hands. Like in *Candāyan*, the nose has been compared with the sesamum flower in *Mirgāvatī* as well. Mirgāvatī understands all the essence of fragrances and perfumes and knows what the six kind of *rasas* are. She is eternally blessed.

In *Padmāvat* the heroine's nose is as thin as the edge of the sword. When it saw her nose, the parrot was filled with shame, as its beak was not as shapely as Padmāvatī's. Here Jāyasī uses standard and traditional metaphors. In the *Padmāvat*, the narrator of the *nakh-śikh* is the parrot Hirāman, who is jealous of Padmāvatī because its beak is not as tender as sesamum flower. Padmāvatī like Candā, has the capacity to enjoy the fragrance of every flower and every kind of scent. A comparison of Padmāvatī's nose with the sesamum flower has been repeated in the second *nakh-śikh* as well (475/4).

In *Madhumālatī* the poet says that Madhumālatī is beyond all descriptions. A parrot's beak, a sword's keen edge, and a sesamum flower could not be compared with her nose. Sweet scents and fragrance keep her alive. The sun and moon serve her day and night. Here Manjhan compares Madhumālatī's nose with the Udayācal mountain, where the sun rises but the moon shines first. Like all other poets of Hindi Sūfī tradition Manjhan also demonstrates some originality in his descriptions but the principal metaphors of *Candāyan* are preserved in *Madhumālatī*.

In *Kanhāvat,* the nose resembles the parrot's beak as well. It is thin and the milkmaids have put on a nose ornament studded with jewels. It appears that Agastya[10] star is risen in the sky. It should be mentioned here that nose ornaments are not described in classical Indian literature. *Kanhāvat* is the first Sūfī text that mentions *nakbesari*, a kind of nose ring (SP 235).

[10] Agastya (the star of Canopas). The name of the star Agastya which appears in the southern part of the sky in the month of Bhādrapada (August-September). Its colour is whitish yellow and is very bright.

LIPS

In *Candāyan* Bājir tells the king Rūpcandra,

O king! Candā's lips frighten people as if they are thirsty for human blood (70/1). They look like the red powder *ingur*. These lips have learnt well to drink human blood. The poet uses another simile as well and says that these lips look like red coral. They are in two pieces as if some one has cut them with a sword in two parts (70/5). When the king heard about them tears of blood flowed from his eyes.

In *Mirgāvatī*, her lips are red as though she has chewed betel leaves, well prepared (60). They match the *ingur*'s red colour. They are softer than butter. Kutuban also compares them with nectar. Like in *Candāyan,* they look like *pravāl* (red coral). The prince Rājkuvār says that these red lips have sucked my blood so much so that I have grown pale. Profound deep *ingur* (a red powder) as the colour of the lips is similar to the red lips in *Candāyan*. They are like red coral. As already referred to, this comparison is found in *Candāyan* too.

In *Padmāvat*, Padmāvatī's lips are scarlet. They are filled with nectar. They look like blood-red wild gourd. The betel within her mouth ever pours new colour into it (106).

In *Madhumālatī*, Madhumālatī's lovely lips are full of nectar; they always remain thirsty for human blood. They are compared here with the red *vimba* fruit. It seems that the creator has squeezed the nectar from the moon and formed them with it. Rājkuvār has a keen desire to obtain them. The poet says 'her two lips were fire but the world regards them as a sea of nectar'.

In *Kanhāvat*, there is no description of lips. *Mirgāvatī*, *Padmāvat*, *Madhumālatī*, all portray lips (*adhar*) differently but their red colour is mentioned in all the texts. They contain nectar but they are not easily available to any one. This has been indicated in all the Sūfī texts of Hindi.

TEETH

Maulānā Dāūd begins the description of Candā's teeth and her four frontal teeth (71) which have become red because she eats well-prepared betel leaves. In *Candāyan* when she smiles opening her lips then lightning flashes in the dark night. They shine like diamonds. Maulānā Dāūd compares them with burning coals in a fire pot. Again he reports that these teeth are like pomegranate.

In *Mirgāvatī*, the heroine's teeth shine like lightning and the four front teeth shine like the bright diamond which are found in Berāgar.[11] Mirgāvatī's teeth are compared with the pomegranate, just as in *Candāyan* (61/3). Her teeth are red because she eats betel leaves. This is described in *Candāyan* as well. Mirgāvatī's teeth are neither big nor small. They are uniform in their size and they give peace to mind when you see them. Kutuban compares them with special jewels (*gajmuktā*).

Following the *Candāyan*, Jāyasī also compares Padmāvatī's teeth with the gleam of lightning. Her teeth are splendid and the sun, the moon, the stars and jewels, diamonds, rubies, pearls, all owe their splendour to it. The pomegranate can not equal her teeth. When she opens her lips, light is scattered all around (Shirreff, p. 77). Padmāvatī's fore teeth strike people as the lightning does.[12]

In *Madhumālatī* (verse 88), the brilliance of Madhumālatī's teeth was beyond all description.

So dazzling were they to the eye. Even when she gave a little smile in sleep, it seemed as if a lightning bolt had fallen from heaven. When she opened her lips, her teeth shone forth so brightly that the saints and sages of all worlds were overcome and lost all recollection of themselves. Mars, Venus, Jupiter, and Saturn were so frightened by the radiance of her teeth that they went off who knows where, and hid themselves within the moon. But were some one to say in these teeth God has revealed Himself, I must explain the nature of the Lord, for he is hidden in this world, and no one has ever seen Him. (88)

In *Kanhāvat* (SP 238), the teeth have been compared to diamonds. The milkmaids' front teeth shine brilliantly and when they smile, they strike like lightning. Their teeth look like pomegranates. These teeth are *nakṣatra*s who appeared on the earth. All the fairies are ashamed because they can not match the milkmaids' beauty. *Candāyan*'s influence can be seen here as well.

THE TONGUE

In *Candāyan* sweet words fall from Candā's tongue. The *padminī*[13] woman Candā tells the tale of love as sweet as delicate leaves and flowers. By her speech she puts people to sleep. They forget their sufferings and sleep

[11] Diamonds from Bairāgar mines used to be very shiny and precious. Someśvara in *Mānasollāsa* refers to Bairāgar in early twelfth century. According to Motīcandra, Bairāgaṛh was in Candā district of Madhya Pradesh on the bank of Bengaṅgā river. Veṇu or Veṇ of classical Sanskrit literature is perhaps the river Bengaṅgā. In Bairāgaṛh of Madhya Pradesh, diamonds are still found. For details, see also P.L. Gupta, *Mirgāvatī*, p. 148.

[12] Agravāl, *Padmāvat*, verse 477; Shirreff, p. 281.

[13] Padminī. In Indian Kāmaśāstra, *padminī* is the most beautiful and benevolent

happily during at night. Her mouth is a pot of nectar and sweet speech flows from it. The tongue, in her mouth is like a lotus flower which touches the leaves of the lips and lives under their shadow. When she smiles and speaks, then flowers fall from her mouth.

The king Rūpcandra has been tricked by this description. He starts crying, 'Catch, catch Candā who is nectar and is delicate like leaves and flowers. I had a glimpse of her but she has run away' (*Candāyan*, 72).

In *Mirgāvatī*, her tongue is full of *rasa*s.[14] When she speaks, she pleases the heart. Her speech is like the chanting of a cuckoo bird, but a cuckoo bird is always sad in its singing whereas Mirgāvatī's tongue utters the story of love (*premkathā*). When Mirgāvatī speaks, flowers fall from her lotus tongue.

In *Candāyan*, Candā tells *piram kahānī*[15] and so does Mirgāvatī. Kutuban uses the word *premkathā*[16] for love story. Her tongue utters sweet words in the same manner as in *Candāyan*. Kutuban compares Mirgāvatī's chanting with the cuckoo bird's songs, which is not mentioned in *Candāyan*. However, there are some clear similarities between the two texts.

In *Padmāvat* (verse108) Padmāvatī's tongue utters words as sweet as nectar. She has stolen the songs from the *cātak* and the cuckoo birds. The melody of the flute and lute can not compare with her sweet speech. Her tongue speaks words filled with the wine of love and he who hears them becomes drunk and staggers in giddiness. Padmāvatī is expert in four Vedas such as Ṛg, Yajur, Atharva and Sāmveda and whatever she speaks contain many meanings. Paṇḍits cannot surpass her at interpreting Amara Kośa, Gītā and Pingala (prosody) and many other works on astrology and grammar. In the first and the second *nakh-śikh* of *Padmāvat* Indra, Brahmā, and Sarasvatī desire to borrow sweet speech from her.

---

woman. She is fair complexioned and is delicate like the yellowish white flower *campā*. Sweet fragrance emanates from her body. Other kinds of women are *śaṅkhinī*, *citriṇī* and *hastinī*. They do not have as many qualities as *padminī* women have, so they are considered to be inferior.

[14] *Rasa* has various meanings such as taste, enjoyment, juice, etc. In literature nine *rasa*s (nine aesthetic experiences) have been defined. Bharata in his *Nāṭya-śāstra* mentions only eight *rasa*s such as, *śṛṅgāra* (erotic), *hāsya* (comic), *karuṇā* (pathetic), *raudra* (furious), *vīra* (heroic), *bhayānaka* (fearful), *vibhatsa* (disgusting), and *adbhuta* (marvellous). Later *śānta rasa* was added to it. As far as food is concerned, six *rasa*s have been described and they are *madhura* (sweet), *launa* (saltish), *tikta* (chillyhot, bitter), *kaṭu* (pungent), *kāśāya* (astringent), and *amla* (sour).

[15] *Candāyan*, 72/1.

[16] *Mirgāvatī*, 62/3.

In *Madhumālatī*, sweet was the tongue within the maidens' mouth. It spoke in pleasant and delightful tones. Hearing this speech as sweet as nectar, even the dead would savour it. It was as though whoever heard the priceless jewels of her speech, themselves began to speak more sweetly in the world, whose life could have been sufficiently austere to have earned the right to touch her tongue with his. Her tongue so rich in all delight, moved languidly, within the maiden's mouth, as though it had passed between two hostile foes and now was pleased to make its dwelling there. So full of pleasure and delight, this tongue within her mouth had truly the taste of nectar. It was like a spring of nectar within the moon-like face (verse 90). In *Kanhāvat*, the poet does not describe the tongues of the milkmaids.

EARS

Candā's ears are like shell smeared with sandal paste. They are red *kumkum* coloured, and are delicate. They are neither long nor short or gross. They shine like a lamp of death (*kāla*). Her two ear-rings (eartops) shine like the flash of lightning in the sky. Her cheeks are as soft as purified butter and they shine like mirrors. They are nectar pots. Nobody knows for whom they have been placed there. Candā's mouth is filled with nectar; therefore her words are immortal. She is the blessed one. When the king heard this from Bājir he became conscious and alert (*Candāyan*, 74).

In *Mirgāvatī*, Mirgāvatī's ears have been described immediately after the eyes. In *Candāyan* Maulānā Dāūd describes them after he has described Candā's tongue. Like Candā's ears, her ears are well formed. They are neither long nor short. They look as if they are shells smeared with gold. They flash like lightning. They glitter like gold put in the fire. Ascetics are always in search for these two brilliant Agastya stars which have appeared along with the moon. The prince Rājkuvār says that these two Agastya stars (ears) have taken away all my blood.

In the description of the ears Kutuban owes much to Maulānā Dāūd. After the two cheeks Padmāvatī's two ears have been described. They are two priceless halves of one orange. Composed of flower pollen and juice of nectar, who has kneaded these sugared comfits fair of hue? (Shirreff, p. 269).

Here the description is short but in the second *nakh-śikh* a detailed description is given. They are like shells, adorned with pendants of Siṃhal-dvīp. They glisten on both sides like the moon and the sun, filled with constellations, they cannot be gagged at. Every now and then they vibrate like lightning; they do not remain covered by the clouds which are her garments. These ears have heard and learnt the Vedas, Purāṇas and all other books. God has given her ears which are a pledge for the delight of music and the charm of song (Shirreff, 282).

It is needless to say that Jāyasī is a great poet and he always demonstrates his poetic skill in giving minute details in his descriptions. He follows Maulānā Dāūd but he always maintains his own originality when he portrays the objects.

MOLE

In *Candāyan*, there is a mole (*til*) between Candā's ears and eyes, as though it is a small drop of the ink as a sign of *virah* placed there. This mole is a sign of good fortune on her face. It looks as if a bee is sitting on the lotus flower and making an attempt to fly there. This mole is like red velvet burned in *virah* and so it is half red and half black. Rūpcandra says 'I am burnt'. 'With the weapon of her mole she has attacked me. The fire of *virah* is burning in my heart every moment and it cannot be extinguished' (*Candāyan*, 74).

In *Mirgāvatī*, there is a mole in the middle of the heroine's cheeks. The creator has made this bee and placed it on top of a lotus flower and thus it cannot fly away. What can a lover do when he is immersed in love?

It seems *virah* separated from its source has come to rest there, and it is attracting the whole world. 'I am lost and cannot find my way', says the prince Rājkuvār.

In *Padmāvat* the mole is on Padmāvatī's left cheek. This mole appears like a fire arrow. Her one sidelong glance slays a million. This mole is never effaced from the cheek and the cheek becomes the source of destruction for the world. When the eyes see it, it is reflected in them and from it they become black and red above it. Seeing this mole on the cheek, the pole star has remained fixed in the sky. It rises one moment and sets in another but it never changes its position in relation to the mole (Shirreff, p. 78).

In the second *nakh-śikh* also there is a mole on her left cheek; this mole is a ray of the spark of love. He who beholds this mole is consumed with fire; let no one see it. It is like a bee which has dropped upon a lotus which has given up its life but is faithful in death. When men see this mole, it becomes fixed in their eyes.

The mole in *Madhumālatī* is described differently.

The mole the princess had upon her face could neither be described nor yet compared. The princess's eyes were so enamoured of its beauty, they become transfixed, and would not leave it even when drawn away. 'It is not a mole' he said, 'but reflection of my eye appears as a beauty spot. Her face is clear and unblemished as a mirror and it is the reflection of my eye soft and dark and on her pure and spotless face it seems to be a mole.' The maiden's lovely face was unblemished as a mirror in which the reflection of the prince's eye had taken on the appearance of a mole. (verse 89)

It becomes clear from the above descriptions that all the four poets in Hindi see the mole from different points of view. For Maulānā Dāūd, the mole is a drop of ink on the cheek which symbolizes *virah*. Red velvet burns from this *virah* and becomes black. Bājir becomes pale when he looks at Candā's mole. This characteristic of *virah* is found in all the Sūfī texts of Hindi.

Mirgāvatī emphasizes that the mole hides death in it. This mole is a poisonous serpent. As in *Candāyan,* the mole is like a bee as well. Mirgāvatī's cheeks where the mole exists are like a stone as well as like a lotus. A bee is sitting there. In *Mirgāvatī, virah* is just suggested without details. In *Padmāvat* a mole is both a symbol of *virah* and death. Red velvet has become black in *virah,* this has been repeated in *Padmāvat* just as in *Candāyan*. In the second *nakh-śikh,* Jāyasī says: 'This mole is the spark of *virah*.' Obviously this metaphor has been borrowed here from *Candāyan*. In *Madhumālatī*, Rājkuvār says that 'this mole is the shadow of my eyes'. Madhumālatī's face is a mirror. Rājkuvār says 'my black eyelids are shining on her clear face'. Madhumālatī's descriptions are different because philosophically Manjhan belongs to a different school of thought, in which God, Muhammad, creation and the world are one and the same entity. There is unity between Madhumālatī and Manohar. They form a part of the same divinity. There is no difference between divine and creation in *Madhumālatī*.

The mole is not found in the *nakh-śikh* described in the classical Sanskrit literature from Kālidāsa to Śrīharṣa (twelfth century). In Persian literature it was very common to describe the mole with *sarāpā* which is head to foot description. This mole in Pesian literatue is mostly the symbol of divine unity, from where the separation of soul begins. Hindi poets are also symbolic in their descriptions of the *til* (mole). Shabistarī, a thirteenth century Persian poet says 'Plurality finds not entrance. There are no two points in the root of unity. I know not if this mole is the reflection of my heart or my heart the reflection of the mole on that fair face' (*Gulshan-i*

Rāz, p. 77). Hāfiz dedicates almost 150 verses on mole in his *Dīvān*.[17] Nizāmī, Jāmī and many other Persian poets describe this extraordinary mole which is called *khāl* in Persian literature. According to these Persian poets this mole is the centre of attraction and beauty as well as that which kills the lovers. This is also a snare in which seekers of love get stuck like birds.

NECK

Bājir tells king Rūpcandra that Candā's neck is charming, as if a potter has shaped it on his wheel. Thirty-three thousand gods praise this neck. From where has this neck been brought and fixed there? Such a beautiful neck has not been found in any other human being. She raises her head and walks straight just like a special horse kayāh, raising its head. God has created such a neck. Nobody knows who will get it.

Following *Candāyan*, Kutuban describes her neck as shaped on a potter's wheel. In *Mirgāvatī*, it looks like the neck of a dancing peacock or a horse raising its head. It is neither long nor short nor thin. Some one with special skill (*vijñānī*) has made it. The prince says she has shown me her neck and tricked me just like sweets (*laḍḍū*) given by a cheat (*ṭhag kā laḍḍū*). In her neck there are three lines and they have put a noose round my neck. I am tricked completely.

In *Padmāvat*, Padmāvatī's neck is like a conch shell. It is like the neck of a vase overlaid with gold thread. A neck which seems to have been turned on the lathe. The peacock is defeated by it. It is like the neck of a horse straining at the bridle. Her neck is again like peacock's and three lines in the necks are found here as well. In the second *nakh-śikh* of *Padmāvat*, many comparisons are common such as her neck stands erect like that of a peacock. It is like a horse straining at the bridle.

In *Madhumālatī*, Manjhan says: 'To whom may I compare her neck which was surely turned on the creator's wheel? Blessed indeed will be he who knows that joy of embracing the neck of Madhumālatī. How could a man retain awareness of his body when he sees the triple creases of her neck' (92).

Candāyan's description, such as the neck has been made by a potter on

[17] See S.M. Pandey, *Hindī aur Fārsī Sūfī Kāvya*, pp. 86-107. Also *Dīvān-i Hāfiz*, trans. by Wilberforce Clarke, Samuel Wiser, INC, New York, 1970 (1st edn. 1891).

a wheel has been changed slightly in *Mirgāvatī* and *Padmāvat*. In these two texts, the necks have been turned on the lathe. Like in *Candāyan,* it has been compared with the neck of a horse in both the texts also but these comparisons are not found in *Madhumālatī*.

ARMS

Candā's arms are unparalleled. Banana trunks can not compare with her arms. Lotus petals are not as tender and beautiful as her arms. The palms of her hands are reddish like the red *hingul*. They look like the tender leaves on a tree. Should she use her arms, then no valiant person could win her. Her finger nails are the top of a spear which a king holds. Her arms are the sharp swords (*kharśāṇ*). Bājir says, 'O king! I was nearly dead by her charms' (*Candāyan*, 76).

Kutuban also compares Mirgāvatī's arms with lotus petals. Her hands are like smooth leaves. Her wrists are unique with bangles on them. Her fingers are sharp. Even a lion's jaws are not as sharp as her fingers (*Mirgāvatī*, 64). *Candāyan's* influence can be seen in the description of Mirgāvatī's arms.

In *Padmāvat*, Padmāvatī's two arms are like golden shafts; they appear to have been turned on a lathe. They are like a pair of young plaintain shoots and the palms of her hands are like lotus flowers. They are steeped in blood. Jāyasī describes Padmāvatī's rings also which are studded with jewels. Lotus stalks can not compare with her arms. In the second *nakh-śikh* in *Padmāvat* her arms are fashioned like golden bars and like lotus stalks. Her upper arms are designed like sandalwood pillars (Shirreff, p. 28). It is needless to say that comparisons of arms with banana shoots and lotus petals are derived from *Candāyan*. Kutuban also follows this tradition.

In *Madhumālatī*, 'the creator formed her arms Himself for, though I have searched and searched, I have found nothing to compare with them', says Manjhan. Her arms were graceful, powerful and strong. The very sight of them gave strength to the feeble and the weak. Her wrists were quite unique, for had not the god of love himself turned them on the lathe? Beneath them were her flawless palms as pure as crystal filled with deep vermilion. So many grieving lovers had she killed that all ten finger nails were red with blood. These lovely arms so strong and graceful, had conquered the three worlds. Blessed indeed would be the man whose neck these arms embraced (93).

Manjhan shows his originality in many ways. Traditional images of banana trunks and lotus petals have been ignored by Manjhan.

In *Kanhāvat* the arms of the milkmaids look like golden sticks. Their ornaments have been described in some detail. Their bracelets, rings and other ornaments such as *tāṃḍ* (an ornament of the upper arm) or *bājū-band* (bracelet), add beauty to their arms, wrists and palms (Pāṭhak, p. 159, verse 241).

BREASTS

Candā's breasts are like plates full of jewels, precious stones and rubies. They are smooth and it seems that some artisan turner (*kunderā*) has shaped them on a lathe. Her nipples are as if bees are sitting on top. These fully developed breasts are like oranges. Neither can sun see them nor wind touch them. It appears her heart has produced two wood apples of ambrosia. After having heard about Candā's nectar like breasts the king Rūpcandra's suffering ended and his heart found peace (*Candāyan*, 7).

In *Mirgāvatī*, Mirgāvatī's breasts are hard and like a pot of nectar well decorated. They are like lotus flowers yet to blossom. They are fully developed and bees are stting on them. People are afraid of being pierced by these breasts and therefore they do not come near her. They are golden vessels filled with infinite *rasa* (enjoyment), but nobody can touch them (*Mirgāvatī*, 67).

The description of the big round breasts are found in all the texts. They compare with oranges, grapes or wood apples and they are full of nectar. These are highlighted in almost all the texts but nobody can touch them. Even the sun cannot reach them and wind cannot penetrate them. Two descriptions of the breasts in *Padmāvat* are very much similar. One of them is as follows:

> A bosom like a tray on which the breasts are like the golden sweetmeat balls, yet they rise like beauteous golden bowls. They are like golden cups fashioned on a lathe; they are two jewelled caskets closed and containing ambrosia. They are like *ketakī* flowers which have impaled humble bees on their thorns; they are ready to pierce through her jacket; they are like arrows of youth impatient of restraint, ready to keep out and pierce the hearts of men.
>
> They are like two fire arrows aimed straight. They would pierce all the world if they were not fastened. They are like limes on a high branch carefully guarded Who would touch the royal garden? They are like pomegranates and grapes whose fruit is yet untasted; for whom have such oranges been kept. Many kings have killed themselves by austerities, placing their head on the ground but none has succeeded in touching, and they have gone away wringing their hands. (Shirreff, p. 80)

There are many things in common to both the descriptions of *Padmāvat* as far as breasts are concerned.

Breasts in *Madhumālatī* are described in the same manner as in other Sūfī texts:

Sharply were her precious breasts, the very sight of them threw three worlds in confusion; these breasts were firm and hard because Lord had placed them against her stony heart, but when another heart should touch her heart, their nipples would rise up to welcome him. It is if youth itself had fetched and given her two perfect but unripened fruits from a wood apple tree. When the lord of her life captures her heart, then nipples will rise up shyly and come out. These firm breasts with their dark tipped nipples were so proud that they would bow before no one. They were like two hostile neighbours divided by a boundary line, who would never come together. (verse 95)

In *Kanhāvat*, these breasts are the pots filled with nectar. They look like *sindhaurā* (vermilion pot). They are hard and pointed and it seems they are like golden wood apples. Fully developed and round they look like oranges, pomegranates or grape fruits. Nobody could touch them (SP, p. 159, PG, p. 198, verse120).

In the description of breasts, these Sūfī poets make use of the standard similes of the classical literature of India. Of course, they make additions and omissions too.

Bājir tells the king Rūpcandra, that Candā's stomach is full of sugar. It is as if *sohārī* bread has been fried in purified butter and like a betel leaf it is thin. In the pond of her navel even valiant people sink; they cannot cross it. Her stomach is so thin that her intestine is not seen in it. It seems that the moon's shadow is reflected there. The lake of her stomach is so profound that nobody can see water there. The king sank into it and he could not reach its shore.

In *Mirgāvatī*, the heroine's stomach is so thin as if her intestine is taken out. Her thin stomach with lines resemble the fried breads *purī* and *sohārī*. Just as in *Candāyan* her navel has been described but here it is like a pond of gold fixed there. Her hair is as though they were bees who have lost their way, there as if whoever sank in her navel, never came out. The prince Rājkuvār submerged in this lake of Mirgāvatī's navel never came out.

In *Padmāvat*, 'the stomach is thin and overspread, as if it were, with sandal paste, of a hair colour, like turmeric and saffron colour. So dainty is it that it does not feed even on milk; its substance is the juice of betel leaves and the scent of flowers.'

The line of hairs, like a black serpent, goes from her navel towards the lotus (her face). It passes between the two oranges (her breasts) but halts in alarm when it sees the peacock (her neck). It is like a line of black bees which had settled there, intoxicated with the fragrance of columns of sandal wood or it is like the Jamuna which distressed by separation makes its way to Prayāg and to (the junction with Ganges at) Arail. In the hollow of her navel is Benares. Who can face it? Death dwells therein. (Shirreff, p. 81)

In *Madhumālatī*, her waist and stomach both have been described together. The line of hair that is beneath her navel was a venomous serpent which seemed to be coming from the waist and moving towards its hair. When it fell into her navel, it curled itself around, but then was quite unable to climb out. Her slender stomach was both graceful and attractive, as though the Lord created it to be without an end. Seeing the narrowness of her waist, one feared lest the buttock's weight might cause it to snap. So slender was it that, however hard it tried, the hand could never grasp it. Indeed one feared lest it may break when touched. Had not the three folds of her stomach given it support, her waist would surely have snapped from the weight of her hips below (*Madhumālatī*, 96).

The attractive stomach and the deep navel have been described in *Candāyan* in which people get sunk (*Candāyan*, 78). *Mirgāvatī* follows *Candāyan*. In *Padmāvat* as well as in *Madhumālatī*, the navel is a symbol of death. In *Padmāvat* it has been compared with the confluence of Gangā and Yamunā in Prayāg where people used to go to be killed to obtain Heaven. In *Padmāvat* and *Madhumālatī* the lines of hair on the stomach are like serpents creeping towards the navel. One who wants to obtain it or have a glimpse of it, must be careful against the danger of death.

BACK AND THE WAIST

Candā's back has been made and placed there by a special craftsman who has cast it into a special mould. Hair on her back creates illusion. Her waist is as thin as a thread of silk Maulānā Dāūd compares her waist with the waist of a wasp which is extremely thin. It seems that if some one blows it then it will break into pieces. This is a standard traditional Indian metaphor used by the poet. People have a great desire to get to her thin waist. He will be a fool who does not know swimming and puts his feet in the lake of her back (*Candāyan*, 79).

In *Mirgāvatī*, her back is as if conch shells have been ground and placed there. This back is like wax which has been cast in mould. In fact, the creator himself has made it with his own accord and with deep interest and dexterity (*Mirgāvatī*, 65). Her tresses, rolling on her back, are like a serpent. Mirgāvatī's beauty from her head to foot along with her tresses make people afraid. They have been created by Murāri (Kṛṣṇa) himself .

In *Padmāvat*, Padmāvatī's back is an enemy which she has put behind her (Shirreff, p. 81). It is like a fully dressed *apsarā*, who has turned round. Her back is like the *malay* mountain whereupon her hair braid climbs like a black serpent; in sinous waves the serpent climbs down her back and the clothing in which she is wrapped is the slough which covers it. For whom has this hair braid been made so beautiful?

In *Candāyan*, as already mentioned the back of Candā is like the betel leaf which is very smooth and like a *sohārī* bread which is again very soft and delicate. Immediately after the back, Hindi Sūfī poets describe their heroines waists which are very thin in all the texts. However, the braids or locks of hair rolling like serpents on the backs of the heroines, which are found in Mirgāvatī and Padmāvatī, is not found in *Candāyan* in this context. In Manjhan's *Madhumālatī*, the description of Madhumālatī's back is not found but Madhumālatī's thin waist is described. It is significant to note that the back of Candā is like a lake. One who does not know to swim would be a fool to step into it. Obviously, this is a suggestion that one should be well prepared if one wants to swim into the lake of divine knowledge.

THIGHS AND FEET

In *Candāyan*, Candā's thighs are like banana trunks and her feet are unique. They are better than the colour of *pravāl* (coral). Many people touched her feet and their sins were washed away. The creator shaped her feet and she was an image of beauty. The God put nails in her feet, and her souls were red as if blood were flowing through them. Bājir says to Rūpcandra, 'I saluted her feet and kept looking at her face but she did not speak a word to me.' The king heard this and he fainted on hearing this (*Candāyan*, 81).

In *Mirgāvatī* also, thighs are like banana trunks which are covered with good clothes. The prince says I could not see through them. They were a golden colour smeared with vermilion. They were as though beautiful and smooth trees from *malay* mountain. Like Bājir in *Candāyan* the prince Rājkuvār wished he could touch her feet.

In *Padmāvat*, Padmāvatī's two thighs attached to her buttocks are exceedingly beautiful, like plaintain stalks planted upside down. The lotus feet are especially rosy; they always remain on her couch and never see the earth; the gods hold these feet in both their hands; where she would place her feet there they laid their heads. What man has such good fortune written in his forehead that he may take those lotus feet and set them on his head?

To add more esoteric meanings Jāyasī adds: 'I have told the tale of charms, yet I know not rightly how to tell of all her members from top to toe, how pure they are. I have not found anything like them in the world which I might offer as a comparison worthy of them.

In *Madhumālatī*, after the description of Madhumālatī's waist her three wrinkles (*tribalī*) are mentioned. These three wrinkles on her waist suggested that the Creator had her there while he was making her being. The poet Manjhan says:

> I have no wish to appear immodest before my elders, I shall not now describe her treasury of love. At the sight of her hips my mind was captivated. The moment I saw them my passion was aroused, while, when I saw her thighs, my being was plunged so deep in confusion I could not bring myself to speak. Her soft and tender legs were red and white like lotuses in bloom; they could be likened to a golden plaintain tree placed upside down or to an elephant's trunk, but, in all truth I feel ashamed to offer any likeness.

In *Kanhāvat*, the milkmaid's two thighs are like the banana trunks as in *Candāyan* and other Sūfī texts. Their feet are smeared with sandal paste; their lotus feet are clean and nail polish adorns their nails. They walk slowly like elephants and from their ornaments' sonorous sounds are produced when they move.

At the end of the *nakh-śikh* Maulānā Dāūd compares Candā's slow walking with the movements of swans. She lifts her steps slowly. Bājir wishes to touch her feet and clean her soles with his tongue respectfully. *Mirgāvatī* and *Padmāvat* both follow *Candāyan* in this respect. In *Mirgāvatī*, the prince wishes to touch and salute her feet and the earth where she sets her feet. In *Padmāvat*, gods hold Padmāvatī's lotus feet in their hearts; they wish to lay their heads where she sets her feet on the ground. On her feet ornaments shine like the moon and the sun. It is clear that all these texts follow *Candāyan*.

WHY *NAKH-ŚIKH*?

It appears that *nakh-śikh* in *Candāyan* and other Sūfī texts have been portrayed for two reasons Since these poets were literary geniouses they wished to convey to their readers or to the public the aesthetics of the poetry, secondly they suggested symbolism of divine love through their heroines. Heroes were the seekers of this divine love. This *nakh-śikh* is found both in Sanskrit and Persian literature. In Sanskrit the aim of the poets is to describe the superb physical beauty of the heroines or hero. In Persian literature it is both, aesthetics and mystic meanings interwoven in *sarāpā* (head-to-foot description). Following the Persian tradition, Hindi Sūfī poets mostly suggest mystical and symbolic meanings although their similes and metaphors are by and large Indian.

In *Candāyan*, Candā like the moon illuminates the four worlds. It seems she is a ruby or jewel (*māṇikya*); she is clever, articulate (*nāgarī*) and sophisticated. Bājir reports this to Rūpcandra. The forehead of Candā is shining with the rays of the rising sun. The pearls on her forehead brighten the universe. Everyone likes to play Holi with her. Her black hair is as if serpents are sitting on nectar. When some one sees the locks of her hair, he is bitten and he cannot be cured even by Gāruṛī who cures snake bites. It is not easy to look at her. People desirous of obtaining her must work hard to achieve her. Her hair brings darkness to the world in the daytime. This is again a cosmic symbol which is described by the poet. Other Hindi Sūfī poets also describe this phenomenon. In *Padmāvat* when Padmāvati loosens her hair darkness prevails upon the whole world (470).

Gods become enamoured seeing her forehead, and they abandon their own families to serve Candā. This forehead is like the second day moon. Maulānā Dāūd compares this forehead with the melting red iron on fire which is difficult to look at. Her eyebrows are compared with Arjuna's bow which was given to him by the god Varuṇa. This bow was unbreakable and very powerful. All these powerful Hindu gods have been referred to show Candā's superhuman powers. Candā has the capacity to kill people with her eyebrows. This is also a mystical symbol which is used by later Hindi poets. Her eyes red and white are a fathomless sea in which many kings have sunk to death with their boats. The poet describes the profundity of Candā's eyes in many ways. Candā is not an earthly human being; she is sitting in heaven. Nobody can reach her easily. From her nose that *padminī* woman, extremely beautiful, enjoys the fragrance of all the perfumed objects created in this world such as *khas*, flower and musk, etc.

Her lips are thirsty for human blood. Again this symbol suggests Candā's destructive power. Her teeth diffuse light in the darkness. From her tongue she narrates sweet tales (*premkahānī*). People forget their sorrows and sufferings through her speech. She is a transmitter of sweet words. In her mouth exists nectar of immortality and thus her words are also immortal. She is a blessed woman endowed with superb divine power.

The description of a mystical mole (*til*) is very important in all the Persian and Hindi Sūfī texts. It symbolizes *virah* (pain of love in separation). From her *virah* berry of shrub (*ghunghucī*) is burnt black. The whole nature separated from its divine source burning from her *virah*, is depicted in this symbolism. The king Rūpcandra himself started burning in *virah* when he heard about this *til*; this was an arrow which killed Bājir. Candā's neck is praised by thirty-three million gods; human beings do not have such beautiful necks. If she used her arms no hero on earth would be saved. The sun can not see her breasts nor the wind touch them. Her navel is deep and no valiant person (*bīr*) can fathom it. In the inner part of her stomach the shadow of the moon is reflected. It is to be remembered that divine lovers are mentioned as *bīr*s in all these texts. Candā's back is like a lake and one should be very clever to set his feet in this lake. He will be foolish who does not know swimming and steps into this lake.

Indra, Gopendra, Brahmā, Viṣṇu, Murārī, *gandharva*s and all other Hindu gods and sages were enamoured by her beauty. Candā is the harbinger of the spring season in this world. The nine parts of the world were filled with fragrance because of her perfumed body. Her ear pendants shine like stars. Her nose ring is like the brilliant Agastya star. The sun abandons other planets and serves Candā. Her ornaments are planets of the sky who have come down to the earth in Gobar where she lives. The inferior status of all these Indian gods in *Candāyan* is just to show Candā's superior divine status and to maintain the divine symbolism.

All these suggestions in *Candāyan* indicate that Candā is not an ordinary human being. Her beauty is divine and Lorik is a seeker of that divine beauty. Hyperboles in *Candāyan* and other Sūfī texts are strategies through which Maulānā Dāūd and other poets of this tradition try to make their subtle symbolic suggestions.

EXTERNAL EVIDENCE

Internal evidence is sufficient to prove the mystical aspects of *Candāyan*. There is external evidence as well which suggests that *Candāyan* was considered a mystical text in the medieval period. It was followed by almost all the Sūfī poets of Hindi. Hazrat Quddūs Gangohī (AD 1456-1537), who composed many *dohā*s in Hindi by the name of Alakhdās before Kabīr, had held *Candāyan* in a great esteem for its mystical context. He translated many portions of *Candāyan* in Persian but except few lines the whole text was lost during the battle between Bahlol Lodī (AD 1451-89) and Hussain Shāh Sharqī. The Persian translation of one verse is given here from the *Lataif-i Quddusī* which was completed by his son Shaikh Ruknuddīn in 1538.

shajar baland ast dar sama
qat' i ummid ast thamar dar ma
zaharā ki ra dast farazī kunad
shakh falaq dastī ki bbazi kunad
roz u shab gashta nigahban i base
kushta shavad chun ki ba binad kase[18]

birikh ūṃc phar lāg akāsā.
hāth caṛhai kai nāhīṃ āsā
kahu jogit ko bāṃh pasāraī
taruvar ḍāli chuvaī ko pāvaī
rāti divas bahut rakhavārā
nayanai dekhai so jāi so mārā[19]

A lofty tree , whose fruit is up in the sky. There is no hope of searching it with the hand. Say who has the power to stretch up his arm to pass on to touch the branches of the tree? Day and night there are many guards and he who with his eyes looks up will be killed.[20]

In the text Candā symbolizes the tree; her breasts are fruits; her arms are branches and her locks are serpents. Shaikh Quddūs Gangohī lectured on *Candāyan* with the same intensity as when he lectured on the works of Ibn al Arabī, Fakhruddīn Irāqī, and Sādī.[21]

Quddūs wrote a letter to Shaikh Jalāl Thāneshwarī on the *Wahdat al Wajud* quoted a verse from *Candāyan* to prove that although lovers sought to meet their beloved they are always thwarted. The verse is immediately followed by lines from a verse of Qurān in which Moses urges God to reveal Himself but his request is rejected on the ground that it was impossible for Moses to see his creator. Hindi *caupāī* (not *dohā* as quoted by Rizvī) from the original letters of Quddūs is as follows:

[18] Simon Digby, '*Abd al Qudd us Gangohī* (AD 1456-1537): *The Personality and Attitudes of a Medieval Indian Sūfī*', in *Medieval India, A Miscellany*, Aligarh: Aligarh Muslim University, 1975, vol. 3, p. 55.

[19] M.P. Gupta, *Candāyan*, 57, pp. 54-5.

[20] Digby, op. cit., p. 55.

[21] Saiyid Athar Abbās Rizvi, *A History of Sufism in India*, Delhi: Munshiram Manohar Lal, 1978, vol. 1, p. 365.

binu kariyā mori ḍālai nāvā
nayan ka thār kant nahiṃ āvaū[22]

In the Bikāner manuscript of *Candāyan* this *caupāī* is like this:

binu kariyā mori ḍālaī nāvā
nigun gārā kant na āvā[23]

The Bikaner text is corrupt and *nigun gārā* does not seem to be an appropriate reading. M.P. Gupta has reconstructed *gārā* as kariyā which appears in the first line too. Quddūs gives a simplified text which means 'my boat has been put in the stream without a boatman. Plates are full of my tears but my beloved has not arrived'. There is some difficulty in interpreting this verse. However, it is significant that Quddūs refers to *Candāyan* as a mystical text and he mentions *Candāyan* along with great Sūfī masters such as Ibn al Arabī and Iraqī, etc.

Badāyūnī, a historian who lived during the period of Akbar, indicates that *Candāyan* was considered a mystical text in the medieval period. It was read in the mosques and people used to fall into ecstasy when they heard its verses. In his *Muntakhābut tawārikh* he quotes:

In the year 772 H. (AD 1370) Khān i Jahān, the vazīr, died and his son Junā Shāh obtained that title; and the book Chandāban which is a *masnavī* in the Hindi language relating the loves of Lurak and Chandā, a lover and his mistress, a very graphic work, was put into verse, in his honour by Maulānā Dāūd. There is no need for me to praise it because of its great fame in that country, and Makhdūm Shaikh Taqi uddīn Waiz Rabbānī used to read some of his occasional poems from the pulpit, and the people used to be strangely influenced by hearing them, and when certain learned men of that time asked the Shaikh saying, 'what is the reason for this Hindi *masnavī* being selected?' he answered , 'the whole of it is divine truth and pleasing in subject, worthy of the ecstatic contemplation of devout lovers, and conformable to the interpretation of the *Āyats* of the *Qurān*, and the sweet singers of Hindustan. Moreover by its public recitation human hearts are taken captive.'[24]

Badāyunī is an orthodox historian but he refers to *Candāyan* and its influence which it had among the Sūfīs. It is apparent that *Candāyan* was considered to be a text of extraordinary importance. In about 1896 when George Ranking wrote the introduction to his English translation, he did

[22] Ibid., p. 365.

[23] Gupta, op. cit., p.50.

[24] Al Badaonī (Abd ul Qadir Ibn i Muluk Shāh), *Muntakhab ut Tawārikh*, trans. by George S.A. Ranking, Patna: Academica Asiatica, 1973 (1st edn., Calcutta, 1898), vol. 1, p. 333.

not have any detailed infomation[25] on *Candāyan* but the above reference is a valuable piece of information, and later scholars who have been interested in *Candāyan* have referred to this extensively.

An Indian Persian text *Haqāiq-i Hindi* which was completed in AD 1566 by Mīr Wāhid Bilgrāmī, outlines the mystical significance of the head to toe description, a summary of which is given here.

If the *māng* (parting of hair) is described in Hindui poems then it refers to the straight path leading to God. The black hair of the heroine alludes to darkness and sinful and corrupt paths. God has said, 'Follow my direct path; other paths lead you to destruction'. If the parting of hair is filled with vermilion then it means a master may get lost on the path by his desires. It may suggest that the master has conquered his ego also. If the veil is described in Hindui texts it means that purity of the lovers is veiled. Vermilion may also mean that god has accepted a seeker of love. If the mole is described in the texts then it means that a seeker of path is anxious and worried. God is hidden and a lover is eager to reach him. Hair is also a disturbing and worrying factor like the *til*. The hair style of a maiden in these texts means pride and hypocrisy.[26]

When the forehead and the head is mentioned in these texts then it means 'What is assigned to the fate of a seeker', and the ornaments refer to the various names of God. A mark on her forehead (*tilak*) means the light of generosity and one's capacity to prostrate oneself before God and pray to him. If the nose is described then it means that the seeker's heart is pure and filled with fragrance of love. Eyes allude to the two worlds and the synthesis of the attributes which are contradictory. Eyebrows and sidelong glances suggest the removal of darkness or light.[27]

If the ears are mentioned it means that one enjoys hearing the preaching of the Koran and religious texts as well as inspired divine words which come from the heaven. A seeker loves to hear gods names (*ziqr*). Cheeks and face represent divine light and the face of God which brings benefits in both the worlds. Lips and their redness indicate the blessings and kindness of god that have come to us through the ages. A garland or necklace in the neck means maintaining ethical and moral values.[28]

[25] Ibid., p. 323, fn. 6.

[26] Mīr Wahid Bilgrāmī, *Haqāiq-i Hindī*, translated from Persian into Hindi by Athar Abbās Rizvī, Kashi: Nāgarī Pracāriṇī Sabhā, 1957, pp. 39-41.

[27] Ibid., p. 43.

[28] Ibid., pp. 43-4.

In a similar manner Bilgrāmī tries to explain the other parts of the body of the heroines in the Hindui texts such as neck, fingers, waists, etc., along with the ornaments that she wears. From the interpretations given by Bilgrāmī it is clear that head-to-toe descriptions in the Hindi texts were not simple erotic descriptions; they contained mystical meanings too. From all the internal and external evidence it becomes clear that these descriptions are not meant to be understood just as pure *śṛṅgāra*. The poets put in them mystical meanings.

In Persian literature, almost all the Persian poets such as Nizāmī (AD 1140-1202), Rūmī (AD 1207-73), Maghrībī (twelfth century), Shabistrī (thirteenth century), have described the beauty of the beloved, in a symbolic language. Here an example of Maghrībī's poetry is given:

Then of down and beauty spots should I speak,
The eyebrows bend and towering statures praise,
Take note of cheeks and cheekbone,
Impudent eyes and teeth, lovely waists;
Of faces and braids should I sing
Or else of cuff and fist insist you listen
At such idioms be flustered not;
Of their object inquire of long and short feet.
Of my phrases, morphology don't ask.
If with symbolists you would be confident
Into hermeneutics an initiate Rectify your eye
You will see staight
Perfect your insight
You will see right
Reject the rind
The nut you find.[29]

At the end of the poem Maghrībī says: 'You should seek its spirit, its flesh reject, its noumenon pursue and Named–Essence adopt, its phenomenon do not; its phenomenon do not claim. Neglect no Minute Particular if in the truths of symbolists you would become adept.'[30]

Shabistarī gives his own explanation for *sarāpā*. He describes of his beloved. In *Gulshan-i Rāz* he describes the curl of the beloved in the following words:

[29] Leonard Lewison, *Beyond Faith and Infidelity*, London: Curzon Press, 1995, pp. 205-6.

[30] Ibid., 207.

The story of the curl of The Beloved is very long
What is it meet to tell of this seeing it is a mystery?
Ask not of me the story of that knotted curl
It is a chain leading mad lovers captive[31]

Another example of mystical eye is like this

From His eyes proceed laughing and intoxication
From His ruby lip the essence of being
Because of His eye all hearts are burning
His ruby lip is healing to the sick heart
Because of His eye hearts are drunken and aching
By His ruby lip all souls are clothed
Though the world is not regarded by His eye
His lip ever anon shows compassion
Sometimes with humanity He charms our hearts
Sometimes with humanity He charms our hearts
Sometimes He grants help to the helpless[32]

Then Shabistarī portrays the mole of the Beloved: 'It is a centre which is the basis of the circling circumference. From that centre is drawn the circle of the two worlds. From that centre Adam's heart and soul. Because of that mole the heart is bleeding sore. For it is a reflection of the point of the black mole.'[33]

Nizāmī in *Makhzanol Asrār* describes the beauty of the heroine from head to toe in the following manner:

The intrigues of that beauty, clothed in the muslin, had burnt the harvest of the moon as a fire burns the reeds. From her tresses she had woven armour to her waist. She was beautiful from head to foot. Since to see her dazzled the eyes, whoso beheld her shed salt tears. Since her savour had been mixed with sweetness, it destroyed the sweetness of the beauties.

The parrot of the garden was put to shame by her sweetness. Her chin had a ring like that on the head of the parrot. Close to that beautiful orange shaped chin, a silvery neck was formed on her breast. Cherisher of drunkards, like the rose of the garden, destroyer of repentance like the wine of a friend. Her lips, had in them like a Tabarī, had the red wood of Taberistan with which they crush the sugar cane. She was a red rose fresher than sugar cane, a dry sugar candy full of rose water. Her black mole which burnt the heart, was the ambergris pounded in the oyster shell of

[31] Shabistarī, *Gulshan-i Rāz*, translated into English by E.H. Whinfield, London, Ludgate Bill: Trubner & Company, 1880, p. 74.
[32] Ibid., p. 73.
[33] Ibid., p. 77.

the dawn. Yearning for that black mole, the full moon became a mole. Her eyes burnt the heart more than the sun; her lips illuminated the night more than the moon.[34]

At the conclusion of this *sarāpā* (head-to-foot description), the poet says 'I have made this journey on the road of certainty. Go thou on the road by which I have travelled. Thou hast not the secret of this road, beware, leave Nezāmī's work to Nezāmī.'[35]

Jalāluddīn Rūmī also portrays the beauty of the beloved. A description of the mole is as follows:

O comrade on the way, dismiss thy weariness for a moment, that I may describe a single mole (grain) of that beauty. The beauty of his state can not be set forth; what are both worlds (temporal and spiritual). The reflection of this mole. When I breathe a word concerning His beauteous mole, my speech would fain burst my body, like an ant, I am so happy in this grannary that I am dragging a burden too great for me.[36]

It is to be remembered that Sūfīs portrayed the beauty of both male and female to express divine concepts. Fariduddin Attar describes prophet Muhammad's beauty in *Ilāhīnāmā* when he went to heaven in *mirāj*:

In the night of (heavenly journey) the Peacock of the Angels was utterly effaced by the raven of his hair. See in his two tresses, two ravens; see in the almonds of his eyes how they 'turned not aside'. The 'two bows' are a symbol of his eyebrows; the ends of those bows are his two tresses. Since the tresses were all light they gave rise to two rainbows. When the ravens of his tresses grow restless; the Peacock of the Heavens is a fitting quarry of them. Hurra for the bow the two thumb and the bow end! Hurra for 'is not' and what He revealed and turned not aside.[37]

In *Yusuf Zulaikhā*, Jāmī describes the superb beauty of Yusuf.

When Joseph in his ear had heard this word
Out of his fountain sweet souls food was poured
I am the great creators work, he cried
With one drop from His ocean satisfied
the heaven is but one dot from perfections reed

[34] *Makhzanol-Asrar* of Nezāmī, trans. by Goolam Hosen Dara, London: Arthur Probsthain, 1945, pp.138-9. For further details on *sarāpā* pp.136-40.

[35] Ibid., 140.

[36] R.A. Nicholson, *The Mathnavī of Jalaluddīn Rūmī*, English translation, London: Luzac and Company, 1972, vol. 2, p. 232.

[37] *The Ilāhī-Nāmā or the Book of God of Farid al Din Attār*, trans. by John Andrew Boyle, Manchester, 1976, pp. 16-17.

The earth but one bud from his beauty's mead
The sun a spark out of his wisdom light
The sphere a bubble from His show of might
Pure is his beauty from all charge of sin
Of the invisible, the screen within
Of worlds atoms He has mirrors made
of his own face on each an image is laid[38]

This cosmic beauty is reflected in each part of the body described in Jāmī's Yusuf and Zulaikhā. One example is given below:

By those musk like spots on thy rosy cheeks
and by that sweet smile when thy rose words speak[39]

The poet describes Zulaikhā's beauty and her mystical mole *(khāl)* as follows:

With mole of the amber fresh upon her face
She to her darling there would state her case[40]
Yes, though she srinks from earthly lover's call
Eternal beauty is the queen of all[41]

Some technical terms used by the poets in *sarāpā* and their symbolic meanings have been explained by a Persian author Muhsin Farīd Kāshānī in the following manner:

Rukh (face, cheek): the revelation of Divine Beauty in Attributes of Grace, e.g. the Gracious, the clement, the Life giving, the Guide, the Beautiful; Light; Divine reality.

Zulf (tress): the revelation of Divine Majesty in Attributes of omnipresence, e.g. the Withholder, the Seizer, the Omnipotent, the death giver, the deluder; Darkness; phenomena as a veil concealing Divine Reality.

Khāl (mole): the point of Real unity, which is concealed and is therefore represented as black.

Khatt (down on the cheek): the manifestation of Reality in spiritual forms.

Chashm (eye): God's beholding His servants and their aptitudes. The eye is said to be *mast* (intoxicated) or *bīmār* (languishing) to indicate that

[38] *Yusuf-Zulaikhā of Jāmī*, trans. by Alexander Rogers, London, 1892, p. 103.
[39] Ibid., p. 142.
[40] Ibid., p. 136.
[41] Jāmī, *Yusuf and Zulaikhā*, trans. by R.T.H Griffith, London, 1881, p. 21.

god has no need of man, and pays no heed to him. The *ghamzā* (glance) of the 'eye' refers to God's granting of spiritual repose after anguish, or anguish after repose.

Abru: (eyebrow): God's Attributes, which veil His Essence.

Lab (lip): the life giving property of God, and his keeping man in existence.The *dahān* (mouth) is said to be *tang* (narrow) as reference to the fact that the source of man's being is invisible.[42]

Kāshānī explains the meanings of *sharāb* (wine), *sāqī* (wine bearer), *jām* (cup), *bahr* (sea) and many other words that Sūfīs use, but they are not relevant in the present context because Hindi Sūfī poets hardly use them. It becomes clear here that a symbolic interpretation was given to each part of the body referred to in the portrayal of the *nakh-śikh* or *sarāpā.*

Description of the divine beauty and its manifestation in the male is found at least in two Hindi Sūfī texts: Shaikh Nabī's *Gyāndīp*, in which Sur gyānī a female character, is the seeker of love and Gyān dīp is the loved one.[43] Shaikh Nasīr's *Premdarpaṇ* in which the story of Yusuf Zulaikhā (AD 1917) [44] has been adopted, is another text in Hindi in which divine beauty is manifested in male but again this is an old Persian tale as already mentioned above.

NAKH-ŚIKH IN SANSKRIT LITERATURE

Sanskrit literature is full of *nakh-śikh* descriptions. Poets in Sanskrit literature delineate extraordinary physical beauty of their heroes or heroines but the kind of symbolism and mystical meanings that we find in Persian and Hindi Sūfī literature is not found in Sanskrit poetry although many metaphors used by Sanskrit poets are used by Hindi Sūfī poets.

Kālidāsa describes Pārvatī's thighs, back, thin waist, three folds (*tribalī*), neck, mouth, red lips, large eyes, sidelong glances, in the first chapter of *Kumārasambhava*.[45] In *Meghadūta* and *Ṛtusaṃhāra*, Kālidāsa gives a

[42] A.J. Arberry, *Sūfism*, London: George Allen & Unwin Limited, 1968 (1st edn. 1950), pp. 113-14.

[43] For a detailed study see S.M. Pandey, *Madhyayugīn Premākhyān,* Allahabad: Lokbhārtī Prakāśan, 1982 (1st edn. 1961), pp. 109-10. *Gyān dīp* was composed in AH 1026. The poet mentions Vikram Samvat also, along with the Hijrī year which is 1676 (AD 1619).

[44] For details see Saralā Śukla, *Hindi Sūfī Kavi aur Kāvya*, Lucknow: Lucknow University, vs 2013 (AD 1956), pp. 565-73.

[45] Kālidāsa, *Raghuvaṃśa*, trans. by Gopala Raghunath Nandargikar, Delhi: Motilal Banarasidass, 1971, pp. 160-2.

detailed description of *śṛṅgāra* without referring to any symbolism. In *Raghuvaṃśa* the charming princes are described in greater detail.

Later, Subandhu of the fifth century portrays in *Vāsavadattā*, heroine's beauty from head to toe and her red face which has the redness of the dusk. Māgha (seventh century) in *Śiśupālavadha* gives details of the *nakh-śikh.* Similarly Bhartṛhari (sixth to seventh century) describes the beauty of women with exotic flashing eyes, youthful pride and voluptuous breasts, with creepers of beauty cresses, twining above their slender bellies. Those few are fortunate whose minds are still unperturbed.[46]

Bilhaṇa a poet of the eleventh century, from Kashmir gives a vivid description of woman's beauty in *Caurapañcāśikā:*

Even now,
I always remember
her neck adorned with
spring jasmine bloom
garlands seductively swaying
at her sides.
Her face more charming than a gleaming moon disc
her salty beauty surpassing elixir in flavour.[47]

After the neck the poet describes his beloved's eyes:

Even now
I see her kohl blackened eyes
burning mouth
laughter weary ears
I see her body weakened
by its own swelling breasts
if it wastes away who is to blame[48]

Śrīharṣa, in the *Naiṣadhīya Caritam* describes Damayantī's beauty in greater detail. Damayantī's locks of hair, her face, eyebrows, her lotus eyes possessing rich lashes, her nose, her lips on the moon-like face, her teeth as pearls and four frontal teeth, ears and other parts of her body are superbly beautiful. The creator, having made all the limbs of Damayantī who is

[46] Barbara Stoler Miller, *Bhartṛhari*: *Poems*, New York: Columbia University Press, 1967, p. 78.

[47] 'Phantasies of a love thief, *The Caura Pañcāśikā attributed to Bilhaṇa*', translated into English by Barbara Stoler Miller, New York: Columbia University Press, 1971, p. 89.

[48] Ibid., p. 231.

softer than the cup of the *śirīśa* flower, and attained perfection in the creation of tender objects, put the final seal of softness on her voice.[49]

But one thing is noteworthy, that Sanskrit poets do not describe the mole in any form. I have elsewhere discussed this in detail. In Persian and Hindi literature this mystical *til* (Persian *khāl*) is very important for its various symbolic meanings. According to Kāshānī this is the point of Real Unity which is concealed and is therefore represented as black. Sanskrit poets do not philosophize their *nakh-śikh.* However they describe physical beauty of their heroes or heroines vividly. In the Sanskrit poetic tradition some scholars have described this as *śṛṅgāra,* which is the king of all the *rasas* or aesthetic enjoyment. Maulānā Dāūd and other Hindi Sūfī poets try to add divine symbolism as it is found in Persian tradition, although they mostly use Indian images.

[49] Cf. *Naiṣadhacarita* of Śrīharṣa, trans. by Kṛṣṇa Kānta Handiqui, Poona, 1965 (1st edn. 1934), pp. 90-4. Also, Śrīharṣa, *Naiṣadhiya Caritam*, Hindi translation, Ṛṣīśvara Bhaṭṭa, 1949, p. 143.

Madhumālatī and *Gulšan-i ᶜišq*
A Question of Originality

PETER GAEFFKE

One always hears complaints about the lack of originality of medieval Indian literature. There is the dependance of the bhakti poetry on the *Purāṇas* and of the Sufi literature on Niẓāmī's *Khamse*, not to speak of the dependance of the Urdu *ġazal* on the metre and imagination of Ḥafīth's poems. This has far-reaching consequences for the acceptance and also funding of work in this period in Western societies.

Therefore, it is a timely endeavour to look closer into the question of 'derivation'. In this case let me start with the comparison of two Sufi *mathnawīs* containing the same story line, i.e. *Madhumālatī* by Mañjhan and *Gulšan-i ᶜišq* by Nuṣratī, but written at a distance of about 113 years apart (1545 against 1658).

The story consists of ten episodes which are:

1. A king has no offspring but gets a son by magic intervention.
2. The first meeting of the young prince with his beloved is brought about by fairies.
3. Separation of the lovers and the prince searches for his beloved.
4. The meeting of the prince with another girl kidnapped by a demon and the killing of the demon.
5. The prince returns this girl to her parents.
6. The second meeting of the lovers.
7. The beloved girl is turned into a bird, captured by another prince, restored to her parents and regains her human form.
8. Wedding of the two lovers.
9. The other two young characters of the story fall in love and get married.
10. Return of the two couples to the cities of the husbands.

These episodes are identical and arranged in the same order in both texts.

The difference starts with the names: The hero and the heroine in both texts have the same names: they are Manohar or Manhar and Madhumālatī or Madumālatī and the place of birth of the hero is identical in both too (Kanaigirī or Kanakgirī, 'The mountain of gold').

But already the name of the city of Madhumālatī (Mahāras) in the poem with the same name becomes in *Gulšan-i ͨišq* the name of the home-town of the girl saved by Manohar.

From here onward all the names are changed. In the order of the story: the father of Manohar is Surājbhānu in Mañjhan's poem, against Bikram; his mother is Kamalā against a blank; also the wet nurse of Manohar is named in the earlier text (Sahajā) but not in the later one. The girl saved by Manohar is called Premā against Campāwatī; her father is Citrasena against Sūrbal. Her mother is called Madhurā against a blank; Madhumālatī's father is Vikramarājā against Dharmrāj. He lives in Kancannagar against Mahāras. Her mother is Rupāmañjarī against Sārikā. The rescuer of Madhumālatī is Tārācand against Candarsen. The female gardener in this episode is Jaunā against Jhūnā.

Tārācand's city is called Pauneri, in the later text no name is mentioned. From this comparison two things become clear: The stability of the names of primary actors and the confusion and changes of the secondary actors' names is typical of an oral tradition. This excludes right from the beginning, a direct dependence of *Gulšan-i ͨišq* from the *Madhumālatī*. The second point of interest is that despite the Muslim environment in which both of the books were created, the changes in names do not deviate from the Sanskrit and Prakrit vocabulary of the earlier text with one exception: The ascetic who provides the king with a magic medicine to heal the infertility of his marriage is called Rošan Dil ('Shining Heart') in *Gulšan-i ͨišq*. In *Madhumālatī*, he does not have a name.

When we now look at the length of the two poems we notice that *Madhumālatī* is much shorter than *Gulšan-i ͨišq*. *Madhumālatī* consists of 538 *pada*s containing 5 *caupāī* and two *dohā*, i.e. seven lines by 538 which is 3766 lines plus two more at the very end.

The manuscript of *Gulšan-i ͨišq* on the other hand, tells the story in 4522 *abyāt* which would translate into 9044 lines. Taking all the *mutatis mutandis* into account, e.g. different word counts per line, a different arrangement of subject matter because of a different structure of meaning in a *bait* and in *caupāī* and *dohā*, by and large it can be stated that the *Gulšan-i ͨišq* is double the length of *Madhumālatī*.

This raises the question as to where the additional lines are placed and what is their nature. The first great difference in both texts is that the introduction of *Madhumālatī* has 301 lines against 1728 lines in

Gulšan-i ᶜišq, There are only two *padas* plus two lines in *Madhumālatī* for the conclusion while *Gulšan-i ᶜišq* has 240 lines. The other great differences in length of the episodes are to be found at the beginning, namely the first and the second episode are 84 against 882 lines and 777 against 1626 respectively.

The beginning and conclusion contain theological matter, etc. It would be interesting to look into both parts in detail but this would lead us into a complicated debate about presenting Islam to different audiences. It is, therefore, more feasible to deal here with the first episode which gives us a clear picture of the different approaches of each author.

The *Madhumālatī* version of this episode is very short. It tells about the city Kanaigiri which is situated north of the Kailāsa and its king is Sūrajbhānu. After two lines devoted to his wealth, the rest of the *pada* (44) tells us that he is old and has no son. The next *pada* (45) states the misery of not having a son. This *pada* contains also a reference to the miseries of the son-less condition in the kaliyuga which among other deficiencies imply that there will be nobody to sacrifice the *piṇḍa* for a deceased father and life will be wasted without a son, the world will be dark. But, so, says the poet, this will not apply to good sons while a bad son is like a sixth finger on one's hand. The Hindu character of this statement in undeniable. The next *pada* (46) tells about the arrival of a *tapā* whom the king approaches and with the necessary devotion he asks him to fulfil his only wish. The *tapā* falls into *samādhi* and the king serves him for twelve years. After the *tapā* emerges from this condition (47), the king repeats his request and the *tapā* fulfils his wish. He cooks a *piṇḍa* and tells the king to give it to his chief queen. After the king's return in *pada* 48 , he tells his wife: 'Eat it, take a bath and go'. Then the next *pada* (49) speaks about the new hope of the king, the birth of a son and his horoscope. This horoscope is extended into *pada* 50.

From this summary we understand that the environment and terminology is of a Hindu *yogī,* called *tapā* (*tapasvin*) who can heal infertility but only after long service to him, and that he is versed in *rasāyana* by which he can produce the effective medicine. The queen gets an order to eat and to purify herself and then we are briefly informed of the result of this procedure.

When we now look at the same episode in *Gulšan-i ᶜišq* we can speak of a thorough Islamization of the story. We shall now not follow the story line, but highlight different layers of Islamic life which find an almost exemplary expression in this very episode, setting the tone for the rest of the poem.

FAMILY LIFE

After a description of the wealth and splendour of King Bikram, which we can omit here, his childless condition is couched in the following terms:

Though God had given him everything
still he suffered bitter pain without a son. (893)
He did not see an escape from his anguish
and nobody shared this secret with him except God. (895)

Then follows a description of a morning of the king: He ascends to his throne and hands out jewels and pearls to his nobles and common people. Then he leaves his throne and goes into his private quarters to meet his queen. She, 'a woman who shared his dignity and fortune', comes with a basin of water and with her friends washes his face and then feeds him. She dresses him and gives him *pān,* especially prepared by her. On one of these mornings the king hears a beggar call outside and he wonders how there could be a beggar left in his prosperous kingdom. So he takes his plate and goes outside to feed him, but the mendicant turns away from him. The king runs after him, puts his head on his feet and asks him why he has turned his back on him. The beggar answers:

It is not proper to take water from the house of a barren woman. (934)

The king goes back into his house in great despair but his queen consoles him and says:

Why did you bare your soul silently to such destruction? (946)
Gird your loins and pull yourself together courageously. (947)
Go and find this derwiš! (948)

She promises him that she would administer the country in his absence and will hang a bell under the roof and when he returns and rings the bell, she will come and receive him even in the middle of the night.

When the king sets out on his search, she spreads the news that the king is sick and can not see anybody. She calls medical doctors and gives them different symptoms and while the people can not bear the 'suffering' of the king, she is the sickest of all:

She walked the fiery path of separation every night
no stars showed her the way. (1130)
Although her body was composed of light exactly like the moon,
it had become blacker than the night (1140)
But while she was alive, the mercy of God rested upon her
and this was the fortunate state of the queen of this country. (1141)
But when the bell sounded

the suffering of the queen had ended. (1142)
She prepared a paradise of luxurious treatment for him
and directed the sources of the Kauthar river into his bad. (1143)
She removed the rags of a mendicant from his body
and washed his limbs so that the sun became jealous. (1144)
She covered his body with fresh clothes
and led him into the lofty beautiful hall to rest. (1145)
She opened her attire and did not close her eyes
and embraced him like a black-eyed Huri. (1146)

And now the text reads: 'Taking the name of God with much earnestness, he gave her the magic fruit.' This passage rests on a *ḥadīth* : 'In the name of a Allah! O Allah, protect me from Satan and protect what you bestow on us from Satan.' When these words are said before intercourse, it is destined that the couple should have a child, and Satan will never be able to harm it.

After this comes a folkloristic image:

The poet speaks about the rains in Spring falling into the ocean of 'Umān and that by Gods 'unlimited mercy' a pearl was placed into the shell, and after 'the immense pleasures in the beautiful bed | they started to ask each other their stories.' (1152)

There were already other references to folklore in the above, namely the reference to the river *Kauthar* of the Paradise and the comparison of the queen with a black-eyed Huri. Moreover, built into this episode is also a whole episode of the encounter of king Bikram with fairies (*parīs*).

When he was searching for the *derwiš* and could not find him, 'by God's command' he entered a garden, a Muslim garden, with an artificial pond in its centre. And while the king rests, suddenly seven *parīs* descend, take off their clothes and enter the lake. The king takes hold of their clothes and when the *parīs* cannot find them after their bath, they implore the king to return their dresses, even offer themselves for sex. But the king wants only to know where the *derwiš* lives and the *parīs* carry him to this abode.

Although everybody may relate this story to the pranks of Kṛṣṇa with the *gopīs*, this trick is here not used as a prank, but as the last resource of a desperate man.

RELIGION

When the king sets out to search the *derwiš*, he acts like a Sufi:

I shall change my royal appearance
and walk as a renouncer through foreign lands. (985)

He put a necklace of heavy toil on his neck
his beggar's bowl revealed his faith. (959)
On his body he wore the ash of resignation
and took with him cries of anguish as his companions. (960)
He put in his ear the seal of patience
and carried a basket of wisdom, filled with better understanding. (961)
He had slain the world of comfort
and went down a lower course of life. (962)
Under his arm he took a mattock of greediness
in order to burn all desires. (963)
He denounced his lower soul which acted like a dog
to awaken its friend by barking. (964)
As a reliable weapon her carried
a massive ring of sharp prayers in his hand. (965)
he mustered courage
and took into his hand unshakable intention as a staff. (966)
He took with him beautiful thoughts as his students
each working earnestly and fast. (967)

When he finally came to the garden of the *derwiš* who has the only Islamic name in the book, namely Rošan Dil ('The Shining Heart') and about whom it is said:

The wine of love flew always through his body
and intoxication had given passion to his mind during all his life. (1080)
He believed only in one God. Except God he did not know another
because one calls anyone a pagan who worships also a second. (1081)
He was never far from the view of union with God
before the eye of his heart this treasure was present in his mind. (1087)

The king stood silently six month before this *derwiš* and then the *derwiš* said to the king:

O royal beggar
above your head there is a tree. Look at it! (1102)
An exquisite fruit has grown on it
look at it carefully! (1102)
When it falls open your hands
take it and go straight back to your city. (1103)
Keep the Trust in God (tawakkul) in your heart
and enjoy the fruit with your queen on a place. (1104)

In addition to the sketched Islamization we find set pieces and formulas from the Islamic literature spread through this piece.

There are the *matla*[c] at the beginnings of each canto (*bāb*). So Chapter 14 starts with

Wonderful are the works of God
His eyes do not cease to look at everybody. (920)
It is good to endure evil which comes from him
for He gives happiness later but first he sorely tries us. (921)

Powerful as this are also the endings of the chapters, e.g.:

The creator of the mysteries of the world is powerful
He is an able nourisher of the world that deserves it. (1052)
Because to one who does not even know the name of his works
he shows him a place to view them (1053)

A larger set piece is the description of a garden and here we find an exuberant example, namely the garden of the Derwiš Rošan Dil. It comes in the shape of a metaphor of a banquet in which the wine of love is flowing freely. Rose apples, lotuses, *campā* flowers, roses, hyacinths are in different stages of inebriation. Red doves, sparrows, peacocks, pigeons, and animals of all kinds join the feast at which the East Wind plays on the tambourine of leaves.

This indicates the other side of the Sufi experience: the inebriating love for God which flows from the *derwiš* to the nature around him.

So we see that a good part of Islamic culture of the middle ages is contained in this one episode. An awareness of Islam is built into an intimate family setting, in the ways in which the king acts in search of the *derwiš*, in the Sufi setting of this man close to God. Moreover, Islamic folklore is also intertwined. So anybody who wants to get a picture of this warm and friendly Islamic life in the middle ages can start from here where its basis and results are shown clearly. There is only one reference to the *tauḥīd* about the *derwiš* together with a line drawn against Hinduism.

Only the skeleton of the story line is identical with *Madhumālatī* while the Ḍakkinī poet fleshed it out, enlarged it and gave it a completely new shape, added family scenes, folklore, and religious experiences of a gentle and peaceful nature and so produced an 'imitation' with innovation.

REFERENCES

Mañjhan kṛt Madhumālatī, sampādak Mātāprasād Gupta, Ilāhābād: Mitra Prakāśan Prāiveṭ Limiṭeḍ, 1961.

Mullā Nuṣratī, *Gulšan-i ᶜišq*, manuscript kept in the Philadelphia Museum of Art.

Visions of the Unseen
Rhetorical Strategies in Bhakti and Sufi Poetry

THOMAS DE BRUIJN

INTRODUCTION

By its nature, religious poetry is an attempt at achieving the impossible: mediating an experience that is beyond human insight and for which language, even in its most sophisticated form — poetry — is but an inapt medium. The study of rhetoric and rhetorical strategy in religious poetry gives us some insight into the tools a poet has, for convincingly making an audience part of his own ineffable experience.

This approach to religious poetry might seem to cast doubt on the truthfulness and sincerity of the poet. Certainly in the Western tradition rhetoric has a connotation of being a manipulative tool. The religious poet's efforts at convincing an audience of his experience of the divine should not be seen as a clever deceit: it is a necessary means to tune in to reader responses in his audience in order to fully express his creative intentions.

This paper intends to discuss some efforts that have been made at studying the rhetoric of bhakti poetry, looking at some of the inherent problems and suggesting a rhetorical concept that is suitable to the specific needs of this tradition. The limited format of this paper will only allow a brief and general discussion, while the remainder will be devoted to a more detailed study of the rhetoric in medieval Indian Sufi poetry as it can be found in the *Akharāvaṭa* by Malik Muḥammad Jāyasī.

RHETORIC OF BHAKTI POETRY

Recent studies of the different rhetorical attitudes and voices that can be distinguished in the poetry attributed to Kabīr and Sūrdās, by Linda Hess (Hess 1983, 1987) and Kenneth Bryant (Bryant 1978), contributed significantly to the understanding of bhakti poetry. Sūrdās subtly uses the audience's perception of the scenes of the Krishna story portrayed in his poems to evoke a religious experience that is not (and cannot be) expressed directly (see Bryant 1978, pp. 45ff). Kabīr uses a dialectic approach as he addresses the intended hearer of the poem directly with seemingly paradoxical images and stinging, cynical remarks on the morals of the religious men of his time. With these direct 'attacks' on the existing order of things the listener should abandon his usual perspective on life, rendering him susceptible for the revelation of another reality. In this state the listener can respond to the images with which Kabīr describes his mystical experience that is induced by the encounter with his *satguru*.

Both strategies operate on the basis of interaction with an audience or with a listener/reader, appealing to a certain degree of familiarity with poetic forms and conventions and with religious concepts involved in the experience that is to be conveyed. The rhetorical stratagems that evoke this interaction seem to be effective, independently of whether the poet himself is reciting his work in front of a 'live' audience, or whether some other person is reciting written or remembered versions of the poems. This effect is also present in private, silent readings of the poems, although there are very few historical records of this form of reception and usage of religious poetry.

The background of the *rasa*-based aesthetics of Sanskrit poetry can also be discerned in the poetry of Kabīr, Sūrdās and other early bhakti poets. The rhetorical address to an audience or reader with enough background information or empathy for the religious concepts involved, however, is the principal factor in the mediation of the poet's experience and vision.[1]

Direct assessment of the rhetoric qualities of bhakti poetry is seriously hindered by the great distance between the medieval poet's creative moment, and the actual record of the reception of his poetry in the form of manuscripts. The attempts at restoring the early collections of bhakti poetry have shown that the influence of scribes and compilers on both the lines of the poems and the rhetorical attitudes has been substantial. In the transmission of Kabīr's and of Sūrdās's poems, especially in a sectarian environment, this distortion is due to changes in the responses to the original rhetoric in the poem and to the conscious imposition of a new rhetorical stamp on the words of the poet. An interesting case is the 'softening' of Kabīr's dialectic style which is typical of the reception in the 'Western' collections which emphasize the Vaiṣṇava-bhakti themes (Vaudeville 1974, p. 55; Hess 1987a, pp. 117, 123-6). A similar reworking

[1] This does not mean that the *rasa*-based aesthetics are not at work in bhakti poetry, but rather that they operate on a different level of creation and reception. The immediate rhetoric effect is a primary level which may give rise to the appreciation of the poetic qualities of the poem in the sense of formal aesthetics.

of the rhetorical effect of bhakti poems can be found in the sectarian collections of Sūrdās poems. The direct and 'unresolved' depiction of scenes from the Krishna story that characterizes the poems that seem to form the core of the Sūr-tradition are, in later collections, enlarged or embedded in poems that explain the doctrinal implications of the scenes, thus bringing the early material in line with sectarian doctrine (Hawley 1979, p. 71).

SAGUṆA/NIRGUṆA AND THE RHETORICAL PERSONA

Another form of distortion that has been described in studies on the early collections of bhakti-poetry is the tendency to attribute separate identities or labels such as *saguṇa* and *nirguṇa* to specific poets and the poems attributed to them. This labelling is also mainly the result of the sectarian adoption of bhakti poets and the compilation of sectarian collections of their poems. In early compilations of bhakti poetry which do not bear a sectarian imprint, Krishna bhakti (*saguṇa*) poems can be found together with Sant (*nirguṇa*) poems. Even within the corpus of single poets, verses of both natures appear together (Hawley 1995, pp. 172ff).

The coexistence of these styles of poetry in the early collections suggests that poems with different doctrinal and rhetorical attitudes appealed to a single audience or instance of reception. The combination of poems of a different nature seems to have presented an array of rhetorical possibilities for approaching the central themes of devotional poetry. Because the specific 'truth' of one *mārga* was probably not the organizing principle of the early collections, their attraction might have been the display of various strategies for expressing the ineffable religious experience.

As the construction of the saintly image of the poet in popular devotion progressed, the room for variation in rhetorical and doctrinal outlook, which seems have been present in the original corpus of the poet, became less. The poet became detached from his original creation and was made into a rhetorical persona, associated with a certain religious outlook and mode of poetic expression. The adoption of the famous poets and their literary heritage by sectarian movements can be seen as a subsequent stage in this development. The figure of the poet and his life-story were by then completely abstracted into a hagiographic stereotype and many verses were added in his name, with characteristics that reflected the later image rather than the actual creation of the historical poet. Like the Cheshire cat, the historical poet had vanished, leaving behind nothing but this persona which was readily implemented by later poets who created many verses in his name.

This development of the image of the bhakti poet implies a concept of authorship in which the poet is not primarily regarded as an original creator of verses, but rather as a mediator of an inspired vision. His individual creativity and skill lie in being a good receptacle for the religious experience and in optimizing the efficiency of existing poetic forms, images and themes for conveying it to his audience. This concept of authorship allows the construction of the poet as a rhetorical persona to whom one can attribute material that is clearly of a later date. The abstraction of the mediatory role of the poet from his historical presence is also the basis for the devotion to the poet as a legendary saintly figure.

SUFI POETRY

For now, this analysis can only be very tentative as there is so little evidence of reader responses and reactions of early audiences of bhakti poetry which can present us with a clear view on the role of rhetoric and rhetorical persona in this kind of literature. Yet, even in this incomplete form, it can act as a basis for comparison with similar concepts in that other important part of medieval Indian poetry: the works of Indian Sufi poets. This tradition came about as the result of the cultural accommodation of Indian Sufis from the times of the earliest Muslim presence in Northern India onwards. Its development is marked by continuous adaptation of models from the Persian and Indian traditions to suit the needs of local Sufi poets. The choice of rhetorical attitudes and the anticipation of reader responses were important elements in this adaptation.

The Sufi poet, like the bhakti poet, was foremost a mediator who relayed a vision of a transcendent truth to his audience. His social and religious position made that this involved the complex communication between Indian and Islamic cultural traditions, the various religious positions within the Indian Muslim audience, and his direct social environment: local Hindu or Muslim courts as patrons, or religious institutions such as the Dargāḥ of his pīr. Each of these social spheres demanded a specific rhetorical mode from the Sufi poet — even within the Dargāḥ, the growing influence of popular Islam and devotion to the pīr's tomb challenged the mystical doctrine and precepts of the originator of the *tārīqa* and forced the poet to adapt to new audiences.

Recent studies of the mystical romances of the Sufi poets have dealt with the poetics and the rhetorical aspects of these creations (de Bruijn

1996; Weightman 1992). The symbolical meaning of the narrative seems to be the most powerful rhetorical element in these works. The story is the main carrier of the message, but its structure offers many opportunities for explanatory passages in which specific doctrinal points can be emphasized. The works are built around the vision of a virtual world that is governed by the logic of its symbolical meaning, which the poet projects on the mind of his audience rather than by natural and worldly principles.

It would create a false impression to say that there were only two distinct rhetorical registers in Sufi poetry in Indian languages: the short mystical *dohā*s or *pada*s as direct reflections of a religious experience, which can be found scattered in various compilations, and the narrative symbolism of the mystical romances. Luckily, a number of works of the sixteenth century poet Muḥammad Jāyasī are extant which give us some insight into the rhetorical bandwidth of medieval Sufi poetry. Besides the romances *Padmāvat* and *Citrarekhā,* he also produced works of a homiletic and didactic nature such as the *Ākhirī Kalām* and the *Akharāvaṭa*. This last work is an interesting source for the study of the rhetoric as intended in this paper.

THE RHETORIC OF THE *AKHARĀVAṬA*

The *Akharāvaṭa* is an acrostic, or rather an *abecedarius*, as it is based on a list of letters of the alphabet which provides keywords for the verses. It is probably the earliest known work of Jāyasī, although there is some discussion on the date of 911 H/AD 1505-6 (Askari 1953, pp. 18ff). The alphabet used for the work is definitely Indian, probably the Kaithī-alphabet which was widely used by scribes for administrative and literary texts which were not composed in Persian (Pandey, 1933, pp. 491ff). The text has been included in the *Jāyasī Granthāvalī*s by R.C. Shukla and M.P. Gupta, based on a printed manuscript, with some notes from another manuscript added in Gupta's edition. After this edition some more manuscripts have been found. The text consists of fifty-three units of seven lines in the *caupāī* meter, followed by a *dohā* and a *soraṭhā*. The style of the verses is comparable with Jāyasī's other works, but the Avadhi seems less refined and contains a great number of uncommon words.

The most striking feature of the *Akharāvaṭa* is the creative use of the rhetorical possibilities of this poetic format. From what can be deducted from a brief look at other acrostics in medieval poetry, the genre is part of a tradition of didactical poetry of which early examples can be found in collections of Gorakhnāthī-poetry. In collections of Sant poetry and in the

Guru-granth, similar didactical verses are found in the *ramainī*-sections (Vaudeville 1982, p. xix).[2] In collections of Kabīr poems, acrostics such as the *Cauṁtīsī Ramainī* (Callewaert and Op de Beeck 1991, pp. 341-2) can be found. Charlotte Vaudeville has expressed doubts as to the authenticity of this poem (Vaudeville 1974, pp. 55ff, 61). It is basically a list of *caupāīs* in which the key-character is the dominant initial letter of the words. In spite of the assonance, there is no apparent coherence between the different stanzas and it lacks the vivid rhetoric of Kabīr's other poems.

In the opening lines of the *Cauṁtīsī Ramainī* one finds a 'motto' for the acrostic which introduces a central concept in the symbolism of this poetic form: in the form of speech, the range of letters of the alphabet represents the entire creation. With the divine gift of speech, everything in the universe can be named and therefore exists. Paradoxically, the *abola* — he who is beyond speech — is the originator of speech and is the only fixed and eternal element (character). Thus the link between Creator and creation is symbolized in speech and in the letters of the alphabet.

Cauṁtīsī Ramainī 1-4:[3]
There are fifty-two characters and everything in the three worlds is contained in them;
all that is here will be destroyed, except for that Indestructible one[4] among them.
Know the *tārīqa* of the Muslim and the *veda*s and *purāṇa*s of the Hindu,
but you only need to learn one bit of knowledge to enlighten your mind.
Where there is speech, that Indestructible one comes; where the Ineffable is, the mind can not reside.

[2] There are many other examples of acrostics in Sant poetry. At the Venice conference David Lorenzen was so kind to point out to me two interesting acrostics [*ke(a)kaharā*] in a collection of poetry from the collections of Sant poetry (Rām Lagan Lāl 1933, pp. 88-9). There must be numerous other acrostics, which I have not yet seen for this paper.

[3] *Cauṁtīsī ramainī* 1-4:
bābana akkhira loka trai sabha kachu iniahīṁ māṁhiṁ |
e sabha ṣiri ṣiri jāhige so akkhira ina mahiṁ nāṁhiṁ ||
turuka tarīkata jānie hiṁdū beda purāṁna |
mana samujhāvana kāranaiṁ kachu eka paḍhie gyāṁna ||
jahāṁ bola tahaṁ akhira āvā jahaṁ abola tahāṁ mana na rahāvā |
bola abola maṁjhi hai soī jasa ohu hai tasa laṣai na koī ||
allaha lahau ta kyā kahau ta ko upakāra |
baṭaka bīja mahiṁ rami rahā jākā tīni loka bistāra ||

[4] Note the pun on akkhira (*akṣara)*: 'indestructible' and 'character'. See also note 12.

He is in between speech and what cannot be said, but nobody can see His true nature.
What good can I do, how can I speak of Allāh: He spans all three worlds but is contained in a seed of pulse.

Jāyasī has taken up the notion of the acrostic as a metaphor for the universal presence of God, but has developed it differently. In his *Akharāvaṭa*, the list of letters as initials for the words of his verses only provides a basic structure for a much more elaborate exposition on the creation of man, his divine origin and the need to know the Creator before life in this world is over. Instead of being a mere list of topoi, the lemmas of his acrostic connect to form a didactic poem that shows how the pupil of the Sufi pīr can use the signs of speech and words to recognize his Creator.

In the *Akharāvaṭa,* Jāyasī introduces the theme of the lost knowledge of God with the story of the creation of Adam and Eve, the betrayal of Iblīs (Nārada) and the subsequent expulsion from paradise. Following the lead given by this tale, the poet explains how the link between man and his Creator was lost through the treacherous work of Nārada. The letters of the alphabet indicate key notions in this didactic and homiletic exposition. Through the events that befell him who was meant to be the vicegerent of God: the first Prophet Adam, Jāyasī arrives at a detailed description of the mystical path that leads back to Allāh.

The story of Adam is a prominent part of the tradition of the *Qiṣāṣ al-Anbiyā'*, the stories of the prophets of Islam, beginning with Adam and ending with Muḥammad, the seal of the prophets. There is no known contemporary source for this material in Avadhi, but it must be assumed that Jāyasī adapted it from an Indian version or an oral account of these tales.[5] In the *Akharāvaṭa* the tale of Adam's fall is connected with the

[5] Comparison with a much later Urdu version of the *Qiṣāṣ al Anbiyā'*, parts of which have been translated by Ralph Russell, shows many similarities in the images used (except for the role of Nārada, see below). Russell quotes from an Urdu 'folktale', which is of much later date, unfortunately without specifying his source other than as *Qasas ul Anbiya*, 'Stories of the Prophets', a work by Ghulam Nabi based upon Persian originals (Russell 1995, pp. 91, 106-12). The *Qiṣāṣ al Anbiyā'* contains the account of the lives of the prophets as they can be found in the Koran, but also from many other sources, which have no canonical status. This material has played a major part in popular Islamic traditions. See also Thackston (1978) on the Arabic sources and versions of the *Qiṣāṣ al Anbiyā'*. Some places in the Koran which mention the story of Adam are: 2.33; 7.12; 15.26-36; 17.64; 18.49; 20.116; see also Encyclopaedia of Islam *s.v.* Ādam (vol. I, pp. 176-8).

universal notion of the acrostic. The poet translates the well-known elements of the story into Indian terms and symbols from Nātha-yogī and Sant mystical theories. In this translation, however, the Sufi ideology and the Islamic connotation of the material is kept intact. The fall of Adam, the first man and direct evidence of God's creative power, and the deceit by Iblīs causing the split between man and God are central notions in the Islamic tradition. By focusing on the role of the local pīr and on the path to insight that is described in the terms of medieval Indian devotional mysticism, Jāyasī brings these notions closer to his own audience.

The *Akharāvaṭa* begins with a description of God as the one entity in which the universe was contained (*Akh.* 1-4). Allāh then desires to create a represėntative (*dūjā*) or double of himself in the form of Adam. After doing so he presents the first man to the angels and demands them to bow down in reverence for this double, who is not immortal like the original. God has hidden the divine origin in man, but he has left a secret passage to this knowledge inside the body which is sealed with the tenth door. Deviating from the Koranic account of this scene, Jāyasī describes how all angels bow, including his favourite servant Nārada, whom God chooses to be the keeper of the hidden path.[6] Nārada seizes this opportunity to seize control of Adam's mind. When Adam sneezes, Nārada enters his mind, and the entrance is shut (*Akh.* 6). From there he seduces Adam and Eve to sin against the rules of paradise. They are expelled and land in the *andhakūpa* of *saṁsāra*. This moment is the start of the acrostic, starting with the letter *ka*.

Akharāvaṭa 7.1-4:
Ka — What the creator wants is done accordingly, he puts his own fault on someone else's head.
They ate the wheat, their minds led astray and fell down to earth and regretted.
They cried for the loss of the heavenly beauty and power: 'How (wonderful) was that place that God expelled us from?'

[6] Nārada is portrayed as the devil, probably because of his background as meddlesome sage who sabotaged the creative activities of Brahmā. In the Krishna-myths this sage is the adviser to Kaṁsa. In his *Kanhāvat*, Jāyasī also portrays the sage in this role. It is remarkable that Jāyasī portrays Nārada as the closest servant (*sevaka ninārā*) of God, while, in the Koranic account, and also in the *Qiṣāṣ al Anbiyā'* version of the story, Iblīs refuses to bow before Ādam. Iblīs denies the superiority of the mortal man over himself and is expelled from paradise for that. The poet combines the two figures, Iblīs and Nārada, to make one coherent account.

The whole world is a dark pit, where is here a man or woman?[7]

In the following verses Jāyasī describes how the body of Adam was created in pairs: two hands, ears, eyes, etc. Heaven and earth were separated and the world is fashioned after the parts of Adam's body. This world is derived from the first man and is a microcosm, representing its Creator. With the creation of life in this world the primal unity of existence was split. Conflict and death appeared and Nārada worked his evil ways to keep man from happiness and realization of his divine origin (*Akh*. 7-11). The duality that reigns the world is also represented in the divisions of humans into various kinds. In stanza 14 Jāyasī describes how 'one tree' produced 'different branches': from the blood of mother Eve sprang the 'Turuka', the Muslims, from the seed of the father the Hindus (*Akh*. 14.2-3).[8]

There is still hope for man if he realizes that he is made in the image of God. His power can deter the devil who keeps man from reaching reunion with God. This argument is supported by extensive descriptions of the body as a microcosm, using images from Nātha-yogī mystical theories (*Akh*. 12-20). Jāyasī is very explicit about the way to reach this insight. In *Akh*. 25 he mentions:

Akharāvaṭa 25.2-4:
2. There are as many roads to God as there are hairs on the body and stars in heaven.
(. . .)
4. Of these I sing the praise of one path, which will bring glory in both worlds.
5. This is the great path of Muḥammad, he is spotless and resides in heaven.[9]

In accordance with Sufi doctrine, the pīr is for Jāyasī the most important guide who puts the pupil on the right track and assists him in achieving the realization of the divine. This point is underlined with a praise, in

[7] *Akh*. 7.1-4:
Kā — karatāra cahiya asa kīnhā | āpana dokha āna sira dīnhā ||
khāeni gohūṁ kumati bhulāne | pare āi jaga mahaṁ pachitāne ||
choḍi jamāla jalālahi rovā | kauna ṭhāṁva teṁ daiu bichovā ||
andhakūpa sagarauṁ saṁsārū | kahāṁ so purukha kahāṁ meharārū ||
[8] *Akh*. 14.2-3:
biricha eka lāgīṁ dui ḍārā | ekahi teṁ nānā parakārā ||
mātu ke rakata pitā ke biṁdū | upane duau turuka au hiṁdū ||
[9] *Akh*. 25.2; 4-5:
bidhinā ke māraga haiṁ tete | saraga nakhata tana rovāṁ jete ||
(. . .)
tehi mahaṁ pantha kahauṁ bhala gāī | jehi dūnau jaga chāja baḍāī |
so baḍa pantha muhammada kerā | hai niramala kailāsa baserā ||

two stanzas, of Jāyasī's own pīr, Saiyid Ashraf Jahangir (*Akh.* 26). The position of this passage, in the centre of the work, indicates that the call to follow the path of the Sufi pīr is the rhetorical focus of the *Akharāvaṭa*. The poet goes on to explain how the pīr lights the lamp of divine inspiration in the pupil. With this light and the right mantra, Nārada can be driven from the tenth door and can the secret channel inside the body be entered (*Akh.* 26ff). Then Jāyasī describes the *tapas* and self-sacrifice needed to play the dangerous game of *prema.* The mystical path is dangerous and difficult, but once the pupil has taken the opportunity and experienced the divine inside himself, he can leave his worldly existence to prepare for death as a *marajiya* and thus become 'immortal' (*Akh.* 37.5).[10]

In the last part of the acrostic, Jāyasī describes the splendour and all-pervasive power of God, the only steady element in the flux of existence. The poet also returns to the main theme of the work as he explains the meaning of meditation on the name Adam. In the style of the acrostic he shows how the three characters (in Arabic script) — the *aliph*, *dāl* and *mīm* — stand for Allāh, Faith (*dīna*) and Muḥammad. Meditation on this name will bring one to the divine essence within:

Akharāvaṭa 40.1-4:

Kha — The play is laid out and this is the way to play it; both the play and the Player are difficult (to understand).

He wanted to show His own true self; so He came and took on the garb of Adam.

The *aliph* is the great and only Allāh; the *dāl* is the Faith which is for everyone in this world.

The *mīm* is Muḥammad which he loves with a deep affection; recognize this meaning in these three letters.[11]

After the acrostic the work continues with verses that further explain the doctrinal points mentioned earlier on. The importance of the guru in the process of distinguishing the divine element within oneself is underlined by the concluding verses of the *Akharāvaṭa* which contain a set of questions put by a *celā* and the answers by the guru. They deal with issues such as: is evil of divine origin; what material fills the space between heaven and earth?

[10] *Akh.* 37.5:
binu jiu die na pāvai koī | jā marajiyā amara bhā soī ||

[11] *Akh.* 40.1-4:
khā — khelana au khela pasārā | kaṭhina khela au khelanahārā ||
āpuhi āpuhi cāha dekhāvā | ādama rūpa bhesa dhari āvā ||
alipha eka allā baḍa soī | dāla dīna duniyā saba koī ||
mīma muhammada prīti piyārā | tini ākhara yaha aratha bicārā ||

REACHING THE RIGHT AUDIENCE

With his version of the acrostic Jāyasī seems to build on the concepts of earlier examples such as the didactic verses in the collections of Sant poetry. The images of the body as a microcosm, the divine essence within man, and the guru's enlightening inspiration are taken from Sant and Nātha-yogī imagery and are used here to express Islamic concepts. The main difference with the earlier acrostics is that Jāyasī places the short phrases of the *nirguṇa* poets in the framework of a longer didactic narrative that fully exploits the metaphor of the alphabet as mirror of the universe. It compares in essence with the symbolism of the acrostic of Sant poets. Kabīr concludes his acrostic with the phrase:

Cauṁtīsī Ramainī 41:
Even if one brings together the fifty-two letters one can not recognize this one letter (the imperishable one).[12]

Instead of stringing up short verses which repeat the same message with different keywords, Jāyasī uses the alphabet and the lemmas it provides to narrate the whole history of man's divine essence, beginning with the creation of Adam and ending with the *celā*'s quest for knowledge and the precepts from his guru. The rhetorical strategy of this adaptation of the acrostic is to make the story convincingly reflect the Sufi poet's inspired vision. Central to this view are the *baraka* of the pīr and the urgency to use this life to gain eternal life in heaven. There is some resemblance with the rhetoric of Jāyasī's later mystical romances. Being a compact poem, the *Akharāvaṭa* combines the directness of Sant poetry with the doctrinal exposé of an extensive homiletic poem. The poet does not hide behind the *tamāśā* of the events in his story, as in the *Padmāvat*, but addresses the conscience and soul of his audience with the voice of the visionary preacher. This register differs from the didactic tone of the mystical preceptor as it allows the poet to translate elements from the mystical discourse of the Dargāḥ to a representation that appeals to a more 'worldly' audience. His verses address the worldview of the devotee (Hindu or Muslim) coming to the grave of the pīr or of a worldly patron who is interested in the *capital culturel* which the religious prestige of the pīr and the Dargāḥ provided. The following passage is a good example:

Akharāvaṭa 19:
Now that paradise is lost, be afraid; hereafter regret is of no use.
He who is arrogant and cannot stop saying: 'I, I' is an enemy of the Lord.

[12] Callewaert 1991; 342, Vaudeville 1982; 417:
bāvana akkhira jore āṁni sakā na akkhira eka pachāṁni |

He who realizes that he is certainly going to die, what use are 'mine' or 'thine' to him.
God gave us eyes, tongue, ears, hands and feet and made us all his servants.
He who enjoys his kingdom and wealth takes pleasure in the world as he wishes.
But He will ask all of them: 'Why did you misuse what I gave to you.'
What answer and what excuse will you come up with then? If one sows acacias, how much rice will one harvest?

dohā
Once something is done, you can not do anything about it; steadily the limit (the Last Day) approaches.
That day will come and when it arises nothing can be done.[13]

This appeal by the poet conveys the homiletic spirit of the poem which tells of the grace of the guru and the fight against Satan in images and concepts from the familiar idiom of Indian devotional poetry. Alternating between visionary descriptions of the transcendent nature of God and direct preaching, the poet is able to reach the various realms of religious experience in his audience. Besides translating a truly Islamic concept to the Indian environment, he also mediates between the spheres of the detached Sufi and of the worldly devotee of the pīr. The acrostic and the homiletic poem provide him with poetic forms and rhetorical personas that enable him to make the message work in his own environment.

CONCLUSION

In connection with the example of Jāyasī's *Akharāvaṭa*, I have tried to investigate the range of rhetorical strategies in medieval Indian religious poems. These approaches to conveying an ineffable religious experience

[13] *Akh.* 19:
ḍā — ḍarapahu mana saragahi khoī | jehi pāche pachitāva na hoī ||
garaba karai jau hauṁ hauṁ karaī | bairī soī gosāiṁ ka ahaī ||
jo jānai nihacaya hai maranā | tehi kahaṁ mora tora kā karanā ||
naina baina saravana bidhi dīnhā | hātha pāṁva saba sevaka kīnhā ||
jehi ke rāja bhoga sukha karaī | lei savāda jagata jasa cahaī ||
so saba pūṁchihi maiṁ jo dīnhā | taiṁ ohi kara kasa avaguna kīnhā ||
kauna utara kā karaba bahānā | bovai babura lavai kita dhānā ||

dohā
kai kichu lei na sakata taba nitihi avadhi niyarāi |
so dina āi jo pahuṁcai puni kichu kīnha na jāi ||

discussed so far seem to converge in the concept of the rhetorical persona. On the one hand this mask may consist of a religious attitude and doctrinal view that is projected on the legendary figure of the bhakti poet; on the other hand it is a tool consciously used by a poet to reach a certain audience, as in the case of Jāyasī's acrostic. The creation of devotional poetry involves mediating between a vision of a transcendent world and the expectations of an audience in a painfully visible world. This by nature impossible communication requires the masks of poetic convention, style, form and rhetoric. Studying these masks may provide a better view on the real face of the medieval Indian poet and his creative work.

REFERENCES

Askari, S.N., 'A Newly Discovered Volume of Awadhi Works including Padmawat and Akharawat', *Journal of the Bihar Research Society*, 39, 1953, pp. 12-40.

Bruijn, Th. de, *The Ruby Hidden in the Dust, A study of the poetics of Malik Muḥammad Jāyasī's Padmāvat*, Leiden: private publication (Ph.D. dissertation Leiden University), 1996.

Bryant, Kenneth E., *Poems to the Child-God: Structures and Strategies in the Poetry of Sūrdās*, Berkeley: University of California Press, 1978.

Jāyasī, Malik Muḥammad, *Jāyasī Granthāvalī, arthāt Padmāvat, Akharāvaṭa aur Ākhirī Kalām*, edited by R.C. Shukla [Nāgarī Pracāriṇī Granthmālā 31] [2nd edn. Banaras: Nāgarī Pracāriṇī Sabhā], 1935.

———, *Jāyasī Granthāvalī, Padmāvat, Akharāvaṭa, Ākhirī Kalām aur Maharī Bāīsī*, edited by M.P. Gupta, Allahabad: Sāhitya Akademi, 1952.

———, *Malik Muḥammad Jāyasī kṛt Kanhāvat*, edited by P.L. Gupta, Banaras: Annapūrṇā Prakāśan, 1981.

Callewaert, W.M. and B. Op de Beeck, *Nirguṇa-bhakti-sāgar, Devotional Hindi Literature, A critical edition of the pañc-vāṇī or Five Works of Dadu . . . and a Complete Word-index* (vols. I-II), New Delhi: Manohar, 1991.

Hawley, John Stratton, 'The early Sūr sāgar and the growth of the Sūr tradition', *Journal of the American Oriental Society,* 1979, 99/1, pp. 64-72.

———, 'The Nirguṇ/Saguṇ Distinction in Early Manuscript Anthologies of Hindu Devotion', in David N. Lorenzen (ed.), *Bhakti religion in North India, Community identity and political action*, New York: State University of New York Press, 1995, pp.160-80.

Hess, Linda and Shukdev Singh, *The Bījak of Kabīr*. Translated by Linda Hess and Shukdev Singh, Essays and Notes by Linda Hess, New Delhi: Motilal Banarsidass, 1983.

Hess, Linda, 'Three Kabīr collections: a comparative study', in Karine Schomer and W.H. McLeod (eds.), *The Sant Tradition of India*, Berkeley: Berkeley Religious Studies Series, 1987, pp. 111-41.

———, 'Kabīr's rough rhetoric', in Karine Schomer and W.H. McLeod (eds.), *The Sant Tradition of India*, Berkeley: Berkeley Religious Studies Series, 1987, pp. 143-66.

Pandey, C., 'Padmāvat kī lipi tathā racanā-kāl', *Nāgarī Pracāriṇī Patrikā*, 13-14, 1933, pp. 491ff.

Rām Lagan Lāl, *Mahātmāoṁ kī bāṇī* (*Bhuḍkuḍā kī sant-paramparā kī racanāeṁ*), edited by Rām Lagan Lāl, Bhuḍakuḍā, 1933.

Russel, Ralph, *Hidden in the Lute, an anthology of two centuries of Urdu literature*, Manchester: Carcanet, 1995.

Thackston Jr., W.M., *The Tales of the Prophets of al-Kisai, translated from the Arabic*, Boston: Twayne, 1978.

Vaudeville Ch., *Kabīr*, vol. I, Oxford: Oxford University Press, 1974.

———, *Kabīr-vāṇī, recension occidentale/western recension*, Pondichéry: Institut Français d'Indologie, 1982.

Weightman, S.C.R., 'Symmetry and Symbolism in Shaikh Manjhan's Madhumālatī', in C. Shackle and Rupert Snell (eds.), *The Indian Narrative*, Wiesbaden: Harrassowitz, 1992.

Jāysī's *Citrarekhā*

MARIOLA OFFREDI

Citrarekhā is one of the minor works attributed to Jāysī. It is a short poem that tells a love story, but, unlike *Padmāvat*, it is not regarded as a romance (premākhyān). It has the same structure as *Padmāvat*, Jāysī's major work, which is believed to have been written in 1540. The stanza structure of *Citrarekhā* is identical to that of *Padmāvat*: seven lines (*caupāī*) of 16+16 mātrās followed by a *dohā*, each line of which has 24 mātrās (13 + 11). In the text I used, edited by Śivsahāy Pāṭhak and published in 1959 (Śivsahāy Pāṭhak, sampādak (ed.), *Citrarekhā* (Malik Muhammad Jāysī kṛt premkāvy), Vārāṇasī: Hindī Pracārak Pustakālay, 1959, 113 pp. [the text covers pp. 65-113]) not all the stanzas are composed of seven *caupāī* verses — some have less, others more — and not all of them are succeeded by a *dohā*. After the final stanza, which consists of seven *caupāī* verses followed by a *dohā*, there are two *dohā*s. The text has a total of approximately 400 lines, whereas *Padmāvat* contains some six thousand lines. The text is not subdivided into parts, and the stanzas are not numbered (it is only for convenience's sake that I have numbered them in this paper). There are 47 stanzas in all (with the irregularities mentioned above), added to which there are a couple of *dohā*s at two points midway through the text, besides the two final *dohā*s. The most regular sequence of *caupāī-dohā* is found in the first 14 stanzas, the first 13 of which constitute the preface, as though, after praising the Lord, the poet had left the story as a rough, unformed draft that he may have planned to develop at a later stage.

Śivsahāy Pāṭhak worked on two undated manuscripts in Perso-Arabic script. The manuscript forming the basis of his work was provided by Candrbalī Sinh, and it belonged to a collection of Jāysī's manuscripts which Candrbalī had been given by a Muslim from Ahmedabad, and which, besides *Citrarekhā*, contained *Kahrānāmā* and *Kanhāvat*. Śivsahāy Pāṭhak combined this manuscript with another manuscript of *Citrarekhā* that is stored in the Sālār Jang Library at Hyderābad. The text edited by Śivsahāy Pāṭhak is preceded by a profile of the poet Jāysī, focusing in particular on his spiritual heritage, together with a synopsis of *Citrarekhā* that briefly summarizes the 13 introductory stanzas and recounts the story itself in fuller detail. (A subsequent edition of *Kanhāvat* [Śivsahāy Pāṭhak (ed.), *Kanhāvat*, Ilāhābād: Sāhity Bhavan, 1981] was treated in greater depth, and included word meanings and etymology).

In his introduction to Śivsahāy Pāṭhak's work, Vāsudevśaraṇ Agrvāl remarks that *Citrarekhā* is 'a minor love story (prem kahānī), but it is very enjoyable to read, and it bears the stamp of Jāysī's language throughout (sarvathā Jāysī kī bhāṣā ke sā̃ce mẽ ḍhalī huī hai)' (p. 13). The tale recounted in *Citrarekhā* is very simple. The actual story is told in 34 stanzas (from stanza 14 to the final stanza, 47, followed by two *dohā*s) which are preceded by 13 stanzas in which Jāysī praises the Lord, the creator of all things, describes the prophet Muhammad and his four companions, and then refers to his spiritual heritage (stating that his guru was Śaikh Burhān) and introduces himself as the poet.

SUMMARY OF THE TALE

The king of Candrapur, Candrabhānu, has 700 queens. Rūprekhā, the principal queen and the fairest of them all, gives birth to a daughter, Citrarekhā. Astrologers predict that she will marry the prince of Kannauj. Citrarekhā grows up into a beautiful girl, and her father dispatches his attendants to seek a husband for her. They arrange for Citrarekhā to marry the hunchback son of Singhandev, king of Sinhad. In the meantime, in Kannauj, after performing much penance King Kalyāṇ Sinh has succeeded in producing a son, Prītam Kunvar. The astrologers foretell that Prītam will rise to glory but will live only to the age of twenty. Just two days before his twentieth birthday, Prītam learns of his fate and resolves to go to Kāśī to die, thus ensuring that he will go straight to heaven. He sets off on horseback, but during the journey, hot and weary, he shelters beneath a tree, where he faints and then falls asleep. King Singhandev appears, bound for Candrapur, with his hunchback son and the wedding procession. When Prītam awakens, Singhandev asks him if, before going to Kāśī to die, he will stand in for his hunchback son at the ceremony in which he is to marry Citrarekhā. Prītam agrees. On the wedding night, he writes down the truth on the sleeping Citrarekhā's añcal, and then resumes his journey on horseback to Kāśī. At dawn, Citrarekhā's companions arrive to find her clothing and headdress untouched, and enquire as to the whereabouts of her husband. When Citrarekhā reads what Prītam has written on her añcal, she decides to kill herself on a burning pyre so that she may join her husband in paradise. In the meantime, Prītam Kunvar has reached Kāśī and built his pyre, but before dying, he lavishly bestows alms upon holy men. One of them is Vyās, who, touched by Prītam's generosity, blesses him with the words, 'May you live long'. Surprised by this blessing, Prītam tells Vyās that he is destined to die, and asks him who he is. Vyās introduces himself and, declaring that his words have been prompted by Brahmā, claims that Prītam has now won back his life. Guessing that Citrarekhā is probably intent on killing herself, Prītam at once steps down from the pyre. He arrives at Candrapur to find Citrarekhā seated on her pyre, torch in hand, waiting for the appointed time of Prītam's death, when she will start the fire and die with him. Their eyes meet; Citrarekhā covers her head in shame, climbs down from the pyre and goes into the palace. 'Today the deity has brought happiness and pleasure into sorrow, for those whose hearts are torn by separation will surely meet' (daī ān uparājā, sog mā̃h sukh bhog | avas te milā̃i bichohī, jinh hiy hoi viyog, 46, dohā).

Main features of the story

In *Citrarekhā*, two stories run parallel, then merge in a third tale.

1.a. King No. 1: Has a daughter.
1.b. King No. 2: Has no children, performs ascetic practices, has a son.
1.c. King No. 3: Has a hunchback son.
2.a. The princess (daughter of King No. 1) grows up to be a beautiful woman.
2.b. The prince (son of King No. 2) grows up to be a valiant young man.
3.a. The princess is betrothed to the hunchback (son of King No. 3)
3.b. The prince is destined to die young.
3.c. The union of the prince and princess, brought about by the hunchback.
The tale of the hunchback serves to bring the couple together.
Happy ending.

In *Padmāvat* there are two parallel tales which eventually merge, but they are far more complex in terms of both narrative and style. In *Padmāvat* we also find negative characters, but the union occurs through a positive figure, the parrot.

Tragic ending.

Scene of the action

In *Citrarekhā* the action takes place in three locations:

1. Candrapur (King No. 1)
2. Kannauj (King No. 2)
3. Sinhad (King No. 3)

In *Padmāvat* the action also occurs in three places:

1. Sinhal
2. Cittaur
3. Dillī

Psychological make-up of the characters

Citrarekhā is an extremely simple tale, suitable for a village audience or female courtiers.

In psychological terms, the story of *Padmāvat* — which is rich in metaphor and wordgames — is highly complex, suited to a sophisticated male audience that was able to appreciate female beauty and muse on the tragic nature of the tale. One of the more stylistically intricate passages of Citrarekhā is the description of its heroine's beauty. Nevertheless, unlike a comparable passage in *Padmāvat*, it could have been understood even by a village audience. The passage from *Padmāvat* contains elements alien to popular culture (the scent of limbs permeating the universe, of southern sandalwood wafting through the air, lips like rubies and teeth like diamonds, etc.).

Of course, a great deal may be said about the shortcomings of *Citrarekhā* as compared with *Padmāvat*. This little poem lacks the sweeping global vision we find in *Padmāvat*, a work which, as (Vijaydevnārāyaṇ Sāhī has remarked, leaves the reader with a sense of complete, unfragmented intellectual cohesion that, whilst akin to a tragedy, is not tragic in the Greek sense of the word (Vijaydevnārāyaṇ Sāhī, *Jāysī*, Ilāhābād: Hindustānī Ekeḍemī, 1993, 1st edn. 1983). Sāhī called this vision 'tragic vision'. Unlike Tulsīdās and Sūrdās, in *Padmāvat* Jāysī does not turn his back in history, but accepts the challenge of confronting his own era. His was an age of fierce strife that saw the conflict between Hindus and Turks matched by the Muslims' struggles amongst themselves for power. Unlike the other Sufi poets, Jāysī sets his fictional world at history's very core. The chief link between the fictional world and history is Padmāvatī, a character of such finely woven complexity as to emerge as the centre of energy that meshes the tale as a whole. The tragic vision emerges from Padmāvatī's very ashes. When, after years of siege, Alāuddīn captures the fortress of Cittaur, and hopes finally to claim Padmāvatī, her body has already turned to ashes. He gathers a handful of these ashes and scatters them into the air, saying, 'Earth is vanity' (chār uṭhāi līnh ek mūṭhī | dīnh uṛāi, pirthimī jhūṭhī, Padmāvatī Nāgmatī sati khaṇḍ, 4.4).

Citrarekhā's character is very different from that of Padmāvatī. While Padmāvatī is part idealized woman, part real woman, Citrarekhā is never idealized. As a result, she lacks the contrast which, in *Padmāvat*, where the two sides of Padmāvatī are portrayed, emphasizes the heroine's ideal nature. However, it is by describing Padmāvatī's uniqueness in terms of her physical beauty, and not of her ideal qualities, that the author highlights and develops this facet of her character. Since Jāysī does not have to make

Citrarekhā an idealized woman, he does not even bother to describe her remarkable beauty in great detail.

In Sufi poems, the hero's love is stronger than that of the heroine. In *Citrarekhā*, on the other hand, the heroine's love is more powerful than the hero's. What is absent is the hero's determination to become an ascetic in order to win the heroine. If the hero does cut himself off from the world, it is not because he wishes to pursue the ascetic's thorny path in order to conquer his loved one. In *Citrarekhā*, the hero isolates himself from the world simply because, two and a half days before he is to die, he learns of his imminent death, and leaves the throne in order to die in the sacred city of Kāśī. When Vyās wishes him a long life, he is delighted to discover that he will not die, but will instead be able to enjoy his bride.

In Sufi poems there are negative characters who make the hero's ascetic path harder and, therefore, praiseworthy. No characters of this kind are found in *Citrarekhā*; indeed, the father of the hunchback bridegroom comes to the hero's aid by suggesting that he stands in for his own son and marry Citrarekhā. Neither can the foe who attacks the hero's kingdom be regarded as a negative character — this is, in fact, a common device used to illustrate a hero's soldierly virtues.

In *Citrarekhā*, unlike *Padmāvat*, no spiritual guide appears. The spiritual guide in *Padmāvat* is the parrot, Hīrāman, whose description of Padmāvatī's beauty inspires the hero, Ratansen, to endeavour to win her heart, the implied symbolism being that of a soul thirsting with love for the Lord. In *Citrarekhā*, the heroine is entrusted first to a wet-nurse and then to a guru, whom Jāysī calls Gaṇeś (gurū Ganesū), under whose tutelage she soon becomes a paṇḍit. Whilst Hīrāman serves to bring the hero and heroine together, Gaṇeś performs no such role.

In Sufi texts, the hero falls in love with the heroine either at first sight or after hearing her being spoken of. In *Citrarekhā*, however, it is the heroine who hears the hero being mentioned, an event that is not even preceded by a description, but by a few extremely succinct words (a single *caupāī*): 'There came her companions, who, seeing the wedding procession, recounted great things to Citrarekhā' (āin sakhiyan dekhi barātā | kahin Citrarekhā sõ bātā, op. cit., p. 102).

In comparison with *Padmāvat*, *Citrarekhā* has the pace of a tale written for a village audience, yet it has all of its charm. It is impossible to say, however, if Jāysī's intention was, in fact, to write a short work, or whether, after beginning the poem, he was dissatisfied with it and put it aside unfinished. This theory is not to be dismissed, and we shall see the reason why.

The preface to *Citrarekhā*, in which praise is sung to the Lord (see above), consists of thirteen stanzas that comprise 117 of the poem's approximately 400 lines. In *Padmāvat*, there is a preface of 24 stanzas, comprising 216 of the total number of lines in the poem — more than six thousand. *Citrarekhā*'s preface is therefore extensively developed, and, when one considers the two works, *Citrarekhā* and *Padmāvat*, it is out of proportion to the length of *Citrarekhā* as a whole. This statement rings particularly true when *Citrarekhā* is compared with *Kanhāvat*. In *Kanhāvat*, a work by Jāysī, or at least attributed to him (and one which, at any rate, was written by someone extremely familiar with his stylistic technique), the preface fills thirteen out of 366 stanzas (in Śivsahāy Pāṭhak's edition), so that in proportion it is less developed than that of *Citrarekhā*. By no stretch of the imagination could *Citrarekhā* be regarded as even remotely religious (it is pointless to search for a spiritual element). It therefore cannot be perceived as an indirect form of sermonising (which in any case would be alien to Jāysī's writing) or as a work in which the poet voices his faith (unlike *Akhrāvaṭ*, for example, which is a religious-philosophical text). For this reason, the lengthy preface would seem to be the start of a work that was planned to be far more extensive.

The fact that the poet does not mention a contemporary king (śāhevaqt) in the preface to *Citrarekhā* may not be of major significance. The contemporary king is mentioned in *Padmāvat* (Śer Śāh), in *Kanhāvat* (Humāyū̃), and in *Ākhirī Kalām* (Bābar), but does not appear in *Akhrāvaṭ*. *Ākhirī Kalām* is a religious text, and, as such, is to some extent comparable with *Akhrāvaṭ*. In *Padmāvat*, *Kanhāvat* and *Ākhirī Kalām*, the poet mentions the year of writing (although I will not dwell on this point, as it has already been the subject of extensive academic debate), but he does not do so in *Akhrāvaṭ* or *Citrarekhā*. Nor does he name the location (the city in which Jāysī lived and may even have been born — another topic debated by scholars) in *Citrarekhā*. Neither, however, is the location mentioned in *Akhrāvaṭ*, whilst it is named in *Padmāvat* (Jāyas nagar dharam asthānū | tahā̃ āi kabi kīnh bakhānū, 'The city Jāyas is a holy spot: there came the poet and told his lay' [Shirreff 1944, p. 19], Stuti khaṇḍ 23.1), *Kanhāvat* (kahā̃u nagar baṛ āpun thā̃u | sadā sohāvā Jāyas nā̃u, 'I speak of my place, a large town, the name of Jāyas always pleases me'), and *Ākhirī Kalām* (Jāyas nagar mor asthānū, 'The city of Jāyas is my place', 10.1). It may be that these technical details are of no significance.

The name of the place in which part of the action occurs — Sinhad in *Citrarekhā* and Sinhal in *Padmāvat* — is possibly more significant. Although Sinhad/Sinhal may be a common name used to denote a far-off location, the fact remains that Sinhad is relatively close to the other places in the story (it can be reached on horseback) while Sinhal is 'beyond the seven seas' (it is reached by ship). Jāysī may have changed Sinhad to Sinhal in order to extend the range of the story.

It is tempting to toy with the theory that *Citrarekhā* was a rough draft from which *Padmāvat* subsequently evolved, but with quite different results. But it is merely a temptation, one that is based on psychological interpretation and not on an exegesis of the work. The fact remains that in some brief passages, the two works are very similar (see example 1), whilst in other, lengthier passages, the same structural form, but different words, are used to express the same concept (example 2); alternatively, the image may actually be reversed (example 3). Generally speaking, the starting point is *Padmāvat*, as it is unquestionably Jāysī's major work. However, the situation could be inverted, in which case images and lines appearing in both works may have been transferred from *Citrarekhā* into *Padmāvat*; in other words, Jāysī may have abandoned *Citrarekhā* in favour of the more important work. In both, however, he reveals himself to be proud of his poetic skills, as the following two quotations illustrate.

Citrarekhā (13.2-3 and *dohā*, 14.1)

ahai Citrarekhā ju kahānī | likhe citrakari kañcan bānī || kañcan kañcan hīrā motī (. . .) Muhmad sāyar dīn duni, mukh ambrit bainān | badan jaïs jag cand sapūran, sūk jaïs nainān || sunaü kathā jas ambrit bānī (. . .)

It is the tale of Citrarekhā, I painted words of gold as I wrote. Each word [is] of gold, diamonds and pearls (. . .) Muhammad (Jāysī) brought poetry to the world, words of ambrosia on his lips, a face like a full moon, eyes like Śukrācārya. Listen to the tale in words of ambrosia (. . .)

Padmāvat (Stuti khaṇḍ 21.1)

ek nayan kabi Muhmad gunī | soi bimohā jehi kabi sunī || (. . .) jag sūjhā ekai navanāhā̃ [nayanāhā̃] (. . .)

Muhammad was skilful, though he had but one eye, and every poet who heard him was entranced. (. . .) With that one eye the poet saw the whole world (. . .). (Shirreff 1944, pp. 17-18)

EXAMPLE 1

The openings of *Citrarekhā* (*caupāī* 1) and *Padmāvat* (*caupāī* 1) are virtually identical (but differ from the openings of *Kanhāvat*, *Akhrāvaṭ*, and *Ākhirī Kalām*).

ādi ek barnāũ so rājā | jākar sabai jagat yah sājā || (*Citrarekhā*, 1.1)

I describe that one and only primal king, who created this entire universe.

Sumirāũ adi ek kartārū | jehi jiu dīnh kīnh sansārū || (*Padmāvat*, Stuti khaṇḍ, 1.1)

I bear in mind that one and only primal Maker, who gave life and made the world. (Shirreff 1944, p.1)

EXAMPLE 2

Citrarekhā (7.1-4)

pem pirīti purukh ek kiyā | nāū Muhammad duhū jag diyā || andhkūp bhayā ahā nirāsā | onke prīti joti parkāsā || āpni joti dipāĩ vai sā̃cā | onke joti sabai parkāsā || hoi pargat path joti anūpā | ghaṭ-ghaṭ pūri bhaeu sab rūpā ||

Out of love he created a man named Muhammad, [and] gave him to the world. There was darkness, there was no hope, out of love for him He created light. He filled the lamp with His light, and that man's light was shed throughout the world. The way became clear, the light was extraordinary, every body acquired its shape.

Padmāvat (Stuti khaṇḍ 11.1-4)

kīnhesi puruṣ ek nirmarā | nām Muhammad pūnau-karā || pratham joti bidhi tākar sājī | au tehi prīti sihiṭ uparājī || dīpak lesi jagat kahā̃ dīnhā | bhā nirmal jag, marag cīnhā || jau na hot as puruṣ ujārā | sūjhi na parat panth adhiyārā ||

Thus made He one without blemish, named Muhammad, glorious as the full moon. It was his radiancy that God first produced, and then for love of him He created the universe. He kindled that light and gave it to the world. The world became clear, and recognized its [true] way. If that bright man had not been, the dark path would not have been visible. (Shirreff 1944, p. 7)

EXAMPLE 3

Citrarekhā (7.6)

jin vah nāū linh au japā | so kabilāsī au baṛ tapā

He who invokes and recites that name [is] worthy of paradise [and is] a great ascetic.

Padmāvat (Stuti khaṇḍ 11.6)

jehi nahĩ līnh janam bhari nāũ | tā kahā̃ kinh narak mahā̃ ṭhāũ

For those who have not taken [refuge in] his name throughout his life, God hath prepared a place in hell. (Shirreff 1944, p. 7)

This *caupāī* from *Padmāvat* appears in almost identical form in *Ākhirī Kalām* (jei nahī̃ līnh janam mahã nāū̃ | tehi kahā kīnh narak mahã ṭhāū̃, *Ākhirī Kalām*, 7.7).

The *nakh-śikh* description of Citrarekhā is certainly not comparable with that of Padmāvatī. This is not simply because the description fills just one stanza of *Citrarekhā* (a stanza that is, moreover, incomplete, since it has only five *caupāīs*), but because not even those who insist on the religious significance of all Jāysī's works would be able to find any spiritual meaning in it.

Citrarekhā, 18.1-5

So it was that when she was ten years old, her body shone like a full moon. Her jewel-like forehead acquired light and radiance. Her tresses were hornets, snakes and Śeṣnāg. The radiance of the lovely girl was the radiance of the autumn moon, her eyes became a pair of khañjan. Her eyebrows [became] a bow that strikes the enemy, her eyelashes [like] arrows aimed to pierce. Her eyelids [became like] the sword that strikes Kāmdev, her lips sought to cut to the quick.

Brief though *Citrarekhā* may be, this *nakh-śikh* is clearly unfinished, for only the head and face are described. The stanza itself is incomplete.

There is, however, a similarity in the mood of Citrarekhā's young female companions in the swing scene (*Citrarekhā*, 20.1-7) and those of Padmāvatī in the sporting scene at Lake Mānsarodak (*Padmāvat*, Mānsarodak khaṇḍ, stanzas 2 and 3). They even share some identical lines.

Citrarekhā, 20.1-7 and *dohā*

mili rahāsi sab caṛhī hiḍorāĩ | jhūli lehu sāg bārī bhaurāĩ || jhūli lehu naihar jab tāĩ | phir kat jhūlan daihāĩ sāĩ || lekai sasur rākhihai tahā̃ | naihar gavan na pāib jahā̃ || kahā yah dhūp kahā̃ yah chā̃hā̃ | rahab rain din mandir mā̃hā̃ || au nit neh harāsahī soī | sādh marab ā̃gan kas hoī || sāsu nanad bolat jiv leī | dārun sasur na nikaran deī || sāsu nanad ke mūhāhī agore | rahab sukhī doū kar jore || kat naihar phir āib, kat sasurāĩ yah khel | āp āp kahā̃ hoihāĩ, jyō̃ pankhin mahā̃ ḍel ||

All the artless damsels meet, mount the swings, and rock themselves. 'Well may you swing whilst you art in your parents' house, for whenever will our husbands allow us to swing? Once married, they will put us in our father-in-law's home, whence we shall not be permitted to go to our parents' homes. Where [will there be] this sunshine, where this shadow, day and night we shall remain indoors. And they are the very persons who love us the least, how can we languish at home? Mother-in-law and sister-in-law, talking, steal our lives, they will not let us go outside our father-in-law's dreadful house. Awaiting the orders of mother-in-law and sister-in-law, we will be content with both hands humbly joined.—Will we visit our parents' homes ever again, will we ever sport this way in our father-in-law's house? Each of us will be alone, as a bird in the fowler's basket.'

Padmāvat, Mānsarodak khaṇḍ, 2 and 3

khelat Mānsarovar gaī̃ | jāi pāl par ṭhāṛhī bhaī̃ || dekhi sarovar hā̃sāi kuleli | Padmāvatī sa͂u kahahī saheli || e rānī! man dekhu bicārī | ehi naihar rahnā din cārī || jau lagi ahai pitā kar rājū | kheli lehu jo khelahu ājū || puni sāsur ham gavanab kālī | kit ham, kit yas saravar pālī || kit āvan puni apne hāthā | kit mili kai khelab ek sāthā || sāsu nanad bolinh jiu lehī̃ | dārun sasur na nisarai dehī̃ || piu piyār sir ūpar, puni so karai dahū̃ kāh | dahu sukh rākhai kī dukh, dahū̃ kas janam nibāh ||2||

milahī rahasi sab caṛhahī hī̃ḍorī | jhūli lẽhī sukh bārī bhorī || jhūli lehu naihar jab tāī̃ | phiri nahī̃ jhūlan deihī̃ sāī̃ || puni sāsur lei rākhihi tahā̃ | naihar cāh na pāub jahā̃ || kit yah dhūp, kahā̃ yah chāhā̃ | rahab sakhī binu mandir māhā̃ || gun pūchihi au lāihi dokhū | kaun utar pāub tahā̃ mokhū || sāsu nanad ke bhaũh sikore | rahab sā̃koci duvau kar jore || kit yah rahasi jo āub karnā | sasurei ant janam dukh bharnā || kit naihar puni āub, kit sasure yah khel | āpu āpu kahā̃ hoihi parab paṅkhi jas ḍel ||3||

Sporting went they forth to the Manasarodaka lake, and stood upon its bank. As they looked at it frolicked they, and cried to Padmavati, 'My Princess, consider in thine heart, but a few days more have we to wait in our fathers' homes. If thou must sport, sport thou to-day, for thou can'st but sport while thou art a maiden in thy father's kingdom. On the morrow must we all depart to our hubands' dwellings,—then where will we be, and where the bank of this fair lake? Where will be our liberty of going and coming at our own sweet will, and where shall we meet together and sport? The husband's mother and sister will kill us with their [jealous] speeches, and his stern father will not let us slip out of doors. — I know that my Love will be beloved and over all but what can he do against them? Keep he us in bliss or in sorrow, still we must live with him.'

Frolicking do they meet, and mount the swing, and happily do the artless damsels rock themselves therein. 'Swing away while thou art in thy parent's house: for, once married, our Lord will no longer let us swing. He will [jealously] guard us in our father-in-law's house, [and put us] where we shall not e'en be able to wish for our parents' homes. Where will then be this sunshine, and where this shade? We shall ever remain indoors, and without our young friends. Some day he will consider and ask questions [of us] and blame us [for to-day's sport]: what answer, what release, shall we obtain? How often will our mothers-in-law and our sisters-in-law contract their brows, and we shall remain shrivelled up, with both hands humbly joined? Where again shall we come to frolic thus? In our husbands' houses shall we have sorrow to bear till our deaths. — How seldom shall we return to our parents' homes. How seldom will there be this sport in our husbands' houses. Each of us will be herself to herself, as a bird fallen into a fowler's basket'. (Shirreff 1944, pp. 44-5)

As I pointed out earlier, *Citrarekhā* is a love story with a happy ending. It lacks the tragic vision that is so striking in *Padmāvat*. Scholars have identified the spurious parts of *Padmāvat*, and the text is now regarded as well determined. *Citrarekhā* has not been scholarly analysed in the same manner. There undoubtedly are several spurious areas in this text, too. The most significant would seem to be the second part of the final stanza, a veritable 'lesson' that fails to blend with the text. The true closing stanza is the one that precedes it: in the concluding *dohā*, the happy ending is actually justified. There follow both stanzas (46.1-7 and *dohā*, 47.1-7 and *dohā*).

'Princess Citrarekhā mounted the pyre after reading the words written on her añcal. When the hour comes, I will light the pyre and die together with my beloved. When the appointed time was due, they decided to set fire to the pyre. In that instant, the bridegroom reached the city, Prītam Kunvar arrived. His eyes met those of Citrarekhā, the torch she was holding remained in her hand. Covering her head in shame, the girl stepped down from the pyre and entered the palace. When it was learned that the bridegroom was alive, they made haste to ring out congratulations, then one hundred congratulations began to be rung. — Today the deity has brought happiness and pleasure into sorrow, for those whose hearts are torn by separation will surely meet.

'Her companions adorned her with jewel-encrusted necklaces, and swiftly gave the bride a small meal. "Today, your bridegroom wishes to meet you, good and evil will be erased." Her companions attended to her toilette, "You must serve your groom, use neither spells nor affectations to win him." Duty to your husband, that is the spell, without duty that spell is malignant. For women whose minds are concentrated on duty, nuptial contentment will grow daily. The idea of duty appeals to the mind of her beloved, who loses interest in beauty and is attracted by lack of beauty. With duty, the husband will not be angered, no blame can be laid on a dutiful person. — Through duty and through order, the tenth state is attained, those who continue to play will later be repentant.'

The first of the two *dohā*s that effectively bring the text to a close is a literary conclusion which matches Jāysī's style, whilst the second and final *dohā* is a typical example of Kabīr's influence, and is probably spurious.

'If someone is a capable writer, his writings will endure for years, the writer is wretched, for he will dissolve and turn to dust.'

'They recited many books and died, [but] no one was a paṇḍit, the person who recites a single word of love becomes a paṇḍit.'

The sixth stanza, which is part of the preface, would also seem false. In it there appear motifs and images that are used by Kabīr or are generally associated with him.

'He who manifestly injures his body, who piously beats his head on the ground, whose hair is left in tangles, [and] who wears ashes, who dons ochre-coloured garments, who elects to walk naked, who falls down onto a bed of thorns, who casts his apparel aside to take a vow of silence, does not remain a goose, but becomes a devotee apart. In the water there are fish and frog, and the bat, too, continues to hang. Animals [and] birds are all unclothed, the potter always has an abundance of ash. The bargad and the pīpal are generously tressed, what will you achieve from this garb, simpleton. —Until there is separation in the body, [and until] love springs forth in the body, there can be no ascetic fervour, moral duty, virtue, [or] truth.'

REFERENCES

Āśā Kiśor (ed.), *Jāysī koś*, New Delhi: Macmillan, 1976.

Campion, Silvia, 'L'*Akhrāvaṭ* di Malik Muhammad Jāysī' (with Italian translation of the poem), *Annali di Ca' Foscari* (Venice), XXXVI, 3, 1997, pp. 303-34.

McGregor, Ronald Stuart, *Hindi Literature from its beginnings to the nineteenth century*, Wiesbaden: Otto Harrassowitz, 1974.

Pandey, Shyam Manohar, '*Kanhāvat*, A Kṛṣṇaite Sūfī text attributed to Malik Muhammad Jāyasī', *Orientalia Lovaniensia Periodica*, vol. 26, Leuven, 1995, pp. 187-98.

———, 'The King and the Guru in early Hindī Sūfī poetry', *Orientalia Lovaniensia Periodica*, vol. 24, Leuven, 1993, pp. 197-211.

———, *Madhyyugīn premākhyān*, Ilāhābād: Lokbhārtī Prakāśan, 1982, 2nd revd. edn.

Rāmcandr Śukl, *Jāysī Granthāvalī*, Vārāṇasī: Nāgrīpracāriṇī Sabhā, 1968, 13th edn.

Shirreff, A.G., *Padmāvatī*, Calcutta: Royal Asiatic Society of Bengal, 1944.

Śivsahāy Pāṭhak, *Malik Muhammad Jāysī aur unkā kāvy*, Ilāhābād: Sāhity Bhavan, 1976.

Śivsahāy Pāṭhak (ed.), *Citrarekhā* (Malik Muhammad Jāysī kṛt premkāvy), Vārāṇasī: Hindī Pracārak Pustakālay, 1959.

———, *Kanhāvat*, Ilāhābād: Sāhity Bhavan, 1981.

Vijaydevnārāyaṇ Sāhī, *Jāysī*, Ilāhābād: Hindustānī Ekeḍemī, 1993, 1st edn. 1983.

PART II

Urdu Drama and Poetry at the Muslim Courts

Heteroglossia in Amānat's *Indar Sabhā*

KATHRYN HANSEN

On the most widely accepted account, the *Indar sabhā* (The Assembly of King Indra, hereafter *IS*) was composed in 1853 by Āghā Hasan Amānat (1816-59), a poet attached to the court of Wajid Ali Shah at Lucknow. The rule of the Nawabs of Awadh, arguably the most celebrated of the successor states that followed the Mughal dynasty, was to come to an inglorious end within a few short years. Nonetheless, during the decade of his reign Wajid Ali was considered a generous and creative patron of the arts, who not only provided for the maintenance of performers but through his personal involvement advanced artistic development in several fields. He nourished Kathak, an Indo-Muslim style of dance, embellished the light classical song form *ṭhumrī*, composed poetry in several languages, and adapted both Persian-style romances (*masnavī*) and dramas based on stories of the god Krishna (*līlā*) for his own royal stage. Famed for his hedonistic habits, among the British he gained notoriety for spending more time in his harem, which he called a *parīkhānā* or 'house of fairies', than attending to affairs of state.

Apparently affected by the activities at his patron's salon, a poet named Amānat Alī created the *IS*, an original work that assimilated Urdu *ghazal*s, Braj Bhasha *ṭhumrī*s, and Awadhi folk songs to a narrative base drawn from several popular *masnavī*s. Composed almost entirely in verse, lacking division into acts and scenes, and constructed as a pageant of song and dance connected by a thread of a story, the *IS* lacks the characteristics of modern drama that Urdu critics would eventually delineate. Yet this late example of premodern culture was both imitative of longstanding traditions and highly innovative. Now viewed by scholars as the first Urdu drama, the *IS* was such a success that it remained a favourite for more than a hundred years. It was one of the first printed texts in the nineteenth century to become a best seller, being reprinted several times in Urdu, transliterated into Hindi, Gurumukhi, Gujarati, and even Hebrew characters, and published in Tamil, Sinhala, Malay, and German translations. Moreover, as a standard item in the repertoire of the Parsi theatrical companies, it was carried to all corners of the subcontinent and even beyond, and it spawned a legion of imitations and adaptations into other languages. In the twentieth century, songs from the *IS* were among the first wax recordings made; several successful screen versions are known. The *IS* is thus both a landmark in the canons of literary history and a foundational moment in the evolution of the popular culture of South Asia.

As part of an explanation for the *IS*'s wide and lasting acclaim, I will pursue in this essay the notion that the text's multiple linguistic registers enabled the drama to address a more diversely configured audience than that associated with either premodern courtly drama or the more widely circulated so-called folk traditions. Code shifting within dramatic texts has generally been understood as a necessary strategy to engage diverse sectors within a heterogeneous audience. The classic example is Sanskrit drama wherein the Sanskrit passages are presumed to have been intended for the high-caste, highly educated, male members of the audience, whereas Prakrit speech was directed toward the lower ranks and women. Multilinguality continues to be a feature of audience composition in South Asia, and the notion that different groups can be catered to and satisfied by the recognition of their 'own' languages still holds sway in the political and cultural arenas. The implications of this argument, however, tend to be divisive and essentializing, insofar as the model of social stratification assumes airtight linguistic communities with rigid boundaries. The alternative would be to consider the idea that multiple linguistic usages are accessible to a range of speakers or auditors, who may respond diversely but are nonetheless interpellated as hypothetical audiences for each type of address. The issue then becomes how socio-economic position, gender, and other variables inflect the reception of language. What did a Sanskrit verse signify to a Brahmin male, a Brahmin female, and a lower-caste individual? What structures of feeling were engaged by the use of Prakrits, and how did these contrast with Sanskrit? Were linguistic shifts recognized as such by the audience, or were moves between different genres or categories of characters more significant to their tracking of a performance?

In bringing this approach to the *IS*, I would start then by questioning the notion that the drama's allegedly 'Hindi' poems and songs were intended for and understood only by Hindi speakers, or Hindus, or the 'middle class', or women, while the 'Urdu' *sher*s and *ghazal*s were exclusively for the king, the court, or the Muslim literati. Similarly I would cast doubt on the common wisdom that only those groups inducted into particular literary practices by virtue of class, community, and gender identity could enjoy 'their' kinds of poetry. Instead of imagining an audience divided by the languages of the day, why not think about a social order and a performative economy at least partially based on inclusion? What will hopefully emerge from this change in perspective is a way of imagining how poetic texts differently structured by language, voice, and imagery, and perhaps even composed originally for separate publics, could be brought together for a common public, albeit one still in formation, and enjoyed and consumed within a shared set of understandings about the pleasures of spectacle and the sung word.

This framework does not deny that speech forms and the poetic structures associated with them are embedded in broader political, ideological, and economic systems, and therefore are inevitably linked to the social relations of speakers. Mikhail Bakhtin, a theorist with a particular interest in language as a field of discourse, distinguishes several ways that linguistic practices can be interlayered in specific communities and times. The synchronicity of multiple languages he identifies as *polyglossia*. I posit as an example the prevalence of English, Marathi, and Hindi in the urban environment of present-day Mumbai. A society characterized by polyglossia, Bakhtin contends, is generally engaged in an ongoing contest among the ideologies, social histories, and identities encoded within the distinct languages. Contrasted with this is *heteroglossia*, referring to the variation within a single language (Bakhtin 1981). Heteroglossia, I suggest, would apply to the range of Hindustani-based registers found in large parts of north Indian society as well as to the diversity in the text of the *IS*. In both cases, a grammatical base of Khari Boli and core vocabulary are shared but dialectal forms and lexical preferences diverge. While the concept of heteroglossia does not rule out contention, it proposes a multilayered field of overlapping language styles with a relatively higher degree of mutual comprehension than that indicated by polyglossia, and thus is more appropriate to analysing the reception of our text.

In an earlier study, I suggested that with the advent of the *IS* in the middle of the nineteenth century, theatre in north India begins to make the transition from the courtly milieu to a popular arena (Hansen 1992). More recently I have explored the idea that the figure of Indar, with his multiple articulations as Vedic deity, post-Mughal Nawab, and sensuous Lord Krishna, is largely accountable for facilitating this movement (Hansen 1998a). Even in the heyday of the British Empire, Indar with his courtly assembly continued to evoke nostalgia for opulence and feudal certainties. Moreover, in his dual position within the drama as participant and patron, he helped to construct the imagined self of the new spectator of the public theatre. In this paper I extend the argument by focusing on how the fluid subjectivity of Indar is to a large extent constructed in the shifting forms of linguistic address with which he is hailed in the drama. The heteroglossia of the text, I hope to show, mobilizes Indar as a multivalent icon of symbolic authority. A similar fluidity accrues to the identity of the fairies, the primary interlocutors in the piece and the foci of the viewers' eroticized gaze. Via the switches among the poetic personae inhabiting genres such as *ṭhumrī*, *horī*, and *ghazal*, the text imbues the fairies with a markedly liminal, androgynous quality. This gender play, linked to the permutations of language and poetic address, is further complicated by the popular practice of using cross-dressed male-to-female impersonators to perform the female roles, particularly in the urban Parsi theatre. Amānat's artfully hybrid language thus allows an incorporation of the available vocabularies of eroticism, without consigning performers, spectators, or the characters within the drama to exclusive categories of gender, class, or community.

The text itself divides into two parts, the second of which comprises the story proper. The events take place in the court of Indar, king of the gods, who sits in state flanked by beautiful fairies. The Emerald Fairy (Sabz Parī) falls in love with an earthly prince (Gulfām), and with the assistance of the Black Demon (Kālā Dev) she smuggles Gulfām into Indar's heaven. Displeased at this infraction, Indar casts Gulfām into a well and clips the wings of the Sabz Parī, who plunges to earth. Undaunted, she disguises herself as a *jogin* (female mendicant) and, singing irresistible songs of separation, gains readmission to the heavens, wins the king's favour, and eventually earns her lover's release. Indar grants his blessings to the couple and they are reunited amidst general celebration.

By late medieval times, the Vedic deity Indra/Indar had evolved into an emblem of the lordly monarch, and his entourage of beautiful dancing girls, whether known as *apsarā*s or *parī*s, symbolized his potency and dedication to sensual pleasure (*vilās*, *kām*). This figurehead of the Hindu pantheon is wedded in the *IS* to the theme of fairy-mortal romance, long a staple of narrative genres in Urdu and Persian (*qissā*, *dāstān*, *masnavī*). Amānat may have modelled his plot on two specific *masnavī*s that achieved particular popularity earlier in the nineteenth century. The romance of Prince Benazīr and Princess Badr-i Munīr as told in *Sihr ul-bayān* by Mīr Hasan (1727-86) was, in 1805, one of the first Urdu books ever printed. It could be the source for such scenes in the *IS* as the fairy's first encounter with the sleeping prince, his befuddled awakening in the fairy world, his imprisonment in the well, and the disguise of the fairy as a *jogin.* A later work, *Gulzār-i nasīm* by Dayā Shankar 'Nasīm' (1837), itself a reworking of the prose tale *Gul-i bakāwalī* or *Mazhab-i ishq* by Nihāl Chand, was said to be an effort at repeating Mīr Hasan's success.

(Schimmel 1975). From it Amānat may have borrowed the description of Indar's court, the king's anger upon learning of the fairy's love for a mortal, and other passages.

What sets the *IS* apart from its antecedents is the very simplicity of the story line. Whereas long *dāstān*s contained embedded worlds with innumerable conquests and love affairs, even the shorter tales generally included a subplot with a second pair of lovers, useful for complications such as jealousy, mistaken identity, and so on. The *IS* story line is restricted to a single pair of lovers, and the only serious obstacle they face is the king's hostility, which is readily overcome by the fairy's enchanting singing. One aspect that the *IS* shares with the earlier narratives is the presence of an active female *āshiq* (lover) in the character of the *parī*. *Parī*s in these stories pursue their male love-objects, declare their infatuation openly, carry them away through the air, and kiss or touch them without invitation. Born of fire, possessed of the ability to appear and disappear at will, they exert a powerful control over the hero, not unlike the demanding, high-status Beloved of the Urdu *ghazal*. The difference is that the Beloved of the *ghazal* remains Other — distant, veiled, unobtainable except in death. The *parī* is all too near, forward, and potentially overpowering.

Debate has long raged regarding the relation of the historical king, Wajid Ali Shah, to the Indar of the play, with one school of opinion contending that not only did the Nawab commission the drama but that he then played the title role. This interpretation gains support from the first (and in certain ways more original) part of the drama, in which Amānat recreates a court that resembles Wajid Ali Shah's own. In the opening scene, Indar is seated on his throne, enjoying himself as he is entertained by a succession of lovely fairies, each of whom performs a set of songs and dances before him. This royal assembly is termed variously *sabhā*, *majlis*, *mehfil*, and *jalsā* in the text. These usages denote the cultural gatherings generally held in the outer, public rooms of wealthy patrons, wherein poetry was recited and/or dance and musical expertise displayed. Such events establish a context in which public honours may be distributed or denied, and in which the mutuality of regard (or its lack) between two individuals may be magnified in intensity by the potential rivalry of the others present within the circle. This could be called a kind of public sphere, but one filled with strong currents of personal and at least partially covert feeling.

It is within this opening assembly that the interplay of languages begins to define the relations between the fairies, the king, and the spectators. In the absence of episodic action, attention is focused upon the serial performances of the first three fairies, each of whom delivers for the king's and the audience's delectation a set of songs accompanied by dancing. (Exactly how the song texts were set to dance is unknown, but both the illustrations that accompany the published editions of the *IS* and internal references establish that the fairies danced as they sang.) Each fairy's set typically begins with an *āmad* or 'entry', an introductory poem lauding the fairy as she enters the stage, presumably enunciated or sung by the stage director or narrator (*sūtradhār*). Then follows a self-descriptive poem, called *sherkhvānī*, in which the fairy depicts her own virtues in first-person *ghazal*-like verses. Next follows a subset of songs that employ Hindi meters and switch the register to Braj Bhasha, most commonly consisting of a *chand* or two, a *ṭhumrī*, and a *horī*, with other song types such as *basant* and *sāvan* occasionally adding a tinge of Awadhi. To conclude the set, the fairy sings three *ghazal*s; the length of each is between ten and fifteen *sher*s. The highly formalized set of pieces, juxtaposed without any connective dialogue, is concluded by a brief comment by the king and summons for the next fairy to appear.

Linguistically these songs may be placed on a continuum whose centre point is the accessible, mixed register Khari Boli Hindustani used for *āmad*s and the king's opening *caubolā*:

A. *CAUBOLĀ*

rājā hū̃ maĩ qaum kā aur indar merā nām
bin pariyõ kī dīd ke nahī̃ mujhe ārām.

King I am of this land, and Indar is my name.
Without the sight of the fairies, I am disconsolate.

suno re mere dev re dil ko nahī̃ qarār
jaldī mere vāste sabhā karo taiyār. (no. 2)[1]

Listen, my giant-servant, my spirit is restless:
Arrange a musical assembly for me right away!

B. *ĀMAD*

mahfil-i rājā mẽ pukhrāj parī ātī hai
sāre māshūqõ kī sartāj parī ātī hai. (no. 3)

The Topaz Fairy enters the king's assembly.
Jewel in the crown of all the Beloveds, she enters.

[1] All citations are from the Urdu text edited by Rizvī 1957. For a Devnagari version of Rizvī's edition, see Husain 1990.

At the 'Urdu' end of the continuum are *ghazals* that employ the stock imagery of the lamenting lover, the cruel beloved figured as an executioner, and various metaphors for beauty such as the rose, the moth and flame, etc. These poems assume a familiarity with the conventions of *ghazal* recitation, and they contain Persian and Arabic words and a somewhat limited used of *izāfat* constructions. On the whole, however, we are in a much simpler world than that of the *ghazals* being written by 'classical' Urdu poets like Ghalib around the same time. Examples from several *ghazals*:

C. *GHAZAL*

ṭakarā ke sar ko jān na dū̃ mãi to kyā karū̃
kab tak firāq-i yār ke sadme sahā karū̃. (no. 11)

What should I do but dash out my brains?
How long should I bear the blows of separation from the Beloved?

lailī-i zulf kā saudā lab-i shīrīn kī hai cāh
kabhī majnūn hū̃ tere ishq mẽ farhād kabhī. (no. 21)

Laila's tresses vie with Shirin's lips in my desires.
Sometimes I am Majnun, sometimes Farhad: such is my love for you.

bhūlā hū̃ mãi ālam ko sarshār ise kahte hãi
mastī se nahī̃ ghāfil hushiyār ise kahte hãi. (no. 66)

I'm oblivious to the world — they call this intoxication.
No stranger to divine madness — they call this intelligence.

At the 'Hindi', or more precisely, Braj Bhasha end of the scale, the poems mostly eschew Persian and Arabic, although they rely much more upon words of indigenous origin than Sanskrit derivatives. Endings may reflect local dialects, and references within the texts are to seasons, plants, and other items from the Indian environment. Some of these poems specifically refer to the romance of Krishna and his sport with the *gopīs* of Vrindavan, while others voice the pain of the *virahinī*, the woman separated from her lover.

D. *HORĪ*

pā lāgī kar jorī
shyām mo se khelo na horī

Clasping your feet I beg of you,
Please Shyam, don't play Holi with me!

gauvẽ carāvan mãi nikasī hũ sās nanand kī corī
sagarī cūnar raṅg mẽ na bhijovo itnī suno bāt morī

I came out to graze the cows, stealing away from my in-laws.
Don't drench my whole garment in dye — this much I ask of you.

shyām mo se khelo na horī (no. 9)

Please Shyam, don't play Holi with me!

E. *SĀVAN*

bin piyā ghaṭā nahī̃ bhāve
rah rah dil raund ho āve
bijarī kī camak tarpāve ḍarāve
bin piyā ghaṭā nahī̃ bhāve. (no. 28)

Without my Beloved/Piya, I cannot endure the rainy season.
My heart is oppressed with longing.
The lightning crashes, my body thrashes.
Without my Beloved/Piya, I cannot endure the rainy season.

F. *ṬHUMRĪ*

rājā jī karo mo se batiyā̃ re
dil tarapat din ratiyā̃ re
hamrī or se tum se din din
sautan jāke lagatiyā̃ re. (no. 18)

Dear king, speak a few sweet words to me.
My heart throbs for you night and day,
Yet day after day, keeping away from me,
You enjoy that other woman's embraces.

As each fairy displays musical and poetic virtuosity, the audience is treated to a medley of compositions, reinforced by special visual effects. Each fairy is named after a monocoloured gemstone — Pukhrāj (topaz), Nīlam (sapphire), Lāl (ruby), and Sabz (emerald) — and each attired in clothes appropriate to her colour. In the songs that describe her beauty, she refers to that colour and its association with seasons, festivals, flowers, trees, and other elements of nature. Thus the Topaz Fairy sings an item known as Basant (spring) in the Rāga Bahār (also spring) celebrating her yellow outfit and referring to marigolds and the new blossoms of the mustard plant (*sarsõ*).

G. *BASANT*

rut āī basant ajab bahār
khile jard phūl birvan kī ḍār
rut āī.

Spring has come, that wondrous season.
Yellow blossoms hang from the tree branches.
Spring has come.

caṭko kusum phūle lāgī sarsõ
phapakat calat guhū̃ kī bār
rut āī. (no. 7)

Clusters of bright mustard flowers burst forth,
Sheaves of new wheat rustle and sway.
Spring has come.

What results is a kind of variety show, or an early Miss India pageant, highlighted by the visual effect of colour coding. Beginning in the 1870s, special lighting was added to accentuate each fairy's colour when she first appeared on the stage. According to Memuna Dalvi, 'To create the effect of the marvellous, *limelight* [Eng.] was used, so that as each fairy entered Raja Indar's court, the entire scene was bathed in the light of that fairy's garments. The spectators were beside themselves and burst into spontaneous applause' (Yusuf 1980).

Kaleidoscopic shifts in poetic persona accompany the movement back and forth between languages and genres. One moment a fairy boasts of her own charms and mastery, constructing a voice like the *parī* of the Urdu *dāstān*, and yet remarkably akin to a saucy Lucknow courtesan demanding her due.

H. *SHERKHVĀNĪ*

gātī hū̃ mãĩ aur nāc sadā kām hai merā
āfāq mẽ pukhrāj parī nām hai merā.

My occupation is forever to sing and to dance.
Throughout the heavens I am renowned as the Topaz Fairy.

mãĩ lākh kī do lākh kī parvā nahī̃ rakhtī
qārū̃ kā khazānā ajī inām hai merā. (no. 4)

I'm not impressed by one lākh or two,
My fitting reward is the treasury of Qarun.

Next she assumes the abject tone of a royal slave or concubine, disclaiming rather disingenuously any interest in wealth.

I. *CHAND*

rājā indar des mẽ rahẽ ilāhī shād
jo mujh sī nācīz ko kiyā sabhā mẽ yād.
kiyā sabhā mẽ yād mujhe rājā ne āj
daulat māl khazāne kī kab hū̃ mai̇̃ muhtāj. (no. 5)

Long live King Indar, and may God bless his reign,
Who remembered this worthless wretch and called her to the assembly.
The king remembered me today —
When have I ever been lured by the promise of gold?

Sometimes she takes on the guise of a *gopī* and chides Lord Krishna playfully, as in the *Horī* already cited. (*Pā lāgī kar jorī | Shyām mo se khelo na horī.*) At other moments, she assumes the pitiable stance of a bereft woman in love, as in the *Sāvan* (above) that purposefully casts her lover as Piyā, one of Wajid Ali Shah's pen-names. (*Bin piyā ghaṭā nahī̃ bhāve.*) These alter egos could be referencing the *nāyikā bhed* classificatory system of premodern Hindi poetry, whereby women are allotted specific roles within an erotic typology. The display of the repertory of *nāyikā*s figures in the structure of the Indian classical dance recital, and this practice could have been established by Amānat's time. Significantly, each of these songs is linguistically marked by the use of the feminine gender in the text, and except for one song (*Bihāg kī cīz*) assigned to prince Gulfām later in the play and Indar's opening *caubolā* (quoted above), it is noteworthy that *all* of the Hindi verse forms (*ṭhumrī, horī, basant, sāvan, chand, caubolā*) are sung by *parī*s.

Beyond these, an alien voice, but one that could be considered dominant, interrupts the succession of feminine images. In the Urdu *ghazal*s that bring closure to each part of the *sabhā* section, the fairy assumes the persona of the *āshiq*, the wronged but devoted lover in pursuit of the unattainable (and possibly divine) Beloved. For example, in a characteristically masochistic pose, the Topaz Fairy complains of her beloved's haughty neglect and threatens suicide: *Ṭakarā ke sar ko jān na dū̃ mai̇̃ to kyā karū̃ | Kab tak firāq-i yār ke sadme sahā karū̃* (no. 11). In another of the *ghazal*s quoted above, the Sapphire Fairy declares herself to be one with Majnun and Farhad, great lovers of yore who exemplified the perfection of *ishq* or pure love (no. 21). The Emerald Fairy is willing to become intoxicated with passion, leaving the world behind: *Bhūlā hū̃ mai̇̃ ālam ko sarshār ise* *kahte hāĩ* (no. 66). In the majority of the *ghazal*s sung by fairies in the *IS*, the persona of the *āshiq* is marked as masculine, and the fairy speaks from this voice, using the first person masculine grammatical endings. (In the Urdu *ghazal*, the Beloved was also traditionally hailed in the masculine gender, as is well known. The convention is preserved in Amānat's *ghazal*s.) In a smaller number of *ghazal*s, the gender of the speaker is not made explicit. Moreover, references to the beloved's hair, eyebrows, etc., although commonly interpreted as pertaining to women, could in fact indicate either gender. I will return to the question of the construction of the fairy's gender in the *IS* as a whole. For the moment, it is sufficient to point out the complementarity provided by the alternation between the Hindi-based songs in the feminine voice and the Urdu *ghazal*s in the masculine voice within each fairy's self-representation.

Corresponding to these shifts, the addressee of the fairies' utterances moves back and forth, both with regard to gender and in respect to social and metaphysical status: from patron to king, from deity to mortal lover, from cruel beauty to Divine Master. An ambiguous blurring of roles is indeed embedded in Indic poetic traditions; kings, gods, and lovers all occupy an eroticized space and easily merge with one other. The *sabhā* section of the *IS* brings these domains into contact, not through density of symbolism or internal references but through the sequencing of heterogeneous linguistic media. The vocalizations of the fairies serially hail the king as Indar, as Krishna, as Piya or the Nawab, and as the Beloved of the *āshiq*. From the heteroglossia of Amānat's text, Indar, the silent but powerful icon, emerges as a multivalent object of desire.

If the success of the *IS* can in some way then be attributed to the fascinated self-identification of the urban spectator with King Indar, what of the fairies, the objects of Indar's and the spectators' gaze? I have already established that the gender identity associated with the language of their songs in the *sabhā* section is fluid, oscillating between feminine and masculine. The narrative portion of the drama now bears some consideration, both with regard to language and gender. In relation to Gulfām, the mortal prince who is the object of the Sabz Parī's affections in this part, the principal fairy's actions and language are remarkably bold. Gulfām, in fact, is a passive figure who spends most of his time on stage imprisoned in a well. His main contribution to the plot is to express his wish to *see* the fairies dance, which pushes the narrative towards the climax of his capture and punishment. The Sabz Parī meanwhile has had her way with him. Leaving Indar and the court after he dozes off during her opening act, she wanders to a garden and spots the sleeping prince:

J. *CAUBOLĀ*

sūrat uskī dekh kar dil se gayā qarār
mūh par mūh maĩ ne rakhā kiyā khūb sā pyār. (no. 37)

Seeing his beautiful form, I lost my heart to him:
I placed my mouth upon his and gave him many kisses.

The Sabz Parī subsequently professes her love to Gulfām verbally, identifying her actions overtly as those of an *āshiq*. In contrast to her voice in earlier Urdu *ghazal*s, she now claims this role in the feminine:

K. *JAVĀB*

tujh par maĩ āshiq huī calte calte rāh
uṭhā māgāyā yā̃ tujhe bhej ke dev siyāh. (no. 51)

I fell in love with you while coming along the way.
I sent for the Dark Demon and had you transported here.

When Gulfām finds himself in heaven against his will, his initial reaction is to burst into lamentation, first in the form of an Urdu *ghazal*, then in a Hindi composition in the Rāga Bihāg. Despite the nominal language switch, the expressions used in the opening lines of Gulfām's laments are very similar:

L. *GHAZAL*

ghar se yā̃ kaun khudā ke liye lāyā mujh ko
kis sitamgar ne sote se jagāyā mujh ko. (no. 44)

Who, for God's sake, brought me from my home to this place?
What oppressor awakened me from my slumber?

M. *BIHĀG*

mujhe kaun ghar se lāyā yahā̃
batāo ye kis kā haigā makā̃. (no. 45)

Who brought me from my home to this place?
Tell me, whose dwelling could this be?

A spirited argument between the prince and the fairy ensues, a series of *savāl-javāb*s (questions and answers) in rhyming couplets. In these passages, there is little variation between the two speakers in language; an intermediate register of mixed Hindi and Urdu is employed by both. Each uses gender endings conventionally, Gulfām employing masculine forms, Sabz Parī feminine forms. None the less, Gulfām's plaintive, victimized posture *vis à vis* the Sabz Parī's obvious domination lends an effeminacy, or perhaps more accurately, a gender indeterminacy to his character, which perhaps finds its equivalent in the undifferentiated linguistic character of this section.

By contrast, finding her wings clipped by the angry Indar, the Sabz Parī assumes the form of a *jogin*, a mendicant singer. *Jogin*s were reputed, like certain *jogī*s, to possess supernatural powers and were commonly associated with the practice of witchcraft. The *jogin* role thus empowers the fairy, supplying a 'heavy' counter-identity to her former 'light' status as a weightless celestial. In this guise, the fairy returns to Indar's court, singing songs of separation to the mournful strains of Rāga Bhairavī in such a way that the king succumbs to her enchantment and offers her a boon. As in the earlier sections, the *jogin* sings several *ṭhumrī*s, a *horī*, and a number of *ghazal*s. Again an assortment of gendered stances are vocalized, with little variation in the overall sentiment of anguish:

N. Ṭhumrī: *mãĩ to shahzāde ko ḍhūnḍhan caliyā̃* (no. 81)
Ṭhumrī: *kahā̃ pāū̃ kahā̃ pāū̃ yār re mãĩ* (no. 82)
Ghazal: *martā hū̃ tere hijr mẽ ai yār khabar le* (no. 83)
Ghazal: *rūh badan mẽ hai tapā̃ jī ko hai kal se bekalī* (no. 84)
Ṭhumrī: *kahā̃ gayo guīyā̃ shahzādā jānī piyārā* (no. 92)
Holī: *jar jāe gayā̃ aisī horī*
bin sayā̃ deh sulagat morī (no. 94)

The final, and apparently most persuasive, song is the one in which the fairy laments in Urdu. Despite the casting of the song in *ghazal* form, she decisively retains the feminine self-identification:

O. Ghazal: *dil ko cain ik dam tahai carakh-i kohan miltā nahī̃*
vo merā gulfām vo gul perhan miltā nahī̃.
jiskī khātir jhā̃ktī hū̃ bahr-i ālam mẽ kuẽ . . .
kartī hū̃ kū kū sadā sehrā mẽ qumrī kī tarah . . .
ṭhokarẽ khāti hūṇ jaṇgal kī khafā rahtā hai dam
jān par ban jāe aisā koī ban miltā nahī̃. (no. 96)

What can one make of this 'return of the repressed [feminine]'? The *āshiq* of the Urdu *ghazal* and the *jogin/virahinī* of Hindi poetry seem to have merged into an androgynous figure whose final triumph is not simply to win back the lover but to appropriate the variously available languages of longing for his/her own expressive ends.

Additional gender-bending possibilities were opened up in performance with the use of female impersonators to play the fairy roles in the *IS*. Even in Amānat's time, beardless youths of graceful figure and sweet voice were trained to take the fairies' parts, as recounted by Sa'ādat Alī Khā̃ Nāsir in his *Tazkirah khush ma'arika-i zibā*. Soon after, the drama reached Bombay from Lucknow, and in the year 1864 it was performed by the Alfred Nāṭak Maṇḍalī, one of the first Parsi companies. Another memorable performance was the 1873 Bombay production by the Elphinstone Dramatic Club under the direction of C.S. Nazīr. In the following year Nazīr introduced the *IS* to Calcutta theatre audiences during a tour of the long-lived Victoria Nāṭak Maṇḍalī. The Victoria went on to tour Hyderabad, Banaras, Delhi, Lahore, and Jaipur, and by the 1880s the company ventured as far as Rangoon, Singapore, Ceylon, and even London. Everywhere the *IS* was a centrepiece and created an impact on local popular culture, leading to the emergence of new styles of theatre.

Once the *IS* was taken up by the Parsi theatrical companies, the female roles were routinely played by men. In the early days, young men of high social standing performed female dramatic parts in the cosmopolitan setting of new institutions like the Elphinstone College. D.N. Parekh, later a medical doctor and Lieutenant Colonel in the Indian Medical Service, who was a close associate of Nazīr, featured in notable roles such as Portia in *The Merchant of Venice* and Mrs. Smart in G.O. Trevelyan's *The Dawk Bungalow*. After 1870, the Parsi theatre entered a stage of increasing professionalization, and young men were systematically recruited and schooled to play women's parts. Pestanjī Jījībhāī Bāṭlīwālā, an outstanding female impersonator, was known as Pesū Pukhrāj, on account of his part as the Topaz Fairy in the *IS*. Similarly Nasharvānjī Frāmjī Mādan became famous as Naslū Tahmīnā for his performance as Sohrāb's mother in *Rustam and Sohrab* (1868). When Jehā̃gīr Khambātā founded the Empress Victoria Theatrical Company in Delhi in 1877, he took full advantage of the talents of a popular female impersonator known as Naslū Sarkārī (Nasarvānjī Ratanjī Sarkārī). Famed for his sweet, 'cuckoo' voice (*kokil kaṇṭh*), Naslū played the Sabz Parī to Kāvas Khaṭāū's Gulfām in the *IS*. Although a few Anglo-Indian women began to appear in female roles in the 1880s, resistance to the employment of women on stage continued well into the twentieth century, most notably in the New Alfred Theatrical Company which for over forty years upheld a ban on actresses. Not surprisingly, the New Alfred acquired the reputation of being one of the most 'respectable' Parsi troupes, and it attracted the likes of Madan Mohan Malaviya and Motilal Nehru to its performances. A number of female impersonators were associated with the New Alfred — Amritlāl (Ambū),

Narmadā Shankar, Master Nisār (who later played opposite actress Kajjan in films), and Motīlāl.

In other work, I have analysed the historical practice of male-to-female impersonation from the standpoint of spectatorial pleasure (Hansen 1998b). The Parsi theatre, as a significant site of gender formation, was faced with the problem of bringing the heretofore invisible woman on to the stage. This constituted a rupture, both with the systemic segregation of respectable women and their exclusion from public life, and with the practices of *mehfil* and court performance, wherein patrons exercised exclusive control over female performers. Working out the issue of female representation on the stage took some years, and to the extent that women's participation in theatrical activity is still suspect in the subcontinent, it is an ongoing process.

The female impersonator phenomenon enabled a long tradition of cross-gender play, one that is visible in courtly dramas like the *IS*, to go on uninterrupted well into the beginning of the modern period. If the language of the *IS* already encoded a polymorphous erotic terrain, the convention of cross-dressing allowed its promise of gendered doubleness to be fully realized. A 'fairy' thus became a sign of a man playing a woman. His/her songs were so alluring precisely by virtue of their shifting modes of address. In underlining the presence of the masculine voice of the *āshiq* within the female form of the *parī*, and then delivering that representation via a male-to-female impersonator, the heteroglossia formed by overlays of diverse song styles reinforced a well-established, popular interest in gender disguise and innuendo. As the *IS* moved from its late premodern origins into the modern period, a heightened consciousness of language and gender informed by the ideologies of class, community, and nation led to other readings of the text. In this new environment, the conjunction of disparate categories fashioned by Amānat acquired overtones of paradox and parody. The *IS* may therefore appear a strange exotic to today's readers, and some would perhaps dismiss it entirely as nostalgia for a world that never was. In its fluidity of linguistic expression and inclusive approach to gendered pleasure, however, the longevity of the *IS* seems entirely legitimate, and it may still make a contribution to this postmodern age.[2]

[2] Since drafting this paper, I learned that the *Indar Sabhā* of Amānat has been successfully revived by the National School of Drama in New Delhi, under the direction of Mohan Upreti. It was first performed in 1996, and in February 1999 I had the good fortune of viewing it at last.

REFERENCES

Bhaktin, Mikhail M., *The Dialogic Imagination: Four Essays*, edited by Michael Holquist, trans. by Caryl Emerson and Michael Holquist, Austin: University of Texas Press, 1981.

Hansen, Kathryn, *Grounds for Play: The Nauṭankī Theatre of North India*, Berkeley: University of California Press, 1992.

———, 'The Migration of a Text: The *Indar Sabhā* in Print and Performance', *Sangeet Natak*, nos. 127-8 (1998a), pp. 3-34

———, '*Strī Bhūmikā*: Female Impersonators and Actresses on the Parsi Stage', *Economic and Political Weekly*, 29 August 1998 (1998b), pp. 2291-2300

Husain, Muḥammad Shāhid, *Indar-sabhā kī paramparā*, Delhi: Sīmānt Prakāshan, 1990.

Rizvī, Masūd Hasan, *Urdū ḍrāmā aur istej*, pts. 1 and 2, Lucknow: Kitāb Ghar, 1957.

Schimmel, Annemarie, *Classical Urdu Literature from the Beginning to Iqbal*, Wiesbaden: Otto Harrassowitz, 1975.

Yūsuf, Ibrāhim, *Indar sabhā aur indar sabhāẽ*, Lucknow: Nasīm Book Depot, 1980.

Dakani's Radha-Krishna Imagery and Canon Formation in Urdu

CARLA PETIEVICH

Piyā te dūr hone mẽ liḍiyā hai nāg birhe kā
Usī kā yād amrit ho nā marnā hai muje bis sũ

Dwelling far from the beloved
The serpent of separation bites me:
Remembering [the Beloved] is immortal ambrosia,
Poison cannot kill me.

'Ali 'Adil Shah II 'Shahi'

Court poetry from the sixteenth- and seventeenth-century Deccan, specifically that of Bijapur and Golkunda, represents the earliest known body of what we could call 'classical Urdu' literature; yet despite the prestige Urdu enjoys in general, Dakani poetry has been neglected woefully in literary scholarship.

Classical Urdu poetry is generally associated with the court culture of northern India, and derives much of its prestige from its linkage, in popular imagination, with the grandeur of Mughal civilization. Much less known about Urdu is that it became a literary language for the Mughals only in the eighteenth century, nearly two centuries after its first flowering in central India. Also practically unknown is that Urdu's star rose in Hindustan (i.e. north India) only after Mughal conquest of the Deccan's once-thriving, Muslim-ruled, kingdoms. It would be plausible to suggest that with this literary gift we see one of many possible examples throughout history where conquered peoples have served to 'civilize' the conquerors. Yet Urdu's literary history having been written largely by somewhat partisan northerners, Dakani's spectacular cultural achievements have gone largely ignored in the official record.[1] It is nevertheless a corpus of literature most

[1] For an expanded discussion of this phenomenon, see Petievich (1990) and 'Making Manly Poetry: the Construction of Urdu's "Golden Age"', in Richard B. Barnett (ed.), *Rethinking Early Modern India*, New Delhi: Manohar (forthcoming).

interesting, not only because it represents 'early Urdu', but also because its contents challenge received wisdom about the Hindustan-centred history of 'Muslim' culture in South Asia.

For some time now scholars of early Indo-Muslim cultural history have recognized that, at the popular level, there was a significant exchange between Islamic and indigenous cultural systems. Sufi missionaries were able to spread Islam among the Indian masses by latching onto concepts and symbols shared by bhakti devotional cults and Sufi mysticism.[2] On the other hand, scholars have generally assumed that not until the great eclectic patrons like the Mughal Emperor Akbar (r. 1556-1605) did significant exchange take place between Hindu and Muslim cultural elites; rather, the assumption has been, the foreign conquerors sought to bolster their hold over vast numbers of subject peoples by remaining distant, aloof, and awesome. While this perception was true at various times, especially the Delhi of eighteenth and nineteenth centuries, there were other times when elite art forms reflected a high degree of dialogue with the Indian environment (for example the Lucknow court during the mid-nineteenth century, shortly before Awadh's 1856 annexation by the British).

For the Deccan, too, there exists much evidence that painting, music and court poetry — all highly elite artistic forms — were enthusiastically supported by the Turkish- and Persian-descended rulers in the Deccan during the sixteenth and seventeenth centuries.[3] There is, furthermore, a consensus that great art was achieved under this patronage; and that the so-called 'Dakani school' is said to reflect a brilliant synthesis of Persian and Indian influences. It is unfortunate — and perennially frustrating — that such pronouncements as these, though abundant, are almost never elaborated in concrete terms for the benefit of those who might not know implicitly what 'Persian' and 'Indian' influences in art happen to be. Since I also subscribe to this theory of synthesis, I will attempt a very basic

[2] See especially Ali Asani, 'Spinning Songs, Yearning Brides and the Bridegroom Prophet: Muslim Literatures in the South Asian Vernaculars', unpublished ms; and Richard M. Eaton, *Sufis of Bijapur*, Princeton, 1978.

[3] Cf. D. Barrett, *Painting of the Deccan*, London, 1958; K. Ebeling, *Rāgamālā Painting*, Paris, 1973; H. Goetz, 'Deccani Paintings: the school of Bijapur', *Burlington Magazine*, 73, August 1938, pp. 74-6; Stella Kramrisch, *A Survey of Painting in the Deccan*, London, 1937; G. Yazdani, 'Two Miniatures from Bijapur', *Islamic Culture*, IX, 2, April 1935, pp. 211-17; and Mark Zebrowski, *Deccani Painting*, Roli/California, 1983.

illustration of what those opaque terms might mean for Dakani poetry.[4] Vocabulary that derives from Sanskrit will be termed 'Indic' as contrasted with vocabulary of Persian or Arabic derivation; similarly, iconography or imagery identifiable as inherited from Sanskritic/Hindu cultural traditions will be distinguished from that of Perso-Arabic/Islamic traditions. A persuasive argument can be made that, at elite levels, there was by no means the system of cultural apartheid which has often been assumed. In the case of Dakani poetry, where patrons were also poets, this point is all the more easily demonstrated. The present essay concentrates on verse by two poet-kings, Muhammad Quli Qutb Shah of Golkunda (r.1580-1612) and 'Ali 'Adil Shah II (r. 1656-72). Issues of central importance are the narrator's persona; the aesthetics and philosophy of mystical devotionalism, both Sufi and Bhakti; the role gender plays in its expression; and the tension (or sympathy) between the 'Indic' and 'Islamic'.

URDU POETRY AS 'ISLAMIC' ART

Urdu poetry is seen as a particularly 'Muslim' art form, serving for many as the central icon of Indo-Muslim culture. Even the most conservative elements within normative Islam have celebrated poetry, for it is the form in which Allah's message came down to Muhammad.[5] On this basis Urdu poetry can be justified as legitimate, despite its primary topic of love and its characteristic extravagance of emotional and passionate expression. This extravagance might well have compromised poetry's legitimacy in Islam's otherwise austere religio-cultural sensibility, were these expressions of passionate love not directed, ostensibly, toward the Divine. It is a happy occurrence that mysticism gave rise to much of the great Perso-Islamicate literature of the past millennium. The legacy of Sufi Persian poetry, dating back to about the twelfth century, served as Urdu's 'Islamic' precedent, both legitimizing and contributing greatly to the 'brilliant synthesis' of Persian and Indic elements attributed to Indo-Muslim literature and visual arts and music.

Given this strong identification in our minds of Urdu poetry with Islam, it can come as something of a surprise to encounter 'non-Muslim' — indeed positively idolatrous — images in Urdu poetry. We can see this in the following Dakani ghazal by Sultan Muhammad Quli Qutb Shah:

[4] I am unable to address myself to Dakani painting in this essay, but a more expanded study is in progress.

[5] In this regard, then, Urdu poetry is far less anomalous to 'Islamic' sensibility than is the rich art of miniature painting developed in India.

I. ***Sakī*** ***bātā̃ shakar kartī vale miṭhā'ī āse nā***
divānī nīshakar mē̃ ko'ī kadhin nābāt bāse nā

My girlfriend speaks in sugared words
but sweetness doesn't come.
O Mad One, there's never the sweetness of rock candy in sugar cane.

Khabar hū'ī shah hu'e savārā yakāyak āye muj ṭhāṛā
nā pūchhe tuk phire bhārā, to ab ***birhā*** *samāse nā*

I heard the news that the king came
riding up to my door.
But suddenly, wordlessly, he wheeled round and took off —
now the pangs of separation are unendurable.

Kahū̃ āpan birah kis kan agin sho'ala paṛe us tan
so muskhil dāṭiyā muj man, haman ***dukh*** *kō'ī sunā se nā*

Were I to speak to anyone
of Separation's burning tumult
its flames would scorch *their* bodies —
so I let it rage only inside.

Magar kho'e khudā yih ***dukh*** *dikhāve us* ***sūraj kā mukh***
andhārī nayan *pāvē̃* ***sukh*** *to muj par* ***dukh*** *dahā se nā*

But let God lose me this sorrow and
show me the face of that sun.
Let solace come to these darkened eyes
and sorrow burn me no more.

Ma'ānī ***thā'ū̃*** *to jāne ghavvāṣ ho kar* ***ratan pāne***
so khālī ***sīpiyā̃*** *liyāne* ***dūjiyā̃*** *sam tuj kū̃ āse nā*

Ma'ani, you know your place:
Be a pearl-diver and bring forth gems!
It's not for you to come up with
the empty shells of others.

To come across lexical 'archaisms' (i.e. Sanskrit-derived vocabulary indicated by bold-face) is not unheard of even in the later, high classical, ghazal of Hindustan. But in this ghazal, authored in the late sixteenth or early seventeenth century[6] the borrowings are more dramatic. The poem's structure is clearly that of ghazal, determined by metre (*bahr*) and rhyme-

[6] Muhammad Quli Qutb Shah (1566-1612) is accepted as the first Urdu *ṣāḥib-i dīvān* [author of a collection of *ghazals*].

scheme (*qāfiyah*).[7] The central theme is love in separation,with the narrator (*'āshiq*) pining for an absent Beloved just as in the Persian, Sufi ghazal. But the narrator's condition (called *'āshiqī* in the Perso-Arabic ghazal) is here expressed in terms strikingly reminiscent of Indic, even Hindu devotional, poetry: it employs the verbal and visual iconography of *viraha* (separation from the Beloved). By combining the poetics of *viraha* with that of Perso-Arabic's *firāq-i yār* (separation from the Beloved), this ghazal not only blends 'Indic' and Persian *vocabulary*,[8] but evokes more fully both the Perso-Arabic and Indic *lyric traditions* as well. What marks the poem's departure from Perso-Arabic poetics, from the *'āshiqī* of the normative ghazal, however, is that its narrator-Lover here is a *virahinī*, expressing herself unambiguously in the grammatically feminine voice.

THE FEMININE AS 'HINDU'

A feminine narrator is standard, of course, in *bhakti* poetry and Sanskrit *kāvya* but absolutely anomalous in the classical Urdu ghazal of eighteenth-nineteenth century north India. Nor has 'she' a counterpart in earlier Persian lyric literature. Secondary literature on Dakani poetry does refer to certain 'Indic' elements in pre-nineteenth century Urdu. Some authors will go so far as to say that these elements are manifest in emotions 'being expressed from the woman's side'.[9] But Urdu scholars have not discussed Dakani's feminine narrator convincingly, in my opinion. I have written elsewhere on this topic and, judging from the response it has prompted, it is safe to say that the issue still remains under debate. (To that debate we will return later.) But while other aspects of our analysis may differ, it is

[7] Here the metre is *hazaj* of Perso-Arabic prosody; and the rhyme-scheme's *qāfiya-radīf is '—āse nā'*.

[8] Indic vocabulary includes: *Sakī* [=*sakhī*: girlfriend/female companion]; *birha* [=*viraha*]; *agin* [=*agni*: fire]; *dukh* [sorrow, grief]; *sūraj* [sun]; *andhārī* [=*andherī*: darkness]; *nayand* [=*naina*: eyes]; *ratan* [jewel, gem]; and *dūjiyā̃* [=*dūtiyā̃*: seconds/others/rivals]. Persian vocabulary: *divānī* [mad one]; *khabar* [news]; *sho'le* [flames]; *tan* [body]; *mushkil* [difficult/y]; *khudā* [God]; *ghavvāṣ* [pearl-diver].

[9] Cf. Sayeda Ja'far (ed.), *Kulliyāt-i Muḥammad Qulī Quṭb Shāh*, Delhi: Anjuman Taraqqi-i Urdu, 1985, pp. 208-12; Jamil Jalibi, *Tārīkh-i Adab-i Urdū*, vol.1, Delhi: Educational Publishing House, 1977; D.J. Matthews, 'Dakani Language and Literature, 1500-1700 AD', unpublished Ph.D. thesis, University of London, 1976, passim.

universally accepted by scholars that this feminine narrator is unique to Indian 'Muslim' poetry. What remains under debate is what 'she' is doing there. Does 'she' represent a 'brilliant synthesis'? A shocking contamination of Islam's sanctioned medium of expression? A paganistic fall from grace? Why would Indo-Muslim lyric poets choose this *virahinī*'s voice over that of the more familiar (masculine) *'āshiq* of Persian lyric? What is the appeal in choosing the feminine voice over the masculine? Those steeped in the literature of bhakti may find it difficult to understand just how extraordinary this feminine voice is for canonical Islamicate poetry.

As rich in possibility as the gender-ambiguous ghazal is, the feminine narrator opens up all sorts of new space to a poet steeped in Perso-Arabic literary aesthetics. While separation from the beloved is central to both the Islamicate ghazal and to bhakti expression, there do seem to be nuances of difference between the *virahinī*'s relationship to 'her' absent lover and the *'āshiq*'s relationship to 'his'. Both are suppliants, it is true; and both await the elusive favour of a 'visit' from their love object. But the whole complex of *śriṅgār ras* in 'Indic' love poetry implies union between the lovers at some previous time in addition to the promise of union in the future; while with the ghazal, especially when the beloved can be construed as divine, this past is far more rare. When it is alluded to at all, there is no physicality imputed to the union. With *śriṅgār ras* it is all around, if not always at centre stage. What is made possible by this implied physical union in the *virahinī*'s past, then, is the conventionalized attitude of *māninī*. This term is defined in Platts' *Dictionary of Urdu, Classical Hindi and English* as 'A proud or disdainful woman; an angry or sulky woman (one who is offended with her lover)' (p. 986).

The standard *'āshiq* is not able to draw quite as freely on the *māninī* aspects of separation. This is not to say that 'he' doesn't complain bitterly of his treatment at the hands of the Beloved — 'he' often does. But the kind of sulking with which we associate the *māninī* persona is predicated, I am convinced, on a richer background of shared experience with the Beloved than we can strictly assume in the case of the ghazal's *'āshiq*. This is especially true if we think about how informed bhakti's *virahinī* has been by Indic love poetry's *nāyikā*.[10] Thanks to the popularity of Krishnaite

[10] See M.A.R. Barker, *Naqsh-i Dilpaẕīr* (Classical Urdu Poetry), Ithaca: Spoken Language Service, Inc., 1969 for a complete poem by 'Ali 'Adil Shah 'Shahi' entitled *Birahani*, written in an adapted *mukhammas* (5-line stanza) form.

bhakti poetry, the *nāyikā* conflates, in our imagination, into the quintessential *virahinī*, Radha.[11]

I speculate that this 'Radha' has been imported into the Dakani ghazal through Bijapur and Golkunda poets' exposure to bhakti poetry. She may have been borrowed from Jayadeva's *Gītagovinda*, which was apparently in wide circulation throughout the subcontinent by the sixteenth century; or from a wealth of Krishna bhakti poetry inspired by Jayadeva, such as that of Vidyapati and Mira Bai.[12] It is not implausible that the *virahinī* was known to Dakani court poets from a variety of sources, both elite and popular. Scholars tell us that by the sixteenth century Krishna bhakti was well known not only in north India, but all over the subcontinent.[13]

Perhaps these poets were even exposed to bhakti poetry via Telugu. Secondary literature tells us that Dakani rulers patronized both Persian and indigenous art forms. H.K. Sherwani, in his *History of the Qutb Shahi Dynasty*[14] describes at some length the patronage of Telugu literature in Golkunda by both Ibrahim Qutb Shah (r. 1550-80) and his successor, Muhammad Quli Qutb Shah (r. 1580-1612) who was also the first *ṣāḥib-i dīvān* in Urdu. Both rulers appointed Poets Laureate for Telugu and Dakani. If they were steeped in Telugu literature, it is quite possible that this might have been a further source of exposure to Krishna bhakti poetry.[15] In any case my purpose is not to establish a direct, causal link between Jayadeva and the Dakani poets, but rather to suggest the possibility of multiple links; to suggest that from the Urdu ghazal's earliest days its composers were aware of parallel literary traditions in their environment; and that the possibilities of expanding Perso-Arabic literature's poetics of love by employing the feminine voice were not lost on Dakani poets.

By way of illustration I offer another ghazal, this one by 'Ali 'Adil

[11] This author recognizes that Radha could not have become the quintessential *nāyikā* had not Jayadeva been steeped in Sanskritic poetics well before he composed the *Gītagovinda*; but for many, his poem represents an introduction, indeed the epitome, of *viraha* as well as of Radha-Krishna poetry.

[12] Barbara Stoler Miller, *Love Song of the Dark Lord: Jayadeva's Gītagovinda*, Columbia, 1977, pp. 3-7; Deben Bhattacharya, trans., *Love Songs of Vidyapati*, Delhi: Hind Pocket Books Ltd., 1963; Edward C. Dimock and Denise Levertov, trans., *In Praise of Krishna,* Doubleday & Co., 1967; and Usha S. Nilsson, *Mira Bai*, New Delhi: Sahitya Akademi, 1969.

[13] Miller, p. ix.

[14] Delhi: Munshiram Manoharlal, 1974.

[15] To speculate even more wildly, recall that Krishna Deva Raya was a Vaishnava.

Shah II 'Shahi', Bijapur's ruler from 1656-1672:

Sajan milne bulā de jo chalūngī pāū̃ kar sis sū̃
Pirit lā piyū te rahne nā pūchhūngī kadhin kis sū̃

When my sweetheart calls me to meet him
I trip off, head over heels.
If I could dwell with my beloved
I'd ask for nothing more.

Piyā te dūr hone mẽ liṛiyā hai nāg birhe kā
Usī kā yād amrit ho na marnā hai muje bis sū̃

Dwelling far from the beloved
The serpent of separation bites me:
Remembering [the Beloved] is immortal nectar,
Poison cannot kill me.

Paṛyā andhkār chak mẽ muj pyāre ke bichhaṛne taī̃
Nayan til roz lāge yū̃ muqābil ho rahiyā nis sū̃

Apart from him darkness befalls my eyes:
In my view the day is vanquished by night.

Nahī̃ paṛā sanvarne kā muje bhukan panā'o mat
Kanchan nainõ mẽ ab mere kamīnah ho dise mis sū̃

I care nothing for adornments — do not deck me in jewels!
In my eyes now, even gold
carries the tinge of copper. [is duller than copper]

Agar kuchh bol kaṛve muj sū̃ bolenge sarījan jo
Phir ūtar na deūngī kadhin bhavā̃ gāṇṭ bhāris sū̃

Even should he utter bitter words to me
I shall not frown and reply in kind.

Jo kuchh haṭ dil sū̃ dho, saṭ sab, karū̃ man bhā'uta piyū kū
Rahūngī sevakī ho mãi, piyā kī rej hai jis sū̃

I'll cleanse my heart of stubbornness
and do my lover's bidding:
I'll stay his loyal servant — that one who infatuates me!

Ḍhanḍāorā mār Shāhī birah ke bol bolīyā jo
Jahā̃ ke 'āshiqā̃ sun to hu'e behosh sab jis sū̃

When Shahi proclaimed the meaning of Separation
His words rendered all
the world's lovers unconscious.

Now to revisit bhakti poetry, let us look at a verse which could be said to encapsulate the devotional aesthetic of Radha-Krishna poetry, and incidentally forms the imagined biography of both Mira Bai and, by extension, any bhakta:

Mira sang ecstatically of Hari's virtues.	
The king sent her a serpent basket	*sāmp pitāre rānā bhejyo*
and placed it in Mira's hands.	*Mīrā hāth diyo jāy;*
When, bathed and washed, she took a look,	*nhāy dhoy jab dekhan lāgī*
she found an image of God.	*sālīgaram gayī pāy.*
A cup of poison was sent by the king	*jahr kā pyālā ranā bhejyo*
it turned into nectar.	*amrit diyo vanāy;*
When bathed and washed, she took a drink.	*nhāy dhoy jal pīvan lāgī*
she achieved immortality. . . .[16]	*amat ho gayī jāy. . . .*

Radha-Mira's echo cannot help but sound in the verses above by Sultan 'Ali 'Adil Shah II of Bijapur. Though none of the verses in his ghazal is likely either a translation or a direct paraphrase, several of the *tópoi* drawn upon echo verses in the *Gītagovinda*, poems of Vidyapati and Mira Bai. Many of the familiar themes from both bhakti poetry and *śriṅgār-ras* of non-devotional poetry are recognized here (the physical torment, the sense of betrayal mixed nonetheless with attestations of eternal devotion); and it is difficult to conclude otherwise than that they are deliberate transplants by sophisticated connoisseur-artists, artists who were open to experimentation across the 'lines' of a range of cultural/aesthetic systems.

In present times — and for quite some time now — communities, their idioms, and their expressive culture are labelled 'Hindu' or 'Muslim' and are presented to us as separate and distinct; as communities, we are given to understand, whose cultures are so profoundly different (based on religious boundaries) as to provide rationales for mutual intolerance. It is increasingly clear, however, that at least in the case of Dakani cultural history, this received wisdom is a misrepresentation. Recent analysis of fourteenth-seventeenth centuries Telugu inscriptions and historiographic poems challenges and complicates the simplistic formulations of conventional wisdom.[17] In a few short sentences justice cannot be done to their

[16] Nilsson, op. cit., poem 14.

[17] See especially Talbot's excellent 'Inscribing the Other, Inscribing the Self: Hindu-Muslim Identities in Pre-Colonial India', *Comparative Studies in History and Society*, 37/4, October 1995, pp. 692-722; Wagoner's '"Sultan Among Hindu Kings": Dress, Titles, and Islamicization of Hindu Culture at Vijayanagara', *Journal of Asian Studies*, 55/4, November 1996, pp. 851-80; and Wagoner, *Tidings of the King: A Translation and Ethnohistorical Analysis of the Rāyavācakamu*, Hawaii, 1993.

work and its implications. But Cynthia Talbot, discussing the Vilasa grant (issued between 1325-50) by post-Kakatiya Andhran leader, Prolaya Nayaka; and Phillip B. Wagoner, examining the Vijayanagara court chronicle[18] entitled *Rāyavācakamu* or 'Tidings of the King'; show that reference to political rivals as 'Muslims' on the part of Hindu rulers—and derogatory reference at that—was in the first place rare. In the second place such reference constituted a deliberate rhetorical strategy in the service of establishing their own legitimacy as rulers of successor states in the aftermath of conquest by Muslim Turkish rulers. Moreover, Wagoner demonstrates that, at the court of Vijayanagara, so-called 'Islamic' styles of dress were deployed in ceremonial functions 'parallel[ing] the appropriation of Islamicate modes of political language, the most striking instance of which appears in the Vijayanagara ṛulers' adoption of the title "Hindu-rāya-suratrāṇa", literally, "Sultan among Hindu Kings"'.[19]

The early poetry of Dakani 'Muslim' courts supports the arguments of Talbot and Wagoner from the 'other' side. Indeed, there are a number of Bijapuri and Golkunda poet-kings who projected the persona of 'Raja among Sultans'. Wagoner shows that Muslim nobles of the Deccan could move fluidly back and forth across this supposed barrier between Hindu- and Muslim-ruled territory in search of patronage; and that, where appropriate, they made symbolic gestures in the direction of 'Hindu' rulership (as, for example, making land grants to Brahmins dwelling within territory they controlled).[20]

The point here is not that any of these rulers or nobles wished to renounce their roots. Rather, they were informed manipulators of a political environment that was complicated and enriched by the interaction of Perso-Turkish culture with that of central and southern India. In the case of the poetry discussed here, it seems clear that these 'manipulations' were successful precisely because they were based upon genuine compatibilities

[18] It must be noted that Wagoner complicates what is implied by 'court chronicle' and makes very clear that the *Rāyavācakamu* is neither a standard court chronicle nor was it actually produced at the court of Vijayanagara. Rather, it was produced at the post-Vijayanagara Nāyaka court of Madurai in the early seventeenth century.

[19] Wagoner, 'Sultan Among Hindu Kings', p. 853.

[20] See the case of 'Ain-ul Mulk Gīlānī (Telugu: Ayyanamalukka) in Wagoner, 'Iqtā' and Nayamkāra: Military Service Tenures & Political Theory from Saljuq Iran to Vijayanagara South India', paper presented at the 25th Annual Conference on South Asia, Madison, WI, 18-20 October 1996.

within the aesthetics of Indic love poetry and that of the Perso-Islamicate ghazal. The *'āshiq*, or protagonist, of the ghazal stood in comparable relationship to the desired Beloved as did the *virahinī* in Indic poetry, viz., that of abject suppliant whose position could thus be seen as feminized. To invoke her allowed poets who worked within even a loosely-framed 'Islamic' environment to concretize their depictions of love's suffering as developed by the concept of *firāq-i yār*; and to simultaneously celebrate the heterosexuality otherwise implied, perhaps, but understandably marginalized in expressions of Muslim devotionalism.

It may not even be necessary to explain further why poets like Muhammad Quli and 'Ali 'Adil Shah II adopted the poetic conventions under discussion here. But we can speculate enough to point out how well it served the imperative that they establish their own legitimacy as Indian kings. After all, the Sultans of Golkunda and Bijapur ruled over large territories, the vast majority of whose inhabitants were considerably more familiar with the conventions of bhakti than with Islamicate lyric poetry. While it is quite reasonable to attribute to these rulers a genuine appreciation of indigenous arts, there is no reason to overlook the cultural capital they could gain by (1) patronizing exponents of Indic arts and (2) visibly adapting themselves to their environment, as in the case of 'Ain ul-Mulk (cited earlier), who made a point of granting tax-exempt land to Brahmins.

To explain why such visible adaptation is less evident from eighteenth and nineteenth centuries north Indian sources, we might look to the conscious process of differentiation between late-Mughal elites and their subject environments.[21] The later Mughals were, arguably, impelled toward different legitimizing strategies — those that would bolster their claims to maintaining the legacy of Perso-Islamicate rulership in India (as against competing claims from successor states and ambitious Afghans). If we accept such a postulated perspective for the Mughals, their increased Persianization of Indo-Muslim culture makes sense, for the operative concept here would be Persianization rather than Indianization as in the Dakanis' case.[22]

[21] See Petievich, 'The Feminine and Cultural Syncretism in early Dakani Culture', *Annual of Urdu Studies*, 8, Winter 1993, pp. 119-30.

[22] Indeed, this could be seen as a parallel to the strategy Wagoner attributes to the author? patron? of the *Rāyavācakamu* in explaining the rather uncharacteristic diatribe that text contains against the Turks. See *Tidings of the King*, pp. 11-12 and passim.

Turning our attention now to the past century, which has been the first century of Urdu literary historiography, we come to the formation of literary canonization. This was a process driven largely by late-nineteenth century Urdu elites' perceptions of what Mughal culture had been all about. This project of constructing a history and literary canon was, as I have argued elsewhere.[23] intricately linked to defining and protecting a distinct 'Muslim' cultural space in British India and in post-colonial South Asia. For the purposes of that project, cultural syncretism or hybridity — especially within Indo-Muslim culture's most prestigious expressive art form — could not be embraced if it (1) appeared to extend as far as 'religious' expression and (2) thus rendered Indian Islam 'feminine' rather than 'masculine' in the eyes of the Raj. Recall that the British engaged in an elaborate process of categorization (and valorization) of 'martial' or 'manly' peoples of the subcontinent; and that they also denigrated those deemed effeminate, e.g. the Bengali Babu and the 'sensualist' Indian rulers such as Wajid 'Ali Shah of Avadh, whom they deposed, allegedly 'without a shot being fired'.[24]

Such an interpretation would seem to shed light on the tension we see manifest in much Urdu literary historiography as well as in such historiography of the Deccan as that of H.K. Sherwani.[25] In both bodies of scholarship we see celebrated the glories of Indo-Muslim culture achieved through the process of synthesis. At the same time there is an ambivalence toward the 'sensualist, Oriental despotism' with which such cultural production is associated, thanks largely to the colonialist discourses in which many of these scholars were educated. Sherwani, e.g. documents tremendous patronage of Persian Telugu and Dakani literature by the Qutb Shahi Sultans. He records Ibrahim Qutb Shah's and Muhammad Quli's love of Dakani culture and their own artistic endeavours as well as their patronage. Yet he also seems to dismiss Muhammad Quli Qutb Shah as a libertine whose court was notorious for moral laxity. The less positive

[23] Petievich, *Assembly of Rivals: Delhi, Lucknow and the Urdu Ghazal*, New Delhi: Manohar, 1992, Chap. 12; 'The Feminine Voice in the Urdu Ghazal', *Indian Horizons*, vol. 39, nos. 1-2, 1990, pp. 25-41; and 'Making Manly Poetry: The Construction of Urdu's "Golden Age"' (forthcoming).

[24] See Premchand's famous short story, *Shatranj ke khilāṛī* ('The Chess-Players') (and Satyajit Ray's 1977 film by the same name) for this construction of the effeminate, sensualist, ineffectual Indian elite.

[25] See his *History of Medieval Deccan*, Govt. of Andhra Pradesh, 1974, vol. 2; *History of the Qutb Shahi Dynasty*, Munshiram Manoharlal, 1974; *Muhammad Quli Qutb Shah: Founder of Haidarabad*, Asia Publishing House, 1967.

construction is offered in a chapter about Muhammad Quli's successor, Muhammad Qutb Shah (r.1612-26) a more austere, rigorously pious, anti-Dakani, Persophilic Shi'a. This ruler rather pointedly did not patronize Dakani poets, though he did patronize Persian literature.[26]

One guesses that Sherwani did not really find Muhammad Quli Qutb Shah's more 'morally relaxed' milieu all that offensive; and that in drawing these comparisons between rulers he was merely following the conventions of this century's cultural historiography. As I have mentioned, his remarks about Muhammad Quli recall the terms in which other lavish patron-poets are typically dismissed.[27] Contemporary Lakhnavis and Dakanis, in my experience, tend to be proud of their eclectic cultural history. But they are also proud to identify these cultural centres (*marākiz*) as Muslim, and this presents a problem.

Twentieth-century Nationalism has promoted conscious differentiation of communities labelled 'Hindu' from those labelled 'Muslim'; the Nationalist movement thereby served to create the self-proclaimed Muslim nation-state, Pakistan, whose name means 'Land of the Pure'. There is room in the notion of 'Land of the Pure' for piety, for a cultural legacy from Persian, and for upright manliness; but not for sensuality, lavishness and the effeminization of Islam blamed on the Indian environment. Given this critical atmosphere it is little wonder that those writing the history of Muslim culture in India would find Dakani poetry, with its *virahinī* and her idolatrous associations, rather problematic; nor that the response would be to sweep the Dakani ghazal under the carpet and all but 'disappear' it from view.

[26] Ghavvasi and Vajhi had to wait for the beneficence of Md. Qutb Shah's successor, Abdullah (r. 1626-72), who was himself a distinguished poet in Dakani.

[27] I allude here especially to the treatment of Lucknow's Asif ud Daula (r.1775-94) as well as Vajid 'Ali Shah (r.1846-56).

APPENDIX

Another Ghazal by Sultan 'Ali 'Adil Shah II 'Shahi'

Avval te dil lagā muj sū̃ itā to kī phirāte hãi
Hamāre sukh bhare jīvan kū̃ tume kī duk me bhāte hãi

First you give your heart to me
And then you turn away?
How can you turn my joy-filled being
to grief?

Sarījan ke chandar muk kū̃ dekhan kū̃ haiyā tāpe hai
Pirit kar aur dū̃ pyāre haman kū̃ kī tapāte hãi

My soul's on fire to see
the moon-face of my sweetheart —
Why, Beloved, do you burn me
with your love of others?

Kamārī chuk nãi kuch haur tumẽ chup chup rukhā'ī kar
Nahī̃ so rīt ki rītõ nipat hamnā khijāte hãi

I've done nothing
to invite your cool indifference.
You vex me completely with your little love games!

Lage hãi sej mẽ aksar dūtan ke hāt ke nakh yū̃
tumāre gāl par chhab sū̃ chandar sūraj dipāte hãi

Often on the bed like this
My rival's fingernails
leave crescent marks shining
on your sunny cheeks.

Bharū par gānṭ bhā piyā ne phirā'e muk dese muj yū̃
Avval te mār kar tirā̃ kaman ab to chhupāte hãi

First he raises his eyebrows
then my Beloved turns away from me:
Having let fly the arrow
he hides his bow.

Dis āvẽ rāt ke sheve tumāre gāt par sāre
Thagāne kū̃ itā hamnā su'ā̃ kī jhūt khāte hãi

The signs of night
mark your body all over
laying false your claims of fidelity.

Rangīle rang bhare Shāhī lagā'e pem kā lāvak
Jagā to rain sārī muj nayan rang meñ rangāte hãi

Shahi, all decked out
created in me a taste for love
Then all night long he colored my eyes red.

REFERENCES

Asani, Ali, 'Spinning Songs, Yearning Brides and the Bridegroom Prophet: Muslim Literatures in the South Asian Vernaculars', paper presented at the University of British Columbia, Vancouver, February 1989

Barker, M.A.R., *Naqsh-i Dilpazir: Classical Urdu Poetry*, 3 vols, Ithaca: Spoken Language Services, Inc., 1968.

Barrett, D., *Painting of the Deccan*, London, 1958.

Bhattacharya, Deben, *Love Songs of Vidyapati*, Delhi: Hind Pocket Books Ltd., 1963.

Dimock, Edward C. and Denise Levertov, trans., *In Praise of Krishna*, New York: Doubleday and Co., 1967.

Eaton, Richard M., *Sufis of Bijapur, 1300-1700: Social Roles of Sufis in Medieval India*, Princeton: Princeton University Press, 1978.

Ebeling, K., *Ragamala Painting*, Paris, 1973.

Goetz, Hermann, 'Deccani Paintings: the school of Bijapur', *Burlington Magazine*, 73, August 1938.

Ja'far, Syeda, *Kulliyat-i Muhammad Quli Qutb Shah*, New Delhi: Anjuman Taraqqi-i Urdu, 1985.

Jalibi, Jamil, *Tarikh-i Adab-i Urdu* (History of Urdu Literature), 2 vols., Delhi: Educational Publishing House, 1977.

Kramrisch, Stella, *A Survey of Painting in the Deccan*, London, 1937.

Matthews, D.J., 'Dakani Language and Literature, 1500-1700', unpublished dissertation, School of Oriental and African Studies, University of London, 1976.

Miller, Barbara S., *Love Song of the Dark Lord: Jayadeva's Gītagovinda*, New York: Columbia University Press, 1977.

Nilsson, Usha S., *Mira Bai*, New Delhi: Sahitya Akademi, 1969.

Petievich, Carla, 'The Feminine Voice in the Urdu Ghazal', *Indian Horizons*, 39: 1-2, 1990, pp. 25-41.

———, 'The Feminine and Cultural Syncretism in Early Dakani Culture', *Annual of Urdu Studies*, 8, 1993, pp. 119-30.

———, 'Making Manly Poetry: the Construction of Urdu's "Golden Age"', in Richard B. Barnett (ed.), *Rethinking Early Modern India*, New Delhi: Manohar (forthcoming).

Platts, John T., *Dictionary of Urdu, Classical Hindi and English*, rpt., New Delhi: Munshiram Manoharlal, 1988 [1893].

Sherwani, H.K., *Muhammad Quli Qutb Shah: Founder of Haidarabad*, Bombay: Asia Publishing House, 1967.

———, *History of Medieval Deccan*, vol. 2, Hyderabad: Govt. of Andhra Pradesh, 1974(a).

———, *History of the Qutb Shahi Dynasty*, New Delhi: Munshiram Manoharlal, 1974(b).

Talbot, Cynthia, 'Inscribing the Other, Inscribing the Self: Hindu-Muslim Identities in Pre-Colonial India', *Comparative Studies in History and Society*, 37/4, October 1995, pp. 692-722.

Wagoner, Phillip B., *Tidings of the King: A Translation and Ethnohistorical Analysis of the Rāyavācakamu*, Honolulu: University of Hawaii Press, 1993.

———, '*Iqta and Nayamkara*: Military Service Tenures and Political Theory from Saljuq Iran to Vijayanagara, South India'. Paper presented at the 25th Annual Conference on South Asia, University of Wisconsin, Madison, October 1996(a).

———, '"Sultan Among Hindu Kings": Dress, Titles and Islamicization of Hindu Culture at Vijayanagara', *Journal of Asian Studies*, 55:4, November 1996(b), pp. 851-80.

Yazdani, G., 'Two Miniatures from Bijapur', *Islamic Culture*, 9:2, April 1935, pp. 211-17.

Zebrowski, Mark, *Deccani Painting*, New Delhi: Roli International / Berkeley: University of California Press, 1983.

PART III
Modern Indian Ismailism

Historical and Religious Debates amongst Indian Ismailis 1840-1920

ZAWAHIR MOIR

During the middle and the later years of the nineteenth century and the early part of the twentieth, a number of writers of Indian Ismaili origin researched and hotly debated the nature, history and origin of their faith, some strongly imbued with the desirability of abandoning it for Shia Ithna Ashari or Sunni Islam or even Hinduism, others equally convinced of its continuing authenticity and power. Today largely forgotten — and easily passed over for their apparent air of antiquarian sectarianism — these writings in fact reveal the extent to which the Ismaili sense of religious identity was rooted in, and carved out of, the complexities and ambiguities of their South Asian past, whilst also responding to the emergent political realities of early twentieth-century Indian national movements. However, before examining these writings in more depth, it is necessary to introduce and contextualize them by briefly recalling firstly, the general socio-religious position of the Ismaili communities in northern India around the middle of the nineteenth century, and secondly, the period of public dissension and turmoil that followed the arrival of the First Agha Khan Hasanali Shah in Bombay in 1845.

BACKGROUND

The Indian Nizāri Ismailis, whose spiritual leader (Imām) the newly-arrived Agha Khan (d.1881) claimed to be, were a mixed and scattered group, not easily categorized as Muslims or Hindus, and not all prepared to acknowledge the Agha's authority. Besides the few hundred families then resident in Bombay in the 1840s — a growing commercial class who were to present the Agha Khan with his most serious challenges — they mostly comprised a scattering of small-scale trader, artisan and agriculturist communities extending northwards through Gujarat, Kathiawar, Kachchh and Sindh as far as Punjab and Kashmir. Following their own traditional accounts, most believed themselves to have been originally converted to the Ismaili faith, generally known as the Satpanth (true path), by a line of charismatic Pīrs or missionaries sent by the Nizāri Ismaili Imāms in Iran from about the twelfth century onwards. In particular many of those living outwardly as Khojas[1] in the southern region from Bombay to Sindh, claimed to have been Lohāṇā Hindus brought to the faith by Pīr Ṣadruddīn in the early fifteenth century (Arnould). By contrast, many others, especially in the northern region of Punjab — the so-called Gupti Ismailis and Shamsis — practised an extreme form of *taqiyya* (concealment), following the Satpanth in secret whilst conforming outwardly to Hindu customs and life-style; they also mostly claimed to have been converted in the thirteenth century by Pīr Shams, the predecessor of Pīr Ṣadruddīn (Aziz 1974).[2] Besides these main divisions, there were also other groups in Gujarat who were specially devoted to Pīr Satgur Nūr (probably a near-contemporary of Pīr Shams), or who, like the Imāmshāhis, had split off from the main Ismaili fold during the sixteenth century, and come under increasing Hindu Mahāmārgi or Swāmi Nārāyan influences (Contractor). To the west of the main Ismaili communities in Gujarat and Sindh, i.e. in Rajasthan, there were lesser-known groups, such as Nizārpanthis and Mahāpanthis, who seem to have been converted to Ismailism in medieval times but to have later become re-Hinduized, or even re-Islamized, whilst preserving tantalising traces of their original affiliation (Khan 1997).

Given the considerable variety of practice amongst the Indian Ismailis, it will be at once apparent that the most striking feature of the Satpanth (and that which proved most baffling to outsiders) was its syncretism: the fact that it managed to combine the basic elements of Ismaili Islam with a range of local Hindu concepts and customs. This defining characteristic can be partly ascribed to the flexible conversion strategies of the founder Pīrs, who, for a variety of reasons — some associated with classical Ismaili philosophy, others perhaps more politically inspired — had sought to project the Satpanth as the completion of Hindu beliefs rather than as a new

[1] The term Khoja is derived from the title *Khwāja*, meaning Lord. For recent general accounts of the Indian Nizāri Ismaili Khoja Satpanthis, see Shackle and Moir.

[2] The Guptis were sometimes referred to as Shamsis. Hollister suggests that the Shamsi communities in Punjab, NWFP and Jammu practised a less extreme form of *taqiyya* than the Guptis, maintaining, for instance, the custom of burying rather than cremating their dead. Some sources also claim that sections of the Shamsis were originally converted not by Pīr Shams of Multan but by a later sixteenth-century Pīr of the same name. It may also be noted here that the recent new converts in Punjab (converted by local missionaries after 1913) were known as Sheikhs. I am grateful to Mumtaz Sadik Ali for this information. See also his latest book *Ismailis through History*, Karachi, 1997.

and alien creed. Most famously, this approach was expressed in the dual identity of the Ismaili Imām as both the direct successor of Ali and the Tenth Avatar (*avatār*) of Viṣhṇu — the long-awaited Nakalank. But the same approach also permeated the whole fabric of the Ismailis' religious and social life. For example, though most Khojas were no doubt vaguely aware of the significance of the Koran, they were far more devoted to the teachings of their own *gināns* — the hymns attributed to their leading Pīrs, which they regularly recited in their Jamā'tkhānas (assembly halls) in the mixed languages of northern India. Similarly, whilst they followed the Shia practice of offering prayers three times daily, professing faith in Allah, Prophet Muhammad and Imām Ali, these prayers, the Sindhi *du'ā*, were largely given over to recitations of the names of their own Pīrs and Imāms (including their Hindu Avatars) and were on regular occasions preceded by the distribution of holy water (Mujtaba Ali).

A comparable combination of Islamic and Hindu forms also characterized their outward life. For instance, many Khojas in Bombay and Gujarat bore Hindu names, dressed like Lohāṇā Hindus and followed Hindu property law, but they also practised circumcision and mostly preferred to arrange their marriages and funerals through local Sunni mullahs. Amongst the Punjab Guptis, as already suggested, the adoption of complete *taqiyya* resulted in what would now be judged as startlingly schizoid life-styles. Thus apart from following the Satpanth in secret, these groups were otherwise indistinguishable from caste Hindus, having Hindu names, participating in Hindu festivals, cremating their dead, intermarrying with Hindus and keeping to a vegetarian diet.

Hasanali Shah's decision to settle in Bombay in the 1840s, formally transferring his headquarters from Iran to India, ushered in a long period of dissension and transformation in the Indian Ismaili community. Although links had always been maintained between the previous Imāms and their Indian followers (especially through the hereditary line of Khoja representatives — vakils in Kachchh responsible for the collection / transmission of tithe monies to Iran), such links had necessarily been loose and intermittent, and after the break-up of the line of Indian Pīrs at the end of the fifteenth century, there had been no centralized authority capable of imposing conformity across the wide range of locally autonomous communities. Almost at once the Agha Khan's arrival on the scene began to challenge this situation.

It is unnecessary here to recount the detailed story of all the successive conflicts that characterized the relations between the Agha Khans and the minority of dissident Bombay Khojas during the next sixty or seventy years. That story is, I think, already sufficiently familiar through the work of various recent scholars (Asani and Masselos). For the present purpose what needs to be brought out is the extent to which most of these disputes focused on the twin issues of the Agha Khan's claims to exercise authority over the Ismaili communities, and the socio-religious identity of those same communities. In particular, representatives of each of the major traditions that had previously quietly combined within the eclectic folds of the Satpanth, began to assert strong claims or viewpoints concerning what each group considered to be the essential character of their faith. Though the intimate character of these movements is sometimes hard to define, the underlying logic was simple: if groups whom the Agha Khan claimed to lead could prove themselves to be Sunnis, Shia Ithna Asharis, or Hindus, then they would be freed from his interference and exactions.

Of these groups, it was perhaps the Sunni Khojas who created the biggest stir in the public life of Bombay in the 1860s (Newspapers). Basing their claim that the Khojas were really Sunni Muslims owing no obligations to the Ismaili Imām, largely on their marriage and burial customs, it was this group which in 1866 boldly challenged the Agha Khan to defend the legitimacy of his position in the Bombay High Court before Justice Arnould. The upshot, of course, was a notable victory for the Agha Khan, in the course of which a wealth of historical evidence was adduced to establish (a) the special position enjoyed by the Ismaili Imām within the broad Shia branch of Islam as the direct descendant of Ali, (b) that the Khojas themselves had originally been Hindus converted to Ismailism by Pīr Ṣadruddīn, and had always acknowledged the Imām's authority, and (c) that such Sunni customs as the Khojas had adopted had been part of their *taqiyya*. As a result of this decision a minority of Sunni Khojas chose to sever their links with the loyalist majority.

By contrast, the later claims advanced by the Bombay Shia Khojas from the 1870s onwards, though potentially stronger than the earlier Sunni Khoja attacks, were in practice weakened in legal terms by the Agha Khan's convincing victory in the earlier case. None the less several ingenious arguments were put forward by this groups to support their contention that the Khoja community were really mainstream Ithna Ashari who had been led astray by the fraudulent claims of the Agha Khan. For example, they put forward evidence (a) that the Agha Khan's claim to an uninterrupted line of descent from Ali was distinctly dubious (a point left unresolved by the earlier Arnould judgement), or (b) that he and the members of his family privately followed Ithna Ashari practice. In the face of strong opposition from the Agha Khan party, many Shia Khojas left the community in 1901, and their claims were also firmly dismissed by Justice Russell in the Haji Bibi case of 1908 in Bombay (Judgement).

Finally, as regards the public expression of Hindu-minded Ismailis, the situation is more complex since for a long time these groups remained muted. In a sense, however, their viewpoint — or rather the Hindu elements in Indian Ismailism — had been partially expressed in the earlier case brought to the Bombay High Court in 1847, when Justice Perry had ruled that Khoja property was subjected to Hindu not Islamic law, as the Agha Khan's party had argued. But it was not really till much later in 1913-14 that a more wholehearted mass expression of Hindu Ismaili opinion was manifested, this time, appropriately enough, not from the sophisticated Bombay Khojas but from the long-forgotten Gupti communities in Punjab and Gujarat.[3] Called upon then by the Third Agha Khan to come out of hiding and openly declare themselves as Muslim Ismailis, some authorities claim that as many as 40,000 eventually came out positively in response to this appeal, leaving perhaps a similar number who felt unable to abandon their traditional Hindu life-style, including some who in a sense followed the logic of their convictions by joining the Arya Samaj (Nizami).

THE ISMAILI WRITERS AND THEIR DEBATES

The dozen or more writers of Ismaili origin whose works reflect and illuminate this long period of religious and legal dissension in the Indian Ismaili community may be roughly divided into four main categories. The first and earliest group includes two writers (a) Khaki Khoja, whose rather mysterious tract *Gupt panth kā shajara* (also called *Shajara*) seems to have appeared around the time the Agha Khan case was being heard in Bombay (1866), and (b) Sachedina Nanjiani whose better-known *Khojā vratānt* was published in Ahmedabad in 1892. Although, as we shall see, these two works vary considerably in sophistication and reliability, they may be associated in so far as they both represent first attempts by Ismaili writers to research and reconstruct the early history of the Satpanth, each providing new — and to the contemporary community — controversial accounts of the nature and origin of its Hindu elements.

The remaining three groups belong to the next generation of Ismaili writers, all emerging more or less simultaneously during the first quarter

[3] I am grateful to Mr. Mahboobali Khoja of Karachi and also to his friend Mr. Sherali (whose family was originally Gupti) for providing the information about the Agha Khan's appeal to the Guptis.

of the twentieth century. Not only do many of these writers in varying degrees seek to respond to the challenging historical material presented in the Agha Khan case and by Khaki and Nanjiani, but each group also articulates — often in open debate with their rivals — one or other of those main viewpoints concerning the essential nature of Ismaili identity, whose more public manifestations in Bombay were briefly described in the introductory section of this paper. That is to say, for the viewpoint of the Shia Khojas, the most vigorous and polemical expression is to be found in the writings of Edulji Dhanji Kaba, a prolific Gujarati author, whose works include *Khojā komnī tavārikh* (Amreli, 1912) and *Khojā panth darpan* (Amreli, 1913-14). As for the third group — representing a range of Hindu Ismaili perspectives — we shall be looking briefly at three writers, all influenced by the Arya Samaj, namely, Pindi Das, Ram Chandar and Radha Krishan, all of Gupti origin, and particularly active from 1913-14 onwards.

Finally — and forming the fourth and the largest category — are what may be best described as the Ismaili revivalists — a group of Agha-Khani loyalists who, acting more or less in concert, sought to create a renewed sense of traditional Ismaili identity, strong enough to hearten and educate their supporters and refute their opponents. Active for several decades from about 1905 onwards, mainly in Bombay, these Gujarati writers included Jaffer Rahimtoola, Master Hashim Bogha, Alimuhammad Chunara and Ebrahim Varteji. Together they produced a stream of publications, ranging from newspaper articles, books about Ismaili history and religion, and educational text books, to polemical replies to Shia and Arya Samaj attacks and even volumes of poetry. Amongst their most significant works are Rahimtoola's *Khojā komno itihās* (Bombay, 1905), Bogha Master's *Asaliyate Khojā* (Bombay, 1912) and Varteji's *Āftābe hakīkat* (Bombay, 1916) and *Vedik Islām* (Bombay, 1921).

Before analysing the positions adopted by these several groups in more detail, that is to say explaining their differences, I must briefly draw attention to two or three general features, which they have in common. First and foremost, of course, was their preoccupation with Ismailism itself. Thus, although their individual and group opinions vary enormously, along with their degrees of certitude, they are all ultimately asking similar questions about the Satpanth. How did it begin? Is it still valid? If not, what should replace it? And if it is still to be accepted, how should it be represented?

The comparative freedom with which these questions were asked also points towards the second common ground shared by these writers, namely, the fact they represent the first generations of Indian Ismaili writers able to take advantage of the general climate of religious freedom associated with the consolidation of the British Raj during the nineteenth century. No doubt there were limits to that freedom — marked by the successive vernacular press acts — but for Ismailis of all sorts, inured to earlier periods of orthodox persecution and accustomed to the need for *taqiyya*, the opportunities opened up to express their views over a range of vital issues, and even to answer their critics, were certainly novel experiences, which several of the writers themselves acknowledge. New, too, was the growing availability of printed vernacular and English translations of many of the major scriptural texts belonging to the different South Asian religious traditions — Hindu, Islamic, Jain, etc. As we shall see, most of these writers, particularly the Ismaili revivalists, made ample use of this newly accessible material to challenge their opponents and identify new sources of support for their own positions.

KHAKI KHOJA

Next to nothing is known about Khaki Khoja, the author of *Gupt Panth kā Shajara*, other than what can be deduced from the internal evidence of his undated work. That is to say, since he quotes extensively from the *ginān*s, and his book is written in Bombay-style Urdu rendered in the Khojki script, it seems almost certain that he was of Khoja Ismaili origin, and may have lived in Bombay. His evident aversion to tithes' payment suggests that he may have been connected with the early Bombay Khoja opposition to the First Agha Khan on that score, whilst some of his sceptical representations of the Ismaili Pīrs and Imāms seem to indicate that he is writing from a Shia perspective. As indicated earlier, it also appears from Nanjiani's later account that the *Shajara* may have come out shortly before the Agha Khan Case in 1866; certainly it makes no direct reference to the historical materials produced in that case, though it does include Hasanali Shah in its lists of Ismaili Imāms.

As the title implies, Khaki's book is largely made up of a series of genealogies or tables detailing the lines of Islamic Prophets, Shia Ithna Ashari Imāms, Ismaili Imāms and Avatars, as well as their 'Indian' Pīrs and assistants (Maheshvaras and vakils). It also includes brief narrative accounts of certain key episodes in the history of the Ismaili mission in India, such as the lives of Satgur Nūr and his disciple Chach, the subsequent alleged foundation of the Satpanth by Pīr Ṣadruddīn and Sohodev Joshi (see below), and the later disputes leading to the separation of the Imāmshāhis in the fifteenth and sixteenth centuries. Unfortunately, unlike Nanjiani, Khaki says very little about the sources of his *Shajara*. However, it seems probable that he drew upon certain older manuscript sources and traditions, especially for his genealogies, and that he may also have investigated Imāmshāhi materials at Pirana and mainstream Khoja materials at traditional centres in Kachchh and Gujarat.

From the point of view of its implications for Indian Ismaili identity, the most intriguing part of Khaki's *Shajara* lies in its dramatic treatment of the secret pact between Pīr Ṣadruddīn and Sohodev Joshi said to have been concluded in AD 1420. According to the *Shajara*, Sohodev Joshi was a former Brahmin prince descended from Chach, the disciple of Satgur Nūr, who is traditionally supposed to have murdered his master before creating his own following amongst the Mahāmārgis in Gujarat and Punjab.[4] Khaki also describes Sohodev as a leading Mahāmārgi, deeply versed in Vaishnavite and Islamic mysticism, who had at one time even being captured by Pathans and forcibly converted to Islam. Helped by a wealthy Lohāṇā named Kapur, Sohodev made the acquaintance of Pīr Ṣadruddīn in Punjab. The two men then engaged in a lengthy dialogue in the course of which they both decided to put away their religious differences and forge a new Ismaili Hindu synthesis, referred to as the Satpanth. As part of the new system, a series of Hindu/Ismaili equivalences were worked out (e.g. Viṣhṇu as Imām, etc.), and a flexible arrangement agreed according to which those who joined the Satpanth but preferred to continue outwardly as Hindus, could do so as Guptis, whilst those who were ready to appear openly as Ismailis became known as Khojas. However, though Khaki's narrative does not explicitly state this, it implies that some sort of Ismaili Gupti-cum-Mahāmārgi community had existed before this agreement, apparently going back to the conversions made by Satgur Nūr and Chach. Finally, it also emerges that Khaki himself views the formation of the Satpanth as amounting to a form of conspiracy, which resulted in the creation of a profitable source of income for the Pīr and his successors (through their implied misappropriation of the money intended for the Imām), while leaving their hapless followers relegated to a limbo between Islam and Hinduism.

In trying to assess the historical significance of Khaki's *Shajara*, a distinction may usefully be drawn between its immediate effects upon

[4] Among present-day Hindu Gujarati writers, Pīr Ṣadruddīn and Sohodev are included amongst the founders of the Mahāmārgi sect, also known as Nizārpanthis. See Mallison and Moir in *Puruṣārtha*, 19, 1996, pp. 265-76.

the Khoja community and its longer-term historical interest. As far as the community was concerned, it appears that the *Shajara*'s critical representation of the Satpanth's origin and abuses initially had strongly negative effects, leading several hundred Khoja families in Bombay and Gujarat to secede. Thereafter, although the work continues to be occasionally cited by later writers, notably Nanjiani and Kaba, it hardly seems to figure — even as an object of criticism — in the writings of the later Ismaili revivalists. What is more, the extraordinary, multi-layered figure of Sohodev disappears entirely from the official Ismaili historiography which those writers helped to create. In particular, at least from the time of Laljibhai Devraj's official edition of the *ginān*s (1904+), the name Sohodev is applied to Pīr Ṣadruddīn himself, with the implication that his adoption of it was part of the Pīr's syncretic approach to Hindu conversions.

As regards to its historical reliability, it is clear that the *Shajara* needs to be treated with considerable caution, not only in view of its author's evident intention to discredit the Khojas but also because of the contrived, story-like quality it deploys. The need for caution is also generally underlined by Nanjiani who, though he gives credit to Khaki for having made a pioneering attempt to collect up Ismaili sources and traditions, considers that many of the *Shajara*'s stories are not to be relied upon. At the same time it would also be a mistake to dismiss the work as wholly lacking in historical credibility. For example, preliminary examinations of the manuscript versions of the *ginān*s (as opposed to the authorized printed copies) suggest that Sohodev may indeed have been an independent personality, not just an alias for Ṣadruddīn, though what exactly his role was remains obscure. Similarly, recent research is beginning to confirm at least some of the broader historical elements hinted at in the *Shajara*'s accounts, namely, the role of the Mahāmārgis in the formation and spread of the Satpanth, the extent to which the early Ismaili Pīrs relied upon Hindu religious and political support, and the significance of the Gupti communities as evidence of those early alliances and accommodations (Kassam).

SACHEDINA NANJIANI

If Khaki Khoja's ancient genealogies and graphic tales of secret pacts and conspiracies seem in some ways to place the *Shajara* in a late medieval setting, Sachedina Nanjiani's *Khojā vratānt*, with its systematic conception and framework and critical use of historical sources, bears more of the hallmarks of modernity. Also, unlike Khaki Khoja, Nanjiani himself is a fairly well-documented figure. Born into what would seem to have been a well-to-do Ismaili family in Kachchh, he himself met the First Agha Khan more than once — first in the company of his grandfather on a visit to Hyderabad in 1842, and later with his father in Kachchh. Pursuing his career as Assistant Revenue Commissioner in Kachchh state, he began to collect material for his history from 1874 onwards. The result, *Khojā vratānt*, was printed in Ahmedabad in 1892 and later reprinted (in abridged form) in 1918; he himself probably died sometime before 1912. Though at some stage — perhaps after the First Agha Khan case, he decided to become a Shia Ithna Ashari, he does not allow his own views to colour his historical judgement. *Khojā vratānt* is a personal exploration of his roots, and a sober, rational attempt to help the Khoja community to overcome its present confusion and division by coming to terms with the full complexities of its past. That it was soon recognized as such is shown by the extent it is later referred to by various government memoirs and gazetteers (Enthoven, Sadiq Ali).

The variety of source material consulted by Nanjiani in his long period of research is particularly impressive, including the *ginān*s themselves, Khaki Khoja's *Shajara*, Arabic and Persian sources cited in the 1866 Agha Khan Case, the Persian text of *Farishta* as well as various works by Western orientalists and Hindu religious texts. He himself also describes visits made to check the archives belonging to the Ismaili Vakils in Bhuj, as well as the traditional Ismaili Sayyid centre at Kera and the Imāmshāhi Dargah at Pirana. With a pioneer spirit somewhat unusual for the period, he also investigated, as we shall see, the *bhajan*s preserved in the oral tradition of the Meghval communities in Kachchh and Gujarat.[5]

Khojā vratānt aims to cover almost the whole history of the Ismaili movement, including the Fatimid and Nizāri/ Alamut periods (909-1256), and also to summarize as much of the Hindu tradition as seems to be relevant. But the core of the work's contribution — and that which concerns us here — is its original investigation into the early history of the Satpanth in Kachchh and Gujarat, and in particular the relations between the first Ismaili missionaries and their Hindu converts. In following this line of research, it also appears that Nanjiani is consciously seeking to advance beyond the two most important previous contributions to the

[5] There seems to be no recent socio-anthropological study of the Mahāmārgi communities, who retain evidence of early contacts with the Nizāri Ismaili mission — contacts which were apparently subsequently broken. Contemporary Indian writers on Gujarati folk literature prefer to derive the term Nizār from *nija* (pure).

subject, namely, (1) the statements made in 1866 Agha Khan Case that the Khojas were originally Lohāṇā Hindus converted by Pīr Ṣadruddīn in the fifteenth century, and (2) Khaki Khoja's tantalizing glimpse into the Mahāmārgi contribution to Indian Ismailism during and before the Ṣadruddīn mission (though it is interesting to note that Nanjiani makes no mention of Sohodev Joshi).

It was Nanjiani's discovery of the oral tradition of *bhajan*s preserved by the Meghval and other Mahāmārgi communities in Kachchh and Gujarat that brought the most significant breakthrough in his research. To his surprise he discovered that these *bhajan*s not only contained the expected references to purely Hindu sacred figures and symbols, but also to the Nakalank, the long-awaited Tenth Avatar, expressly described as due to arrive from Daylam (Alamut) in the West in Muslim garb to establish the reign of truth and justice. Above all these same *bhajan*s spoke devoutly of the Nizārpanth and recorded stories about Satgur Nūr and Chach Mātang which closely paralleled the accounts given in the Ismaili *ginān*s. Extending his fieldwork to cover the Mahāmārgi religious practices and rituals, Nanjiani also encountered holy water ceremonies and forms of prayers bearing close resemblances to the Khoja rituals.

Although Nanjiani is cautious about making deductions from his material, he appears to recognize that it pointed in two main directions, firstly suggesting that Nizāri Ismaili missionaries had been active making converts in these areas probably as early as the twelfth century (or middle Alamut period); and secondly that many of the basic Khoja concepts and rituals still practised had been originally borrowed from or at least influenced by the Hindu Mahāmārgis. In other words, using a source independent of the *ginān*s, Nanjiani though he had found evidence of an Ismaili presence in Western India several centuries before Justice Arnould had supposed, and that the syncretic conversion methods previously credited to Pīr Ṣadruddīn had apparently been employed in Gujarat much earlier. At the same time Nanjiani was careful not to speculate beyond the main area of his research. For instance, he certainly knew about the Ismaili communities in Punjab and Kashmir becoming Ithna Asharis but frankly admitted that he had no material concerning their origin.

In drawing attention to the strong Hindu influences that had helped to shape the Satpanth, Nanjiani himself, though by this time adhering to Shia Ithna Asharism, never suggests that the Ismaili Pīrs went too far in accepting and incorporating Hindu influences: on the contrary, he rather commends the success of their achievements. None the less it is also clear that other aspects of his research — particularly into the questionable line of descent of the Ismaili Imāms during the Alamut period — had played a part in his decision to move towards a mainstream Shia position. Hence all these different elements in his research are reflected in the final conclusions of *Khojā vratānt* when he tells the Khojas that the time had now come for them to abandon their Hindu practices and join the rest of the Shia. But characteristically there is nothing strident about his conclusion: rather the tone is calm and matter-of-fact. The Hindus, he says, 'will not accept us back, and we should join the Shias' apparently for the sake of the unity of Islam (p. 264).

EDULJI DHANJI KABA, ETC.

Although Nanjiani and, as far as we can tell, Khaki Khoja both opted to abandon their given identity as Ismaili Khojas in favour of Shia Ithna Asharism, and these personal moves are to some extent reflected in their respective works, it would be clearly misleading to characterize them as Shia apologist writers. Nanjiani's work in particular (as we have seen) has an objective rather than a sectarian quality, and this quality becomes even more apparent when compared with the writings of an outright Shia polemicist like Edulji Dhanji Kaba, and other minor Shia propagandists such as those writing under the pen-names of Mr. Jim, Mr. Ain and Mr. Gain.

Like Nanjiani, Kaba belonged to an Ismaili Khoja family, and was probably born in Amreli (Baroda) in the late nineteenth century. In his youth he too joined the Ithna Ashari Khoja group but unlike Nanjiani he became increasingly outspoken and fanatical in his new-found faith, and determined to use his journalistic skills (he was for a while editor of a Gujarati newspaper) to expose his former Ismaili co-religionists as crypto-Hindus and polytheists. Besides his newspaper articles, he was especially active between 1907 and 1920, producing more than half-a-dozen books and pamphlets, printed in Amreli, and mostly attacking Ismailis (e.g. *Hasan bin Sabbāh* (1907), *Khoja komnī tavārikh* (1912) and *Khojā panth darpan* (1913-14). Moreover, as we shall see later, several of his publications were issued in response to counter-attacks by Ismaili revivalist writers in what became an increasingly heated contest. At one stage Kaba was even prepared to collaborate with the Arya Samaj Gupti writer Radha Krishan to discredit their common enemy (Varteji 1919).

Although Kaba's later writings seem at times to go over the top in making wild accusations, it is none the less possible to identify certain more coherent elements in his general critique of Ismaili Khojas. Making use of his knowledge of the *ginān*s, plus a wide reading in contemporary religious and historical literature (including Nanjiani and Khoja), Kaba attempts to deconstruct the Khoja Ismaili tradition, making it possible for Ithna Asharis to reclaim what he sees as their lost ground. Thus his critique is directed at two closely-related targets: the Ismaili Khojas' own claim to a distinct and authentic religious identity, and the legitimacy claims of the Agha Khan himself. In tackling the Khojas, he adopts a partly historical approach, making particular use of a recently published account by the caretaker of the Satgur Nūr Dargah in Gujarat (Dargahvala 1914). On this basis he argues (contrary to Nanjiani) that Satgur Nūr was not an Ismaili at all but a Twelver Shia missionary, active before the Alamut period, who obliged his converts to abandon their Hindu practices and accept full Islam. It was only later, he held, that Pīr Ṣadruddīn (and apparently Pīr Shams before him) allowed their Khoja followers to revert to or continue with their Mahāmārgi beliefs and customs, especially their belief in the Imām as the Vaishnavite Avatar, and thereby (in Kaba's view) to lose their Islamic identity. Only a return to Shia Ithna Ashari Islam would thus ensure their salvation (Kaba 1912).

In seeking to delegitimize the Agha Khans, Kaba's main line of attack is less original and more personal, concentrating principally on the alleged breaks in the line of Ismaili Imāms, and a variety of evidence to show that, despite their pretensions, the Agha Khans' personal religion was Ithna Ashari Shia (Kaba 1913-14). This latter evidence, however, for Kaba was not enough to redeem the Agha Khans as Muslim leaders, since (and here he brings the two sides of his critique together) they continued to project themselves as the Nakalank for their benighted Khoja followers. Incidentally, in labelling the Khojas as Hindus and their Imāms as fallen Shia, polluted by polytheism, Kaba's ingenious argument finally seeks to invert the two main conclusions reached in Arnould's judgement, namely that the Khojas were converted Hindus and that their Imāms were Shia leaders.

GUPTIS

In contrast to the substantial and long-standing movement amongst certain Khojas to convert to Shia Islam, a tendency reflected in Kaba's fierce attacks on Ismailis, those Indian Ismailis who were closest to Hindu traditions were slow to assert their own distinct identity claims. Of course, one of the ironies attached to Kaba's contention that the Ismailis were really Hindus not Muslims, was that it opened up the possibility, in theory at least, that such people might as well publicly declare themselves as Hindus, as join the mainstream Shia. In practice, however, the groups most likely to be attracted to the former possibility were not amongst the Agha Khan loyalist Khojas, who openly practised their Satpanth (and for whom, as Nanjiani had pointed out, the option of returning to Hinduism would not be easy) but among the Gupti and Shamsi communities in Punjab, Kashmir and Gujarat, who had practised *taqiyya* for centuries. Since almost by definition these communities were bound to be reticent, it required the shock of the Third Agha Khan's 1913-14 appeal to them to come out as Ismaili Muslims, to induce at least some of them to declare their contrary allegiance, encouraged by tactical support from the Arya Samaj (according to one report as many as 20,000 were re-Hinduized).

As already suggested, further research is needed before we can form a clear picture of the overall outcome of the Agha Khan's appeal, particularly as regards the respective numbers of those who accepted and rejected his call. Essentially, for those who opted to declare themselves Ismailis, it was mostly a matter of adopting Muslim names, changing their marriage and funeral customs, developing their organization, etc. (Mohamed). But for those who chose to remain Guptis, the position was perhaps rather more difficult.[6] Ostracized or excommunicated by the Ismaili authorities, the pressures on these people to assimilate completely to Hinduism were probably considerable, and it was here that the strong influence exerted by the Arya Samaj becomes apparent. Well established in Punjab since the 1890s as a proselytizing force, these groups took advantage of the Guptis' predicament in 1913-14 to persuade some to join their movement, at the same time encouraging them to undergo the Shuddhi (purification) ceremony to regularize their religious identity. Here again we encounter a case in which the peculiar social patterns associated with Ismaili syncretism challenge conventional notions about the Hindu/ Muslim divide, especially as conceived by groups such as Arya Samaj. Thus given that the Guptis still closely conformed to Hindu caste and ritual practices, in what sense could they be said to have left the Hindu fold and therefore be in need of purification?

So far I have found three main Gupti spokesmen with Arya Samaj affiliations, who chose to speak out and write publicly against the Agha

[6] I am grateful to Alwaez Noordin H. Baksh of Karachi for showing me his collection of materials on Guptis, and on the families who did not join the Ismaili fold. I also understand that Alwaez Abu Ali of Vancouver is writing an account of some of these re-Hinduized families.

Khan's appeal: Radha Krishan, Pindi Das, and Ram Chandar (all incidentally addressed as Pandit by their Ismaili interlocutors). Little is known about the origin of these men, except that the first two were both from Peshawar, where 400 families had openly declared for Agha Khan; whilst the other one, Ram Chandar came from Surat, where some 250 families had similarly come out. Although it is possible that they all joined the Arya Samaj around the time of the Agha's appeal, it is of course also possible that they may have had earlier connections with the movement. Anyway, between 1914 and 1916 all three published strong appeals to their fellow Guptis to reject the Agha Khan's advice, Pindi Das's view being argued in an Urdu pamphlet, Ram Chandar's articulated in the Gujarati press, while Radha Krishan — the most committed Gupti-publicist actually produced a book entitled *Āgākhāni khudāī aur uske karashme*. As we shall see, Ismaili revivalist writers were quick to respond to these attacks, even extending invitations to the dissident Guptis to join them in open debate. Predictably, the resultant encounters became emotional and bitter, and had to be discontinued. Meanwhile Radha Krishan engaged in a campaign of speeches in Punjab, even joining forces with E.D. Kaba in an attempt to widen public opposition to their common foe by publishing articles in Punjabi newspapers designed to inflame Sunni opinion against the so-called polytheist Ismailis. Not surprisingly, Radha Krishan's vehement attacks at one point resulted in a religious riot, leading to his own eventual imprisonment by the British authorities.[7]

It is difficult to provide a complete representation of the dissident Gupti viewpoint partly because of the limited availability of their literature and partly because they themselves were unable or unwilling to reveal the full extent of their traditions. For instance, so far I have only been able to trace Pindi Das's pamphlet, and for the other writers I have had to rely mostly on the lengthy quotations from their works given by Ismaili respondents (Varteji 1919). However, these several sources suggest that their approach was rather to commiserate with those who had unwarily joined the Agha Khan's followers — to find themselves compelled to pay tithe money and other exactions. Still devoutly awaiting the arrival of the Tenth Avatar, the dissident Guptis could not accept the Khojas' proclamation that the awaited one was now present in the shape of Agha Khan, whose luxurious European life-style seemed to the Guptis quite incompatible with his meta-

[7] The articles of Alwaez Aziz Fidai and Alwaez Noordin H. Baksh provide vivid accounts of these debates. See Kamaluddin.

messianic claims (Pindi Das). As regards their own origins and traditions, they were in general predictably reticent, though it is intriguing to find Pindi Das invoking at one point the name of Sohodev Joshi, whose *gināns*, he asserts, had been appropriated by Pīr Ṣadruddīn (without however mentioning Khaki Khoja's tract). It also seems clear from the unpublished account of a later Ismaili of Gupti origin that the Guptis claimed to have been originally converted by the elusive Pīr Shams, the predecessor of Pīr Ṣadruddīn, who was placed in the thirteenth century (Aziz 1990).

ISMAILI REVIVALISTS

The formation in the first few years of the twentieth century of a small but very active group of Ismaili writers and editors, able to answer their Shia Ithna Ashari and Arya Samaj critics and to articulate a unified vision of the Satpanth, roughly coincides with the ending of the long period of dissension and confusion that had beset the community since the arrival of the First Agha Khan in 1845. As we have seen, it was during these years (1901-8) that the main body of Shia Khoja dissidents finally left the parent body, and their legal challenge was removed by the Russell ruling in the Haji Bibi case (Judgement). Also it was around this time that the Third Agha Khan, Sultan Muhammad Shah (d. 1957) began to project himself strongly as a leading figure on the Indian political stage, holding the position of President of the Muslim League from 1905 to 1913. While the revealing conflicts and the defections associated with his call to the Guptis were yet to come (1913-14), it is apparent that those defections were seen by the Agha Khan as a minor disappointment, not seriously detracting from the triumphant accession of fresh support from the majority Gupti groups.

It was during this period too that the Agha introduced an important series of reforms and new initiatives transforming the internal structure and ethos of the Ismaili community. A set of community councils was created with their constitutions carefully defined (1906); a network of religious schools was established, with committees formed to provide the necessary textbooks and training, etc. (1901); a project for printing the entire corpus of *gināns* in Khojki was inaugurated (1904); fresh conversion programmes were undertaken (1913); and in 1903 the Ismaili Literary Society (Ismāili sāhitia utejak mandal) was founded in Bombay to publish books in Gujarati and also to produce monthly and bi-monthly newspapers to report the activities of the Imām and the community (Hooda 1927).

The kind of writers who now emerged to play a leading role in the Literary Society and other community projects did not come from the old

Sayyid families of Kachchh and Sindh in whom the responsibility for religious instruction and the *ginānic* composition had traditionally been vested. Instead they represented the new social elements in the community that had come to the fore, especially in Bombay, during the previous half century or so. For example, some of these men were successful in Bombay business, such as Lalji Devraj (d. 1930), who masterminded the printing of the *ginān*s and other publishing projects, and also Alimuhammad Chunara (d. 1966), a Bombay factory owner, who edited Khoja newspapers from 1911 onwards, and, having taught himself Urdu, Arabic and Sanskrit, embarked on writing a series of books about Ismaili history and religion. Another prominent contributor, Jaffer Rahimtoola, the author of a *History of the Khojas* (Bombay, 1905), was a Bombay lawyer who had qualified as a barrister in London, acquiring a taste for research and an ability to present arguments with legal precision.

Two other writers brought a more individual talent and background of study to their community work. Master Hashim Bogha (d. 1913) came from a humble Gujarati background and was largely self-educated. Eventually qualifying as a school-master in Bombay, he became a kind of teacher for the whole community, producing a series of textbooks and other religious and historical studies. Similarly, Ebrahim Varteji (d. 1953) had been a brilliant Gujarati student and also a poet, with a knowledge of Sanskrit, Marathi, Arabic, Urdu, Persian and English. Joining the Shia Ithna Ashari Khojas in his boyhood, he spent nearly twenty years exploring a variety of Indian religious traditions before returning to the Ismaili fold in 1913. His subsequent literary work for the community runs to more than a dozen books, including poetry, expositions of the Satpanth and replies to Shia and Gupti / Arya Samaj critics. At its best his work has a vibrant and zestful quality unusual in this type of literature.

In attempting to revitalize the Satpanth and project it as a coherent system, not just a mishmash of conflicting beliefs and practices, the Ismaili revivalist writers were fully aware that they had to address the different concerns of three main groups: their Gupti / Arya Samaj and Twelver Shia opponents as well as their fellow Khojas. As we shall see, each group required not exactly a different message, but a different kind of emphasis.

In the case of the Ithna Ashari Khojas, the Ismaili writers generally sought to combine reassurance and persuasion by stressing as far as possible their shared Islamic values. For example, the Shias were reminded that they and the Ismailis both accorded fundamental importance to the living Imām. It was true that they differed as to whether the Imām was hidden or manifest, but, so the Ismailis contended, their conception of the

Imām-e Mubīn (the living and manifest Imām) had the benefit of Koranic authority (36:12), as well as providing a source of authority through which the Koran itself could be interpreted in changing circumstances. Hence, as true Muslims, Ismailis claimed they had always followed the Imām's Farmāns and injunctions, whereas they believed the Shia Ithna Asharis had in a sense succumbed to a form of static idolatry (*bhūtparastī*) in privileging the occulted Imām (Varteji 1917, Hooda 1920).

With considerable ingenuity, the Ismaili writers also sought to invoke the true spirit of Islam to persuade the Ithna Asharis of the validity of their doctrinal and ritual accommodations with Hinduism — especially the identification of the Imām with the Nakalank Avatar which writers like Kaba had so much deplored. They therefore stressed that the essential purpose behind such moves was to represent Islam as the completion of Hinduism, just as early Islam had projected itself as the completion of Christianity and Judaism. Instead of criticizing Khojas and seeking to convert them, the Ismaili writers urged the Ithna Asharis to have a go themselves at converting the recalcitrant Hindus. They would then perhaps better appreciate the wisdom of the Ismaili methods (Bogha 1912, Varteji 1921).

Whereas in their debates with the Ithna Asharis the Ismaili writers had implied that their representation of Ismailism as the completion of Hinduism was to be seen as a method for facilitating the conversion of Hindus to Islam, their attempts to win back the dissident Guptis understandably represented the same notion in terms of its intrinsic truth, i.e. the Satpanth was indeed the completion of Hinduism. This after all had been the original basic belief of the Guptis, and from the Ismaili point of view, it was essential to try to reassure them of its continuing validity. Hence, using a variety of quotations from different Sanskrit texts, including the Upanishads, the Gita, etc., the Ismaili writers tried to hammer home their traditional messages, namely, (1) that the Imām was the Tenth Avatar for the Kaliyuga, also referred to in the *ginān*s as the Nakalank Avatar; (2) that the Avatar or Guru Nakalank was always available, and without him there could be no salvation (*mukti*); and (3) that the *ginān*s — standing in for the Koran — were the Atharvaveda for the Kaliyuga. To reinforce these eschatological equations, the Ismailis also liked to point to particular key lines in the *ginān*s which also occurred in Sanskrit texts, such as 'bhagat kāraṇ hari āviā' (The Lord has arrived for the devotees), which appears both in the *ginān* of Imām Shah and in the *Bhagavadgītā* (Varteji 1919).

On a more worldly level they also warned those Guptis attracted to Arya Samaj (such as Radha Krishan) and those who sought to represent the

Ismailis as polytheists to incite Sunni or Shia criticism, that they would soon discover that such Muslim groups considered all Hindus to be infidels (*kāfir*), unlike the true Satpanthis who consciously stood in spiritual relation to the Hindu tradition. In a final ingenious twist of the argument aimed at the Arya Samajs the Guptis were also reminded that the real Satpanthi Ismailis were like Hindus who did not consider Muslims as barbarians (*mleccha*).

Whilst in their responses to Shias and dissident Guptis, the Ismaili writers gave a somewhat tactical expression to the notion of the Satpanth as the completion of Islam and Hinduism, they felt able to project this concept in a more wholehearted and emotional way in their writings aimed at the community itself. Ismailis, they say, are *hakīkī momin* (believers in the ultimate truth), who recognize the unique position of the Imām/Nakalank as revealed in the Koran/Vedas, and accept his Farmāns as authentic interpretation of both traditions. They also represent the Satpanth as a religion of inner transformation and spiritual progress. Whilst other Muslims are said to follow *sharia*, contenting themselves with worldly happiness and good deeds, Ismaili Satpanthis seek to transcend their desires not through asceticism but by seeking the ultimate truth of religion as revealed by the Imām, and defined variously in terms of *moksha/fanāfillāh* (liberation or losing oneself in Allah's essence) (Bogha 1910). History in general is also viewed by the Ismaili writers as the medium through which the *nūr* (Light) of the Imām/Avatar — conceived of as a single spiritual personality — is made accessible to human kind. Also on more human scale, the Ismailis tried to illustrate how down the ages the individual Imām/Avatar had struggled to reveal the true path of spiritual progress in the face of all sorts of opposition, comparing, for example, Ali's struggles with those of Krishna Avatar (Bogha 1909).

Imbued with the sense of Ismailism as containing the essence of both Islam and Hinduism, the Ismaili revivalists have no problem about continuing to accept the Hindu-related religious practices that so much outraged their more orthodox Muslim opponents. The *du'ā* (prayer) and the *ginān*s themselves are all seen as integral parts of the Satpanth, having symbolic or inner meanings which the writers are happy to expound (Varteji 1917).

As already suggested, the Ismaili revivalists' treatment of their history reflects the basic conception of the guiding role performed by the Imām/Nakalank through the ages and by the Pīrs who transmitted his message. Full hagiographical accounts of the lives and achievements of these figures were therefore presented for the community's edification. These accounts also incorporated and interpreted the considerable body of new information about the earlier phases of Ismaili history during the Fatimid and Alamut periods, mainly brought to light from Sunni and Western sources through the evidence presented in the 1866 case, and subsequently added to by writers such as Nanjiani. It is not, however, till the 1920s that a more creative boost to Ismaili history was given following W. Ivanow's pioneering research into newly-discovered Arabic and Persian manuscript materials for the Fatimid and Alamut periods (Chunara). Meanwhile, in the Ismaili revivalist writings, it is also interesting to note that despite their positive acknowledgement of their spiritual links with Hindus, those elements from their Hindu past which Khaki and Nanjiani had excavated were not now dwelt upon. Thus the Mahāmārgi and Gupti contributions were largely forgotten, and the mysterious, ambiguous figure of Sohodev Joshi only survived in the purified form of Pīr Ṣadruddīn.

In conclusion we may say that, although the Ismaili revivalists of this period preferred not to investigate the early formation of Indian Ismailism, none the less, on a broad religious level, they did succeed in asserting or reasserting the original syncretic vision of the Satpanth despite strong opposition from Ismaili dissidents. In recognition of this concept many Ismaili publications for this period depict a logo in which the mantra *OM* read in Sanskrit can also be read backwards as *ALI* in Arabic.

At the same time it has to be said that for most non-Ismailis in contemporary South Asia this syncretic concept remained mysterious and alien. For instance, when the poet Ebrahim Varteji tried to explain to Gandhi in 1918 that the Ismailis were both Hindus and Muslims, and that the Agha Khan was not just a Muslim but a universal Indian leader, the bemused Mahātma is reported to have remained silent for two whole minutes before sweetly confessing: 'I cannot say anything about these matters' (Varteji 1919). Somewhat similarly, Jawaharlal Nehru could not help wondering out loud in 1935 how far the Agha Khan and his community could be regarded as leading participants in the movement for Islamic solidarity, as understood by Muhammad Iqbal. The fact was that for all his immense personal prestige, the third Agha Khan remained a somewhat ambiguous figure: too Muslim to be accepted as a leader by Indian Hindus, too Hindu and heterodox to be considered a satisfactory leader for orthodox Islam.[8] This, of course, is a larger subject that cannot

[8] It appears that the third Agha Khan was denounced as a heretic in a *fatwa* issued by orthodox Muslims. This judgement was, however, condemned by writers such as Nizami. Unfortunately I have so far been unable to trace this *fatwa*.

be fully gone into here. Enough to say that as the strong forces of communal nationalism drove South Asia forward through Partition into future conflict, the fragile sound of *OM/ALI* could not easily be heard, even within the Ismaili community itself.

REFERENCES

I am grateful to the Institute of Ismaili Studies, London for allowing me access to some of the Gujarati books referred to in this paper. In a few cases the title covers of these books are missing, hence publication dates are not available (dna).

Aga Khan, Sultan Muhammad Shah, *The Memoirs of Aga Khan: World enough and Time*, London, 1954.

Arnould, Joseph, *Judgement by the Hon'ble Sir Joseph Arnould in the Khoja case, otherwise known as the Aga Khan Case*, Bombay: Bombay Steam Press, 1867.

Asani, Ali, 'The Khojas of Indo-Pakistan: the quest for an Islamic Identity', *Journal of the Institute of Muslim Minority Affairs*, vol. 8, 1983, pp. 31-41.

Aziz, Abualy, 'Autobiography of a Dā'i', pt. 1, unpublished, Vancouver, 1990.

———, *A Brief History of Ismailism*, Dar-es-Salaam: author, 1974.

Bogha, Hashim, *Asaliyat-e Khojā*, V.P. Parpiya, Bombay, 1912 (2nd edn.).

———, *Ismāilī darpan*, Bombay: author, 1906.

———, *Ismāilī prakāsh*, pts. 1 and 2, Bombay: author, 1906-8.

———, *Jauhar-e hakīkat*, Bombay: author, 1910.

———, *Nūr-e vahadāniyat*, pts. 1 and 2, Bombay: author, 1909.

Boivin, Michel, 'The reform of Islam in Ismaili Shi'ism 1885 to 1957', in *Confluence of Cultures*, edited by Françoise N. Delvoye, New Delhi: Manohar, 1994, pp. 197-216.

Bombay Government, *Gazetteer of the Bombay Presidency*, vol. IX, pt. II, Gujarat population: Musalmans and Parsees, Bombay: Bombay Government Press, 1899.

Contractor, Ramjibhai, *Pirānā satpanthni pol*, Ahmedabad: author, 1926.

Chunara, Alimuhammad, *Ādamthī ali*, Bombay: Ismāili sāhitia utejak mandal, dna.

———, *Ālamotano yodho*, Bombay: Ismāili Sāhitia utejak mandal, dna.

———, *Arebiyā ane imamat*, Bombay: Ismāili Sāhitia utejak mandal, dna.

———, *Fātamī khilāfat*, Bombay: Ismāili Sāhitia utejak mandal, dna.

———, *Khuli ciṭhinun bhopāruṅ*, Bombay: Ismāili Sāhitia utejak mandal, dna.

———, *Noorum Mubin*, Bombay: Khoja Printing Press, 1936.

Dargahvala, Ṣadruddīn, *Tavārikh-e pīr*, pts. 1 and 2, Nausari: author, 1914 and 1935.

Devraj, Laljibhai, *Tapasil buk*, Bombay: author, 1915 (2nd edn.).

Enthoven, R.F., *Tribes and Castes of Bombay*, vol. II, Bombay: Government Central Press, 1922.

Fyzee, Asghar Ali, *Cases in the Muhammadan Law of India and Pakistan*, London: Oxford Clarendon Press, 1965.

Hollister, Normana, *The Shiᶜa of India*, London: Luzac and Co., 1953.

Hooda, Vallimuhammad, *Asatya arop yāne khojā gṇātinuṅ gorav*, Kathiavar: N. Budhavani, 1927.

———, *Imām-e maujud*, pts. 1 and 2, Bombay: Ismāili sāhitia utejak mandal, 1920.

Howard, E.I., *The Shia School of Islam and its branches, especially that of Imāmee-Ismailies*, Bombay: Oriental Press, 1866.

Jones, Kenneth, *The New Cambridge History of India*, vol. III, pt. I, Cambridge: Cambridge University Press, 1908.

Judgement of Judge Russell, *The Bombay Law Reporter*, vol. XI, Bombay, September 1908.

Kaba, Edulji Dhanji, *Hasan bin Sabbāh*, Amreli: author, 1907.

———, *Khojā komni tavārikh*, Amreli: author, 1912.

———, *Khojā panth darpan*, Amreli: author, 1913-14.

Kamaluddin et al. (eds.), *Wāezin digest*, nos. 60 and 64, Karachi: Shia Imāmi Ismaili Tariqa and Religious Education Board for Pakistan, dna.

Kassam, Tazim, *Songs of Wisdom and Circles of Dance, An Anthology of Hymns by the Satpanth Isma'ili Muslim Saint Pīr Shams*, New York: Sunny Press, 1996.

Khaki, Khoja, *Gupt Panth kā Shajara*, Bombay: author, dna.

Khan, Dominique-Sila, *Conversions and Shifting Identities: Ramdev Pīr and the Ismailis of Rajasthan*, New Delhi: Manohar, 1997.

———, 'The coming of Niklank Avatar: 'A messianic theme in some sectarian Traditions of North-Western India', *Journal of Indian Philosophy*, Netherlands: Kluwer Academic Publisher, 1997, pp. 401-26.

Masselos, J.C., 'The Khojas of Bombay: the defining of formal membership critieria during the nineteenth century', in *Caste and Social Stratification among Muslims in India*, edited by Imtiaz Ahmad, New Delhi: Manohar, 1978, pp. 97-116.

Mohamed, Sultanali, *Heroes of Surat*, Kenya: Shia Imāmi Ismailia Association for Kisumu, 1968.

Mujtaba, Ali, *The Origins of the Khojas and their religious life today*, Bonn: Ludwig Rohrscheid, 1936.

Nanjiani, Sachedina, *Khojā vratānt*, Ahmedabad: Samasher Press, 1892.

Nehru, Jawaharlal, 'His Highness the Aga Khan', *Modern Review*, Calcutta, Nov. 1935, pp. 505-6.

Newspaper, *Times of India*, Bombay, 1862-8.

Nizami, Hasan, *Fatimī da'wat-e islām*, Delhi: author, 1925 (2nd edn.).

Oddie, Geoffrey, *Religion in South Asia: Religious Conversion and Revival Movements in South Asia in Medieval and Modern Times*, New Delhi: Manohar, 1977.

Perry, Erskine, *Cases illustrative of Oriental Life and the Application of English Law to India*, London, 1853.

Pindi Das, *Āghākhāni izam ke hathkande*, Rawalpindi: Lala Dhanpat Rae, 1926 (2nd edn.).

Rahimtoola, Jaffer, *Khojā komno itihās*, Bombay: author, 1905.

Rattansi, Diamond, 'Islamization and the Khojah Ismaili Community of Pakistan', Montreal: McGill University Ph.D. dissertation (unpublished), 1987.

Roohkash, Noormuhammad, *Momin komno itihās*, Bombay: author, 1936.

Sadiq Ali, *A short sketch of Musulman Races found in Sind, Baluchistan and Afghanistan*, Karachi: Commissioner's Press, 1901.

Shackle, C. and Z. Moir, *Ismaili Hymns from South Asia — An Introduction to the Ginans*, London: SOAS University of London, 1992.

Schimmel, Annemarie, *Islam in the Indian subcontinent*, Leiden: E.J. Brill, 1980.

Vafa, Ghulam Ali, *al-Shams yāni nūr-i imāmat*, Multan: Sultan Bakhash, 1924.

Varsi, Salim, *Izhār-e hakīkat*, Bombay: Khojā sindhī chapakhānā, 1921.

Varteji, Ebrahim, *Āfatāb-e hakīkat*, Bombay: Ismāili sāhitia utejak mandal, dna.

———, *Āraya prakāshnī uḍhatai*, Bombay: Ismāili sāhitia utejak mandal, dna.

———, *Āraya samāji panḍitonun pokar*, Bombay: Ismāili sāhitia utejak mandal, dna.

———, *Duānā dushamanne zaṭako*, Bombay: Ismāili sāhitia utejak mandal, dna.

———, *Hājar imāmani hidāyat*, Bombay: Ismāili sāhitia utejak mandal, 1917.

———, *Ismaīlī cābuk*, Bombay: Ismāili sāhitia utejak mandal, 1913.

———, *Kābānun ṭhekānen āvelun bhejun*, Bombay: Ismāili sāhitia utejak mandal, dna.

———, *Khudāi kitabani samāntā*, Bombay: Ismāili sāhitia utejak mandal, 1919.

———, *Vedik islām*, Bombay: Khoja Sindhi Press, 1921.

A voice from India: Being an appeal to the British Legislature by a Khojah, 1864, London.

PART IV

Social Values and Modes of Devotion in Bengal

Textual Confrontations with Female Transgression in the Behulā Legend

MANDAKRANTA BOSE

Spirituality is often a process played out in the arena of social action. While the encounter with the concept of energy known as Śakti takes profoundly metaphysical turns in the sacred texts of Hinduism, popular culture seeks to understand it in terms of social relationships and conduct. A striking example of this grounding of the supranormal in social experience is the maṅgala-kāvya that tells the story of Manasā, the goddess of snakes, and Behulā, a woman of exemplary wifely virtue. The prevalence of the literary genre known as the maṅgala-kāvyas is one of the most distinctive signs of the intersection of popular culture and folk spirituality in early Bengali society. Maṅgala-kāvyas are narratives of the boons that worshippers receive from gods and goddesses to whom they prove their devotion. Ironically for tales purported to celebrate the beneficence of divine beings, the stories are intimidating in their portrayal of deities who are as overwhelming in their gifts when placated as in their vengefulness when displeased. Reward and punishment are the two poles between which the perception of the spirit world grows in these tales. As discourses for the masses, the formulations of these perceptions are not arguments of abstract reasoning but models of concrete, worldly action. Grounded as they are in felt experience, it is hardly surprising that these perceptions should be organized into a literary format and their rhetoric moulded in terms of human interactions on social and emotional levels. This makes the genre particularly interesting when we see the homage the kāvyas pay to female deities as well as to mortal women, because this emphasis makes these stories pre-eminently women's narratives. While this aspect of the genre has been generally recognized,[1] the complexity of its representation of the feminine remains to be thoroughly explored so that we may find a key to the understanding of power, status and conduct, to questionings of the idea of faith and justice, and to the conceptualization of the unknown

[1] Bhudeb Chaudhuri, *Bāṅglā Sāhityera Itikathā*, vol. 1, Calcutta: Dey's Publishing, 1978.

in the world of the kāvyas. In popular Hinduism, these tales serve as instruments to explore the mysterious power of *śakti*, conceived at once as the autonomous devī and as the convention-bound woman.

Within the genre, the earliest text is the *Manasā-Maṅgala*, which enjoyed wide popularity for centuries from the 13th till the 18th. In the present century it has survived in a form that is significantly truncated but still capable of drawing large audiences. Especially in the Birbhum district of West Bengal, the tale continues as a dramatic performance consisting of songs, dances and play-acting presented by rural performers on the fifth day of the first quarter of the moon in the Bengali month of Bhādra to mark the ritual worship of Manasā, the goddess of snakes.[2] While the ritual requires the recitation of the entire life story of the goddess, including her origin, her struggle for recognition in the society of gods and the establishment of her rite in human society, the dramatic performances focus almost exclusively upon only one part of the long tale. That part is the trial of Behulā, the virtuous wife who wins back the life of her husband, who was killed on Manasā's command in order to force his father to submit to Manasā. This narrowing of the tale has thus placed the suffering and struggling woman in its centre, a familiar figure, and has removed the goddess into the dark zone of the mysterious doings of gods and goddesses. This, then, is the most recent turn the tale has taken in its long history of transmission, through which it has appeared in many versions.[3] Despite the multiplicity of renderings, the story has not changed substantially in its main constituent events, including the shortened version of present times. Rather, the alterations reflect the differing sympathies of different story-tellers. In this essay I shall examine the principal older versions of the story from different regions and by a number of narrators, focusing on the particular narrative of Behulā rather than on the entire kāvya.

The plot of *Manasā-Maṅgala*, the tale of Manasā, the deity of snakes and daughter of Śiva, is a contest narrative centring on the efforts of Manasā to claim a place for herself in the pantheon of deities worshipped in the human world and the refusal of the everyman figure Cānd to accept her. The crucial moment of the conflict is reached when in her attempt to intimidate Cānd, Manasā has his youngest son Lakhindar killed by one of her snakes on the night of his wedding to Behulā. This tragic climax is none

[2] Barunkumar Chakrabarty (ed.), *Baṅgīya Lokasaṁskṛtikośa*, Calcutta: Aparna Book Distributors, 1995, pp. 292-3.

[3] A succinct and complete account of the versions of the story is given by W.L. Smith, *The One-eyed Goddess*, Stockholm: Almqvist & Wiksell, 1980.

the less reversed by the resolute action of Behulā who sets out with her husband's corpse to win back his life and after overcoming many perils she succeeds in doing so by obtaining Manasā's servant Neto's aid in pleasing the gods and appeasing Manasā. Her achievement also brings closure to the larger story of Manasā because Manasā relents only when Behulā promises and secures Cānd's capitulation and conversion. In many versions the real closure occurs in the wider framework of divine affairs because the Behulā episode turns out to be the penance required for re-entry into heaven by Behulā and Lakhindar who are actually the semi-divine beings Ūṣā and Aniruddha consigned to earthly existence under Indra's curse. On this broad outline of events different narrators have plotted twists and turns of the story according to the different emphases they have placed. But before we begin to look at their manipulations we must note that at this point of the story the *Manasā-Maṅgala* has changed direction decisively. What had started as an instructive chronicle of Manasā has now become a celebration of Behulā, equally didactic but aimed at a different objective. We must also note that she overcomes all difficulties because her virtues stand up to any challenge. Thereby the tale undergoes a radical change from a contest narrative to a trial narrative. Thus, the whole Behulā episode is framed as a test of character, constructed as a series of moral challenges to which Behulā is subjected by the storytellers. Particularly interesting are those versions in which she is revealed to be a denizen of heaven itself, because this adds a whole new layer to her tasks of proving herself. Her tests as Behulā qualify her for fame on earth; but gaining fame on earth is in fact the higher test she must pass to be re-admitted to heaven.

In her journey of six months on a raft with her husband's corpse Behulā travels with faith, determination and conviction that she will bring back her husband to life. She confronts many obstacles which not only include animals who are eager to devour the decomposing body of her husband but there are also men eager to enjoy her body. Her achievements are phenomenal. In her journey she succeeds in every task, bringing back her husband and her brothers-in-law to life as well as restoring the entire wealth of her father-in-law. Finally, she succeeds in establishing the pūjā of Manasā on earth by converting her father-in-law to the Manasā cult. With this kind of success one hopes she will have nothing but praise when she returns home and will live happily ever after. Surprisingly, not only does this not happen, but she actually faces blame for her bold transgression of the code of her social world. It is obvious that the conflict between the demands of a fixed social code and those of a crisis constitutes a problem for the storyteller if she is to be held up as a role model. Why, then, tell the story this way? Why does Behulā have to face not one but two sets of tests? I shall argue that this is a necessary narrative strategy for the narrators to rationalize the conflict between the demands of a fixed social code and those of a crisis.

The tests Behulā faces are numerous and varied. They are physical, moral and social, and are calculated to build up her persona as a particular ethical model. Even a brief and random review of the textual tradition will show by the ubiquitousness of ordeals how essential they are to the story.

In a western version of the story, by Bişṇu Pāl, Behulā is required to undergo a series of ordeals specifically to prove her chastity after her return from heaven to earth, which she does in Campaka. Another western poet, Bipradāsa, takes this even farther by making the same demand originate with Indra after Behulā has returned to heaven, having already proved her purity on earth.

Eastern poets also demand Behulā to submit to ordeals for the same reason. In the versions by Nārāyaṇadeva, Bamśīdāsa, Sukanāni and Rādhānāth Roy Choudhury, Behulā is commanded by the merchants of her community to go through a series of ordeals after her six-month long trip. She does so and survives them all. A striking twist occurs in the better known and fuller narrative by Bijay Gupta, who spares Behulā from submitting to the ordeals the merchants demand and leaves with Manasā for heaven. In a slight shift, a version from Bihar shows Behulā subjected to ordeals by her own brothers on her return to Campaka.

This insistence on putting Behulā on trial is such a standard element of the Behulā plot that it suggests a general agreement as to the fragility of a woman's chastity, particularly when it is placed against the larger backdrop of the ordeals required of Sītā. But we must not forget that in Behulā's case, the ordeals occur in two parts: the hazards she faces in her task of reviving her husband comprise the first level of her ordeals; the tests of her chastity comprise the second. The point made by the storytellers in adding this second level of tests is that no achievement by a woman is as valuable a moral commodity as her chastity. What these trials serve to establish is that Behulā is the ideal wife because not only does she dedicate herself to her husband's well-being but retains her honour in the process. It is worth noting that within the Bengali cultural domain, of all models of womanly virtue in the Hindu tradition, Behulā has received the strongest and most sustained attention. She represents the ideal of Indian womanhood as an exemplar of wifely devotion who is no less important than either Sita or Savitri of the pan-Indian Hindu tradition. Again, it is important to note that all these women are celebrated because they pass tests of wifely devotion and honour.

But these tests can be of the widest variety. The qualities of the perfect wife are not limited to absolute devotion and chastity but include physical attributes as well, be it beauty or plain physical stamina. Behulā gets high marks on both. First of all, she can be inducted into the story only because she is physically attractive and possesses high qualifications for a desirable bride, including her skill as a dancer, not a conventional virtue but one that proves to be the key to her success in the assembly of gods. The physical demands made upon her as she floats down the river guarding her husband's rotting corpse are obvious but they are made the more hazardous by the sheer physical threats represented by the beasts of water and land who may tear her to pieces and are prevented only by her courageous presence.

These physical hazards merge neatly into others related to Behulā's body that prove to be moral tests. Like the beasts hungering after her flesh, men lusting after her body attempt to coerce or entrap her but are similarly repulsed. The gravity of this particular type of hazard is made plain from the moment she sets out to regain her husband's life. Indeed, the threat to her virtue is so crucial to the ideology behind the story that it is expressed universally in the tales. In Tantrabibhuti's *Manasā Purāṇ* Behulā's mother-in-law shows a touching concern for the young woman's safety as she sets out on her journey, thinking of the ordeals she will face from the swarming 'susu matsya ghariāla' in the river (Tantra 519). But the mother-in-law is also worried about the loss of Behulā's honour and, through her, the loss of the family's status, lamenting: 'kibā jāti kula majaile' (she has destroyed her caste and her family).

Similarly, the Oriya poet Dvārikādāsa has the mother-in-law worried about the threat to Behulā's virtue:

kulera nandinī tumi kula badhū nārī
anāthinī haiyā kothā yābe ekeśvarī. . .

You are the daughter of a good family and the daughter-in-law of one
Where are you going all alone without a protector?

(Dvārika 84)

Here Sanakā is charging Behulā with behaviour improper to a woman of good breeding, taking it for granted that her unchaperoned journey will irrecoverably stain her virtue. Her emphasis is on the rules of 'kula' which Behulā flouts as she assumes the ways of an 'ekesvari', that is, her own mistress. Sanakā's misgivings also parallel Manu's view, deeply ingrained in Hindu society, that a woman can never win independence: 'na strī svātantramarhati' (Manu IX, 3). To Sanakā, not only is female independence unthinkable, it is also morally and socially ruinous. The potential pollution here is twofold: first, Behulā's bodily purity is placed in doubt because her unprotected state simply invites violation; secondly, her 'ekesvari' persona transgresses the moral boundaries set for a 'kulabadhu' by custom.

Nor is this the only account concerned with Behulā's sexual purity. Bisṇu Pāl and the more talented Bijay Gupta and Ketakādās all deal with the theme. In Bisṇu Pāl's somewhat crude treatment of the story, the revived Lakhīndar does not express his gratitude to her but harsh censure:

natini haina bāpāra jāta majāili . . .
debasabhāya uluṅgu kāpara kene para

By becoming a dancer you have corrupted your father's caste . . .
Why did you wear revealing clothes in the assembly of gods?

(Bisṇu 123)

Of all the chroniclers of Behulā, Ketakādāsa Kṣemananda is the most sympathetic. But even he does not dare to bring back Behulā and Lakhīndar to place them in their earlier station after their return from heaven. Although he portrays Behulā's innocence, faith and conviction with much tenderness, yet even in his version she has to prove her chastity at every stage. While Ketakādāsa scrupulously avoids any erotic element to taint his description of her beauty and emphasizes her divine origin to stress her virtue, yet he too has to admit the problem of her sexual purity. The sexual trial to which Ketakādāsa subjects her is the demand of a doctor who promises to revive Lakhīndar if Behulā will yield to him for three days and three nights.

The question of sexual purity is ever-present. In Bijay Gupta's lengthy account of Behulā's reception when she returns victorious with her husband brought back from the dead, the key element is the general suspicion about her chastity. Her husband, whom one might expect to be thankful for his wife's courage and initiative, indulges in a long monologue about women's nature, stressing their frailty and the impossibility of a woman on her own maintaining her chastity:

lakhāi bale strī jati kibā karma bujhe
. . . . .
svatantara haile tāra nānā doṣa theke
satī pativratā hauka dharmete tatpara
svatantara haile narī phale athāntara

Lakhai says, what do women know of right action
. . . . .
On their own they fall into many improprieties

Even if she is devoted to her husband and firm in *dharma*,
When a woman becomes independent, only disaster follows.
(Bijay II 240)

Lakhīndar's discontent is noteworthy because it is directed not merely at his wife but at the female sex itself. His repeated indictment of 'svatantara' equates independence with waywardness. Clearly, in his view Behulā has been guilty of unwomanly behaviour. If submissivness is the true definition of womanly virtue, then Behulā is guilty indeed because throughout the story she acts in a manner irreconcilable with submissive modesty. Not only in taking on her grim task alone, but in achieving success in it she transgresses her gender role. She wins Śiva's support against Manasā not through devotion but by dancing alluringly and by her foresight in producing unanswerable evidence of Manasā's guilt. Neither ability falls within the bounds of conventional feminine virtues. Dancing in particular is suspect. Behulā's skill in the art is noted from her childhood — indeed she is known as nācni, a dancer. If we are to take into account the divine origin ascribed to her, then she is Ūṣā the divine dancer who is responsible for introducing dance to women of earth.[4] But in her world this is not an art of repute, being associated with courtesans. As a devoted wife (pativratā, a much valued concept) Behulā is not expected to dance for the pleasure of men and even though her audience is divine, her honour is seriously compromised. Her use of her dancing ability underscores the fact that her success does not come through the conventional woman's method of supplication. It is interesting that her parallel figure in Hindu mythology, Sāvitrī also succeeds in regaining her husband's life not through supplication but by outwitting Yama.

Whatever turns the portrayal of Behulā may take in its numerous versions, she remains a problem as both a saviour figure and a threat to established social order. Her boldness, her independent spirit and her readiness to venture her body and mind to the performance of her task are alien to the concept of the virtuous woman. My point here is that in the society that produced the story these are all real concerns and the audience have to resolve the problem of Behulā's paradoxical status. If she is a truly devoted wife, then she must undertake the awesome task of bringing her husband back to life. But if she is a woman worth respecting, she cannot expose herself to the threats to her chastity, even if that threat is merely one of wandering about the world alone, without a male protector. How, then,

[4] Nandīkeśvara's *Abhinaya Darpaṇam*, verses 4-7, edited by M.M. Ghosh, Calcutta: Firma K.L. Mukhopadhyay, 1957.

are we to judge her? This unavoidable question thus tests the audience's moral acumen as well. Several problems have to be confronted. Can a woman be beautiful and not the target of lust? Can a woman be on her own and chaste? Can she be a good woman and transgress the requirements of accepted social behaviour? Can she overstep the essential timidity of her gender and act with unwomanly fortitude and tactics to achieve her end? If she is permitted to do so, would she still be worthy of praise? Each of these questions underlies one or the other of the trials of Behulā, and all are answered by the same affirmation, namely, that whatever a woman does in the service of her husband is virtuous. In other words, in the hierarchy of women's dharma, wifely devotion pre-empts all social custom and dispensation. Thus, these questions at once try the moral perspicacity of the reader/listener and affirm Behulā as a model of absolute virtue. The first of these two functions is perhaps the more important, given the didactic aim of the narrative. Overflowing the bounds of fiction, the act of narration here relocates the imagined problems of Behulā within a historical social reality. How do the readers/listeners learn about morality? Obviously by witnessing Behulā's predicament and her response to it. Behulā's moral profile is the key to the didactic function of the story. The critical question the audience have to resolve is, how can Behulā's actions be moral behaviour on the part of a model wife? Clearly, there must be justification by a higher rationale, and the doubts expressed by people around her are in fact tests set by the storyteller as much for the reader/listener as for Behulā, who shows us by her resolute ignoring of the criticism her understanding of where true virtue lies and how well she attains to it. That higher rationale by which we must absolve Behulā is consistently displayed as the unquestioned necessity for a wife to place her husband's good above every other consideration, social, moral or physical. Not a surprising lesson, it none the less requires argument and demonstration because its affirmation is put into jeopardy by conflicting values governing women's nature and duty. The conflict is in fact an opportunity for the storytellers to exploit the ambiguity because by showing the force of the social code they may validate it for ordinary circumstances and at the same time allow the possibility of transgression by individuals empowered by some higher enabling legislation. It is by taking Behulā through her trials that her chroniclers keep her bound within the code even as they acknowledge her transcendence over it.

What I have tried to argue here is that the narrative variants in Behulā's story are responses to the need for bringing the paradox of a required rebellion within the control of the social code. The differing turns in the story and the moral emphases they imply are strategies to demonstrate that female transgression is in fact female submission to gender roles, whereby the female adventurer can be re-affirmed as the devoted wife. No matter who tells the story or when or with what emphases of sympathy or criticism, all versions of Behulā's tale make their point by viewing the harnessing of female energy as a precondition to personal, social and cosmic stability. One does not have to look too deep to discover in the tale a systemic fear of the feminine, explicit in the devouring possessiveness of Manasā and implicit in the ambiguous heroism of Behulā. Instead of the metaphysical rationalization of the feminine that high culture might effect, the story of Manasā and Behulā assimilates the power of the female within the framework of rules for everyday living.

REFERENCES

Bhattacharya, Ashutosh, *Bāṅglā Maṅgalkāvyera Itihāsa (A History of Medieval Bengali Narrative Poetry)*, Calcutta: A. Mukherjee & Co. Private Ltd., 1968.

Bhattacharya, Ashutosh, *Bāṅglā Sāhityera Itihāsa*, Calcutta: Calcutta Book House, 1950.

Bhattacharya, Hamsa Narayan, *Bāṅglā Maṅgalkāvyera Dhārā*, Calcutta: House of Books, 1970.

Bhattacharya, Tarapada, *Baṅgasāhityera Itihāsa*, Calcutta: S. Gupta Brothers (Private) Ltd., 1962.

Bhattacharya, Yatindramohan (ed.), *Ketakādās's Manasā-Maṅgala*, Calcutta: University of Calcutta, 1949.

Chakrabarty, Barunkumar (ed.), *Baṅgīya Lokasaṁskṛtikośa*, Calcutta: Aparna Book Distributors, 1995.

Chakrabarty, Purnachandra (ed.), *Baṁśīdās's Śrīśrīpadmapurāṇa*, Calcutta: University of Calcutta, 1951.

Chaudhuri, Bhudev, *Bāṅglā Sāhityera Itikathā*, vol. 1, Calcutta: Dey's Publishing, 1978.

Das, Ashutosh and Surendrachandra Bhattacharya (eds.), *Manasāmaṅgala: Jagajjīvana viracita*, Calcutta: Calcutta University, 1984.

Dasgupta, Jayantakumar (ed.), Bijay Gupta's *Padmapurāṇa*, Calcutta: University of Calcutta, 1962.

Ghosh, M.M. (ed.), *Abhinaya Darpaṇam*, Calcutta: Firma K.L. Mukhopadhyay, 1957.

Gupta, Ksetra, *Bāṅglā Sahityer Samagra Itihāsa*, Calcutta: Granthanilaya, 1992.

Jha, Ganganath (ed.), *Manusmṛti*, Delhi: Parimal Publications, 1992.

Kayal, Akshay and Chitra Dev (eds.), *Manasāmaṅgala: Ketakādāsa Kṣemānanda viracita*, Calcutta: Lekhapara, 1978.

Poddar, Arabinda, *Bāṅglā Sāhitya: Saṁkṣipta Itihāsa*, Calcutta: Indiana Publishers, 1962.

Roy Chaudhurī, Rādhānāth, *Padmapurāṇa (Manasā-Maṅgala)*, Calcutta: University of Calcutta, 1975.
Sen, Dinesh Chandra, *Baṅgasāhityera Paricaya or Typical Selections from Old Bengali Literature*, pt. 1, Calcutta: University of Calcutta, 1914.
Sen, Sukumar, *Bāṅglā Sāhityera Itihāsa*, Calcutta: Eastern Publishers, 1940.
———, *History of Bengali Literature*, New Delhi: Sahitya Akademi, 1971.
Sen, Sukumar (ed.), *Bipradāsa's Manasā-Vijaya*, Calcutta: Asiatic Society, 1953.
——— (ed.), *Biṣṇu Pāla's Manasā-Maṅgala*, Calcutta: Asiatic Society, 1968.
Sen, Uma, *Prācīna o Mạdhyayugera Sadharan Manuṣa*, Calcutta: Jijnasa, 1971.
Smith, William, *The One-Eyed Goddess: a study of the Manasāmaṅgala*, Stockholm, Sweden: Alqmvist and Winkell International, 1980.
Tantrabibhuti, *Bāiśa Kabira Manasā Maṅgala*, edited by Ashutosh Bhattacharyya, Calcutta: University of Calcutta, 1962.

The Theology of a Lovers' Quarrel Classical and Contemporary Interpretations of Krishna's Humiliation

DONNA M. WULFF

Several of the episodes in the story of Rādhā's and Krishna's love, as it has been told and enacted for centuries throughout Bengal, contain striking elements of theological as well as social reversal.[1] Among these, perhaps the most perplexing is the story of Rādhā's angry rejection of Krishna. In this well-known episode, called *Khaṇḍitā*, 'The Woman Offended', Rādhā gradually comes to realize that Krishna has just spent the night with her rival, Candrāvalī. Although Rādhā's expressions of anger and hurt are entirely comprehensible in human emotional terms, her reaction is hardly consonant with the behaviour one would expect of a divine consort toward her Lord, or of an Indian woman toward her man, as indicated, for example, in Manu and the other *Dharmaśāstra*s.[2]

In order to understand something of the range of meanings that Rādhā's reproach and humiliation of Krishna have had for Vaiṣṇava devotees, we shall focus on the portrayal of this episode in a form of dramatic musical devotional performance called *padāvalī kīrtan*. We shall examine a portion of a single, fairly representative performance of the episode by the late, eminent performer Nanda Kishor Das, and then consider the differing interpretations of Rādhā's harsh treatment of Krishna by the sixteenth-century theologian Rūpa Gosvāmī in his Sanskrit treatises, by Nanda Kishor in the course of his performance, and by two other contemporary *kīrtan* singers. Our concern will be to identify certain fundamental meanings, in both theological and social terms, of a story in which Rādhā —

[1] This article has benefited from the close reading and insightful suggestions of two friends and colleagues, Timothy Cahill and Rupert Snell.

[2] In Bengal, Rādhā is generally considered to be Krishna's lover rather than his wife; see note 23, below. For a text setting forth the traditional ideal for a married woman, see Julia Leslie, *The Perfect Wife: The Orthodox Hindu Woman according to the Stridharmapaddhati of Tryambakayajvan*, Delhi: Oxford University Press, 1989.

traditionally said to be a cowherd woman but also revered as a goddess—thoroughly dresses down and humiliates her lover, the Lord of the universe. What attitudes toward deity and toward gender do interpretations of this episode reveal?

It is not my intention to compare these interpretations wholesale, as if they were on a par with one another, but rather merely to note points of continuity as well as certain shifts in the interpretation given to Rādhā's audacious treatment of Krishna. As we shall see, the continuities are greater than one might expect, given the enormous disparities in time period, language, and degree of learning.

The relation between Rādhā and Krishna is discussed in the Sanskrit works of Rūpa and the other learned disciples of Caitanya, known collectively as the six gosvāmīs, but by far the largest body of material that we have about their love is in the vernacular languages of north India. Especially significant are the medieval song lyrics (*padas*) composed on the Rādhā-Krishna theme in a medieval form of Hindi known as Braj Bhāṣā, in medieval Bengali, and in an artificial hybrid language that combines these two, Brajabuli.[3] Although most of these songs date from the fourteenth through the seventeenth centuries, those in Bengali and Brajabuli in particular continue to be sung today, especially in West Bengal, in a complex but widespread form of devotional performance. Because its structuring elements are the lyrical songs known as *padas*, this musical form is called *padāvalī kīrtan*. Its two broad themes are the love of Rādhā and Krishna and the life of the ecstatic mystic Caitanya. Episodes (*pālā*s[4]) depicting the first of these themes show a somewhat different and far more widely disseminated portrait of Rādhā than the one presented in the Sanskrit writings of Rūpa and the other gosvāmīs.[5]

[3] In Hindi, Braj Bhāṣā literally means the language of the Braj region; Brajabuli means the same thing in Bengali. However, whereas Braj Bhāṣā was spoken over a wide area of present-day Uttar Pradesh, Brajabuli was solely a poetic language, never a vernacular.

[4] The term *pālā*, literally, 'turn', refers to the *kīrtan* performance, the three-to-four-hour exposition and elaboration of a given theme. However, it also refers to the episode or 'play' itself, a generally-accepted story line independent of any given rendering. The fact that the literal meaning of *pālā* is 'turn' suggests that these episodes were conceived as a cycle, to be performed on successive days or nights. The term 'play' is the closest English equivalent, but it is somewhat misleading, for these are dramatic musical renderings with elements of dance, not fully staged plays.

[5] In 1980, there were an estimated 250 *kīrtan* troupes in West Bengal alone. The number today would be significantly lower.

The analysis of a single episode of *padāvalī kīrtan* carries us to the very heart of Rādhā-Krishna devotion in Bengal. The term *khaṇḍitā*, like the other Sanskrit terms designating the different aspects of Rādhā in her relation to Krishna, and the various phases of their love, were adapted by Rūpa Gosvāmī from the classical aesthetic theory worked out by philosophers of aesthetics such as Abhinavagupta (tenth-eleventh centuries) and Mammaṭa (eleventh-twelfth centuries). These same terms were used by the anthologists of the medieval Bengali and Brajabuli poetry collectively termed Vaiṣṇava *padāvalī* as headings for classifying the individual poems of this vast corpus. Terms such as *khaṇḍitā* are also used by *kīrtan* singers and their audiences as designations for the episodes they perform. These shared categories and the collection of episodes they designate presuppose the existence of a common reservoir of stories that has been drawn on through the centuries by poets and performers alike.

Although we have no direct access to this reservoir, the substantial agreement on the broad lines of each story among *kīrtanīyā*s of different regions and lineages, the essential convergence of the Vaiṣṇava *padāvalī* on each theme, and the existence of an early Bengali text, the *Śrīkṛṣṇakīrtan*, containing a number of the episodes represented in *kīrtan* and commented upon by the *padāvalī*, provide evidence for the existence of such a narrative source. The portrayal of a given episode by a widely respected traditional performer, such as Nanda Kishor Das, may thus approximate to the form in which the story has been handed down through the last several centuries. The theological interpretations of Rūpa and the comments of the contemporary *kīrtan* singers I have interviewed take this basic story as their starting point. Although Nanda Kishor's rendering of the story in performance is itself an interpretation, I shall therefore treat it as more nearly primary than the other interpretations we shall consider.

A brief look at the main ingredients of a *kīrtan* performance will give us a context for understanding the episode in question. A *kīrtan* troupe typically consists of a lead singer, termed a *kīrtanīyā*, who may be either male or female, several supporting singers, who are usually of the same sex as the lead singer, and two or sometimes three male drummers, who play on both ends of elongated, two-headed drums[6] suspended from straps around their necks. In a performance, the lead singer and his or her troupe present a kind of musical drama — containing elements of dance — that centres on a single devotional episode. For some three or four hours, the

[6] These drums, called *khol* (or, respectfully, *śrīkhol*), are shaped much like the *mṛdaṅgam* of the Karnatak music of south India.

lead singer spins out a narrative to the nearly constant rhythmic background of drums and small brass hand cymbals, punctuating the story at intervals with songs based on the lyrical medieval poems called *padāvalī*. The performance area, often in the centre of an audience of devotees who sit on the floor in a circular arrangement, is bare of scenery, and the only props used are the lead singer's shawl, sometimes put over the head to resemble a sari, and perhaps the garland of flowers with which a lead singer is often honoured.

Operating within these spare means, however, a skilled singer can create a powerful drama through effective timing, the expressive power of such musical means as variation in tempo and dynamic level, the subtle or expansive use of gesture, and the visual and kinesthetic reinforcement of aurally perceived rhythms through dance. It is mainly the lead singer who tells and enacts the story, but the supporting singers also use gesture as they echo the lines of the lead performer in antiphonal fashion. The drummers' highly trained fingers beat out intricate patterns on the two leather heads of their slender drums,[7] and the drummers augment these at intervals by sharply articulated vocal sounds. These include the elaborate mnemonic patterns (*bol*s) that imitate the sounds of the different drum strokes, as well as such exclamations as '*hāiyā*' — sounds apparently drawn from boatmen's songs. In addition to their strong hand and arm movements and the dramatic swings of their heads, the drummers often dance vigorously with the lead singer during the songs, and the supporting singers, most of whom keep time with hand cymbals, sometimes join in the dance as well.

Kīrtan performers portray Rādhā in a web of emotional relationships in which her love for Krishna unfolds. The successive phases of their love provide the themes of some of the most popular episodes sung and enacted in *kīrtan*. These include episodes in which the two are united, as well as those portraying different forms of separation. Even though Rādhā and Krishna are physically together for much of the time during the episodes of Rādhā's jealous anger, these episodes, portraying emotional distance, are classified as modes of separation.[8]

[7] These rhythmic patterns equal in complexity those of the major classical traditions of north and south India.

[8] Rūpa in his *Ujjvalanīlamaṇi* discusses four varieties of love-in-separation (*vipralambha śṛṅgāra*), infatuation (*pūrvarāga*), love before first full union; pique (*māna*), Rādhā's ambivalent feelings of hurt, anger, jealousy and yearning that follow her discovery of Krishna's betrayal; bewilderment (*premavaicittya*), Rādhā's temporary delusion, brought on by the singular intensity of her love; and lastly,

I have chosen an excerpt from the transcription of a performance of *Khaṇḍitā* given in 1980 by Nanda Kishor Das, the most famous male *kīrtanīyā* of his generation, who continued to perform regularly until 1990, when he was well into his seventies. The theme of the story is a familiar one in Bengal. It takes place in the grove in which Rādhā and her friends have been waiting all night for Krishna, who had earlier indicated to Rādhā that he would meet her that evening. Instead, he spends the night with Rādhā's chief rival, Candrāvalī. At dawn, when Candrāvalī, exhausted from their lovemaking, has fallen asleep, Krishna remembers his appointment with Rādhā and sets out in search of her. He arrives at her grove with his body covered with the signs of the night's enjoyment. As Rādhā comments to her friends on each of these telltale signs in turn, she gradually constructs for the devotee a mental icon — a *mūrti*[9] — of Krishna. It is, however, a highly ambiguous image, for however beautiful the marks look on Krishna's body, each one is an eloquent reminder to Rādhā of his betrayal.

In addition to the gradual revelation of Krishna's nature as a universal — and thus inconstant — lover, this section of the performance contains reflections by Krishna, and more especially by Rādhā, on their feelings toward one another. The dialogue also communicates certain attitudes and values of the Vaiṣṇava community, such as the view that bhakti renders stringent ascetic practices unnecessary.

Rādhā's utterances throughout the section are laced with irony and sarcasm. At points she employs words with double meanings: thus she seems to say of the red nail-marks on Krishna's chest that he deserves such

---

abandonment (*pravāsa*), the final, permanent separation brought about by Krishna's departure for Mathura. See my *Drama as a Mode of Religious Realization: The Vidagdhamādhava of Rūpa Gosvāmī*, Chico, Calif.: Scholars Press, 1984, pp. 150-3. This and three of the preceding paragraphs are slightly modified from my 'Rādhā: Consort and Conqueror of Krishna', in John S. Hawley and Donna M. Wulff (eds.), *Devī: Goddesses of India*, Berkeley, Calif.: University of California Press, 1996, pp. 109-34.

[9] The term *mūrti* refers to the form — often but by no means always anthropomorphic — in which a deity is worshipped. The marks to which Rādhā refers, spanning Krishna's entire body from his forehead to his ankles, form a composite image for the devotee to contemplate. This dramatic device brings to mind the *nakh-śikh* convention of Hindi poetry (or, as here, its reverse: *śikh-nakh*), in which the poet describes the beloved woman's beauty, literally from her toenails to the crest of her hair (or, in the case of *śikh-nakh*, vice versa). The significance of the gender reversal is also worth pondering.

adornment (*shājā*) because he is her lover, but what she is saying at a deeper level is that he deserves such *punishment* (also *shājā*) because he is *her* lover (and he was unfaithful to her). She later ironically calls Krishna a virtuous lover, at which point the seemingly surprised *kīrtanīyā* breaks into the dialogue that he is reporting to remark that this is no laughing matter. Such irony proves to be a repeated source of amusement for the devotees in the audience. At the same time, however, the genuineness of her pain, clearly born of deep love, leads these same devotees to weep through much of the profoundly moving performance.

In the section that I give below of my translation of the transcription of one of Nanda Kishor Das' performances of this episode, there are numerous repetitions, chiefly of lines in the songs. I have eliminated almost all these repetitions, and I have omitted a long passage in which Rādhā accuses Krishna of making her lose face in Brindavan. Otherwise, what follows is a fairly literal rendering of the transcription of the portion of the performance in which Rādhā comments, feature by feature, on Krishna's appearance. The characters or voices in order of appearance are as follows:

R	Rādhā, Rādhārāṇī ('Queen Rādhā')
NK	Nanda Kishor, the lead singer, who functions as narrator and commentator
K	Krishna, also called Govinda and Madan Mohan[10]
L	Lalitā, Rādhā's girl friend

R: (to Krishna, after she has recognized him)
If you have taken pity on this unfortunate woman, then why are you looking the other way? Turn around. Let me see that face for the last time in this life.[11] Turn this way with that face of yours smeared with vermilion powder and black eye shadow. Turn around.

NK: There, she's saying, 'smeared with vermilion powder and black eye shadow'. She really did say it. My Govinda felt terribly ashamed. And what did he do? Govinda is saying to himself,

K: What did I do? I am ruined. If I had realized that I had black eye shadow and vermilion powder smeared all over my face, I would have wiped them off before I came. What have I done? What should I do now?

R: O Lord of my life, don't be frightened. Turn your face this way. Are you

[10] Govinda, 'cowherd', is a common epithet of Krishna from the Harivaṃśa onward; Madan Mohan, literally, 'the enchanter of Kāmadeva (god of love)', is also fairly common.

[11] Rādhā is indicating that her death is imminent, due to the extremity of her suffering at Krishna's betrayal.

ashamed? Don't worry. Don't you know you can come to me any way you please, just as you have done now? You can also come in some other getup.[12] There's no harm in that. But since you are standing with your face turned away from me, I have to tell you this: turn your face this way. If I see your face, will it be diminished? Turn around.

Ah, the beauty of black eye shadow enhances your (dark) beauty![13]

Oh, yuck, red and black makeup all smushed together!

My lover's face is all smeared with red and black makeup!

The vermilion mark on your forehead would be the envy of ascetics.[14]

Alas, Lord of my life, what is this? Your body is covered with the bites of sharp nails. Who has made nail scratches on your breast? This adornment/punishment is what you deserve, because you are my lover. Friends, say, do we know this? We do. Do we know how to adorn him like this/arrange such a punishment? The hand shakes when applying sandal paste to the soft bosom.[15] The body is softer than a lotus. The mark of her bracelet is on your forehead and heart.

Lord of my life, is that a sari that you are wearing? A blue silk sari.[16] Is this your silk sari? Is it because we've never seen it that you've come to show us? How nice that you've come to show us! Friends, take a good look. By my lover's grace I got to see a silk sari. Who else has a lover with such virtues?

NK: I say, why did she call him a virtuous lover?[17] It's no laughing matter!

R: (as if she is responding to Nanda Kishor) Don't laugh, friends; this is no laughing matter. Do you know why I called him my virtuous lover? He who is someone's well-wisher and friend, when he finds something remarkable, secretly brings it and shows it: 'I love you so much. See what a beautiful thing I've brought. An amazing thing.' But suppose we find an expensive

[12] Rādhā here refers to Krishna's numerous disguises, which he assumes in order to deceive her in-laws so that he can meet her.

[13] This assertion constitutes a triple paradox. First, as God, Krishna's beauty is unsurpassable. Second, what is here said to enhance it is a (messy) smear of eye shadow. Finally, Krishna is already black; the black eye shadow should thus be indistinguishable from his black skin.

[14] The first and last of these four statements, which contain classical figures of speech, are in a highly Sanskritized form of Bengali, whereas the middle two, in which Rādhā forcefully indicates her displeasure, are in a village dialect.

[15] This is a hint that Krishna is soft-hearted; however, it is clearly ironic in the present context, because he was hard-hearted toward Rādhā.

[16] Rādhā is referring to Candrāvalī's sari, which Krishna has absent-mindedly put on as a loincloth.

[17] The term *guṇ* (Sanskrit, *guṇa*) means virtue or (usually good) quality. *Guṇī* refers to a person who possesses virtues or good qualities.

thing, say, a sari. Suppose the cloth is checked or patterned. O Lord of my life, I could not do that. With my fate, such saris don't come my way. Tell me—I'm just a cowherd's daughter — where would I find one? I am poor. Well, you (after all) are my love.

Well, where'd you get it? Is it your chief queen's silk sari?[18]

NK: Govinda is now hiding. (to Krishna) Don't hide.

R: Not just the sari — the way the pleats are folded. Oh, take a look at how my lover has worn a sari.

NK: Lalitā says, 'Now Rādhā, what's there to see in a sari?'

R: Can't you see? This one, who has spent his whole life wearing a simple loincloth, is now sporting pleats!

Oh, what's this? Whose lover were you last night?

NK: This is what she said. Much has been said to Govinda.

R: She dressed you as she pleased. Madan Mohan's neck is covered with garlands.

NK: Rādhā looks at his body carefully, to see how he's been decorated.

R: She's made scratches. I can see that much. And I can see a light shining. Oh, friends, what is this light coming from my lover's chest?

NK: They say, 'What shall we see?'

R: That red light shining.

L: Rādhāraṇī, a light is shining, it's true. What's the glow from? No, ask him.

R: O Lord of my life, what's that red light coming from? Let me see — move, move. Oh, it's bright red lac.[19] How did lac get on your breast? Tell me — I can't accept this. It could be the mark of lac-dye powder. Oh, no, no, it's not that lac. This is a bright line of lac. The outline of feet in lac. The lac from someone's feet has rubbed off on his breast. O Madan Mohan, how did that mark get on your breast? Come now, some people like to make marks on their bodies.

NK: Do you understand? Everyone paints a mark on the forehead, and some make the mark of feet on their bodies, in twelve places. They make a *tilak*.[20] And everyone makes the sign of feet. I think he's put on those foot-marks.

R: (once again as if she is responding to Nanda Kishor) But the foot-mark is not like a *tilak*. It's the lac used for feet that has left its mark on your breast. The question is, how did the lac from someone's feet get on your breast? This is strange. Let me explain. When the marks of her feet were made on your breast, did you embrace them voluntarily or did she put them there forcefully? 'Please, please, put your two feet on my heart, let me cool this

[18] Rādhā here puns on the obscurely related terms *pāṭ* (silk) and *pāṭrāṇī* (chief queen); again, she speaks in two sharply contrasting idioms.

[19] Lac is a red resinous substance applied to the feet of women especially for weddings and other auspicious occasions.

[20] A *tilak* is a sectarian mark usually applied to the forehead, but sometimes to other parts of the body as well.

burning breast' — did you say this as you pressed her two feet to your heart? Madan Mohan, you are the ocean of love, the crown-jewel of lovers. Did you take onto your breast the impression of the feet of the one for whom your body burned, and perhaps find peace? Or did she put her feet there forcefully? Tell me, tell me.

NK: And can Govinda say anything now? It happened. What he'd done came back to him fourfold. No, how could it be just fourfold? It returned to him a hundredfold.

R: Did you draw her feet to your heart or has she put them there? You don't have to say — let me explain. I think she put them on your breast. It seems she struck you with her feet after having triumphed over you.

NK: Saying these things in front of the *gopīs* of Brindavan — such offensive words!

R: She must have struck you with her feet after conquering you in the battle of lovemaking. That's why you have the marks of her feet on your breast.

NK: Madan Mohan realized, 'I've been severely punished. They said, "Bright lac looks attractive on your chest".' He is quiet. What's the matter? Has he found the words sweet? Well, let him be — he doesn't have to answer.

THE THEOLOGY OF THE OFFENDED GODDESS/WOMAN

The preceding excerpt illustrates a striking aspect of *kīrtan* performances: the subtle, varied way in which the voices relate to one another, creating a richly textured whole. These voices intertwine and interact in certain ways that one would expect, as well as in some ways that are initially surprising. In addition to conversations that take place among the characters of the story, the characters hear and respond to the performers and even to the medieval poets who wrote the lyrics of the songs being sung, and the performers in turn speak to the characters. Similarly, the lead singer addresses questions to the devotees present, drawing them as well into the story's complex fabric. There is likewise a certain blurring of distinctions among the characters, especially between Rādhā and the other *gopīs*, who often give voice to her inner conflict. The performance also incorporates the words of different poets as well as several different languages (Sanskrit, Brajabuli, and medieval and modern Bengali, the modern Bengali largely quite colloquial). Finally, *kīrtanīyās* especially of previous generations have responded — often extemporaneously — to the poets' words, interpolating lines called *ākhar*[21] according to certain patterns among the lines

[21] See my 'Internal Interpretation: The *Ākhar* Lines in Performances of *Padāvalī Kīrtan*', in K.I. Koppedrayer (ed.), *Contacts between Cultures*, vol. 2, *South Asia*, Queenston, Ontario: The Edwin Mellen Press, 1992, pp. 317-24. Reprinted in the *Journal of Vaiṣṇava Studies*, vol. 4, no. 4, Fall 1996, pp. 75-86.

of the original poems. The use by present-day *kīrtanīyā*s of *ākhar* lines composed by earlier singers brings these earlier singers' interpretations into the performance as well.

In the light of this complex, multi-layered texture, it is not surprising that interpreters have found different, even opposed meanings in the events represented in Nanda Kishor's rendering of *Khaṇḍitā*. Indeed, my questioning of *kīrtanīyā*s and devotees who listen regularly to *kīrtan* elicited a wide range of responses. In the present section, we shall consider interpretations of Rādhā's defiant posture by the sixteenth-century theologian Rūpa Gosvāmī and by two contemporary *kīrtanīyā*s apart from the episode's performer. Before doing so, we would do well to reflect on certain statements made by Nanda Kishor in the excerpt itself for clues to its meaning for him. What is his attitude toward Rādhā's and her friends' seemingly heartless enumeration of the telltale marks on Krishna's body?

Throughout the episode, Nanda Kishor's treatment of Rādhā and Krishna is remarkably impartial, and at one point elsewhere in the performance he even states explicitly that they are equal. At times, as we have seen, he openly sides with Rādhā and her friends, as when he admonishes Krishna not to hide when Rādhā points out that Krishna is wearing a sari. At others, however, he takes Krishna's part, as when he offers an alternative explanation for the bright red lac footprints on Krishna's chest. Similarly, he expresses sympathy for Krishna at the end of the excerpt, but he never chastises Rādhā and her friends for their relentlessness in revealing the evidence of his lovemaking with Candrāvalī; instead, he expresses the view that Krishna's punishment at their hands is well deserved. The intimacy he feels with both Rādhā and Krishna is underlined by his repeated use of the pronouns 'my' and 'our'[22] before their names, as well as by his use of such affectionate diminutives as Rai (for Rādhā).

Rūpa Gosvāmī, the sixteenth-century disciple of Caitanya who reworked the classical theory of aesthetics into an aesthetic theory of devotion (*bhaktirasa*), dedicated an entire treatise, the *Ujjvalanīlamaṇi*, to the successive phases and diverse aspects of Rādhā's and Krishna's love. Rūpa's relevance to *kīrtan* is twofold. First, as we have already noted, the categories he adapted from the classical theory of aesthetics to refer to the phases and modes of Rādhā's and Krishna's love serve as headings for the anthologies of songs that structure *kīrtan* performances, as well as providing the titles for many of the episodes represented in *kīrtan*. Secondly, Rūpa's

[22] The genitive forms are *āmār* and *āmāder*, yielding phrases such as *āmār Kṛṣṇa* and *āmāder Rādhā*.

Sanskrit treatises are frequently quoted and cited by *kīrtan* singers, even though few if any of these singers know Sanskrit. Two general assertions that Rūpa makes about Rādhā in her relation to Krishna have important bearing on the episode under consideration. The first is the claim — reiterated by his influential nephew Jīva — that Rādhā is the blissful energy (*hlādinī śakti*) of Krishna. Such an understanding diminishes the scandal of their illicit love (*parakīyā rati*[23]) by interpreting its movements as an oscillation between separation and union within the Godhead.

The second claim about Rādhā emerges in the context of a discussion of her chief rival, Candrāvalī. Rūpa contrasts Candrāvalī's deference and excessive respect (*ādara*) for Krishna with Rādhā's boldness and spontaneity, and he goes on to claim that Krishna strongly prefers Rādhā's love to that of her rival.[24] In the first of his two full-length Sanskrit plays, the *Vidagdhamādhava*, he has Krishna tell Candrāvalī that he prefers 'the sweet wine of your angry words to this poison of respect (*gaurava*).'[25] It is Rādhā, however, whom Rūpa portrays in the play as actually uttering such angry words.[26] As in the *kīrtan* episode that we have just reviewed, she does so most forcefully when she discovers that Krishna has just betrayed her.[27] Remarkably, for a writer who might well be thought to represent the patriarchal elite,[28] Rūpa praises Rādhā's independence, willfulness, and the tenacity with which she persists in the posture of angry rejection known as *māna*.[29] He contrasts Rādhā's stubbornness in this

[23] On the distinction between *svīyā* or *svakīyā rati,* love within the confines of marriage, and *parakīyā rati*, love for someone not one's own, as this distinction is discussed by Bengal Vaiṣṇava theologians, see S.K. De, *Early History of the Vaiṣṇava Faith and Movement in Bengal*, 2nd edn., Calcutta: Firma K.L. Mukhopadhyay, 1961, pp. 205-6.

[24] Wulff, *Drama*, pp. 138-43.

[25] Rūpa Gosvāmī, *Vidagdhamādhava* IV.12.5-6, as discussed in my *Drama*, p. 139.

[26] See, for example, *Vidagdhamādhava* VII. 49.9-50.23, in my *Drama*, pp. 88-90.

[27] Although her language in Rūpa's play is direct, it is never so earthy as in the rebukes found in Nanda Kishor's and other *kīrtan* singers' versions of the story. See my 'Rādhā: Consort and Conqueror of Krishna', in *Devī*, pp. 127-8.

[28] See, for example, Sumanta Banerjee, *Appropriation of a Folk-heroine: Rādhā in Medieval Bengali Culture*, Shimla: Indian Institute of Advanced Study, 1993.

[29] The discussion occurs in a section of the *Ujjvalanīlamaṇi*, his treatise on *madhura bhaktirasa*, in which he is delineating the different types and qualities of heroines.

phase of their love with the docility of her rival, noting the ease with which Candrāvalī can be cajoled out of her pique.

In the course of an extended interview with Tribhanga Das, a male *kīrtanīyā* who lives in the village of Radhakund, in the Braj region of U.P., I inquired about Rādhā's reproachful behaviour and its relation to a woman's scolding of her husband in ordinary society. I began by asking him why Rādhā reproaches Krishna during episodes of *māna* (Bengali, *mān*).[30] Drawing in a general way on the terminology appropriated by Rūpa from classical Indian aesthetic theory, Tribhanga Das responded that *māna* is a *rasa*, an aesthetically relishable decoction or 'mood'.[31] In response to my next query, about why Krishna likes scolding more than praise, he replied that *māna* is *madhura rasa*, the sweet 'mood', specifying further that *madhura* is the highest *rasa*. He then refined his original formulation, stating that *māna* is a division of *rasa*. Although Rūpa does not include *māna* in his list of five primary and seven secondary *bhaktirasa*s, of which he indeed ranks *madhura bhaktirasa*, the erotic mode of aesthetic devotion, as the highest, he does classify *māna* as one of the four forms of separation of *madhura bhaktirasa*.[32] Tribhanga Das' assertion that *māna* is a division of *rasa* is thus broadly consistent with Rūpa's theory. What he appears to be arguing is that Krishna likes scolding because *māna*, as a *rasa*, is enjoyable to him, just as it is to the spectators of a performance portraying it.

My next question, however, about the relation of Rādhā's scolding to a woman's reproaching of her husband, elicited a very different response. Tribhanga began by stating categorically that such reproach is not a *rasa*. He then illustrated his point by means of an elaborate narrative comprising a story within a story. In the frame story, an upper-caste, well-educated man from Calcutta was being driven crazy by the incessant quarrelling and abuse of his two wives. Seeking peace of mind, he came to the region of Braj, where he began to attend recitations and discourses on the *Bhāgavata Purāṇa* given by a certain pandit.[33] One day, the pandit was talking about

[30] Although my interview of Tribhanga Das was in Bengali, I shall continue to use the Sanskrit forms for the sake of consistency.

[31] On Rūpa's understanding of *rasa* and his theory of *bhaktirasa*, see my *Drama*, pp. 25-38.

[32] See note 8, above.

[33] The recitation and exposition of excerpts from the *Bhāgavata Purāṇa*, a mode of performance called *Bhāgavat Pāṭh*, is common in Bengal as well as in Braj.

a quarrel between Rādhā and Candrāvalī. In utter dismay, the Calcutta gentleman told the pandit that it was precisely in order to get away from quarrelling wives that he had come to Braj. If the same sort of quarrelling goes on between Rādhā and Candrāvalī in Brindavan,[34] he argued, then Brindavan is no different from Calcutta!

The pandit's reply took the form of another story, a narrative concerning the way members of a Bengali household ridicule a new son-in-law. The new bride's younger sisters prepare a meal of snake, scorpion, and tiger's head, together with *chānā* (a ricotta-cheese-like substance) and fruits, and they set it before the son-in-law, who grows very angry. The pandit in the frame story then asks the Calcutta gentleman whether the things the sisters served their new brother-in-law are snake and tiger, or *chānā* and fruit. Tribhanga, the narrator, answers the question himself, asserting that quarrelling in Calcutta is just like snake and tiger's head, whereas quarrelling here in Brindavan, although it may look just like snake and tiger's head, is really *chānā* and fruit. The one is disgusting, whereas the other is delectable.

At the end of these two stories, Tribhanga Das returned to the matter of Rādhā's reproach of Krishna. After narrating in brief the episode of Rādhā as the offended woman he ended his commentary with what he termed his most essential point: that Rādhā's scolding of Krishna is undertaken for the purpose of giving Krishna pleasure. In specifying Rādhā's motive in this way, he takes a major step beyond Rūpa's simple assertion that her scolding gives him pleasure.

The view that Rādhā does everything for Krishna's pleasure likewise stands behind the somewhat different interpretation offered to me in an interview by Nimai Mitra, a *kīrtan* singer of north Calcutta. In his view, Rādhā's anger, rather than being caused by her jealousy over the fact that Krishna had made love with Candrāvalī, arises out of her concern for Krishna's pleasure. Rādhā grows angry because she knows that Candrāvalī would not be able to serve Krishna adequately in their lovemaking, as she herself would. This idea, too, builds on the views of Rūpa and the other gosvāmīs, though it goes beyond them in attributing to Rādhā an attitude of altruistic servitude.

[34] Especially in earlier texts, the terms Brindavan and Braj are often used interchangeably to refer to the area in which Krishna grew up among the cowherds. Modern-day Brindavan (official spelling: Vrindaban) is a pilgrimage town in the Braj region of Uttar Pradesh.

DIVINE LILA, HUMAN SOCIETY, AND DEVOTIONAL PERFORMANCE

The dramatic portrayals of 'The Woman Offended' by *kīrtan* singers play on the theological and social reversals in Rādhā's humiliation of Krishna. The interpretations of Rūpa and the two *kīrtanīyās* whom I interviewed on this issue seem to be attempts to square the story with certain accepted doctrinal positions. However, their claims are at variance in certain respects with the portrayal of the story in *kīrtan*. In particular, Nanda Kishor's rendering of this episode calls into question Rūpa's assertion that Krishna likes Rādhā's stubborn persistence in the posture of jealous anger (*māna*). In his version of the episode, as we have seen, Krishna gives every indication that he is thoroughly uncomfortable: he twice tries to hide from the scrutiny of Rādhā and her friends, and he expresses anguished regret for not having washed the telltale marks from his face before coming to meet her. Moreover, Nanda Kishor's sympathetic comments at the conclusion of the excerpt, in which he portrays Krishna as thinking, 'I've been severely punished', would scarcely be necessary if Krishna had been enjoying Rādhā's and Lalitā's verbal drubbing.

Nanda Kishor's performance of this episode likewise provides no evidence to support Tribhanga Das's claim that Rādhā's motive for scolding Krishna is to give Krishna pleasure. Not surprisingly, therefore, it also fails to support Nimai Mitra's contention that Rādhā's anger arises from her altruistic concern for Krishna's pleasure, rather than from her jealousy of Candrāvalī. These interpretations appear to be based in theological and social concerns that are at odds with the story, as we have seen it in Nanda Kishor's rendering, which depicts Rādhā's and Krishna's emotions in convincingly human terms. In concluding, we shall consider certain of the theological and social aims that these interpretations appear to serve.

Even though Rūpa goes beyond the evidence of the narrative, as we have it in Nanda Kishor's rendering, in declaring that Krishna likes Rādhā's angry words, his interpretation is otherwise more harmonious with Nanda Kishor's rendering than are those of Tribhanga Das and Nimai Mitra. First, his theological doctrine that Rādhā is Krishna's *hlādiṇī śakti*, and thus an integral part of the Godhead, accords in a general way with Nanda Kishor's representation of Rādhā and Krishna as equal. Secondly, Rūpa's celebration of the greater intensity and intimacy of Rādhā's love with Krishna over that of Candrāvalī, because it incorporates spontaneity and willfulness rather than being constrained by excessive respect and deference, appears to be echoed in Nanda Kishor's frequent expressions of his own intimacy with Rādhā and Krishna. Although Rūpa's description of the intimacy of Rādhā's and Krishna's love is couched in theological terms, whereas Nanda Kishor's utterances appear to be spontaneous expressions of his devotional experience, the two may be seen to participate in a common religious ideal. Indeed, it is possible that Rūpa's admiration for the intimacy shared by Rādhā and Krishna hints at the mode of his own devotion, a mode akin to the intimacy and delight revealed in performance by Nanda Kishor.

Tribhanga Das and Nimai Mitra follow Rūpa's interpretation in certain respects, but they go beyond his views in demarcating the realm of Rādhā and Krishna in fundamental ways from the world of human relations. Moreover, both depart from Rūpa in subordinating Rādhā to Krishna. The views expressed by both these singers have theological as well as social implications.

Although Tribhanga Das couches his thoughts in a village idiom, his ideas are remarkably close to Rūpa's. Like Rūpa, he has a marked preference for Rādhā's love for Krishna over Candrāvalī's, and he expresses this preference in the aesthetic language of *rasa*.[35] He also echoes Rūpa's view that Krishna likes Rādhā's state of jealous anger, asserting that Krishna prefers her scolding to praise. However, in claiming that Rādhā reproaches Krishna for Krishna's pleasure, Tribhanga departs significantly from Rūpa, establishing Krishna's supremacy — both theologically and socially — over his consort. In so doing, he replaces spontaneity, which Rūpa enshrines as a supreme characteristic of their love, with a fixed and indeed subservient purpose. Tribhanga thereby recasts Rādhā, both as divine consort and as human lover, in the familiar mold of the *pativratā*, the woman whose highest purpose is to serve her lord.[36] By contrast, the story of Rādhā's humiliation of Krishna in Nanda Kishor's representation is powerful precisely in its deviation from — and challenge to — such stereotypes.

Whether deliberately or not, Tribhanga, in representing Rādhā as a societal and devotional ideal, places distance between her and human

[35] Although the terms of comparison used by Tribhanga, *ciṭā guṛ* (coarse brown sugar) and *cini* (refined white sugar), are different from those used by Rūpa, namely, *ghṛta* (clarified butter) and *madhu* (honey), the effect of the comparison is in certain respects quite similar.

[36] One must, of course, bear in mind that Rādhā's and Krishna's love is *parakīyā rati*, love outside the confines of marriage, whereas the *pativratā* ideal applies to *svakīyā rati*, that is, to the love of a married woman for her husband. See fn. 23, above.

women. We saw how he uses the story of the Calcutta gentleman with quarrelling co-wives in a parallel way to demarcate Brindavan from the world.[37] His aim would seem to be practical as well as apologetic: he calls the behaviour of women who scold their husbands disgusting, presumably in order to discourage such behaviour.

Nimai Mitra continues Tribhanga's project of cordoning Rādhā off from human women. Like Tribhanga, he asserts that Rādhā acts out of a concern for Krishna's happiness. Differentiating her still further from ordinary women, he claims that her anger is not the product of jealousy, but rather the result of her realization that Candrāvalī would not be able to make Krishna happy. In denying such an ordinary human emotion as jealousy to Rādhā, Nimai Mitra's interpretation also seems aimed at discouraging devotees from emulating her.

CONCLUSION

The issues raised by the example we have been considering are many: the relation — in Braj and in Bengal — of Sanskrit and vernacular, and medieval and modern sources; and of text and performance, narrative and theology, and goddesses and women; as well as the nature of religious authority in a remarkably pluralistic tradition. Our exploration of an excerpt from Nanda Kishor's performance of *Khaṇḍitā* in fact leaves us with more questions than answers. How, for example, has Tribhanga Das — a contemporary *kīrtanīyā* from a small village in Braj, in Hindi-speaking U.P., who speaks and performs in Bengali, but who, so far as I know, does not read Sanskrit — come to know so much of the aesthetic-devotional theory of Rūpa Gosvāmī, which is enshrined in difficult Sanskrit treatises?[38] How is it that Tribhanga's understanding, although it

[37] Paradoxically, by introducing a story of quarrelling co-wives in an attempt to distinguish such worldly squabbling from the quarrelling of Rādhā and Candrāvalī in Brindavan, Tribhanga shows that he sees them as integrally related.

[38] There are any number of possible answers to this question; I shall merely adumbrate three. First, much of Rūpa's theory has been incorporated into the Bengali *Caitanyacaritāmṛta* of Kṛṣṇadāsa Kavirāja, the most influential of the biographies of Caitanya, and this work has been widely circulated and quoted in Braj as well as in Bengal. Secondly, some of the Bengali Vaiṣṇava preceptors, such as the gosvāmīs who preside over the temple of Rādhāramaṇ in Brindavan, regularly expound and interpret Rūpa's theory in religious gatherings. Finally, some especially learned teachers and performers of *padāvalī kīrtan* quote Rūpa's Sanskrit works at key points, such as the definition of each of the eight types of

is formulated in village language and illustrated by village stories, extends to such complex concepts as *madhura rasa* and *māna*? For me, this process demonstrates the permeability of cultural layers and the relativity of such categories as elite and popular, Sanskrit and vernacular, 'classical' and 'folk', *mārgī* (pan-Indian) and *deśī* (regional).[39] At the very least, we must see each such pair, not as a binary opposition, but rather as a set of two fluid, overlapping domains.

Finally, our investigation reveals how complex the matter of religious meaning is. For example, whether a given woman who hears and sees Nanda Kishor's dramatization of *Khaṇḍitā* will be empowered in her own personal relations with men by witnessing Rādhā's humiliation of Krishna depends — in part, at least — on the degree to which she identifies emotionally with Rādhā. This in turn may depend, at least partly, on the theological interpretation she has internalized. For those women who follow the tradition represented by Tribhanga Das and Nimai Mitra in maintaining a clear line between the realm of Rādhā's and Krishna's *līlā* and the world, identifying with Rādhā or looking to her as a role model would be tantamount to blasphemy. For others, whose emotional participation in the story is not constrained by such dogmatic strictures, the line separating their feelings from Rādhā's would be far less sharp. Such women might well be inspired to emulate Rādhā's assertive, uncompromising behaviour in their relations with their husbands. In a preliminary survey of women attending a *kīrtan* performance in south Calcutta,[40] I found roughly equal numbers of women in these two groups.

The distinction between the world of Krishna's *līlā* and the realm of humans has been drawn at least since the eighth century: in the *Bhāgavata Purāṇa*, the bard Śuka answers King Parikṣit's query about the apparent immorality of Krishna's love-play with married women by explaining that because Krishna is God, his actions are not immoral; humans, on the other hand, are not to imitate them.[41] The orthodox Bengal Vaiṣṇava tradition has expanded this injunction to include as well the actions of Rādhā and

---

heroine (*khaṇḍitā* and so forth), and instruction in the pertinent elements of Rūpa's theory is thus part of the traditional process of learning to be a singer of *kīrtan*.

[39] For the relevance of the terms 'classical', 'folk', *mārgī*, and *deśī* to Indian performance genres, see Kapila Vatsyayan, *Traditional Indian Theatre: Multiple Streams*, New Delhi: National Book Trust, 1980, pp. 1-14.

[40] The interviews were conducted in January 1996, during a month-long 'Gītājayantī' celebration in Triangular Park, on Rash Behari Avenue in south Calcutta.

[41] BhP 10.33.27-37.

the other close associates of Krishna. However, some Bengali women whom my assistants and I interviewed expressed the view that emulating Rādhā in her strong, uncompromising stance toward Krishna, especially if their husbands should be unfaithful, is entirely legitimate.

In our discussion of Nanda Kishor's representation of 'The Woman Offended', we have traced some of the Sanskrit and vernacular sources of its various interpretations. There is also the intriguing possibility that *kīrtanīyās* and others who sharply dissociate Rādhā's and Krishna's realm from that of humans are responding to yet another element in the religious complex of eastern India, one emanating from pre-Victorian and Victorian England. From at least the end of the nineteenth century many Western-educated Bengalis have felt a great deal of embarrassment about the erotic content of the Krishna *līlā*.[42] The strong British presence in Bengal from the early nineteenth century may help account for the vehemence with which Tribhanga Das and Nimai Mitra maintain the sharp distinction between the love of Rādhā and Krishna and the world of human relations. Such a moralistic current, however, seems not to have diminished the natural, easy affection that Nanda Kishor expresses in his performance of *Khaṇḍitā*. His comfortableness with the story of Rādhā's and Krishna's love undoubtedly contributed to his enormous appeal — to English-educated Bengalis[43] and others alike — as a singer of *padāvalī kīrtan*.

Even Nanda Kishor, however, repeatedly points up in his commentary the startlingly deviant nature of Rādhā's accusations. The story of her defiance gains much of its power from the fact that her dressing down of Krishna constitutes a reversal — both theologically and socially — of what is expected. The interpretations of Tribhanga Das and Nimai Mitra, in emphasizing the discontinuity between the realm of Rādhā's and Krishna's love and the everyday world, illustrate the extent to which the episode of Rādhā as offended heroine has posed a challenge to recent Bengali sensibilities. Nevertheless, the enormous popularity of the episode, a perennial favourite of *kīrtan* troupes and their audiences, has resulted in the widespread availability through several centuries in Bengal of a model of womanly conduct that stands in sharp contrast to the *pativratā* ideal of wifely submission.

[42] This point was made by Tirthankar Bose during the discussion that followed my presentation at the Conference on Early Literature in New Indo-Aryan Languages held in August 1997, in Venice.

[43] Two of the most influential newspaper editors in Calcutta during the second half of the twentieth century, Tushar Kanti Ghosh and Ashok Kumar Sarkar, were great patrons of *kīrtan* and especially of Nanda Kishor, whom they regularly invited to perform in their homes.

Caitanya's Performances

BOŻENA ŚLIWCZYŃSKA

Ekadina Prabhu balilena savā-sthāne. 'Āji nṛtya karibāṅa aṅkera vidhāne.' (CB, M, XVIII, 6) — *One day the Master said to everyone there: Today I shall dance in a sequence of acts*. With these words Caitanya announced to his companions his desire to present a performance, a dance drama. Then his orders concerning costumes followed. Buddhimata Khān was responsible for preparing and fetching them. *Kāca sajja kara giyā* — ordered the Master (CB, M, XVIII, 7) and gave a more precise command to bring conch (bracelets), bodices, silk saris and ornaments (CB, M, XVIII, 8). However, it was not going to be a solo performance. Caitanya was accompanied by his followers whose parts were assigned by him, except for one. Thus, Gadādhara was to play Rukmiṇī and Brahmānanda–her eldery friend (*buṛī sakhī*) Suprabhā (CB, M, XVIII, 9), Nityānanda–Baṛāi and Haridāsa–a (Vaikuṇṭha) policeman/guardian (CB, M, XVIII, 10), Śrīvāsa–Nārada and Śrīrāma–Snātaka (a young Brahmin) (CB, M, XVIII, 11), Gopīnātha–a male hero (*pātra*) on a throne (CB, M, XVIII, 12). Advaita was the only one who could chose a part to play according to his will.[1] So he decided to play a Jester–Vidūṣaka (CB, M, XVIII, 36). Caitanya himself danced in Lakṣmī's dress.[2] The preparations were finished, all participants, both performers and spectators, ready for enjoying a wonderful event taking place in a house of the fortunate Ācāryaratna Candraśekhara. Verily was he fortunate as in his abode the Master revealed his divine grace — *Śrīcandraśekhara-bhāgya tāra ei sīmā. Yāra ghare prabhu prakāśilā e mahimā* (CB, M, XVIII, 31). Let us stop here for a while, just before the beginning of this significant performance.

Praising the deity with music, songs, dance is a very emotional way of expressing devotee's feelings towards an object of his/her adoration;

[1] *karayoṛe advaitā balilā bāra-bāra.*
'more āgñā prabhu kon kāca kācibāra?' CB, M, XVIII, 33
prabhu bale,—'yata kāca, sakali tomāra.
icchā-anurūpa kāca kāca' āpnāra'. CB, M, XVIII, 34

[2] *lakṣmīveśe aṅka-nṛtya kariba ṭhākura.* CB, M, XVIII, 20a
Lakṣmīveśe — in Lakṣmī's dress, dressed as Lakṣmī, in Lakṣmī's role.

praising the god with enacting his deeds — his *līlā*s is to participate in them, is to participate in the eternal. Caitanya's fervent devotion full of ecstatic states needed to be fostered and expressed in a unique way referring to emotionally intensive media. Dancing, singing, reciting or listening to stanzas from favourite works are often mentioned as activities very much enjoyed by the Master and provoking his moments of ecstasy. Recitation from works of great Vaiṣṇava poets — Jayadeva's *Gītagovinda*, Caṇḍīdāsa and Vidyāpati's poems as well as of his pupil Rāmānanda Ray's drama[3] — pleased him a lot and created a perfect ambience for his euphoric and frenzied states. Enacting *Kṛṣṇa-līlā*s was an important part of the devotional practice of Caitanya and his circle. Participating in their presentation was considered as a special privilege which could be shared by pious and pure people free from worldly bonds and delusion, by the initiates.

Just before the performance in Candraśekhara's house, Caitanya told his friends that only a man who subdued passions and controlled senses (*jitendriya*) could watch him playing and dancing the primordial female energy nature.[4] Those words caused sadness as some of the Vaiṣṇavas did not feel worthy enough to witness the performance and to participate in it. Advaita and Śrīvāsa were among those who hesitated to join the unusual gathering in the house of Candraśekhara, because their senses were not controlled and passions not subdued (*ajitendriya*) (CB, M, XVIII, 21-3). Smiling said the Master to them: 'If you do not go, whom shall I dance with?'[5] And then he consoled them: 'Nobody should worry. Today you will be great ascetics. Watching me (dancing) nobody will be seized by delusion.'[6] Thus the presence of Caitanya purified minds and souls, and made the event sacred. All Vaiṣṇavas, men and women[7] became happy and went to the place of the performance.

[3] *caṇḍidāsa vidyāpati rāyera nāṭaka gīti karṇāmṛtaśrīgītagovinda*
svarūpa rāmānanda sane mahāprabhu rātridinaṁ gāya śune parama ānande.
Caitanyacaritāmṛta, comp. Das Gupta 1934, p. 100.

[4] *prakṛti-svarūpā nṛtya haibe āmāra.*
dekhite ye jitendriya, tā'r adhikāra. CB, M, XVIII, 18-19

[5] *tomrā nā gele nṛtya kāhāre laiyā?'* CB, M, XVIII, 24b

[6] (. . .)*'kāro cintā nāi.*
mahāyogeśvara āji tomrā haibā.
dekhiyā āmāre keha moha nā pāibā.' CB, M, XVIII, 25b-26

[7] Śacī, Caitanya's mother, as well as his wife Viṣṇupriyā participated in the event, and together with them other pious and dedicated Vaiṣṇava women (*pativratā*); Mālinī, Śrīvāsa's wife was also among them.

Although Caitanya's interest in dramatic art is often mentioned,[8] there are not many description of his performances. Vṛndāvanadāsa in his Bengali biography *Caitanyabhāgavata* gives a relatively lengthy account[9] of Caitanya's performance taking place in Ācārya Candraśekhara's house in AD 1507.[10] Another reference to Caitanya's stage presentation is by Kavikarṇapurā in his written in Sanskrit drama *Caitanyacandrodaya* (*nāṭaka*). In the third act called *Dānavinoda* there is an inset play enacted by Caitanya and his companions (who are also *dramatis personae* of the drama proper) reflecting the fact of presenting *Kṛṣṇa-līlā*s by the Master. The inset play about the *Dānalīlā* of Kṛṣṇa and Rādhā seems to be the poet's version of the same performance.

Caitanya's performances are considered to create a very important stage in the development of the histrionic art in Bengal, of Bengali drama. For some scholars the performances of Caitanya made the beginning of the Bengali drama,[11] for others *Bengali drama [. . .] revived in the time of Lord Śrī Caitanya.*[12] Undoubtedly, those spectacles reflected indigenous performing tradition around. Since the sources concerning them are rather poor, we can only try to define their presumable form and structure. The account of Vṛndāvanadāsa is of a descriptive nature and the main intention

[8] Caitanya was also vividly interested in creating dramas praising Kṛṣṇa. Thus, for example, one day he asked Rūpa Gosvāmin to create such. *Ethā prabhu āgñāya rūpa āila vṛndāvana. Kṛṣṇalīlā nāṭaka karite haila tā̃ra mana.* (CC, Antya, I, 29.)

[9] The Aṣṭadaśa Adhyāya of the Madhyakhaṇḍa of the *Caitanyabhāgavata* contains 234 stanzas (couplets in a *payār* metre), of which verses 38-209 present the description of the performance proper. (Verses 1-4: an introductory hymn to Caitanya; 5-37: the announcement of the spectacle and preparations of different kind for it; 210-34: a sort of commentary on the event.)

[10] Centuries later Hemendranath Das Gupta writes: *This performance by the brightest jewel of Bengal with his noble followers was indeed wonderful. The performance took place in AD 1507.* Das Gupta 1934, p. 95.

[11] *Die Theaterstuecke, die Caitanya mit den Seinen in Navadvipa improvisierte, bilden den Anfang des Dramas in der Bengalisprache.* Eidlitz 1968, p. 318.

[12] *Bengali drama, however, revived in the time of Lord Śrī Chaitanya. Śrī Chaitanya himself was fond of drama and was highly skilled in dramatic performance. His performance was of such a finished character that the audience was kept spell-bound by his acting and dancing. Being inspired by His example many devout poets wrote several religious plays. After this, Bengal learnt to appreciate drama, and almost all the Bengali dramatists were the followers of Lord Gouranga.* Das Gupta, 1934, p. 92. This opinion is very much in favour of Caitanya's histrionic skills and his further influence on Bengali drama.

of the author is to display the marvel of the event, however it contains some details of stage presentation. As there is no formal division of the play enacted, we shall propose propose such an arrangement while presenting the performance of Caitanya and his companions.

(Invocation):

To start with, the performance Mukunda initiated *Kṛṣṇa-kīrtana* and the rest of the Vaiṣṇavas joined him loudly shouting-singing divine names: *Rāma Kṛṣṇa Bala Hari Gopāla Govinda* (CB, M, XVIII, 38).

After that auspicious beginning, which we can compare with and treat as a *maṅgalacāraṇa* or *nāndī* (invocation), a prologue (*prastāvanā*) — announcement of the subject-matter followed.

(Prologue): Haridāsa–Vaikuṇṭha policeman/guardian.

Haridāsa playing a Vaikuṇṭha policeman entered the stage with a stick in his hand.[13] He told everybody about the dance of Caitanya (*Jagatera Prāṇa*) in Lakṣmī's dress (CB, M, XVIII, 41). Haridāsa was dressed in dhoti, a big turban crowned his head and he had huge false mustaches.[14] His appearance and gestures provoked laughter. He lauded *Kṛṣṇa bhoja, Kṛṣṇa seva, bala Kṛṣṇa nāma* (CB, M, XVIII, 43) and informed the onlookers that the Master left Vaikuṇṭha for Nadīyā to spread *premabhakti*, devotional love, everywhere.[15]

The sequence of scenes (*dṛśya*)[16] came next.

(Scene 1): Śrīvāsa–Nārada, Advaita–Vidūṣaka, Śrīrāma–Snātaka (standing at the back of the stage with a waterpot in his hand).

Śrīvāsa–Nārada entered the stage much to the delight of the public. Long bearded, dotted all over his body, with the *vīṇā* on his arm and *kuśa* grass in his hand he walked around.[17] At the sight of that strange looking

[13] All references concerning a drama character's appearance (dress, ornaments, etc.) as well as his/her stage behaviour (a way of walking, etc.) could be treated as 'stage directions'.

[14] *prathame praviṣṭa hailā prabhu haridāsa.*
mahā dui gōpha kari' vadane vilāsa. CB, M, VIII, 39
mahā pāga śobhe śire dhaṭī paridhāna.
daṇḍa haste savāre karaye sāvadhāna. CB, M, XVIII, 40

[15] *vaikuṇṭha chāṛiyā prabhu āilena ethā.*
premabhakti loṭāiba ṭhākura sarvvathā. CB, M, XVIII, 46

[16] Although Caitanya himself announced to dance in a sequence of acts (*nṛtya karibāṅa aṅkera vidhāne*) the spectacle presented consists rather of succeeding scenes (*dṛśya*) than of acts proper (*aṅka*).

[17] *mahā-dīrgha pākā dāṛi, phōṭā sarvva gāya.*
vīṇā-kāndhe, kuśa-haste cāridike cāya. CB, M, XVIII, 51

figure Advaita–Vidūṣaka asked: 'Who are you, what is the reason of your coming here?'[18] And the reply:

My name is Nārada, Kṛṣṇa's singer.
I wander through the eternal world of Brahman.
I went to Vaikuṇṭha to see Kṛṣṇa,
there I heard Kṛṣṇa had gone to the town of Nadīyā.
I saw empty Vaikuṇṭha houses,
There were no housewives and husbands, no families there.
As I could not watch Vaikuṇṭha deserted,
I came here remembering Lord.
Today the Master will dance dressed as Lakṣmī,
That is why I appear in this gathering.[19]

Nārada's words full of devotion (how simply beyond a doubt the identification of Caitanya and Kṛṣṇa is displayed!) were heartily greeted by the Vaiṣṇavas who exclaimed with sounds of triumph (*jayadhvani*). When Śacī saw Śrīvāsa–Nārada, she was greatly astonished and fainted overwhelmed by joy (*ānande parilā āi haiyā mūrcchitā*) (CB, M, XVIII, 66a). At the sound of Kṛṣṇa's name she revived. Emotions envoked were so intensive that many pious participants wept, shook or collapsed.[20]

(Scene 2): Caitanya–Rukmiṇī.

While Caitanya was dressing up in Rukmiṇī's robe he was so engrossed in Rukmiṇī's emotion[21] that he could not recognize himself. His absorption

[18] *'ke tumi āilā ethā, kon vā kāraṇe?'* CB, M, XVIII, 55a

[19] *'nārada āmāra nāma kṛṣṇera gāyana.
ananta brahmāṇḍe āmi kariye bhramaṇa.* CB, M, XVIII, 56
*vaikuṇṭhe gelāṅa kṛṣṇa dekhibāra tare.
śunilāma kṛṣṇa gelā nadīyā-nagare.* CB, M, XVIII, 57
*śūnya dekhilām vaikuṇṭhera ghara-dvāra.
gṛhiṇī-gṛhastha nāhi, nāhi paribāra.* CB, M, XVIII, 58
*nā pāri rahite śūnya-vaikuṇṭha dekhiyā.
āilāma āpana ṭhākura saṅariyā.* CB, M, XVIII, 59
*prabhu āji nācibena dhari' lakṣmīveśa.
ataeva e sabhāya āmāra praveśa.'* CB, M, XVIII, 60

The part of Nārada is a very important one in Kṛṣṇa-yātrās. He usually appears at the beginning of a yātrā-play announcing its subject-matter, preparing the audience for it. He is also a sort of comic personage in yātrās.

[20] *bāhya nāhi sphure, save karena krandana.* CB, M, XVIII, 69b

[21] *rukmiṇīra bhāve* — in Rukmiṇī's emotion; in this (Gauḍīya Vaiṣṇava) context *bhāva* — emotion (state, nature) is to be understood as the *emotional role*. Comp. Haberman 1988, p. 73, *passim*.

in Rukmiṇī was complete, he was Rukmiṇī.[22] With eyes drawned in tears he/she was writing a letter to Kṛṣṇa containing seven stanzas from the *Bhāgavatapurāṇa* (Bh, X, 52, 37-43).[23] Those seven stanzas with some other interspersed verses were sang in the melody (*rāga*) *Kāruṇyaśāradā* by Caitanya-Rukmiṇī. That melodious recitation started with 'When one hears about your virtues, o Beauty of the World! — his/her carnal austerity is gone away, triple austerity — difficult to keep.'[24] Touched till the tears came all the Vaiṣṇavas observed Caitanya's absorption in Rukmiṇī (*Rukmiṇī-āveśa*). Their loud shouting of the name Hari sounded everywhere.

The participants' enthusiasm was tremendous. Haridāsa screamed, Śrīvāsa–Nārada danced. And in such a way the first three hours of the performance passed, three hours of joy and fun.[25]

The second part of three hours opened Gadādhara.[26]

(Scene 3): Gadādhara–Rukmiṇī, Ramā (Lakṣmī), Cowherdess (Rādhā), Lakṣmī; Brahmānanda–Suprabhā Baṛāi, Haridāsa–Policeman, Śrīvāsa–Nārada, Gaṅgādāsa, Caitanya.

Gadādhara-Rukmiṇī and his/her old friend Suprabhā walked around the stage. Brahmānanda–Baṛāi was dressed in a muslin robe, with a stick in his/her hand and a basket on his/her shoulder.[27] The Vaiṣṇavas were curious about the identity of two women. It turned out that both women on their way to Mathura wanted to stop in Nadīyā and they asked for a place to stay. Haridāsa–Policeman, Śrīvāsa–Nārada, Gaṅgādāsa[28] queried them

[22] *gṛhāntare veśa kare prabhu viśvambhara.*
rukmiṇīra bhāve magna haila nirbhara. CB, M, XVIII, 70
āpanā nā jāne prabhu rukmiṇī-āveśe.
vidarbhera sutā yena āpanāre bāse. CB, M, XVIII, 71
āveśa— entering, entrance, taking possession of, absorption of the faculties in one wish or ideas, devotness to an object, possession; 'absorption in'. Comp. Haberman 1988, p. 75.

[23] *nayanera jale patra likhiye āpane.*
pṛthivī haila patra, angulī kalame. CB, M, XVIII, 72
rukmiṇīra patra— saptaśloka bhāgavate.
ye āche, paṛaye tāhā kāndite kāndite. CB, M, XVIII, 73

[24] *'śuniyā tomāra guṇa bhuvansundara.*
dūra bhela aṅgatāpa trividha duṣkara.' CB, M, XVIII, 76

[25] *prathama prahare ei kautuka-viśeṣa.* CB, M, XVIII, 101a

[26] *dvitīya prahare gadādhara-paraveśa.* CB, M, XVIII, 101b

[27] *hāte naṛi, kā̃khe dālī, neta paridhāna.*
brahmānanda ye-hena baṛāi vidyamāna. CB, M, XVIII, 103

[28] His part in the performance is not stated in the text.

quite severely (a very exemplary piece of a simple stage dialogue (CB, M, 104-10). Finally Advaita was irritated with such a questioning the poor women who should had been treated like mothers. Suggesting a way of 'payment' for staying in Nadīyā he said: 'The Master is very much pleased with dance and songs.'[29] Gadādhara happy with those words danced manifesting love (*nṛtya kare gadādhara prema parakāśe*) (CB, M, XVIII, 111b). While he was dancing as Ramā (Lakṣmī), Brahmānanda was singing (CB, M, XVIII, 112). All were impressed by Gadādhara's dance. From his eyes flew a river of love, the earth became wet and verily blessed.[30] Then 'Gadādhara was like Gaṅgā manifested. Truly Gadādhara was Kṛṣṇa's *prakṛti* (female energy).'[31] Thus Caitanya kept repeating: 'Gadādhara is my Vaikuṇṭha's wife.'[32] Gadādhara continued dancing to the delight of everybody. Some Vaiṣṇavas sang, some observed, all were overflowing with love.[33] The participants happily shouted the name of Hari and Gadādhara danced as Cowherdess (Rādhā).[34]

(Scene 4): Caitanya–Ādyāśakti,[35] Nityānanda–Baṛāi, Kṛṣṇa.

Caitanya appeared as Ādyāśakti[36] and Nityānanda as old Baṛāi walked crook-backed. All the Vaiṣṇavas made a circle and cried 'Triumph! Triumph!' They did not recognize the Master and wondered who was there just in front of their own eyes — Kamalā or Sītā (Janakī), Mahālakṣmī or Pārvatī, Rādhā[37] or Gaṅgā (Bhāgīrathī), Rūpavatī or Dayā? (CB, M, XVIII,

[29] *nṛtya-gīte priya bāṛa āmāra ṭhākura.* CB, M, XVIII, 110a

[30] *premanadī bahe gadādharera nayane.*
pṛthivī hailā sikta, dhanya kari' māne. CB, M, XVIII, 114

[31] *gadādhara hailā yena gaṅgā mūrttimatī.*
satya satya gadādhara kṛṣṇera prakṛti. CB, M, XVIII, 115

[32] *āpane caitanya baliyāche bāra bāra.*
'gadādhara mora vaikuṇṭhera paribāra.' CB, M, XVIII, 116

[33] *ye gāya, ye dekhe, sava bhāsilena preme.* CB, M, XVIII, 117a

[34] *caudike śuniye kṛṣṇapremera krandana.*
gopikāra veśe nāce mādhavanandana. CB, M, XVIII, 119.

[35] *Ādyāśakti* — primordial energy, nature; a name of *Brahmāṇḍajananī* — Mother of the World.
See *Gauṛīya-bhāṣya* to *Caitanyabhāgavata*, CB (1934: 715)
In the text analysed all female deities and energies are various manifestations of the one primordial energy — Ādyāśakti (Lakṣmī).

[36] *henei samaye sarvva prabhu viśvambhara.*
praveśa karilā ādyāśakti-veṣadhara. CB, M, XVIII, 120

[37] Her name is not directly stated. She is described as: *vṛndāvana sampatti mūrttimatī.* (Vṛndāvana's fortune manifested). CB, M, XVIII, 127b

126-8). Even his mother Śacī was confused — 'Did Lakṣmī come to dance?' Or Mahāyogeśvarī, Bhakti Itself–ŚrīHari? (CB, M, XVIII, 131b-2). The illusion was complete. Finally motherly emotion (*jananī-bhāva*) filled everybody entirely (CB, M, XVIII, 135). They sank in the ocean of Kṛṣṇa-love while watching the Master. Then Caitanya danced as Mother of the World (*Jagata-Jananī*) (CB, M, XVIII, 138). Caitanya assumed one nature after another in his dance-acting. So the bhaktas were greatly bewildered all the time guessing what (female) energy's emotion he danced in (*kon prakṛtira bhāve nāce nārāyaṇa?*) (CB, M, XVIII, 139b). He was Rukmiṇī (*Vidarbhera bālā*) while asking about Kṛṣṇa's arrival (CB, M, XVIII, 140). Then Gaṅgā's manifestation (141), or Mahācaṇḍī (142), or Revatī (Śrībaladeva's *śakti*) (143). He was Rādhā (*Gokula-Sundarī*) saying 'Go Baṛāi! Let's go to Vṛndāvana' (144), then Yogeśvarī (145). Caitanya danced — acted all *śaktis*.[38] The Vaiṣṇavas 'swam in the waves of the ocean of love, those who watched, those who listened to, those who sang together with the Master'.[39] While Caitanya was dancing as Ādyāśakti, the bhaktas shed tears of joy, shook, thrilled with delight, all gathered at his feet like a swarm of bees. Caitanya embodied bhakti-devotion (*mūrttimatī bhakti*).[40] Ecstatic emotions heightened with every minute. Caitanya continued his dance taking Nityānanda's hand (156). Nityānanda was no longer old Baṛāi, he was absorbed in Kṛṣṇa (*kṛṣṇa-āveśe*).[41] Śrīmān kept the light all the time, Haridāsa carefully looked around. Kṛṣṇa-love emotion (*Kṛṣṇaprema bhāva*) fulfilled everybody. Nityānanda fainted and fell on the ground. The Vaiṣṇavas wept, they hugged each other, cried loudly, grasped each others' feet. Caitanya in Mahālakṣmī's emotion embraced Gopīnātha and together with him sat on the cot (throne) (CB, M, XVIII, 163). The rest of the Vaiṣṇavas stood before them with folded hands (CB, M, XVIII, 164). At the order of the Master they sang hymn to Jagata-Jananī (Mother of the World), Lakṣmī

[38] *sarvva-śakti-svarūpe nācaye viśvambhara.* CB, M, XVIII, 151a

[39] *ye dekhe, ye śune, yevā gāya prabhu-saṅge.*
savei bhāsena prema-sāgara-taraṅge. CB, M, XVIII, 152

[40] *ādyāśakti-veṣe nāce prabhu gaurasiṁha.*
sukhe dekhe tā̃ra yata caranera bhṛṅga. CB, M, XVIII, 154
kampa, sveda, pulaka, aśrura anta nāi.
mūrttimatī bhakti hailā caitanya-gosāñi. CB, M, XVIII, 155

[41] *kothāya vā gela buṛi-baṛāira sāja.*
kṛṣṇāveśe vihvala hailā nāgarāja. CB, M, XVIII, 159
Nāgarāja = Nityānanda

and Caṇḍī praising their grace and divine power. They sang in the *Mālaśī* melody pattern (*rāga*) (CB, M, XVIII, 167-82, 185). The hymn pleased the Master greatly. In such a way homage was paid by all the Vaiṣṇavas — men and women (Śacī-mātā was all the time among them). Joyful weeping sounded around. Enormous delight fulfilled the house of Candraśekhara.[42] Rejoicing the very thrilling moments nobody noticed that the night was over and the dawn came. The dance, the performance had to be finished. Everybody became sad, their hearts deeply hurt, pierced with an arrow.[43] The bhaktas wept bitterly 'Oh, why did the night pass? (*āre rātri kene pohāile?*) (CB, M, XVIII, 200a).

Thus it seems that the end of the performance might be announced. However, if we consider the theory of Indian drama, we know that it could not be the end. Since in accordance with the rules of the dramatic theory a spectacle should always finish with the sentiment of enchantment, of wonder (*adbhuta rasa*);[44] there is no place for an unfulfilled desire and sadness. Thus, we can expect the continuation. Well, and we shall not be disappointed!

(Scene 5): Caitanya–Mother of the World.

When Caitanya — Son of Śacī (*Śacīnandana*) — saw the great dispair of the Vaiṣṇavas, he favoured them with filial emotion (*pūtrabhāva*) (CB, M, XVIII, 202). They could enjoy their sonship while the Master was engrossed in motherly emotion (*mātṛbhāva*) and gave them his breast to suck.[45] Caitanya was Kamalā, Pārvatī, Dayā, Mahā-Nārāyaṇī, Jagata-Jananī (CB, M, XVIII, 204). He sang: 'I am the father, the grandfather, I am the father — the sustainer, I am the mother' (CB, M, XVIII, 205b).[46] Joyfully the bhaktas sucked milk from his breast, their worry about separation went away. They were full of love sentiment (*premarasa*) (CB, M, XVIII, 208). They already knew that Caitanya's *līlā*s would never end;

[42] *ānanda haila candraśekhara-bhāvana.* CB, M, XVIII, 187b

[43] *pohāila niśi, haila nṛtya-avasāna.*
bājila savāra buke yena mahābāṇa. CB, M, XVIII, 190

[44] *sarveṣāṁ kāvyānāṁ nānārasabhāvayuktiyuktānām.*
nirvahaṇe kartavyo nityaṁ hi raso'dbhutastajjñaiḥ. NS, XVIII, 43

[45] *mātṛbhāve viśvambhara savāre dhariyā.*
stana pāna karāya parama snigdha haiyā. CB, M, XVIII, 203

[46] *'āmi pitā, pitāmaha, āmi dhātā, mātā.'* (CB, M, XVIII, 205b). This fragment refers to the *Bhagavadgītā*, IX, 17a:
pitāhamasya jagato mātā dhātā pitāmaha.

they would appear and disappear (to appear again).[47] The *līlā*s of Caitanya are eternal.

Thus, there was the end of the outstanding performance of the Master in Nadīyā–Navadvīpa.[48]

However, there was not the end of joy and wonder. For seven days in Candraśekhara's house[49] the enchanting light shone. The glow was extremely bright. 'The moon, the sun and the lightening meet to shine in one place. The pious Vaiṣṇavas were entranced.'[50] For a long time the event was much commented by all inhabitants of Nadīyā who wanted to know what had really happened in the house of Candraśekhara. But the Vaiṣṇavas, the bhaktas, just smiled and did not reveal the truth[51] as *that* could be shared and understood by the initiates only.

The performance described was probably one of many staged by Caitanya and his companions. Those performances were a part of Vaiṣṇava ritual practice.[52] We could guess that they were similar in form and structure to the one presented above. It perfectly reflects the emotional needs and expectations of the Vaiṣṇava community. From its very beginning, in fact, from the moment of its announcement, the performance was greeted with great enthusiasm and it invoked fervent emotions of devotional nature till its very end. Taking part in enacting the divine dalliance everybody could experience the presence of the ultimate and rejoiced in Kṛṣṇa-bhakti entirely. Both, actors and spectators, created that performance. Both of them could be called performers. As we could notice there was no scene without active participation of 'the audience' whose spontaneous response was a vivid element of the performance. The Vaiṣṇavas cried and shook with joy, exclaimed God's names, sang and danced. Their rapturous reactions influenced and supported stage actions of the main performers

[47] *e sava līlāra kabhu abadhi nā haya.*
'āvirbhāva, tirobhāva' bede mātra kaya. CB, M, XVIII, 209.

[48] *mahārāja-rājeśvara prabhu viśvambhara.*
ei raṅga karilena nadīyā-bhitara. CB, M, XVIII, 210.

[49] *saptadina śrīācārya-ratnera mandire.*
parama adbhuta teja chila nirantare. CB, M, XVIII, 226.

[50] *candra, sūryya, viduyat ekatra yena jvale.*
dekhiye sukṛti-sava mahā-kutuhale. CB, M, XVIII, 227.

[51] *(. . .) vaiṣṇavagaṇa mane mane hāse.*
keha āra kichu nāhi karaye prakāśe. CB, M, XVIII, 230.

[52] It is quite possible that the early Caitanya's performances of a similar kind gave rise to the *rāgānugā* practice according to which a bhakta assumes a role of one of Kṛṣṇa's beloved companions from Vraja (*Vrajaloka*).

(actors) — Caitanya and his very close companions. The *līlā* of God, invoking the most ultimate sentiment of devotion, is to be enacted and shared by those completely absorbed in it.

The performance is quite clearly divided into two parts, each of three hours duration. The first part contains the invocation, the prologue and two scenes. It is preparatory in character. The main event of the performance is announced (Caitanya's dance in Lakṣmī's dress = Ādyāśakti's dress). Almost all main personages (except for Gadādhara) are introduced. There is a sort of descriptive and narrative action. The atmosphere of delight is already created. All participants are prepared to witness and experience the eternal. The second part containing three scenes deals much more with presenting different emotional roles (*bhāvas*) assumed, first by Gadādhara, then by Caitanya. From the very beginning of the performance every scene leads to the final one, in which the unique intimacy of the Vaiṣṇavas is displayed. The fruit of the dramatic action is attained (*phalaprāpti*) and devotional love triumphs.

The performance described is very much of the Kṛṣṇa-yātrā type. It resembles the yātrā in its structure of succeeding scenes and in the intensity of emotions engaged in. The very passionate acting and re-acting of all the participants are crucial features of both, the performance presented and the yātrā. Depending on rather scarce information, we shall not go too far calling Caitanya's performances the Kṛṣṇa-yātrās proper, although, we must admit, we are very tempted to do it.[53] The ambience they both operated in as well as their social context could also support our opinion in favour of this identification.

APPENDIX

Let us briefly comment on the Third Act of the *Caitanyacandrodaya-nāṭaka* by Kavikarṇapūra. This act called *Dānavinoda* contains an inset play about the dalliance of Kṛṣṇa and Rādhā, *Dānalīlā*.

In the *praveśaka* scene (an interlude) two allegorical characters, Maitrī (Friendship) and Premabhakti (Devotional Love), announced enacting Kṛṣṇa-Rādhā play by Caitanya and his companions. The main actors are

[53] Let us mention two fragments from the *Caitanyabhāgavata*.
kṛṣṇa-yātrā-mahotsava-purvva nāhi kare.
vivāhādi-karme se ānanda kari' mare. CB, Ādi, VIII, 204.
kṛṣṇa-yātrā, ahorātri kṛṣṇa-saṁkīrttana.
ihāra uddeśa nāhi jāne kon jana. CB, Antya, IV, 412.

known to us. Thus Haridāsa is to play a *sūtradhāra* (stage manager), Mukunda–his assistant (*pāripārśvaka*), Nityānanda–Baṛāi (Yogamāyā Bhagavatī), Kṛṣṇa; Śrīvāsa–Nārada, Śrīrāma–Snātaka, Caitanya–Rādhā (Vṛndāvaneśvarī),[54] Advaitā–Vidūṣaka.[55] The performance takes place in the house of Ācāryaratna (Candraśekhara). The play describes an episode of offering flowers to Gopīśvara Śiva[56] by Rādhā.

(Invocation): A nāndī stanza is recited behind the scene (*nepathya eva nāndī paṭhitā*).[57] The sounds of mṛdaṅga drums could be heard from there.

(Prologue–*Prastāvanā*): Sūtradhāra-Haridāsa, Pāripārśvaka–Mukunda, Premabhakti and Maitrī. Premabhakti stressed the importance of enacting the *līlās*. Listening to the *līlās* was not so much admirable as enacting them. (CCN, III, 18); the annoucement of the subject-matter (CCN, III, 23).

Then the play itself begins. We can mark off the following scenes:

(Scene 1): Nārada–Śrīvāsa, Snātaka–Śrīrāma, Premabhakti, Maitrī. It is a long scene containing a discussion on *Kṛṣṇa-līlās* in Vṛndāvana and their praise. At the end of this scene Kṛṣṇa-Nityānanda entered the stage.

Two short scenes — (Scene 2): Kṛṣṇa and his friends — Suvala, Śrīdāman, Sudāman and Kusumāsava, Vidūṣaka, Nārada. (Scene 3): Kṛṣṇa, Suvala, Kusumāsava.

(Scene 4): Rādhā–Caitanya, Kṛṣṇa, Rādhā's friends — Jaratī (Baṛāi) and Lalitā, Suvala, Kusumāsava, Premabhakti, Maitrī.

Rādhā and her friends plucked flowers for the pūjā of Gopīśvara. Suddenly Kṛṣṇa with his friends appeared demanding from Rādhā an adequate price for the flowers collected in his forest. This can be called the main scene of the play. At the very end of it Nityānanda emboding Yogamāyā's emotion regained his own nature.

[54]In the performance described by Vṛndāvanadāsa Caitanya played different manifestations of Ādyāśakti, Rādhā was just one of many. In the *Caitanya-candrodayanāṭaka* Caitanya plays only one female energy — Rādhā.

[55]CCN; Act III, a prose portion after the ninth stanza, then the twelfth-thirteenth stanzas and prose portions following them (pp. 44-7).

[56]In the course of the play it turns out that the true Gopīśvara is not Śiva but Kṛṣṇa himself.

[57]A prose portion following the seventeenth stanza (p. 48). The fact that the nāndī śloka is recited behind the stage gives rise to an opinion that the play is of *bhāṇa* or *vyāyoga* type (a prose portion following the sixteenth stanza). However, it is not right as the both mentioned types represent different dramatic features than the inset play in the *Caitanyacandrodayanāṭaka*.

Then the end of the play about the *Dānalīlā* of Kṛṣṇa and Rādhā was announced.

The plot of the inset play is rather weak. The main concern of it is to display the glory of Kṛṣṇa- and Caitanya-*līlā*s and to praise Kṛṣṇa-bhakti.

REFERENCES

Bharatamuni, *Nāṭyaśāstra*, with the commentary *Abhinavabhārati* by Abhinavaguptācārya, vol. 2, Delhi: Parimal Publications, 1988 (NS).

Das Gupta, Hemendranath, *The Indian Stage*, vol. 1, pt. 1, Calcutta: Metropolitan Printing and Publishing House, 1934.

Eidlitz, Walther, *Kṛṣṇa-Caitanya, Sein Leben und Seine Lehre*, Stockholm: Almqvist ans Wiksell, 1968.

Haberman, David L., *Acting as a way of Salvation. A Study of Rāgānugā Bhakti Sādhanā*, New York; Oxford: Oxford University Press, 1988.

Kavikarṇapūra, *The Chaitanyacandrodaya: A Devotional Drama*, edited by Paṇḍit Kedāranātha and Vāsudev Lakṣmaṇ Śāstrī Paṇsikar, 2nd edn., Bombay: Nirṇaya-Sāgar Press, 1917 (CCN).

Kṛṣṇadāsa Kavirāja, *ŚrīŚrīCaitanyacaritāmṛta*, with the Sanskrit commentary of Viśvanātha Chakravartī and a Bengali interpretation by the editor Mākhanlālā Dās Bhāgavatabhūṣaṇ, vol. 3, Calcutta, 1908 (CC).

Vṛndāvanadāsa, *ŚrīŚrīCaitanyabhāgavata*, with the *Gauṛīyabhāṣya*; *Ādikhaṇḍa,* 1928; *Madhya-, Antyakhaṇḍa*, 1934, edited by Gauṛiyā Maṭha, 2nd edn., Calcutta (CB).

PART V

Modes of Transmission of Religion in Gujarat

Bārahakkhara-kakka of Mahācandra Muni

H.C. BHAYANI AND PRITAM SINGHVI

An Early Old Gujarati Didactic Jain Poem in the Genre Mātṛkā ('The Alphabet')

Old Gujarati-Rajasthani literature began about the twelfth century BC. Up to the fifteenth century the literary language was common for western Rajasthan and Gujarat.[1] Later on because of the different directions of linguistic development we find some works specifically in the regional languages, while some continue to be written in the common literary medium.

For some seven centuries, hundreds of works have been written in old western Rajasthani-Gujarati, both in prose and verse. It is therefore natural that there would be numerous types, forms and genres. Naturally, our modern notion of literature and literary types and forms will not be applicable to the literary works written in Indian regional languages during the medieval period. Therefore, we shall have to take into consideration the types of actual works written in various regions, towards which some efforts have been already made. But much remains to be done. So far as the old Rajasthani-Gujarati literature is concerned, some valuable work to classify its literature has been done. Researchers have distinguished some one hundred to two hundred various literary types and forms. Even though the subject still needs to be critically surveyed, whatever work has been done so far by three or four scholars is quite useful.[2] For example, in Nahta's work mentioned in the note, 117 different designations of various medieval types, forms, etc., are counted and described. From this, it is quite obvious that these traditional designations were based on several norms of classification, e.g. (1) Metrical form, (2) Social festival or occasion, (3) Subject-matter, (4) Religious contexts, (5) Number of verses,

[1] For the historical development and description see (1) The pioneering efforts of L.P. Tessitori, *'Notes' on Grammar of the Old Western Rajasthani*, 1914-16; (2) *Gujarātī Sāhitya no Itihās*, pt. 1, Ahmedabad, 1973.

[2] See the list of reference works given at the end.

(6) Biography of individuals or hagiography. These are mentioned only as pointers.

In this multiplicity of types, forms, etc., there is one genre variously called *Mātṛkā, Kakka, Kakaharā* or *Bāvnī*. In this type of work every verse begins sequentially with each letter of the Sanskrit Varṇamālā in order. This will be clear from the following citation from Nahta's work mentioned earlier.

मातृका, बावनी, कक्क

वर्णमाला के अक्षर ५२ मानते हुए प्रत्येक वर्ण से प्रारम्भ करके जब पद्य रचे जाते हैं तब ऐसी रचनाओं की संज्ञा 'बावनी' होती है। अपभ्रंश से इस प्रकार की रचनाओं का प्रारम्भ होता है। इसकी अन्य संज्ञा 'बावनी' है। हिन्दी में इसे 'अखरावट' भी कहते हैं। तेरहवीं-चौदहवीं शताब्दी की ऐसी चार रचनाएं—'शालिभद्र कक्क', 'दुहामातृका', 'सम्यक्त्व-माई-चौपाई', 'मातृका-चौपाई'—'प्राचीन गुर्जर काव्यसंग्रह' में प्रकाशित हैं। ये बावनी के पूर्व रूप हैं। सोलहवीं शताब्दी से ऐसी रचनाओं का नाम बावनी व्यवहृत हुआ है, यद्यपि आदि अंत में कुछ अन्य पद्य जोड़ने से पद्यों की संख्या ५५, ५७ या ६० तक पहुँच गई है। कुछ रचनाएं मातृकाक्षरों के क्रम पर नहीं की गई हैं। उनकी पद्य संख्या ५२ से कुछ ही अधिक होने पर उनको भी बावनी कहा गया है। हिन्दी, राजस्थानी, गुजराती इन तीन भाषाओं में जैन कवियों द्वारा रचित पचास के लगभग बावनियां हैं। भिन्न-भिन्न छन्दों में रची होने से इनके नाम दूहाबावनी, सवैयाबावनी, कविताबावनी, कुण्डलियाबावनी आदि रखे गए हैं और कुछ के नाम विषय के अनुसार धर्मबावनी, गुणबावनी इत्यादि मिलते हैं। टीकमगढ़ से प्रकाशित 'मधुकर' पत्रिका में कई वर्ष पूर्व 'बावनी-संज्ञक हिन्दी रचनाएं' शीर्षक लेख प्रकाशित हो चुका है। हिन्दी भाषा की कतिपय बावनियों, बारहखड़ियों, बत्तीसियों आदि का विवरण लेखक द्वारा संपादित 'राजस्थान में हस्तलिखित ग्रन्थों की खोज', भाग ४ में दिया गया है। इनमें वर्णमाला के अक्षरों का क्रम इस प्रकार रखा गया मिलता है:

ओं (न मो सि द्धं) अ, आ, इ, ई, उ, ऊ, ऋ, ॠ, ऌ, ॡ, ए, ऐ, ओ, औ, अं, अः, क, ख, ग, घ, ङ., च, छ, ज, झ, ञ, ट, ठ, ड, ढ, ण, त, थ, द, ध, न, प, फ, ब, भ, म, य, र, ल, व, श, ष, स, ह, क्ष।

The earliest known reference to this 'Alphabet' genre is from the Buddhist work *Lalitavistara* (about seventh-eighth century). In its tenth chapter it is said that when the teacher started to teach the alphabet to the boy (who was to be later the Buddha) the latter recited Subhāṣitas, each of which began with a letter of alphabet in sequence. Besides, in musicological texts, Mātṛkā figures as one of the musical Prabandhas. In Mataṅga Muni's *Bṛhaddeśī*, Mātṛkā is defined as that composition in which each verse begins with the Varṇas of Mātṛkā in sequence (Chap. 6, Prabandha no. 40; pt. 2, p. 238).[3] So also in Someśvara's *Mānasollāsa* (or

[3] In the *Bṛhaddeśī* (Chap. 1, v. 6) Mātṛkā is said to be the matrix of varṇas consisting of vowels and consonants and is praised as the light of the world.

In Hemavijaya's *Kathāratnākara* (AD 1600) Mātṛkā is called *Veda-mātā*.

	Name	Author	Date	Extent, Metre	Language	Published or not	Remarks
1.	अष्टापद-तीर्थ-बावनी	जयसागर उपाध्याय	१५वीं शताब्दी	गाथा ५४			
2.	आत्मबोध मातृका	अज्ञात	१६वीं १७वीं शताब्दी	गाथा ६४			भले से प्रारंभ
3.	उपदेशकारक कक्को	जिनवर्धन	१५८५ करीब			प्रकाशित	
4.	उपदेश-बावनी	विजयानन्द सूरीश्वर					
5.	कक्का	भोजो	१९वीं शताब्दी		पुरानी गुज.		
6.	कक्कानां कीर्त्तनो	कृष्णाराम महाराज	१९वीं शताब्दी		पुरानी गुज.	प्रकाशित	एक एक को लेकर बाराखडी के अनुसार कीर्त्तनों की रचना की गई है। प्रत्येक व्यंजन के अकार और आकार वाली अलग-अलग कडियाँ यहाँ है।
7.	काकबंधि चौपई	देवसुन्दरसूरि शिष्य	१३९४ के करीब	कडी ६९			
8.	कृष्ण उपासनानुं धोळ	प्रीतमदास	१८वीं शताब्दी			प्रकाशित	
9.	केशव-बावनी अथवा मातृका-बावनी	केशवदास अथवा कौशलसागर	१६८०	६० सवैया	हिन्दी	अप्रकाशित	ऊँकार से आरंभ और 'क्ष' कार से अन्त
10.	जसराज-बावनी अथवा ऊँकार बावनी,	जिनहर्ष					
	मातृका-बावनी अथवा कवित्व बावनी	जसराज	१६८२	५७ सवैया	हिन्दी	प्रकाशित	ऊँकार से आरंभ।

Name	Author	Date	Extent, Metre	Language	Published or not	Remarks
11. दीपक-माई	अज्ञात		६४ चउपई, ५२ वर्ण			रास के स्वरूप में नागलपुर में पार्श्व जिनालय में रास खेलने के लिए रचना की गई है।
12. दूहा-बावनी	लक्ष्मीवल्लभ अथवा हेमराज	१६वीं शताब्दी				इस कृति के बारे में और कोई सूचना नहीं है, लगता है कि यह कक्कहरा के रूप में न हो। सिर्फ ५२ दोहे की रचना हो। क्योंकि इसी कवि की 'कुंडलिया बावनी' 'उपदेशबत्तीसी' जैसी रचनाओं का नामकरण छन्द के नाम के आधार पर किया गया है।
13. दोहा-मातृका अथवा धर्म-मातृका	पउम	१३वीं शताब्दी	५७ कडी			सारे व्यंजन अकार और आकार से युक्त दिये गये हैं।
14. शालिभद्र-कक्क	पउम	१३वीं शताब्दी	७१ कडी			इनके लिये अलग अलग कडियां हैं। स्वर नहीं लिये गये हैं। दोनों का छन्द दोहा है।
15. दोहा-बावनी अथवा मातृका-बावनी	जिनहर्ष अथवा जसराज	१६६४	दोहा ५३	हिन्दी	प्रकाशित	अन्त्य वर्ण 'क्ष' है और अकार तथा आकार युक्त वर्ण दिये गये हैं।

	Name	Author	Date	Extent, Metre	Language	Published or not	Remarks
16.	धर्म-(भावना) बावनी	धर्मवर्धन अथवा धर्मसिंह पाठक	१६६९	५७ कडी छन्द सवैया	हिन्दी	प्रकाशित	
17.	बावन-अक्षरी	भोजो	१७३२	५९ तुक	ब्रजभाषा	प्रकाशित	
18.	बाराखडी	अज्ञात	१९वीं शताब्दी	४० दोहा	हिन्दी	अप्रकाशित	
19.	माइ-अक्षर-बावनी	मतिशेखर वाचक	१४५८	गाथा ५३			भले से आरंभ होता है।
20.	मातृका	जयमूर्तिगणि	१५वीं शताब्दी	६४ चउपई			
21.	मातृका चउपाई	अज्ञात	१२७१	६४ कडी			जो जगडू की कृति में है वही वर्णमाला है। मगर 'ॐ' के पहले मींडू अधिक है। इस तरह बावन वर्ण हैं। और कवि ने स्वयं भी कहा है कि ५२ अक्षर की रचना मैं करता हूँ।
22.	मातृका-प्रथमाक्षर-दोहक अपरनाम रसविलास	पुहवीचन्द	संवत १३७० के करीब	दोहा ५४			५२ अक्षर, भले से आरंभ बाद में मीडूं दो रेखा बाद में ओमकार। दोहा के पहले अर्ध में एक वर्ण और दूसरे अर्ध में दूसरा वर्ण ऐसा रचनाक्रम है।
23.	मातृका-फाग	अज्ञात	१५वीं शताब्दी				

	Name	Author	Date	Extent, Metre	Language	Published or not	Remarks
24.	मातृका-बावनी	अज्ञात	१४वीं शताब्दी	गाथा ६४			'भले' से आरंभ होता है।
25.	लखा-भगतना छप्पा	अ० क० खबरदार	२०वीं शताब्दी		अर्वाचीन गुज.		
26.	वैशंपायननो कक्को	करसनदास माणेक	१९५४		अर्वाचीन गुज.		
27.	स्थूलभद्र-काकादि	स. आत्माराम जाजोडिया	१९६८				राजस्थान पुरातन ग्रंथमाला
28.	स्थूलिभद्र-काक	देपाल	१४३५	दोहा ३६			जोधपुर, क्रमांक ६७ आरंभ भले मींडू और दो रेखा से होता है। प्रत्येक दोहे में अकार और आकार क्रमशः व्यंजन दिये गए हैं और 'ह' के बाद 'क्ष' दिया गया है।
29.	सम्यक्त्व-माइ-चौपाई	जगडु	१२७५ करीब	६४ कडी		प्रकाशित	
30.	संवेग-मातृका	अज्ञात	१२९४	६१ कडी		अप्रकाशित	उसका आरंभ भले और मींडू से होता है।
31.	ज्ञान-कक्का	अखो	१७वीं शताब्दी		पुरानी गुज.	प्रकाशित	दोहाबद्ध रचना, क, ख, ग, इत्यादि क्रम से।
32.	ज्ञाननो कक्को	जीवनदास	१८वीं शताब्दी		पुरानी गुज.		चौपाईबद्ध है।

Abhilaṣitārtha-cintāmaṇi, dated 1163), Mātṛkā is similarly defined (IV, 16, 310).

Below is given a list of known works of this genre. The list is not exhaustive. It is compiled mainly on the basis of the reference works.

The earliest available work of the 'Mātṛkā' type in the post-Apabhraṁśa regional language of Gujarat-Rajasthan is called *Bārahakkharia-kakka* (also called *Bārahakkhariya*), written by Muni Mahācandra in possibly about the thirteenth century. This name is given in view of the form of the poem. It is composed in the Dohā metre. Besides, in the third verse, the poet has also called his poem *Dohāvelli.* Its significance is that the poem is composed in a continuous series of Dohās. *Velli* means a creeper. *Velli* is known as a literary genre in medieval Rajasthani-Gujarati literature. For information on this type of poem, see H.C. Bhayani, *Rāula Vela of Roḍā* (1994), Introduction, pp. 30-1. At the end of the text in the manuscript the concluding stanza remarks: इति दोहापाहुडं समाप्तं. This implies that traditionally the work was also known as *Dohāpāhuḍa*. It is obvious that this name became current under the influence of Rāmasiṁha's *Dohāpāhuḍa*, which was possibly written before the eleventh century AD and which has considerable similarity with Mahācandra's poem in subject-matter, ideas and metre.

There are 331 verses in all in this work. The author himself has stated that there are 324 Dohās in his poem. The poem begins with a Sanskrit verse as Maṅgala. Thereafter he has mentioned in introductory five Dohās the name of the poem, its form, its extent and author's name. A final verse expresses the conclusion of the poem. In this way 6+324+1 make up a total of 331 verses.

The Dohā is well known as one of the standard Apabhraṁśa metres used for several literary types, and later on we have a vast body of literature written in this metre in Rajasthani, Gujarati, Hindi and other regional languages.

The subject-matter of the poem can be briefly stated as follows: In keeping with the tenets of the Jain religion one should observe self-control, practise religious vows and austerities, avoiding false religion, false Gurus and false gods, etc., giving up attachment to worldly things; importance should not be given to external practices like pilgrimage, physical cleanliness, and sensuous enjoyment; one's mind should concentrate on Samādhi and Yoga and not remain tied up by scriptural knowledge; concentration on self (Ātman) would thus destroy the Karmans through internal purity and achieve absolute knowledge and ultimate release. This instruction has been given in clear and simple words and it is made interesting by illustrations from the experience of ordinary familiar world.

From about the eighth century onwards, we have a series of Jain works emphasizing the spiritual point of view and meditation with regard to instructions of the tenets of Jainism. We can mention *Paramātmaprakāśa* and *Yogasāra* of Yogīndudeva, *Dohāpāhuḍā* of Rāmasiṁha and the works on Yoga of Haribhadra, Hemacandra, etc., in the Śvetāmbara Jain tradition. In fact the tradition goes back to the works (principally in the Dohā metre) of the Bauddha Siddhas Sarahapāḍa, Kṛṣṇapāda, etc. The tradition of writing works under the profound influence of the spiritual vision of the Siddhas and Yogīndudeva continued uninterrupted down to the nineteenth century, as shown for example by the poems of the poets like Ānandaghana.[4] Mahācandra's poem is an important early link in this chain.

Mahācandra Muni has introduced himself as the disciple of Vīracandra. We have no knowledge about the life and the time of both of them. In view of the comparative position of the *Bārahakkhara-kakka* and language of the work our inference is that the work can be placed about the thirteenth century AD. We find in the language of the poem many Apabhraṁśa words and forms along with those that are characteristic of early medieval Indo-Aryan regional languages: in numerous expressions we can clearly trace the influence of old Rajasthani. This fact suggests that Mahācandra Muni must have been a Digambara Muni from Rajasthan. It is also quite clear that the *Bārahakkhara-kakka* is to be dated after the works like *Paramappapayāsa*, *Dohāpāhuḍa*, *Sāvaya-dhamma-Dohā*, etc.[5]

[4] In a recently published poem *Jinastuti* in praise of the Jina (ed.) Jagaccandravijay-gaṇi, *Anusandhān*, 8, 1977, pp. 125-6, each of the letters of the Varṇamālā is used as an adjective of the Jina and its meaning is given on the basis of Ekākṣara-kośas.

The tradition of composing the Alphabet type of poems is living till today. See B.N. Goswami's *Ranga Roop, Gods, Words, Images* (Neelkanth Books, 1996) in which along with the pictures of Purāṇic gods and goddesses a verse in Hindi is given, the order of the pictures follows the order of the letters in the Hindi Varṇamālā.

In their edition of its *Bṛhaddeśī* the editors in their note on the Mātṛkā type of musical Prabandha have remarked that this type of the Prabandhas (based on the varṇas of Mātṛkā) are current in the present-day Odissi folk music (*Bṛhaddeśī*, 2, p. 320).

[5] The *Bārahakkhara-kakka* with the original text, Hindi translation, Introduction and notes has been edited by the authors of this paper and it is to be shortly published. The information given here is based on the only known manuscript from Āmer Śāstra Bhaṇḍār, Jaipur. We are thankful to the Apabhraṃṣa Sāhitya Academy and to its Director Dr. Kamal Chand Sogani for making the Ms. available for our use.

REFERENCES

Āpaṇā Kavio, K.K. Shastri, pt. 1, Ahmedabad, 1989.
Amanaska-yoga of Gorakhanātha.
Jain Gūrjar Kavio (revd. edn.), pt. 7, 1991.
Gujarātī Sāhitya nā Svarūpo, Manjulal Majmudar, Baroda, 1954.
Gujarātī Sāhitya no Itihās, pts. 1 and 2, Ahmedabad, 1973, 1976.
Gujarātī Sāhitya Kośa, pt. 1, 1989.
Prācīn Kāvyo kī Rūp-paramparā, Agarchanda Nahta, Bikaner, 1962.
Bṛhaddeśī of Śrī Mataṅga Muni, edited by P.L. Sharma, A.B. Beohar, pt. 1, 1992; pt. 2, 1994.

A Unique Unison of the Saguṇa and the Nirguṇa in the *Agamnā Bār Mahinā* (The *Bārmāsī*) by Kāyamuddīn Ciśtī

BALVANT JANI

BACKGROUND

In the long tradition of the Muslim saints of Gujarāt, Kāyamuddīn Ciśtī has always been held high in esteem as one of the towering saints. A good number of Muslim saints who came to India primarily as preachers or preceptors, succeeded in persuading and drawing even the aborigines towards Islamic ideology. Largely owing to this sort of religious conversion, there came into existence quite a good number of 'converted communities', such as: Khojā, Vohrā, Mūmnā, Molesalām, Mīr, Matwā and the like, all of whom, as a matter of fact, had formerly belonged to various Hindu castes, originally known as: Lohāṇā, Brāhmin, Kaṇbī, Rājput, Bāroṭ and Bharwāḍ, etc. Consequent upon their conversion to Islam, however, all of them acquired a sort of new identity and nomenclature, as cited above. Right from the outset, this 'newly converted' population tended to differ from the Muslims in many respects. Some of their customs and conventions in regard to inter-dining and matrimonial relationships and caste-dinners, etc., were strictly limited to their respective groups only, that is to say, — a good number of inhibitions and taboos were imposed upon them.[1]

From an intensive study of the Indian culture undertaken by the Muslim saints and preachers, who preached to all these communities, along with the various methods of preaching adopted by them, a fine example, can be obtained of their patience and composure, besides that of the mental disposition of the local population.

Such preachers and preceptors, who were, indeed, well-versed and conversant in the acquisition of profound knowledge in regard to the Indian culture and Indian literature, considered it greatly convenient to

[1] *Studies in South Asian Devotional Literature*, edited by A. Entwistle and F. Mallison, 1994, p. 222.

utilize the heritage of ancient Indian literature and its various literary forms, which they found to be a very potential medium for the purpose of their didactic verses. A number of metrical compositions akin to *Pada-Bhajans*, etc., came into existence, following the above tradition, which had been composed by Muslim saints and preachers, and these are widely known as: *Ginan*, *Kāsīdā* compositions, *Prabhātiyāṅ* (morning hymns or songs), *Garbi* and *Āratī*, — all of which are highly significant. The mode of their expression as well as their subject-matter is both basically of Indian origin and reflecting a native touch, though certain linguistic variations and the script, are either Arabic or Persian.[2] Nevertheless, in the case of all these compositions, the overwhelming influence of the medieval Gujarātī language can be seen everywhere. Thus, it can be observed that, instead of preaching their proposed ideology, these Muslim saints successfully tended to be rather preoccupied with a close study of the culture, literature, as also the mentality of the people, to whom they hoped to preach and admonish, and thereafter, through its own media, they strove to claim a sort of recognition to their self-identity and also to establish their personality in the midst of an altogether strange social circle.

Thus, it can be observed that in the long tradition of the Muslim saints, the place occupied by Kāyamuddīn Ciśtī is no less significant.[3] Though the year of his birth is not certain, it is an established fact, however, that he died in the Hījrī Era year 1187, that is, in AD 1768. He died at a village named Dhokḍā near Naṅdurbār, and in keeping with his last wish, he was buried in the village Ekalbārā, on the bank of river Mahī. There also stands his Dargāh (mosque) on that spot,[4] which is visited daily by throngs of both Hindu and Muslim devotees along with their families.

KĀYAMUDDĪN CIŚTĪ: ANCESTORS AND TRADITION

A city named Ciśt exists near the river Herāt in Iraq. In this city, there happened to flourish, one by one, four venerable Ciśtī Khwājās. From amongst these four, in the traditional sequence of generations of Ciśtī Khwājās, one of them has ever been held in great prominence as Bābā Farīd-Sāheb Pīr. This Pīr had cultivated a close and intimate relationship with the Emperors of India, where he used to stay most of the time. He was married to the daughter of Sultān Gyāsuddīn, who was the son of Samsuddīn

[2] Karim Master, *Mahāgujarātana Musalamāno*, pts. 1, 2, 1969, p. 200.

[3] Balvant Jani, *Oral Traditional Literature of Gujarāt*, 1995, p. 9.

[4] Ardesar Phrāmjī Khabardār, 'Pīrasāheb Kāyamuddīn Ciśtī', in Ambālāl Bulākhirām Jānī (ed.), *Forbes Gujarātī Sabhā Mahotsava Grantha*, 1940, p. 991.

Altamas, the Sultān of Delhi. In this way, over and above his reputation as a learned man, he was also prominent as one of the members of the Royal family of Delhi.

The descendants of Bābā Farīd migrated to Gujarāt, after three hundred years, and settled in Pāṭaṇ, and later on, started their residence in Kaḍī. Along with the tradition of pīrs, the name of Hazrat Badruddīn Sāheb, too, is very prominent. His son, Kāyamuddīn, had acquired the knowledge of the Korān right from his childhood days, and had learnt it by heart at the age of eight years.[5] He was greatly fascinated and impressed by the cultural rites, rituals and conventions of the Indian people. Succeeding his father, he attained the dignified status of a pīr. He exercised great command over the Arabic, Persian, Sanskrit and Gujarātī languages. Pīr Sāheb Kāyamuddīn was a staunch vegetarian. Even today, there is not a single stall selling meat, nor is any non-vegetarian diet served in the precincts of his Dargāh!

He was a profound scholar of Indian Yoga-Vidyā and Vedānta. He was not merely concerned with the study of the science of Yoga, but he strongly believed in their thorough application to life, and himself practised it, that is to say, he was greatly advanced in his accomplishments. After assimilating the mysticism of the Yoga, he was also successful in imbibing yogic exercises and processes, such as: *ṣaṭcakrabhedana*, as a result of which, he had acquired certain occult powers as well. Among his followers, there were Hindus as well as Muslims alike.

THE DISCIPLE-TRADITION OF KĀYAMUDDĪN CIŚTĪ

Among his pupils, one named Ebrāhīm is widely popular and known as Abhrām Bhagat throughout the region of north Gujarāt. In like manner, another, named Panjābāpā is equally famous.

Then, there are other disciples, such as: Nirānt Bhagat, the disciple of Aman Sāheb, who was himself a disciple of Kāyamuddīn, a Pāṭīdār devotee named Jīvan Mastān, and his cousin sister, Ratanbai, are also well-known. In fact, the tomb of Ratanbāi is situated just near the stairs leading to the Dargāh of Pīr Sāheb.[6] This brilliant tradition of disciples has always remained inclined to the composition and recitation of *pada*s or *bhajan*s and other devotional songs, thereby following in the footsteps of Pīr Sāheb Kāyamuddīn himself.

[5] Ibid., p. 89.

[6] Ibid., p. 91.

CONTRIBUTION OF KĀYAMUDDĪN CIŚTĪ

Dil-e-Rośan and *Nūr-e-Rośan* are considered to be the two volumes of verses composed by Kāyamuddīn Ciśtī. It has not been possible to undertake a study of *Dil-e-Rośan*, but while going through *Nūr-e-Rośan*, we invariably come across an idea that all its compositions are akin to the medieval Gujarātī-Hindī-Braj devotional songs or *bhajans*.

In this instance, it is quite apparent that in the case of all these compositions, the tune, the metre, the mode or the style of singing and all such aspects invariably reflect the medieval Gujarātī origin.[7] Moreover, as regards the literary or metrical forms employed here, they are very well-known among Gujarātī people, as for example, *Garbī*, *Bāramāsī*, *Pada*, *Bhajan*, etc. And, as for the subject-matter, in the majority of cases, there is obviously an unmistakable application of Indian Yoga and Vedānta. It has been intended to present here the translation and interpretation of at least one of the compositions of Kāyamuddīn Ciśtī, titled *Agamnā Bār Mahinā*,[8] answering to the requirements of the form known as *Bārmāsī*.

AGAMNĀ BĀR MAHINĀ: THE *BĀRMĀSĪ* COMPOSED BY KĀYAMUDDĪN CIŚTĪ

Caraṇe satagurune ramiye, jhīṇā thai muraśadane namiye,
Tyāre to alakha dhanīne namiye . . . (Ṭek)
Suratā sunamāṁhīṁ lāgī, ke vaṁsaḷī aganamāṁ vāgī,
Khumārī prema taṇī jāgī . . . Caraṇe satagurune . . . (1)

Kāratake kāyāmāṁ jāgī, śabda agama jāya lāgī,
Ke hyam nahīṁ veda kitāba, kājī . . . Caraṇe. (2)

Māgasare mana māruṁ mohyuṁ, darśana nūra taṇuṁ joyuṁ,
Ke meṁ to Āpa-paṇuṁ khoyuṁ . . . Caraṇe. (3)

Poṣe piṇḍa māruṁ khoyuṁ, mana to sataguruse mohyuṁ,
Ke meṁ to arasa-kurasa joyuṁ . . . Caraṇe. (4)

Māhe mahāsunamāṁ phoḍī, suratā sāhebaśuṁ joḍī,
Ke śuddha meṁ to dehī taṇī choḍī . . . Caraṇe. (5)

Phagaṇe Brahma thayo prakāśa lāgī mane antaraghaṭamāṁ āśa,
Ke ghaṭamāṁ pote thayā prakāśa . . . Caraṇe. (6)

[7] *Gujarātī Sāhityakośa*, *Madhyakāla*, pt. 1, edited by Jayanta Koṭhārī et al., 1989.

[8] *Nūr-e-Rośan*, ed. by Vakīl Ratansāh Koyājī, 1924, p. 138.

Caitare caraṇa jai lāgī, dhūna mārī sāhebśuṁ vāgī,
Ke bhrānti mana tanī bhāgī . . . Caraṇe. (7)

Vaiśākhe mana sunamāṁ mohyuṁ, ke Darśana nūra tanuṁ jayuṅ,
Ke te to sāhebśuṁ mohyuṁ . . . Caraṇe. (8)

Jethe jagatamāṁ jāgī, tāḷī ābhamaṇḍala lāgī,
Cittamāṁ cetana thai jāgī . . . Caraṇe. (9)

Aṣāḍhe aleka rahyo bharapūra, huṁ to jai ūbhī hajhūra,
Ke vājāṁ vāge anahada tūra . . . Caraṇe. (10)

Śrāvaṇe suratā jai lāgī, meṁ to mana mamatā tyāgī,
Piyujīse raṅga kesarī bāndhī . . . Caraṇe. (11)

Bhādarve varabhaṇḍane phoḍī, suratā gai vaikuṇṭha choḍī,
Darasa meṁ to jīvatāṁ jāḍi . . . Caraṇe. (12)

Garabo agama taṇo kīdho, bheda Śāha Kāyamdīne līdho,
Āso mahīne Hari-rasa pīdho . . . Caraṇe. (13)

CONTENTS OF THE *BĀRMĀSĪ*

In the Beginning of *Bārmāsī*, there are details of homage to Guru (or Preceptor), instead of homage to Saraswati, goddess of learning. It has been stated here that salutation to God is offered, in all humility, only after paying homage to the Guru. (In fact, the sight of God seems to have become possible only through the agency of Guru, and that is the reason why the first place is offered to the Guru.) In the next stanza, the state of deep concentration and the state of being engrossed in deep meditation (or trance) have been indicated. During this sort of trance, the sound of the flute is heard, in the element of lustre, which creates a sort of intoxication saturated with love for God. There is an indication of being completely absorbed in love for God. In the Sūfī tradition, God is deemed to be the Beloved (*Māśukā*), while in the tradition following devotion to Kṛṣṇa, it is the devotee himself who feels the sentiment of being the *Māśukā*.[9]

(In the present instance, Kāyamuddīn Ciśtī has followed the tradition, where the devotee feels the sentiment of being a Gopī, during the course of his devotion to Kṛṣṇa, instead of following the Sūfī tradition.)

During the month of *Kārtik*, it is shown how the state of *Anāhata* (i.e. Unbeaten) is created (which is, in fact, beyond the perception of senses),

[9] *Madhyakālīna Gujarātī Jnānamārgī Kavitā*, edited by Balvant Jānī, 1991, p. 31.

that is, a peculiar sort of affection towards the incomprehensible element gets awakened in the body, and this kind of experience is described at length here. This peculiar state is incomprehensible, which is deemed to be the state of *Anāhata* (or the 'Unbeaten' state). One who attains this state, does not require the services of either the Vedas or the Korān, or at best, of the Kājī who teaches the *āyāt*s (verses of the Korān).

During the month of *Māgśar*, the mind has become rather infatuated on account of the sight of the element of Lustre. It means that it has lost its own identity. One tends to reach the state, where the ego or self-consciousness gets effaced altogether as a result of the sound of *Sohaṁ*, and this kind of self-experience is described here.

During the month of *Poṣa*, there is an indication of the loss of physical consciousness, when the mind becomes absorbed in *Sadguru*. On account of this position, everything appears to be tasteless, dull and devoid of any charm or interest, and accordingly, it has been pointed out that we feel two kinds of experience: *A-ras* (tastelessness), and *Ku-ras* (bad taste). Thus, it is a revelation of *Aras-Kuras* experiences. After having felt this, one does not even find any sort of interest in worldly pleasures. It has also been felt that the consciousness towards body is forgotten altogether and the *Turīya* state or *Amanībhāva* state is attained. This kind of position is the outcome of regular and repeated recitation of the mantras (or incantations) such as: *Sohaṁ-Sohaṁ*.

During the month of *Mahā*, there is an indication of how the absorption or obsession towards body-awareness is severed, and how, after breaking off ties with the world, — which state is analogous to an absolute void, — a new relationship is established with the *Parama-Tattva* (or *Mālik*) or the Supreme Being.

During the month of *Phāgaṇ*, an acute longing is generated in the heart to have a glimpse or Darśan of that 'Divine Lustre' and it is shown here as to how this 'Divine Lustre' gets transmitted to the human body causing supreme contentment.

During the month of *Caitra*, the unbeaten tune of *Sohaṁ-Sohaṁ* leads us to the feet of *Mālik* or the Almighty. And, the hallucinations of Body, World, Egotism, etc., are all broken. It is also indicated, how these ties are severed, followed by the details of how the state of non-duality or Advaita is attained which is akin to the state of the Śiva-Gaurī sentiment.

During the month of *Jeṭh*, the *Ābhamaṇḍala*, i.e. the blue vault of the sky is described, as it is found in the Chāndogya Upaniṣad. From which it becomes manifest that all the names and forms are included in the same Supreme Spirit and, therefore, they are akin to *Parabrahman*. Moreover, in Taittirīya Upaniṣad, the sky is symbolized as pure delight, which also affirms a close affinity to *Parabrahman*. And so, it has been duly described here as 'Cosmos'.[10] There is also an indication of the way in which it is totally engrossed in it, and how deep sentiments are developed in the heart as a *Caitanya* form.

During the month of *Āṣāḍha*, there are ample details of completeness, or *Ahālek* (that is, 'Brahman is felt everywhere, in all directions'). It is a situation like where a maid is present, waiting upon the 'Beloved' personally, to offer here humble services. There is an experience of the Ecstasy of Unbeaten Light, and listening to the musical instruments, speedy and swift as wind.

During the month of *Śrāvaṇ*, it is shown how deep concentration and absorption in the Beloved is achieved, as a result of which the mind tends to abandon 'affection' and adopts or assumes the saffron colour, which is the colour symbolizing the entity of the Beloved, and ultimately there happens to be a complete identity of the mind in it, and the experience of non-duality or of one-ness is achieved.

During the month of *Bhādarvā*, the devotee gets a vision of God by *aparokṣānubhūti* (directly visible experience), while living in flesh and blood, consequent upon the breaking up of the Cosmos. So, he is now free from the anxiety of attaining Vaikuṇṭha (the abode of Lord Viṣṇu), it has been stated here.

During the month of *Āso*, by singing a Garbā of the incomprehensible *Parabrahman*, it is shown how Kāyamuddīn has learnt the secret and drunk deep the ecstatic joy of *Hari-rasa*, that is to say, he has obtained intense personal delight resulting from his intuitive perception of God.

INTERPRETATION OF THE *BĀRMĀSĪ*

At this juncture, it is curious to observe a happy and harmonious blending of both the streams, such as: *Premalakṣaṇābhaktimārga* or *Saguṇa* (having attributes), and *Jñānamārga* or *Nirguṇa* (without attributes). But for a few Arabic and Persian words, there is a complete manifestation, almost everywhere, of Indian Philosophy and Yoga-Sādhanā through the language and also through the subject-matter. In this way, this *Bārmāsī* has

[10] Balvant Jānī, 'Upaniṣadonī Sāthe Bhajanavāṇinuṁ Anusandhāna', in Balvant Jānī (ed.), *Santvāṇī, tattva ane tantra*, 1996, p. 141.

(1) Chāndogya Upaniṣad 8-14-11: 'Ākāśo vai nāmarūpayonirvahitā, the yadantarā tadbrahma'.

(2) Taittirīya Upaniṣad 2-7, 'Yadesa ākāśa ānando na syāt'.

been attributed with various phases of *anubhūti* (experience) as well as *sākṣātkāra* (perception or realization) in regard to the Yoga-Sādhanā.

Further, from amongst the various sects of Lokadharmasanskṛti, the achievement of one of its aspects, known as *saṭcakrabhedana*, has been identified as accomplishment of *ulaṭ* and that of *palaṭ*. At this juncture, such terms are employed, as: *Alakha-Dhanī*, *Sāheba*, *Ghaṭa*, *Varbhaṇḍa*, and the like, which are also found in various sects and sub-sects of the Loka-Sanskṛti (Folk Culture), such as: Mahā-Pantha, and Ravi-Bhāṇa-Pantha. In this way, it can be easily asserted that the present *Bārmāsī* composition might have been associated with the peculiar tradition, having close affinity with the sect known as Lokadharma — which happens to be its Creator. The method of worship known as *Ghaṭa-Paṭa* is also observed in Pīr-Paramparā (i.e. the tradition of Pīrs). Thus, we get a glimpse of the process of accomplishment called *saṭcakrabhedana*, following fundamentally the process of *ulaṭ* — which is cited above.

The figure of 12 (twelve), which is a suggestive numeral of the term *Bārmāsī*, is the *Paricāyaka* of the Fourth Cakra. This Fourth Cakra, in turn, is identified by the name of *Anāhata*. The number of petals of the lotus in this Cakra is 12 (twelve). And, an indication of these twelve petals can be obtained through twelve numerals of the *Bārmāsī*. The indication of *Anāhata* is obtained first in the month of *Kārtak*, and thereafter, in the number of months, following it. Śiva-Gaurī are the Presiding deities of the Fourth Cakra. There is an indication of this fact in the months of *Caitra* and *Śrāvaṇ*. The location of this Cakra is the heart. This is indicated in the months of *Phāgaṇ*, *Jeṭh*, etc. And the humming sound of this Cakra is presented as *Sohaṁ-Sohaṁ*, which has been indicated in the months of *Poṣa*, *Mahā*, *Caitra*, etc. The chief element of this Cakra is 'Lustre' (or say, 'Supreme Lustre') and this fact has been indicated in the months of *Māgśar*, *Vaiśākh*, *Jeṭh*, *Āṣāḍh*, *Bhādarvā*, etc.

In this manner, the present composition is an eloquent expression of the experience of *Anāhatabheda* pertaining to the Fourth Cakra *bheda*. The person who rises to such an ultimate height of accomplishment, whether male or female, is endowed with the dignified status of a Sādhu if a male, and of a Sadh if a female. Looking from this perspective, the present composition may be looked upon as an ideal expression of Kāyamuddīn's experience while attaining the dignified status of a Sādhu. Such type of practice or achievement is known as the Indian Yoga-Sādhanā and in Loka-Sampradāyas it is known as the *ulaṭ* accomplishment. In this way, the personal experience as felt by the creative artist himself in respect of the Indian Yoga-Sādhanā and the resultant experience lies at the centre.

Over and above the Yoga-Sādhanā, it can also be seen that a good number of examples reflecting Indian philosophy are also included here. The concept of being a small entity and thereby to develop a concept of smallness, the element of Guru-Mahimā (i.e. the Greatness of Guru) etc., are highlighted. The viewpoint of a sense of realization or consciousness towards the body, the details of elimination of egotism or self-esteem, the concept of Advaita or non-duality,[11] and the depiction of concentration, one-ness and of void, etc. — all these things have been described, along with their correlation with Indian philosophy Vedānta-Vicāra (ideology of Vedānta), as envisaged in the Vedas and Upaniṣads.[12] In this way, it can be stated here that in the present *Bārmāsī* composition, a curious combination of Indian philosophy and the Indian Yoga-Sādhanā has been included to a considerable extent.

On account of this curious blending of the Indian philosophy and the Indian Yoga-Sādhanā, the present *Bārmāsī* composition has occupied a unique position as an exquisite composition which ideally follows the *Jñāna-Mārgī* tradition. But, at the same time, there are also details which reflect the feelings of intense love and the experience of the sense of being a *Gopī* (known as *Gopībhāva*), towards the *Parama-Tattva* or the Supreme Being. Further, it is shown how the maid remains ever present and ready to serve the Beloved in person and to look after Him with sufficient care and concern, as a result of which, it has become possible to attain the stage of one-ness, and be dyed in His own colour, and to seek unification with Him. All these things have been described here in an effective manner. On account of such portrayal and description, this *Bārmāsī* has also been endowed with quite a new dimension of Premalakṣaṇābhaktimārga. Looking from yet another perspective, it can be observed that in the Fourth Cakra, the differentiation between Premalakṣaṇābhaktimārga and Jñānamārga is altogether destroyed and therefore both the methods cited above have been aptly included here.

If we examine this fact in the context of the medieval Gujarātī Literature, we invariably get an idea that the present *Bārmāsī* composition

[11] Ibid., Makaranda Dave, 'Yoganī Sāthe Bhajanonuṁ Anusandhāna', in *Santvāṇī, tattva ane tantra*, edited by Balvant Jānī, 1996, p. 132.

[12] (1) Ṛgveda 10-129-1 and 3: Mantra - Ṛcā

'Nāsadāsīnno sadāsīttadānīṃ . . .' and 'Tama āsīttamasa gūdhamagre . . .'

(2) Amanībhāva: depicted in the Yoga-Darśana, over and above in the *Gauḍapādakārikā*.

(3) Due consideration is made of *Śūnya* (O) in Bauddha-Darśana: 'Sarvaṁ Śūnyaṁ' is a sign in vogue.

as well as its creator, Kāyamuddīn Ciśtī, occupy an equally significant place in the field of literature, amidst the conglomeration of compositions of other poets, who have followed the medieval tradition of Jñānamārga, such as Akho, Bhojo, Bāpusāheb, Vasto, Kewalpurī, and the like. In other words, we also get a glimpse of the concept of Premalakṣaṇābhakti, just as we tend to find the same in the leading compositions of Narsiṁh, Mīrāṁ, Dayārām, etc. In this way, both the traditions, namely, Jñānamārga and Premalakṣaṇābhaktimārga of the medieval Gujarātī literature have been well reflected in the present *Bārmāsī* and that is the reason why it is deemed so unique and full of literary significance. In the context of Indian tradition, we distinctly find a connection between this tradition and the tradition of Sūrdās and Kabīr.

It is curious, indeed, to observe that a Muslim preacher saint may tend to accomplish a harmonious blending of the Indian Yoga-Sādhanā and Indian philosophy, in an effective manner (in other words, between the *Saguṇa* and the *Nirguṇa*), and to give it an eloquent expression, and may choose to employ the Indian names of months, instead of their Muslim names; and owing to this sort of fusion, both the *Bārmāsī* composition and its Creator have occupied a very significant position among the medieval Indian traditions, which, all of us will agree, they fully deserve, indeed!

GLOSSARY

[The first numeral indicates the serial number of the stanza; the second numeral indicates the serial number of the line.]

Sadguru (1, 1): Guru
Murśada (1, 1): Guru
Alakha Dhanī (1, 2): Paramātmā
Suratā 1, 3): Ekāgratā
Agana (1, 3): Tej
Śūnmāṁhī (1, 3): Samādhi Avasthā
Khūmārī (1, 4): Kef-Naśo
Agama (2, 1): That which is not perceptible by senses
Veda (2, 2): Volumes of Indian Philosophy
Kitāb (2, 2): Muslim Scripture: 'The Korān'
Kājī (2, 2): One who teaches the Verses of 'The Korān' and judge also.
Nūr (3, 1): Lustre of Parama-Tattva
Āpa-paṇuṁ (3, 2): Egotism, Body-consciousness
Piṇḍa (4, 1): Body
A-rasa (4, 2): Tasteless
Ku-rasa (4, 2): Having a bad taste
Mahāsūna (5, 1): World, Mahaśunya (Great Zero)

Sāheba (5, 2): God, Mālik, Master, Owner
Śudha (5, 2): Awareness, Consciousness
Antarghaṭa (5, 1): Heart
Ghaṭa (6, 2): Body
Bhrānti (7, 2): Illusion, Sentiment of Ego
Tālī Lāgī (9, 1): To become engrossed, raptured
Ābhamaṇḍala (9, 2): Celestial abode, Vault of Heaven
Cetana (9, 2): Chaitanya, living
Aleka (10, 1): Ahālak, Brahmalaya
Tūra (10, 1): Ecstasy, Paramānanda
Darasa (12, 2): Aparokṣānubhūti, Direct vision/perception
Varbhaṇḍa (12, 1): Brahmāṇḍa, Cosmos
Jīvatāṁ (12, 2): In Person; Living; In flesh and blood
Bheda (13, 1): Secret, Mystery
Hari-Rasa (13, 2): Unity with the Almighty

The Saraju-songs

A Living Tradition within the Devī-worship Ritual of the Vaiśya Sutār and Sorathiā and Bhopā Rabārī of Saurashtra

HASU YAJNIK

Gujarati folk-tradition of Devī-worship includes the various forms and kinds of Devī-stotra, such as Chand, Aṣṭaka, Vadhāi, Garbā, Āratī, Āraṇyu, Regdi and Saraju. The bravery and the beauty of the various Devīs and their subtle forms are being described, praised and invoked in such stotra-type poems. Compared to Chand, Aṣṭaka, Garbā and Āratī the three forms of the Devī worshipping devotional songs namely, Āraṇyu, Regdi and Saraju are most remarkable for not being common or general, but provincial and ethnic. The basic content of these three forms is similar to that of Chand and Aṣṭaka. Here too, the valour and the subtle forms of the Devī are worshipped. But these forms are specially related to ethnic groups. Āraṇyu are sung only by the Rāval community. The Regdi is mostly sung by the Pātanvādia Rabārī of north Gujarat.

Saraju is sung by two communities Vaiśya Sutār and Sorathiā and Bhopā Rabārī of Saurashtra. The geographical area of the Saraju is the seacoast of Saurashtra, from Dwarka to Div. The areas covered are mainly Okhamandal, Baradi and Ghed. The main cities are Dwarka, Jamnagar, Porbandar, Madhavpur, Mangrol, Chorvad, Verāval, Kodinar and Div. The main block is in Junagadh district and its Verāval and Keshod tālukās. The map of the area of the Saraju-songs is given on page 243.

ETYMOLOGY

Saraju has been derived from the Sanskrit word 'Caryā': *Caryā—Caraju—Saraju*. In colloquial Gujarati 'Ch' is often pronounced as 'S' so the 'Charaju' has been pronounced as 'Saraju'. The Cāraṇs of Rajasthan and Gujarat sing Caraju, which is also a traditional Devī-worship and the form is known as 'Caraja Gīt'.[1] The Cāraṇs have a very long ancient tradition

[1] Dr. Govardhan Sharma and Dr. Bhavana Mehta, 'Mātṛśaktinuṃ stavana: Caraja', *Śabdasṛṣṭi*, December 1995, Gujarat Sahitya Akademi, pp. 40-5.

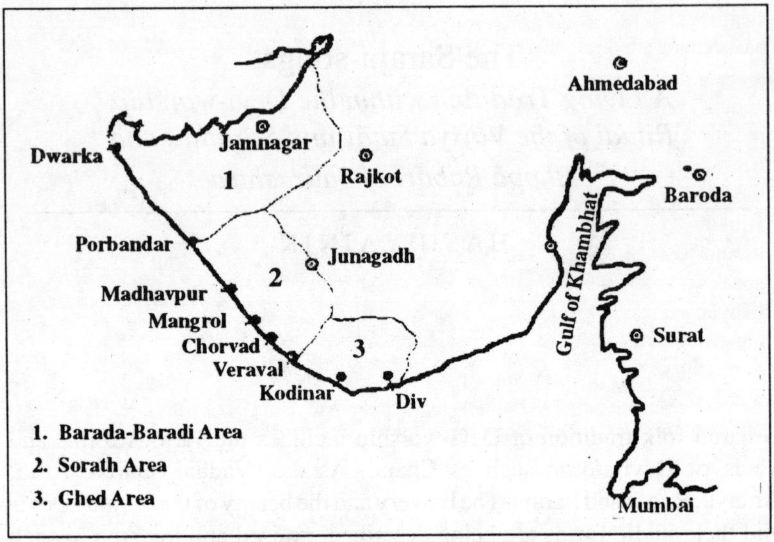

Map 1: Area of the Saraju-songs.

of Devī worship and are known as Ḍevī Putras. But there is no specific relation between the Caraju and Saraju, which is being studied here. The origin, tradition, and singing style of the Saraju of Vaiśya Sutār and Bhopā Rabārī is quite different from the Caraju of the Cāraṇs. The tradition of the Saraju-songs of Vaiśya Sutār and Rabārī of Saurashtra would have its roots in Saurashtra since the tenth century, according to the story of Jālaṇ:[2]

Vaiśya Sutār Parasottam Mehtā and his wife Gangā were living in Jariāvāḍā, a small village on the seacoast of Saurashtra. They had a son by the blessings of a sant. When the child was five years of age the sant came again to the village and named him 'Jālhaṇ' which was pronounced as Jālaṇ. On seeing the palm of Jālaṇ, the sant forecast that he was destined to die by snakebite at the age of twenty. To protect, instruct and save him from this misfortune, the sant took Jālaṇ with him to Mānsarovar near the mount Kailāś, in the Himālaya and handed him over to the Priest of the Devī-Pārvatī-Temple, Sāre Rāval. Jālaṇ learnt Sāma-veda. While collecting a blue lotus at the age of twelve Jālaṇ was bitten by a snake. Sāre Rāval called for the sant, who prayed to Mātā Pārvatī to save Jālaṇ's life. Pārvatī cured Jālaṇ. On completion of his learning of Sāma-veda, Jālaṇ started to go to his hometown in Saurashtra and brought five conch-shells, a peacock and a

[2] Shri Devajibhai Vaja, 'Śakti Upāsak Jālaṇ', *Akhand Anand*, May 1984, Ahmedabad, pp. 55-7. Reprint *Janakalyan*, July 1996, Ahmedabad, pp. 10-11.

swan, which he carried on a kāvad (a pole carried on a shoulder, with a bamboo basket hanging at each ends). At the request of Jālaṇ, Devī Pārvatī also accompanied him on condition that she would walk behind him, but he should not doubt her veracity and should not turn back to see her. Jālaṇ came to Saurashtra. In the early morning the brightest sun rose in the East. Jālaṇ felt that there was a brilliant light behind him in the West, so he turned his face and saw the brilliant Devī Pārvatī on the surface of the ocean. As he had broken his promise, Pārvatī returned to the Himālaya but at the request of Jālaṇ, she promised to come and bless and guide him as and when called for. But she said that she would remain mute and would not speak to him, but would assure him of her presence. Jālaṇ hung the kāvad on a banyan tree and went into a vāv (a step well). Some Rabārī-boys came and out of curiosity took down the kāvad and opened the basket. The conch-shells fell on the earth, the swan flew to Mānsarovar and the peacock who tried to fly was killed by a dog. Jālaṇ came back and on seeing the loss of the pious symbols was grieved, and began to fast till death. The older Rabārīs came and worshipped their Kul Devī Cāmundā, who gave them a pot of nectar. The Rabārīs brought back to life the dead peacock, which tried to fly. The Rabārī held on to its feathers to prevent it. The peacock shed his feathers and flew away. The Rabārīs requested Jālaṇ to give up his fast and explained that where the pious symbols had fallen, on this site, he should build a Madh (small temple of Devī). Jālaṇ agreed and built a Madh of Mammāī Mātā, which is the pioneer Madh at Sangavadi Derī, and the conch-shells, the Morpicch Dhājā (A Flag of the Devī, made of peacock feathers) and a symbol of a swan were kept in it. Jālaṇ taught saraju to the Vaiśya Sutārs and Rabārīs.

Jālaṇ took *samādhi* and a platform named *otto* (a small shrine erected over the dead body of a sant) was built in Jariāvāḍā. While repairing the *otto*, an inscription was found on which the year has been inscribed and read as Vikram Saṃvat 1018, i.e. AD 962.[3] This has been visited and checked by history researchers[4] of Porbandar. This shows that the tradition of the Saraju-gān seems to have started during the tenth century. But no other details are available about the time and life and works of Jālaṇ.

A Cāraṇ poet of Junagadh, Jetho Amara Udhāc,[5] living before 300 years, narrated the story of Jālaṇ and gave some more details of how the Vaiśya Sutār named Mātaro was first met, how other Madhs were built and

[3] Ibid., p. 57 ('Śakti Upāsak Jālaṇ').

[4] Narottam Palan gave me some details during my fieldwork, on 21 December 1996, at Porbandar. The researchers have published a short note on it, which was not available at that time. Photocopy of the inscripted writing was requested but the result of the photo was so poor that it did not help in reading.

[5] I got this poem during my field work at Surendranagar on 19 October 1996, and this has been edited and published.

how the Rabārī Ujavo was made the first Bhuvā by the Devī. Jetho Udhāc himself was a follower with deep faith in Mammāī Mātā. The Rabārī tradition is evidenced in this poem.

MAMMĀĪ MĀTĀ

Etymologically the word 'Mammāī' is derived from the Sanskrit word 'Mohamāyā'. Devī Mammāī or Totara is the worshipped deity form of Pārvatī. She is believed to be virgin and so instead of kumkum (vermilion), gulāl (pink powder) is offered. Kumkum stands as symbol for married women and Devīs. The Dvārpāl (the doorkeeper) is believed to be Batuka Bhairava, a childhood form of Hanumān. And in worshipping Devī Mammāī, ākado (a kind of shrub) which is specially used in Hanumān Pūjan, is offered and used. The other name of Mammāī is 'Totara-Devī' which according to Devjibhai Vaja is derived from 'stotra' which seems etymologically not acceptable. Shri Amritlal Laljibhai Vadhiya[6] says that Devī Parvatī when invoked by Jālaṇ, agreed to come, but on condition that she would not utter a word. From this event the word 'Totara' came into vogue. But we may note that the word 'Totaḍuṃ' means stammering, not dumb or silent.

ORGANIZATION OF MADHS AND MAIN RITUALS

The tradition of Saraju-song has been developed in the well organized institutional form of Madh. There is one pioneering Madh at Sangvada Derī and seven others at Praśnāvāda, Sutārej, Chorvad, Shidokar, Takhat, Loj and Balej. According to *Pragatya*,[7] two Madhs established by the Kānteliyā Bhuvā at Praśnāvāda (in AD 1836) and Sutārej (in AD 1843) are also believed to be *svayambhū* (self created) because the symbols kept in Sāngāvāda Derī Madh are original and brought by Jālaṇ himself from Mansarovar and the symbols kept in Praśnāvāda and in Sutārej which were brought by Sāmaji Kānteliyā and Devdās respectively, were directly and miraculously found from the sea. The sub-branches of the Madhs are at Vadodara (Jhala) Chur, Bhuvā Timbi, Fatāṇā, Zariavādā, Sodhānā, Āntroli and Vadnagar. The authority of each Madh is well defined and its branches are fixed areawise.

[6] Well-educated informant and Saraju-singer.

[7] A booklet on Vaiśya Sutār and Mammāī Mātā, published by Shri Visvakarma Vaiśya Jnati Bhajan-Mandal, London, 1987.

According to the poem written by the Cāraṇ poet Jetho Amarā Udhāc, when Jālaṇ came, the Rabārīs named Sāmbado Cāvado, Ulavo and Chelano followed him and are worshipped out of four conch shells, the first at Chorvad, the second at Shidokar, the third at Loj and the forth at Balej. The Devī declared Ulavo as her permanent Bhuvā. The Bhuvās of these four Madhs walked carrying peacock feather flags; they could cure snake-bites by brushing with these flags the body of the diseased. They established the fifth Madh at Odedar near Takhat Chāyā.

All these Madhs are places of Pilgrimage for the Vaiśya Sutārs and the Rabārīs. The Madh at Balej, Odedar are of Shikotar Mātā of Rabārīs, rest of Mammāī Mātā of Vaiśya Sutārs.

THREE CATEGORIES

The main Bhuvā is designated as Bhuvā Ātā under whom the first assistant is Padhiār and thereafter a Pinchidhar. The Bhuvā Ātā is the supreme priest of the Madh who speaks and orders on behalf of the Devī. The main ritual 'Pūj' can only be sanctioned by Bhuvā Ātā who proceeds to the test of the juvār-seed.[8] The second category is of the Padhiār who is believed to be a Vāhan (Vehicle) of Bhuvā Ātā. After the ritual ceremony is over, the Bhuvā Ātā's body quivers heavily feeling the entry of the deity in his body, and running to the Padhiār, he climbs onto his shoulders and scatters juvār seeds over the followers in token of the Devī's blessings.

[8] Juvār-seed Test: Any ritual can only be performed after obtaining the permission and sanction order of the Devī through the Bhuvā who uses of the specific method of the Juvār-seed Test. The Bhuvā spreads a clean woollen cloth before the Devī and puts a heap of the juvār-seed (sorgho grains) on it. A virgin and five respectable gentlemen — a Panch — sit before the heap and one of them asks, 'If the Devī permits us to perform the ritual wished by us (Chelan, Kaḷaś or Pūj) give us the Vadhāvo'. The 'Vadhāvo' means the odd number of the total seeds given to each person. The Bhuvā gives a pinch of juvār-seed to the virgin and Panch. They count. If the total of each comes to an odd number, it is believed that the Devī permits them to perform the ritual. To make it doubly sure, they may again ask, 'Your sanction is final, please give us Vācā this time'. 'Vācā' means an even number of the total. The Bhuvā again picks up the corn effortlessly and gives it to the six persons. Everybody counts the juvār-seed and if now the total comes to an even number the sanctions of the Devī are believed to be final. Even after the ritual is over, this very same method of testing with juvār-seed is adopted to make sure that the Devī has accepted this worship.

THREE RITUALS

There are three main rituals: Chelan, Kaḷaś and Pūj. Chelan is the smallest ritual signifying some vow (*bādhā*). When the vow is to give a feast to 5, 10, 15, 20 or 125 persons, it is called Chelan Pāvī. The person qualified to be a *chelan* must wear the sacred threads 'janoi', as formerly the Vaiśya Sutārs were the Purohits of the Rabārīs. Later on a Sompurā Brāhmin worked as Purohit at the time of the marriage of the Rabārīs.[9] But in Chelan, the Rabārīs only invite Vaiśya Sutār to be a *chelan*. This ritual being a small vow, any Pinchidhar can give the sanction on behalf of the Devī and can perform the duty of the Bhuvā. This ritual lasts four to five hours. Saraju is sung with each Pūjan-vidhi and the *chelan* are feasted with rice piṇi made of pure ghee (clarified butter) molasses and rice.

'Kaḷaś' is a ritual of two days and the community is invited to participate. The Bhuvā sanctions the ritual by 'Āshā ni juvār' (juvār-seed of hope). At midnight on a heap of *kāng* or rice, a holy water pot (*kumbha*), and a coconut are placed near the 'Jyot' or sacred flame. A peacock feather flag and other symbols are also established on a *pāṭ*, a small square wooden stool. The *sthāpan* and Pūjan-vidhi is performed with the Saraju-songs till morning. Rice piṇi is offered. In the early morning, after Āratī is over, the Bhuvā climbs on the shoulder of the Padhiār and sprinkles the blessed seeds on the followers. A community feast takes place at the end.

'Pūj' is the biggest ritual and it can be performed only in the Madh and not in anybody's house. The Bhuvā Ātā gives permission and performs the ritual. If the Devī permits the arrangement of a Pūj a messenger, known as 'Sāmo', goes from village to village with a peacock flag in hand, and is welcomed by the followers. This ritual lasts for a full two days and nights. People of the followers caste gather from each corner in the Madh. The expense is borne by the whole community and never by the Madh or anyone individually. The common contribution to the expense is known as 'dhupedo'. October 20, 21 and 22 of the year 1996 are considered historic for the 'Pūj' because the Devī permitted Rabārīs to celebrate the 'Pūj' in all the five Madhs on these dates. It should be noted here that the Vaiśya Sutārs have stopped the rituals of 'Pūj' for some time now.[10]

[9] The Sompura Brāhmins, Vaiśya Sutārs and Rabārīs seem to have come to Saurashtra from the Himālaya via Sindh, Punjab, Rajasthan and Kutch. They seem to belong to the larger group of the Gujars who would have given its name to Gujarat.

[10] According to the information given by Shri Devjibhai Vaja, on one occasion some years ago, a Bhuvā died while mounting a horse. The followers think that the Devī did not wish to celebrate the Pūj.

PĀṬ PŪJĀ

Most remarkable element in these rituals is Pāṭ Pūjā. It is also noteworthy that in the Madhs no idol of Devī is kept. Only the holy symbols and the Jyot are worshipped. In the rituals of Chelan, Kaḷaś and Pūj, Pāṭ Pūjā is accepted. These Mammāī rituals follow the Bījmārgī Pāṭ Pūjā, which is not secret but open to all. Only the text of Saraju is kept secret. The Bījmārgī and Mammāī Pāṭ use the Gujarati language in their Vidhi Mantras.[11] Pāṭ Pūjan seems to have its origin in Rāmdev cult. Most of the castes and tribes of Gujarat such as Rabārī, Wāgher, Harijan, Sagar, etc., are the followers of Rāmdev. It is possible that the influence of the Rāmdev cult, is still accepted in Chelan, Kaḷaś and Pūj.

SARAJU AND SNAKEBITE

Saraju-songs are believed to be most effective and life-saving for poisonous snakebites. Even today the people believe that Saraju can regain and sustain life after a cobrabite. Mostly Mammāī and Sikotar Devīs' Madh, Sarpa Derī of Dudhrej near Surendranagar known as the Rabārīs' Vadvāḷi Jagyā,[12] the Ghoghājī's Temple of Rabārīs at Unāva near Gandhinagar and other various small temples or Sthānakas of Vachadādā[13] (Vatsarāj Solanki) in Gujarat are places renowned for the treatment of snakebite. This practice is mostly connected with Rabārīs who have to live and wander in the jungle with cattle. It is a strong belief in the community that, as they are the sons of the goddess Pārvatī, even a poisonous snake cannot kill them.

The story of Jālaṇ is also significant in this regard as he himself was treated and made alive after a cobrabite. In the Madh they treat the snakebite with peacock feather flags and Saraju-songs. This miracle has also been cited by Jetho Udhac:

Nāg ro dans to jari lopé nahi

'The snake bite becomes ineffective on spreading the peacock flag.'

[11] For a detailed study see Dr. Niranjan Rajyaguru, *Bīj Mārgī Gupta Pāṭ Upāsanā ane Mahāpanthī Santonī Bhajan Vāṇī*, Gandhinagar: Gujarat Sahitya Akademi, 1995.

[12] Dr. Nagaji Kesar Bhatti, *Shri Sadguru Jivāṇ Prakash*, Shri Vadvālā Mandir, Dudhrej, Surendranagar District, 1994, pp. 135-7 (The story of Snake).

[13] *Gujarātī Lok-Sāhityamāṃ Kathā-gīto*, edited by Hasu Yajnik (Padabhajana Sūcīkaraṇa, vol. 10), Gandhinagar: Gujarat Sahitya Akademī, 1994, pp. 18-19 for the story of Bhāthījī.

In Āratī of Mammāī Mata it has been mentioned:

Mrityu loka mān Mātājī āvyā, thayo jay jaykār,
Bhoring ne bhāgvuṃ padyuṃ, letā nām niradhār,

meaning, when the Devī came on earth, people welcomed her with joy. On the arrival of the Devī, the snake had to escaped as the utterance of the Devī's name is sufficient to make the snake run away. Saraju-songs also describe how Jālaṇ was saved after a snake bite him.

CARYĀPADA AND SARAJU

Saraju is derived from 'Caryā' and this tradition is believed to have come down from the Mānsarovar of Kailāś, near Tibet. Buddhist Siddhas would have composed the *Caryāpada* on which critical study is available.[14] In these *Caryāpada,* there are various tricks to hide their inlearning from the outsiders, like adding some irrelevant words and matter. Those are discussed by Dr. H.C. Bhayani.[15] The Saraju text has also been kept secret and words like Ha-Ho-He are being incorporated while singing. The text of the *Caryāpada* is in Apabhraṃśa. These stylistic similarities may show some relation between Saraju and Buddhist *Caryāpada,* which would require a separate detailed study.

SĀM-GĀN AND SARAJU-GĀN

While singing Saraju the words like Ha-He-Ho which might have been derived from the Bīj Mantra Hram-Hre-Hro, are incorporated between the letters of each or most of the words. This resembles Sām-gān. The Saraju has been believed to be written, sung and taught by Jālaṇ, who learnt *Sām-veda* from Sāre Rāval as the story goes. The Late Shri Jaymalbhai Parmar, folklorist of Gujarat, has also mentioned that Saraju resembles Sām-gān.[16] This requires detailed research, based on the comparative study of the notations of Sām-gān and Saraju-gān. When I first heard Saraju-gān[17] on

[14] Per Koaerne, *An anthology of Buddhist Tantrik Songs*, Bangkok: White Orchid Press, 2nd rpt. 1986.

[15] Dr. H.C. Bhayani's book on the restoration of the text of the *Caryāgīti* is expected to be shortly published in the Prakrit Text Society Series.

[16] Jaymall Parmar, 'Lok-gīt', in *Gujarat ek Paricaya*, p. 198.

[17] My first fieldwork on Saraju was when I attended 'Kaḷaś' at Dwarka on 1 December 1987, at the residence of Prof. Kaḷubhai and Nanges Hardhol Laxaman (a Bhopā Rabārī).

1 December 1987, at the ceremony of changing the flag at the Temple of Dwarka, a short note was published on Saraju, stating that the tunes were based on the Indian classical Rāg Bairāgī, as recited in Vedic Mantras mostly in south India. The basic tunes of Bairāgi are C, D, E flat, G, B flat with F and A completely omitted. But after enjoying more opportunities of hearing Saraju and analysing its tunes, I have changed my opinion: it is not in Rāg Bairāgī and F and A are not omitted, as I previously believed.

NOTATION

Today there are three main traditions of Saraju singing (1) Vaiśya Sutār, (2) Sorathiā Rabārī, and (3) Bhopā Rabārī. The Vaiśya Sutār and Sorathiā Rabārī residing in the same geographical area of Ghed, have the same tradition whereas the tunes of Bhopā Rabārī differ to some extent. To a common hearer, both the types of singing would seem the same, but technically there is a basic difference between these two traditions.[18] In both the traditions F (Madhyama) and B (Nishad) are omitted and C, D, E, G, A are used. But the Vaiśya Sutār uses E sharp, A sharp (Suddha Gandhar and Suddha Dhaivat), whereas Bhopā Rabārī uses E flat (Komal Gandhar) and A Flat (Komal Dhaivat), which is the major difference.

SUBJECT MATTER AND KINDS OF SARAJU

Saraju describes the creation of universe by the creator. Cāraṇ poet Jetho Udhac narrates in the beginning of his poems:

आदिया शक्ति कमलथी ऊपनी, केतरां जोगणी रुप कीधां
जला बोल मांहेथी अलखने जगाडीआ, बार ब्रह्म ईशने साथ लीधां
पयोणरा पान पर चार देव प्रगाटीआ, धरावण आभ ते दन्न धरियो
परमाणे आभने रचावी प्रथमी, कमकरो थंभ ते मेरू धरीओ

'Ādya Śakti was first born in a lotus and she took the various forms of Jogaṇī.

[18] In Bhopā Rabārī the notations are: CD$\underline{E}$-$\underline{E}$-D—$\underline{E}$D-CD$\underline{E}$DC-CD$\underline{E}$D$\underline{A}$CD—CD—CD—D$\underline{E}$CD-C—C—CD—CD$\underline{E}$DC$\underline{A}$G-C$\underline{A}$B-A—C (• indicates Lower Scale) Basic Tunes: $\underset{\bullet}{G}$ $\underset{\bullet}{\underline{A}}$ C D $\underline{E}$ G $\underline{A}$.

In Vaiśya Sutār: CDE—DE—DED—GDE—DE—DGA-GA-A—GE—GA—E—DE-C—E-DE—DE—E—E—DE-D-ED-G-A-A-GA-GA—AE—GA—A—AG—G—EG—A—G—A—GA—AE—G—A—G—A—A—A—G—GA—G—G—A—E—DE—DE—D—E—CDC—DE—CDE—EDC—D-CDE—DE—GA—GA—GA (Basic Tunes: C D E G A—all sharp, no flat)

From the water she awakened Alakh and kept along with her twelve Brahmas. Four Devas, born on a leaf of lotus, created the sky without earth. Thereafter they created the earth to match proportionately with the sky, and it rested on Golden Meru.'

Bījmārgī Pāṭ of various communities and tribes like Bhīl Garāsīās[19] also give a similar story of the creation of the creator, sky and earth.

According to Bījmārgī Naklang Rāmdev Pāṭ, the creator first of all made an egg of five basic elements and broke it into pieces. From one part the sky was created, and the earth from another part. Ādivāsī Garāsīā Bhīl of Khedbrahma describes the earth as being created from water. The Saraju songs too deal with creation while establishing the Pāṭ Pūjā and praying the Devī Totarā to come on the Pāṭ:

अन्न जागे, देवता जागे, जागे पवन ने पाणी,
दहेरे दहेरे देवारा जागे, जागे मानसरोवरनी राणी.
जती जागे सती जागे, जागे नवनाथ,
झांपे हनुमान जती जागे, आदर्यां सुधरे काज.
शिव जागे शक्ति जागे, जागे गोपी ने कान
गौरी पुत्र गणेष जागे, नक्खंडमां आगेवान
राम लक्ष्मणने जानकी, त्रीजी तारादे नार
चोथा तेडावो देवां तोतरां, कंकोत्री लखे कैलाश
स्वर्गलोकमांथी भवानी ऊतर्यां, साथे लाव्यां हेमनो पाट,
पाट पधारो देवां तोतरां चोखा चोडे चौद भुवननो नाथ.

'The corn may awake, Devas may awake, wind and water may awake, Devas of each temple awake with them, the Queen of Mānsarovar may also awake. Jatī and Satī awake. The nine Nāths awake, on the door Hanumān may awake and finish our unfinished work. Śiva and Śakti awake, Gopī and Kṛṣṇa awake, the son of Gaurī, Gaṇeś who is the leader of nine *khaṇḍ*, may also awake (We have the occasion of Pāṭ Pūjan so) we first invite Rām Jānakī, second, Laksman, third, Tārāde and fourth, an invitation is sent to Kailāś for the Devī Totarā. (On receiving and accepting the invitation) Bhavānī Mātā comes from *svarga* and with her a Pāṭ made of gold (We pray now). Goddess Totarā, now please be seated on Pāṭ, the king of fourteen Bhuvans himself is ready to welcome you by sprinkling rice on you.'

Likewise, there are Saraju to invoke Ganesh. Pāṭ Sthāpan-vidhi is performed with Saraju. The subject matter of these kinds of Saraju is related to Pāṭ.

Over and above such ritual Sarajus, there are Sarajus on Rāmkathā and

[19] Dr. Bhagavandas Patel, *Toḷī Rāṇī nī Vāratā*, Ahmedabad: Navbharat Prakashan, 1994 (for details about Bīj no Paṭ Pūjā of Garāsīā Bhīls of Khedbrahma).

Kṛṣṇakathā. The Bījmārgī Pāṭ ends with a Bhajan known as Āgam Vāṇī. Such Vāṇī (Speeches) are mainly of three kinds (1) Āgam (2) Agam and (3) Aval. Āgam means Bhajan dealing with Adhyātma Vidyā and Yoga Sādhanā. When the subject matter is very technical and based on some kind of realization, it has to use its own terms, the meaning of which is deliberately obscure and secret. Such words and realization are not understood and felt by common people, so they remain, 'Agam' meaning, a place or realization where every one cannot go. Such Bhajans and their terminology deal with complex Yogic Sādhanā. Even the Caryāpada of Bauddh Siddhas of Tibet have such typical 'Āgamya' element. The basic verb 'Car' has also other specific meaning such as casually think, to take into consideration, to discuss, to follow.[20] Certain Bhajans deal with forecasting as to what is to happen in the future. Such Bhajans are called Āgam Vāṇī.[21] Āgam means the things to come in future. Āgam Bhajans of Rāmdev, Sarvāṇ Kāpadi, Devāyat Paṇḍit, Sahdev are popular and mostly sung at the end of the Pāṭ Pūjā. Some of the Saraju songs also deal with Āgam Vāṇī and are sung at the end of the Pāṭ. Aval Vāṇī is a kind of satire, ridiculously projecting a result as a cause and vice versa, as in Kabīr 'Nav men nadiā dubjay' rivers sink into a boat.

FORM AND KINDS

Most Sarajus are in Dohā-Chopāī or in similar traditional metres. The two lines of a Saraju stanza are known as kadi or kadā. While singing, the syllables Ha-He-Ho are incorporated between every two letters of each word and in between two words. Only the Saraju singer knows where to add such words. As a result of such additions the smallest Saraju takes a very long time in performance. Most of the Saraju have four to ten stanzas, depending on the subject matter.

The Saraju sung at the time of various Pāṭ rituals such as 'Sthāpan' and 'Pūjan' have mostly four to twelve stanzas, whereas the Sarajus on Rāmkathā, Kṛṣṇakathā or other legends are proportionately long. These Sarajus resemble an Ākhyān or narrative poem, and not to a Pad, though any Pad can be sung in the style of the Saraju singing. A part or a chapter of any Gujarati Ākhyān is known as 'Kaḍavuṃ'. According to Dr. H.C.

[20] G.V. Devasthali, *Sanskrit English Dictionary*, Bombay, 1936, p. 483.

[21] Dr. Nathalal Gohil, *Āgam Vāṇī*, Ahmedabad: Navbharat Sahitya Mandir, 1994.

Bhayani this Kaḍavakbandh form has come from Apabhraṃśa.[22] Kaḍavakbandh form started during the tenth century. If the Saraju had its origin in the tenth century, it would be possible that Saraju adopted Kaḍavakbandh from Apabhraṃśa, but it might as well have been influenced by Ākhyān. As in the Ākhyān form there is a 'Valaṇ' or 'Uthalo' stanza for summarizing the narrated event at the end in the Saraju. But the Valaṇ or Uthalo of Ākhyān is known in Saraju as Dhoḷ. In this tradition, Dhoḷ means the summary of the Saraju. Kaḍavās of Ākhyān are in various Deśīs, singable in various tunes of Rāg, which is known as 'Ḍhāḷ'. The singable Deśī and its Ḍhāḷ have been evolved by adding rhythmic phases like Re, Lol, Jī, Hanke, etc. Deśīs are basically the chanted form of the metre. In Saraju there are no Deśī nor Ḍhāḷ. Because the singing style itself includes the Ha-He-Ho, any metre can be sung in Saraju style. The singing has 4, 8, 12, 14 or 16 beats. With the stress at the beginning of the rhythm, they give a beat of Jānz.

There are different rhythm beats and tunes. Such changes are known as 'Suvedo'. There are five main kinds of Saraju: (1) Bhar nī Vāṇ (2) Otar nī Vāṇ (3) Utar nī Vāṇ (4) Āmbārāyaṇa and (5) Suvedo. Each is sung at a special time. The Āmbārāyaṇa Saraju are sung during the fifteen days of Śrāddha. Suvedās are sung during Navrātri.

Thus, the Saraju-songs are the oldest ethnic and provincial devotional Devī worshipping Stotra, believed to have their roots somewhere in Sām-gān. Saraju is thus a holy Gangā of Śakti Stotra flown down from Kailāś Mānsarovar to the west sea coast of Saurashtra.

[22] *Gujarātī Sāhityano Ithihās*, Ahmedabad: Gujarati Sahitya Parishad, 1973, pt. 1.

Sant-vāṇī and Harijan, Mahāmārgī *Bhajan* and Ismaili *Ginān*

A new appraisal of popular devotion in Saurashtra

FRANCOISE MALLISON

It is not easy for a conscientious worker in the field of Gujarati literature to dig out references concerning a type of work which seemingly belongs to the area of poetry, to judge from its name, i.e. *sant-vāṇī*. Indeed when I started trying to appreciate its scholarly references, I could not really find what I was looking for. To which section of a *History of Gujarati Literature* ought these songs belong to? The *Gujarātī Sāhitya Koś́*, even the most recent ones,[1] hardly mention more than a few names of authors of *sant-vāṇī*, no history of the literature bears witness to their existence. What might be the reason?, — their orality, beyond doubt, as there are no manuscripts, — or the use of the Saurashtrian dialect. Yet, since the appearance of the printed book, i.e. for quite some time now, everywhere, and even in northern Gujarat, one finds booklets containing collections of *sant-vāṇī*. It looks as if the status of a *literary work* were denied to lyrical religious compositions created and sung among the low castes and untouchables of Saurashtra and yet appreciated paradoxically by the whole of the Gujarati-speaking public.

Kanaiyalal Munshi (1887-1971), a follower of Gandhi, when dedicating his History of Gujarati Literature to the Mahatma, had asked him to write a preface. The result was startling. I cannot quote it here *in extenso*, but it surely is an appeal to recognize *another* literature, not the one belonging to the middle class, Munshi's only subject matter according to Gandhi who pleaded for the recognition of the literature of *the people*, and for an official birth of this literature:

> Shri Munshi's estimate of our literary achievement appears to me to be very faithful. The survey naturally confines itself to the language understood and

[1] The last one was published by the Gujarati Sahitya Parishad, Ahmedabad, vol.1, edited by J. Kothari and J. Gadit, 1989.

spoken by the middle class. Commercially-minded and self-satisfied, their language has naturally been 'effeminate and sensuous'. Of the language of the people we know next to nothing. We hardly understand their speech. The gulf between them and us the middle class, is so great that we do not know them and they know still less of what we think and speak. . . .

Gandhi adds:

There is an awakening among the masses. They have not begun with thought but with action, as I suppose they always do. Their language has yet to take definite shape. It is to be found somewhat, but only somewhat, in the newspapers; not in books. . . . The unquestionable poverty of Gujarati is a token of the poverty of the people. But no language is really poor. We hardly had time to speak since we have begun to act. Gujarat like the rest of India is brooding. The language is shaping itself. There is enough work awaiting writers like our author.

One must not forget in this context that Gandhi hails from Saurashtra. He knows what he is talking about, and behind his considerations looms the entire corpus of the so-called *sant-vāṇī* literature of Kathiawar which, in spite of what he says, touches also the local middle class.

Maybe due to their success — unless it was its consequence — the *sant-vāṇī* came to be collected, preserved and commented as texts belonging to folklore; here and there a few were admitted into the big *pad* collections of the folklorists, especially by the great Gandhian and folklorist whose centenary has just been celebrated: Javerchand Meghani (1897-1947) who was the first to devote a whole study to the *sant-vāṇī*.[2] It is clear that Meghani was struck by the aesthetic aspect of this literature of which he was himself an extraordinary performer. In his mind, the whole culture of Saurashtra stood to benefit from his publications,[3] whatever their religious tendency. Already in 1928 he had drawn the attention of the reading public to the intense religious activity of the Gurus and the Sants in the rural areas of his province.[4]

The aesthetic and cultural pleasure these texts provide does not entirely explain the success of the *sant-vāṇī*. A deeper link attaches those who listen, to the performers of the *bhajan*, even although their social origin may be different. At London, on 4 September 1993, the Sahitya Akademi had invited a group of *bhajankār* from Surendranagar to perform for a

[2] By the way, Gandhi evokes his contribution in the preface to Munshi's volume, p. v.

[3] For instance, see *Soraṭhī santavāṇī*, Ahmedabad: Gurjar Grantharatna Karyalay, 1947 (rpt. 1960).

[4] His volume *Soraṭhī Santo*, had five editions up to 1946 and seven reprints. The last one is by Prasar at Bhavnagar in 1994.

public of London Gujaratis. It lasted the whole night, a video recording preserved it. The piously acquired video cassettes show not only the singers and their Guru but also their public, London middle class, enthused. The *sant-bhajan* evidently constitutes in itself a salutary religious practice, a true *sādhanā*. Makrand Dave (born 1922) is generally recognized to be the most learned of the *pad-bhajan* specialists in Gujarat right now. We owe him several collections such as the precious *Sat kerī vāṇī* (1970).[5] He is the Guru of an āśram, the Nandigrām or Ātmānuṃ-ānandadhām, where he teaches the *bhajan-sādhanā* and where he tries to establish an academic training of the *pad-bhajan*. Through his activity the religious literature of the *bhajan*, including the *sant-vāṇī*, has acquired a generally recognized status, and his enthusiasm provoked the positive echo of the academic specialists. For some years now, ten years or more, thanks to the work done by the Department of Gujarati Language and Literature at the University of Rajkot and its director Professor Balvant Jani, thanks also to a combined and unprecedented effort of the Gujarati Sahitya Akademi of Gandhinagar under the heading of Dr Hasu Yajnik, a systematic overall study of this literary genre imperilled by the modern way of life, has been undertaken. Taking into account the whole body of *pad* literature, the entire corpus was catalogued, and under the guidance of professor Bhayani who had started the project, several index volumes have been published; but as far as the *sant-vāṇī* of Saurashtra are concerned, the work of systematic collecting has been undertaken by the University of Rajkot within the framework of a general project for the Oral Popular Literature of Saurashtra. The most recently published volume, *Santvāṇī, tattva ane tantra*, edited by B. Jani[6] is the result of a seminar held at Bhīmorā (tālukā Coṭilā, district Surendranagar) and gathering specialists such as Makrand Dave, Niranjan Rajyaguru, Nathabhai Gohil, Mohanpuri Goswami, Narottam Palan, Rajul Dave, Manoj Raval, Hasu Yajnik, Rajendrasinh Rayjada. It includes the publication of an anthology of 76 *pad*, and a reference list of 160 collections of *bhajan*.

Who are the Sants, and which are their *vāṇī*? In Gujarat the word *sant* does not have exactly the same meaning as in northern India, i.e. the great Gurus of the *Nirguṇa* Bhakti. In Saurashtra it refers to Gurus belonging to the lower castes and who more often than not are untouchables.[7] They

[5] There is a second edition in 1991. Both editions are published at Bombay by Navbharat Sahitya Mandir.

[6] At Gandhinagar: Gujarati Sahitya Akadami, 1996.

[7] Cf. the book by Nathabhai Gohil, *Saurāṣṭranā harijana bhaktakavio*, Keshod: the author, 1987.

adhere generally to one of the three following important Sampradāy:

— The group of the Mahāpanthīs, or Mahāmārgīs or Nijārpanthīs, more numerous and more ancient than the remaining two: as a tantric movement with secret rites, open to all yet dominated by the untouchable caste of the Meghvāḷs, the Mahāmārgīs indeed belong to the Nirguṇī group of Bhakti movements in as much as they recognize the Non-Qualified Absolute as the supreme principle which they adore in the shape of the *jyot-agni-nūr*, the light and sun, the equivalents of the primeval energy. Their *bhajan* are their only public manifestation to which the non-initiates may be admitted, with a proselytizing aim in mind, as it seems. The authors are the poet-saints of the sect, the more or less mythological founders of the movement: Rāmdeopīr, Sahadev Jośī, Devāyat Pāṇḍit, Dharmrājā; and women of equal rank to the male Gurus: Toral, Loyaṇ, Līrlābāī, Gaṃgāsatī; divine authors like Śiv and Śakti; or mythological saints such as the Mahābhaktas Dhruv, Prahlād, Draupadī, Kuntī, Markaṇḍ Ṛṣi.

— The second most important group is formed by the Nāthpanthīs and their local Gurus. Around Mount Girnar, in the region of Pancal (Gebīnāth near Thān, district of Surendranagar) and in Cutch (Dharamnāth at Dhīṇodhar) stay important Nāth communities, and the *bhajan* of the *sant-vāṇī* of even different denominations advocate all the *hāṭh-yog* notions of the Nāths.

— The third group belongs to the Kabīr movements, the Ravibhāṇpanth, named after two of the Gurus: Bhāṇ (1698-1755), a disciple of Kabīr and rather late propagator in Gujarat of the Kabirian message, and his disciple Ravi (1727-1804). Their successors, Khīmsāheb, Trikamsāheb and Dāsī Jīvaṇ are authors of very popular *pad*.

There are no differences between these groups as far as the stucture of the *bhajan* and the type of text are concerned. For instance Trikamsāheb or Dāsī Jīvaṇ are sung in the *bhajan* of the Mahāpanthīs but the latter of course predominate. The *pad*, short lyrical pieces sung according to a fixed tune, eventually called a *deśī rāg*, fall into different categories according to the fonction of their content or the timing of the *bhajan* during which they are sung.

The Mahāpanthī *bhajan* take place every day but especially on *bīj* days (i.e. the second day of the two fortnights of the lunar months). They last the whole night, structured by vigils of two hours' length from 7 pm to 7 am, each vigil bearing a name which may also indicate the genre of the *pad*:

Sandhyā pad	7 pm
Gaṇapati pad	9 pm
Guru mahimā	10 pm
Māḷā	between 9 and 11 pm
Pyālo or *Kaṭārī*	between 9 and 11 pm
Ārtī-Thāḷa	12 pm
Ārādha	12 pm or 2 am
Āgama	2-3 am
Helo-Helī	*idem* (for Rāmdeopīr)
Baṃsarī	*idem*
Paraj	3-4 am
Rāmagarī	4-5 am
Prabhātī	5-7 am

Certain important themes are specific to the *sant-vāṇī* of Saurashtra and of the Mahāpanthīs, and have become genres:

— *Guru-mahimā* (the greatness of the Guru) : an entire submission to the will of the Guru who alone is able to lead the disciple towards the abolition of his self and passions, is one of the compulsory principles of the Mahāpanthīs; the Guru's greatness knows no limits. Thus for instance, according to Rūkhi Rāmdās (1907-43) (sometimes taken for Markaṇḍ Ṛṣi), 'The greatness of the mantra of my Guru [is such that] the *jap* he recites is not even known by the four Vedas.'[8]

— *Raveṇī* (the title alludes to the churning of the milk ocean) describes the secret of the creation of the world, often as a dialogue between Śiv and Pārvatī (*Śiva Śakti Saṃvad*) where Śiv reveals this secret to the goddess (the dialogue may also happen between Sītā and Rām). These *pad* are also called sometimes *Sṛṣṭinī utpatti*.

— *Pyālo or Kaṭārī* (the cup) celebrates the joy of spiritual meeting when the *śiṣya* receives from the Guru the mantra of salvation thanks to which he accedes to supreme bliss, such as a secret water called *amṛt ras*. In a famous *pyālo* attributed to Dhruv and Prahlād, *Thoḍe thoḍe piyo*, it is said:

O my brother, anything immortal cannot be easily digested
Taste holiness drop by drop.

[8] This is quoted from a version sung by Kalīdās Mahārāj at Keshod (district Junagadh) in the house of Professor Nathabhai Gohil, on 3 December 1995. The version published in *Saurāṣṭranā harijana bhaktakavio* (see n. 7 above), p. 417, is slightly different.

Your body is the horse, your mind the rider.

. . .

With the sword of good conduct, and with truth as your weapon,
Start fighting the Ego.[9]

or according to Gaṃgā Satī reminding her servant and disciple:

Drink Pānbāī, this *ras* is ready for taking,
The cup has come forward just now.

If you let it pass, you will regret it, Pānbāī,
as without a warning death will swallow you.[10]

— Another type of *vāṇī* tells (or alludes to) legendary lives, exemplary for the Mahāpanthī faithful, the stories of which have outgrown the limits of their Sampradāy and come to concern the culture of anyone living in Saurashtra. There one may meet often unmarried couples such as the spiritual lovers Jesal-Toral or Lakho-Loyaṇ, or rajputs like Rupaṇḍe Malde, or Gaṃgā Satī (who, actually, lived in the nineteenth century).

For instance the story of Rupaṇḍe Malde attributed to Meghadhāru reads as follows:

Rupaṇḍe of Gujarat married prince Malde of Rajasthan. She was converted to the Mahāpanth by her untouchable Guru, the great Meghdhāru. Her husband tolerates this strange situation (which is not without recalling Mīrābāī's plight), but then is upset by the practice of the secret rites such as the *paṭ-pūjā*. The mystic powers acquired by Rupaṇḍe enable her to undo her husband who, convinced of the vanity of his violence equally opts for conversion.

— *Ārādh* (adoration) is a prayer which is sometimes used as a liturgic formula in the rites of the Mahāpanthīs, such as the complex and elaborate ritual of the *pāṭ-pūjā*.[11] One of the most famous is the *Delamī-ārādh* by Devāyat Pāṇḍit. A famous *ārādh* is attributed to Toral who, reproaching Jesal for having died before her, finally brings him back to life through her prayer so that they might die together as they had promised each other. The *ārādh* sometimes resemble the *āgam*.

— *Āgam*. They are maybe the most surprising of the *vāṇī, they* describe the end of the Kaliyug and the accompanying events: the undoing of the

[9] Jh. Meghani (ed.), *Sorațhī santavāṇī* (see n. 3), p. 31.

[10] M. Jadeja (ed.), *Śrī Kahaḷasang bhagata Gaṃgā satī ane Pānabāīnī saṃṣodhana paraka saṃkṣipta jīvanakathā*, Ahmedabad: the author, 1993, p. 124.

[11] Cf. N. Rajyaguru, *Bījamārgī gupta pāṭa-upāsanā ane Mahāpanthī-Santonī bhajanavāṇī*, Gandhinagar: Gujarati Sahitya Akademi, 1995.

dharmic order, the upsetting of natural phenomena . . . , they announce the end of the world as well as the arrival of the saving *avatār*, Naklaṃk-Kalki (corresponding to the tenth *avatār* of Viṣṇu in a Hindu context), who shall abolish untouchability and restore a new golden age together with a new cycle of four *yug*.[12] Follows the text of an *āgam* by Devāyat Pāṇḍit, of the thirteenth or fourteenth century:

Listen, Devalḍe, my wife,
Our guru said the truth,
He does not lie, not even a little bit,
It was written, it was said, this day will come.

At first, the wind will rise,
And there will be no water in the rivers,
From the North the Lord will arrive,
In front, the hero Hanumān.

On the roof of the world will advance a chariot of gold and fire,
And in the deserted cities
The goods of the people will be looted,
Nobody will listen to the orders of the king.

. . .
Untrue the books, untrue the bills,
Untrue the Coran of the kazi,
The girls of noble birth will wear bangles,
These are the signs of the time to come.

The Lord of life will come from the North,
He will kill the demon Kaliṃga,
He will bear the name of Naklaṃka,
He will undo the Kaliyug, install the Satyayug.

So said Devāyat Pīr.[13]

As already mentioned, the *pad* of the *sant-vāṇī* are shared by different Nirguṇī communities of Saurashtra. More astonishing still is the fact that they are shared also with the community of the Ismaili Nizārīs, called locally Khojās or Satpanthīs. Precisely in the section of the *āgam-vāṇī* one meets with texts and authors in common, with the difference that the

[12] Cf. Nathalal Gohil, *Āgamavāṇī*, Ahmedabad: Navabharat Sahitya Mandir, 1994.

[13] N. Gohil (ed.), ibid., p. 66, and J. Parmar and R. Dave, *Sevādharamnā amardhām*, Amreli: Dr Jivraj Mehta Smarak Trust, 1990, p. 510.

Mahāmārgīs admit to the fact of the borrowing, even admitting that they do not always know the meaning of the Islamic terms used by the Ismaili *ginān* they sing, whereas the Ismaili ignore the fact of the use made of their *ginān* by the Mahāmārgīs.[14] The doctrine of the *das avatār*, developed by the Satpanthī Ismailis (even though this is not any longer openly admitted at present) constituted the central element of the Nizārī preaching in the north-west of the Indian subcontinent: it announced the arrival of the tenth *avatār* of Viṣṇu, Kalki, under the name of Naklaṃki and assisted by several epic Hindu heroes, but arriving as an incarnation of 'Ali, the son-in-law of the Prophet, from Alamut in the country of Dailam, in order to signify the end of the world and the final resurrection (*Qiyama*), as well as the Last Judgment. Exactly this was told by the *āgam-vāṇī* of the Mahāmārgīs and their very authors Devāyat Pāṇḍit, Sahadev Jośī, Harcand Jośī (who are often held to be identical with Pīr Sadr-ud Din).

The strange eschatological context, especially touching when giving hope to the Untouchables of delivery from their social condition, seems to have been borrowed from an Ismaili Islamic belief based itself on a Hindu myth.[15] Indeed for anyone familiar with what is called the *sant-vāṇī* of Saurashtra, a strong resemblance of style, metaphors and teaching exists between not only the *āgam* compositions but between the totality of the *bhajan* of the Mahāmārgīs, and a great part of the corpus of the *ginān* attributed to the Khojā Pīrs and Sayyids. It is true that both communities show marked esoteric tendencies. But it would be necessary to dispose of a historical explanation to account for the phenomenon. Until it becomes available, I propose a tentative interpretation:

The Ismaili Pīrs might have converted a sizeable part of the Meghvāḷs or other Untouchables while borrowing, according to their particular technique, from the latter's Hindu culture. In time, these groups might

[14] Cf. F. Mallison and Z. Moir, 'Rencontrer l'Absolu, ô Ami . . . Un hymne commun aux hindous tantriques et aux musulmans ismaéliens du Saurashtra (Gujarat)', in J. Assayag and G. Tarabout (eds.), *Altérité et identité, islam et christianisme en Inde*, Paris: Éditions de l'École des Hautes Études en Sciences Sociales, collection *Puruṣārtha*, no. 19, pp. 265-76.

[15] See the recent article by Dominique-Sila Khan, just forwarded to me after the Conference: 'The Coming of Nikalank Avatār: A Messianic Theme in Some Sectarian Traditions of North-Western India', *Journal of Indian Philosophy*, 25, 1997, pp. 401-26, and her book: *Conversions and Shifting Identities, Ramdev Pir and the Ismailis in Rajasthan*, New Delhi: Manohar and Centre de Sciences Humaines, 1997.

have ceased to be a part of the Khojā community when the latter structured itself in the middle layers of society,[16] maybe after a first wave of reforms tending to diminish the Hindu influence had taken place in the sixteenth century. At that time the need made itself felt of consigning in writing the teaching of the Pīrs and thus the *ginān* were attributed to the missionaries who had come from Iran. It seems likely that those one calls the Hindu Pīrs such as Rāmdeo Pīr, Sahadev Jośī, Devāyat Pāṇḍit, etc., at that time more or less disappeared from the authorized body of writings, but continued to be known and recited, credited sometimes with the qualification of Guptī Mukhīs, as there are Guptī Khojās: Ismailis — but outwardly Hindus.[17] However this might be, the tradition of the *sant-vāṇī* of Kathiawad is flourishing and well appreciated by all levels of Gujarati society, and the Mahāmārgī *bhajan* seem to generate the same emotion in their Hindu public as the *ginān* do among the Khojā faithful. The Untouchable Sant-Kavis call their *āgam-vāṇī* the 'Fifth Veda', exactly as do the Ismaili Pīrs for the *ginān*.

The tradition of the *sant-vāṇī* appears as a common Hindu, tantric and Untouchable, lyrical heritage, indeed a component of the religious culture of Saurashtra and, certainly, as an important chapter of the Gujarati literature, as well as of the Sant poetry of north India.

[16] Cf. the considerations of Mumtaz Ali concerning the mission of Ramdeo Pir in Rajasthan: 'Randeo Pir: A Forgotten Ismaili Saint', *Sind Review*, 32, 1995, pp. 24-6, 27-8.

[17] Cf. the article by Zawahir Moir, to appear: 'Ismaili Hagiography and History in the Ginans of Sayyid Nur Mohammad Shah', especially the part on 'Mahesvara Avatar and Guptis'.

PART VI

Religious and Literary Traditions in Maharashtra and the Konkan

Jñānadeva's Six-Handed God Gaṇeśa

GANGADHAR MORJE

INTRODUCTION

It is customary, according to Indian traditions, to pray and praise god Gaṇeśa, before beginning any work. It is generally believed that god Gaṇeśa is a remover of obstacles, a protector who showers happiness on his devotees. Historically, it seems that the concepts underlying god Gaṇeśa have changed over time, and at different levels, according to different groups of people. Similarly, the forms of the idol of Gaṇeśa have undergone change.

In this context, I would like to analyse an idol of Gaṇeśa with six hands which is described and prayed to by the Marathi saint-poet Jñānadeva (AD 1290) at the beginning of his Marathi commentary on the *Bhagavadgītā* generally known as *Jñānadevī* or *Jñāneśvarī*. It is worth noting that saint Jñānadeva, through the six-handed god Gaṇeśa, is experiencing or enjoying himself, his Guru and Brahman, at one and the same time. He also experiences the Oṃkārasvarūpa through the same idol. The other point is that a reading of the history of Marathi saint-poets reveals that Jñānadeva is the only saint-poet, who praised the six-handed Gaṇeśa at the beginning of his monumental work. No other saint-poet, either before or after him has prayed to the six-handed Gaṇeśa, i.e. god of Obstacles (*Vighnarāju*).

It is historically well known that saint Jñānadeva originally belonged to the Nātha Sampradāya, which followed Tantric systems and rituals, and his forefathers were traditionally devotees of Viṭhobā of Pandharpur. It is also well known that saint Jñānadeva expounded the Vārakarī or Māḷakarī cult as it is presently known in Maharashtra. All the saint-poets respected and honoured saint Jñānadeva for his poetry and exemplary life. But it is a wonder that no saint-poet other than Jñānadeva prayed to the six-handed god Gaṇeśa. Saint Ekanātha from the same vicinity — Paithan — came 300 years after Jñānadeva, prayed to the four-handed Gaṇeśa.[1] Saint Ekanātha researched and edited *Jñānadevī* and did pioneering work in

[1] 'A man sees you, his life turns into happiness that is why you are respectfully called the god of obstacles. Your face is joy and your four hands represent the four

preaching the Vārakarī cult. Rāmadāsa and the other saints prayed to the four-handed Gaṇeśa.[2] According to them, that is the expression of Oṃkāra, the origin of the whole universe.

POINTS FOR CONSIDERATION

In the light of the above information, there are certain questions which need to be answered:

- Why does saint Jñānadeva praise the six-handed god Gaṇeśa?
- How and why has he experienced the whole universe through the said idol and expressed it in figurative language?
- Which religious traditions was he following?
- Was he rejecting the previous religious traditions and did he want to establish new traditions?
- Did he want to propound a new concept of religion in accordance with his time and place?
- Did he want to expound Bhaktidharma or Bhaktipremadharma, based on his worldly life and religious experiences, taking into account the previous religious traditions?

After answering these questions, it is possible to draw some conclusions. In Appendix A an English translation of Jñānadeva's *Gaṇeśa Namana* (prayer) is given. The important points according to Jñānadeva's *Gaṇeśa Namana* are as follows:

- God Gaṇeśa is the cause of all our intellectual expressions.
- Gaṇeśa is the Śabda-Brahman, universe of words. He expressed himself in words.
- The Smṛti literature is his physical expression.
- The Purāṇas are the ornaments which adorn an idol of Gaṇeśa.
- Literary works such as poems and dramas are the small ornaments adorning his feet.
- The idol of Gaṇeśa with six hands represents the six schools of Indian philosophy.

---

means of life (dharma, artha, kāma, mokṣa). You are the cause of light and your tusk is shining.' *Ekanāthī Bhāgavata*, Maharashtra Govt., 1971, p. 1.

[2] 'Having four hands and a large belly, wearing yellow cloth to the waist, a snake on his large belly moving with a kind of noise.' *Dāsabodha*, K.B. Dhavale, 8th edn., Mumbai, 1950.

Further, he describes the objects which he holds in his six hands, giving their symbolic meaning.

- Logic = an axe.
- Ethical difference = aṅkuśa.
- Juicy knowledge from the Vedas = modaka (sweet-balls).
- Bauddhamata = Broken tooth.
- Satkāryavāda (Sāṅkhya philosophy) = lotus flower.
- A hand giving promise to protect = Abhaya hasta.

Jñānadeva also adds that the straight trunk of Gaṇeśa is a symbol of the power of discrimination.

The point at issue is why Jñānadeva called Gaṇeśa 'king of obstacles' (Vighnarāju), an epithet which is not in conformity with tradition. In fact, in accordance with his teachings, he does not appear in favour of breaking tradition. He often preached that 'Everybody should follow his own traditions, and should not be unworldly. Observance of one's duties enables to have whatever one wishes.' With this understanding, why did saint Jñānadeva pray to Vighnarāju?

It seemed that Jñānadeva wished to propound a new concept of religion in accordance with the demands of his time, without rejecting the earlier religious traditions completely. He gave much importance to Vedic, Tantric and Lokāyata traditions. In order to understand the new concept of his Bhaktidharma and the texture of his new religious construction, it is necessary to see how the concepts of god Gaṇeśa have changed from time to time, at the Vedic, Tantric and Lokāyata levels.

GAṆEŚA — GOD OF OBSTACLES

According to Vedic tradition, Gaṇeśa is a god or a leader who creates obstacles. In the Brahminical literature (*Mānavagṛhyasūtra*, *Yājñavalkya-smṛti*, *Manusmṛti*, etc.) Gaṇeśa is described as follows:

(a) According to Yajñavalkya, Vināyaka is another name for Gaṇeśa, and god Rudra created Vināyaka to destroy the plans of people.

(b) Manu, the author of *Manusmṛti*, known for his disrespect and disregard towards non-Brahmins, shudras and women, has condemned god Gaṇeśa throughout his literature.

(c) In the *Baudhāyanasūtra*, Gaṇeśa is considered a god of obstacles, and given the epithets: Vighnarāja, Vighnakṛt, Vighneśa.

(d) In other Brahminical literature, Gaṇeśa is known as a leader of a group or god of a group, who himself is an obstacle or the creator of obstacles.

The sculptures of the Vedic and Buddhist periods testify that god Gaṇeśa is accorded a low status, as he is put at the feet of the deities (e.g. the Buddhist Mañjuśrī and Mahākāla Buddha).An examination of these evidences reveals that, in the Vedic and Buddhist traditions Gaṇeśa was a leader or a god of destruction and a creator of obstacles.

TANTRIC GOD GAṆEŚA

According to Tantric literature, god Gaṇeśa plays an important role in religious rituals. Tantric tradition is known as Vāmācāra, as woman enjoys an important place in rituals. Most of the Tantric traditions are based on the matriarchal life pattern. In this tradition, Gaṇeśa is known as Vṛṣabhadhvaja, Vṛṣniketana, Dvijihvā, etc. It appears that during the Tantric period, the concept of Gaṇeśa as god of obstacles tended to shift to that of remover of obstacles, protector or happiness giver.

GAṆEŚA OF LOKĀYATA OR LOKADHARMA

In the second maṇḍal of Ṛgveda, Bṛhaspati is called Gaṇapati, and in the Aitareya Brāhmaṇa the mantra 'Gaṇanamatvām Gaṇapate', is addressed to Bṛhaspati, who is believed to be the propounder of Lokāyata also known as Bṛhaspati-mata. In this respect scholars have shown that Gaṇeśa was a tribal god. In Lokāyata, Gaṇeśa was conceived as:

(a) A leader of a group.
(b) A guardian of a group of people.
(c) The elephant-headed god.

According to this tradition, he is variously known as Gaṇeśa, Gaṇanāyaka, Varāhamihira, Lokabandhu, etc.

Lokāyata thought is connected with the matriarchal system, which is peculiar to the primary stage of human life, and it is thus considered a kind of protomaterialism. The religious rituals of the Lokāyata were not so sophisticated as other developed traditions.

GOD OF OBSTACLES TURNED INTO A REMOVER OF OBSTACLES

The period of Gaṇeśa revival is still controversial. It is however believed that it might have taken place under the Gupta dynasty. Kālidāsa does not mention god Gaṇeśa. It is certain that the presently-known elephant-headed god Gaṇeśa cannot be placed before the fourth century. From the fifth century onwards, an elephant-headed god Gaṇeśa, having a mouse as his vehicle, became known. In the same period, Puranic literature was revived and transformed. References in praise of Gaṇeśa are found in *Brahmavaivarta Purāṇa* and *Skanda Purāṇa*, while new literature on Gaṇeśa also appeared in the course of time (*Gaṇeśa Purāṇa*, *Gaṇeśa Upaniṣad*, *Gaṇeśa Gītā*, etc.). In this literature we can find some references to the greatness of god Gaṇeśa. During this period god Gaṇeśa became to his devotees Brahmasvarūpa, 'incarnation (avatāra) of the supreme god', a form of Oṃkāra, and even the writer of the epic *Mahābhārata*.

Taking into account the changes in the concept of god Gaṇeśa at different levels and in different traditions, we can understand the circumstances under which saint Jñānadeva had to pray to Vighnarāju, god of obstacles, in the form of Brahman or Oṃkārasvarūpa. The following information will further clarify the situation.

Around the middle period (after the fourth century onwards), Puranic literature contributed largely in making compromises in religious traditions, particularly in making adjustments to the concept of deities. Puranic literature gave new forms and meanings to the earlier traditional deities. During that period, most of the Puranic literature had been reconstructed and rewritten in the changed context of time and life of the people. In order to establish their superiority over other religious traditions and deities, each religious tradition tried to add acceptable attributes to its deities. With the help of Tantric traditions and rituals, deities like Śiva, Viṣṇu and Śakti were popularised. In that popularisation process, Tantric Vāmācāra was given place inside the 'high' tradition.

According to historical records, at the end of the fourth century, vital reconstructions and revivals took place both in Hinduism and Buddhism. The leaders of both religions tried their utmost to attract the common people to their fold. The development of Mahāyana from inside Buddhism forced the Hindus to search for a new path so as to face the new challenge, and the Purāṇas and the *Mahābhārata* played a vital and effective role in repelling the attacks of Buddhism. According to orthodoxy, the Vedic cult was restricted to the three varṇas, but the Purāṇas opened the doors of Vedic religious traditions to all castes and creeds, and to people at all levels. For the salvation of man, the Purāṇas described three ways:

(a) Vedic traditions.
(b) Tantric tradition.
(c) Mixture or combination of the two traditions, i.e. Miśra.

By practising these traditions, any person belonging to any caste and creed, without much effort and with minimum expense, could qualify for salvation. Therefore, mantra, tantra, vrata, japajāpya, became increasingly important in the religious life of the time. It should be noted that these methods were already being practised by the common people, Śiva, Viṣṇu, Śakti and Kṛṣṇa had become popular. During this period the Purāṇas honoured or accepted the ways of Tantric worship (Vāmācāra and Dakṣiṇācāra). They tried to propagate that all deities were part of the Vedic religion, i.e. Hindu religion, so it was not necessary to turn to Buddhism. In the same way, Brahminical literature tried to give the Puranic religious traditions Vedic form. But the deeply rooted Tantric nature of worship could not be uprooted completely. On the other hand, Vyāsa was known for compiling the Purāṇas, thus acceptance of the Purāṇas amounted to the acceptance or sanction to Tantric rituals and ways of worship, because Vyāsa was respected by all religious groups at all levels. In this context, it is important to note that the Bhāgavata Sampradāya which was motivated for the salvation of the common man, accepted Tantric ways of worship. This is obvious from the *Viṣṇu Purāṇa*, *Bhāgavata Purāṇa*, *Nārāyaṇīya Pañcarātra Saṃhitā*, etc. From this, we can infer that Hinduism was dominated by the Tantric ways of worship from the middle of the fifth to the tenth centuries.

Under these circumstances, it was necessary to reconstruct the religious and cultural life of Maharashtra of that time. Keeping this in view saint Jñānadeva launched his historical religious movement. For that purpose, he analysed the religious problems, social life, contradictions in religious worship process and beliefs. His concept of a new Bhaktidharma was based on ethical, religious and worldly practical life. Accordingly, he tried to ensure: (a) religious equality, (b) humanism, (c) healthy social life, (d) ethical behaviour, (e) svadharmācaraṇa, and (f) lokasaṅgraha. Thus, he imparted a new meaning to his religious concept.

Against this background, we can see saint Jñānadeva's Vighnarāju in the light of a new transformed meaning and form, which is in the form of Oṃkāra, the giver of all desires. Gaṇeśa's straight trunk is *viveka* and his hand suggesting protection is the symbol of Sāṅkhya philosophy. Though the early Purāṇas worked in that direction, Jñānadeva wanted to give a fresh interpretation to his newly organised religion. He wished to bring all religious traditions under his newly organised Bhaktidharma umbrella. He accommodated Gaṇeśa, a god of destruction with transformed meaning and allowed all, including shudras and womenfolk, into his new religion.

WHY A SIX-HANDED GAṆEŚA?

In the light of all these explanations, one question remains unanswered. Why did Jñānadeva praise the six-handed Gaṇeśa only? A simple answer is that the idol represents the six theories of the Indian schools of philosophy, and saint Jñānadeva used it figuratively to symbolise the six theories, in the form of six hands. Though Indian philosophy accepted the six theories, the names and theories are not the same. These theories differ from school to school. The saint-poets before or after Jñānadeva, believed in the six Darśanas even though they praised the four-handed god Gaṇeśa. If the Vārakarī cult respects and honours saint Jñānadeva as a propounder of the cult, why did other saints not follow Jñānadeva?

God Gaṇeśa: around the vicinity of Paithan

Though the transformation of god Gaṇeśa took place after the fifth century, and Gaṇeśa became a popular deity amongst most of the groups, with names such as Vighnaharta (remover of obstacles), Siddhidātā (able to give whatever you want), and Gajamukha (having the head of an elephant), there was one religious tradition, which was the worship of the formerly destroyer god Gaṇeśa, in the vicinity of Paithan, at the time of saint Jñānadeva — a worship still popular amongst a few local families.

During recent fieldwork (19 October 1996), in the vicinity of Paithan, the following information was obtained from a scholar and descendant of the family of saint Ekanātha, Shri Balasaheb Patil of Paithan. According to him, in Paithan there is a tall pillar known as Vijayastambha (pillar of victory) (Plate 1) which is supposed to have been constructed by the then Sātavāhana kings (second century). On that pillar a figure of the six-handed Gaṇeśa has been carved.

In this area god Gaṇeśa was perceived as a protector god and he protected the town of Paithan in all four directions. In support of this belief there are idols of Gaṇeśa in all four directions of Paithan. These are:

- An idol of god Gaṇeśa at Narlan, to the north of Paithan.
- To the south at Pategaon.
- On the eastwards road at Apegaon.
- To the west at the village of Kavsal.

From these sculptural traditions, it can be deduced that god Gaṇeśa was a popular deity in the vicinity of Paithan before and at the time of Jñānadeva.

The informant Shri Balasaheb Patil was kind enough to list the names of some families in the area who traditionally worship the six-handed god Gaṇeśa even today. These families are:

1. One branch of the Barabhatti family now known as Panabhatti.
2. A Kulkarni family from Kannad.

An idol of Tantric Gaṇapati is in the Maṭh of Shivdinkesari, an eminent scholar and saint of the Nātha Sampradāya after saint Jñānadeva.

On the basis of this information, we can say that saint Jñānadeva had to accommodate god Gaṇeśa considering the popularity and respect he enjoyed in the community of the time. For his new concept of Bhaktidharma, he could not ignore any group of people or tradition, because his Bhaktidharma was meant for all.

Considering the vicinity and the beliefs in respect of god Gaṇeśa, we will discuss the personal life and family religious tradition of saint Jñānadeva. The village of Apegaon is to the east of Paithan town, at a distance of 11 km. His forefathers from Tryambakapanta were devotees of Viṭhobā of Pandharpur, the centre or the Vārkārī cult. An elder brother of Jñānadeva, Nivṛttinātha, who was his religious guru and belonged to the Nātha Sampradāya, was the disciple of Gahinīnātha — a well-known Nātha Sampradāya authority. Though Jñānadeva was born in a traditional religious family, he had undergone instruction and experience through the Nātha Sampradāya such as Yoga and other systems and ways of worship.

In support of this, there is sufficient material available from the literature of Jñānadeva. At Apegoan, a house or *wāḍā* is described as the birthplace of Jñānadeva (Plate 2). It is an old building.

In that building on the right hand side after the entrance, there is a samādhi which is believed to be the samādhi of Tryambakapanta, grandfather of saint Jñānadeva (Plate 3).

Next to the samādhi, there is an idol of the six-handed god Gaṇeśa. (Plates 4, 5, 6).

From this, it can be inferred that in saint Jñānadeva's family there was probably a tradition of worshipping the six-handed god Gaṇeśa. Traditionally, his family and members of the generations worshipped the six-handed god Gaṇeśa. In keeping with the family tradition, saint Jñānadeva must have prayed and praised the six-handed god Gaṇeśa. On the other hand, he was strengthening his new concept of religion, i.e. 'self religion' or Svadharma. According to him, one can get everything one desires, if one performs one's duties sincerely according to one's family traditions.

To conclude, saint Jñānadeva prayed and praised the six-handed Gaṇeśa in keeping with his family tradition. He teaches the perception of Guru and Oṃkāra in the one idol of god Gaṇeśa. In respect of other saints before or after Jñānadeva, none of them have the family tradition of worshipping the six-handed god Gaṇeśa. None of them prayed or praised the six-handed god Gaṇeśa before beginning any work.

APPENDIX A

Jñāneśvara begins his text with a panegyric to Gaṇeśa, identifying the elephant-faced lord with the totality of sacred texts and knowledge:

The Vedas in their perfection are the beautiful image of the god, of which the flawless words are the resplendent body.

The Smṛtis are the limbs thereof, the marking of the verses shows their structure, and in the meaning lies the veritable treasure-house of beauty.

The eighteen Purāṇas are the rich ornaments, and the theories propounded in them are the gems, for which the rhythmic style provides the settings.

The fine material form is his many-coloured garment of which the composition is the fine shining texture.

So the epic poems and dramas in it, read with delight, are as jingling bells giving out the music of the sense.

The various principles carefully expounded in them and the aptness of the words expressing them appear as precious jewels set in the bells.

The wisdom of Vyāsa and others is the waist cloth, its tassled end gleaming with purity.

The six systems of philosophy are the six arms, and the different theories propounded in them are the six weapons held in his hands.

The art of reasoning is the hatchet, logic the goad, the Vedānta philosophy is the luscious sweetmeat (held in the hand).

In one hand is held the broken tusk, symbolizing the rejection of the teachings of the Buddha, refuted by the Vedānta commentaries.

Then the doctrine of the Universal Spirit is the lotus-like hand of blessing; the establishment of religion is the hand of reassurance.

Pure discrimination is the straight trunk, wherein dwells the highest joy of supreme bliss.

Impartial discussion is the pure white tusk of (Gaṇeśa), the small-eyed elephant-god, king of obstacles (representing the subtle eye of wisdom).

I regard the two systems as his ears, and the bees (hovering over his temples) as the sages who taste of the nectar of their own teaching.

The themes of duality and non-duality come together on the temples of his elephant head as lustrous corals.

The fragrant flowers adorning the crown of the head are the ten Upaniṣads, containing in full the honey of knowledge.

The A of the Om (*Aum*) is the legs, U is the large belly, and the M is the great circle of the head.

When these three are united, the sacred word is formed. Through the grace of my preceptor, I salute this, the primal cause of all being, the Om.

[English translation of Marathi *Namana* (*Jñaneśvarī* 1:3-20) — taken from *Gaṇeśa Lord of Obstacles, Lord of Beginning*, by Paul B. Courtright, New York: Oxford University Press, 1985, pp. 165-6.]

REFERENCES

Jñānadeva's *Gaṇeśa Namana*, Appedix A.

Gadgil, S.R., *Lokāyata*, Mumbai: Lokvynmay Prakashan Grih.

———, *Madhyayugīn tantrasādhanā ani Jñāneśvara praṇit Bhakti Yoga*, Pune: Dastane Ramchandra ani Co., 1979.

Plate 1: Paithan. Vijayastambha.

Plate 2: Apegaon. Birthplace of Jñānadeva.

Plate 3: Apegaon. Samādhi of Jñānadeva's grandfather Tryambakapanta.

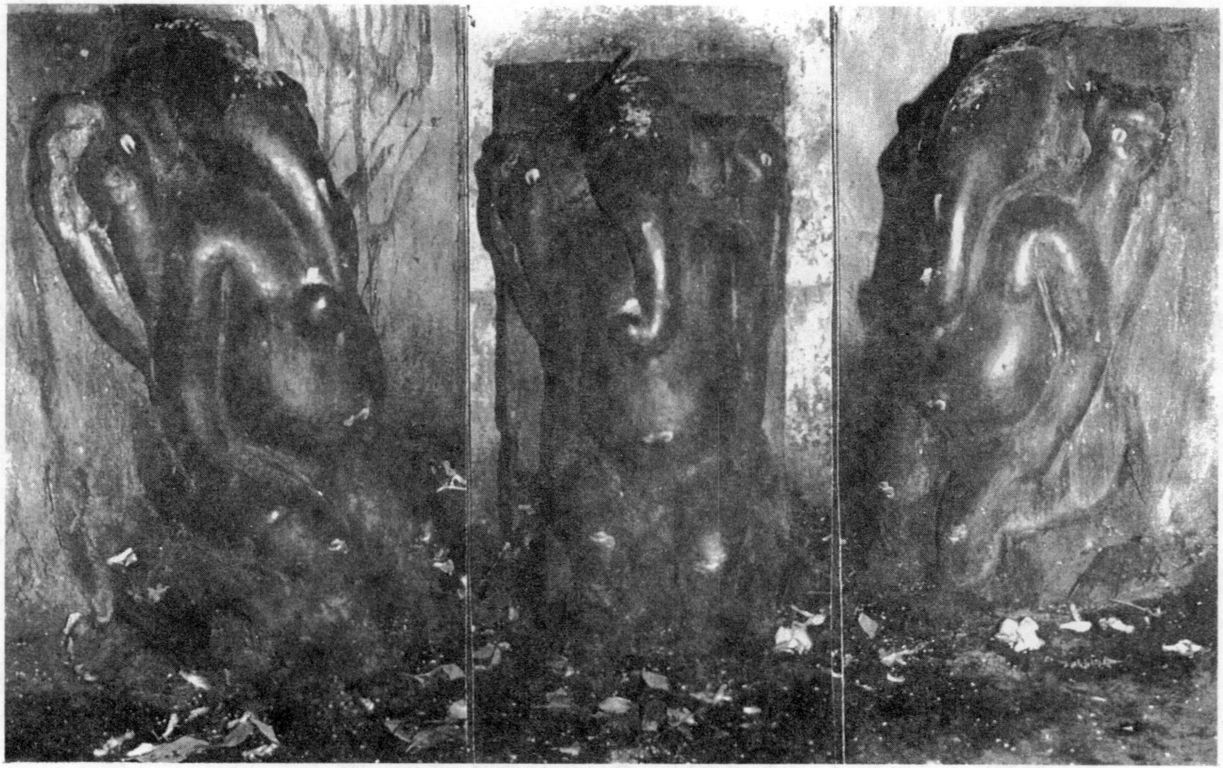

Plates 4, 5, 6: Apegaon. Six-handed god Gaṇeśa.

Vitthal: Sometimes Adored, Sometimes Rejected
Changes in Theological Pattern

IRINA GLUSHKOVA

The god Vitthal (Viṭṭhal) alias Vithoba (Viṭhobā) alias Panduranga (Pāṇḍūraṅga) of the sacred town of Pandharpur at the Bhima river in south Maharashtra is a pivot of the Varkari[1] Panth which is the most illustrious variety of Maharashtrian bhakti. The significant features of this tradition as seen today are: the unbroken succession of saint prophets from Dnyaneshvar in the thirteenth century to Tukaram in the seventeenth century along with the uninterrupted flow of the literature created by them, and a collective pilgrimage with *pādukās* of great saints carried in palanquins to Pandharpur at the eleventh day of the bright half of the month of *āṣāḍh*.[2] Both features are closely connected with a priority of visual images (*saguṇ rūp*) of Vithoba. The saints unceasingly and in the smallest details, praised the beauty of the favourite god, and modern pilgrims of mostly low origin while moving to Pandharpur for his *darśan* and *padasparśa* sing hymns created by saints in glory of Vithoba:

How beautiful is the image of the god
Standing on a brick, his hands on his hips. (1)
A garland of tulsi-beads is round his neck
A yellow silk cloth is round his loins,
I love continuously this very image. (2)
On his ears the fish-shaped pendants shine,
And his throat is decorated with the kaustubha jewel. (3)
Tuka says: All my joy [is in this image],
I am gazing with love at its sacred face. (4)

(Tukaram, 3)

[1] Vārkarī [*vār(ī)+karī*] is traditionally understood as 'one who performs *vārī*', i.e. goes on regular pilgrimages to Pandharpur.

[2] I have reported my impressions on the pilgrimage (*vārī*) to Pandharpur and the changes in the Varkari Panth in my papers read at the Twelfth European Conference on South Asia (Berlin, 1992) and the International Symposium on 'Tradition: Transmission or Invention' (Pondicherry, 1997). Some preliminary observations have been published in the Russian language editions and issues.

THE SAINTS AND THE GOD

Notwithstanding the clearly spelt adoration, there are well-known cases of explicit or implicit rejection of Vitthal by some of the Varkari saints. Addressed in favourable circumstances as a loving mother (*māūlī*), Vithoba is sometimes really treated as a member of the family: he is scolded and beaten, abused and neglected, but is still adored. This might appear as the third distinctive feature of the Varkari tradition testifying to the unique character of its bhakti, devoid of the slightest fear, individualized and intimate to the utmost.

Namdev (13th-14th cent.) was probably the first among the Varkari saints who bluntly expressed his dissatisfaction with Vithoba. He stated that the god 'worked [him] into fury', and that he wanted to 'seize hold of [the god's] legs roughly' instead of touching them with affection as was the routine practice. He accused the god of 'selfishness' and 'guile', and called him different names including 'a thief' and 'a whore'. He blamed the god for refusing to help other bhaktas and in perplexity questioned him, 'What good have you ever done to anybody?' concluding afterwards that 'if a fame of [the god] is to be narrated [it will be a story] of his disgrace' (Namdev, 1625-1649).

According to Namdev's statements, his mother, Gonai, was very critical about his surrender to Vitthal and acted as a classical vixen: she called the god a 'destroyer of the house', compared him to a 'blood-thirsty tiger' with the cow-Namdev bound to the tiger's neck, blamed for 'impudence' and 'duplicity' and 'for butter thefts in order to fill his own belly'. She also repeatedly stated, addressing Vithoba, that 'nobody is able to say that you are good', and named bitter examples of different prominent figures of Indian mythology — Narada, Mayurdhvarna, Bhishma, Upamanyu, etc. — who suffered because of the god to prove her point. She even threatened Vithoba once, 'I shall swallow [the whole] Pandharpur along with you' (Namdev, 1264-1294).

Tukaram, one of the most renowned poets of the Varkari tradition, who composed the above-quoted lines about the striking beauty of the god, is also the author of broadly known blasphemous poems in which he expressed a mixture of childish surprise and frenzied fury in view of his own failure in mystic cognition of the god. He called Vithoba many names such as 'a thief', 'cruel', 'shameless', 'dishonest', 'provoking a quarrel', 'a harlot', 'a frog', 'a donkey', 'a dog', and even the most obscene, 'an ass' and 'a fucking prick' (Tukaram, 1469-1553).

According to Mahipati, the eighteenth century biographer of all Varkari saints, Tukaram's wife Jijabai, famous for her peevish character, 'refused to go to the temple to see God [in the temple of Dehu - I.G.]. She used to say, 'I do not want to see that Black fellow' (Abbot 1986, p. 111). The woman was desperate because of her husband's indifferent attitude toward family problems, and wishing to injure Vithoba, treated his image in their native village of Dehu with boiling milk as *naivedya* [Abbot 1986, p. 166]. A rain of reproaches and abuse is hurled at Vithoba by Tukaram's younger brother Kanheya who blamed the god for Tukaram's mysterious disappearance from Dehu. Among the epithets showered at the god were 'a thief', 'shameless', 'false', 'importunate', 'a destroyer of a home', 'a hectoring debtor', 'devoid of name and mercy' and again 'a fucking prick' (Kanheya, 5-46).

THE DEVOTEES AND THE GOD

The temple of Pandharpur and its image, albeit anthropomorphic, but viewed as self-existent (*svayaṃbhū*), are usually accepted as main sacred objects by the devotees of Vithoba. This fact is by no means an obstacle for construction of a great number of other temples of smaller size and significance dedicated to Vithoba throughout Maharashtra. These temples are looked upon not as sacred sanctities for worshipping god, but rather as an accommodation for the joint singing of *bhajan*s, performance of *kīrtan*s based on saints' poems, *pravacana*s illustrating the fundamental tenets of saints' world outlook and *parāyaṇa*s. The latter are the non-stop recitation of *Dñyāneśvarī* (*Bhāvārthadīpikā*), an expanded poetic commentary to *Bhagavadgītā* written by Dnyaneshvar who is traditionally recognized as the founder of the Varkari panth. This *Dñyāneśvarī* along with *Bhāgavata* (the Marathi commentary on the XI chapter of the *Bhāgavata-purāṇa*) of Eknath of the sixteenth century and *Gāthā* of Tukaram are treated as sacred canons (*traysthī*) of the Varkari tradition. Nevertheless, some temples of Vithoba, especially connected with famous promoters of the Varkari ideas, start to function as self-efficient centres of ritual and pilgrimage activity, drawing off a number of pilgrims from the main temple in Pandharpur. The Bombay temple of Vithoba in Vadala founded by an authoritative preceptor of the tradition some 150 years ago is an example of this trend. The aged teacher was finding it difficult to continue the practice of travelling 400 km to Pandharpur. He happened to discover an image of Vithoba during ablutions on the way to Pandharpur, so he built a temple, installed the idol and stopped visiting Pandharpur. His followers too stopped going to Pandharpur and started elaborate celebrations of calendar festivals in Vadala coinciding in time with those celebrated in Pandharpur, including the *ekadaśī* of the bright half of *āṣādh* (*Census 1961*, pp. 71-3).

THE BRAHMINS AND THE GOD

Everyone born in the Varkari family or initiated into the Varkari Panth is supposed to worship Vithoba and go on regular pilgrimages to Pandharpur,[3] but not every devotee of Vithoba is a bhakta and a varkari. Representatives of the so-called 'Brahminic' and 'folk' traditions, who made a substantial contribution to the formation of the cult of the god of Pandharpur[4] and who have their own ideas about and claims of Vithoba are neither bhaktas in the strict meaning of the word nor varkaris. The roots of Vithoba's origin are traced in the prehistoric and historic past of pastoral nomadic tribes. On the other hand worship pattern in the temple of Pandharpur goes in line with Brahminic norms. None other than Brahmins had been responsible for incorporation of Vithoba into the frame of 'normative Hinduism' and they still continue to define the climate around the god. Each modification or innovation introduced into the Pandharpur temple tenor or liturgy during the last two centuries is known by the name of its initiator.

In 1947 after the ten days hunger-strike by Sane Guruji, a famous Marathi writer, the temple in Pandharpur was officially opened for untouchables. Under the pressure of the indisputable authority of a local pandit Bhagavanshastri Dharurkar, the Brahmins of Pandharpur set up a boycott against the 'defiled god' (*dev bāṭla*) and stopped entering the temple. The most surprising thing about this much-talked-of boycott was its support by a number of hereditary Varkari leaders, including Sopankaka Dehukar, the direct descendant of Tukaram in the seventh generation. According to Tukaram, he himself was not a 'twice-born' but a shudra from the Kunbi caste,[5] and his poems, echoing the poems of other Varkari saints, are full of statements about the equality of all bhaktas in the eyes of god. Parallel to this boycott, a number of rank-and-file varkaris too refused to take *darśan* of Vithoba as a protest against the intensive process of Vithoba's 'Brahminisation'.

[3] For description of varkaris see Deleury 1960.

[4] For discussion of the formation of the cult of Vithoba see Deleury 1960, Dhere 1984, Raeside 1965, Sand 1990, Sontheimer 1981.

[5] Tukaram's descendants hold a different view of their great ancestor's origin, and are ranked at present with the Maratha caste (of Kshatriya status).

'Vithoba of Pandharpur', a well-known essay by Durga Bhagwat, is usually referred to as the first articulated suggestion of the pastoral origin of Vithoba and his links with the nomadic tribe of Dhangars. But the introductory part of this essay in which Bhagwat states that Pandharpur is her ancestral place is also worth intent attention:

> In his childhood my grandfather had witnessed his mother's death which resulted from his father's cruel and unjust treatment. He swore that he would never step back on the earth stained with blood and left his home once and for ever. In advanced age, he, full of sincere bhakti feeling, started reading 'Dñyāneśvarī', 'Bhāgavata' of Eknath, 'Gāthā' of Tukaram and other books and strictly observed *ekadaśī* fast, but never did he visit the temple of Vithoba. He would have gone for *darśan* of Vithoba but he was sticked to his prejudice and he never approached the image of the god . . . My grandfather rejected everything — the ancestral house, his fields, and kinsmen. His father's name was Panduranga, and he rejected the name, too. Love of the ancestral god (*kuldevatā*) could not emerge among us devoid of adherence to ancestral rules (*kulācār*). But still Vithoba backed my grandfather and ultimately drew him back. My grandfather rejected the temple Vithoba, but he, though by stealth, placed by his side the bookish Vithoba of Dnyaneshvar and Tukaram. . . . (Bhagwat 1970, pp. 32-3)

The main postulates of Prārthanā Samāj, a monotheistic association founded in 1867 in Maharashtra, were: 'God is one and without form. It is proper and it is our duty to worship him in a spiritual way. Idolatry is an aberration; it is an insult to God, debases man and leads him to evil practices' (cited from Lederle 1976, p. 80). The religious reformists, including R.G. Bhandarkar and M.G. Ranade, attempted to combine a single father-god with an observance of the basic social rules of Hinduism. Looking for reasonable and convincing means to achieve their goals they turned to the treasures of the past, and above all to the Marathi saint-poets and Tukaram in the first place ('Tukaram was at the centre of the awakening process of nineteenth century Maharashtra', More 1996, p. 240). Accepting his poems saturated with longing for Vithoba, the reformists sang them at their prayer-meetings as the highest example of a realization of a personal God, but they did not ever adopted Vithoba as the embodiment of divinity. Nevertheless, the members of the Prārthanā Samāj could not completely escape the magnetism of Vithoba, and though their activity was mainly concentrated in Pune and around, they took over a foundling home (1881) and an orphanage (1881) at Pandharpur and added a maternity home and a refuge home for the homeless as a token of their zeal, for social reform but not for the visual form of Lord of Pandharpur.

THE *PHAḌS* AND THE GOD

Stepping back into the hold of the Varkari Panth of the twentieth century one can not but come across evidence and feel that the Panth can neither as the order nor as the ideology be called a monolithic structure. It actually reveals itself through its *phaḍ*s which are a kind of amorphous constituting body and are still very little known to an outsider.[6] Most probably *phaḍ*s began to emerge from the eighteenth century onwards to consolidate institutionally separate varkaris around 1. the personality of a prominent varkari saint (such as Dnyaneshvar, Namdev, Eknath, Tukaram, etc.); 2. personalities of the founder of the *phaḍ* (*mūḷpuruṣ*) who can be either descendants or pupils or popular *kīrtankār*s and their successors; 3. main relic which is either an object attributed to the saint or more often, a manuscript which is believed to be that of the saint himself or rewritten by the *mūḷpuruṣ*; and 4. a temple or some temples to shelter a religious activity. Along with dates and arrangements common and sacred to all varkaris, there exists a separate annual programme of each *phaḍ* which specifies particular festive days, weeks and months, independent pilgrimages and accompanying rituals. Different *phaḍ*s have accepted different editions of saints' literature as normative and different inventories of routinely performed hymns; each *phaḍ* holds its own position regarding the sequence of performed hymns, their articulation, interpretation of obscure parts and usage of ritual exclamations. Song programmes of each *phaḍ* are based mainly on the hymns of the more revered saint, and other saints' poems are used as additional illustrations.

The exact number of *phaḍ*s embracing practically all Maharashtra and the number of members of each *phaḍ* are not known. To make a rough estimate, there exist around fifty *phaḍ*s — some of them recognize each other, some do not consider other *phaḍ*s as legitimate. The Dehukar and Vaskar *phaḍ*s were the first to establish themselves. The Dehukar *phaḍ*, as its name shows, was founded by Tukaram's grandson and great-grandson who had moved from Dehu to Pandharpur with a manuscript of Tukaram's *Gāthā* rewritten by the eldest son of the saint. The founder of the Vaskar *phaḍ* was a lingayat Mallappa Vaskar (1709-99) who had adopted Varkari views being impressed by Dnyaneshvar's literature. Contemporary members of this *phaḍ* form their own *diṇḍī*, the structural

[6] There is some scarce data on *phaḍ*s in Bahirat and Bhalerav (Bahiraṭ and Bhālerāv 1972) and some fragmentary and perfunctory information in the unpublished Ph.D. dissertation of Nalini G. Sontakke (Soṇṭakke 1992) dedicated by the author to 'the feeling of bhakti towards Tukaram'.

unit of the Pandharpur pilgrimage, and take the closest place to the palanquin with Dnyaneshvar's *pādukā*s. The Dehukar *phaḍ* has split into six *phaḍ*s by now, all of them give priority to poems of Tukaram; one of these *phaḍ*s claims that it has the original *ciplyā* — a kind of musical instrument used by Tukaram — and his original *pādukā*s are in its possession. The reasons why these new *phaḍ*s have detached themselves are differences of opinions on some philosophical, ritual and practical matters and the numerical increase of Tukaram's (and other saints') descendants making claims of leadership, but the latter reason is not pronounced. *Dṛṣṭānta*s and *sākṣātkār*s — mystical visions and instructions revealed to authoritative Varkari personalities are a stimulating motif and a convenient pretext, too. The Vaskar *phaḍ* has also split into various *phaḍ*s. One of them, the Ajrekar *phaḍ* got detached due to the discord arising out of whether the god of Pandharpur is mentioned or not in the text of *Dñyāneśvarī*. Different regions of Maharashtra are under the impact of respective *phaḍ*s in their perception of Vithoba and the saints' literature. For example, the town of Kolhapur, its vicinity and even the adjoining parts of Karnatak have for long been under the influence of the Ajrekar *phaḍ*. In the temples raised by the members of this *phaḍ* which are known as Hari temples (*harīmandir*), not the image of Vithoba, but the books, namely *Dñyāneśvarī* and *Bhāgavata* of Eknath, are the main sacred objects. In this way, the traditional *saguṇ* worship of the Varkari Panth is replaced in some places by the *nirguṇ* devotion. It is argued that one of the most prominent leaders of the Prārthanā Samāj, M.G. Ranade who had spent his childhood in Kolhapur and around, was deeply influenced by the Ajrekar *phaḍ* and its leader of those days, Govindababa (More 1996, p. 241). The same model of attributeless worship has been adopted by followers of Kisan Sakhre-maharaj, who represents a stable trend in the context of Marathi devotional literature. He and his followers do not enter the temple of Vithoba in Pandharpur, finding an authoritative support to what has taken a form of a principle, in a new interpretation of an *ovī* from the *Dñyāneśvarī*. According to them, this *ovī* contains the recommendation to substitute the *darśan* of the god for the *darśan* of the pinnacle of the god's temple.[7] This group, not accepted as a *phaḍ* by some other *phaḍ*s,

[7] It is well known that the name of Vitthal is not mentioned in the *Dñyāneśvarī* and other works of Dnyaneshvar but in *abhaṅga*s of doubtful authorship which are traditionally attributed to Dnyaneshvar. In this light almost any *ovī* of the *Dñyāneśvarī* can be subjected to a new interpretation and it is being regularly done for many reasons (one of these is stimulated by tracing a Dravidian, and not Aryan, origin of obscure words with consequent shifting of the meaning of the whole context).

has ordered the making of copper plates with the complete text of the *Dñyāneśvarī* (9000 *ovīs*) engraved on them, and now is collecting money for building the temple which will be decorated with those plates.[8] It is interesting to note that this group (the Sakhre-Sampradāy) along with a number of other *phaḍs* too is led by Brahmins who are not habitual members of the Varkari Panth. They also generally give more attention to those works of Varkari devotional literature which were composed by Dnyaneshvar and Eknath, both Brahmins.

By the beginning of the twentieth century contradictions between some *phaḍs* started to take the form of clear-cut opposition (Dandekar 1988, p. 62). In these circumstances an authoritative expert in saints' literature Vishnu Narasimha Jog, popularly known as Jog-maharaj, and his co-thinkers founded the Varkari School (*Vārkarī śikṣaṇ saṃsthā*) in the small town of Alandi. Alandi had already established its fame and religious importance due to the *samādhī* of Dnyaneshvar located there and the temple complex around it; it had already by that time become a starting point for the procession of pilgrims who go to Pandharpur grouping around the palanquin with Dnyaneshvar's *pādukā*s. The goal of foundation of the Varkari School was formulated as follows: 'To study philosophy expressed in the *Dñyāneśvarī*, *Amṛtānubhava*, Tukaram's *Gāthā* and other works of the Varkari saints and to train advocates for giving impetus to the Varkari Panth and Maharashtra Dharma' (Dandekar 1988, pp. 62-3). In spite of an attempt to bring unity into the varkaris' views, the still greatly active Varkari School has turned into another *phaḍ* with its own main personalities, ideas and rituals. Tendencies towards dissociation among different Varkari *phaḍs* have survived and are not getting any milder.

Veneration of saint preachers and their literature takes even more extraordinary forms: take for example a recently published book by Sadananda More *The Darshan of Tukaram* (More 1996). Sadananda More is a professor of philosophy in the University of Poona and a descendant of Tukaram in the tenth generation. He made an attempt to systematically expound a 'Tukaram-centric' view on the cultural history of Maharashtrian

[8] Over twenty years Kisan-Sakhre-maharaj (who maintains a spiritual tradition established by his predecessor Nana-Sakhre-maharaj in the nineteenth century) has been running a monthly periodical (*Svastiśrī*) propagandizing his vision of Varkari values. His 'Sādhakāśram' is situated in Alandi, in a prestigious locality on the bank of the Indrayani river almost opposite to the temple of the *samādhī* of Dnyaneshvar. If Kisan-maharaj gets a new temple built within his own premises it will certainly result in an outburst of rivalry of the two temples with far-reaching consequences for the future of the Varkari community.

society, believing that a man and his ideas are decisive factors in the formation of human relationships. Almost eight hundred pages of his book deal with the reconstruction of socio-cultural processes in Maharashtra in terms of Tukaram's personality and his poetry, which has, indeed, enriched the Marathi language and literature and is still very popular among Maharashtrians.[9]

THE MODERN POETS AND THE GOD

Rejection of Vithoba — either permanent or provisional — has become a peculiar device used in the literature of secular circles related to no tradition constituting the cult of the god but which easily resort to regional symbols of faith and devotion. Dilip Chitre, a poet, begins his poem in the following way:

I have never seen the lustre of Vitthal, only vanishing shadow of Tukaram.[10]

For Chitre the image of Vithoba is of semiotic significance only, being a source of inspiration of the great Tukaram. The importance of the latter is incontestable not because he was a devoted bhakta but due to his poetic genius. In one of his poems, Bhalchandra Nemade, a famous man of letters, rejects Vithoba quite harshly (cited from More 1996, p. 525):

Let your brick be broken, Vitha,[11] let the Chandrabhaga dry up,[12] let your leg be fractured.[13] Drive away this Vitthal from our home, get rid of this Vitthal, let a sin and a merit be smashed . . . I want him to leave our house in peace and that is all. . . .

Unlike Chitre, Nemade makes a confession in his closing lines, that a visit

[9] More himself gives the following explanation to the concept of his book: I was writing this book presuming that Tukaram was a cultural phenomenon of Maharashtra (*mahārāṣṭrāce saṃskṛtīpuruṣ*). Resting on the evaluations of Tukaram made by different persons and groups at different times, it is possible to get a picture not of Tukaram alone, but of those persons and groups, too. This picture quite naturally leads to analysis of causes and effects that make either person and either group view Tukaram in their own ways (More 1996, p. 739).

[10] Quoted from the manuscript handed to me by D. Chitre.

[11] The brick under the feet is a specific feature of Vithoba which inspired many legends and became an eagerly venerated symbol of the god.

[12] The Bhima river in Pandharpur vicinity is called Chandrabhaga due to its crescent curve.

[13] This might be the reminiscence of an actual fact which took place in 1873 when a Gosavi mendicant deliberately broke one of the image's legs.

to Pandharpur 'has made him soft' and 'he felt himself a branch of the tree'. According to the logic of Nemade, 'the tree' he mentions is nothing else but the Marathi language and the great Marathi literature composed to glorify Vithoba, but it is not the god.

INTERPRETATION

All these facts testify to two reasons for the rejection of Vithoba—to dissatisfaction with events taking place around one's own self and to non-agreement with events taking place around the god.

In the history of religions, blasphemy and abuse of gods are not unknown behavioural patterns, sometimes fraught with grave consequences including severe punishments and court trials (e.g. the case of Socrates, the case of John Taylor 1676, in England, etc.). Antinomianism is labelled with less irrevocability whenever mystics are involved, as their exclamations and judgements are looked upon as after-effects of their exalted state. Moreover, this longing for a divine substance accompanied by spiritual turmoil is referred to as 'the Dark Night of the Soul' (the expression formulated by St. John of the Cross), and 'On the whole, however, it remains true that the Dark Night is more or less a necessary ingredient, and it seems that mystical healthy-mindedness is never reached, or can never be fully appreciated, unless it is preceded by a mystical sick-mindedness' (Ranade 1988, p. 18, Preface). Understood as 'necessary ingredient', though absent in other varieties of Marathi bhakti, the provisional rejection of the beloved god by Marathi mystics, even supported by their closest relatives albeit for different, mostly very profane reasons, does not change or break the religious system of their world-outlook.[14]

Other cases of rejection based on personal perception, relate to individuals and bodies within the Varkari Panth (the flock of the Vithoba temple in Vadala, and Durga Bhagwat's grandfather), and to those not belonging formally to the latter (Prārthanā Samāj, such as D. Chitre and B. Nemade — this list can be easily enlarged) who have devaluated the significance of the god from Pandharpur in a cardinal way, giving priority to their own temples and/or placing the devotional literature inspired by the image of Vithoba as the independent and even the sole object of veneration. This is

[14] Dealing with other issues, W. Doniger suggests: On the theological level, the human experience of the abandoning mother or wife [which literally occurred in the lifespan of some Varkari saints - I.G.], and the theological hypothesis of an abandoning god (otiose, absconditus, or deist) serve as metaphors for one another (Doniger 1996, p. 43).

also the basic principle laid down as the theological foundation of those Varkari *phaḍ*s in which neither Vithoba nor even a pilgrimage to Pandharpur[15] seem to be considered as essentials. Dissatisfied with the activity around the god, some leaders and their followers aimed their protest against the god and later substantiated it with scriptural reasoning and ritualistic practice. Deviations of this kind signify a structural and functional modification in the theological pattern of the units of the diffuse Varkari Panth bringing the god-abandoning persons and *phaḍ*s in the hold of 'holy book' traditions. On the whole, some implication for this split can be found in the hymns of the Varkari saints who looked upon *saguṇ* and *nirguṇ* forms as two subsequent (and not mutually exclusive) stages of the realization of God.

In these circumstances, Vithoba, sometimes neglected or rejected by his bhaktas, but still famous for his mercy towards them, like a mother's unconditional love for her children, continues to stand on the brick in Pandharpur. He is witnessing the tireless activity around the devotional literature which glorifies him and around the creators of this literature.

[15] It looks as if the Pandharpur pilgrimage (at least in its form of *pālkhī soholā*, 'a festival of palanquins', is exceptional (may be along with the Pushti Marga pilgrimage to Krishna's homeland in Braj) in its evident emphasis on the journey 'It has great importance itself as a spiritual discipline' rather than the actual meeting with the god (Englblom 1987, pp. 27-8). My own experience throughout the whole pilgrimage confirms this point of view. I remember, for example, that Mandutai, who had been in charge of my *dindī* (*Śegḍe-dindi* no. 3) for almost fifteen years did not care much about visiting the temple on arrival to Pandharpur (probably because of the huge queues), but she personally did not object to *darśan* in principle, and was glad when I managed to get hold of a two-persons pass for the night *mahāpūjā*.

REFERENCES

Abbot, Justin E., *Life of Tukaram*, translation from Mahipati's Bhaktalilamrita, Chapters 25 to 40, Delhi:Motilal Banarsidass, 1986 (rpt.).

Bahiraṭ, Bh.P. and Dn. Bhālerāv P., *Vārkarī sampradāy: uday va vikās*, Puṇe: Vhīnas Prakāśan, 1972.

Bhāgwat, Durgā, Pāṇḍhrīcā Viṭhobā, *Pais*, Mumbai: Mauj Prakāśan, 1970.

Census of India 1961, vol. X, Maharashtra, pt. VII-B, *Fairs and Festivals in Maharashtra*, Bombay: Government Central Press, 1969.

Dāṇḍekar, S.V., *Vārkarī sampradāyāce thor pravartak vai. Jogmahārāj-caritra*, Nagpur: Vārkarī Prakāśan Maṇḍaḷ, Śake 1910 (1988).

Deleury, G.A., *The Cult of Viṭhobā*, Poona: Deccan College Postgraduate and Research Institute, 1960.

Dhere, R.C., *Viṭṭhal: ek mahāsamanvay*, Puṇe: Śrīvidyā Prakāśan, 1984.

Doniger, Wendi, 'Sexual Masquerades in Hindu Myths: Aspects of the Transmission of Knowledge in Ancient India', in *The Transmission of Knowledge in South Asia.* Essays on Education, Religion, History, and Politics, edited by Nigel Crook, Delhi: Oxford University Press, 1996.

Engblom, Ph.C., (translated with introduction) D.B. Mokashi, *Palkhi: An Indian Pilgrimage*, New York: State University of New York Press, 1987.

(Kanheya), *Śrīsakaḷsantgāthā*, Khaṇḍ dusrā, sampādak Kāśīnāth Anant Jośī, Puṇe: Śrīsantvāṅgmay Prakāśan Mandir, 1967 (*avṛttī dusrī*).

Lederle, M., *Philosophical Trends in Modern Maharashtra*, Bombay: Popular Prakashan, 1976.

More, Sadānanda, *Tukārām darśan*, Ahmadnagar: Gaj Prakāśan, 1996.

(Namdev), *Śrīsakaḷsantgāthā*, Khaṇḍ pahilā, sampādak Kāśīnāth Anant Jośī, Puṇe: Śrīsantvāṅgmay Prakāśan Mandir, 1967 (*avṛttī dusrī*).

Raeside, I.M.P., 'The Pāṇḍūranga-Māhātmya of Śrīdhar', *Bulletin of the School of Oriental and African Studies*, vol. 28, 1965.

Ranade, R.D., *Mysticism in Maharashtra: Indian Mysticism*, Delhi: Motilal Banarsidass, 1988 (rpt.).

Sand, E.R., 'The Legend of Pundarīka: The Founder of Pāṇḍharpūr', in *The History of Sacred Places in Traditional Literature*, Papers on Pilgrimage in South Asia, edited by Hans Bakker, Leiden, New York, København and Köln: E.J. Brill, 1990.

Sontheimer, G.-D., *Gopjanāñcā Dev*: *Śrīviṭṭhal: Mahārāstrācī sattvadhārā*, Dr. R.C. Dhere Abhinandagranth, sampādak G.M. Kulkarṇī and V.T. Śete, Puṇe: Dāstane rāmcandra āṇi kămpanī, Śake 1903 (1981).

———, *Pastoral Deities in Western India*, translated by Anne Feldhaus, New York and Oxford: Oxford University Press, 1989.

Sonṭakke, N.G., *Tukārām uttarkālīn vārkarī sampradāy — phaḍ āṇi paramparā* (*Tukārām te Dhundā mahārāj Deglūrkar*), Nagpur: Nagpur Vidyāpīṭh, 1992.

(Tukaram), *Śrītukārām mahārājāncī sārtha gāthā*, sampādak H.Bh.P.S.K. Neūrgāvkar, Puṇe: Prācārya Dāṇḍekar Dhārmik va Sāṃskṛtik Vāṅgmay Prakāśan Māṇḍaḷ, 1978.

The Untouchable Women Saint-Poets of Maharashtra

ELEANOR ZELLIOT

We all know that the bhakti movement, the spread of devotional religion in medieval India, was the most inclusive of the many facets of Hinduism. And I tried to prove in my paper for the conference preceding this[1] that Maharashtrian bhakti was not only open to all castes and many women but also, almost exclusively, was a householder phenomenon. Both points are illustrated by the stories and songs of Soyrabai and Nirmala, two women from the untouchable caste of Mahars, the wife and sister of Cokhamela, a saint-poet well known to Maharashtrians. As far as I know, there are no other songs by a woman bhakta from an untouchable caste in the medieval literature of any Indian language.

Nirmala and Soyrabai lived in the late thirteenth, early fourteenth century, Nirmala in Mehunpuri near Aurangabad and Soyrabai probably in Pandharpur, the centre of Maharashtrian bhakti. Whoever preserved their songs is unknown, and there are no early manuscripts, but their *abhaṅgas* (the flexible metre used in Marathi for devotional songs) ring true in terms of the Maharashtrian tradition of that period and what we know of the place of women and the role of caste in early Maharashtra. Theirs seem to be true women's voices in the Marathi style. For instance, there is no great personal passionate love for Krishna as in the case of Mirabai and Antal; there is no scathing (and amusing) denunciation of husbands as in the poetry of Mahadeviyakka, the three best known women poets from other language areas.[2] The typology developed by A.K.

[1] 'The Householder Saints of Maharashtra' was given at the 1994 conference in Seattle, and has been published in *Studies in Early Modern Indo-Aryan Languages, Literature and Culture*, edited by Alan W. Entwistle and Carol Salomon with Heidi Pauwels and Michael C. Shapiro, New Delhi: Manohar, 1999, pp. 415-26.

[2] Mirabai sang in Rajasthani Hindi, Antal in Tamil, Mahadeviyakka in Kannada. For a compilation of many women saint-poets, see the tenth anniversary triple issue of *Manushi*, 50, 51, 52 (January-June 1989) on the theme of Women Bhakta Poets. The Maharashtrian women sants included are Muktabai, Janabai and Bahinabai.

Ramanujan for women saints: early dedication to God, denial of marriage, defying societal norms, initiation, marrying the Lord, does not apply to either Soyrabai or Nirmala as it does not to Muktabai or Janabai, other women poets of the period, nor do they qualify as 'superior to their husbands' which Ramanujan notes is the pattern of saints' wives. Like others of the many women bhaktas of the Marathi tradition, Soyrabai and Nirmala write of family, of their devotion to the god Vithoba, of the joyous pilgrimage to Pandharpur, of the ways to maintain household and still find true freedom.

Although sixty-two *abhaṅga*s of Soyrabai and twenty-four of Nirmala appear in the collected works of all the saints,[3] they have received very little popular or scholarly attention. Only two of Soyrabai's *abhaṅga*s have found their way into the popular Maharashtrian tradition. Vinayak Lakshman Bhave, in the first edition of his *Mahārāṣṭra sāraswat* (introduction to Maharashtra), used the third and fourth lines of Soyrabai's first *abhaṅga* in the *Śrīsakalsantgāthā* as an invocation:

I'll place a leaf before you and I will serve you family food. (3)
O God, it's not fit for you, but imagine it sweet and accept it. (4)

The lines well illustrate Soyrabai's humility (as well as the Brahmin Bhave's), but the whole *abhaṅga* indicates another quality: Soyrabai's knowledge of *Mahābhārata* legends:

Come, come, you who bear the flag of Garuda,
I will worship you along with the brick. (1)
O Gopala, I will present you with incense, lights and garlands. (2)
I'll place a leaf before you and I will serve you family food. (3)
O God, it's not fit for you, but imagine it sweet and accept it. (4)
Vidhur served watered broken rice, O my mother and father, O Lord. (5)
O Narayana, Draupadi's one leaf smeared with leftover food
satisfied you. (6)
It's just like that here, says the Mahari of Cokha. (7)[4]

Another of Soyrabai's *abhaṅga*s has been widely sung and recorded by

[3] *Śrīsakalsantgāthā* in 2 vols. collected by Nanamaharaj Sakhare, edited by Kashinath Anant Joshi, Pune: Srisantwangmay Prakashan Mandir, 1967 (1923).

[4] *yeī yeī garuḍadhvajā viṭe sahit karīn pūjā.* The flag of Garuda is a symbol of Vishnu and Narayana is another of his names. Vithoba is almost always referred to in Vaishnava terms. The brick is a symbol of Vithoba, who stood on a brick thrown him by the devotee Pundalik to keep his feet from the mud while Pundalik finished his loving attention to his parents. It symbolizes Vithoba's patient love for his devotees.

The poems of Soyrabai were translated primarily with the help of Vijaya Deo.

Bhimsen Joshi, Maharashtra's beloved classical and *bhāvgīt* (devotional songs) singer.

Sing this joyous Name lovingly, chant a prayer to Vithoba. (1)
This worldly life will be happy if you chant the Name again and again. (2)
Lust and anger become helpless; look! Desires and longings flee. (3)
Say Hari Hari lovingly, says Cokha's Mahari. (4)[5]

These well known songs illustrate some of the message of Soyrabai: her sense of her own poverty although she will give God all she has, the common Maharashtrian understanding of God as father *and* mother (*māy-bāp*, written as one word), chanting the Name of God as the cure for the emotions and woes of *sansār*, the worldly or married life. There are other themes in Soyrabai's songs. Among the *abhaṅga*s which deal with the 'dark night of the soul', a sense of the inaccessibility of the divine common to all saints, is one which interests me especially because one of my interpreters, Jayant Karve, said while we translated: 'She's speaking to God as if he were a Brahmin, not really angry-sounding, just reproachful':

Why have you saddened me so?
Who would call you the Just? (1)
We sit at your doorstep
asking for alms, saying 'Give, give'. (2)
And you have taken from so many.
How can you feel good about it? (3)
This is not decent conduct
says the Mahari of Cokha. (4)[6]

There seems to be nothing specific of caste in the song above, unless sitting at God's doorstep refers to the fact that the Mahar could not enter the temple of Vithoba while asking for alms indicates a low status. In fact, caste does not enter into the majority of her songs. However, in some *abhaṅga*s Soyrabai is very conscious of her low status and her untouchability. In one *abhaṅga* she clearly protests the very basis of untouchability, pollution, in explicit and moving terms:

A body is unclean, they say, only the soul is untainted. (1)
But the impurity of the body is born with the body.
By which rule has a body become pure? (2)

[5] *sukhāce he nām āvaḍīne gāve | vāce āḷvāve viṭhobāsī*. *Abhaṅga* 43 in *Śrīsakalsantgāthā*. Giving a human quality to the deadly sins of lust and anger and the desires and longings which hinder devotion, is typical of Soyrabai. She sometimes signs her work in her own name, more often as her husband's wife.

[6] *kā bā udās maj kele | koṇ mhaṇe tumhī bhale*. *Abhaṅga* 28 in *Śrīsakalsantgāthā*.

Not a creature in the world has been born
    except in a gory womb. (3)
This is the glory of God: defilement exists within. (4)
The body is polluted from within.
Be sure of it, says the Mahari of Cokha. (5)[7]

There is no stronger statement of the bhaktas against the very idea of hereditary pollution except for the anguished cry of Soyrabai's husband in one of his *abhaṅgas*, 'O Lord, who is born pure?' However, the Marathi for 'untouchable' or 'untouchability' is not used. Soyrabai refers to herself as *hīn*, i.e. low or base. But she does refer in a backhand way to the restrictions Mahars were subject to. Both Nirmala and Soyrabai speak joyfully of coming to the Great Door of the temple at Pandharpur, implying but not saying directly that they could not go inside to see the image itself. Indeed, the *samādhi* of Cokhamela is at the very foot of the steps leading to the Great Door and until Independence (and the fasting of a Brahmin reformer, Sane Guruji), no Untouchable could go further than that memorial stone. In many *abhaṅgas* Soyrabai refers to 'leftover food', food ritually and perhaps actually unclean, which was one of the Mahar's perquisites after higher caste feasts and rituals. The word is used in a religious context in addressing God, 'I will accept your leftovers' (*abhaṅga* 32) and 'I can only wish for your discarded food' (*abhaṅga* 55).

Perhaps one should not wonder that there is so little reference to untouchability. The songs of the saints must have been kept orally for generations, sung by pilgrims going to Pandharpur, so those specifically about untouchability might have been considered inappropriate for the joyous pilgrimage. There is, however, a curious partial story in *abhaṅga* 19 that begins with trouble in Pandharpur from the temple priests but then ends very happily:

The Brahmans of Pandhari harassed Cokha;
    God was surprised at this. (1)
Everyone gathered at Cokha's house;
    Wealth and Power stood at the door. (2)
Rangoli at the entrance, flags on the gate,
    Joyous *kīrtan* of the Vaisnavas. (3)
The celebration was like Divali and Dasara
    Soyra waves the lights of *āratī* before Cokha. (5)[8]

[7] *dehāsī viṭāḷ mhaṇtī sakaḷ | ātmā to nirmaḷ shuddhbuddh. Abhaṅga* 6 in *Śrīsakalsantgāthā*.

[8] *paṇḍharīce brahmaṇe cokhapāsī chaḷīle | tayālāgī kele naval deve. Abhaṅga* 19 in *Śrīsakalsantgāthā*. Temple priests in Pandharpur are not often

One of the most unusual characteristics of Soyrabai's poetry is that she often refers to her sister-in-law, Nirmala, Cokhamela's sister. Although she calls herself Cokha's Mahari, she does not really refer to her husband in any meaningful way. For instance, Soyra tells us that she and Cokhamela and their son Karmamela went to see Nirmala in her far away village of Mehunpuri, but then her attention turns solely to Nirmala. Soyra embraced her feet saying, 'Great is the woman of Mehunpuri' (*abhaṅga* 12). As Soyra and Nirmala sit together, 'By the grace of the Father, Vithal and Nirmala became one' (*abhaṅga* 13). She sees God in her husband's sister. And she sings in *abhaṅga* 15 'Taking a bath at Nirmala's place is like visiting Prayag crores of times.' The affection between the two women and the clear religious guidance of Nirmala brings a sense of realism to the lives of these women and an idea of the importance of the extended family relationships.

Nirmala herself is also an accomplished poet and bhakta. She speaks of her brother, Cokhamela, as her guide, although she does not hesitate to chide him when he leaves Soyrabai as she is about to give birth to their son. She never mentions her husband Banka, even though he is thought to have been Soyrabai's brother, and does not use his name in her signature line, although she does occasionally end, 'the sister of Cokha says'. Banka himself was also a poet and a bhakta, and when Prabhakar Mande, a folklorist, my research assistant Sudhir Waghmare, and I went to Mehunpuri, we found that both Banka and Nirmala were remembered as if they had died yesterday. The spot in the river where they took *samādhi* was obliterated in a flood, but a hut where a contemporary guru came to set himself up as a modern Cokhamela is still preserved. The villagers also think that Cokhamela lived there, although it is two hundred miles from Pandharpur as the crow flies. At one time a *pālkhī* (palanquin bearing the footprints of the saint) left Mehunpuri for Pandharpur, but since the great conversion of Mahars (and some others) to Buddhism in 1956, such devotion to Pandharpur has ceased.

Nirmala seems to have a more personal relationship with the God Vithoba than Soyrabai. In one *abhaṅga* she sings:

---

bhaktas in the Maharashtrian tradition and they do not join in the pilgrimage. The other references in this song are to *kīrtan*, the song and sermon sessions common to bhakti groups; to the Hindu holidays of Divali and Dasara; to *āratī*, the ceremony of waving a tray of lights in circles before the face of someone being honoured; and to the chalk drawings made for special occasions called *raṅgolī*.

I am certain of you; I surrender to your feet. (1)
Now, do what you think is right; I have put down my burden. (2)
I have put my head in your lap, knowing what the future holds. (3)
Nirmala says, Save me or kill me; now the burden is yours. (4)[9]

She often compares the closeness of her brother Cokhamela to God with her sense of less worth but just as much need:.

You have protected Cokha then and now, bearing all his faults. (1)
O merciful one, tell me, after that, why are you weary of me? (2)
I am low-born and poor, a heap of sins, but with heart and soul
I fall at your feet. (3)
Nirmala says, You are merciful so take care of me. (4)[10]

I read Nirmala's poetry with the late S.G. Tulpule, whose work on classical Marathi literature is indispensable.[11] He had not read the *abhaṅga*s of the untouchable saints before, although he is very familiar with other bhakti literature. I was touched and amused when he looked up at me after we worked on the following *abhaṅga* and said, 'This is a very intelligent woman!'

People say you should gain the ultimate goal, but they don't
have the skill at all. (1)
Pure bhakti feeling, meditation on the name—this is the
source of spirituality. (2)
Censure, fault finding, praise, honor, dishonor—treat all these
as vomit! (3)
In spirituality, others' food, others' money, others' women
should be considered polluting. (4)
Nirmala says, This is the way to the ultimate goal: the companionship
of the saints night and day. (5)[12]

[9] *tumcā bharaṅvasā dharonī mānasī | draḍh pāyāsī śaraṇ āle. Abhaṅga* 23 in *Śrīsakalsantgāthā.*

[10] *ājivarī tumhī tayāsī pāḷile | aprādh sāhile cokhiyāce. Abhaṅga* 21 in *Śrīsakalsantgāthā.*

[11] *Classical Marāṭhī Literature from the beginning to AD 1818* (A History of Indian Literature, vol. IX, Fasc. 4), Wiesbaden: Otto Harrassowitz, 1979. The late Dr. Tulpule refers only briefly to Cokhamela and quotes one *abhaṅga* but his work sets the bhakti literature in its historic place. S.G. Tulpule is also the author of *Mysticism in Medieval India* (Wiesbaden: Otto Harrassowitz, 1984).

[12] *parmārth sādhāva boltīā goṣṭī | parī na ye hātvaṭi kāhī tyācī. Abhaṅga* 10 in *Śrīsakalsantgāthā. Parmārth* has here been translated both 'ultimate goal' and, in accordance with Tulpule's suggestion, 'spirituality'.

There is nothing in this *abhaṅga* that could not be sung by any high caste saint, except perhaps the rather vulgar word *vomit*. Like Soyrabai, Nirmala rarely refers to her untouchable status except in a roundabout way, here perhaps with the word 'polluting' for the sin of covetousness, a use very different from the idea that a human could be polluting by birth.

An *abhaṅga* which illustrates why the Mahar untouchable saints have been rejected in the modern movement of untouchables led by B.R. Ambedkar is this one which indicates Soyrabai's belief in rebirth. The Ambedkar movement, which culminated in a Buddhist conversion,[13] totally rejected the concept that untouchable status was the result of karma, birth according to past deeds. It is not clear whether Soyrabai traces her status to 'sin' or whether she simply is using the traditional idea of many many births before *mokṣa* (salvation or freedom) can be reached.

The name of Hari is on the lips only of the one who has merit
tied in his garments throughout innumerable births. (1)
The name of Hari is on the lips only of the one who carries
in his purse the good deeds of innumerable births. (2)
The chanting of Narayan's name is only for the one who has practised
discipline throughout innumerable births. (3)
The sweetness of Harinama is only for the one who has left
worldly attachments throughout innumerable births. (4)
Nirmala says, the sin of innumerable births disappears
as you chant the Name. (5)[14]

Here Nirmala speaks of 'innumerable' births rather than the traditional number of eighty-four hundred thousand births before one reaches *mokṣa* the ultimate union with *brahman*, the universal substance. She also presents us with a contradiction in the final stanza, since the Name itself removes sin and the implication is that one does not have to suffer birth after birth!

[13] See my *From Untouchable to Dalit: Essays on the Ambedkar Movement*, New Delhi: Manohar, 1998 (1st edn. 1992), for the story of the long path to conversion.

[14] *anaṅdā janmāce sukṛt paṅdari | toci uccārī harināṃ. Abhaṅga* 9 in *Śrīsakalsantgāthā*. The early Mahar movement rejoiced in the presence of a Mahar saint, Cokhamela, as an important part of the Pandharpur pantheon of religious figures. Cokhamela, however, explained in one *abhaṅga* that his untouchable status was due to previous sin, and this means he no longer serves as a religious icon or source of pride. Ravidas, the untouchable saint of the north, does fill the role of one who allows a claim of religious worth for the Maharashtrian Chamarkars (*cambhār*s).

In contrast to most of the Maharashtrian bhaktas, Nirmala does not use the stuff of her daily life in her poetry. Gora the potter refers to pots, Janabai the maidservant to her daily work, but Nirmala's *abhaṅgas* (and Soyrabai's for the most part) contain no household images. What both women do, and this may be in part the reason for the neglect of their work, is to sing of their daily life, their *sansār*, as a great burden. Nirmala indicates that she has some understanding of meditation in this *abhaṅga*, but that her daily existence prevents her for reaching the presence of God:

Ocean of mercy, listen to my prayer.
　Let me lay my head at your feet. (1)
There are many ways, but I do not know them.
　I can only embrace your feet with all my strength. (2)
My body, my mind, my thoughts are restless.
　What can I do? I have no strength to quiet my mind. (3)
I cannot free myself from *sansār*;
　it embraces me, it takes you far from me. (4)
Nirmala says, what shall I do? You have left me far behind. (5)[15]

Nirmala is even more tormented by *sansār* in this *abhaṅga*, in which not even Cokhamela is called upon to relieve her weariness:

Oh God, the forest fire blazes all around;
　why don't you have pity on me? (1)
I am caught in the midst of *sansār*;
　help me now, O mother and father. (2)
Oh God, I am weary to death of this *sansār*;
　Oh Keshava, come now! (3)
Who is my family other than you?
　Oh God, you are my support. (4)
Nirmala says, embracing your feet,
　don't send me away, you who are mother and father. (5)[16]

Soyrabai has an even more negative *abhaṅga*, but one which offers also a sense of her imagination and of the possibility that the power of the mind can overcome meaninglessness:

House and home are meaningless; *sansār* is meaningless,
　the corporeal body is meaningless. (1)

[15] *kṛpecyā sāgarā parisā vinvaṇī | mastak charṇi aso mājha. Abhaṅga* 5 in *Śrīsakalsantgāthā*.

[16] *cahukaḍe devā dāṭlā vaṇva | kā na ye kanvā tujlāgī. Abhaṅga* 1 in *Śrīsakalsantgāthā*.

Your name is meaningful, all else is meaningless;
 if people don't drown it is only because of the Name. (2)
All things are meaningless.
 Ideas are meaningless.
 Great wisdom is meaningless. Who cares? (3)
The science of words is meaningless.
 Words themselves are meaningless.
 Knowledge is meaningless.
 Why speak of these things? (4)
If your mind is not steady, that's also meaningless
 and then how will you come to Hari? (5)
Till then, there's no meaning in speaking speech
 says Cokha's Mahari. (6)[17]

The antidote to all this misery is the chanting of the name of God. But there are also other kinds of relief which these women sing of. One is the great pilgrimage to Pandharpur, that joyous occasion which has in this century become the central event in Maharashtrian religious life for many people, and the culmination of that pilgrimage in the celebrations near the temple or at the river which flows by the city. Soyrabai begins *abhaṅga* 18 with 'There's a celebration of joy in the month of Ashad in Pandhari, *kīrtan* and shouting on the river's sands' and ends the song with 'Soyra prostrates herself with devotion'. Another *abhaṅga* sparkles with joy as she describes the dancing and singing of the bhaktas:

They shout, they dance, they sway in joy.
 They bubble up the name of Viṭhṭhal with love. (1)
Even Brahma and all those Gods don't know such happiness —
 this Pundalik has them in ecstasy. (2)
They dislike Vaikuntha, dislike jewels, dislike household comforts. (3)
Sri Hari dances in the shouts, in the *kīrtan*, says Cokha's Mahari. (4)[18]

[17] *vāuge ghardār vāugā sansār | vāuge śarīr nāśivaṅt. Abhaṅga* 10 in *Śrīsakalsantgāthā*.

[18] *garjatī nāctī ānaṅde ḍoltī | saprem phuṅdatī viṭhṭhal nāme. Abhaṅga* 17 in *Śrīsakalsantgāthā*. The three classic sources of information on the Pandharpur pilgrimage are: G.A. Deleury, *The Cult of Vithoba*. Poona: Deccan College Postgraduate Research Centre, 1960; Irawati Karve, 'On the Road', *Journal of Asian Studies* 22 (1962), pp. 13-29, reprinted in *The Experience of Hinduism: Essays on Religion in Maharashtra*, edited by Eleanor Zelliot and Maxine Berntsen, Albany: State University of New York Press, 1988; D.B. Mokashi, *Palkhi: A Pilgrimage to Pandharpur*, translated by Philip C. Engblom, Albany: State University of New York Press, 1987, reprinted in India by Orient Longman, 1990.

While reading the entire book of Soyrabai, one also occasionally has a feeling that she is a true mystic, finding at times the words to describe the indescribable, words that recall the poetry of mystics in many cultures. A fourteenth century untouchable woman seems to have risen above the problems of *sansār* and the humiliation of low birth to sing of immersion in the divine:

All colours have merged into one. The Lord of Colour himself
    is immersed in that colour. (1)
When I saw the Lord of Pandhari, the I–you feeling also disappeared. (2)
Distinctions have no work here. Anger and lust have run away. (3)
You who have a body are not embodied. Look! You are
    always in *samādhi*. (4)
I who look and the looking itself are one, says Cokha's Mahari. (5)[19]

[19] *avaghā raṅg ek jhālā | rangī raṅgalā śrīraṅg. Abhaṅga* 5 in *Śrīsakalsant-gāthā. Samādhi* here means a state of immersion in the divine that transcends consciousness.

Janābāī as a Mystic and Hagiographer

CHRISTOPHER SHELKE, SJ

INTRODUCTION

The mother-bird flies to the ends of the horizon and brings grain to her little ones,
The mother-kite, though flying high in the sky, jumps suddenly down to her little ones,
The mother, though busy in her work, pays attention continuously to her baby,
The mother-monkey leaps from tree to tree, holding tightly at the belly her little one.
In such a way also is Viṭṭhala the mother to us all, so considers Jani always.[1]

Through these verses of the poet-saint, Janābāī, Maharashtrian children in primary school are introduced to the motherly care of the divine providence. The poet-saint, Janābāī follows chronologically after Mahadambā (1228-1303), the first woman biographer in the Marathi literature and after Muktābāī (1279-93), the first woman saint of the Vārkarī tradition. Janābāī took *samādhi* on the third of July in the year 1350. We are sure of the date not because the biographical data of Janābāī is available to us, but rather because of the availability of the biographical data of Nāmadeva, at whose death she took *samādhi*.

In this paper I shall investigate Janābāī's *Abhaṅgas* to see her mystical experience and to observe the events of her life. Through the description of the events of her life, she has recorded for us God's working in her. As I investigate her life, I shall also investigate how she describes the lives of some other saints. In the narration of her own mystical experience she has given us her own portrait as a woman mystic, and has also depicted short biographical sketches of other saints. Thereby she has become an autobiographer and a hagiographer.

JANĀBĀĪ AS A SAINT

The first biographical sketch of Janābāī is found in the *Abhaṅgas* of Nāmadeva where he also had sketched life stories of other saints like, Gorā Kumbhār, Chokhāmelā and Sāvatā Mālī. However, in comparison with

[1] Shri Nanamaharaj Sakhare, Janābāī, *Abhaṅga*, 92, *Shri Namdeva Gatha*, Pune, 1999.

the other saints, the biographical data of Sant Janābāī is rather scanty. We don't know with certainty how Janābāī came into the house of Nārnadeva. He tells us:

At the house of Nāmadeva there is a maidservant, called Janābāī. She is pleasing to *Chakrapāni*.
During performance of her daily work, she fixes her mind day and night on Nārāyana.
Having seen her devotion and trust, Pānduranga helps her in her duties.
He comes at night to the house of Jani and helps her in grinding.[2]

Later on we find that Ekanātha in the biography of Nāmadeva mentions that Jani was a maidservant of Nāmadeva and she had such a devotion to the Lord of Pandhari that she has become the beloved of God.[3] In the *Bhaktavijaya*, Mahipati has stated that Janābāī, at the age of seven, came along with her parents to Pandharpur; she refused to return home along with them because she had intense attraction to Pānduranga and she remained in the temple. Nāmadeva found this child and 'feeling compassion' he brought her to his home and told Gonāi, his mother, how the girl was found. Mahipati relates this story saying that such a story is quoted by God's servant, Paramānanda.[4] Some scholars do state that Janābāī was older than Nāmadeva and she was brought in his house not by Nāmadeva but by his father. Such a tradition has a support from one of the *Abhaṅga*s of Janābāī herself which tells the story of Nāmadeva's birth.

Gonāi made a vow asking for a son; Give me a devoted son who would have a liking for *Pandharināth*.
Lord having seen her trust and devotion, had put Nāmadeva in her womb.
Damasheta was very happy and Dasi Jani has welcomed him with an *Owālani*.[5]

In these verses, Janābāī mentions that she has done the traditional *owālani* for the newborn babe. Actually by these verses she starts relating the biography of Nāmadeva. In another place she also gives an account of the birth of Nāmadeva's son stating:

A son was born to Nāmadeva; Viṭho came for the naming ceremony;
He brought a little frock and a cap for the child, so also a dress and a turban for Nāmadeva.

[2] Ibid., Nāmadeva's *Abhaṅga*, 2195.
[3] Shri Nanamaharaj Sakhare, *Abhaṅga*, 3619, *Shri Eknath Gatha*, Pune, 1990.
[4] Justin, B. Abbot, *Stories of Indian Saints*, 1988 (19th edn.), vol. I, p. 338.
[5] Janābāī, 282.

You are Life of my life, Nārāyana, you must name him.
Jani says to Pānduranga, please say what name should be given. [6]

Through the analysis of these verses we see how Janābāī is playing with words and giving different meanings. Her literary and creative style is certainly to be admired. She merely states, *Māzhyā jivanāchyā Jivanā, Nām thevi Nārāyana mhane Pānduranga, Nāva kāya thevu sāngā.* This phrase could be interpreted in three different ways. First, it could be translated and mean, 'Nārāyana, you give a name to the life of my life'. Secondly, it could be also read, 'Nārāyana, you are the life of my life and you, please, name this child', and thirdly one could also interpret as that the two requests are made by Nāmadeva, and then Janābāī adds her own request to Pānduranga asking Him to suggest the name. Even today, it is customary in Maharashtrian society for the maternal uncle to first pronounce the child's name. Usually the uncle is asked by one of the very close relatives of the child, either by the elder sister of the child or by a younger sister of the father of the child, to give a name to the child. In the episode which Janābāī narrates, the very name which is given suggests the various relationships in the household. The child is named Nārāyana. It is Viṭhobā who comes to name the child. The child is named Nārāyana and Jani's question of naming the child has been addressed to Pānduranga, who is Viṭhobā and Nārāyana himself. Therefore one could conclude that Janābāī is actually not giving us the facts or the information of the naming ceremony, but wants to say that through the child's birth Nārāyana has arrived in the house of Nāmadeva.

She is not setting down events as she actually saw them, but interpreting the events of the life of Nāmadeva and showing how God has been close to him. In the same way, in the verse describing the birth of Nāmadeva she is telling us that Nāmadeva is a gift of God, and that, Jani by making *owālani* accepts and welcomes this gift. Naturally, in order to accept or to welcome this gift she has not necessarily to be present at the birth of Nāmadeva. But as she tells the story of the birth, she would like to show her relationship with this birth and thereby she represents herself as a person who is making the *owālani*.

Therefore one could doubt, whether Jani as a child was actually present at the birth of Nāmadeva. Janābāī could have been found in the temple and brought into the house by Nāmadeva himself. This assumption certainly goes along with the tradition of Paramānanda who says that Nāmadeva had found Jani as a young girl and brought her in the house. However the fact

[6] Janābāī, 142.

remains true that Jani is a servant girl in the house of Nāmadeva.

LITERATURE OF JANĀBĀĪ

Today, we have about 351[7] *Abhaṅga*s and *Owi*s of Janābāī in published form, and these are normally incorporated along with the *Abhaṅga*s of Nāmadeva in the *Nāmadevagāthā*. Besides we find also about 43 *Abhaṅgas*[8] in unpublished form in various manuscripts in different places. The manuscripts of Janābāī's *Abhaṅga* are found in Rājawade Sanshodhān Mandir, and Samartha Vaṅgamaya Mandir, Dhule, Bhavani Chitra-sangrāhalaya and Granthālaya, Aundh and Sarswati Mahāl Granthālaya, Thanjavur. These manuscripts belong to different times. Therefore, the authorship of Janābāī, in the case of many verses, could be questioned. Till today, many of the editors have accepted her authorship for the *Abhaṅga*s and *Owi*s, because she signs her name in every verse. She quotes her name as 'Jani' in the most of verses, in other verses she calls herself *Namyachi Jani* and in a few verses she had even named herself as a *Dasi Jani*.

THE CLASSIFICATION OF HER LITERATURE

The entire of literature of Janābāī, both *Abhaṅga* and *Owi*s, I would classify in six categories.

1. *Nāmsankīrtan* containing the *Abhaṅga*s 1-71,[9] where she has praised the divine name.
2. Viṭhobā's loving attitude is expressed in the *Abhaṅga*s 72-168.
3. Janābāī's spiritual experience is narrated in 183-262.
4. Hagiographical *Abhaṅga*s: 169-82 and 271-97.
5. Episodical poems: 298-320 and 321-33.
6. Occasional literature containing different themes: 334-51.

In the second category of her poetry, she states that the divine name has taken the form of Viṭhobā and has made its abode at Pandharpur, where the saints can take refuge by praising the name and by making the pilgrimage and *kīrtan*. In the third category of *Abhaṅga*s Janābāī tells us the story of

[7] The Sarkari Prata Edition of *Namdeva-gatha* has only 348 *Abhaṅga*s of Janābāī.

[8] Dr. D.B. Bhingarkar published for the first time the unpublished *Abhaṅga*s of Janābāī in his book, *Janābāī, Charitra, Kāvya āni Kāmagiri*, Bombay, 1989.

[9] I have used the edition of Sakhare Maharaj.

her own devotion to Nārāyana and how this very Nārāyana abides in the form of Viṭhobā, whom she praises and worships. Through the analysis of these *Abhaṅgas* we can follow her spiritual development. However one would not be able to give chronological stages of development because the *Abhaṅgas* and *Owis* do not have any chronological order. Yet they are sufficient to give us an insight into the spiritual life of Janābāī. They certainly point out the spiritual height she had achieved.

Through the visit of Viṭhobā, my body has been transfigured; It is a meeting of two, a meeting of salt with water.

Blessed is Nāmadeva, who is father and mother to me; He showed me the Lord of Pandhari.

Day and night I lay at the feet of Viṭhobā; My mind is lost in his depth.

Jani of Nāmadeva has truly become happy; Pānduranga has come to meet her.[10]

The fourth category is of the hagiographical *Abhaṅgas*. In these she states how the saints through their devotion and trust and by praising God's name have overcome their shortcomings and trials and have become *jīvanmuktas*. Here she refers to an individual saint, like Dñyāneshwara, Senā Nhāvi and Nāmadeva. Then she points out how they had helped others and praised God in the form of his divine name.

The fifth part of her literature is named as *ākhyānakāvya* because in it two stories from the *Mahābhārata* are recounted. The first story is that of King Harischandra and his queen Tārāmati. The second story is given under the title *Thālipāk* narrating the event when Durvāsa Rishi had asked from Draupadī and the Pāṇḍavas the *icchyābhojan*, the desired meal. The fourth category, in comparison with other parts, is rather short. However in these two stories Janābāī has shown her creative and literary talents. She does not merely repeat the *Mahābhārata* stories but records them in her own way. The original story of Harischandra and Tārāmati narrates how the king and the queen remain faithful to the promised word in keeping with their royal status. They go through many sacrifices and undergo extreme sufferings to keep the promise. In this episode, like many other Marathi poet saints, Janābāī narrates that God protects the truthful ones and helps the righteous. However Janābāī has given a little more twist to the story. At the end of the story the disguised Vishwāmitra asks her to make a request. He promises to grant her a boon. She asks that in every birth she should have a son like Rohidās, a husband like Harischandra and further says that she would also like to have someone like Vishwāmitra to

[10] Janābāī, 81.

make such requests.[11] This is totally a new aspect in the narration. Janābāī has described Tārāmati as not only patient and faithful like Harischandra, but also how the generosity of Tārāmati surpasses the normal behaviour pattern. Out of such generosity she even asks to have a person like Vishwāmitra who had caused so much pain, once more in their lives. But this very twist in narrating the story gives us an insight into her spiritual height.

The second narrative story is of Durvāsa. At the suggestion of Duryodhana, the sage Durvāsa goes to the forest where the Pāṇḍavas are staying and requests from them an *icchyābhojan*, the desired meal for a Rishi. The Pāṇḍavas and Draupadī are dismayed. Draupadī takes the initiative and makes a prayer to Krishna. Her prayer is heard by Rukhminī and Krishna. Rukhminī requests Krishna to help Draupadī. Krishna comes to help the Pāṇḍavas and Draupadī. He himself offers the sage the desired meal.[12] At the end of the narration Janābāī does not forget to narrate that God is father and mother. By bringing Rukhminī into the picture Janābāī indirectly suggests that the divine couple resides at Pandharpur.

In the narration of both of these stories, Janābāī has shown extreme poetic qualities and literary characteristics. Her descriptions are concise and full of compassion. In her style, she is lofty, natural, creative and independent. We realize that later on, two Marathi poets, Vishnudāsnāmā and Mukteshwara, have imitated her.[13] Certainly, as a poet and saint she has not merely been the shadow of Nāmadeva.

In the sixth category[14] she has given us occasional *Owis* and *Abhaṅgas* like *Pālaṅā*, *Ārati* and *Tirthāwali* and some small poems.[15]

JANI AS A *DĀSĪ*

In 1972, a controversy was raised about the origin of Janābāī and thereby also about the relationship between Nāmadeva and Janābāī. As it is said above that some of the *Abhaṅgas* she signed her name as *Jani Dāsī*. The controversy was raised on account of the word *Dāsī*, suggesting that this word could mean that Janābāī had been a Devadasi and probably a devotee of Khandoba. She comes in contact with Nāmadeva and through him she

[11] Janābāī, 319.

[12] The desire of a guest and a priest for meal should be fulfilled.

[13] Bhingarkar 1989, p. 223.

[14] The *Abhaṅga* and *Owis* that cannot be classified are included here.

[15] Some verses, *palana* and *owis* are included here.

has been brought into the service of the temple of Viṭhobā where she does menial work. Like any other Murali or a devadāsī she must have been in the temple and courtyard doing manual work, cleaning the temple, giving a bath to God and making him sleep. As a devadāsī she, when desired, must have been offering herself sexually to the disciples or the main devotee. Naturally in such a case the first person in the question would be Nāmadeva himself.

In one of her *Abhaṅgas* (291) Janābāī calls Nāmadeva as a *dāsī Janichā ātmasakhā*, 'the beloved of maid Jani'. Surely this is the most endearing term which Jani ever used for Nāmadeva. When we study the text of this *Abhaṅgas* in the context, we get the clear idea of Jani's thought.

It was the eleventh day of the bright fortnight of *Āṣhāḍha*, Nāmadeva was fasting severely,
God sent an eagle to call him; It is better that I remain here; let me know who calls me?
Such is the excellent devotee, the beloved companion of Dāsī Jani.[16]

Certainly, the beloved companion is Nāmadeva. However this companionship and endearment are not on account of earthly and carnal pleasures. It is a joyous term of endearment on account of his excellent devotion and fidelity. In the words, 'the beloved companion', Jani expresses her admiration and gratitude for Nāmadeva. She praises him in these words on account of his concern for her and also on account of his love for Viṭhobā. Every hagiographer interprets an event and a happening in the life of the saint, not to merely give a historical fact or a chronological record but to support his own personal view and to highlight the attitude of a saintly person. This is what Janābāī is doing when she speaks about Nāmadeva. She is actually narrating to us, the fellowship, *satsang* of Nāmadeva, that was helping her tread on the path of devotion.

TERESA AS A SPOUSE OF CHRIST

Let us take a hagiographical parallel from Christianity. We read in the life of St. Teresa of Avila that one day she had a vision of Jesus in His Majesty. In this vision He gave her wedding-ring and told her that He would take her as a chosen bride. She even told Jesus in the vision that His chosen beloved is Mary Magdalene. Thereupon Jesus replied that in His majestic heavenly life, He has given Teresa the privilege of being His beloved. Certainly none of her hagiographers searches for the wedding ring. The vowed nun is

[16] Janābāī, 2.

considered to be the bride of Christ. This is symbolic of the unity with the Divine person of Christ. Secondly, St. Teresa of Avila tells us how she felt before the vision and what her prayer was. 'Often His Majesty says to me, as a sign of His great love: "now thou art Mine and I am thine". There are some words which I am in the habit of repeating to myself — and I mean what I say. They are: "What do I care about myself, Lord, or about anything but Thee?".'[17] Further she also speaks, 'again, my God, I speak to Thee and beg Thee, by the blood of Thy Son, to grant me this favour: "let Him kiss me with a kiss of His mouth". For what I am, Lord, without Thee?'[18]

It is this experience of the union with God that St. Teresa of Avila tries to express in her human words. It is the union with the Divine that makes her consider that vowed virgins are the brides of Christ. The communion railing becomes a spousal bed. It is the sublimation of the human experience by the transcendence and this transcendence enables her to be in union with God.

Janābāī describes often how the Lord of Pandhari comes to help her. He helps her in all her work whether it is cleaning or grinding grains early in the mornings. He gives her company when she is alone in the fields. He even comes as a loving mother to bathe and to clean her hair. Janābāī through these *Abhaṅgas* is telling us that there is not a moment when Viṭhobā is not with her. This union with the Lord, she expresses in her womanly language saying that after helping her in the work, the Lord gives her companionship in the bed.

One day God hastened to me at night; with happiness he lay beside me.
He revealed to me the secrets, and as he revealed, he fell asleep.
At dawn Jani got up and said, 'Chakrapāni, get up, get up; it has already dawned.'[19]

SAINTS AS IDEALS

There is another example of quite a different nature from Christian hagiography. The very first biography of St. Aloysius Gonzaga (1568-91) was written by Fr. Virgil Cepari, with the material gathered from persons who had been in contact with him. In the biography, Fr. Cepari states,

Aloysius did not even like talking to his mother alone. When it chanced that while he was with her, either in the drawing room or in her own private room, those who

[17] E. Allison Peers, *The Complete Works of St. Teresa of Jesus*, London, 1957, p. 287.

[18] Ibid, pp. 287-8.

[19] Janābāī, 152.

were with her chanced to leave, he either sought for some excuse to go away or if could not go he blushed deeply, so exceedingly careful and circumspect was he.[20]

Further the same biographer says,

> St. Aloysius Gonzaga watched over himself and his senses with a constant and extraordinary diligence, and especially with regard to his eyes, which kept in check in order that they might never transgress by looking at anything which could at all be a source of disquiet to him. This was one of the reasons why he ever passed through the streets with down cast eyes.[21]

This biography was published in the year 1605, a few years after the death of this young nobleman. The biographer before stating the facts of the life and the behaviour of Aloysius states how St. Jerome, St. Benedict, St. Equitus and St. Thomas Aquinas acquired the virtue of chastity. Then he states that for Aloysius it was not merely a 'natural gift', but rather he had 'cultivated the angelic habits'. Naturally the author does not forget to state the aim of the biography. 'I am writing for the good of religious and devout persons, and the life is that of a religious man and not of some great captain or prince. It describes moral actions for our imitation.'[22]

OBJECTIVES OF A HAGIOGRAPHY

The biography was written a few months before the beatification of the saint. The biographer and the act of the beatification have placed Aloysius before the Christian world as the ideal and the excellent example for the practice of Christian purity. He is the patron of youth and later on many Catholic youth organizations were named after him. In the year 1591, the whole of Italy was afflicted by a widespread mortality, that was caused by the great scarcity and famine. A pestilence had spread in Rome. Serving the sick, Aloysius caught plague fever and died within few months. He died serving the sick. This heroic aspect of his death and service is mentioned in the biography but not stressed. From this example we can see that a hagiographer uses available facts, events and documents for his own purpose. It is usually to show how the saint practised virtues, how he cooperated with God's grace and how he used his talents. The framing of a biography depends on the objectives that the biographer has in mind. What kind of an ideal the hagiographer would like to put before his readers,

[20] Goldie, Francis, *St. Aloysius Gonzaga*, Einsiedeln, 1891, p. 19.
[21] Ibid., p. 18.
[22] Goldie 1891, p. xxii.

is an important factor. There is no doubt that the very life of the saint whose biography he writes, offers him this ideal. However, the interpretation which the hagiographer gives, becomes a very important factor in portraying the person.

JANĀBĀĪ'S OBJECTIVES IN WRITING

When Janābāī writes about Nāmadeva, her primary concern is to express her own spiritual experience to the reader or to the audience. Further she would like to show how Nāmadeva has led her on the path of devotion. He becomes the beloved because he has done this. She speaks of him out of gratitude and certainly not with the intention of writing his biography. Moreover we know from her own writings that she has experienced hardship and difficulties in the house of Nāmadeva. But these difficulties and hardships are not worth of mentioning before the goodness of Nāmadeva. When she mentions them, she has done so that she could show how God was helpful to her.

Janābāī explains her spiritual path, her practice of devotion and the grace of God which she had experienced, in such a way, so that her *Abhaṅga*s do not remain merely poetry but turn out to be autobiography. In such an autobiography some historical facts, social changes and some particular events do enter. But they are not intended to give historical data. These have the sole aim of relating the spiritual experience and God's working in the life of the saint. Therefore, the real Bhakti and its practice become the objectives of her writings.

Bhakti does not require any affiliation to a particular caste or a family. It does not require any rank or office. God accepts all who take refuge in him. Janābāī tells us that God honours the casteless as he has once done for Chokhāmelā.[23] This is her firm belief. Janābāī has mentioned the castes of some saints, not so that her audience should know the castes of the saints, but rather she wants to show how God comes to the help of all and how he has been gracious to them all. When she mentions one particular saint, she gives us the circumstances of his life and then mentions the great deeds the Lord has done for him. In this way she has mentioned the castes of some saints. However, she has not mentioned anywhere her own caste or even her family background. Certainly, when at the age of seven she was found at the temple of Pandharpur she was old enough to know her caste and to clearly remember her family background. Why does she keep silent about

[23] Janābāī, 110.

her family background and about her caste? When she speaks of herself, she always mentions that she is the maidservant in the house of Nāmadeva, who belongs to the tailors' caste. Once she does mention her family saying that the deity of her father is the Lord of Pandhari and it is he who gives meaning to her life.[24]

In another place, she indirectly mentions her family background, which has created the suspicion of her being a *devadāsī*. She says that Vidur belongs to her kuḷa. By this statement she does not want to say that she has been born in the family of Vidur for no one can with certainly state his or her affiliation to any puranic family or to any puranic vansha. Why does the affiliation to Vidur enter her writings? Is it to point out that she has been born like Vidur out of wedlock or to show that her devotion and her righteousness are like that of Vidur?

Vidur is the famous sage and is well known for his righteousness and uprightness. He appears in the *Mahābhārata*, as the most intelligent among the intelligent ones. He is one of the few *Mahābhārata* figures who chides Duryodhana and does not approve his evil doings. However Vidur is a half-brother of Dhritarashtra and Pandu. He is actually the son of a female slave of Ambikā. He does not approve of the behaviour of Kauravas because he is considered to be *jīvanmukta*. I suppose, when Janābāī mentions that Vidur belongs to her kuḷa, she certainly stresses her situation as a servant, and it is not a reference to her either being a child of a *devadāsī or* being herself a *devadāsī*, as Mr. H.S. Ghonge presumes. Besides Vidur if he ever has experienced discrimination then it is not because he was born out of wedlock but because he was born of a slave. In the *Mahābhārata* period, marriages with slave women were an accepted phenomenon. The family background of Janābāī must have been that of a normal village poor woman whose parents were on a pilgrimage to Pandharpur.

Moreover, in the same *Abhaṅga* she refers to women in general. She is not unhappy on account of her female birth. She affirms very consciously that in spite of being a woman she has become like saints and sages. Therefore she advises all women not to be disappointed or disheartened, but rather to give themselves to devotion.

On account of woman's birth, one should not be disappointed.
He has made us like sages and saints.
I am merely a maidservant in subjection at the house of Nāmadeva.
Yet Viṭhobā has offered me his loving care and concern.
The righteous Vidur belongs to my family. God has accepted his devotion.

[24] Janābāī, 230.

God saved Ganikā, without enquiring into her family-background.
The power of the Name surpasses all three worlds.
It has constituted families of sages; it has made its abode in the heaven.
Jani of Nāmadeva is ever ready for devotion; He who stands on the brick is my real treasure.[25]

The verse makes it clear that Janābāī considers Viṭhobā to be her real treasure and this treasure has been given to her by the special grace of Viṭhobā himself. It is Viṭhobā who is the treasure and also the very donor of such a treasure. She has received it not because she was worthy of it. In spite of her being merely a servant girl and in spite of her unworthiness she has received it on account of Nāmadeva. He has enabled her to sit among sadhus and saints. Therefore we cannot say that in these verses Janābāī is speaking about her family background or about her caste. She merely states that in spite of her being worthless, she has been graced by God. Therefore Janābāī could not possibly be a girl child offered at Pandharpur by her parents, nor could she be a devadāsī. And certainly she did not have any contact with Nāmadeva as a devadāsī.

Mahipati, the hagiographer narrates the incident of how this child was found. He says,

being only seven years of age, how she hás obtained such spiritual knowledge? The mother and father were greatly troubled by her resolve but would not listen to anything. When Shri Hari casts upon anyone the eyes of compassion, the love of that which is ones own does not arise in the heart. Seeing her determination, however her parents were comforted. They left their daughter at the great door of the temple and returned to their home.[26]

It is neither the desire of Janābāī nor any other human attraction that makes her resolve to be at Pandharpur, but it is the Lord who puts in her the holy desire and moves her to action. Exactly, the same way the hagiographer, Fr. Cepari, says about Aloysius Gonzaga.

This holy absence of bodily feeling, this purity of mind in St. Aloysius cannot be attributed to him because any natural coldness or sluggishness, for he was full of life and spirit, activity and alertness, as all know who were acquainted with him. We are obliged then to own that it was the result of an extraordinary grace from God.[27]

A hagiographer, as he describes the experiences of a saint and the

[25] Janābāī, 181.
[26] Abbot 1988, p. 339.
[27] Goldie 1891, p. 18.

incidents in the life of a saint, wants to tell us how the saint has received the gifts of God, how as a human, he has accepted these gifts and how he has used these gifts. When Janābāī narrates her own spiritual experiences or when she narrates about her life, she is telling us what she has received from her Hari in Pandharpur and what she has done with those gifts which she had received. She is not primarily writing her autobiography but rather relating her mystical experience. It is the experience where she tells us of her sinfulness and weakness.

We have heaps of sins, and we have taken refuge at your feet;
Do with us, whatever may please you;
Now, you may save us or you may kill us;
Jani says that you alone are truly the Lord in the Universe.[28]

Out of consciousness of personal sins and weakness, she moves to God and takes refuge in him. She acknowledges that He alone has power to save her. She says with humility that it is the Lord who takes away this sinfulness. Further she goes on to say that when she suffers, it is not she who suffers, but it is the Viṭhobā who suffers in her. Here we see the significance of her statement that the meeting of the devotee and the Lord is like salt and water. It is not the human person who suffers but the Lord who suffers in the human because the Lord abides in the Naradeha. The main cause of her suffering is that she has not served the Lord. She had not been in union with him.

I have not served you; I feel pain in my heart;
I am an unfortunate and clumsy sinner; I have not remembered you;
Whatever pain I have suffered, that you yourself have suffered, O Viṭṭhala;
Forgive me, Lord God, your servant Jani lies at your feet.[29]

HAGIOGRAPHICAL CHARACTERISTICS

Janābāī has portrayed some biographies in her *Abhaṅgas*, especially three biographies seem to have interested her most, those of Dñyāneshwara, Nāmadeva and of Senā Nhāvī. In the biography of Dñyāneshwara, she praises his wisdom and the way that he has shown the path of salvation to men through his commentary on the *Bhagavadgītā*. His relationship with his brothers and sister is unique because he has been a guide to them in obtaining *Mukti*. In the same way in the biography of Senā Nhāvī, she lauds him on account of his devotion to God's name. Then she relates the

[28] Janābāī, 219.
[29] Janābāī, 46.

incident of the Lord of Pandhari substituted for him in the court and performed the service which the saint was supposed to perform. In this way the Lord saves his devotee. The story has been often repeated by other saints. But through this story, once more Janābāī reminds her listeners of how the Lord acts for his servants. In the biography of Nāmadeva she describes his birth, his household, the persons in his family and the way these persons serve God and the trust they have in God. She relates to us through episodes, how God had come to help Nāmadeva when he was in difficulties. In time of danger God had always come to rescue him.

The most interesting phenomenon in these biographies is that for Janābāī, these persons don't remain historical persons. Their earthly existence is of secondary importance. They are avatars. It is God who acts through them and who through them meets her.

The Avatār of Sadāshiva is the generous master Nivritti. The Avatār of Mahāvishnu is my beloved Dñyāneshwara;
The Brahma has become Sopan and has given joy to the devotees.
The Ādishakti has become Muktābāī; the maidservant Jani is at their feet.[30]

However in the very next verse, she narrates to us the dates of birth of these saints. By quoting their birth dates in the next *Abhaṅga* she certainly portrays them as historical persons. But she would like to stress that God works in the world through his saints and since God is acting through them they are to be considered as avatars.

In the same way, at the end of the biography of Nāmadeva she states,

Hear, O people, the story of Nāmadeva's birth and origin;
In the family of Hiranyakashyapa Nāmā is Prahlād and my own name is Padmini, the greatest maidservant.
In the second birth he is Rama's devotee Angad. And I am Mantharā who was kicked by him.
In Dwāraka in the service of Krishna he is born as Uddhava, where my name is Kubjā, whom God has saved.
In this Kaliyuga, Nāmadeva is lost in the devotion of Viṭhobā and for his service is born the servant Jani.[31]

This *Abhaṅga* gives the impression that Janābāī believes in the theory of the rebirth. We cannot conclude that Janābāī had any mystical or parapsychological knowledge of Nāmadeva's previous birth. Certainly, she does not have any interest in the metaphysical problem of the rebirth.

[30] Janābāī, 277.
[31] Janābāī, 297.

The doctrine of the rebirth might have been for her a matter of fact as it is for any Hindu believer. The *Abhaṅga* points out primarily her satisfaction with this life and the events that have taken place in this life, in spite of all hardship. She has achieved this satisfaction through the company of Nāmadeva, and out of this gratitude she has the extreme desire to be his servant so that she may be always on the path of salvation.

When self-consciousness disappears totally, one enjoys the joy of being selfless.
Those, who have experienced such ecstasy, don't have the consciousness of the world.
Such ecstasy has been granted to me; I have been overjoyed;
In his oneness I have been united; the maidservant Jani exists no more.[32]

Mukti means losing oneself and not having one's own desires. By achieving such a state in life, one becomes the *jīvanmukta*, who does not distinguish in life between mine and thine. He is always free of self and ready to serve others, which is to say that he is ready to be with others. This service does not mean that he is doing some good to others but rather he is at the disposal of others because the other person is not a stranger due to the fact that the other person is in God. This is the characteristic of the *satsang*. Janābāī would like to bring this experience of oneness to men and women and therefore she must proclaim the great name of the Lord of Pandhari and all that he had done to her. With this attitude she loses her fear of the world. Freed from all bonds and fears, she seeks nothing but sings the praises of the Lord before men so that she can be in a continuous *satsang* with them. Therefore she loudly and firmly tells God,

I will uncover my head and stand in the open marketplace,
having a Veena on my shoulder and cymbals in hands. Who will prevent me?
In Pandhari's market-yard I have fixed my tent; I am resolved with firm resolve;
O God, I have become a prostitute, I am coming to visit you.[33]

It is through this holy service of the *satsang* that she can achieve God. In this resolve she shows such firmness, that God has to surrender to her. Ultimately the maidservant Jani makes God the servant.

God has become the servant of his devotees; He is ever ready to do their work;
He suffers that they lack nothing; He becomes their protector;
Jani says the true devotion means God as a servant has united with the human.[34]

[32] Janābāī, 152.
[33] Janābāī, 232.
[34] In original *Jīva*. Janābāī, 104.

In all her *Abhaṅga* and *Owi*s, as she describes her unity with the Lord of Pandhari, who has helped her, she has not forgotten that she is a woman. She remains always very conscious of her being a woman. It is this womanhood, she brings before the Lord of Pandhari and it is through this womanhood she praises him. By her life and poetry she gives a testimony that before the Lord there is no distinction between man and woman. He accepts all and he gives duty to all according to his or her individuality. Therefore she declares firmly her resolve of proclaiming the name of the Lord, in spite of her being only a maidservant and a woman:

Truly, I am the maid of the powerful One; I embrace his feet.
This is my firm resolve that I will celebrate the festival of the Name.
This very work has been entrusted to us maidservants; we pronounce the Lord Viṭṭhala's Name.
All happiness lies at his feet; It is Viṭṭhala, who reveals himself to Jani.[35]

Janābāī, by describing her mystical experience, has given us her own biography and also the biographies of other saints. She has shown how the proclamation of the Divine name has been the aim of her life.

[35] Janābāī, 229.

Reconstruction of the History of Medieval Maharashtra through *Lāvaṇīs*

VARSHA S. SHIRGAONKAR

Lāvaṇī is a form of poetry of Maharashtra in western India. It has been an integral part of *shāhirī*, the folk literature of Maharashtra. It originated in medieval Maharashtra through religio-cultural folk traditions. It developed not merely as a type of poetry but also as a component of folk theatre. In Maharashtra many dramatic forms existed as folk theatre. Forms like *Dashāvatār*, *Gondhaḷ* were in existence before *lāvaṇī*. *Dashāvatār* was a dramatic exposition while *Gondhaḷ* was the poetic and musical presentation. *Gondhaḷ* was generally composed in the name of the goddess Amba Bhavani of Tuljapur and the performers were called *Gondhaḷī*s. The *Gondhaḷī*s were both bards and priests.[1] Gradually they also started composing ballads celebrating war heroes. These songs were in praise of Shivaji and the other Maratha leaders. Since the composers eulogized the military and other actions of their leaders they came to be known as *shāhīr*s (poets or bards) and their compositions obtained the name *shāhirī*. These *shāhīr*s were generally travelling minstrels. *Shāhirī* gradually took two forms, namely, *povāḍā* and *lāvaṇī*. Of these, *povāḍā* was a song applauding bravery while *lāvaṇī* popularly presented the erotic aspect of human life. On the basis of their literary contents these two forms within the *shāhirī*, together were called *Kāvyamay Jodpe* or a poetic couple.[2] While, the *povāḍā*s tended to be very long, the *lāvaṇī*s were short. The present paper deals with the value of *lāvaṇī* as a source of the history of medieval Maharashtra. The paper has emphasized the literary aspect of the *lāvaṇī*s.

*The researcher is indebted to Mr. V.Y. Kelkar of Pune, Maharashtra, for giving away the original *lāvaṇī*s from the personal collection of his father, Late Mr. Y.N. Kelkar.

[1] Harry A. Acworth and Shankar T. Shaligram (collected, arranged and annotated), *Povadas or Historical Ballads of the Marathas*, Poona: Aryabhushan Press, 2nd edn., 1911, Introduction, p. 4.

[2] Y.N. Kelkar, *Tantakavi tahta Shahir*, Pune: The Teachers Ideal Publishing House Limited, 1952, p. 9.

Before discussing the utility of *lāvaṇī*s as historical sources, it would be worthwhile to understand the meaning and implications of the word *lāvaṇī*. The earliest reference to it has been made by Harry Acworth and Shankar Shaligram. They interpret *lāvaṇī* as a sensual love-song.[3] This was because most of the *lāvaṇī*s are erotic. They focus on the description of the beauty of woman and the physical aspect of love between a man and a woman. Some of them are quite titillating. Interestingly, the popular derivation of the word *lāvaṇī* is from the word '*lavaṇ*' meaning salt. Just as salt lends flavour to food, beauty enhances woman's personality. Hence, popularly *lāvaṇī* was interpreted as a poem describing a woman's beauty. But a careful analysis of *lāvaṇī* as a form of poetry shows many similarities of subject with the earlier poetic forms called *Goulaṇī*s and *Virahiṇī*s. These two forms were devotional, not erotic in nature; they showed devotion to Lord Krishna and the pure love towards him was their subject-matter.[4] There are also *lāvaṇī*s on cities, Hindu deities and famines. Many times, the *shāhīr*s used the word *lāvaṇī* in a different manner. To them, *lāvaṇī* meant connecting two things or ideas. Therefore, it is to be noted that words like *shāhirī* or *lāvaṇī* are not used in the strict sense of the terms. There is much flexibility in their usage. The *lāvaṇī* is sometimes taken to be inclusive of *povāḍā*s and *abhanga*s (devotional songs).

Lāvaṇī is a type of folk literature. In fact, every piece of folk literature is first an oral story. It attains the status of literature much later. There is a direct contact between the narrator and the audience. The narration becomes a medium through which this contact may be established. The effectiveness of the narration depends upon the adaptability of the narrator to pick up words from the local language of the audience. A careful analysis of the words mentioned in the *lāvaṇī*s may throw light upon the different linguistic groups who resided in Maharashtra. The folk literature always shows a potential for change. *Lāvaṇī*, being basically a part of the oral tradition included other forms of poetry too. It assimilated various local words in accordance with the audience-response.[5] The chief motive of the *shāhīr*s was to appeal to the masses and make the performance lively and effective. The *shāhīr*s performed at the village-fairs as well as in the

[3] Acworth and Shaligram, op. cit., Introduction, p. 2.

[4] H.S. Shenolikar, *Prachin Marathi Vangmayache Swaroop*, Pune and Kolhapur: Moghe Prakashan, 5th edn. 1975 (1st edn. 1956), p. 224.

[5] Gangadhar Morje, *Lokasahitya-Aakalan ani Aaswad*, Pune: Dastane Ramchandra aani Company, 1993, p. 21.

courts of the Peshwas and their sardārs. In Maharashtra, even today, most of the fairs are held during the festivals of Dashahrā and Guḍhī Pāḍvā which fall in October (at the end of the rainy season) and in April (the beginning of summer season) respectively. The village-fairs are organized not merely for entertainment but are also the occasions for carrying out transactions and business. It is thus a conglomeration of different sections of population. Two crops are harvested in the period from the festival Dashahrā to Guḍhī Pāḍvā. Good harvests mean overall prosperity. Performances by *shāhīr*s should be seen in this light. It was a great opportunity for them to earn. There were different performing troupes of *shāhīr*s. The performing skill of the *shāhīr*s was tested in competitions. The practice even today is that the village *pāṭīl* (chief) invites the winning troupe to participate in the next year's performance, by presenting them with a coconut and a betel leaf.

The strong association of many *lāvaṇī*s with an erotic sentiment is undeniable. It is very difficult to establish the approximate period in which *lāvaṇī* came to be taken as a dance form. But it is certain that when it did become a dance form, it reflected erotic feelings, which means that *lāvaṇī* as a performance had become erotic.

An analytical explanation as to why it became so, and before what kind of spectators it was performed, may be given after first peeping into the political conditions of medieval Maharashtra. Ala-ud-din Khilji was the first north Indian Muslim ruler to attack a Deccan state of the Yadavas towards the end of the thirteenth and the beginning of the fourteenth centuries AD. Maharashtra then came into contact with a totally different military camp culture. The military tents of the Muslim soldiers were located in Maharashtra. The first interaction of this racially and religiously different group must have been with some of the migrating groups around Maharashtra. These groups may be identified as Shikalgārs, Kolhāṭīs, etc.[6] The Shikalgārs were those who followed the occupation of polishing weapons. The term *shikalgār* is derived from the word *sikal* which means to polish the weapons. There were several sub-groups of the Shikalgārs. They were found in small numbers all over the Deccan and Karnatak. Many of them were Muslim converts. Even to the present day they celebrate Hindu festivals.[7] Kolhāṭīs were the street performers who

[6] Prabhakar Mande, *Gavgadyabaher*, Aurangabad: Parimal Prakashan, 1983.

[7] R.E. Enthoven, *The Tribes and Castes of Bombay*, vol. III, Bombay: Government Central Press, 1922, p. 115.

obtained money by exhibiting their skills in balancing on sticks. The term *kolhāṭī* is derived from the Kannada words *kolu* and *aṭig*, *kolu* meaning stick and *aṭig*, a player. The Kolhāṭīs were mostly dependent upon the prostitution of their women. The Kolhāṭī women attended to the sexual needs of men at fairs and in the military camps. It is learnt that Gopālgaṇī (a sub-caste of the Kolhāṭīs) women were well-versed in seducing men and making them pay well.[8] They selected the best-looking girls who were called *sonchedịs* or golden daughters. These girls then were taught dancing and subsequently they became the concubines and mistresses of some rich men. In the twentieth century some of the Kolhāṭī women have established *faḍs* (dancing troupes). It is quite likely that the Kolhāṭī women had learnt some crude dance forms to entertain the Muslim soldiers. Some lines from the *Dnyāneshwarī*, the famous literary work of the saint-poet Dnyaneshwar, contain references to this entertainment. He says,

> In the localities of the Mlechchas (Muslims), in the forests, on the unholy land and in the military camps in the evening time, the cheap women entice the men with their body, beauty and dance. The music of the *Bhāṭ*s (bards) is heard on this occasion. The men present there, shower their money collected by foul means on these women generously.[9]

This description shows that some 'cheap' women and bards regularly entertained the Muslim menfolk in the military camps. These bards were the *shāhīr*s. Thus, certain type of entertainment emerged in medieval Maharashtra.

The chief form of entertainment in medieval Maharashtra came to be known as *tamāshā*. *Tamāshā* is a Persian word. This does not, however, mean that *tamāshā* as a form of entertainment originated on account of the interaction of Maharashtra with Islamic culture. On the contrary, it may be noted that *tamāshā* was the new term used for an already existing form of entertainment. At the same time, the word *tamāshā* does establish the contact of the *shāhīr*s with Islamic culture. Initially when the *tamāshā* originated it was probably not of any regular structure. But it included music, dance, humorous dialogues, etc. By and large there was a subtle

[8] Ibid., vol. II, pp. 242-3.

[9] Dnyaneshwar, the saint-poet of Maharashtra was born in AD 1271 and passed away in AD 1296 and was thus a contemporary of the Yadava dynasty of Devagiri. He wrote the *Dnyaneshwari* in AD 1290 at Newase on the bank of the river Godavari. He was an eyewitness to the first attack of Ala-ud-din on Devagiri (AD 1294). Verses 294-8, Chapter 17, Vinayakbova Joshi Sakhare (ed.), *Sartha Dnyaneshwari*, Mumbai: Publisher Balkrishna Pathak, dna, pp. 692-4.

eroticism in this form and the spectators were exclusively male. The conversation of the characters in *tamāshā* was prevented from becoming monotonous and boring by introducing song and dance sequences. The language of the song had erotic words to promote the popular appeal of the *tamāshā*. This song was *lāvaṇī*. In this manner, to add flavour, *lāvaṇī* must have entered *tamāshā*. Since the overall nature of *tamāshā* was full of eroticism, *lāvaṇī* became erotic. The *tamāshā* troupe was called *faḍ*. Hence, the *lāvaṇī*s presented in *tamāshā*s came to be known as *Faḍāchyā Lāvaṇyā*.

Secondly, eroticism in *lāvaṇī*s may be related also to the changing life-styles of the top-ranking officials in Maharashtra. The boom period of the erotic *lāvaṇī*s could be identified as that of the reigns of the last two Peshwas. Most *lāvaṇī*s coupled eroticism with the portrayal of the royal life. There were about one hundred and twenty-five *shāhīr*s who have recorded their names in their *lāvaṇī*s, whereas the actual number of the *shāhīr*s could be four hundred.[10] The important *shāhīr*s who obtained patronage under these Peshwas were Honaji Bala (1754-1844), Parshuram (1754-1844), Ramjoshi (1762-1812), Prabhakar (1769-1843), Anant Phandi (1774-1819) and Saganbhau (1778-1840). All of them got recognition at the time of the last two Peshwas. Some of them were present in the court on special occasions. The Peshwas celebrated festivals like Hoḷī (Spring) and Dashahrā (Autumn) with grandeur when the *shāhīr*s were specially called to present the *lāvaṇī*s. The *shāhīr*s received cash payments and other gifts on such occasions. They usually got Rs. 10 or Rs. 15 for the presentation of their *lāvaṇī*s.[11] Anant Phandi was felicitated by Ahilyabai Holkar, the chief of Indore.[12]

An analytical inquiry into the politico-cultural life of Maharashtra may provide certain explanations as to why the *shāhīr*s were writing such *lāvaṇī*s. The background of a new cultural life may be traced from the arrival of king Shahu into Maharashtra (AD 1707). He was the son of king Sambhaji. In 1689 when Sambhaji became a captive of the Mughals and was subsequently killed, his wife Yesubai and son Shahu were taken as captives and were kept in Mughal custody. Shahu at that time was nine

[10] Yashwant N. Kelkar, *Marathi Shahir ani Shahiri Vangmay*, Pune: Pune University, 1974, p. 47.

[11] Honaji Bala, *Lavanya*, S.N. Shaligram (coll. and ed.), Pune: Chitrashala Press, 5th edn., 1972, Preface, Y.N. Kelkar, pp. 7-8.

[12] Anant Phandi, *Kavita va Lavanya*, pt. 1, Pune: Chitrashala Press, 4th edn., 1921, Preface, not numbered.

years old. According to the orders of the Mughal emperor, Aurangzeb, both of them were kept in the enclosed quarters near his daughter's and his own residential tent. Since Shahu spent the formative years of his life in the Mughal camp the atmosphere there did have a certain impact on his life and personality. On the one hand his long imprisonment in the Mughal seraglio had enervated him and had made him incapable of leading armies on the battlefields, while on the other hand he was induced into an appreciation of music and dance. Shahu entrusted the administration to the Peshwa or the Prime Minister. His regime, thus, marked the beginning of the rule of the Peshwa. The Marathas had started campaigning in central and north India since the time of Peshwa Bajirao I (1720-40). The campaigns became more frequent at the time of Nanasaheb Peshwa (1740-61). The rapport of the Peshwas and their sardārs (officers) with the northern states resulted in the gradual adoption of a different lifestyle. To a certain extent, they wished to imitate the luxurious life of the Mughals and the Rajputs. The Peshwa rulers and the Maratha sardārs desired to cultivate a taste for cultural things. Historical documents like *Peshwe Daftar*, *Peshwe Diaries* contain the orders sent by different Peshwas to their northern officers who were posted to the newly obtained territories. These were regarding the Peshwas' demands for items of luxury, delicacy and beauty. Practically all the Peshwas right from Nanasaheb demanded things like fancy clothes,[13] curtains of *khus*,[14] ivory, etc.[15]

During his lifetime Peshwa Bajirao I had obtained the right over some territories and also over the diamond-mines in Bundelkhand.[16] The next Peshwa Nanasaheb frequently sent orders to Govindpant Bundele, the Maratha officer-in-charge of Bundelkhand for the acquisition of diamonds.[17] Gold and silver articles were also asked for.[18] There are also the instances of the demands placed by Peshwa Madhavrao I (1761-72) for precious stones and pearls.[19] The Peshwas also developed a taste for creating orchards and gardens like their Mughal counterparts. They enjoyed fruits

[13] Ganesh Chimnaji Wad (Prepared), *Selections from Satara Rajas' and Peshwas' Diaries* (*SSRPD*), vol. II, pt. 2, no. 238, Bombay: Induprakash Press, 1906, p. 147.

[14] G.S. Sardesai (ed.), *Peshwe Daptaratun Niwadlele Kagad* (*PD*), vol. 18, no. 60, Bombay: Government Press, 1911, p. 35.

[15] Ibid., p. 95.

[16] Dattatray B. Parasnis (ed. and pub.), *Govindpant Bundelyanchi Kaifiyat*, Pune: Dnyanprakash Press, 1897, p. 5.

[17] *SSRPD*, vol. II, pt. 2, no. 235, p. 146.

[18] Ibid, p. 154.

[19] *PD*, vol. 32, no. 77, p. 42; ibid., no. 80, p. 45.

such as pomegranates, sweet-limes, oranges, etc., which were initially mostly grown in the north and subsequently in Burhanpur when it came under the Mughals. The Peshwas asked for the plants of these fruits and the fragrant flowers including a variety of roses.[20] The Peshwas, thus, attempted to enrich their lives in various ways. During the reigns of the last two Peshwas namely, Sawai Madhavrao (1774-95) and Peshwa Bajirao II (1795-1818), the luxurious lifestyle seems to have fully matured. Besides, in this phase there was a craze for maintaining the nāṭakshāḷās (seraglio). The celebrations of Hoḷī (colour-festival) started anew. Fireworks were brought into Maharashtra for the first time. The *shāhīrs* who wrote *lāvaṇīs* witnessed this atmosphere. Raghunathrao, the uncle of Madhavrao Peshwa had a fascination for keeping dancing girls and patronizing singers and musicians. There are some documentary evidences pertaining to this. In the course of his northern campaigns before the third Battle of Panipat (1761), Raghunathrao brought dancing girls from the north and kept them in Poona. These girls were paid from the government funds. The names of these women and their salaries were as follows. Gahina: Rs. 15, Umeda: Rs. 6, Yamani: Rs. 30, Mother of Vasanti: Rs. 40, Mother of Keshri Chapala: Rs. 45.[21] These salaries were on monthly basis. The last two Peshwas had a similar craze. Nana Phadnis, the caretaker of Sawai Madhavrao, had given instructions to his officers to bring the proficient singers and dancers to the city of Poona (the capital city of the Peshwas) from different places in India like Delhi, Lucknow, Hyderabad and Karnatak. They were brought on high salaries and were granted presents on the occasions of festivals. The kalāvantin (a female performing artist) called Chandri was brought to Poona on a monthly salary of Rs. 1,000.[22] In 1802, Peshwa Bajirao II invited a dancer called Venkat Narsi. For her exclusive dance performance for consecutive three nights she was paid Rs. 26,000.[23] Such evidences show that the city of Poona became the meeting point of many performing artists. The grand celebrations of festivals and other occasions soon lured the *shāhīrs* to Poona. Previously, they had to wait for the village fairs to be able to earn a livelihood. But, now

[20] Ibid, no. 77, p. 42; ibid., no. 120-1, pp. 68-9.

[21] Yashwant N. Kelkar, *Itihasatil Sahali*, Khanda II, Pune: Chitrashala Press, 1964, p. 108.

[22] D.B. Parasnis, *Junya Aitihasik Goshti*, pt. 2, D.B. Parasnis (ed.), *Itihas-sangraha*, vol. II, pub. not mentioned, 1910, pp. 10-11.

[23] V.V. Khare (comp.), *Aitihasik Lekh Sangraha*, pt. 13, Y.V. Khare (ed.), Meeraj, 1926, p. 6896.

many of them could aspire to the regular patronage of the Peshwas. The *lāvaṇī*s which they presented came to be known as *Baiṭhakīchyā Lāvānya* or the *lāvaṇī*s reserved for aristocrats. The composition of their *lāvaṇī*s then obviously presented a picture of royalty along with eroticism. Quite often they painted the rich and luxuries life of their patrons. One remarks the tone of admiration for the Peshwas in their *lāvaṇī*s. The *shāhīr*s eulogized the overall lifestyle of the Peshwas replete with amorous activities. They also described the glamorous life of the city of Poona. Two lines from a *lāvaṇī* of the *shāhīr* Saganbhau are very significant:

The town of Poona of Rāobājī is exclusive.
Every day and night there are amorous activities.[24]

रावबाजीचे शहर नमुना पुणे ग्राम वस्ती।
अहोरात्र अहो दिवस होती इष्काची कुस्ती॥

The term Rāobājī used here is applicable to Peshwa Bajirao II. In this *lāvaṇī* the Peshwa is never censured but is highly praised for his romantic conquests.

Interestingly, while describing the Peshwa it was common for the *shāhīr*s to attach divinity to the Peshwas. This is evident from their comparisons of the Peshwas with the gods. The *shāhīr*s bestowed upon them the epithets like 'Indra', 'Krishna', etc., which they used while describing them. The Peshwa was expected to enjoy life in the same way as the gods enjoyed themselves. The *shāhīr*s advocated such a life for the Peshwas. This is evident from the portrayal of the life-style of the Peshwas through their compositions. Shāhīr Prabhakar has composed many *lāvaṇī*s wherein Shrimant (literally a rich person but commonly a lord) is the hero. This epithet used to be commonly applied to the Peshwa. A *lāvaṇī* of *shāhīr* Prabhakar has the following description of the Peshwa:

(He has) the bracelets studded (with gems), diamond-rings in his fingers... (he has) necklaces of emeralds and pearls, has applied *kesharī gandha* (saffron paste) and *kasturī ṭilak* (musk mark on his forehead). Has the *choukaḍā* (an ear-ornament made of pearls set on a square-shaped disc of gold) in his ears and *turā* (ornament generally made of pearls) in his turban.[25]

[24] C.S. Jahagirdar and G.G. Adhikari (comp.), *Saganbhaukrut Lavanya va Powade*, Pune: Hanuman Press, 1924, p. 22.

[25] Shankar N. Joshi (pub.), *Prabhakarkrit Kavita, Pade, Powade va Lavanya*, Pune: Chitrashala Press, 1920, p. 92.

कडी जडीताची मुद्रिका हिज्याच्या बोटीं।
हार पाचुचे मोत्याच्या माळा कंठी।
केशरी गंध कस्तुरी टिळक लल्लाटी।
चौकडा कानीं शिरपेंच तुरा पागोटी॥

The Peshwa here is described as 'the moon and an honest and chivalrous king whose fame is established in the whole of universe'.

There is a striking similarity between this description and that of the *lāvaṇī* of Honaji Bala.

Like the moon in the sky I have seen the Lord. . . . His turban has a ring, his personality is emanating vivacity, dressed in the nobly way; his stick is decorated with flowers. (He has worn) *turā* of pearls, has the *choukaḍā*, has worn many necklaces of emeralds and also has the finger-rings of diamonds. In what words should I praise him! He is Indra himself sitting in the court. He has applied *kasturī ṭilak* on the forehead and has smeared his body with *kesharī gandha*.[26]

जसा आकाशी चंद्र तसा राजेंद्र पाहिला।
. . . पगडी कंगणीदार आंगावर ज्वाहार छबे ल्या गडी॥
करुन सज्ज पोषाख घेतली हातीं फुलाची छडी।
मुक्त तुरा शिरपेच कानी चौकडा . . .
गळा पाचूचे हार सदोदित एकाहून एक चढी।
हाती हिज्याच्या आंगठया . . .
काय सांगू तारिफ जसा कोणी इंद्र बैसला सभे।
. . . भांळी कस्तुरी टिळा गंध केशरी सर्वांगी उटी॥

Usually in such *lāvaṇī*s the description of the Peshwa's palaçe is cited. The above *lāvaṇī* of Prabhakar illustrates thus:

The colourful *havelī* (palace) has decorated ceilings with mirrors in pink frames. The centre of the floor has the decorated pillars. The silken ropes hold up the swing. The soft and clean carpets (bring grace to the palace). It is as if the court of Indra. The fountains are at many places. The stalks of the *gulchhabu* (a fragrant flower) are cleaned and the *jāī* (jasmine) are in bloom at various places. The foreign chandeliers of crystal glass are dazzling with the candles therein. There are curtains of exquisite *kinkhāb* (silk worked with gold and silver flowers and brocade) and *mashrū* (a silk and cotton stuff with the waving stripes). The lighting arrangements make the simple walls shine.

केली मजसांठी रंगीत हवेली खासी।
छते आरशांची बशिवलीं रंग गुलबासी॥
खांब चौगर्दा सरुदार मधिल मजल्यासी।

[26] Honaji Bala, op. cit., p. 134.

रेशमीं दोऱ्या शोभतात झोपाळ्यासी ॥
रुजामे खालीं मऊ साफ स्वच्छता त्यासी।
सभा इंद्राची आणिली यास ठांयसी।
हवाशिर उडति कारंजी ठांई ठांई।
छड्या निट केल्या गुलछबूं फुलल्या जाई ॥
. . . फाणसें झाडें फिरंगाणी काम बिलोरी।
लाऊन मेणबत्या भंवताल्या हारोहारी।
पडदे किनखाबी मशरूचे भारी भारी।
रोगणी भिंती लखलखाट वर तय्यारी ॥

The scene lit by chandeliers like the stars light up the night sky is described in other *lāvaṇī*s of Prabhakar. There is a mention of the mirror-hall[27] and also of the mīnā-work (inlay-work of gold or silver). The palace or the hall with mīnā-work is referred to as *kānchanbandī mandir* (the hall with the inlay-work of gold).[28]

The palace that is often mentioned in the *lāvaṇī*s is Shaniwārwādā in Pune. The construction of this palace started in the year 1730 during the rule of Peshwa Bajirao I. It was completed in the regime of Peshwa Nanasaheb. Nana Phadnis, the caretaker of the Peshwa Sawai Madhavrao beautified it by setting up fountains and gardens. Of the various halls, Gaṇpatī Rangmahāl (the hall where the idol of Lord Ganesh was installed), Dance-Hall and the Mirror-Hall especially attracted the attention of the visitors. Nana Phadnis had made arrangements to employ artisans from Jaipur in Rajasthan to do the mīnā-work in the palace.[29] Some of the European officers, posted in Bombay Presidency, have left their accounts of Shaniwārwādā and the Peshwa. These accounts strikingly corroborate the descriptions in the *lāvaṇī*s. For instance, Lt. Col. Fitzclarence visited Shaniwārwādā on 31 January 1818. He has given a picturesque description of the Gaṇpatī Rangamahāl of the palace. According to him, the palace was decorated with the mirror-pieces set in artistic wooden frames. The grandeur of the hall was augmented by chandeliers of crystal glass.[30] Robert Mebon, an European painter, was impressed by Peshwa Sawai Madhavrao when he visited him in the Gaṇpatī Rangmahāl. The Peshwa had worn a necklace of exclusive pearls; it hung from his neck to his waist. He had also worn a pendant of a big diamond. His turban ornament was

[27] Prabhakar, op. cit., p. 97.
[28] Ibid, p. 232.
[29] D.B. Parasnis, *Itihassangraha*, vol. II, pub. not mentioned, 1910, p. 38.
[30] D.B. Parasnis, *Poona in the Bygone Days*, Bombay: Times Press, 1921, p. 18.

studded with emeralds and the precious gems. Strings consisting of pearls and rubies hung from the side of the turban. A British officer named Major Price visited Shaniwārwādā on 7 April 1791. He has also left an account. According to him, the ornaments of the Peshwa were unforgettable. He specifically mentions the necklace made of diamonds and emeralds each being of the size of a nutmeg and immensely priced.[31] Along with these accounts the descriptions in the *lāvaṇīs* show striking similarities with material evidence such as the paintings. The paintings of the Peshwas depict fabulous necklaces and the turban ornaments. As already mentioned, the Peshwas had ordered precious stones from the north for the purpose of making ornaments. They were particular in ordering the Hormuzi Persian pearls which had a yellowish lustre. They were required for the ear-ornament called *choukaḍā*. In 1766 Peshwa Madhavrao I had written to Nana Phadnis asking him to send the *choukaḍā* of the pearls 'having the yellowish lustre like that of jaggery'.[32] He had also asked for the *shirpench* (turban ornament) studded with diamond and rubies.[33] Quite often, the Peshwas made demands for the precious stones from Shinde and Holkar, their officers stationed in the north Indian territories. We have instances of bargaining between them and the Peshwa over the jewels. After the death of Mahadaji Shinde, his grand-nephew Doulatrao claimed authority over Gwalior. When he appealed to Sawai Madhavṛao, Nana Phadnis shrewdly demanded a necklace of hundred pearls each of the size of a *jāmun* (purple plum) from him, after obtaining which, his request would be considered.[34] All these historical documents show a close resemblance with the descriptions of the *lāvaṇīs*. The historicity of the *lāvaṇīs* thus increases. There is yet another piece of evidence which may increase the historicity of the *lāvaṇīs*. The portraits of the Peshwas and also some of the wall-paintings establish the authenticity of the descriptions cited in the *lāvaṇīs*.

For the *shāhīrs*, if the Peshwa was the god Indra or Krishna it was logical that he was surrounded by the mistresses who used to dote on him. As stated earlier, the practice of maintaining *nāṭakshālās* (seraglio) had become a regular feature. The presence of such women would enhance the prestige of the Peshwa and establish his manliness. However effeminate it may seem to see a hero sporting among dancing girls, the *shāhīrs* appear

[31] Ibid., no. 80, p. 21.

[32] *PD*, vol. 32, no. 77, p. 42

[33] Ibid, no. 80, p. 45.

[34] R.V. Herwadkar (ed.), *Krishnaji Vinayak Sohonivirachit Peshwyanchi Bakkar*, Bombay: Venus Prakashan, 1975, p. 165.

to be delighting in the portrayal of the Peshwa amongst women boosting his personality as a virile man. In this sense a definite sexuality is reflected in the Peshwa's right to enjoy women. So the *lāvaṇī*s reveal a lot of eroticism. The following lines from a *lāvaṇī* of Honaji Bala may be cited:

Ascended on the muscular horse this sardār (officer) is handsome. Has worn the *turā* (turban-ornament made of pearls) and is reckless and colourful in romance. He looks like the moon in the sky on a full moon day. He is the incarnation of god and does not have any shortcomings. He is the mine of gems, is well-featured and possesses the lustre of the Sun. He is at the centre and is surrounded by the *nāṭakshālā*s (mistresses). They have decked themselves and are enticing him in all the possible ways. One of them presses his lotus-like feet. The other is winking at him (i.e. to induce him into the love-sports). They are all simultaneously enjoying his love. (These women) are beautiful like tiny diamonds, have voice like a cuckoo. One of them sings for (the lord) in the hall while the other dances in joy. Yet another tells a joke. All of them are lively and are displaying their special arts.[35]

जरद्या छोड्यावर स्वार शिपाई सरदार तो छेल छबेला।
मस्तकी फुलाचा तुरा शिपाई झुरा इष्की रंगेला॥
पौर्णिमेस तारांगणी जसा बाई गगनीं चंद्र उदेला।
हे भगवंताचे लाल सदा खुशियाल न्यूनता नाहीं॥
केवक रत्नाची खाण सुस्वरूप दिनमान राजबीज पुतळा।
मध्यभागीं आपुण भोंवत्या नाटकशाळा।
श्रृंगार करुनी कामिनी नित्य अवध्याजणी मिळूनी वेल्हाळा।
एक आपत्या हातीं एकान्तीं चुरिती पदकमला।
एक आजूबाजू एक सन्मुख धाली डोळा।
त्या मुशाफराच्या संगे भोगिती सोहळा॥
एकीहून एक देखण्या हिरकण्या स्वर कोकिळे प्रमाणें।
एक दिवाणखान्यामश्चे आनंदे मंजुळ गाती गाणें।
एक आनंदांत डोलती एक विनोद बोलती गोजिरवाणें।
दाउनी आपआपुत्या खुब्या सभोंवत्यां उभ्या करुनी चतुराई॥

Another *lāvaṇī* of Honaji Bala reflects more or less the same picture. The Peshwa is surrounded by his mistresses in this manner:

One (of us) has the spitoon in hand while the other is standing at the door like Padmini. All of us hold the delicious betel leaves in hand. We have got ready to put them one by one in your mouth (Oh, our Lord). One (of us) is fully adorned; the other holds the garlands of flowers while yet another is holding the door (of your inner chamber). This is a family of romantic persons. —You are our Lord. You are the galaxy, we are the constellations. You are the very *kalpavriksha* (an imaginary

[35] Honaji Bala, op. cit., p. 148.

tree which is supposed to fulfil every wish) we the weak (women) under your shadow. We feel as if we have obtained a pitcher of wealth in our poverty.[36]

येकीचे हातीं पाकीपात्र येक द्वारांत पद्मिनीपरी।
नाना नक्षीचे विडे घेउनिया पुढें आपआपले करीं।
मुखीं छालावयासी सिद्ध होउनिया प्रसिद्ध सदनांतरीं॥
येक उभी करून शृंगार। येक घेउनी फुलांचे हार।
येक उभी धरुनिया द्वार।
हा इष्काचा परिवार। तुम्ही निधान आमचे पती।
तुम्ही अमृतकर नभीं शुद्ध आम्ही नक्षत्रें प्रभुभोंवतीं।
तुम्ही कल्पवृक्ष प्रत्यक्ष दुर्बल आम्ही छायेखालतीं।
धनकुंभ लाभला असें वाटतें आम्हां दारिध्राती॥

Interestingly, in the same *lāvaṇī* the Peshwa is praised for keeping up such a romantic atmosphere. The number of women he kept elevated his status. One line of the *lāvaṇī* says, 'This action is worthy of a king, it is not at all a misdemeanour.' Towards the end there is an appeal to the Peshwa through the *lāvaṇī* to rate all these women equal so that all of them share his love.

The practice of maintaining a seraglio was much in vogue in medieval times. It is a well-known fact that this practice increased at the time of Raghunathrao. He had appointed Gulabrao Khoja as the manager of his harem.[37] The mistresses as a rule were not women proficient in performing arts. The descriptions in the *lāvaṇīs*, however, interestingly project a combined picture of the mistresses and the courtesans who were the female performing artists. Therefore, there was merely a hairline difference between a mistress and a female performing artist. The overall picture projected through the *lāvaṇīs* shows that the kept women were well trained in the performing arts. They entertained royalty in all possible ways.

There are some *lāvaṇīs* associated with Holi festival (the festival of colours) of Maharashtra. Hoḷī was also known as Shimga. In pre-Peshwa times this festival involved only the worship of Holikā goddess and fire. The festival of colours was an addition. In the later Peshwa period (i.e. from the period of Peshwa Madhavrao, 1761-72 onwards) generally, the pomp and show in the celebrations of the Hindu festivals increased. Dance became an essential aspect of the celebrations. Even in pre-Peshwa times the festival of colours was celebrated in north India on a large scale. The sardārs (officers) of the Peshwas in the north like Shinde and Holkar were

[36] Ibid., pp. 116-17.
[37] *PD*, vol. 32, pp. 28-9.

so fascinated by the exchange of colours between the sexes that they also started celebrating it in their states of Gwalior and Indore. Krishnaji Vinayak Sohoni's *Peshwyānchī Bakhar* states as to how Mahadaji Shinde, a northern sardār during the rule of Peshwa Sawai Madhavrao, described the grandeur of the Holī festival of Jaipur, Udaipur, Mathura, Agra, Gokul and Vrindavan to Sawai Madhavrao. The Peshwa desiring to enjoy the festival, willingly introduced it in Maharashtra.[38] Playing with *gulālgoṭā* was a very important action during this festival. *Gulālgoṭā* was a small ball made by putting *gulāl* (dry red powder) in the hollow of mica. When it dashed against surface it broke splashing the powder in the air. Other colours were mixed in water and the tanks were filled with such coloured waters. The nature of the festival was deeply rooted in the mythological tradition according to which there was a congregation of Lord Krishna and the Gopis (female companions of Krishna) on the occasion of the colour festival. In the *lāvaṇīs* of the *shāhīrs* there was a superimposition of the personality of Krishna onto that of the Peshwa. The Peshwas' women appeared to the *shāhīrs* as gopis participating in and enjoying the colourful moments. The atmosphere of this festival was particularly conducive to sexual arousal. The following *lāvaṇī* of Shāhīr Prabhakar may be cited as an example:

Here is the time of Shimgā festival. Let us get up in joy and play with colours. Please wear the white *chanderi shela* (a sort of scarf or a cloth of very thin material from the place chanderi in Madhya Pradesh, slung loosely over the shoulders loosely over the body). . . In your company, oh dear, I'll play with colours with love. I'll put *vidā* (the roll of betel-leaf) in your mouth with pleasure. . . . Oh Lord of kings take the *gulālgoṭa* in hand and fling it on my breast. . . . This is the (important) festival of the year. Add sweetness to it. . . . Please be seated on the swing. I keep the colours in front of you. I'll put the mirrors on the four sides. I'll sprinkle the saffron colour on you and decorate your head with the *turā*. . . everywhere there is the crowd with *gulāl*. . . .[39]

सण शिमग्याचा आला।
उठा आनंदामधें रंग खेळूं चला॥
सफेत शेला चंदेरिचा पांघरा। . . .
सख्या तुझ्यारे संगतिनें।
सुखाचा रेग खेळेन प्रीतिनें।।
. . . मुखामधीं विडी घालीन शांतीनें॥ . . .

[38] V.M. Kulkarni, A.R. Kulkarni and A.N. Deshpande (eds.), *Krishnaji Sohonikrit Peshwyanchi Bakhar*, Pune: Deshmukh Publication, 1963, pp. 119-20.

[39] Prabhakar, op. cit., p. 98.

गुलाल गोटे हातिं घ्या राजेश्वरी।
फेंका छातीवरी॥
. . . वर्षाचा हा सण।
करावा गोड सख्या आपण।।
. . . बसा झुल्यावर झोंपाळा हलवितें॥
रंग पुढें ठेवितें।
आरसे भंवते चौगर्दा लावितें॥
पिचकाऱ्या आणवितें।
रेग केशरी तुम्हावरी उडवितें॥
तुरा शिरीं खोवितें॥ . . .
जिकडे तिकडे गुलालगर्दी . . .

One anonymous *shāhīr* gives a detailed description of the celebration of the first festival of colours in the city of Poona in his *povāḍā*. It was celebrated for the first time in the year 1793. He states that it was Paṭilbāvā (Mahadaji Shinde) who brought the festival to Poona for the first time. He also narrates in a poetic way that Nana Phadnis made arrangements like filling the tanks with coloured water for the festival. The following line of the *lāvaṇī* would show as to how the Peshwa was placed on the level of Lord Krishna:

'In this way Shrimanta (Peshwa) and Paṭilbāvā (Mahadaji Shinde) played with colours in the Kali era like Lord Krishna played in the Dvāpara era.'[40]

According to Hindu mythology, the time-span of this universe right from the beginning is divided in four yugas (eras). They are Satya, Dvāpara, Tretā and Kali. Usually Lord Krishna is said to be of the Dvāpara Yuga.

Such *lāvaṇī*s appealed to the Peshwas because they suited their taste and hence they patronized the *shāhīr*s. It appears that even the Peshwas took pride that they were enjoying life to the fullest. Obviously, therefore, there was a boom in such erotic *lāvaṇī*s. A close analysis of the *lāvaṇī*s of this period shows that there must have been a competition amongst the *shāhīr*s to compose these erotic *lāvaṇī*s and obtain more and more patronage. This is because there are many similar *lāvaṇī*s by different *shāhīr*s the illustrations of which have been given earlier in this text. The similarity is not merely on the basis of subject-matter but also on the basis of the expressions used to describe the Peshwa. The erotic *lāvaṇī*s, thus, established a relationship between the patrons and the poets. The more

[40] R.B. Kapdi (coll.), *Lavanya*, Bhag Pahila, Bombay: Bapu Harshet Devlekar Press, 1854, pp. 57-8.

the *shāhīr*s painted the royal life the more they had an opportunity to earn their living. Hence, the overall degradation of morality, the unstable political conditions, etc., hardly had any coverage in their compositions. Paradoxically, this was a period of the gradual downfall of the Peshwa and also of the Maratha rule. Political instability and anarchy increased especially in the regime of Peshwa Bajirao II. The two out of three Anglo-Maratha Wars (Anglo-Maratha War II—1802 to 1805 and Anglo-Maratha War III—1815 to 1818) which culminated in the total downfall of the Peshwas were fought during the rule of Peshwa Bajirao II. The *shāhīrs* remained unmoved by these developments. Interestingly, there are some *povāḍā*s of the *shāhīr*s which reflect the utter loss that Maharashtra experienced after these wars. But, these are only lamentations after the downfall. Of course, one cannot blame the *shāhīrs*. It was their expediency which made them play the role of mere bards. There are many more *lāvaṇī*s which reflect the economic and cultural life of contemporary Maharashtra. But each of these aspects affords a separate study.

The foregoing account of the *lāvaṇī*s may be interpreted in the framework of the post-structuralism of Foucault, the philosopher of history. The linguistic analysis of the *lāvaṇī*s shows that the *shāhīr*s were drawn into a structure of linguistic expressions. Interestingly this structure reflects the hegemony of the political power of the Peshwas. The cultural life enjoyed by the Peshwas was a model of the best and the richest life according to the *shāhīrs*. They recreated this model in their *lāvaṇī*s since it fetched them monetary gains. Their poetic expressions and language point to their association with the power-structure. This is observed in the case of the *lāvaṇī*s presented before the Peshwas and in the case of those presented before the common folk at the time of the village-fairs, etc. Thus their language acted as a method[41] of reaching out to people in a courtly mode. The *shāhīr*s moved back and forth from the courts to the people. Their mobility offered them the possibility of imbibing the new linguistic expressions of the aristocratic culture and conveying them to the people. Unconsciously they carried these expressions with them to the new sites of performance. Thus the *shāhīr*s were the agents of widening the linguistic framework of the Marathi language. Through their language they could also present a picture of the contemporary culture. In this way the *lāvaṇī*s do not merely remain folk-performances but serve as the indicators of a changing culture. The *lāvaṇī*s therefore become an important source of cultural history of medieval Maharashtra.

[41] Alan Sheridan, *Michael Foucault: The Will to Truth*, London and New York: Tavistock Publications, rpt. 1986, p. 90.

Plate 1: Holi Festival.

Plate 2: Sawai Madhavrao Peshwa. *Shirpench* on the head along with *tura* (the pearl-ornament). He is wearing white pearl-necklace and the emerald necklace. He has applied *kasturi ṭilak* on the forehead.

The Beginnings of Konkani Literature

JOSÉ PEREIRA

THE KONKANI LANGUAGE

Konkani is the southernmost Indo-European speech that is linked without a break in the Indo-European continuity with the northernmost Indo-European tongue, Norwegian. The Singhalese of Sri Lanka is Indo-European too, but is separated from the Indo-European continuum by a stretch of Dravidian territory and by a channel in the Indian Ocean.

Indo-Aryan speech appears to have been brought into the Konkan by the Brahmins and Tsad-ddi (Chardos, Kshatriyas), who evidently arrived from the Indo-Gangetic Plain in northern India, by travelling through lands where the Shauraseni and Nagara Prakrits were current, as their features occur in Konkani. The Konkani that came to be the standard was based on the vernacular of the Sarasvat Brahmins, who derived their name from the Sarasvati, a river that flowed between the Indus and the Ganges. They had lived along its banks and moved southwards when the river had begun to dry around the first century BC. Passing through the Deccan peninsula they adopted the Maharashtri Prakrit, and appear to have reached Goa during or before the rule of the Shilahara dynasty (*c.* AD 765-1020). From Maharashtri, two New Indo-Aryan languages emerged, the older and more disadvantaged Konkani and the younger and more successful Marathi.

Evidently in existence by the eleventh century AD, Konkani gave little sign of its presence in the middle of India's west coast for five centuries. But it burgeoned into literary activity in the early sixteenth century, thriving under the patronage of the Catholic religious orders, especially the Jesuits and the Franciscans, who had landed in India at that time. But before two centuries were over, the high flood of Konkani literary activity abated, with the official suppression of the language in Goa, in 1684 by the order of the Portuguese viceroy. In addition, the habitat of Konkani was divided between four kingdoms, in all of which the official speech was not Konkani, but (starting from the north) Marathi, Portuguese, Kannada and Malayalam. These speeches had flourishing literatures, but were culturally dissociated from one another, and also employed entirely dissimilar scripts. Such a political partitioning inhibited the creation of a uniform literary tradition in Konkani, whose habitat, moreover, extended over a long strip of coastal territory scenically beautiful but broken by numberless streams and thickly wooded hills. The official attitude of the Konkan's rulers to Konkani, when not actively hostile, was one of unbenign neglect, or at best indifference, which was not propitious to the development of a language whose survival (given the paucity of its speakers) was always precarious. While these misfortunes only increased Konkani's will to survive, they were further aggravated in the early nineteenth century by the launching of a controversy based on the claim that Konkani was no more than a dialect of Marathi. As there is little incentive to write in a dialect, Konkani-speaking writers had an added reason for composing their poems and novels in the successful literary languages dominating their habitat, particularly in Portuguese, Marathi and Kannada.

But things began to change in the middle of the twentieth century. The Konkani Bhasha Mandal was founded in 1939 to promote the language's development; the first Konkani schools were set up in 1964, and the Konkani Bhasha Prachar Sabha was established at Cochin in Kerala in 1966, to agitate for the official recognition of the language. In 1975, India's prime literary institution, the Sahitya Akademi, created in 1962, recognized Konkani as an independent language with its own literary tradition. In 1987, the State of Goa made Konkani its official language. And finally, in 1992, Konkani was included in the Eighth Schedule of the Indian Constitution as one of its official languages. There ensued a renaissance of literature in Konkani, a language finally sovereign on its own soil.

THE EARLIEST EVIDENCE OF LITERARY KONKANI[1]

In this essay, we shall limit ourselves to the first burgeoning of Konkani literature, which occurred in the sixteenth and seventeenth centuries. Before we do that, however, it will be pertinent to comment upon the fragmentary evidence, preceding those centuries, of Konkani's existence. The items of this evidence are basically four. *First*, a one-line inscription of the early twelfth century, dated AD 1116-17, at the foot of the colossal monolith of Bahubali at Shravana Belgola,[2] identifying its patron,

[1] See my *Literary Konkani. A Brief History*, Panaji, Goa: Konkani Akademi, 1992, and my *Konkani Mandakini* (An Anthology of Classical Konkani Literature, in Konkani), Panaji, Goa: Konkani Akademi, 1996.

[2] S.G. Tulpule, *Prachin Marathi Koriv Lekh*, Pune: Vidyapith Prakashan, 1963, pt. 1, p. 18.

Gangaraja, who 'caused it to be made', *karaviyalem*. Here we have both the Marathi (*-vi-*) and the Konkani (*-ya-*) causative affixes. For it was not long that Konkani and Marathi had branched off from a common Prakrit, and were still morphologically close to each other.

Second, a couplet (again of the early twelfth century), recorded in the encyclopedia *Abhilaṣitārthacintāmaṇi* (The Wishing-Jewel of Desirable Objectives) of the Chalukya King Someshvara III (r. 1126-38),[3] a consummate votary of the arts and the earliest known collector of folk-songs in the New Indo-Aryan languages. He has a couplet in praise of Vishnu, which he says is in Maharashtri, but it contains a word with the *-ka* dative (*Manu-śivāka*), and so is evidently Konkani. It describes the god's Fish incarnation, in which form Vishnu brought the Veda up from the underworld and revealed it to Manu and Shiva.

Third, a poem, conceivably of the thirteenth century, preserved among the *abhanga*s of the Marathi poet Namdev (*c.* 1270–*c.* 1350).[4] The child Krishna has stolen the clothes of five cowgirls bathing in a stream, and they beg the god, in their five languages — Marathi, Kannada, 'Musalmani', Konkani and Gujarati — for the return of their loin-cloths. The Konkani plea is evidently a folk-song, where the speaker uses the masculine form of the verb (*melom, padllom*), and offers to give the god a large knife (*koito*) in return for the clothes; exactly the kind of prayer one would expect a rustic Konkani peasant to utter, and not one of Krishna's pretty girlfriends.

Fourth, the Konkanisms found in the Marathi inscriptions and official documents in Goa. Marathi seems to have been introduced as an official language into the Konkan by the Marathi-speaking Yadavas (*c.* 860-1317) in the thirteenth century. They invaded Goa under their foremost King Singhana (r. 1209-47), temporarily vassalizing Goa's Kannada-speaking Kadamba dynasty (960-1310), then in decline. Marathi was retained as Goa's official language by the Yadavas' successors the Muslim Bahmanis (1347-1527; in Goa, 1356-70 and 1471-95), the Hindu Vijayanagara (1354-1674; in Goa, 1380-1471), and the Muslim Adilshahis (1490-1686; in Goa, 1495-1510). The following Marathi inscriptions in Goa contain, or may contain, Konkanisms: the Mhapxem copper plates of Nagadeva

[3] Someśvara, *Mānasollāsa*, *vinodaviṁśati*, adhyāya 16, unnumbered verse following verse 339, in Shrigondekar (ed.), Gaekwad's Oriental Series, 138, which is vol. 3 of the book, p. 38.

[4] T.H. Avte (ed.), *Shri Namdev Maharaj Yanchya Abhanganchi Gatha*, *abhanga* 2290. *Shrivitthala Gathapanchaka*, *gatha* 2, Pune: Vijayadashami Shaka, 1830, pp. 664-5.

(1236?),[5] the Malkornnem virgal of Vajjadeva (thirteenth century),[6] the Verem copper plates (of the Bahmani minister Timanna, 1348)[7] the Bannavali/Benaulim inscription of the reinstalment of the idol of Baneshvaradeva (fourteenth century),[8] and the Bandivanda stone tablet of the Nageshi temple (1474).[9] In addition to the inscriptions, are the Marathi records (replete with Konkanisms) of the sixteenth and seventeenth centuries of the Goan village communities, in Candevi, a variety of the Halekannada script.[10]

THE BEGINNINGS OF HINDU KONKANI LITERATURE

The history of Konkani literature opens with the phenomenal figure of Krishnadas Shama or Shamraj, who flourished in the early sixteenth century. A Brahmin of Kellxi/Quelossim in Saxtty/Salcete, a priest in the Shantadurga temple in his native village, and a devotee of the god Vithoba of Pandharpur, he completed a poem in Marathi, the Tale of the Deeds of Krishna (*Srikrishnacharitrakatha*)[11] in 1526, based on the tenth *skanda* of the *Bhāgavata Purāṇa*, one of Vaishnavism's pre-eminent scriptures. In his time there was a tradition, nearly four centuries old, of Konkani-speaking poets writing their poems in Marathi, the more widely diffused language of the Ghats, which had practically substituted Sanskrit as Goan Hinduism's sacred speech. As readership in Konkani was limited, there was little incentive to write in the latter speech, particularly in a cultivated literary idiom aiming at correctness and elegance, and subjected to the exacting discipline of prosody.

However, Shamraj's immemorial religious heritage was one which had enshrined its ideals in two great epics, the *Mahābhārata*[12] and the

[5] Mentioned in B.D. Satoskar, *Gomantak: Prakruti anni Saunskruti*, *Khand* 2, *Prachin va Madhyayugin Govyatsa Itihas*, Pune: Shubada Sarasvat Publications Pvt. Ltd., 1982, p. 383.

[6] Mentioned ibid., p. 384.

[7] Cf. Alfred Master, *A Grammar of Old Marathi*, Oxford: Clarendon Press, 1964, pp. 162-4.

[8] Mentioned in Satoskar, op. cit., p. 386.

[9] Cf. V.N. Kudva, *History of the Daksinatya Sarasvats* (Ms.), vol. 2, Chap. 13.

[10] Gajanan Ghantkar. *An Introduction to Goa Marathi Records in Halakannada Script*, Margão, Goa: Srinivas S.B. Caculo, 1973.

[11] V.B. Prabhudesai and B.N. Mundi (eds.), *Shamavirachit Shrikrishnacharitrakatha*, Mumbai: Mumbai Marathi Sahitya Sangha, 1975.

[12] L.A. Rodrigues (ed.), *Mahabharot (Adi Porv)*, Goa: Avertano Furtado, 1988. Portion of *Shamabharata*, in Roman script.

Rāmāyaṇa[13] and our Konkani-speaking devotee of Krishna was anxious to communicate a knowledge of them to those of his countrymen who knew no Marathi or Sanskrit. All Indian languages came to see the vernacularizing of the two epics as an indispensable condition for attaining literary respectability. Well before the New Indo-Aryan, the Dravidian literatures, particularly the Tamil and the Kannada, had possessed variants of the epics. Already in the tenth century, the first great Kannada poet, Pampa (902-42 . . .), had composed his *Pampabhārata* (AD 942), and in the twelfth century Nagachandra (fl. 1105), also known as Abhinavapampa, had written his *Pamparāmāyaṇa*. As for Marathi, its literature was languishing in Shamraj's time under Muhammadan persecution, and had not yet produced its vernacular version of either epic. A younger contemporary of Shamraj, Vishnudas Nama (fl. 1530-95), was to write a Marathi *Mahābhārata*, in 13,000 verses, in the second half of the sixteenth century; and in the seventeenth century, the poet Mukteshvar (1609-90), composed a short Marathi *Rāmāyaṇa* in 1,725 ovis (as well as a longer *Mahābhārata*, on which his reputation mainly rests).

In this scene appeared the meteoric Shamraj, and created two events apparently without parallel is most New Indo-Aryan tongues: vernacular versions of both epics, and expressed in prose. We may call these versions the *Shāmabhārata* and the *Shāmarāmāyaṇa*. No other writer of New Indo-Aryan (except, subsequently, the Marathi Mukteshvar) appears to have written on both epics together, and never in prose. Shamraj did not base his prose on the only accomplished Indo-Aryan prose then in existence, that of Sanskrit — which, at any rate, had too singular a syntax and too elaborate a sentence structure, for any of the younger and lighter speeches to imitate. Shamraj took as his model the cultivated spoken idiom of his time. Such a practice was initiated in Europe by the Romantics in the eighteenth century — in Shamraj's day European prose was still being patterned on the Latin. A prose comparable to Shama's, fluent and supple, and based on the spoken idiom, was introduced into modern Indian languages only in the nineteenth century by the great British Orientalist William Carey (1761-1834) in his monumental project of translating the Bible into Indian languages. Shama's own achievement was to be the solid basis for the transformation of Konkani prose, by the writers of the seventeenth century, into a medium consummately malleable and elegant, and expressed in measured cadences.

Was there any Hindu writing besides Shama's in the early phase of

[13] Olivinho J.F. Gomes (ed.), *Sollavea Xekrhea-Adlem Konknni Ramayonn*, Goa: Goim Vidyapith / Goa University, 1996.

Konkani literature? If we are to believe the testimony of the poet and linguist John Leyden (1775-1811)[14] — the initiator of the Konkani-Marathi controversy — it appears that there was, though we cannot date it precisely, except to say that it antedates the nineteenth century. In 1804 Leyden visited Kerala, including the towns of Cochin and Quilon. There he met Konkani Brahmins, descendants of those who had fled Goa from Muslim persecution, launched by the Bahmanis, in the mid-fourteenth century, and from Christian persecution, promoted by the Portuguese Inquisition from the mid-sixteenth century. These men claimed to possess what they said were Konkani translations of the *Mahābhārata* and *Rāmāyaṇa* (Shamraj's two works?), and of the *Liṅga* and *Bhāgavata Purāṇas*, as well as original works, among which were the *Virabhadracheritra* and the *Parasarāmacheritra*. Manuscripts of these works may still be stored in the libraries of the Konkani temples of Kerala. Not long ago a manuscript of a Konkani *Rāmāyaṇa*, of uncertain date[15] was discovered in one of these temples, composed in couplets each line of which is normally of fourteen syllables. This *Rāmāyaṇa* is still chanted in Kerala today, accompanied by drumbeats, for a period of thirteen nights.

It is also worth noting that we have a Konkani document, dated Shaka 1597 (AD 1674), which has scant literary value, but is important as the oldest dated text in the Konkani of Kerala. It is a testimonial, in Devanagari, given to Henricus van Rheede (*c.* 1637-91)[16] by three Konkani physicians living in Kerala, guaranteeing the authenticity of the information contained in the Dutch botanist's monumental classification of south Indian plants in his *Hortus Malabaricus Indicus* (1674). This information was supplied by the physicians themselves — Apu Bhatta, Ranga Bhatta and Vinayaka Pandita.

THE CODIFICATION OF STANDARD KONKANI

In 1510, Catholicism arrived in Goa, bearing with it the command of its Founder, to 'make disciples of all nations' (*Matth.* 28: 19). The bearers of

[14] John Leyden, *Plan for Investigating the Languages, Literature, Antiquities and History of the Dekkan*, London: British Museum, Additional Mss., 26,566, fls 69/37-69v/37v.

[15] Cf. Olivinho Gomes, op. cit., p. ix. The Konkani *Rāmāyaṇa* has been edited by R.K. Rao as *God-dde Ramayann* (*Konknni Lokgit*), Cochin: Konkani Bhasha Institute, 1989.

[16] Cited by Xennoi Goimbab, *Konknni Bhaxechem Zoit*, Mumbai: Gomantak Press, 1930, p. 68.

Christ's message, however, did not speak Konkani, the language of their potential disciples, and so had to acquire it laboriously, through dictionaries and grammars. But no grammars or dictionaries were available.

Indeed, they had not been available in Portuguese itself (the language of most of the bearers of Christ's message), since the inception of that language around the ninth century. But the spirit of the Renaissance, blowing in Europe since the fifteenth century, inspired scholars to produce grammars not only of Latin but also of the living tongues of Europe. Moved by that spirit, the first two grammars of any modern European languages were written — of Spanish, in 1492, by Antonio de Lebrija, and of Portuguese, in 1536, by Fernão de Oliveira (1507-81. . .). Quickly following them was a second Portuguese grammar, by the renowned historian João de Barros (1497-1562). Thirty years later came the first dictionary of Portuguese-Latin and Latin-Portuguese, the work of Jerónimo Cardoso (died 1569). Now the Catholic scholars in Goa, both foreigners and natives, had models to follow when they set to work to articulate the linguistic structure of Konkani.

The work was begun in an institution for the training of priests, the first academy of higher learning on the Western model anywhere in Asia, the Seminary of the Holy Faith, later known as the College of St. Paul's, founded in 1541. In 1556, a printing press, Asia's first, was set up in one of the College buildings. In Saxtty/Salcete, the province assigned to them, the Jesuits established the College of the Holy Spirit at Morhgoum/Margão, which they transferred to Raichur/Raitur/Rachol in 1610, naming it the College of St. Ignatius (today the Patriarchal Seminary). This College, also furnished with a printing press, became the powerhouse of Konkani linguistic and literary activity.

The presses belonged to the Jesuits, the chief promoters of Konkani. But not less assiduous in their study of Goa's language were the Franciscans, though they unfortunately had no printing facilities, so that nearly all their Konkani production remained in manuscript.

It was in the College of St. Paul that the grammatical formulation of Konkani was initiated by a Goan lay brother, 'the Grammarian of St. Paul's',[17] whose name may have been André Vaz. By 1563, only about twenty-five years since the publication of the first Portuguese grammar, he had already composed a grammar of Konkani, apparently the first

[17] Mentioned in a letter of Padre Lourenço Peres (17 Dec. 1568). António da Silva Rego, *Documentação para a história das missões do Padroado Português no Oriente*, Lisbon, 1953, *India*, vol. IX, pp. 236-7.

of its kind in any New Indo-Aryan speech, and certainly the first, on any Indian language, based on Western-style grammars. In the Dravidian south, a Tamil grammar was begun by the brilliant Jesuit philologist Henrique Henriques (*c.* 1520-1600). Around 1565, he had started work on a Konkani grammar by interviewing two native speakers at Cochin, and had completed much of it by 1567[18] It was judged to be better than the one of the Grammarian of St. Paul's. No copy of either work has been traced.

Shamraj had chosen the speech of the *xennais* (or pandits) of Kut-tthalli/Cortalim to be the language of his version of the two epics. This speech was to remain, for two centuries, the standard form used by Konkanis anywhere, and is therefore deservedly identified as the *Pramann*, or norm, of Konkani. (Modern Konkanis, on the other hand, have seven literary dialects, in addition to spoken ones.) It was the *Pramann* that three scholars set out to codify. They were the English Jesuit Thomas Stephens (1549-1617), the Portuguese Jesuit Diogo Ribeiro (1560-1633), and, the greatest of the three, the Portuguese Franciscan Gaspar de S. Miguel (fl. 1595-1637). The Jesuit grammar, written by Stephens and enlarged by Ribeiro (and four other, anonymous, priests), was printed in 1640.[19] (In contrast, the first printed Marathi grammar appeared in 1778, but it was based on the Koli dialect of Bombay. The first printed Marathi grammars, two in number, having as their basis the standard dialect of Pune/Poona, only came out in 1836, the work of Gangadhar Shastri Phadke and Balshastri Jambekar/Dadoba, 1810-46, respectively.) The grammar of Gaspar, ready by 1635, remained in manuscript. It contained two parts, the first an accidence and the second a syntax, exhaustively treated (which I published in 1967).[20] Other scholars who worked on Konkani grammar were the Jesuit Leonardo Cinnamo (fl. 1623-44) and the Franciscans João de S. Matias (fl. 1595-1624) and Cristóvão de Jesus, whose Ms. is dated 1635.

[18] Joseph Wicki, S.J., *Documenta Indica* (*Monumenta Historica Societatis Iesu*, vol. 89). Rome, vol. VII, letter 95, p. 442.

[19] Thomas Stephens, *Arte da lingoa canarim*, 2nd edn. by Joaquim Heliodoro da Cunha Rivara, *Grammatica da lingua concani . . .*, Nova Goa: Imprensa Nacional, 1857.

[20] '*Gaspar de S. Miguel, O.F.M., Arte da lingoa canarim, parte 2a. Sintaxis copiosissima na lingoa bramana e pollida*. A Syntax of Standard Konkani. Edited with an Introduction by José Pereira', *Journal of the University of Bombay*, September 1967, Arts Number.

(It is interesting to note that just as Konkani's standard form was fixed by an Englishman, Stephens, in the seventeenth century, so was Marathi's by another Englishman, Major Thomas Candy, 1806-77, in the nineteenth century.)

Our scholars were dedicated students of Marathi also, for it was in that speech that they produced their *purāṇas*. Intended as these extended poems were for a larger potential readership than was available in Goa, it was thought wise to compose them in a language that had acquired a hieratic aura, and possessed an established literary form, lacking in Konkani, a form judged apt for sacred themes — the *purāṇa*. Yet these scholars produced no Marathi grammars, except in 1778, as noted. But the Jesuit Ignazio Arcamone (1615-83), the first Italian Orientalist[21] organized a comparative grammar of Marathi and Konkani, the first of its kind, in Latin, the Indian Gate (*Ianua Indica, sive pro Concanica et Decanica linguis, manuale*, no date)[22], a manual of the Konkani and Deccani (or Marathi) languages for Jesuits recently arrived in India. (Arcamone was also an accomplished Latinist: one of his works in that language is an epic on Portuguese heroic adventures in the East, *Lusiadis leoninae*, the manuscript of which is dated 1678.)

Work on Konkani vocabulary was started by the Jesuits of the Rachol College, and their compilation was enriched with idioms by Diogo Ribeiro (in 2 vols.) in 1626.[23] The Jesuit António de Saldanha (1598-1663) continued the organization of Konkani vocabulary,[24] which appears to have been brought to perfection by his co-religious Miguel de Almeida (1604-83)[25] who based his own work on the Jesuit Benedito/Bento Pereira's (1605-81) vast Latin-Portuguese-Spanish dictionary, the *Prosodia in vocabularium trilingue* (1634) of nearly 50,000 entries. Other compilers of vocabularies were Leonardo Cinnamo, the Franciscan Manuel Banha (fl. 1649-54) and the omnicompetent Gaspar de S. Miguel. We have, in addition, six anonymous vocabularies, which may contain the works of the above-mentioned scholars. I have identified them with the following Latin titles:

[21] José Pereira, 'Ignazio Arcamone (1615-83): First Italian Orientalist?', *East & West*, 24, nos. 1-2, Rome, Mar.-Jan. 1974, pp. 153-7.

[22] Arcamone, *Ianua Indica*, Codex 3049, Lisbon: Biblioteca Nacional.

[23] Diogo Ribeiro, *Vocabulario da lingoa canarym*, Panaji, Goa: Central Library, 403 fls.

[24] Ribadeneira, Alegambe and Sotvellus, *Biblioteca Scriptorum Societatis Iesu*, Rome, 1676, tom. 1, p. 84.

[25] Ibid., p. 611, col. 2.

Lexicon Racholense (or *Bonaventurianum*; Public Library, Panaji, Goa).

Lexicon Bracarense (Public Library, Braga, Portugal).

Lexicon Lisbonense/Ulyssiponense 3044 (Biblioteca Nacional Lisbon, Portugal, Codex 3044).

Lexicon Lisbonense/Ulyssiponense 3195 (Biblioteca Nacional, Lisbon, Codex 3195).

Lexicon Lisbonense/Ulyssiponense Junta (Arquivo Histórico Ultramarino, Junta de Investigações do Ultramar, Lisbon, facsimile edn., 1973).

Lexicon Romanum (Archivum Romanum Societatis Iesu, Rome, Opera Nostrorum, 354).

The opinion has been voiced that the two volumes of the *Lexicon Racholense* are not the work of the Jesuits, but of the Franciscans. The ascription to the Jesuits of Rachol is by a later librarian, while an earlier inscription in the Ms. identifies it as belonging to the Frânciscan Colégio de S. Boaventura in Velha Goa (in which case it may more properly be identified as the *Lexicon Bonaventurianum*). Be that as it may, with the dismantling of the printing presses in 1674, with the deaths of the *Pramann*'s chief scholars by 1683, and by the official suppression of Konkani in 1684 referred to above, Konkani writing came to a halt. A chill wintry wind terminated the summer of Konkani linguistics and literature.

But the *Pramann* was to have a short autumn, which was ushered in by two Goan laymen, of Tsodnnem/Chorão, toward the end of the seventeenth century. Simão and Lourenço Álvares, respectively son and father, and continued by the Jesuits into the eighteenth (until their expulsion from the Portuguese colonies in the East in 1761). In 1694 Simão wrote a Konkani grammar and, in the following year, in collaboration with his father, compiled a Konkani vocabulary.[26] It is possible that both father and son may have known or even been trained by Miguel de Almeida and Ignazio Arcamone. The age of the *Pramann* closed with two younger Jesuits, the Portuguese Diogo de Amaral (1699-1762) and the Czech Karel Przikryl (1718-85). Diogo produced the last dictionary of the *Pramann*[27] and Karel

[26] Joaquim Heliodoro da Cunha Rivara, *Ensaio historico da lingua concani*, Nova Goa: Imprensa Nacional, 1857, p. cxvii.

[27] C. Sommervogel, A. de Backer and A. Carayon (eds.), *Bibliothèque de la Compagnie de Jésus. Bibliographie*, tom. 6, col. 1265.

a Latin summary of its grammar,[28] based mostly on the 1640 book of Stephens and Ribeiro.

These philological investigations suggested ideas which were to become basic in the later science of Comparative Linguistics. In 1583, Stephens intuited the fundamental notion of the science when he observed that Konkani and Marathi were related to Latin and Greek. Arcamone, in his *Ianua Indica*, noted that the syntax of Konkani and Marathi was very nearly that of Latin. The methodology of a comparative study of languages was worked out by the French Jesuit Gaston Laurent Coeurdoux (1691-1779) in 1767, and Comparative Linguistics finally emerged as an autonomous discipline around 1786 with William Jones (1746-94).

THE BEGINNINGS OF CHRISTIAN KONKANI LITERATURE

Now with the linguistic norm established, and Shamraj's matchless prose providing them with a model, the Christian writers proceeded to create a literature that expressed their religious beliefs. As a result of their efforts, Konkani became the first Asian language to employ Western literary genres — today a practice in general use the world over, and included types like the lyric, the epic, the novel, the short story, the essay and the journalistic report. However, as evangelization was the primary motive of the first Christian writers in Konkani, the types adopted by them, all derived from Europe, mostly responded to religious needs, and include the following:

1. Catechisms
2. Pastoral tracts
3. Doctrinal tracts
4. Polemical tracts
5. Bible translations
6. Lives of saints
7. Mystical and devotional treatises
8. Sermons

Most of the works classified under these headings are either in Ms. or known from reports. Not until they have been examined shall we be able to decide whether they are correctly classified, or whether the classifi-

[28] Karel Prikryl, S.J., '*Principia linguae brahmanicae*, A Grammar of Standard Konkani. Edited with an Introduction by José Pereira', *Archív Orientální*, Prague, 36 (1968), pp. 625-84.

cation itself can be made more neat. As it stands, it is rather fluid, with categories overlapping. Many of the works discussed below are translations. Original works are relatively few and are sometimes intermixed with the translations.

Catechisms — or treatises for instruction in the elements of the Christian religion in the form of question and answer — are the most numerous of these types. The best-known of them are translations of three writers (here mentioned along with their works): the celebrated Spanish Dominican orator and mystic Luis de Granada (1504-88), *Compendium of Christian Doctrine* (1559); the Portuguese Jesuit moral theologian Marcos Jorge (1524-71), *Compendium of Christian Doctrine* (1561); and the Italian Jesuit Doctor of the Church Roberto Bellarmino (1542-1621), *Most Copious Explanation of Christian Doctrine* (1598). Granada's book was translated by Gaspar de S. Miguel, Jorge's by Thomas Stephens (posthumously published 1622),[29] and Bellarmino's by Gaspar and Diogo Ribeiro (published 1632).[30] Other catechisms, some of which may be original, are those by the Jesuits Leonardo Cinnamo, Miguel de Almeida (1658) and Teotónio Joseph/José (1758), and by the Franciscans Manuel do Lado, Manuel Baptista and Domingos de S. Bernardino, the latter cast in the form of the explanation of the Apostles Creed: it is not clear if he used the question-and-answer format.

Next are the *pastoral tracts*, or works containing advice on the spiritual care that 'pastors' (priests) can provide their Christian 'flocks' (congregations). These tracts sometimes appear to be no more than instructions in Christian doctrine that dispense with the catechismal format. Such may have been the pamphlet of Domingos referred to. Such may also be António de Saldanha's *Pastoral Praxis*, where the mysteries of Christianity are explained in vivid metaphors drawn from Konkani life. But the pastoral tracts as a rule seem to be handbooks for the use of the clergy, with titles like *The Pastoral Staff* (or *Crozier*; Gaspar, Saldanha) and *Manual for Parish Priests and Rectors* (Gaspar). There are also confessionaries, texts with instructions on how sins are to be confessed to a priest (João de Pedrosa, Simão & Lourenço Álvares). In addition, there is a handbook that gives guidance to the dying and those condemned to death, by Arcamone, published in 1663.

[29] Mariano Saldanha (ed.), Facsimile edition of Thomas Stephen's *Doutrina christam*, Lisbon: Agência Geral das Colónias, 1945.

[30] Parts of Ribeiro's *Catechism* printed in V. B. Prabhudesai, *Satravea Shatakantil Gomantaki Boli*, Mumbai: University of Bombay, 1963, pp. 189-91.

Doctrinal tracts treat particular themes of Christian doctrine, such as Purgatory and the Sacraments. Arcamone published his *Short Commentary on Purgatory* (1663).[31] Gaspar wrote a treatise *On the Seven Sacraments*.

Polemical tracts attack Hindu beliefs and practices. There are at least two such Konkani works, Gaspar's pamphlet *On the Rites of the Gentiles*, and Cinnamo's more extended *Apology for the Mysteries of the Faith with a Refutation of the Pagan Sects and Superstitions*. The information such books could provide would be invaluable for a cultural anthropology of Konkani Hinduism.

The category of *Bible translations* is represented by a single work, Arcamone's *Gospels of the Entire Year*, published in 1667.[32] Though it has renderings of selected Biblical passages only, and not complete translations of the Bible or of any of its books, this is the first work, in any Indian language, that offers a translation of the Christian scriptures at all, and the only one of its kind until Carey's project of the nineteenth century.[33]

The preceding categories (except that of Biblical translation, which is a class by itself, best described as inspirational) comprise works that are more for instruction than for edification. The remaining headings relate to instruction, edification, and increase of devotion; they provide more opportunities for a cultivated aesthetic expression. Devotional works include lives of the saints and mystical treatises. Finally, the entire spectrum of religious teaching, infused with eloquence and emotional exaltation, is consummated in sacred oratory, given expression to in sermons.

Of the *lives of saints*, the most popular in our time appears to have been *The Flower of the Saints* (1599 and 1601) by the Spanish Jesuit hagiographer and Church historian Pedro de Ribadeneyra (1526-1611). It was translated both by the Jesuit Diogo Ribeiro and the Franciscan Amador de Santana (published in 1607, the only Franciscan Konkani book printed in the age of the *Pramann*).[34] Leonardo Cinnamo has a book on the lives of the saints,

[31] Copy of Arcamone's *Short Commentary* in the Biblioteca Casanatense, Rome.

[32] Arcamone, *Sagallea Varussanche (Vangel).* Sommervogel et al., op. cit., tom. 3, p. 513.

[33] *The Holy Bible . . . translated . . . into the Kunkuna Language*, Serampore: Mission Press, 1818-21.

[34] Copy of Amador's *Flos sanctorum* in the Bibliothèque Nationale, Paris.

perhaps a translation. An original saint's life is António de Saldanha's *Miracles of the Wonder-Working Saint Anthony* (1655); Saldanha's raciness of Konkani expression could not have been excelled by Shamraj himself. Finally, the Franciscan João de S. Matias is reported to have written a life of Christ (who, of course, is the Lord of all the saints).

Mystical and devotional treatises include translations and original works. In 1660, João de Pedrosa (1615-72) published a Konkani version of the *Divine Soliloquies* (1632 ?)[35] of the Spanish Jesuit moral theologian Bernardino de Villegas (1592-1653). Apparently original, or original intermixed with translations, are the following works of Saldanha and Miguel de Almeida. Saldanha has three books: *Eminent Benefits Deriving From the Guardian Angels*; *The Delectable Roses and Daisies From the Pleasant Rose-Garden of Mary*; *and Nectarine Fruits of the Tree of Life* (which seems to contain some sermons too).[36] Miguel de Almeida's book is the *Narrative Instances and Miracles Confirming the Mysteries of the Faith That are Explained in the Catechism* (1658).

Finally, *sermons*, eminently represented — besides Saldanha — by Arcamone, Gaspar de S. Miguel and Miguel de Almeida. Gaspar had four manuscript volumes of *Sermons for the Feasts of the Liturgical Year and on the Saints*. He also had *Homilies Which the Parish Priests Ought to Deliver to Their Flocks, in Which are Taught the Mysteries of Our Holy Faith and the Seven Sacraments and Precepts of the Decalogue*. Arcamone had *Sermons for the Feasts of the Solemnities of the Entire Year* (1668); his book on the *Gospels for the Entire Year*, mentioned earlier, also contained indices for Lenten sermons. But the supreme orator of the age of the *Pramann* is Miguel de Almeida, an accomplished Latinist and the author of several unpublished manuscripts of Konkani homilies for the feasts of the liturgical year, for Lent and on the saints. He also has two published homiliaries. First, the *Five Homilies on the Words 'Mary Set Out'* (to meet her cousin Elizabeth, *Luke* 1: 39). And second, five volumes of *The Garden of the Shepherds* (1658-9), the monumental masterpiece of

[35] João de Pedrosa, *Devachim Yecangra Bolannim*. Copy in the Central Library, Panaji.

[36] António de Saldanha, *Zivitva Vruqheachim Amrutam Phallam*, Ms. in the Library of the School of Oriental and African Studies, London, Marsden Collection, n. 12.175.

[37] Miguel de Almeida, *Onvalleancho Mallo*. Of the five volumes, the second is preserved in the Central Library, Panaji, and the fifth in the Library of the School of Oriental and African Studies, S-XII, Misc. 11,937.